SHAKESPEARE'S SONNETS

SHAKESPEARE CRITICISM
VOLUME 20
GARLAND REFERENCE LIBRARY OF THE HUMANITIES
VOLUME 1988

SHAKESPEARE'S SONNETS
CRITICAL ESSAYS

EDITED BY
JAMES SCHIFFER

GARLAND PUBLISHING, INC.
A MEMBER OF THE TAYLOR & FRANCIS GROUP
NEW YORK AND LONDON
2000

First paperback edition published in 2000 by
Garland Publishing Inc.
A Member of the Taylor & Francis Group
29 West 35th Street
New York, NY 10001

Copyright © 1999 by James Schiffer

10 9 8 7 6 5 4 3

Library of Congress Cataloging-in-Publication Data

Schiffer, James.
     Shakespeare's sonnets : critical essays / edited by James Schiffer.
        p.   cm. — (Garland reference library of the humanities ; v. 1988.
  Shakespeare criticism ; v. 20)
     Includes bibliographical references.
     ISBN 0-8153-2365-4 (alk. paper)
     ISBN 0-8153-3893-7 (pbk)
     1. Shakespeare, William, 1564–1616. Sonnets. 2. Sonnets, English—History
and criticism. I. Schiffer, James. II. Series: III. Garland reference library of the
humanities. Shakespeare criticism ; v. 20.
PR2848.S46 1999
821'.3—dc21   98-40426
                                                    CIP

Cover photograph of Agnes Wilcox performing selected Sonnets, April 28, 1998; The
   New Theatre, St. Louis, Missouri.

iv

GENERAL EDITOR'S INTRODUCTION

The continuing goal of the Garland Shakespeare Criticism series is to provide the most influential historical criticism, the most significant contemporary interpretations, and reviews of the most influential productions. Each volume in the series, devoted to a Shakespearean play or poem (e.g., the sonnets, *Venus and Adonis*, the *Rape of Lucrece*), includes the most essential criticism and reviews of Shakespeare's work from the late seventeenth century to the present. The series thus provides, through individual volumes, a representative gathering of critical opinion of how a play or poem has been interpreted over the centuries.

A major feature of each volume in the series is the editor's introduction. Each volume editor provides a substantial essay identifying the main critical issues and problems the play (or poem) has raised, charting the critical trends in looking at the work over the centuries, and assessing the critical discourses that have linked the play or poem to various ideological concerns. In addition to examining the critical commentary in light of important historical and theatrical events, each introduction functions as a discursive bibliographic essay that cites and evaluates significant critical works—essays, journal articles, dissertations, books, theatre documents—and gives readers a guide to research on the particular play or poem.

After the introduction, each volume is organized chronologically, by date of publication of selections, into two sections: critical essays and theatre reviews/documents. The first section includes previously published journal articles and book chapters as well as original essays written for the collection. In selecting essays, editors have chosen works that are representative of a given age and critical approach. Striving for accurate historical representation, editors include earlier as well as contemporary criticism. Their goal is to include the widest possible range of critical approaches to the play or poem to demonstrate the multiplicity and complexity of critical response.

In most instances, essays have been reprinted in their entirety, not butchered into snippets. The editors have also commissioned original essays (sometimes as many as five to ten) by leading Shakespearean scholars, thus offering the most contemporary, theoretically attentive analyses. Reflecting some recent critical approaches in Shakespearean studies, these new essays approach the play or poem from a multiplicity of perspectives, including feminist, Marxist, new historical, semiotic, mythic, performance/staging, cultural, and/or a combination of these and other methodologies. Some volumes in the series even include bibliographic analyses that have significant implications for criticism.

The second section of each volume in the series is devoted to the play in performance and, again, is organized chronologically by publication date, beginning with some of the earliest and most significant productions and proceeding to the most recent. This section, which ultimately provides a theatre history of the play, should not be regarded as different from or rigidly isolated from the critical essays in the first section. Shakespearean criticism has often been informed by or has significantly influenced productions. Shakespearean criticism over the last twenty years or so has usefully been labeled the "Age of Performance." Readers will find information in this section on major foreign productions of Shakespeare's plays as well as landmark productions in English. Consisting of more than reviews of specific productions, this section also contains a variety of theatre documents, including interpretations written for a particular volume by notable directors whose comments might be titled "The Director's Choice," histories of seminal productions (e.g., Peter Brook's *Titus Andronicus* in 1955), and even interviews with directors and/or actors. Editors have also included photographs from productions around the world to help readers see and further appreciate the way a Shakespearean play has taken shape in the theatre.

Each volume in the Garland Shakespeare Criticism series strives to give readers a balanced, representative collection of the best that has been thought and said about a Shakespearean play or poem. In essence, each volume supplies a careful survey of essential materials in the history of criticism for a Shakespearean play or poem. In offering readers complete, fulfilling, and in some instances very hard to locate materials, editors have made conveniently accessible the literary and theatrical criticism of Shakespeare's greatest legacy, his work.

Philip C. Kolin
University of Southern Mississippi

For Samuel G. Schiffer, 1915-1997

Contents

Contents

Illustrations

Preface

This collection of essays has been assembled with a special "dispensation" to diverge from the usual content for volumes in the Garland Shakespeare Criticism series. Unlike most of the other volumes in the series, this one does not have a section for essays and reviews devoted to performance issues. Furthermore, this collection has many more new essays than reprinted ones, sixteen to four, and the four reprints are recent essays, all from the 1990s. In other words, this volume concentrates solely on contemporary interpretations. At one point the plan had been to offer fewer new essays and to include criticism going back to the eighteenth and nineteenth centuries, and the first ninety years of the twentieth. One disadvantage of that plan was that it would be difficult—if not impossible—to represent all the important interpretations of the Sonnets that have been proffered over the last two hundred years.

Limiting this volume to new and recent essays has given it greater coherence and a stronger reason for being than it otherwise would have had: to the best of my knowledge, this is *the* collection of essays on the Sonnets (at least in English) of the 1990s. The last important critical anthologies were Harold Bloom's in 1987 and a long section of volume 10 of the Gale Shakespeare Criticism series edited by James Person and Sandra L. Williamson, which was published in 1990. Bloom's edition consists of a brief introduction and reprints of five important "modern interpretations" by C. L. Barber (1960), Rosalie Colie (1974), Stephen Booth (1977), Thomas M. Greene (1985), and Howard Felperin (1985). The Gale volume includes excerpts (rarely complete essays) from the writings of approximately eighty authors, from Francis Meres (1598) to John Kerrigan (1986). It was to avoid overlap with these two anthologies—as well as several earlier ones—that the Garland editors and I decided finally to limit this collection to essays from the present decade. My one regret about the new plan was that the book would no longer include selections by Stephen Booth, Eve Kosofsky Sedgwick, or Joel Fineman. My consolation is that the importance of the work of all three authors is universally recognized by scholars today. Judging from the many times they are cited in the essays that follow, I think it is fair to say that the spirits of Booth, Sedgwick, and Fineman inhabit these pages.

The 1990s have been a time of important new investigation of Shakespeare's Sonnets, and there is exciting work being done by a number of different scholars who use a great variety of methods and come to an equally varied set of conclusions. The nineteen essays gathered here demonstrate the validity of many different contemporary approaches, as well as the high quality of work being done today on these fascinating poems. These contributors, some in disagreement with others in the volume, address an exciting range of topics, from Shakespeare's relation to Petrarch to early modern codes of maternity to *A Lover's Complaint* as a commentary on and conclusion to the story the Sonnets tell. Most of the essays in this volume, by the way, were completed before publication in late 1997 of Helen Vendler's *The Art of Shakespeare's Sonnets* and Katherine Duncan-Jones's New Arden edition; therefore, few of the new essays refer to these works. I have tried in my introduction to address issues raised by these two books and more generally by these two important scholars. New work comes out all the time on the Sonnets, and there can never be a volume that is entirely up to date. (I have just learned, for example, of Michael Innes's book, *Shakespeare and the English Renaissance Sonnet* [Macmillan/St. Martin's, 1997]).

A brief note on style: all the new essays follow slightly modified MLA guidelines for documentation style and other related matters; however, the four reprinted essays retain the spelling, punctuation, and documentation styles of their original publications, with the following exception: throughout the volume, references to the "Sonnets" (i.e., the collection as a whole) will be capitalized but not italicized; references to individual sonnets (e.g., sonnet 24) will not be capitalized. The essays by Peter Stallybrass, Margreta de Grazia, and Heather Dubrow have been updated by the authors for this publication; George T. Wright's essay is actually a new essay that will be published for the first time in a separate collection just before this one.

For this project I have relied on the kindness of both friends and strangers. First of all, I wish to express a tremendous debt to my nineteen authors for their excellent work and for their discipline in helping to keep this project on track—indeed, ahead of schedule. To David Bevington and Heather Dubrow I owe great thanks for recommending possible contributors when I was just getting started. In fact, several colleagues represented in this volume participated in the seminar on Shakespeare's Sonnets organized by Dubrow and Inga-Stina Ewbank for the 1996 World Shakespeare Congress: George T. Wright, Joyce Sutphen, Michael Schoenfeldt, Lars Engle, Rebecca Laroche, and Bruce R. Smith (essays in this collection by Engle, Laroche, and Smith, however, were not based on papers presented at the World Congress). I would also like to thank Stephen Greenblatt, Dorothea Kehler, Katherine Eisaman Maus, Marianne Novy, Clark Hulse, and Linda Boose for suggesting the names of scholars I might invite to contribute. Bruce R. Smith also assisted by recommending possible reprints for this volume and by contacting more than one author on my behalf; his enthusiasm about this book has been important to me from the start.

I began work on this project in July 1995, while I was in Oxford helping to direct the Virginia Program at Oxford. I am grateful to the librarians at the Bodleian Library for their assistance. In the summer of 1996 I worked at the Folger Shakespeare Library, and I was fortunate to return for three months in 1997 thanks to a short-term Folger fellowship combined with professional development funds from Hampden-Sydney College. At the Folger, I wish to thank fellowship coordinator Carol Brobeck, head librarian Richard Kuhta, reference librarian Georgianna Ziegler, librarian Betsy Walsh, and the rest of the fabulous Folger staff. I am also indebted to the librarians in the Rare Book Room at the Library of Congress, as well as to Margaret Kieckhefer of the Library of Congress's Photoduplication Department. While at the Folger I profited from many stimulating discussions about the Sonnets (and many other matters) with Valerie Traub, Richard A. Levin, Bruce R. Smith, Marvin Hunt, Goran Stanivukovic, Gail Kern Paster, Barbara Mowat, Jeffrey Masten, Mark Bland, Janice Devereux, David Harris Sacks, Marshall Grossman, Jay Halio, and (by phone) Joseph Pequigney: several of these colleagues read and commented on a section of my introduction that I presented as a paper at the Patristic, Medieval, and Renaissance Conference (PMR) at Villanova University in September 1997. My good friend Carole Levin encouraged me with this project in countless ways; it was she, for example, who invited me to present my essay at PMR. I am obliged as well to Tom Olsen, who chaired the session and lively discussion at the conference.

At Garland I have enjoyed working with editors Phyllis Korper (who left at the end of 1997) and Kristi Long, as well as with computer specialist Chuck Bartelt. I would also like to express my gratitude to series editor Philip C. Kolin for assigning me this project. At Hampden-Sydney College, I owe thanks to many. The Professional Development Committee approved two summer research grants and a year's sabbatical in 1997-1998 to work on this project, and I received funds as well from the William W. Elliott Professorship endowment. My colleagues in Shakespeare Diana Rhoads and Scott Colley, former dean of the faculty, have been supportive in many ways, and I have learned much from Hassell Simpson's work-in-progress on the Psalms and the Sonnets. To my students in Shakespeare classes over the years I think I can attribute many of my insights into these poems. I would also like to recognize assistance from the librarians at Hampden-Sydney, especially Gerry Randall, Catherine Polari, and Sharon Goad. I am grateful as well to Sherry Giles in the Hampden-Sydney Computing Center for her help with many technical matters and for allowing me to use her laser printer. Jane Mahne, heroic secretary of Morton Hall, also let me use her printer. My colleague in philosophy Patrick Wilson gave me a valuable lesson in using Word 6, while Pam Fox of our Fine Arts Department very generously and skillfully printed my illustrations. Other close friends who have helped along the way include Steve Shapiro, Richard Stern, and Rosalind Hingeley. I have also been blessed with the loving support of my stepmother, Dolores Schiffer, and inspired by my brothers, Stephen and Fred. To my children, Tanja and Toby, and to my wife, Susan, as always, I owe the greatest thanks of all.

James Schiffer

Figure 1. Agnes Wilcox performing selected Sonnets. The New Theatre, St. Louis, Missouri. April 28, 1998. Photo by Kevin Lowder. Reproduced by permission of The New Theatre.

PART I

Introduction

Reading New Life into Shakespeare's Sonnets
A Survey of Criticism

James Schiffer

> What is your substance, whereof are you made,
> That millions of strange shadows on you tend?
>
> —Sonnet 53.1-2[1]

A common practice in many accounts of the reception history of Shakespeare's Sonnets is to complain, often in tones of comic despair, about the crushing volume of criticism, the mountain of essays, dissertations, chapters, books, poems, plays, and novels on these most problematic of poems—a mountain any surveyor must attempt to climb. Even at the start of the biographical debates in the early nineteenth century, James Boswell the younger protested: "There are few topicks connected with Shakespeare upon which the ingenuity and research of his criticks have been more fruitlessly exercised, than upon the questions which have arisen with regard to the poems before us, the individual to whom they were principally addressed, and the circumstances under which they were written" (20: 218). And by the end of the last century, Swinburne could write: "Upon the Sonnets such a preposterous pyramid of presumptuous commentary has long since been reared by the Cimmerian speculation and Boeotian 'brain-sweat' of sciolists and scholiasts, that no modest man will hope and no wise man will desire to add to the structure or subtract from it one brick of proof or disproof, theorem or theory" (62). That "structure" is much greater now, of course, after another century of voluminous discussion, and modern commentators often lament the uneven quality of much of what has been written as well as the outright insanity of more than a few interpretations.

W. H. Auden, for example, begins his 1964 introduction to the Signet edition of the Sonnets by stating, "Probably, more nonsense has been talked and written, more intellectual and emotional energy expended in vain, on the Sonnets of Shakespeare than on any other literary work in the world" (xvii). In his survey of criticism for the Penguin edition in 1986, John Kerrigan notes that Herbert S. Donow's "admirable but inevitably incomplete" bibliography of the sonnet in England and America, published in 1982 and covering criticism through 1981, lists 1,898 items on Shakespeare's Sonnets alone, but, Kerrigan adds, "much of the literature tends to lunacy and is dispensable" (65).[2] More recently, Helen Vendler has written of "the highly diverting, if appalling, history of the reception of the *Sonnets*" ("Reading" 29). She recalls the first time she realized "with trepidation, that the *Sonnets* are a lightning rod for nuttiness. There is even a man in the *Variorum* who thinks the Dark Lady was a wine bottle, and that the later sonnets record Shakespeare's struggles with alcoholism" ("Reading" 24). Vendler alludes here to J. F. Forbis's *The Shakespearean Enigma and an Elizabethan Mania* (1924), a work worthy to succeed German scholar D. Barnstorff's *A Key to Shakespeare's Sonnets* (1860), which argues that Master W. H., to whom Thomas Thorpe dedicated the 1609 Quarto volume, stands for "William Himself." Father to a line of esoteric/allegorical interpretations, Barnstorff himself is worthy successor to George Chalmers, who argued in 1797 that all the Sonnets, even those directed to "a lovely boy," are in fact addressed to Queen Elizabeth.

Reading the history of the Sonnets' reception can be the occasion of easy laughs, and sometimes disgust, at the blindness of our predecessors. Yet as Vendler also notes, "Earlier methods of reading the *Sonnets*, on display in the *Variorum* and elsewhere, of course teach us a philosophical humility before our own" ("Reading" 39). This same point is made more emphatically—and perhaps more genuinely—by Brian Vickers in volume 6 of *Shakespeare: The Critical Heritage.* In asking that we not judge eighteenth-century critics too harshly for their dislike of Shakespeare's Sonnets and of the sonnet form, he writes:

> In studying the reception of Shakespeare, or of any other major writer, over a long historical period the modern reader is involved in

a constant series of adjustments and comparisons. We work with a triangle, consisting of Shakespeare in his age, the eighteenth century critics in theirs, and ourselves in our own: which, no less than the others, has a critical and aesthetic system that is inherited, consciously or not, and shaped by many influences. We can juxtapose our understanding of Shakespeare with the eighteenth century's understanding of him, and with our understanding of them. This triple process of comparative interpretation ought to make us see that our position is time-bound, and culture-bound, ought to prevent us from feeling any easy sense of superiority. Another age will arise that may look at our Shakespeare criticism with reactions ranging from indulgent apology to disbelief and contempt. . . . We will not be led into a complacent sense of progress. (41-42)

Becoming aware of the cultural, intellectual, and historical "influences" that have shaped responses to the Sonnets in the past should lead us to a greater understanding of how comparable factors shape our changing responses to the Sonnets today.

THE 1609 QUARTO

The first thing to learn about the Sonnets—the first of the ironies, one might call it—is that despite the vast quantity of Sonnets criticism, there is very little agreement about these poems, especially about the circumstances of their composition and first publication as a collection. This is a major theme of the second volume of Hyder Rollins's magisterial 1944 *Variorum* and of Stephen Booth's masterpiece of sardonic brevity, his appendix to his 1977 edition of the Sonnets titled "Facts and Theories." G. Blakemore Evans's 1996 New Cambridge edition offers a similar listing of the key, and as yet unresolved, issues. Most editions of the Sonnets over the last century, in fact, offer detailed discussions of "the problems."

   Scholars have been—and remain—deeply divided on a number of issues regarding the Quarto volume published by Thomas Thorpe in 1609; all subsequent texts of the Sonnets as a collection ultimately derive from this edition, also known as "Q."[3] And virtually every contemporary theory about these poems is based either directly or indirectly on one or more intensely contested assumptions about this publication. In *The Fickle Glass: A Study of Shakespeare's Sonnets*, Paul Ramsey describes the interconnectedness of the various issues:

"The problems of the sonnets may not be entirely solvable; but they cannot be evaded. They loop and twist into each other, and to tug at one is to tighten others. Nor can one bypass the problems to come at aesthetic judgment. Aesthetic judgments about the sonnets necessarily presume and imply stated or unstated, lucky or dubious, judgments about the problems" (3).

The 1609 Quarto consists of 154 consecutively numbered sonnets, followed by *A Lover's Complaint*. All but three sonnets in the collection are in the Shakespearean form (also known as the English form introduced in England by Henry Howard, the Earl of Surrey, early in the sixteenth century) of fourteen lines of iambic pentameter organized into three quatrains and a final couplet, all with the same rhyme scheme of abab cdcd efef gg. The exceptions are sonnet 99, which has fifteen lines; sonnet 126, which has twelve lines consisting of six rhymed couplets; and sonnet 145, which is in iambic tetrameter. The issues that arise from Q 1609 can be listed briefly:

1. AUTHENTICITY

The vast majority of commentators have accepted Shakespeare's authorship, even though no autograph manuscript has survived (a situation comparable to virtually all the plays and other poems). Some accept that the 1609 Quarto is primarily Shakespeare's, but have questioned specific sonnets in the collection, usually on aesthetic grounds, though as Booth observes, which sonnets get challenged has varied from disintegrationist to disintegrationist (most often questioned are the last two sonnets, 153 and 154, followed closely by 145) (*Sonnets* 545); J. M. Robertson, for example, rejected as many as one-third of the poems, largely on the grounds that they are inferior to others in the collection and are therefore unworthy of their author (271); Robertson also argued, as have many others, that *A Lover's Complaint* was not authored by Shakespeare (257). As Hyder Rollins details in volume 2 of the *Variorum*, some commentators have speculated that other personages such as Raleigh, Sidney, the first and second Earls of Essex, "Anne Whateley," Elizabeth Vernon, and the Earl of Pembroke wrote all or some of the Sonnets (2: 45-46). Needless to say, those who reject Shakespeare as author of the plays also reject his authorship of the Sonnets, instead favoring their own candidates (usually Francis Bacon or the Earl of Oxford, Edward de Vere).

Those who accept Shakespeare's authorship base their opinion on the following evidence: (1) obviously, Shakespeare's name on the title page (with the implication of authorship in the title *Shake-speares Sonnets*; see Figure 2 in this volume), as well as the entry in the Stationers' Register on May 20, 1609, by publisher Thomas Thorpe of "a Booke called Shakespeares *sonnettes*"; (2) the fact that there is no evidence Shakespeare protested the attribution or tried to suppress the publication when the work appeared in print; (3) we know Shakespeare was writing sonnets because in 1598 Francis Meres wrote the following praise in *Palladis Tamia*: "the sweet witty soul of *Ovid* lives in Mellifluous & hony-tongued *Shakespeare, witnes his *Venus* and *Adonis*, his *Lucrece*, his sugred Sonnets among his private friends, &c.*"; (4) the presence of versions of sonnets 138 and 144 along with poems from *Love's Labor's Lost* in the first edition of *The Passionate Pilgrim* (see below); (5) parallels in diction, imagery, thought, and style with other works (both dramatic and nondramatic) assumed to be by Shakespeare; and (6) the presence of sonnets, also in the English form, in plays known to be by Shakespeare, for example, *Love's Labor's Lost, Romeo and Juliet, Henry V*, and *All's Well That Ends Well*.

2. DATE OF COMPOSITION

Commentators have long been at odds on this issue, some favoring a date as early as the mid-1580s to the early-to-mid-1590s (when the sonnet-writing vogue was at its height), others favoring a later starting point, from the last years of the 1590s to the obvious *terminus ad quem* of 1609. At least some sonnets were written by 1599, since two were published that year in *The Passionate Pilgrim*, an unauthorized volume attributed to Shakespeare (even though most of the contents were by other authors), published by William Jaggard.[4] Francis Meres's reference in *Palladis Tamia* to "Shakespeares sugred Sonnets among his private friends" may or may not refer to the poems in the 1609 Quarto (most scholars think it does refer to at least some of them). If Meres is referring to sonnets that would later be included in Thorpe's collection, then at least some of the Sonnets had to have been written by 1598. As Rollins observes, theories about date of composition have often been proposed to support specific candidates for the identity of the young male friend, rival poet(s), and dark lady on the assumption that the Sonnets are autobiographical (2: 57). Those favoring Henry Wriothesley, the third Earl of Southampton, as the young friend, for example, have traditionally argued for a date in the early to mid-1590s, while those favoring William Herbert, the third Earl of Pembroke, have tended to posit a date in the late 1590s to early 1600s, since Herbert was not born until 1580 and probably did not move to London until 1598. Some commentators have discovered topical references to historical events in individual sonnets, the most often cited being sonnet 107; unfortunately, scholars disagree about which events, if any, this sonnet might refer to; the line "The mortal moon hath her eclipse endured" has been interpreted by some to allude to the death of Queen Elizabeth in 1603, by others to the defeat of the Spanish Armada in 1588. Yet another possibility is that the line alludes to the Queen's surviving her grand climacteric when she reached the age of sixty-three in 1596 (Rollins 1: 264, 267f., 269).

Studies based on internal evidence have supported theories for both early and late dating; scholars have found strong verbal parallels both with *Love's Labor's Lost* and *Venus and Adonis*, on the one hand, and with *King Lear* and *Timon of Athens* on the other, and with *All's Well That Ends Well* in between. Over the last decade, something like a consensus has emerged that Shakespeare was writing, or at least revising, sonnets up to the time of publication in 1609. Thus, a computer-assisted study by A. Kent Hieatt, Charles W. Hieatt, and Anne Lake Prescott of rare word occurrences in the Sonnets and in plays whose dates are presumed to be known concludes that Shakespeare composed sonnets 1-60 in the first five years of the 1590s and then revised many of them after the turn of the century; sonnets 61-103, they find, were also composed early, but received "little or no revision"; sonnets 104-126 were probably composed around 1600; and sonnets 127-154 were written in the first half of the 1590s, but were probably not revised (92-93). In his examination of rare word occurrences and "lexical influence," meanwhile, Donald Foster has concluded that "most of the sonnets were written later than 1598" and completed by 1608 ("Reconstructing" 27). While both of these recent studies conclude that Shakespeare was working on at least some of the Sonnets into the 1600s, they reach very different conclusions about the initial date of composition for most of these poems. In other words, the issue is still far from settled (see also Evans 113).

3. AUTHORIZATION AND ORDER

There is no direct evidence that Shakespeare authorized the 1609 Quarto, or even that he arranged the poems to form a single collection. For most of the Sonnets' critical history, theorists assumed (and some still do) that the publication was not authorized and that Thomas Thorpe pirated the manuscript, perhaps, but not necessarily, a manuscript that Shakespeare had arranged into a unified collection. They have assumed lack of authorization for a variety of reasons, the most important being the potentially embarrassing story many believe the Sonnets tell, as well as the apparent lack of narrative coherence in the 1609 ordering (of course, not everyone agrees that the order lacks coherence). In addition, some scholars take Francis Meres's statement in *Palladis Tamia* to indicate that Shakespeare circulated sonnets in manuscript—probably singly or in small groups—"among his private friends"; thus, they claim, these poems were never intended to be collected and published in a single volume. They observe as well the lack of an author's dedication (such as Shakespeare provided for the publication of *Venus and Adonis* and *The Rape of Lucrece*) or prefatory letter to the reader. Skeptics also point to the high number of obvious spelling and punctuation errors as proof that Shakespeare did not authorize the 1609 Quarto, and even most critics who believe the publication may have been authorized assume such errors prove that Shakespeare took no part in seeing the manuscript through the printing process.[5]

A serious challenge to received opinion was issued in 1983, however, by Katherine Duncan-Jones in her essay "Was the 1609 *Shake-speares Sonnets* Really Unauthorized?" Duncan-Jones boldly argues that the Quarto was authorized; she speculates that Shakespeare sold the collection to Thorpe when the theaters were closed because of the plague in 1609. She bases her views on the following evidence: (1) far from being the "disreputable pirate" claimed by scores of commentators (including Rollins), Thomas Thorpe was a respected publisher, responsible for printing, among other important works, Ben Jonson's *Sejanus* and *Volpone*; (2) far from seeming incoherent, the collection—along with *A Lover's Complaint*—closely resembles several other sonnet collections published in the 1590s, collections that also often end with a narrative complaint. Furthermore, she argues, "Within the 1609 text many elements of thematic and structural coherence are to be found which commentators have failed to recognize." For example, she observes that the Sonnets fall into "recognizable numerological units" (155).[6] Such structural evidence would seem to refute arguments that Q is an unauthorized, random miscellany. Although Duncan-Jones has persuaded a number of scholars to rethink the issue of authorization, she has not succeeded with everyone. Arthur Marotti takes issue with Duncan-Jones's hypothesis on "several key points"; among other things, he notes that her theory "ignores the facts that the dramatist was undoubtedly more prosperous in 1609 than he was in 1592-94, that the publisher's payment for the text would not have been very great, and that there is no evidence in the presentation of the text that the author was appealing to a patron for economic assistance" ("Sonnets as Property" 171 n. 34). Heather Dubrow has also declared herself a skeptic on the question of Q's authority. The point here, again, is not to take sides but to show that the issue is still unresolved, and is likely to remain so unless the unlikely occurs and new evidence comes to light.

The issue of authorization has obvious relevance to order, as well as to smaller matters of editing, like the extent to which spelling and punctuation in the Quarto can or should be trusted. If it could be demonstrated that the 1609 Quarto was authorized, the order of sonnets—and much else—could also be confirmed. That confirmation, for example, might support Edmond Malone's 1780 division of the Sonnets into two subsequences, the first 126 directed to a young man, the last 28 to or about a dark lady. If, on the other hand, Q was not authorized by Shakespeare, "manifestly there can be no assurance that it represents with any degree of accuracy his own classification of the poems. Yet exactly the opposite assumption—that we have the sonnets printed entirely or with unimportant variations in the sequence Sh[akespeare] himself sponsored—underlies the arguments of most defenders of the existing order" (Rollins 2: 75). Not all of these defenders of the order, of course, argue that Shakespeare authorized the publication; some speculate that Thorpe obtained a manuscript that had been previously arranged by Shakespeare.

Among those who do not trust that the order of Q reflects Shakespeare's design, there have been many attempts to rearrange the Sonnets to provide them with greater narrative or thematic coherence, the most recent by J. W. Lever (1956), Brents Stirling (1968), and John Padel (1981); none has been widely accepted by Sonnets scholars, except, of course, by those who have done the rearranging. The 1609 order has been accepted by most scholars, often if only by default and for ease of reference. In recent years, the order has been supported by John Kerrigan and Katherine Duncan-Jones, as we would expect since both believe the Quarto to have been authorized, or at least shaped by the author for publication. In his study *Such Is My Love*, Joseph Pequigney offers a spirited defense of the narrative coherence of Q. In an essay reprinted in this volume, however, Heather Dubrow questions both the authority and order of the Quarto, as well as Malone's division of the Quarto into two subsequences. Once again, there is no consensus.

4. THORPE'S DEDICATION

The following dedication appears at the front of the 1609 Quarto, after the title page (see also Figure 3 in this volume):

TO.THE.ONLIE.BEGETTER.OF.

THESE.INSVING.SONNETS.

MR.W.H. ALL.HAPPINESSE.

AND.THAT.ETERNITIE.

PROMISED.

BY.

OVR.EVER-LIVING.POET.

WISHETH.

THE.WELL-WISHING.

ADVENTURER.IN.

SETTING.

FORTH.

T.T.

Rollins remarks that "practically every word, every letter and point, of the dedication have caused acrimonious disputes" (2: 166). The chief issues in regard to Thorpe's dedication are the meaning of "ONLIE.BEGETTER" and the identity of "MR.W.H."; the two issues are almost certainly related. Those who believe "ONLIE.BEGETTER" means "inspirer" also usually assume that "MR.W.H." refers to the young man addressed in many of the Sonnets. As we shall see below, a number of candidates with those initials—or with those initials reversed—have been proposed. A different reading of "ONLIE.BEGETTER" as "procurer" was first proposed by George Chalmers in 1799; with this reading, "MR.W.H." indicates the initials

of the person who obtained the manuscript for Thorpe. Again, a number
of different candidates have been proposed: William Hall, a London
stationer and possible friend of Thorpe's (perhaps the dedication's
"W.H. ALL." is a misprint for "W. HALL."); William Hathaway,
Shakespeare's brother-in-law; and William Hervey, Southampton's
stepfather. Yet another guess, first conceived by A. E. Brae in 1869 and
reported by C. M. Ingleby in 1873, and then revived in the twentieth
century by J. M. Nosworthy (1963) and Donald Foster (1987), is that
"ONLIE.BEGETTER" refers to Shakespeare and that "MR.W.H." is a
misprint for "MR.W.SH." or "MR.W.S."[7]

5. LYRIC VERSUS NARRATIVE VERSUS DRAMATIC

Critics have long disagreed about whether or not the Sonnets tell a
coherent, continuous story (Pequigney, *Such Is My Love* and "Sonnets
71-74"; Crosman); or if in fact they should be read simply as lyric
poems, "internalized meditations unconnected to a narrative line"
(Dubrow "Incertainties"); or if at least some sonnets are dramatic
(Hunter) or imply immediate real life or dramatic situations (Barber;
Schalkwyk). In other words, scholarly opinions vary about whether
these poems should be read as a poetic novel, as a series of dramatic
monologues, as letters, as journal entries, as silent meditations, or as
disparate, unrelated groups of related sonnets in a poetic miscellany.

The great majority of readers, even those who resist reading the
Sonnets as a narrative, agree to the presence of the following characters
and situations in the sequence: the poet-speaker; a beautiful, younger
male friend whom the poet first urges to marry and to beget children
(sonnets 1-17), and whom he later promises to immortalize in his verse;
a "rival poet" (or poets) who competes for the young man's affections,
and perhaps for his patronage as well (sonnets 78-86); and a "dark
lady," the poet-speaker's mistress, who the speaker suspects may also
be having an affair with the young male friend (sonnets 40-42, 133,
134, 144, and perhaps others as well). Malone's division of the Sonnets
into two subsequences—the first 126 written to the young friend, the
last 28 to or about the dark lady—has been accepted by most
commentators, but has also frequently been challenged, most recently
by Heather Dubrow, who notes that most of the sonnets in both
subsequences do not have gendered pronouns that would allow us to
determine the addressee ("Incertainties"; *Echoes of Desire* 122-23; see
also Robertson 258). On the other hand, defending the logic of

Malone's division, Booth writes that "[a]lthough the sex of the beloved is unspecified in most of the sonnets, all those that are specifically and exclusively addressed to a man precede [Sonnet 126] in the Q order, and all those specifically and exclusively addressed to a woman follow it" (*Sonnets* 430).

Readers who discern a continuous narrative can be further subdivided according to their stands on various issues. For example, there is considerable difference of opinion about the social class of the fair youth: whether he is an aristocrat or is simply of a slightly higher social class than, or the same social class as, the poet.[8] Deep fault lines also separate readers of the Sonnets on the issue of the kind of love that apparently exists between the two men. Are these poems reflections of the Renaissance cult of male friendship, as Malone and legions of scholars since have maintained? Are they, that is, celebrations of Neoplatonic, nonsexual affection? Or are the sonnets to the young friend, in fact, the poetic record of homoerotic attraction, or even of a consummated homosexual relationship? As we shall see, thinking about these sexual issues has shaped, and in many instances deformed, criticism of the Sonnets for at least the past two hundred years.[9]

The disagreements over the issues of social class, patronage, and sexuality are best illustrated in the contrast between recent work on the Sonnets by Arthur F. Marotti and Joseph Pequigney. Marotti situates the Sonnets in the context of English Renaissance manuscript culture at a time of transition to print culture; he maintains that the poems were initially written to an aristocratic patron and that their language and imagery of courtly love should be read as conventional rather than as genuinely amorous ("Love Is Not Love"). In *Such Is My Love*, however, Pequigney insists that there is no evidence to support the idea that the young friend is an aristocratic patron, or a patron of any kind; for him the language of amorous affection serves the cause of sexual courtship at first and later reflects coded references to a consummated sexual relationship (12). Before either Marotti or Pequigney published their studies, Booth nicely captured the difficulty of interpretation: "the widespread implication that the speaker is addressing a man of high rank" is "an implication that could just as well derive from the courtly love tradition of addressing beloved ladies as if they were feudal lords" (*Sonnets* 547). In other words, Booth suggests, the use of a trope common to the discourses of courtly love and of English Renaissance patronage neither confirms nor disproves a sexual or a patronage relationship, or some combination of the two.

Regarding the so-called "dark lady," there has been disagreement about exactly how dark a lady she is: whether a Caucasian brunette with dark complexion, or a woman of African or West Indian descent (see Marvin Hunt's essay in this volume). Although no one questions the affair between poet and dark lady, furthermore, critics are not unanimous about whether the young friend has a sexual relationship with her as well (Pequigney thinks not; see *Such Is My Love* 147, 153-54).

6. RELATION TO SHAKESPEARE'S LIFE

More has been written on this issue than on any other related to the Sonnets. Those who believe the Sonnets are autobiographical base their view on the assumption that these are the only poems Shakespeare wrote in first person, as well as on the fact that the poet-speaker says his name is "Will," puns many times upon that name ("Will" may also be the name of the young friend and perhaps of the dark lady's husband as well), and perhaps alludes to Shakespeare's profession as an actor-dramatist in sonnets 110 and 111. Furthermore, under the influence of the Romantic aesthetic that for a poem to be good it must also be sincere, many readers have concluded that only genuine feeling based in actual life experiences could produce such powerful rhymes (see Rosmarin). Finally, proponents of the so-called "personal theory" (i.e., the Sonnets as autobiography) maintain that if Shakespeare had wanted to invent a story, he would have done a much better job of telling it. The allusions to events so inadequately rendered in the sequence suggest to these readers an origin in real-life experience; Shakespeare, they argue, must have been writing to people who participated in or at least knew about such events and who therefore did not need them to be explained. To this last argument, A. C. Bradley adds that "No capable poet, much less a Shakespeare, intending to produce a merely 'dramatic' series of poems, would dream of inventing a story like that of these sonnets, or, even if he did, of treating it as they treat it. The story is very odd and unattractive" (331).

Proponents of the personal theory disagree among themselves about the identities of the friend, the rival poet(s), and dark lady. The main theories have been summarized by a number of commentators, from Edward Dowden to R. M. Alden to J. M. Robertson to Hyder Rollins to Samuel Schoenbaum to Kenneth Muir, and more will be said about the major candidates later in this introduction.

A number of readers have also lined up with great certainty against the personal theory. Often these deniers are motivated by a desire to protect Shakespeare's reputation by divorcing Shakespeare from the desires and actions of the speaker-poet, though clearly many skeptics are also unpersuaded by the evidence offered to support specific historical identifications of the rest of the dramatis personae. The failure of scholars to agree on even a single identification of the friend, dark lady, or rival poet(s) has become for some an indication that these poems are not about real people and situations. Even readers who believe that the Sonnets are autobiographical disagree about the extent to which these poems reflect the details of Shakespeare's life. Rollins quotes Robert Bell (1855) with approval: "All poetry is auto-biographical. But the particle of actual life out of which verse is wrought may be, and almost always is, wholly incommensurate to the emotion depicted, and remote from the forms into which it is ultimately shaped" (2: 139).

In summary, then, despite all that has been written about the 1609 Quarto and more generally, about the Sonnets, in many ways we are still very much in the dark. "After nearly two hundred years of speculation and scholarship," writes Donald Foster,

> we have made remarkably little progress toward uncovering the "true story" behind Shakespeare's *Sonnets*, if indeed there is a story to be uncovered. The poems tease us with what appear to be references to real persons, persons who knew the man, Shakespeare, much better than we. Yet we still have no plausible candidates for the role of the dark lady (or ladies), or of the rival poet (or poets), or of the speaker's young friend (or friends). We do not know whether all the sonnets are to be taken as spoken by a single speaker or whether the speaker in each poem is Shakespeare, a fictional lover, or a man. We do not know that the "sugred Sonnets" mentioned by Francis Meres in 1598 . . . are those published in the Quarto, whether we have all the sonnets written by Shakespeare, whether they are all by Shakespeare, whether they are arranged as Shakespeare wished, or when any one of them was written. We do not even know that William Shakespeare wrote a single one of these poems, however likely that surmise may be. ("Master W. H." 51)

BENSON'S 1640 EDITION

Perhaps the second great irony about the huge volume of criticism on the Sonnets is that these poems were virtually ignored for their first 170 years of existence. No second edition of the 1609 Quarto appeared during Shakespeare's lifetime, or for that matter, during the entire time Thorpe was active as a publisher until 1625; thirteen copies of Q have survived. Furthermore, there are fewer allusions to the Sonnets in the seventeenth century than to any other work by Shakespeare, with the exception of *A Lover's Complaint* and minor poems like "The Phoenix and the Turtle." By contrast, *Venus and Adonis* and *The Rape of Lucrece* enjoyed enormous popularity during this time, and both works went through several editions during the seventeenth century. Various explanations have been offered as to why the 1609 Quarto did not achieve more initial success. The most dramatic theory, offered by John Dover Wilson and others, is that the "unauthorized" volume was suppressed by Shakespeare, with the help of a powerful friend (in Dover Wilson's theory, that friend is William Herbert, the Earl of Pembroke), presumably because of the embarrassing true-life story the Sonnets presumably reveal (25).[10]

Yet there is no factual evidence to support the suppression theory. More likely is the explanation that by 1609 the sonnet vogue of the early-to-mid-1590s had long since passed and that therefore interest in sonnets had diminished. Marotti also reminds us of how "ephemeral" publications like Thorpe's were; thirteen extant copies is actually "an unusually large number" for a "poetical pamphlet" of this kind ("Sonnets as Property" 157).[11] We should remember as well that Shakespeare's name then, though clearly growing in importance (or publishers would not have placed it on title pages), did not have anything like the cultural valence it has enjoyed for the last two centuries. Shakespeare did not begin to assume his dominance of the English Renaissance literary-critical field for another hundred years after the publication of Q, and the Sonnets did not begin to rise in the public's estimation, according to Gary Taylor, until the late eighteenth century as "a by-product of the rise of Milton and Spenser" and "the steady expansion, in both popular interest and cultural respectability, of biography and autobiography and of literary biography in particular" (*Reinventing* 155).

In any case, commentators also attribute the silence about the Sonnets during the later seventeenth century and through much of the eighteenth to the fact that most readers did not have access to these poems in their "original" (that is, 1609) form. Instead, if they read Shakespeare's Sonnets at all, it was most probably in John Benson's 1640 edition *Poems: Written by Wil. Shake-speare. Gent* or in an edition based on Benson's collection, a form that would not encourage biographical speculation, much less, in the opinion of many, aesthetic appreciation.[12] Through most of its literary history, Benson's edition has been condemned as a piratical desecration. Benson reprinted all but eight of the 154 sonnets, but in a jumbled order, intermingled with "The Phoenix and the Turtle," *A Lover's Complaint*, and the entire 1612 *Passionate Pilgrim* (most of which is not by Shakespeare), and other works by numerous poets, including Herrick, Jonson, Beaumont, and Milton. In addition, Benson sometimes combined two, three, four, or five sonnets into a single poem to which he affixed a title. Perhaps the most serious charge of all against Benson is that he also made "verbal changes designed to make the verses apply to a woman instead of a man" (Rollins 2: 20).

Benson provided the following preface to his collection:

To the Reader:

I Here presume (under favour) to present to your view, some excellent and sweetely composed Poems, of Master William Shakespeare, Which in themselves appeare of the same purity, the Authour himselfe then living avouched; they had not the fortune by reason of their Infancie in his death, to have the due accomodatio[n] of proportionable glory, with the rest of his everliving Workes, yet the lines of themselves will afford you a more authentick approbation than my assurance any way can, to invite your allowance, in your perusall you shall finde them Seren, cleere and eligantly plaine, such gentle straines as shall recreate and not perplexe your braine, no intricate or cloudy stuffe to puzzell intellect, but perfect eloquence; such as will raise your admiration to his praise: this assurance I know will not differ from your acknowledgement. And certaine I am, my opinion will be seconded by the sufficiency of these ensuing Lines; I have beene somewhat solicitus to bring this forth to the perfect view of all men; and in so doing, glad to be serviceable for the continuance of glory to the deserved Author in these his Poems.

I. B.

In the statement above, Benson is clearly "trying . . . to conceal his thievery," Rollins pronounces (2: 25); according to W. G. Ingram and Theodore Redpath, Benson here displays "the cool impudence to pretend that he was publishing the poems by Shakespeare for the first time"; he is "willing to resort to deceit, and, no less, to misdescription" (xx). This view of Benson and his 1640 edition is shared by most commentators, among them Alden, Dover Wilson, and most recently, Duncan-Jones.

Yet, just as Thorpe has recently been defended against the charge of piracy, so has Benson.[13] While not denying that Benson based his text of the Sonnets on Thorpe's edition without acknowledgment, for example, Marotti contends that if we examine what Benson did "in the context of the more liberal practices of the early stages of the print era," we would see that there was nothing illegal, or even unusual, about Benson's rearrangement: "Not only was he well within his rights as a publisher, but also he was exercising the kind of creative control over acquired texts that collectors, editors, and printers had in this period" ("Sonnets as Property" 158). Benson's letter to the reader, Marotti asserts, reveals not an attempt to deceive the public but rather Benson's desire to offer "his volume as the completion of *The Complete Works of William Shakespeare*, as it were. Despite what critics have assumed, he did not actually say that the *Sonnets* had never been published—after all, Thorpe's quarto was evidently one of his copy-texts—but that they lacked the 'due accommodatio[n] of proportionable glory, with the rest of his everliving Workes,' that is they were not in print in a format that was suitable for preserving the poems for succeeding generations" ("Sonnets as Property" 159).

Even the claim that Benson made verbal changes to conceal that many of the sonnets were addressed to a male beloved has been challenged by a number of scholars (including J. B. Leishman and Dover Wilson), most recently by Margreta de Grazia in "The Scandal of Shakespeare's Sonnets," an essay reprinted in this collection. Thus, de Grazia writes:

> Benson did not attempt to convert a male beloved to a female. To begin with, the number of his alterations has been greatly exaggerated. Of the seventy-five titles Benson assigned to Shakespeare's Sonnets, only three of them direct sonnets from the first group of the 1609 Quarto (sonnets 1-126) to a woman. Furthermore, because none of the sonnets in question specifies the

gender of the beloved, Benson had no reason to believe a male addressee was intended. As for the pronominal changes, Rollins himself within nine pages of his own commentary multiplies the number of sonnets 'with verbal changes designed to make the verses apply to a woman instead of a man' from 'some' to '*many*'. Rollins gives three examples as if there were countless others, but three is all there are and those three appear to have been made to avoid solecism rather than homoeroticism.

De Grazia claims that Benson's edition, rather than an attempt to hide homoeroticism, "would appear to present the first editorial and critical response to the need for a frame of reference for the Sonnets"; Benson saw—or at least presents—the poems as self-contained units, with each poem contributing to "an expansive, generalized understanding of love" ("Locating" 441).

What is most unsettling about the revisionism of Marotti, de Grazia, and others is that it destabilizes the notion that Benson distorted Shakespeare's text (presumed to be the 1609 Quarto). What Marotti is really contending is that "[t]here is *no* text of the *Sonnets*, in either manuscript or print, that can be shown to represent the ideal of old-fashioned textual critics, the 'author's final intentions'"; freeing criticism of this delusion, he asserts, finally allows us "to perceive in the poems the kind of fascinating textual instability that appeals to a postmodern sensibility" ("Sonnets as Property" 165). Just as not everyone has been convinced by Duncan-Jones's arguments that Shakespeare authorized the 1609 Quarto (Marotti, of course, is one of the important dissenters), it is hardly surprising that Duncan-Jones has not been persuaded by revisionist arguments regarding Benson's integrity. In her opinion, "Benson's edition was even more outrageously piratical and misleading than Jaggard's 1612 *Passionate Pilgrim*, whose material it incorporated. . . . For well over a century, Benson succeeded in muddying the textual waters. It was his edition that was read and edited, almost exclusively, until the superb work of Malone in 1780" (*Sonnets* 42-43).

EDMOND MALONE AND THE BIOGRAPHICAL READERS

In virtually all accounts of the reception history of the Sonnets, Edmond Malone holds pride of place as this collection's most important editor. It was Malone's edition of the Sonnets in 1780 as part

of the *Supplement* to the edition of the plays published in 1778 by
Samuel Johnson and George Steevens, as well as Malone's 1790
edition, that firmly established the 1609 Quarto not only as the basis of
Benson's text, but also as the basis for all important future editions of
the Sonnets. Although the 1609 Quarto had been reprinted in 1711 and
1766, Malone's edition was the first to provide Q with textual notes
and critical commentary, thus for the first time bringing the Sonnets
into the Shakespearean canon.[14] According to Rollins, "No nineteenth-
century or twentieth-century editor has done textual work at all
comparable in importance to Malone's; few have surpassed him as an
annotator; and dozens have taken credit for details borrowed from him
without acknowledgment. Truly, one knows not whether to marvel
more that he in that misty time could see so clearly, or that we in this
supposedly clear age walk so stumblingly after him. He will be praised
of ages yet to come" (2: 39).

Malone's editing of the Sonnets coincided with his work on a life
of Shakespeare and with the wave of bardolatry that had commenced
with the Stratford Jubilee of 1769. Of crucial importance, according to
Margreta de Grazia, was Malone's assumption that the "I" of the
Sonnets and Shakespeare were "one and the same." In "The Scandal of
Shakespeare's Sonnets," de Grazia writes: "Malone's driving project of
identifying the experience of the Sonnets with Shakespeare's own is
evident in all his major editorial interventions. Unlike Benson who
expanded their contents to accommodate the experience of all lovers by
giving them generic titles, Malone limited them so that they applied
exclusively to Shakespeare." But the act of identifying Shakespeare
with the "I" of the Sonnets also created a serious dilemma; it threatened
to implicate Shakespeare in transgressive acts and desires: perjury,
adultery, homosexuality, miscegenation. As Rollins explained long
before de Grazia, "One objection to any strict personal interpretation of
the sonnets is that Sh[akespeare]'s character and morals come off
badly—to the distress of many hero-worshipers" (2: 136). Responses to
this dilemma, as we shall see, have greatly affected interpretation of the
Sonnets for the last two centuries.

The textual notes in Malone's 1780 and 1790 editions, as well as in
the edition of 1821 completed by Boswell, take the form of frequent
exchanges between Malone and George Steevens, whom Malone had
invited to contribute; Steevens had himself edited the Sonnets in 1766,
though without notes or commentary. In the sometimes acerbic
dialogue between the two editors, some of the faultlines that would

divide later critics of the Sonnets begin to appear. Like Malone, Steevens had based his edition on the 1609 Quarto, but unlike Malone, Steevens was not an admirer of these poems. His objections were both aesthetic and moral, and strong objections they were indeed. Of the sonnet form, for instance, he has the following harsh words:

> A Sonnet was surely the contrivance of some literary Procrustes. The single thought of which it is to consist, however luxuriant, must be cramped within fourteen verses, or, however scanty, must be spun out into the same number. On a chain of certain links the existence of this metrical whim depends; and its reception is secure as soon as admirers of it have counted their expected and statutable proportion of rhimes. . . . That a few of these trifles deserving a better character may be found, I shall not venture to deny; for chance co-operating with art and genius will occasionally produce wonders. (Malone *Supplement* 1: 682)

And of Shakespeare's particular artistry his judgment is in fact even harsher; for example, he complains of "laboured perplexities of language, and . . . studied deformities of style" in sonnet 30 (Malone *Supplement* 1: 606), and later he remarks, "Perhaps indeed, quaintness, obscurity, and tautology, are to be regarded as the constituent parts of this exotick species of composition. But, in whatever the excellence of it may consist, I profess I am one of those who should have wished it to have expired in the country where it was born" (Malone *Supplement* 1: 682).

But perhaps Steevens's harshest objections are moral—he cannot condone the idea that many of these love poems are addressed to a man. Of the phrase "the master-mistress of my passions" in sonnet 20, he writes: "It is impossible to read this fulsome panegyrick, addressed to a male object, without an equal mixture of disgust and indignation" (Malone *Supplement* 1: 596). So strong was Steevens's dislike of the Sonnets (and of *Venus and Adonis*, incidentally), that he chose not to include them in his 1793 edition of *The Plays of William Shakespeare*. In his preface he states:

> We have not reprinted the *Sonnets*, &c. of Shakespeare, because the strongest act of Parliament that could be framed, would fail to compel readers into their service; notwithstanding these miscellaneous Poems have derived every possible advantage from the

literature and judgement of their only intelligent editor, Mr. Malone,
whose implements of criticism, like the ivory rake and golden spade
of Prudentius, are on this occasion disgraced by the objects of their
culture.—Had Shakespeare produced no other works than these, his
name would have reached us with as little celebrity as time has
conferred on that of Thomas Watson, an older and much more
elegant sonneteer. (103)

Though most commentators in the nineteenth century would have a
much higher opinion of these poems and would condemn Steevens for
his, Steevens was by no means the last to express such strong moral
revulsion. Thus, half a century later Henry Hallam would write:
"Notwithstanding the frequent beauties of these sonnets, the pleasure of
their perusal is greatly diminished by these circumstances; and it is
impossible not to wish that Shakespeare had never written them. There
is a weakness and folly in all excessive and misplaced affection, which
is not redeemed by the touches of nobler sentiments that abound in this
long series of sonnets" (264; see also William Kerrigan).

Malone's aesthetic defense of the Sonnets, his justification for
providing them a full critical apparatus and thus incorporating them
into the Shakespearean canon, was lukewarm. "I do not feel any great
propensity to stand forth as the champion of these compositions," he
wrote in reply to Steevens. "However, as it appears to me that they
have been somewhat under-rated, I think it incumbent on me to do
them that justice to which they seem entitled" (*Supplement* 1: 684). In a
later paragraph he writes:

When they are described as a mass of affectation, pedantry,
circumlocution, and nonsense, the picture appears to me overcharged.
Their great defects seem to be a want of variety, and the majority of
them not being directed to a female, to whom alone such ardent
expressions of esteem could with propriety be addressed. It cannot be
denied too that they contain some far-fetched conceits; but are our
author's plays entirely free from them? Many of the thoughts that
occur in his dramatick productions, are found here likewise; as may
appear from the numerous parallels that have been cited from his
dramas, chiefly for the purpose of authenticating these poems. Had
they therefore no other merit, they are entitled to our attention, as
often illustrating obscure passages in his.

> I do not perceive that the versification of these pieces is less smooth and harmonious than that of Shakespeare's other compositions. Though many of them are not so simple and clear as they ought to be, yet some of them are written with perspicuity and energy. A few have been already pointed out as deserving this character; and many beautiful lines, scattered through these poems, will, it is supposed, strike every reader who is not determined to allow no praise to any species of poetry except blank verse or heroick couplets. (*Supplement* 1: 684-85)

Responding to Steevens's comments about the phrase "master-mistress" in sonnet 20, Malone offers the following explanation in his 1790 edition:

> Some part of this indignation might perhaps have been abated if it had been considered that such addresses to men, however indelicate, were customary in our authour's time, and neither imported criminality, nor were esteemed indecorous.... To regulate our judgment of Shakespeare's poems by the modes of modern times is surely as unreasonable as to try his plays by the rules of Aristotle.
>
> *Master-mistress* does not mean *man*-mistress, but *sovereign* mistress. (10: 207)

Malone's explanation has satisfied thousands, perhaps millions, of later students of the Sonnets, many perhaps reluctant to think that the Bard's poems express passionate affection for a beautiful young man. Indeed, a version of Malone's explanation—that the loverly language of the sonnets addressed to the male friend may reflect the Neoplatonic (i.e., nonsexual) Renaissance cult of male friendship—appears in David Bevington's 1980 edition of the complete works, which is quoted in Anthony Hecht's introduction to the New Cambridge edition of the Sonnets (Bevington 1582; Hecht 18).[15] But Malone's explanation has not seemed plausible to everyone; Steevens is only the first of many who have espied more than Neoplatonic friendship.

Malone's inference of autobiography led directly to Wordsworth's insistence in 1815 that in the Sonnets "Shakespeare expresses his feelings in his own person" ("Essay") and to his famous claim in his sonnet "Scorn Not the Sonnet" (1827) that "with this key, / Shakespeare unlocked his heart" (2-3). Meanwhile, in Germany the same biographical assumptions were popularized by the von Schlegel brothers, August Wilhelm in 1796 and Friedrich in 1812. Most of the commentary that runs through the nineteenth century and much of the twentieth attempts to discover the key to that key by identifying the various actors in the tenuous narrative of poet, friend, rival poet(s), and dark lady. Thus were born the innumerable skirmishes in the wars between those who think the young friend is the Earl of Southampton and those who think he is the Earl of Pembroke, or Willie Hughes, or any of a number of other candidates.

Henry Wriothesley, third Earl of Southampton, was first nominated in 1817 by Nathan Drake, and the Southampton cause has subsequently been championed by a host of others, including Sidney Lee at the turn of the twentieth century. According to Rollins, Southampton has also been from the first the leading candidate among German scholars (2: 187). Supporters point out that Shakespeare dedicated both *Venus and Adonis* and *The Rape of Lucrece* to Southampton (these are the only works by Shakespeare to which he affixed dedications); Drake and others have found a strong resemblance between Shakespeare's dedicatory epistle to *Lucrece* (the tone of which, they claim, is noticeably warmer than the dedication to *Venus and Adonis*) and sonnet 26. Furthermore, as a young man, Southampton refused to marry Lady Elizabeth Vere, preferring instead to pay a fine of £5,000; some have speculated that Shakespeare was originally commissioned by a relative of Southampton's (perhaps his mother or stepfather) to write the procreation sonnets (1-17) to help persuade the recalcitrant young man to marry and breed male heirs. Supporters of Southampton as the young friend tend to favor a date of composition for the Sonnets in the early-to-mid-1590s since by 1598 Southampton was too old to be called a "lovely boy" (he was born October 6, 1573).

Most Southamptonites have also tended to accept George Chalmers's gloss of the phrase "onlie begetter" in Thorpe's dedication to mean "procurer" or "obtainer" of the manuscript rather than "inspirer"; however, some have proposed that Southampton's initials, H. W., were transposed by Thorpe "as a blind" to conceal the young man's identity and to shield him from possible scandal. Most opponents of the Southampton theory doubt that Shakespeare wrote the Sonnets as early as 1594, and they note also that there is no evidence that Southampton's patronage continued beyond the early 1590s when it is assumed Shakespeare was still writing or revising sonnets. Others have questioned that Southampton was a handsome man or that he had a reputation for sensuality. As James Boaden observes, Southampton was "a great Captain, at Cadiz and in the Azores," and "went with his friend Essex to Ireland" in 1598; in 1596 he was thrown into prison for his marriage with Elizabeth Vernon; yet no mention is made of these events (23-25). Finally, those who think Thorpe's phrase "the onlie begetter" refers to the "inspirer" observe that Henry Wriothesley has the wrong initials, and they are not convinced by the suggestion that "Mr. W. H." represents Southampton's initials transposed. In any case, they find it highly unlikely that Thorpe would address the noble Southampton as "Mr."

The case for William Herbert, the third Earl of Pembroke, was first published by Boaden in 1832 (although it was independently articulated in private correspondence in 1819 by B. H. Bright), and since that time it has also had many supporters. The Pembroke faction reached its height in the late 1880s with Thomas Tyler's presentation of his case for the earl, which included his assertion that the dark lady was Mary Fitton, lady-in-waiting to Queen Elizabeth; however, the identification of Fitton was subsequently refuted in 1891 by F. J. Furnivall's discovery of a portrait of Fitton which showed her to have gray eyes and a fair complexion (Rollins 2: 263-64; see Figure 5 in this volume). In recent times, Leishman, Dover Wilson, and Duncan-Jones have favored Pembroke, and even Rollins, who remains an agnostic on the question, states that the case for Pembroke seems to him stronger than the one for Southampton (2: 196). Supporters of Pembroke as the young friend point to his initials, "W. H.," of course, as well as to the fact that the First Folio was dedicated to him and his brother, perhaps suggesting that he had been Shakespeare's patron. Furthermore, like Southampton, Herbert as a young man was violently opposed to the attempts of others to force him to marry. Known for his personal beauty and for his patronage of poets, Herbert also had a reputation for lascivious behavior. Supporters of Pembroke's candidacy have generally favored an initial dating of the Sonnets around 1598, when Pembroke was eighteen (he was born April 8, 1580). Objections to Herbert's identification as the friend begin with the fact that there is no evidence that he was ever Shakespeare's personal patron, or even that he knew Shakespeare personally. Skeptics also doubt that Thorpe would have dared to address Herbert as "Mr."

In addition to Southampton and Pembroke, many other candidates for the young friend have been proposed. In his 1780 edition, for example, Malone reports that Richard Farmer had identified "W. H." as William Harte, Shakespeare's nephew, an idea Malone rejects because

Harte was only twelve in 1598 (Drake would later show that Harte was not baptized until 1600). Instead Malone endorses the theory of Thomas Tyrwhitt that "W. H." is someone named "W. Hughes," a guess based on a possible italicized pun in line 7 of the Quarto version of sonnet 20: "A man in hew all *Hews* in his controwling." Rollins observes dryly that in his endorsement of Hughes, Malone "created a spook harder to drive away than the ghost of Hamlet's father" (2: 181), "a man who is a figment of the imagination" (2: 184). Will Hughes would later appear as the favorite musician of the old Earl of Essex (C. E. Browne, 1873) and (as "Willie Hughes") as the young actor in Oscar Wilde's fiction "The Portrait of Mr. W. H." (the love between the two men in Wilde's homoerotic fantasy is idealized and nonsexual). William Hughes reappears yet again, as a sea cook, in Samuel Butler's account; Butler informs his readers that Hughes lured the young Shakespeare into a love that was, "though only for a short time, more Greek than English" (159). Percy Allen claimed Hughes was born around 1574, the illegitimate actor son of Queen Elizabeth and the Earl of Oxford (Rollins 2: 184).

Other candidates with the initials "W. H." include William Hathaway, Shakespeare's brother-in-law; William Hart, another brother-in-law; William Hervey, Southampton's stepfather and his mother's third husband; William Hammond (to whom Middleton's *Game at Chess* is dedicated); and William Hatcliffe, a Lincolnshire lawyer. Candidates with initials other than "W. H." include Henry Willowbie (apparent author and protagonist of *Willowbie His Avisa*, which some scholars have attempted to link to the Sonnets—*Willowbie* has a character named "W. S.," an actor, who encourages his friend's attempt to seduce a virtuous married woman); Robert Devereux, the second Earl of Essex; Edmund Shakespeare, the poet's brother; Hamnet Shakespeare, the author's son who died in 1596; actor Richard Burbage; actor Will Kemp; Prince Hal; and, as was mentioned earlier, Queen Elizabeth (Rollins 2: 223-26, 248).

Candidates for the rival poet or poets are often tied to the proposer's candidate for friend. Malone thought he was Spenser, others that he was Chapman, or Marlowe, or Jonson, or Daniel (who grew up near Herbert and dedicated poems to him), or Drayton (who dedicated poems to both Southampton and Pembroke), or Gervase Markham, or Barnabe Barnes (Lee's choice), or a small army of others. Though by comparison there have been fewer candidates for the dark lady, theorists have been just as dogmatic, often on evidence even less persuasive than that supporting various theories for the young man or rival poet(s). Past contenders for the dubious honor include Elizabeth Vernon, whom Southampton first impregnated and later married; Mary Fitton, whom Pembroke impregnated but refused to marry; Lucy Negro, a prostitute also known as the Abbess of Clerkenwell (G. B. Harrison); Penelope Devereux, Lady Rich, the woman who inspired Astrophil's Stella; and Mistress Davenant (Arthur Acheson's theory). The case for Mary Fitton, as we have seen, was strongly championed by Thomas Tyler and later discredited by Furnivall's discovery of two portraits of Mary that show her to be quite unlike the dark lady described in sonnets 127, 130, and 136. Fitton was the dedicatee of a book by Will Kemp, perhaps suggesting that she had close ties to Shakespeare's acting company, but Kemp gets her first name wrong in his dedication (how well could he have known her?). Furthermore, Fitton was not married when she had her affair with Pembroke, yet in sonnet 152 the poet states that the addressee, presumably the dark lady, "In act thy bed-vow broke and new faith torn" (3). More recently, A. L. Rowse put forward the name of Emilia Bassano Lanier. Even after most of his so-called evidence was discredited (see Marvin Hunt's essay in this volume, as well as Samuel Schoenbaum's account in *Shakespeare's Lives* and in "Shakespeare's Dark Lady"), however, Rowse persisted in claiming that he had solved "the most mysterious, the most tantalising and elusive problem of them all" (x).

DENIALS OF AUTOBIOGRAPHY

Almost from the start of the frenzy, there was resistance to biographical readings: claims that the Sonnets are fictitious, mere literary exercises, conventional patronage poems, or allegories unrelated to incidents in or material conditions of Shakespeare's life. Sometimes "damaging sonnets were assigned to another voice" (de Grazia, "Locating" 438) or author. Such denials, it seems, were often prompted by moral panic at the thought of an adulterous bard with an undeniable attraction to a beautiful young man. But moral fastidiousness has not been the only motive for questioning the autobiographical assumption. To some, the biographical theory seems illogical. John Halliwell-Phillipps (1865) found it impossible to imagine that "a man of Shakespeare's practical wisdom . . . would have had the incredible folly to record the story of his indiscretions" (Rollins 2: 140). These doubters remind those persuaded by the poems' seeming sincerity that Shakespeare was, and remains, the greatest dramatist to write in the English language; through the power of "negative capability," he made a career of creating believable characters obviously different from himself. Plays, after all, are also works entirely in first person. If the Sonnets are autobiographical, the antipersonalists ask, why is there no evidence of their being read that way for their first 170 years?

Professional and aesthetic reasons, rather than moral squeamishness, prompted Robert Browning to object to Wordsworth's image of Shakespeare filling his poems with his private woes. In the last stanza of his poem "House," Browning replies to Wordsworth's "Scorn not the Sonnet":

> 'Hoity toity! A street to explore,
>   Your house the exception! *"With this same key*
> *Shakespeare unlocked his heart,"* once more!'
>   Did Shakespeare? If so, the less Shakespeare he! (37-40)

As a poet who often assumed the personae of despicable egotists in his dramatic monologues, Browning had a lot invested in this issue. Naturally, he wanted to deflect readers from viewing his poetry as a window on his life, his "I" narrators interpreted as self-portraiture. The poet-speaker in "House" is besieged by a mob intent on prying into every aspect of the poet's private life. It was one thing for Wordsworth to discern his own autobiographical practice in Shakespeare's Sonnets, but for Browning, it would be best if Shakespeare kept his loves and sorrows separate from his poems. Artistic objectivity and distance, in Browning's opinion, create the higher form of art.

Those who have actively opposed the autobiographical theory have often done so, of course, on moral grounds. Thus, James Boswell the younger writes: "Upon the whole I am satisfied that these compositions had neither the poet himself nor any individual in view; but were merely the effusions of his fancy, written upon various topicks for the amusement of a private circle, as indeed the words of Meres point out: 'Witness—his sugred Sonnets among his private friends.' The Sonnet was at that time a popular species of poetry, and was a favorite mode of expressing either the writer's own sentiments, or of embellishing a work of fiction" (20: 220). Boswell's conclusion was based on his a priori assumption of the poet's high moral character. Such a man could not be guilty of adultery:

> I trust it will not require much argument to show that this picture could not be put for gentle Shakespeare. We may lament that we know so little of his history; but this, at least, may be asserted with confidence, that at no time was the slightest imputation cast upon his moral character; and that, in an age abounding, as Mr. Steevens has observed, with illiberal private abuse and peevish satire, the concurring testimony of his contemporaries will confirm the declaration of honest Chettle, that "his demeanour was no less civil, than he excellent in the quality he professed." (20: 220)

Regarding the possibility that the poet-speaker expresses pederastic longings for the young man, Boswell follows Malone's line: in the context of Shakespeare's time, there was nothing improper or inappropriate about the way the poet addresses the young man. Boswell attributes such amorous language from one male to another to Shakespeare's "fondness for classical imitation" and finds Shakespeare's source in the second eclogue of Virgil (20: 221).

By declaring that the Sonnets are "merely the effusions of [Shakespeare's] fancy," Boswell made it morally acceptable to appreciate them as poetry. In fact, he finds Malone's response to Steevens does "scanty justice to these beautiful compositions" (20: 363). As Peter Stallybrass shows in his essay reprinted in this volume, Boswell's response of denial was repeated many times and took many forms over the next century. Homophobia (even more than outrage about adultery and mendacity or possible mixing of races) would again and again call forth ever more desperate denials. The "specter of sodomy," to use Stallybrass's phrase, was also the motivation for efforts to read the Sonnets as allegory or esoterica. Thus, in 1879 Hermann Conrad wrote that it is "our moral duty" to prove that Shakespeare was not homosexual; he was, rather, "a Platonist in the best sense of the word" (Rollins 2: 233). With many esoteric theories, reason and love of the Sonnets keep little company—yet their moral imperative is usually very clear. Thus, Barnstorff rescues Shakespeare from being dragged through the dirt by proposing that "the subjects of the poet's muse . . . is [*sic*] no Earl of Southampton, no Earl of Pembroke, no Queen Elizabeth, no Mrs. Varnon [*sic*]—no corporeal friend, no corporeal mistress, but *Genius* and the *Drama*." Rollins notes that Barnstorff's "interpretation, still usually mentioned with ridicule, reads like dry, established fact when compared with various later sonnet-keys" (2: 157). In addition to the many efforts to read the

Sonnets as a Platonic allegory, there is one interpreter, J. A. Heraud (1865), who maintains that the young man is the Messiah and the dark lady is His Church, while B. R. Ward (1929-30) proposes that the young man is Shakespeare's son and the dark lady is the poet's wife. Rollins exclaims, "No more astounding explanation has ever been printed" (2: 157, 161). The sometimes ludicrous attempt to protect Shakespeare's good name drew the ridicule of L. P. Smith in *On Reading Shakespeare* (1933): "The story Shakespeare recounts of his moral—or rather his immoral—predicament between these 'two loves' [of sonnet 144] . . . must certainly, in the interests of the British Empire, be smothered up; the business of proving and re-proving, and proving over again . . . that our Shakespeare cannot possibly mean what he so frankly tells us, has become almost a national industry" (Rollins 2: 149).

Those who doubt that the Sonnets are autobiographical have pointed to the conventionality (or, as often, to the deliberate anticonventionality) of many of the Sonnets' themes, images, and, "characters." To these scholars, the friend is a "creature of the imagination," as are the rival poet(s) and dark lady. The source studies of M. J. Wolff and Sidney Lee were especially influential in the early part of this century. Both investigated the relation between the Sonnets and classical and Renaissance sources, including Petrarch and his Italian, French, and English imitators. Wolff's essay "Petrarkismus und Antipetrarkismus in Shakespeares Sonetten" contends that many motifs in the Sonnets, including the poet-speaker's self-abasement and his love of a man, can be frequently discovered in Italian lyric sequences. Lee's work on links between the Sonnets and Ovid, and between the Sonnets and the sequences of other continental and English sonneteers, has (at least indirectly) enabled many later source studies, including Gordon Braden's essay commissioned for this volume.[16] While these studies have illuminated many aspects of Shakespeare's art, the fact that the Sonnets exploit conventional images and themes does not in itself prove that the poems are "literary exercises" rather than the key to Shakespeare's heart. As H. C. Beeching, Alden, Rollins, and many others have observed, there is nothing mutually exclusive about conventionality and sincerity: "a poet (or a freshman writing a love letter)," Rollins explains, "can be thoroughly sincere, can deal with real people, real events, real emotions, even while he is borrowing nearly all his subject-matter" (2: 241).

Sidney Lee is a fascinating figure; his career illustrates how slippery are the slopes of Sonnets scholarship. In his *Dictionary of National Biography (D.N.B.)* articles on Mary Fitton (1889), Lady Pembroke (1891), and William Herbert (1891), Lee had supported Pembroke's candidacy, but in his 1897 *D.N.B.* entry on Shakespeare, without prior warning or subsequent explanation, Lee suddenly became a Southamptonite. Lee reversed himself yet again (from the London to the New York editions of the *D.N.B.* in the same year), this time denying that the Sonnets were in any significant sense autobiographical.[17] His change on the issue of autobiography was clearly prompted by a desire to wash clean Shakespeare's good name. In his 1905 facsimile edition of Thorpe's Quarto, Lee acknowledges that "the whole collection is well calculated to create the illusion of a series of earnest personal confessions," which is why so many readers believe the sequence records the poet's personal feelings, as well as incidents from his life (8). Yet an autobiographical Shakespeare, Lee asserts, "is to a large extent in conflict with the habit of mind and method of work which are disclosed in the rest of Shakespeare's achievement" and "credits the poet with humiliating experiences of which there is no hint elsewhere" (9). More specifically, Lee states, "a purely literal interpretation of the impassioned protestations of affection for a 'lovely boy', which course through the sonnets, casts a slur on the dignity of the poet's name which scarcely bears discussion" (11). After all, Lee explains, we are not talking about "friendship of the healthy manly type" of which his plays and biography give "fine and touching examples" (11). Rather than reveal Shakespeare's "morbid infatuation with a youth" (12), these are poems written in what Shakespeare called "the liver vein"; that is, conventional poems of obeisance and flattery to a noble patron (17). Thus, writes Robertson, "Lee had taken up successively, with equal confidence, three positions, the Pembrokian, the Southamptonian, and the 'impersonal,' standing finally for the last view, with a resort to the Southampton connection as explaining Shakespeare's original resort to sonneteering; but never setting forth his reasons for abandoning, in turn, each of his former positions, which had been unreservedly held, and which remained on lasting record" (6).

AGNOSTICISM, NEW CRITICISM, AND THE QUESTION OF ARTISTIC MERIT

Around the end of the nineteenth century, as it became increasingly clear that not a shred a factual evidence existed to prove or disprove any of the prevailing biographical theories, a sense of exhaustion and futility began to set in, and an attitude of agnosticism about (and sometimes of indifference, contempt, or hostility to) the "personal/impersonal" debate began to emerge. Thus, Walter Raleigh introduces his remarks on the Sonnets with the following warning:

> There are many footprints around the cave of this mystery, none of them pointing in the outward direction. No one has ever attempted a solution of the problem without leaving a book behind him; and the shrine of Shakespeare is thickly hung with these votive offerings, all withered and dusty. No one has ever sought to gain access to this heaven of poetry by a privileged and secret stairway, without being blown ten thousand leagues awry, over the backside of the world, into the Paradise of Fools. The quest remains unachieved. (86)

Raleigh is actually certain the Sonnets originate in Shakespeare's experience, but he goes on to say:

> It would help us but little to know the names of the beautiful youth and the dark woman; no public records could reflect even faintly those vicissitudes of experience, exultations and abysses of feeling, which have their sole and sufficient record in the Sonnets.
>
> Poetry is not biography; and the value of the Sonnets to the modern reader is independent of all knowledge of their occasion. That they were made from the material of experience is certain: Shakespeare was no puny imitative rhymster. But the processes of art have changed the tear to a pearl, which remains to decorate new sorrows. The Sonnets speak to all who have known the chances and changes of human life. Their occasion is a thing of the past; their theme is eternal. The tragedy of which they speak is the topic and inspiration of all poetry; it is the triumph of Time, marching relentlessly over the ruin of human ambitions and human desires. (91-92)

Such attention to theme divorced from (some would say sublimated from) biography, while not exactly new, would become a dominant note as Sonnets criticism moved into the twentieth century.

Not just thematic but aesthetic criticism received new life from the agnostics. After acknowledging that the search in the Sonnets for clues about Shakespeare's life holds a certain interest, George Wyndham in 1898 submitted that this interest is nevertheless "alien from, and even antagonistic to, an appreciation of lyric excellence" (ci). In distancing himself from the biographical critics, Wyndham is careful also to stand apart from those who advocate the "impersonal" view:

> I do not mean that the Sonnets are 'mere exercises' written to 'rival' or to 'parody' the efforts of other poets. Such curiosities of criticism are born of a nervous revulsion from conclusions reached by the more confident champions of a 'personal theory'; and their very eccentricity measures the amount of damage done, not by those who endeavour, laudably enough, to retrieve a great life lost but, by those who allow such attempts at biography to bias their consideration of poems which we possess intact. If, indeed, we must choose between critics, who discover an autobiography in the Sonnets, and critics, who find in them a train of poetic exhalations whose airy iridescence never reflects the passionate colours of this earth, then the first are preferable. (ci-cii)

But Wyndham's point is that a choice here is unnecessary. Neither the autobiographical reading nor various readings against autobiography (e.g., theories about "literary exercises" or "Neoplatonic allegory") lead to the aesthetic appreciation these poems deserve. The "wonder" of Shakespeare's Sonnets, Wyndham writes,

> lies in the art of his poetry, not in the accidents of his life; and within that art, not so much in his choice of poetic themes as in the wealth of his Imagery, which grows and shines and changes: above all in the perfect execution of his Verbal Melody. That is the body of which his Imagery is the soul, and the two make one creation so beautiful that we are not concerned with anything but its beauty. (cxlvi-cxlvii)

For virtually the first time, states Hallett Smith in his account of the Sonnets' reception in his book *The Tension in the Lyre*, someone "is reading the sonnets as poetry" (155).

From such intimations of formalism as Wyndham's one can draw a straight line to New Critics like L. C. Knights and William Empson, critics who employ the technique of close reading to understand and appreciate how these poems work *as poems* and to explore the relationship between their form and meaning. Empson's celebrated explorations of ambiguous language and imagery in the Sonnets in *Seven Types of Ambiguity* and in *Some Versions of Pastoral* introduced readers to complexities undreamed of by earlier readers, even readers like Steevens who found not complexity but obscurity. A "flaw" had been turned into a source of aesthetic appeal. In his essay "Shakespeare's Sonnets," Knights cautions that the "attempt to isolate the original stimulus (which in any case *may* have been an imagined situation) . . . is not only hazardous, it is irrelevant" (178). Knights finds that the "most profitable approach to the Sonnets is . . . to consider them in relation to the development of Shakespeare's blank verse," something he proceeds to do, making acute observations about such things as tone, prosody, and imagery. The first sixty years of the twentieth century, in fact, produced many other studies that make a point about *not* being biographical and instead explore such topics as wordplay (Empson, Mahood), genre (Colie), structure (Nowottny,) imagery and theme (Mizener, Knight, Spurgeon). Despite such studies in the New Critical vein, detached from the biographical question, A. Nejgebauer's 1962 survey of twentieth-century Sonnets scholarship was more than a little dispiriting:

> On the whole . . . criticism of the sonnets will not stand comparison with that of the plays. The former has not developed anything like the great new ways of approach to the text, the poetic qualities and the dramatic and theatrical values of Shakespeare's dramas; on the contrary, it has largely been amateurish and misplaced, often attempting to answer too many questions at once. Thus the criticism of the sonnets during the last sixty years has left the 'problems' unsolved and many aspects of the poetry incompletely examined. (18)

Nejgebauer concludes with a call for further study of the "interaction between the English Renaissance sonnet tradition and Shakespeare's individual poetic gift." He also predicts that "[w]holesale interpretations of the sonnets will have to give place to a careful examination of individual sonnets or natural groups of them before new syntheses, based both on historical considerations and on assessments of intrinsic merits, can be profitably attempted. As regards the use of language, stanzaic structure, metre, tropes and imagery, these demand the full tilth and husbandry of criticism" (18; see also Vendler, *The Art* 13).

During the next three decades, important work on the Sonnets continued to appear, some of it perhaps even realizing Nejgebauer's call for "great new ways of approach." Major new editions were published by Martin Seymour-Smith (1963), W. G. Ingram and Theodore Redpath (1964), Barbara Herrnstein Smith (1969), Stephen Booth (1977), and John Kerrigan (1986)—this is just a partial listing—as were important critical studies by J. B. Leishman, Giorgio Melchiori (1976), and, again, Stephen Booth (1969). Leishman's book appeared in 1961; in fact, Nejgebauer has a note welcoming its recent publication. Hilton Landry also wrote a study in the New Critical vein in 1963, as Edward Hubler had done in 1952; both also edited critical anthologies (1976 and 1962, respectively), as did Gerald Willen and Victor B. Reed (1964), Barbara Herrnstein [Smith] (1964), Peter Jones (1977), and Harold Bloom (1987). Except perhaps for Hubler's inclusion of Oscar Wilde's "The Portrait of Mr. W. H.," these collections tend to de-emphasize or even ignore the biographical questions. Booth is an even more radical agnostic, as his oft-quoted 1977 statement about Shakespeare's sexuality reveals: "William Shakespeare was almost certainly homosexual, bisexual, or heterosexual. The sonnets provide no evidence on the matter" (*Sonnets* 548).

Booth's important work owes an acknowledged debt to Empson's explorations of the Sonnets' multivalent language; at the same time it also looks ahead to deconstruction and other forms of post-structuralism that explore the slipperiness of language and indeterminacy of authorial intent. In *An Essay on Shakespeare's Sonnets*, Booth describes how "Shakespeare copes with the problem of the conflicting obligations of a work of art by multiplying the number of ordering principles, systems of organization, and frames of reference in the individual sonnets." Booth finds that the result "of that increase of artificiality is pleasing because the reader's sense of coherences rather than coherence gives him both the simple comfort of order and the comfort that results from the likeness of his ordered experience of the sonnet to the experience of disorderly natural phenomena" (171-72). His 1977 edition and commentary "are determined by what [he

thinks] a Renaissance reader would have thought as he moved from line
to line and sonnet to sonnet in the Quarto" (ix); what such a reader
might have thought turns out to be a bewildering complexity of
possible alternative meanings and overlapping linguistic and rhetorical
structures, a complexity that makes any paraphrasable statement of
theme seem reductive and unsatisfying. "It is the complexity," he
writes, "that gives the sonnets what critics of eras less ambitious than
this one for the clinical precision of natural science called the magic of
the sonnets, the sense they give of effortless control of the
uncontrollable. The notes to this edition investigate the particulars of
the complexity" (xiii).[18]

It is, perhaps, something of a surprise that the harshest attack on
the Sonnets in the twentieth century comes from American poet and
close reader John Crowe Ransom, less of a surprise that the best
responses have come from other New Critics and formalists. Ransom's
1937-38 essay "Shakespeare at Sonnets," which has often been
anthologized, contends that "generally [the Sonnets] are ill
constructed"; in about half of them the "logical pattern" usually fails to
fit the "metrical pattern" (200). "Structurally," he pronounces,
"Shakespeare is a careless workman"; his is a "poetry of feeling" (as
opposed to a "poetry of knowledge"), a Romantic "associationist
poetry" that uses figurative language that is "rich and suggestive even
while it is vague and cloudy" (203-04). Shakespeare aspired to
metaphysical effects, but all too often failed because, Ransom states,
"Shakespeare's imagination is [not] equal to the peculiar and
systematic exercises which Donne imposed habitually upon his" (207-
08).

Ransom's salvo has called forth numerous responses in defense of
Shakespeare's artistry. One of the most important came from Arthur
Mizener in his essay "The Structure of Figurative Language in
Shakespeare's Sonnets." Mizener disagrees that even the late
Shakespeare is attempting to be a metaphysical poet, at least in
Ransom's sense of the term; therefore it is unfair to judge Shakespeare
in light of Donne's poetic achievement. Shakespeare's method,
Mizener explains, is fundamentally different from the metaphysical:
while Donne surprises the reader with "an apparently illogical figure
which can be understood only if its logic is followed, Shakespeare
surprises you with an apparently logical vehicle which is
understandable only if taken figuratively" (221). Using sonnet 124 to
illustrate Shakespeare's method, Mizener shows how a single phrase

like "child of state" evokes several meanings: "the purpose is to make the reader see them all, simultaneously, in soft focus. . . . If any one of these emergent figures had been realized in full, all the rest would necessarily have been excluded" (225). In their analysis of sonnet 129, Roman Jakobsen and L. G. Jones reveal the complex matrices of parallels and contrasts between lines, quatrains, and couplet. This famous essay ends with a glance back at Ransom: "After an attentive inquiry into Shakespeare's Sonnet 129 with its amazing external and internal structuration palpable to any responsive and unprejudiced reader, one may ask whether it is possible to affirm with John Crowe Ransom that far from being a true sonnet this is only a fourteen-line poem, 'with no logical organization at all' except that it has a little couplet conclusion" (214). In Helen Vendler's hands, the Sonnets find their most aesthetically attuned reader of the century. One of her favorite tactics is to quote a Ransom-like dismissal of some aspect of the Sonnets (e.g., their artificiality, their "unnecessary" lines and phrases, or "disappointing" couplets) as a way of demonstrating their artistry (see "Reading" and the introduction to *The Art of Shakespeare's Sonnets*).

It is difficult to generalize about valuation of the Sonnets at any given length of time over the last 200 years because at any given time there seems to be more than one strong opinion. Here, for example, is part of Gary Taylor's brief account of the Sonnets' reception in *Reinventing Shakespeare*:

> Throughout the nineteenth century the sonnets had been admired as romantic lyrics and studied as biographical documents; in the twentieth century they rose toward the summit of Shakespeare's artistic achievement. I. A. Richards defended *The Waste Land* by reference "to Shakespeare's greatest sonnets or to *Hamlet*," taking it for granted that the short sonnets belong alongside the longest and most famous of the plays. "Bare ruined choirs, where late the sweet bird sang" in Sonnet 73 was the first exemplary line of poetry quoted and analyzed in *Seven Types of Ambiguity*. (251)

Although admirable for tracing important trends, this account nevertheless tends to simplify. The Romantics poets, for example, were not all of an admiring mind, and even some admirers changed their minds more than once. Wordsworth offers praise in 1815 and 1827, but his comments in 1803, scribbled into the margins of the second volume of Robert Anderson's *A Complete Edition of the Poets of Great Britain*, show his ambivalence: "These sonnets beginning at CXXVII to his mistress, are worse than a puzzle-peg. They are abominably harsh obscure & worthless. The others are for the most part much better, have many fine lines very fine lines and passages. They are also in many places warm with passion; their chief faults and heavy ones they are, are sameness, tediousness, quaintness, & elaborate obscurity."

The association between life and art may have appealed to some romantic sensibilities, but, as Peter Stallybrass shows in an essay reprinted in this volume, it troubled Coleridge, especially the notion that Shakespeare could write passionate love poems to a man; such uneasiness inevitably affected valuation. Not all dislike, however, can be traced to homophobic panic. In 1843 Walter Savage Landor seems not to have thought much of their style: "Among all Shakespeare's [Sonnets] not a single one is very admirable, and few sink very low. They are hot and pothery: there is much condensation, little delicacy; like raspberry jam without cream, without crust, without bread, to break its viscidity. But I would rather sit down to one of them again, than to a string of such musty sausages as are exposed in our streets at the present dull season" (qtd. in Rollins 2: 354). Later in the century, Oscar Wilde's "charmed fascination" with the Sonnets "and his invocation of them in his own defence on the final day of his third trial, in May 1895, had a lasting, and deeply inhibiting, effect on their subsequent reception" (Duncan-Jones, *Sonnets* 79; see also Laroche in this volume). In other words, the Sonnets were not always appreciated as "romantic lyrics" during either half of the nineteenth century.

Nor can one say that the Sonnets have enjoyed an unqualified rise in the estimation of critics and scholars during the twentieth century. In 1905 Lee declared the Sonnets "unequal in literary merit"; "many reach levels of lyric melody and meditative energy which are not to be matched elsewhere in poetry," but "a few of the poems sink into inanity beneath the burden of quibbles and conceits" (7). As was earlier observed, Robertson thought one third of the Sonnets were so bad they could not have been written by Shakespeare (271), an opinion as damning as Ranson's judgment that the Sonnets are failed attempts in the metaphysical vein. William Kerrigan recalls a more recent instance of critical hostility to the Sonnets: one day at Stanford in 1963 he heard Yvor Winters tell "the thirty-five undergraduates enrolled in 'The English Lyric' that he knew Shakespeare had had to write these embarrassing sonnets, but wished that the author had thrown his manuscript into the fire" (43). In his 1964 introduction Auden concedes "their haphazard order" and "their extremely uneven poetic value" (xxiii). "No serious critic of poetry," he writes, "can possibly think that all the sonnets are equally good." Auden thought forty-nine of the poems are "excellent throughout," while many others have "one or two memorable lines, but there are several which [he] can only read out of a sense of duty" (xxiv). Taylor, in fact, states that "as isolated individuals only a handful of the 154 have ever attracted or rewarded as much enthusiasm as the story told outside and between them" (*Reinventing* 158). It is against just this sort of resistance to the artistry of *all* the Sonnets that Helen Vendler aims her lance in *The Art of Shakespeare's Sonnets*. She attempts brief close readings of each sonnet because "critics tend to dwell on the most famous ten or fifteen out of the total 154" (13), and "many, if not all, of the sonnets deserve close and writerly scrutiny" (37).

Though appreciation of the Sonnets has not been universal in the twentieth century, Taylor is correct about one source of their appeal during this time: their complexity, which for centuries had either been denied (as with Benson) or condemned (as with Steevens, Wordsworth, and many others). Although Taylor's account is tinged with satiric exaggeration, the pattern he discerns of each generation of readers' discovering more complexity than the one before is undeniable. The trouble, according to Taylor, begins with Empson: "His influential taxonomy of literary double-talk found multitudes of meaning packed into what had seemed simple sonnets. Only a professional reader could unravel the intestinal contortions of Empson's own poems or those he praised." Taylor asserts that Empson, Richards, and Q. D. and F. R. Leavis made English studies "respectable" by making it "difficult"; these critics perceived Shakespeare's writing to be "intrinsically difficult . . . in difficulty lay its claim to our intellectual attention" (*Reinventing* 246). The trend, in Taylor's opinion, has continued beyond the old New Critics:

> [John] Kerrigan observes that "the sonnet as a form . . . most aptly finds resolution in a critical apparatus." The 400-page "analytical commentary" of Stephen Booth's edition of *Shakespeare's Sonnets* . . . unravels (and restitches) a bewildering compressed complexity of reference in poems that were once celebrated as a transparent window onto Shakespeare's heart. Booth's commentary makes the sonnets more difficult to read than ever before. Ten years later [in *Voice*

Terminal Echo] Jonathan Goldberg, deliberately abandoning "literary tact," makes his own criticism of those poems as difficult to read as Booth's sonnets. (*Reinventing* 365)

And then there is Joel Fineman's *Shakespeare's Perjured Eye: The Invention of Poetic Subjectivity in the Sonnets.*

Fineman's is perhaps the most brilliant, original study of the Sonnets of the last twenty-five years, if not of all time; it is a work that is difficult to describe because Fineman's complex thesis is throughout the book in a state of continuous revision. At once a source study, an application to literature of Lacanian theory, and an important chapter in the history of the early modern subject, Fineman's analysis describes the Sonnets as Shakespeare's response to "the burden of belated literariness," the dilemma of arriving at the end of the Petrarchan tradition (48). In his first 126 poems, Shakespeare writes an idealized poetry of praise, a poetry of narcissistic, homosexual sameness founded in visual identification (Lacan's "Imaginary"), while sonnets 127-154 produce a poetry of mourning and anguish and satire, a poetry of heterosexual difference figured in the duplicitous tongue (Lacan's "Symbolic"). The result is Shakespeare's invention of a new kind of poetic subjectivity, one engendered by misogynistic heterosexual desire. As Taylor explains,

> Fineman's thesis depends upon his sense of Shakespeare's belatedness in his own time. Shakespeare writes his sonnets at the end of a long wave of European sonneteering that stretches back to Petrarch, and a more immediate English wave initiated by Sidney. . . .
> This is also, of course, though Fineman does not say so, the general situation of a Shakespearean critic in the late twentieth century: how do you praise persuasively when so much praise has already been written? . . .
> Shakespeare, finding himself at the end of an exhausted tradition, rewrites the sonnet. Shakespeareans, drowning in their own dismayed abundance, rewrite criticism. (*Reinventing* 365)[19]

Taylor implies that the complexities of the Sonnets are largely the invention of readers like Empson, Booth, and Fineman. Maybe so. Yet the work of these writers has persuaded most scholars today that this richness of meaning and effect really does reside in these poems. Furthermore, of the nuances of sound and meaning, wordplay, and "occult structures" within each sonnet that she discovers in her recent commentary, Vendler would argue that the praise has not "already been written," or if it has been, praise has often been offered for the wrong reasons.[20]

THE CONTEMPORARY FIELD

Exactly 400 years after Meres's *Palladis Tamia*, serious scholarly as well as popular interest in the Sonnets seems never to have been greater. During the 1980s and 1990s, the International Shakespeare Bibliography published each year in *Shakespeare Quarterly* has continued to report a steady stream of books and critical essays, as well as translations into many different languages (in 1995 and 1996 alone: Croatian, Italian, German, Spanish, Russian, Bulgarian, Azerbaijani, Dutch, French, Hungarian, Portuguese, Chinese, Finnish, and Hebrew). In addition, each year brings reports of theatrical productions, videotapes, and recordings by performers around the world. The last two decades have also witnessed the publication of several important new editions of the Sonnets, two in the last two years (Evans and Duncan-Jones)—actually three if one counts Helen Vendler's commentary as an edition for advanced readers, since her book also reprints each sonnet in Quarto and modernized forms. In a review, Richard Howard called Vendler's book "the most valuable critical performance in recent American literature on classic texts."

Significant criticism on the Sonnets during the last two decades ranges from Thomas M. Greene's exploration of economic language and imagery ("Pitiful Thrivers") to George T. Wright's exposition of Shakespeare's metrical virtuosity in *Shakespeare's Metrical Art* to Heather Dubrow's tracing of the interplay between psychological and rhetorical patterns in *Captive Victors* to Anne Ferry's exposition of "inward language"; from feminist, gay, and lesbian excavations of early modern gender constructions that continue the work of Eve Kosofky Sedgwick to explorations of the Sonnets for signs of class and race stimulated by recent studies by Margreta de Grazia and Kim Hall; from psychoanalytical readings by Richard P. Wheeler, Sara van den Berg, and Jane Hedley to bibliographic forays by Randall McLeod and Gary Taylor. The Sonnets, in other words, have become an extremely important site of contemporary discussions of early modern ideas about sexual, class, and racial differences; moreover, these poems are often mentioned in accounts of the history of subjectivity, of Elizabethan and

Jacobean composing and printing practices, and of Renaissance patronage systems. Much of the liveliness of today's criticism of the Sonnets, of course, is fueled by scholarly disagreement; the only complete agreement seems to be on the value of affording careful study of these poems and the cultural conditions from which they emerged.

Since Rollins's *Variorum*, a virtual *Dunciad* of scholarly folly, and certainly since Booth's appendix to his 1977 edition, there has been a marked decrease in the number of readings that touch directly on biographical issues (either in support or in opposition). Yet some forms of the old biographical criticism have persisted. For example, in 1964 Leslie Hotson came forth with the last significant "new" theory about the young friend: that he was William Hatcliffe, a Lincolnshire lawyer who was "Prince of Purpoole" during Christmas celebrations at Gray's Inn in 1587-88. Schoenbaum reports that Hotson's "case for the dating has been enthusiastically rejected by most scholars. Nor does he demonstrate any connection between Shakespeare and Hatcliffe or between the poet and the Gray's Inn festivities. . . . A chief limitation of Hotson's later work, including this study, is his proneness to attach the same evidential significance to a literary inference (say, the interpretation of an ambiguous topical allusion) as to an irrefutable documentary discovery" (*Lives* 746-47 [1970 ed.]). The flaw in evidential logic that Schoenbaum describes is a frequent problem in the biographical criticism. As we have seen, A. L. Rowse continued until his recent death to insist on identifying Emilia Bassano Lanier as the dark lady even after most of his "evidence" had been discredited. And there are scholars like T. W. Baldwin and R. J. C. Wait who have continued to champion the cause of Southampton (as did Rowse). In her introduction to the New Arden edition of the Sonnets, Duncan-Jones offers extensive support for Pembroke's identity as the young friend (53-69).[21] The anti-Stratfordians, meanwhile, continue to use the Sonnets to make the case for their favorite authorship candidates. Most recently, Joseph Sobran has presented evidence of Edward de Vere's bisexuality as proof of de Vere's authorship of the Sonnets and, of course, of everything else usually attributed to the inadequately educated, socially deprived glover's son from Stratford.

Though biography has not by any means been their emphasis, the recent work of Hieatt, Hieatt, and Prescott and of Foster ("Reconstructing") on the dating of the Sonnets may indeed lead to more informed speculation about the relation between Shakespeare's life and these poems in the future. As Rollins states, the issue of the date of the Sonnets' composition "is in many respects the most important of all the unanswerable questions they pose. If it could be answered definitely and finally, there might be some chance of establishing to general satisfaction the identity of the friend, the dark woman, the rival poet (supposing that all were real individuals), of deciding what contemporary English sources Sh[akespeare] did or did not use, and even of determining whether the order of Q is the author's or not" (2: 53). For Rollins, however, the attainment of such certainty about dating remained "an idle dream" up to the time he was writing (2: 53). Since his time computers have been enlisted in ever more sophisticated ways. What separates Duncan-Jones's speculations about Pembroke from the wild conjecture of earlier biographical theories is that they are grounded in the latest computer-based stylometric research about dating, as well as in Duncan-Jones's historical research into the publishing milieux of early seventeenth-century England. Still, there are many points in her introduction that, by her own admission, are highly conjectural, and many readers will no doubt remain unconvinced by her biographical hypotheses.

The more prevalent critical attitude over the past few decades has been what David Schalkwyk has termed the "revulsion against biography" (398). One can hear that tone of revulsion, for example, in Auden's claim that the Sonnets serve to separate "those who love poetry" from "those who only value poems as historical documents." It makes no sense to Auden to "spend time in conjectures that cannot be proved," given the paucity of solid historical evidence. Even if such evidence did exist, answering the biographical questions would not "illuminate our understanding of the Sonnets" (xvii). Over the past two decades, Schalkwyk observes, avoidance of all issues touching on the relationship between the poet's life and the Sonnets (even arguments that attempt to prove that the Sonnets are *not* autobiographical) has extended into several strains of poststructuralism, especially deconstruction and Lacanian explorations of subjectivity like Fineman's in *Shakespeare's Perjured Eye*. According to Schalkwyk, this "recent trend . . . begins with New Criticism and culminates in poststructuralist theory of the past decade"; often it involves rejecting not only biographical but also "dramatic accounts of the Sonnets in favor of their textually self-reflexive and self-enclosed nature. This critical agenda not only emphasizes the multiple and irreducible complexities and ambiguities of the language of the Sonnets (witness Stephen Booth) but also sacrifices the Sonnets' objects of address to the overriding idea that the poems are interesting above all for the way in which they constitute the subjectivity of their creator" (381).

Not everyone has been content with the recent critical agenda Schalkwyk describes. One of the first to protest the restrictiveness of the orthodoxy of agnosticism was C. L. Barber, who (along with his coauthor in *The Whole Journey*, Richard P. Wheeler) insists on identifying "links between Shakespeare's art and what is known about his life from the biographical record" (xvii). It is essential, Barber contends, to recognize these poems as actions, directed at real persons. "To exclude consideration of the human context," he writes, "is an understandable, though misconceived, response to the quagmire of biographical speculations" (159). Barber does not propose another round of "pin the tail on the dark lady" (the joke is Booth's)—as he states, "it is one thing to read the sonnets by thinking you have discovered their 'story' (like so many—most vociferously, A. L. Rowse) or by making it up (like Oscar Wilde), another thing to read them with an awareness of what they themselves convey about the use Shakespeare is making of them" (159-60).

Others have followed Barber's lead in relaxing the prohibition against the personal theory. In his introduction to his 1986 edition of the Sonnets, for instance, John Kerrigan offers the following pragmatic approach, which is quoted with approval by Dubrow in her essay in this collection: "The text is neither fictive nor confessional. Shakespeare stands behind the first person of his sequence as Sidney had stood behind Astrophil—sometimes near the poetic 'I', sometimes farther off, but never without some degree of rhetorical projection" (11). Along similar lines, Donald Foster has recently observed that:

> the poet himself often seems unsure whether to present his verse principally as literary artifice or as personal chronicle. His text dwells, as it were, in the twilight of both autobiography and fiction, with metrical feet in both worlds. But then again, if these, the most private of Shakespeare's poems, were only one or the other, they would doubtless be far less interesting. The sonnets are in large measure defined for us by their very ambiguity. If we were someday to discover the "facts" concerning Shakespeare's relationship with the persons alluded to in this work, what we have always known as Shakespeare's *Sonnets* would, in a sense, cease to exist, to be replaced by another book of the same title. ("Master W. H." 51)

In Foster's opinion, "biographical questions are not irrelevant to the criticism of these poems," but "any interpretation that seeks to recover intended meanings must remain essentially speculative" (52). Finally, Schalkwyk's recent essay in *Shakespeare Quarterly* attempts to "reveal how humanly and ideologically confined and confining the criticism is that refuses to interrogate or move beyond what is conceived as the internal moral and poetic symbolism of the texts conceived in a formalistically disembodied way" (398).

Although the New Critical tendency to treat the Sonnets as self-contained, self-reflexive artifacts has been compatible with forms of post-structuralism most concerned with the subjects of language, interiority, and subjectivity, it has run counter to the historicizing practice of many other varieties of postmodern interpretation. Marotti's work, for example, reveals the young man sonnets to be deeply embedded in the sociopolitical dynamics of the English Renaissance manuscript culture of poets and patrons at a crucial point of transition to print culture (see also Kernan; Barrell). The same historicizing tendency has, of course, informed a number of recent cultural studies—particularly feminist, gay, bisexual, and lesbian explorations of such issues in the Sonnets as gender definition, sexuality, homosociality, and misogyny, and cultural materialist readings of the Sonnets for economies of class and race. These studies do not attempt to read the Sonnets for clues to the identity of the young friend, but they do attempt to reveal the cultural life in the literary, sexual, social, economic, and historical discourses that shaped Shakespeare and that Shakespeare shaped into poems.

Perhaps the most interesting development of the last decade or so has been the emergence—and general acceptance—of gay and bisexual readings of the Sonnets, thanks mainly to studies by Eve Kosofsky Sedgwick, Joseph Pequigney, Bruce R. Smith, Jonathan Goldberg, Gregory Bredbeck, Marjorie Garber, and others. Sedgwick's chapter on the Sonnets in *Between Men* has been especially influential.[22] Reading the Sonnets in what she concedes is "a simplified because synchronic and ahistorical form," Sedgwick illustrates "some of the patterns traced by male homosocial desire" (29). The Sonnets, she goes on to say, "record and thematize misogyny and gynephobia"; in the Sonnets "women are merely the vehicles by which men breed more men, for the gratification of other men" (33). Pequigney's 1985 study, *Such Is My Love*, argues that the Sonnets are "the grand masterpiece of homoerotic poetry" (1) and that the Sonnets depict the story of a consummated sexual relationship between the poet-persona and young male friend, as well as the poet's affair with the dark lady. Pequigney's main conclusions have subsequently been seconded by Bruce R. Smith and, I might add, have also been attacked by Goldberg for being "banalizing and dehistoricized" (*Sodometries* 21). Following the work of Michel Foucault and Alan Bray, Goldberg and other "social constructionists" insist that the categories of "homosexual" and "heterosexual" did not then exist and that notions of sexuality were radically different from those of the last 100 years (people in early modern times, they assert, did not define themselves according to the objects of their sexual preferences).[23] Yet even Goldberg approves of Pequigney's insistence on the sexualities implicit in the sequence, so long denied by readers. The homoerotic interpretation had, of course, been offered before the mid-1980s, as early as Oscar Wilde and Samuel Butler in the late nineteenth century, but few had openly espoused it or taken it as far as Pequigney has. Even just a generation ago, W. H. Auden wrote dismissively of the "homosexual reader . . . determined to secure our Top-Bard as a patron saint of the Homintern" (xxix).

Not everyone writing on the Sonnets today agrees with Pequigney and Smith that the Sonnets depict the story of a consummated sexual relationship between poet and male friend, but no serious reader can any longer make the facile assumption that the relationship between poet and friend is nonsexual or assume as Malone did (and as many have argued since) that the amorous tone of so many of the Sonnets is typical of the way Neoplatonic male friends spoke to one another in Elizabethan times.[24] What has changed? Obviously, part of the explanation lies in the persuasive power of these recent studies, but it is also clear that cultural forces are at work, especially as a result of the feminist and gay pride movements. Such cultural forces, first of all, created the social and intellectual climate that made possible such studies, and these same forces have also shaped an academic culture that is no longer as troubled by the idea that the Sonnets might depict a bisexual love story. One of Pequigney's important contributions is that he uncovers the shameful history of denial and homophobia that has distorted discussion of the Sonnets for the last 200 years. Following Pequigney, Peter Stallybrass's essay "Editing as Cultural Formation: The Sexing of Shakespeare's Sonnets," reprinted in this collection, reveals the great explanatory power of gender studies when combined with reception history.

The political implications of recent gay readings are both complicated and fascinating. When Auden wrote sardonically in 1964 of efforts by homosexual readers to appropriate Shakespeare as one of their own, he did so—he told friends at a dinner party—because "it won't do just yet to admit that the top Bard was in the homintern" (Pequigney, *Such Is My Love* 79-80). Apparently Auden—who was himself homosexual—did assume that the Sonnets are autobiographical and also that they reveal the truth about Shakespeare's own sexuality, but in 1964 Auden saw this as dangerous knowledge and hid what he really thought from the public. Even in the very different political climate of the last decade, Pequigney and Smith have been extremely cautious about moving from the story the Sonnets seem to tell to making inferences about Shakespeare's life and sexual orientation. In the first chapter of *Such Is My Love*, Pequigney states that "since outside documentary corroboration is lacking, no certainty on the matter [of the biographical question] is attainable" (5); in his final chapter he returns to the issue and speculates tentatively that the Sonnets probably do reflect Shakespeare's experiences in love (220-21), as he does again in his essay commissioned for this volume. But the emphasis of his book is the story the Sonnets depict, not the relation between that story and Shakespeare's life.

What is so curious is the way a number of reviewers and scholars have misread Pequigney on this issue. (I am thinking especially of Denis Donoghue's 1986 review in *Raritan*, which repeatedly characterizes Pequigney's argument as biographical.) Some readers perhaps already believed the Sonnets to be autobiographical; thus, if they were persuaded by Pequigney's account of the story the Sonnets tell, they might naturally assume that Shakespeare's sexuality is reflected in the persona's. After all, they must reason, who but a bisexual would write poems about hetero- *and* homosexual love? In her recent book *Vice Versa*, Marjorie Garber notes that readers today are more willing to admit the homoeroticism of the Sonnets "partly for political or 'identity politics reasons'" (511). The "Shakespeare of the Sonnets," she notes, has long been claimed as a gay author, but few claim him as a bisexual (she acknowledges that Pequigney does [514]). "Why avoid the obvious?" she asks. "*Because* it is obvious? Or because a bisexual Shakespeare fits no one's erotic agenda?" (515). Until Garber, that is, who has a political-erotic agenda of her own.

Helen Vendler has speculated about the cyclical nature of Sonnets criticism: "Biographical, allegorical, historical, and thematic methods of reading return in perpetual recrudescence, no matter the dubiousness of their results, and one can only conclude that something in literary response as it has evolved among us ensures that in every century some group of people will try to reidentify the *Sonnets'* dramatis personae, will allegorize (morally, historically, or dramatically) the import of the series, and will debate the psychology and sexuality of the intrigue" ("Reading" 39). She might well have pointed to sonnet 59 as a prophecy of such unproductive, repetitive critical practices:

> If there be nothing new, but that which is
> Hath been before, how are our brains beguiled,
> Which, lab'ring for invention, bear amiss
> The second burthen of a former child! (1-4)

Yet perhaps we can take some solace in Vendler's recognition of the cyclical pattern; there is something refreshing, if not entirely new, in her awareness of the Sonnets' critical past and her heightened sense of the futility of most theories about these poems.

Some critics today—like de Grazia, Stallybrass, and Adena Rosmarin—actually read the interpretative history of the Sonnets itself as a text, as a slice of social and cultural history. Students of the ever-changing ways these poems have been valued, interpreted, and appropriated, many of today's Sonnets critics seem better able to understand the transitory, culturally influenced nature of their own critical positions, and therefore they often make a point of declaring their ideological and methodological assumptions. Many of those writing on the Sonnets are clearly not afraid to question conventional wisdom (witness Dubrow and Pequigney), and thus, they are open to new ideas and approaches. Most of them, like Donald Foster in his essay on "Master W. H.," are honest, sometimes painfully honest, about what they do not know and are more comfortable living with uncertainty and ambiguity than many previous generations of scholars have been; indeed, today that uncertainty is often celebrated and anatomized. The consciousness of the past (which can become anxiety of influence) and the awareness that perceptions and valuations of the Sonnets will change (which *is* anxiety about the future) lead to a heightened and entirely new kind of metacritical awareness.

Given all that has been written about Shakespeare's Sonnets, it is a wonder that we still know so little about them. I suppose a second wonder is that we keep giving birth to new readings of these wonderful, enigmatic poems. Those of us who have written on the Sonnets are the ironic, unintended (who could have imagined our numbers?) fulfillment of the poet-speaker's desire for his friend to live forever, expressed in the very first line of the first sonnet, "From fairest creatures we desire increase." We are the millions of strange shadows that on the Sonnets tend, descendants of the passions perhaps inspired by an actual young male friend and an actual dark lady, the end of a generative cycle encouraged by Thorpe's mysterious dedication to "Mr. W. H., the onlie begetter of these insuing sonnets," a cycle that proceeds through the first seventeen poems and the speaker's wish that the young man beget a child—or several children, preferably sons—to protect his beauty against the ravages of Time. Refusing to beget copies of himself within some happy maiden womb, the young man instead inspires, inseminates, the poet to write sonnets that celebrate and thus preserve the friend's beauty. In their turn, in *their* beauty and enigmatic complexity, these poems inspire commentary from critics, and that commentary breeds further critical response, a self-perpetuating Talmudic chain. It all begins with the beauty of the young friend. And, again ironically, we do not even know if he existed, or if the rival poet and the dark lady existed. If they did exist, we do not know their names.

SHAKESPEARE'S SONNETS: CRITICAL ESSAYS

The essays in this collection confirm the great variety and high quality of work being done today on the Sonnets. Of course, we do not claim to represent every recent approach to the Sonnets or to have exhausted all that might be said from any single perspective, but it is our hope that these essays contribute to a number of important, ongoing discussions. No book, even a collection of essays by twenty authors, can present the full picture of work written today just in English. What we offer instead is a snapshot, or rather twenty snapshots, of the contemporary scene of Sonnets criticism. Most of the contributors are American, but all are connected to a discourse about the Sonnets that includes scholars from around the world.

In her introduction to *The Art of Shakespeare's Sonnets*, Vendler writes that the Sonnets "represent the largest tract of unexamined Shakespearean lines left open to scrutiny" (13). Of course, she is thinking of examining these poems from her perspective, the high-aesthetic-formalist perspective, which Vendler carefully distinguishes

from merely thematic approaches ("Ways into" 7) or recent
"jaundice[d]" social and psychological criticism of the Sonnets (*The
Art* 1). "The appeal of lyric," she writes, "lies elsewhere than in its
paraphrasable statement" (*The Art* 14). Vendler consciously follows in
the path of formalist critics like Giorgio Melchiori, Rosalie Colie,
Caroline Spurgeon, William Empson, Stephen Booth, and "among the
linguistically trained," Winifred Nowottny, Roman Jakobsen, and Brian
Vickers ("Ways into" 7-8), all critics who attempt to examine "the
fundamental act of a Shakespearean poem, which is to unfold itself in a
developing dynamic of thought and feeling marked by a unifying play
of mind and language" (*The Art* 5).

Yet there is no need to be mutually exclusive about approaches. I
will paraphrase a friend who does not wish to be identified: formalist
readings are a wonderful thing, especially when practiced with the
brilliance of a Helen Vendler, but they are not the only thing. To fish
the ocean of these remarkable poems, one needs to use several different
kinds of net. Something of Vendler's aesthetic sensibility can be found
in George T. Wright's essay in this volume, which has also just
appeared in a collection of essays from the World Shakespeare
Congress in Los Angeles in 1996. Wright traces the phenomenon of
silent speech (as both theme and medium) in Shakespeare's Sonnets:

> It may even be claimed that this unsounded speech, perfectly familiar
> to all of us because we generate it constantly every day of our lives,
> is the basic "voice" of the Sonnets, at least of 1-126, and a great
> range of other lyric poetry, and that by scrutinizing this dimension of
> language we can understand better not only what sort of poems the
> Sonnets and later English lyric and meditative poems are but how
> thoughtful speech of a different kind—sounded and public—appears
> in Shakespeare's dramatic writing. To watch Shakespeare's mastery
> of both is, to say the least, instructive.

Wright's essay connects the Sonnets to Shakespeare's development as a
dramatist and to the development of the English lyric over the last four
centuries, a line of inquiry that dates back at least as far as L. C.
Knights in 1934. Joseph Pequigney's essay, meanwhile, offers close
readings and aesthetic judgments of sonnets 71-74, while also treating
them as a carefully related dramatic sequence. As Pequigney shows, it
is possible to combine aesthetic criticism with other forms of
interpretation; in his case, the combination includes New Critical and

deconstructive close reading, queer theory, bibliographic observations about the design of the 1609 Quarto, and biographical speculation.

The reprinted essays by Peter Stallybrass, Margreta de Grazia, and Heather Dubrow are among the most influential publications on the Sonnets of the 1990s. Each is concerned with editing practices and their cultural implications, particularly their implications regarding gender and sexuality. Stallybrass retraces the nineteenth century's "cultural hysteria" regarding the idea of Shakespeare as potential sodomite; this hysteria, he claims, helped lead to the construction of heterosexuality "as a back-formation . . . the belated defense" against pederasty. In a note Stallybrass acknowledges his debt to Margreta de Grazia's *Shakespeare Verbatim*, which offers a cultural materialist reading of Malone's 1780 edition of the Sonnets. In turn, de Grazia's "The Scandal of Shakespeare's Sonnets" cites Stallybrass's essay, and in a sense goes beyond it in observing that the real scandal of Shakespeare's Sonnets (at least for readers in Shakespeare's time) "is not Shakespeare's desire for a boy; for in upholding social distinctions, that desire proves quite conservative and safe. It is Shakespeare's gynerastic longings for a black mistress that are perverse and menacing, precisely because they threaten to raze the very distinctions his poems to the fair boy strain to preserve."

In her essay, Dubrow interrogates the widespread critical acceptance of Malone's division of the Sonnets into two subsequences, the first 126 to a male friend, the last 28 to or about a woman. Thus, she attempts to render "unstable" all claims about the Sonnets that are based on that division. Dubrow cites de Grazia's observation that approximately 80 percent of the 154 poems lack addressees who are gendered by pronoun, and Dubrow further argues that Thorpe's edition is "imperfect in many ways."[25] Once one stops trying to make what is uncertain certain regarding the order and direction of address, she contends, other possible interpretations of individual sonnets and of the sequence as a whole open up—for example, that some of the eternalizing love poems in 1-126 were written to the dark lady, or that some of the angry, "misogynist" poems in 127-154 are in fact addressed to the young man. Such alternative readings, she cautions, "are as impossible to establish as they are intriguing to consider." Dubrow's real purpose is not to establish new readings but to unhinge the old and to question the "curiously positivistic claims" many scholars continue to make about the Sonnets despite the many uncertainties that surround them. Finally, from a feminist perspective, she offers possible reasons why Malone's division has so rarely been questioned in recent years.

Several of the new essays take their starting point from the reprinted essays by Stallybrass, de Grazia, and Dubrow. Valerie Traub begins her essay with two epigraphs, one a quote from de Grazia's essay in this volume. Marvin Hunt answers de Grazia's call for critics to "entertain the possibility that these poems express desire for a black woman rather than desire for a boy." Rebecca Laroche's essay on Oscar Wilde and the Sonnets draws on Stallybrass's discussion of the nineteenth century's homophobic response to the Sonnets, while Naomi J. Miller takes seriously (as one of several interpretive possibilities) Dubrow's suggestion that the mother in sonnet 143 may represent the male friend rather than the dark lady; by the same token, Dubrow's token, Hunt imagines sonnet 128 as addressed to the young male friend. Of course, some of the new essays challenge important ideas in the articles by Stallybrass, de Grazia, and Dubrow, just as the three of them at times disagree with one another. In a challenge to Dubrow's argument, Joyce Sutphen's essay discovers that imagery about memory in the Sonnets supports Malone's division into two subsequences: "Before sonnet 126, keeping averts loss; preservation of the beloved is accomplished ('such virtue hath [his] pen'), whereas in the sonnets that follow, such as 133, keeping has to do with taking away (as in being kept), and obliteration of the poet's very self is always a possibility."

Ilona Bell's essay, founded on Duncan-Jones's and John Kerrigan's belief that Shakespeare shaped the 1609 Quarto (that is, all the Sonnets and *A Lover's Complaint*) and authorized its publication, offers the starkest contrast with Dubrow's. Olga L. Valbuena quietly states her disagreement with the antinarrative thrust of Dubrow's work on the Sonnets generally. Some contributors of new essays also take on earlier work by other contributors. Thus, Gordon Braden and Valerie Traub both register critical disagreements with specific arguments in Joseph Pequigney's *Such Is My Love*. Obviously, there has been no editorial effort to make everyone begin with the same set of assumptions or reach the same conclusions. Serious scholarly disagreement on many issues is what enlivens Sonnet criticism today; that disagreement is often reflected in this volume.

The influence of Joel Fineman's *Shakespeare's Perjured Eye* is a leitmotif of the volume. Fineman is cited by almost every author in this collection (only Stephen Booth, perhaps, is cited with greater frequency). While acknowledging the obvious brilliance and complexity of Fineman's thesis, many of these essays attempt to refine, or even to refute, his work. In his comparative study of Shakespeare and Petrarch, Braden states that the cogency of many aspects of Fineman's thesis is not matched by his "handling of the lyric precedents that are said to be Shakespeare's starting point"; his "knowledge of this tradition looks skimpy and secondhand." Positing a very different relationship between Shakespeare's art and Petrarch's than Fineman does, Braden asserts that "Shakespeare's sequence is in certain ways one of the most Petrarchan sequences of the age." In fact, Braden later concludes, "It is part of the distinction of Shakespeare's sequence to enact Petrarch's *sententia* more fully than any intervening practitioner." Tracing the language and imagery of usury in the first twenty sonnets, Peter C. Herman's essay expresses an obvious debt to Thomas M. Greene's interpretation of economic language, "Pitiful Thrivers: Failed Husbandry in the Sonnets"; in addition, Herman challenges the strict division between the two subsequences that Fineman (at least in the first two chapters of his book) posits. Herman finds that "the opening poems are as marked by 'linguistic difference' and *mise en abymes* as the poems addressed to the dark lady."

Lisa Freinkel offers what she describes as "a post-Reformation reading" of the Sonnets that both builds on and revises Fineman's post-Petrarchan interpretation: Shakespeare's poems, she states, "recast Petrarchism within a Lutheran universe," a universe that poses "a devastating challenge for Christian allegory." In examining Shakespeare's use of the figure of the rose through the sequence, Freinkel shows that "no redemptive logic enriches Shakespearean temporality." Rejecting the "before and after" sequence posited by Fineman's theory, Freinkel insists the Sonnets present instead "a vision of wasteful time." Michael Schoenfeldt begins his essay by questioning theories like Fineman's, which discover "in the Renaissance prefigurations of modernity"; instead, Schoenfeldt attempts to "highlight some of the considerable differences and surprising similarities that exist between the early modern language of interiority and our own, and to show some of the interpretive dissonance that has been generated from our inability to apprehend these differences and to clarify these similarities." He attempts a pre-Freudian, pre-Romantic close reading of sonnet 94 to show how modern interpreters "unintentionally vex" this poem "with an anachronistic model of self and desire"; unlike Empson, Hubler, and most other modern readers, Schoenfeldt emphasizes "the premium that Shakespeare's own articulations of desire place on self-control, as well as the medical and moral culture from which they derive." Finally, Valerie Traub faults Fineman's "distinction between ascetic homosexuality and erotic heterosexuality" for being "blind to the eroticism suffusing the first 126 poems" and for imposing "modern identity categories onto early modern eroticism."

Essays like Schoenfeldt's, Freinkel's, and Herman's are, of course, deeply committed to the methods of the New Historicism, though each examines a different aspects of early modern life and different areas of discourse. The same could be said of the essays by Naomi J. Miller and Olga L. Valbuena, which combine feminism with historicist methodology. Valbuena focuses on the material implements of the early modern poet's craft to figure forth the failure of the speaker's project to immortalize the young friend. She traces a sequence that "involves not the affirmation of an overarching subject but, instead, tells the story of how the formal and material conditions of that subject dissolve in the very ink that writes them." Miller reveals the ways early modern codes of maternity are reflected in the Sonnets, as well as how the Sonnets use those codes "to explore how conflicts between authority and sexuality frame the progress of desire." Every major character in the Sonnets, Miller writes, "plays the mother's part, from the young man who is enjoined both to procreate and to produce 'children nursed, delivered from thy brain' ([sonnet] 77), to the dark lady who certainly stands as one figure for the 'careful housewife' ([sonnet] 143), to the poet who acknowledges himself both 'an unperfect actor' and a 'fierce thing' with 'speaking breast' ([sonnet] 23)."

Bruce R. Smith also sails a historicist tack; he opens his essay by marveling at critics who are willing to recognize homoeroticism in Shakespeare's plays, but not in the Sonnets. "The cause for readers' continuing anxiety," he writes, "has to do, at bottom, with pronouns, with transactions among 'I,' 'you,' 'he,' 'she,' and 'we.'" These reference points are "historically constructed and . . . are interrelated in these poems in ways that are different—sometimes radically different—from today." Traub, meanwhile, develops Jonathan Goldberg's comment that the real sodomitical relationship in the Sonnets takes place between the speaker and the dark lady, not between the speaker and the young man. Her essay is a sustained attempt "to unravel in historical terms the convergence in Shakespeare's poems of male homoerotic desire and misogyny," a theme Eve Kosofsky

Sedgwick had treated in an admittedly dehistoricized way in *Between Men*. "Through the use of tropes of getting, increase, tillage, husbandry, engrafting, printing, copying, and issue," Traub writes, "the collection appropriates the rhetoric of biological and mechanical reproduction for male-male love."

Historicizing in this collection takes other forms as well. John Klause goes against most recent trends (beginning with Mizener's 1940 response to Ransom) when he "follow[s] older commentators in attempting to identify the 'fools of time' whose testimony is crucial to the poet's case" in sonnet 124. Arguing that the poet in fact sympathizes with the "fools of time," Klause goes on to identify them with the Catholic martyrs executed in England during the late 1580s and early 1590s, described in Jesuit Robert Southwell's *Humble Supplication to Her Majestie* (1591) and *Epistle of Comfort* (1587). (Klause traces the influence of Southwell's pamphlets, which circulated in the Catholic underground and were not printed until 1600, to *Titus Andronicus* as well, evidence that supports his reading of sonnet 124.) The essays by Rebecca Laroche and Marvin Hunt investigate the cultural implications of different periods in the history of the Sonnets' reception. Laroche's essay examines how Wilde "negotiates his own relation to literary history through the Sonnets of Shakespeare"; in her view, his "fictional essay"—*The Portrait of Mr. W. H.*—"provides an allegory of literary relations so compelling that its presence is still felt in much current criticism on the Sonnets." Building on the careful scholarship of Samuel Schoenbaum, Hunt provides a semiotic reading of efforts by Thomas Tyler, George Bernard Shaw, A. L. Rowse, and others to deny or contain the possibility that the dark lady of the Sonnets might be a black woman. Ilona Bell's essay is informed by her careful study of Daniel's practice, as well as that of other Elizabethan sonneteers, while Joyce Sutphen's depends upon her close familiarity with Renaissance tropes of memory, a familiarity that relies on the work of Mary Carruthers.

I will paraphrase my earlier paraphrase of my friend's comment about aesthetic formalism: historicizing is also a wonderful thing, but it is not the only thing either. Though he begins by referring to Erasmus's "On the Education of Children," Lars Engle's essay considers the distinction between shame and guilt in the Sonnets from the vantage point of contemporary philosophers Bernard Williams and Richard Wolheim. Shame, Engle contends, is "a component of the reflective adult self-consciousness, the moral-psychological complexity, for which the Sonnets are justly famous." Engle is not the only contributor to swim against the current of contemporary fashion. Ilona Bell notes that "[m]ost studies of the Sonnets ignore *A Lover's Complaint*, as this collection itself illustrates," thus setting herself apart from the other contributors. She follows up on earlier work by Katherine Duncan-Jones and John Kerrigan, maintaining that *A Lover's Complaint* is Shakespeare's "authorized" conclusion to the edition Thorpe published in 1609 as *SHAKE-SPEARES SONNETS*. According to Bell, "the female complainant's speech and the male lover's persuasion embedded within it provide a commentary on and reader's guide to the drama enacted by and concealed within the Sonnets." Few contributors, I believe, would disapprove of her attention to *A Lover's Complaint*, but some might take issue with Bell's certainty that Shakespeare's Sonnets, like those of Spenser and Donne, "veil allusions to actual persons or events in ambiguity and obscurity." On the biographical issue, at least in the company of the other contributors, Bell stands in the minority, as does Joseph Pequigney when he examines the 1609 Quarto for suggestions of an "affinity between the historical author and the poet inscribed in the text." It may be, he suggests, that the title *SHAKE-SPEARES SONNETS* meant to early modern readers that "in addition to being *by* him they are also *about* him, and he is the leading personage in the work." Though Duncan-Jones agrees about the significance of the title (*Sonnets* 86), many scholars would counter that there is no documentary evidence to corroborate any biographical theory, or they might insist biography is irrelevant to an appreciation of lyric beauty.

Thoughtful disagreement and variety of methods create new knowledge. This seems to be Duncan-Jones's view as well. For example, in her introduction to the New Arden Sonnets, she considers the effect of Stephen Booth's revolutionary 1977 edition:

> Though Booth explores an unprecedentedly wide range of coexistent semantic readings in his 'analytical commentary', he does not by any means exhaust these possibilities, which are, in truth, inexhaustible. Indeed, this is one of the joys of *Sonnets* for modern readers. Here, even more than in the rest of Shakespeare's work, it is open to each and every reader to arrive at an individual and original response. The notorious truism that no two people ever concur in interpreting *Sonnets* is not cause for despair, but for rejoicing. (96-97)

As long as we can hold to such modest wisdom, I think we can indeed speak of a well-earned, as opposed to a complacent, sense of progress, one that I think should carry us well into the twenty-first century.

It is in the same spirit of openness to diverse and sometimes contending voices that the following essays are offered.

NOTES

1. All of my quotations of the Sonnets are from Stephen Booth's 1977 edition.

2. There are 2,503 entries in Tetsumaro Hayashi's *Shakespeare's Sonnets: A Record of 20th-Century Criticism* (1972).

3. Variant versions of sonnets 138 and 144 appeared in the unauthorized *The Passionate Pilgrim* (1599 and 1612). Some scholars (for example, Gary Taylor, "Some Manuscripts") speculate that Shakespeare revised some poems written before 1599 for inclusion in the 1609 Quarto. There is also the chance, of course, that neither version of 138 and 144 represents the author's "final" intentions.

4. Shakespeare's name was removed from the title page of the 1612 edition of *The Passionate Pilgrim*, most probably as a result of Thomas Heywood's objection in "An Apology for Actors" to Jaggard's inclusion of some of Heywood's poems in the volume. Shakespeare, Heywood reported, was "much offended with M. Jaggard that (altogether unknowne to him) presumed to make so bold with his name" (see Marotti, "Sonnets as Property" 152-53).

5. Most authorities agree that Shakespeare probably did not proofread *Venus and Adonis* or *The Rape of Lucrece* while either work was in press. The number of errors discovered in the 1609 Quarto varies from editor to editor; Rollins agrees to thirty-six probable cases of misprints (not counting probable errors of punctuation) (see 2: 6-18). George Wyndham is one of Q's strongest defenders, while Sidney Lee remains one of its harshest judges. Since Duncan-Jones believes Shakespeare authorized Thorpe's publication, her New Arden Sonnets follows the 1609 Quarto "more closely than in any previous modernized edition" (103). Obviously, the issue of the authority of Q is crucial to problems of editing. See Graves and Riding; Booth, Preface to *Sonnets*; Greene, "Anti-Hermeneutics"; and Duncan-Jones, "Filling."

6. See also Duncan-Jones, *Sonnets* 97-101; and Fowler 183-97.

7. Evans writes that "Foster's argument founders on what I feel is a forced interpretation of God as 'our.ever-living.poet'" (115). For Brae and Ingleby, see "*Athenaeum*, July 5 [1873], pp. 18 f." (cited in Rollins 2: 216).

8. That the youth "belonged to a much higher class than the poet's can hardly be reasonably denied," writes Dover Wilson, " though many critics have denied it" (30). See also 32-34.

9. Some scholars would begin the deformation with Benson, who made verbal changes that altered direction of address from a man to a woman in a few sonnets; those who copied sonnets into private manuscript collections also often changed the gender of the beloved. See Taylor, "Some Manuscripts"; and Bruce R. Smith, *Homosexual Desire* 239.

10. See also Robertson (257. Rollins writes that he finds the suppression theory plausible. It perhaps accounts for the lack of references to the dark lady and others, as well as the "total silence [about the Sonnets] of Sh[akespeare]'s contemporaries." (2: 327).

11. Marotti mentions "about a dozen" extant copies of the 1609 Quarto ("Sonnets as Property " 157); the *Short Title Catalogue,* however, lists thirteen, as do Evans (275-76) and Duncan-Jones (*Sonnets* 8).

12. Benson's volume was, in fact, published in 1639. His text was followed in the eighteenth century to Gildon (1710, 1714), Sewell (1725, 1728), Ewing (1771), Gentleman (1774), Evans (1775), and others. The last text based on Benson was Durrell's New York edition in 1817-18 (Ingram and Redpath xix-xxi).

13. In addition to Marotti and de Grazia discussed below, see Bennett.

14. The 1609 Quarto was reprinted by Bernard Lintott in 1711 ("Lintott's description of the volume, however, announcing it to contain 'One hundred and Fifty Four Sonnets, all of them in Praise of his Mistress', was clearly still under the influence of Benson's volume" [Ingram and Redpath xxi]). It was reprinted again in 1766 by George Steevens. Edward Capell had prepared an edition with notes in 1766, but it was never published; Malone apparently consulted Capell's notes as he prepared the 1780 edition.

15. In his most recent introduction to the Sonnets (1997), Bevington repeats the following from the 1980 edition: "His [Shakespeare's] emphasis on friendship seems new, for no other sequence addressed a majority of its sonnets to a friend rather than to a mistress, but even here the anti-Petrarchan quest for spontaneity and candor is in the best Elizabethan tradition of Sidney and Spenser. Besides, the exaltation of friendship over love was itself a widespread Neoplatonic commonplace recently popularized in the writings of John Lyly" (1622). However, later in his 1997 introduction, after mentioning Pequigney's *Such Is My Love,* Bevington concedes that "the bond between poet and friend is extraordinarily strong, and certainly there is a danger that traditional scholarship has minimized the erotic bond between the poet and friend out of a distaste for the idea" (1663).

16. Among the most important source studies of this century are J. B. Leishman's *Themes and Variations in Shakespeare's Sonnets,* Claes Schaar's *An Elizabethan Sonnet Problem: Shakespeare's Sonnets, Daniel's Delia, and their Literary Background,* T. W. Baldwin's *On the Literary Genetics of Shakespeare's Poems and Sonnets,* J. W. Lever's *The Elizabethan Love Sonnet,* Katherine Wilson's *Shakespeare's Sugared Sonnets,* Anne Ferry's *All in War with Time,* Carol Thomas Neely's "The Structure of English Renaissance Sonnet Sequences," Joel Fineman's *Shakespeare's Perjured Eye,* Thomas P. Roche's *Petrarch and the English Sonnet Sequences,* Sandra L. Bermann's *The Sonnet over Time: A Study in the Sonnets of Petrarch, Shakespeare, and Baudelaire,* and Heather Dubrow's *Echoes of Desire.*

17. See Robertson 5-6; Rollins 2: 144-45; and Schoenbaum *Lives* 509-10 (1970 ed.).

18. Booth has been criticized by Hallett Smith for overexplaining the Sonnets: "The reader Booth tries to evoke is a post-Empson reader, and there was no such thing in 1609" (158). Vendler is also critical. She shares Booth's appreciation of the complexity of the Sonnets, but, she states, "Booth gives up too easily on interpretation. Even in the richness of Shakespeare's language, we are not left afloat on an uninterpretable set of 'ideational static,' not when the formal features of the *Sonnets* are there to guide us. It was her awareness of those formal features that made the late Winifred Nowottny the best guide to the sequence" (*The Art* 40).

19. I am indebted to Rebecca Laroche for making me aware of Taylor's survey of criticism, from which she also quotes in her essay in this volume.

20. The phrase "occult structures" is taken from Kermode's review of Vendler's *The Art of Shakespeare's Sonnets* (30). It aptly describes not just Vendler's "micro" interpretations, but also the "macro" claims about numerological structure made by Fowler and by Duncan-Jones.

21. Thus, Duncan-Hones writes: "Once it is accepted that the publication of Q was authorized by Shakespeare, and that it was in the Jacobean period that he put the sequence into its final form, an identification of Pembroke as the dedicatee and addressee of *Sonnets* becomes overwhelmingly attractive." However, she goes on to acknowledge that "[i]f some of the 'fair youth' sonnets, or versions of them, were written as early as 1592-5, these may indeed originally have been associated with Southampton.... But as completed and published in 1609 the sequence strongly invites a reference to Pembroke" (69).

22. Jonathan Goldberg praises Sedgwick's analysis as "the only satisfying reading of Shakespeare's sonnets" (*Sodometries* 23). Calling for the need to rethink early modern friendship from the ground up, Goldberg writes, "That

ground might well be the sonnets, and it is about time that criticism followed Sedgwick's reading of them in *Between Men*" (*Sodometries* 142).

23. See also Masten 5-6; Bredbeck argues that "what has been thought of as 'homosexual' and 'gay' in these sequences [by Shakespeare and Richard Barnfield] is not at all; instead it is part of a more complicated strategy of subject construction" (29).

24. In their introductions to their recent editions, Vendler (15-16) recognizes and Duncan-Jones strongly emphasizes (throughout) the homoeroticism of the first subsequence. Hecht's introduction to Evans's edition is by comparison much more cautious (17-18). See also Hecht's discussion in "The Sonnet: Ruminations on Form, Sex, and History" 140-44. In *Echoes of Desire*, Heather Dubrow credits recent gay studies like Bruce R. Smith's *Homosexual Desire in Shakespeare's England* for offering "a valuable corrective" to traditional claims that the relationship between the poet and the friend "exemplifies asexual friendship." However, she cautions, "students of early modern literature currently risk allowing the pendulum to swing too far: if the assertion that these poems are indubitably heterosexual is too dogmatic (as defensive observations so often are), so too is the assertion that they are unquestionably the product of a homosexual relationship" (121-22).

25. Not all scholars come up with the same count. For example, in "Shakespeare's Sonnets as Literary Property," Marotti writes that "of the first 126, the vast majority, some 112 poems, seem clearly addressed to the young man," five have a "problematical addressee," and nine refer to the male friend in third person (156).

WORKS CITED

Acheson, Arthur. *Mistress Davenant: The Dark Lady of Shakespeare's Sonnets*. London: Quaritch, 1913.

Alden, Raymond Macdonald, ed. *The Sonnets of Shakespeare*. Boston: Houghton Mifflin, 1916.

Auden, W. H. Introduction. *The Sonnets*. Ed. William Burto. New York: New American Library (Signet), 1964. xvii-xxxviii.

Baldwin, T.W. *On the Literary Genetics of Shakespeare's Poems and Sonnets*. Urbana: U of Illinois P, 1950.

Barber, C. L. "An Essay on Shakespeare's Sonnets." *The Sonnets of Shakespeare*. New York: Dell, 1960. Rpt. in *Shakespeare's Sonnets: Modern Critical Interpretations*. Ed. Harold Bloom. New York: Chelsea House, 1987. 5-27.

————, and Richard P. Wheeler. *The Whole Journey: Shakespeare's Power of Development*. Berkeley: U of California P, 1986.

Barnstorff, D. *A Key to Shakespeare's Sonnets*. Trans. T. J. Graham. London: Trubner, 1862. Trans. of *Schlussel zu Shakespeares Sonnetten*. Bremen: J. Kuhtmann, 1860.

Barrell, John. "Editing Out the Discourse of Patronage and Shakespeare's Twenty-ninth Sonnet." *Poetry, Language and Politics*. Manchester: U of Manchester P, 1988.

Beeching, H. C. *The Sonnets of Shakespeare*. Boston: Ginn, 1904.

Bell, Ilona. "'That which thou hast done': Shakespeare's Sonnets and *A Lover's Complaint*." *Shakespeare's Sonnets: Critical Essays*. Ed. James Schiffer. New York: Garland, 1998. 455-74.

Bennett, Josephine Waters. "Benson's Alleged Piracy of *Shakespeare's Sonnets* and Some of Jonson's Works." *Studies in Bibliography* 21 (1968): 235-48.

Benson, John, ed. *Poems: Written by Wil. Shake-speare. Gent.* London, 1640.

Bermann, Sandra. *The Sonnet over Time: A Study in the Sonnets of Petrarch, Shakespeare, and Baudelaire*. Chapel Hill: U of North Carolina P, 1988.

Bevington, David, ed. *The Complete Works of Shakespeare*. [3rd ed. 1980.] Updated 4th ed. New York: Addison Wesley Longman, 1997.

Bloom, Harold, ed. *Shakespeare's Sonnets: Modern Critical Interpretations*. New York: Chelsea House, 1987.

Boaden, James. *On the Sonnets of Shakespeare*. 1832. London: Rodd, 1837.

Booth, Stephen. *An Essay on Shakespeare's Sonnets*. New Haven: Yale UP, 1969.

————, ed. *Shakespeare's Sonnets*. New Haven: Yale UP, 1977.

Boswell, James, et al., eds. *The Plays and Poems of William Shakespeare*. Vol. 20. London, 1821.

Braden, Gordon. "Shakespeare's Petrarchism." *Shakespeare's Sonnets: Critical Essays*. Ed. James Schiffer. New York: Garland, 1998. 163-83.

Bradley, A. C. "Shakespeare the Man." *Oxford Lectures on Poetry*. London: Macmillan, 1909. 311-57.

Bray, Alan. *Homosexuality in Renaissance England*. London: Gay Men's P, 1982.

Bredbeck, Gregory W. *Sodomy and Interpretation: Marlowe to Milton*. Ithaca: Cornell UP, 1991.

Browning, Robert. *The Poetical Works of Robert Browning*. London: Oxford UP, 1905; rpt. 1964.

Butler, Samuel. *Shakespeare's Sonnets Reconsidered*. 1899. London: Jonathan Cape, 1927.

Carruthers, Mary. *The Book of Memory*. Cambridge: Cambridge UP, 1990.

Chalmers, George. *An Apology for the Believers in the Shakespeare-Papers.* London, 1797.

———. *A Supplemental Apology for the Believers in the Shakespeare-Papers.* London, 1799.

Coleridge, Samuel Taylor. *Specimens of the Table Talk.* 2nd ed. London: John Murray, 1836.

Colie, Rosalie L. *Shakespeare's Living Art.* Princeton: Princeton UP, 1974.

Crosman, Robert. "Making Love out of Nothing at All: The Issue of Story in Shakespeare's Procreation Sonnets." *Shakespeare Quarterly* 41 (1990): 470-88.

de Grazia, Margreta. "Locating and Dislocating the 'I' of Shakespeare's Sonnets." *William Shakespeare: His World, His Work, His Influence.* Ed. John F. Andrew. Vol. 2. New York: Scribners, 1985. 433-44.

———. "The Motive for Interiority: Shakespeare's *Sonnets* and *Hamlet*." *Style* 23 (1989): 430-444.

———. "The Scandal of Shakespeare's Sonnets." *Shakespeare Survey* 46 (1994): 35-49. Rpt. in *Shakespeare's Sonnets: Critical Essays.* Ed. James Schiffer. New York: Garland, 1998. 89-112.

———. *Shakespeare Verbatim: The Reproduction of Authenticity and the 1790 Apparatus.* Oxford: Oxford UP, 1991.

Donoghue, Denis. "Shakespeare in the Sonnets." *Raritan* 6 (1986): 123-37.

Donow, Herbert S. *The Sonnet in England and America: A Bibliography of Criticism.* Westport: Greenwood, 1982.

Dowden, Edward, ed. *The Sonnets of William Shakepere.* London: Kegan Paul, 1881.

Drake, Nathan. *Shakespeare and his Times.* London: Cadell and Davies, 1817.

Dubrow, Heather. *Captive Victors: Shakespeare's Narrative Poems and Sonnets.* Ithaca: Cornell UP, 1987.

———. *Echoes of Desire: English Petrarchanism and Its Counterdiscourses.* Ithaca: Cornell UP, 1995.

———. "'Incertainties now crown themselves assur'd': The Politics of Plotting Shakespeare's Sonnets." *Shakespeare Quarterly* 47 (1996): 291-305. Rpt. in *Shakespeare's Sonnets: Critical Essays.* Ed. James Schiffer. New York: Garland, 1998. 113-33.

Duncan-Jones, Katherine. "Filling the Unforgiving Minute: Modernizing SHAKE-SPEARES SONNETS (1609)." *Essays in Criticism* 45 (1995): 199-207.

———, ed. *Shakespeare's Sonnets.* The Arden Shakespeare. Nashville: Nelson, 1997.

————."Was the 1609 *Shake-speares Sonnets* Really Unauthorized?" *Review of English Studies* 34 (1983): 151-71.

Empson, William. *Seven Types of Ambiguity*. London: Chatto and Windus, 1930.

————. *Some Versions of Pastoral*. 1935. New York: New Directions, 1974.

Engle, Lars. "'I am that I am': Shakespeare's Sonnets and the Economy of Shame." *Shakespeare's Sonnets: Critical Essays*. Ed. James Schiffer. New York: Garland, 1998. 185-97.

Evans, G. Blakemore, ed. *The Sonnets*. Cambridge: Cambridge UP, 1996.

Ferry, Anne. *All in War with Time: Love Poetry of Shakespeare, Donne, Jonson, Marvell*. Cambridge: Harvard UP, 1975.

————. *The "Inward" Language: Sonnets of Wyatt, Sidney, Shakespeare, Donne*. Chicago: U of Chicago P, 1983.

Fineman, Joel. *Shakespeare's Perjured Eye: The Invention of Poetic Subjectivity in the Sonnets*. Berkeley: U of California P, 1986.

Forbis, John F. *The Shakespearean Enigma and an Elizabethan Mania*. New York: American Service Library, 1924.

Foster, Donald W. "Master W. H., R.I.P." *PMLA* 102 (1987): 42-55.

————. "Reconstructing Shakespeare Part 2: The Sonnets." *The Shakespeare Newsletter* (Fall 1991): 26-27.

Fowler, Alistair. *Triumphal Forms: Structural Patterns in Elizabethan Poetry*. Cambridge: Cambridge UP, 1970.

Freinkel, Lisa. "The Name of the Rose: Christian Figurality and Shakespeare's Sonnets." *Shakespeare's Sonnets: Critical Essays*. Ed. James Schiffer. New York: Garland, 1998. 241-61.

Garber, Marjorie. *Vice Versa: Bisexuality and the Eroticism of Everyday Life*. New York: Simon and Schuster, 1995.

Goldberg, Jonathan. *Sodometries: Renaissance Texts, Modern Sexualities*. Stanford: Stanford UP, 1992.

————. *Voice Terminal Echo: Postmodernism and English Renaissance*. New York: Methuen, 1986.

Graves, Robert, and Laura Riding. "A Study in Original Punctuation and Spelling: Sonnet 129." *The Common Asphodel: Collected Essays on Poetry 1922-1949*. London: Hamish Hamilton, 1949. 84-95.

Greene, Thomas M. "Anti-Hermeneutics: The Case of Shakespeare's Sonnet 129." *The Vulnerable Text: Essays on Renaissance Literature*. New York: Columbia UP, 1986. 159-74.

————. "Pitiful Thrivers: Failed Husbandry in the Sonnets." *Shakespeare and the Question of Theory*. Ed. Patricia Parker and Geoffrey Hartman. New York: Methuen, 1985. 230-44.

Hall, Kim F. *Things of Darkness: Economies of Race and Gender in Early Modern England*. Ithaca: Cornell UP, 1995.

Hallam, Henry. "Sonnets of Shakespeare." *Introduction to the Literature of Europe in the Fifteenth, Sixteenth, and Seventeenth Centuries*. Vol. 3. London: Murray, 1892. 261-64.

Harrison, G. B. *Shakespeare under Elizabeth*. New York: Knopf, 1933.

Hayashi, Tetsumaro. *Shakespeare's Sonnets: A Record of 20th-Century Criticism*. Metuchen: Scarecrow, 1972.

Hecht, Anthony. Introduction. *The Sonnets*. Ed. G. Blakemore Evans. Cambridge: Cambridge UP, 1997. 1-28.

———. "The Sonnet: Ruminations on Form, Sex, and History." *Antioch Review* 55 (1997): 134-47.

Hedley, Jane. "Since First Your Eye I Eyed: Shakespeare's *Sonnets* and the Poetics of Narcissism." *Style* 28 (1994): 1-30.

Herman, Peter C. "What's the Use? Or, The Problematic of Economy in Shakespeare's Procreation Sonnets." *Shakespeare's Sonnets: Critical Essays*. Ed. James Schiffer. New York: Garland, 1998. 263-83.

Herrnstein [Smith], Barbara, ed. *Discussions of Shakespeare's Sonnets*. Boston: Heath, 1964.

Hieatt, A. Kent, Charles W. Hieatt, and Anne Lake Prescott. "When Did Shakespeare Write *Sonnets* 1609?" *Studies in Philology* 88 (1991): 69-109.

Hotson, Leslie. *Mr. W. H.* London: Hart-Davis, 1964.

Howard, Richard. "Total Immersion." Rev. of *The Art of Shakespeare's Sonnets*, by Helen Vendler. *New York Times Book Review* 17 Nov. 1997: 6.

Hubler, Edward. *The Sense of Shakespeare's Sonnets*. Princeton: Princeton UP, 1952.

Hubler, Edward, et al., eds. *The Riddle of Shakespeare's Sonnets*. New York, 1962.

Hunt, Marvin. "Be Dark but Not Too Dark: Shakespeare's Dark Lady as a Sign of Color." *Shakespeare's Sonnets: Critical Essays*. Ed. James Schiffer. New York: Garland, 1998. 369-89.

Hunter, G. K. "The Dramatic Technique of Shakespeare's Sonnets." *Essays in Criticism* 3 (1953): 152-64.

Ingram, W. G., and Theodore Redpath, eds. *Sonnets*. London: U of London P, 1964.

Jakobsen, Roman [with L. G. Jones]. "Shakespeare's Verbal Art in 'Th' Expence of Spirit.'" *Language in Literature*. Ed. Krystina Pomorska and Stephen Rudy. Cambridge: Belknap/Harvard UP, 1987. 198-215.

Jones, Peter, ed. *Shakespeare: The Sonnets: A Casebook*. London: Macmillan, 1977.

Kermode, Frank. "Millions of Strange Shadows." Rev. of *The Art of Shakespeare's Sonnets,* by Helen Vendler. *New Republic* 17 Nov. 1997: 27-32.

Kernan, Alvin. "Shakespeare's Sonnets and Patronage Art." *Shakespeare, the King's Playwright: Theater in the Stuart Court, 1603-1613*. New Haven: Yale UP, 1995. 169-87.

Kerrigan, John, ed. *The Sonnets and A Lover's Complaint*. Harmondsworth: Penguin, 1986.

Kerrigan, William. "Would He Had Blotted a Thousand." *Raritan* 17 (1997): 38-48.

Klause, John. "Politics, Heresy, and Martyrdom in Shakespeare's Sonnet 124 and *Titus Andronicus."* *Shakespeare's Sonnets: Critical Essays*. Ed. James Schiffer. New York: Garland, 1998. 219-40.

Knight, G. Wilson. *The Mutual Flame*. London: Methuen, 1955.

Knights, L. C. "Shakespeare's Sonnets." *Scrutiny* 3 (1934): 133-60. Rpt. in *A Casebook on Shakespeare's Sonnets*. Ed. Gerald Willen and Victor B. Reed. New York: Crowell, 1964. 173-97.

Landry, Hilton. *Interpretations in Shakespeare's Sonnets*. Berkeley: U of California P, 1963.

——, ed. *New Essays on Shakespeare's Sonnets*. New York: AMS, 1976.

Laroche, Rebecca. "The Sonnets on Trial: Reconsidering *The Portrait of Mr. W. H."* *Shakespeare's Sonnets: Critical Essays*. Ed. James Schiffer. New York: Garland, 1998. 391-409.

Lee, Sidney, ed. *Shakespeare's Sonnets, Being a Reproduction in Facsimile of the First Edition, 1609*. Oxford: Clarendon, 1905.

Leishman, J. B. *Themes and Variations in Shakespeare's Sonnets*. New York: Harper and Row, 1961; Harper Torchbook ed., 1966.

Lever, J. W. *The Elizabethan Love Sonnet*. London: Methuen, 1956.

Mahood, M. M. "Love's Confined Doom." *Shakespeare Survey* 15 (1962): 50-61.

Malone, Edmond, ed. *The Plays and Poems of William Shakspeare*. Vol. 10. London, 1790.

——, ed. *Supplement to the Edition of Shakspeare's Plays Published in 1778*. Vol. 1. London, 1780.

Marotti, Arthur F. "'Love Is Not Love': Elizabethan Sonnet Sequences and the Social Order." *ELH* (1982): 396-428.

——. "Shakespeare's Sonnets as Literary Property." *Soliciting Interpretation: Literary Theory and Seventeenth-Century English Poetry*.

Ed. Elizabeth D. Harvey and Katherine Eisaman Maus. Chicago: U of Chicago P, 1990. 143-73.

Masten, Jeffrey. *Textual Intercourse: Collaboration, Authorhip and Sexualities in Renaissance Drama*. Cambridge: Cambridge UP, 1997.

McLeod, Randall [as "Random Clod"]. "Information on Information." *Text*. Vol. 5. Ed. D. C. Greetham and W. Speed Hill. New York: AMS Press, 1991. 241-81.

Melchiori, Giorgio. *Shakespeare's Dramatic Meditations: An Experiment in Criticism*. Oxford: Clarendon, 1976.

Miller, Naomi J. "Playing 'the mother's part': Shakespeare's Sonnets and Early Modern Codes of Maternity." *Shakespeare's Sonnets: Critical Essays*. Ed. James Schiffer. New York: Garland, 1998. 347-67.

Mizener, Arthur. "The Structure of Figurative Language in Shakespeare's Sonnets." *Southern Review* 5 (1940): 730-47. Rpt. in *A Casebook on Shakespeare's Sonnets*. Ed. Gerald Willen and Victor B. Reed. New York: Crowell, 1964. 219-35.

Muir, Kenneth. *Shakespeare's Sonnets*. London: Allen and Unwin, 1979.

Neely, Carol Thomas. "The Structure of English Renaissance Sonnet Sequences." *ELH* 45 (1978): 359-89.

Nejgebauer, A. "The Sonnets" in "Twentieth-Century Studies in Shakespeare's Songs, Sonnets, and Poems." *Shakespeare Survey* 15 (1962): 10-18.

Nosworthy, J. M. "Shakespeare and Mr. W. H." *Library*. 5th Series. 18 (1963): 294-98.

Nowottny, Winifred M. T. "Formal Elements in Shakespeare's Sonnets I-VI." *Essays in Criticism* 2 (1952): 76-84.

Padel, John. *New Poems by Shakespeare: Order and Meaning Restored to the Sonnets*. London: Herbert, 1981.

Pequigney, Joseph. "Sonnets 71-74: Texts and Contexts." *Shakespeare's Sonnets: Critical Essays*. Ed. James Schiffer. New York: Garland, 1998. 285-304.

———. *Such Is My Love: A Study of Shakespeare's Sonnets*. Chicago: U of Chicago P, 1985.

Raleigh, Walter. *Shakespeare*. New York: Macmillan, 1907.

Ramsey, Paul. *The Fickle Glass: A Study of Shakespeare's Sonnets*. New York: AMS, 1979.

Ransom, John Crowe. "Shakespeare at Sonnets." *Southern Review* 3 (1937-38): 531-53. Rpt. in *A Casebook on Shakespeare's Sonnets*. Ed. Gerald Willen and Victor B. Reed. New York: Crowell, 1964. 198-219.

Robertson, J. M. *The Problems of the Shakespeare Sonnets*. London: George Routledge and Sons, 1926.

Roche, Thomas P. *Petrarch and the English Sonnet Sequences*. New York: AMS, 1989.

Rollins, Hyder Edward, ed. *A New Variorum Edition of Shakespeare: The Sonnets*. 2 vols. Philadelphia: Lippincott, 1944.

Rosmarin, Adena. "Hermeneutics versus Erotics: Shakespeare's *Sonnets* and Interpretive History." *PMLA* 100 (1985): 20-37.

Rowse, A. L., ed. *Shakespeare's Sonnets: The Problems Solved*. New York: Harper and Row, 1964; 2nd ed. 1973.

Schaar, Claes. *An Elizabethan Sonnet Problem: Shakespeare's Sonnets, Daniel's Delia, and Their Literary Background*. Lund: Gleerup, 1960.

Schalkwyk, David. "'She never told her love': Embodiment, Textuality, and Silence in Shakespeare's Sonnets and Plays." *Shakespeare Quarterly* 45 (1994): 381-407.

Schoenbaum, Samuel. "Shakespeare's Dark Lady: A Question of Identity." *Shakespeare's Styles: Essays in Honour of Kenneth Muir*. Ed. Philip Edwards, Inga-Stina Ewbank, and G. K. Hunter. Cambridge: Cambridge UP, 1980. 221-39.

———. *Shakespeare's Lives*. Oxford: Clarendon Press, 1970; rev. ed., 1991.

Schoenfeldt, Michael. "The Matter of Inwardness: Shakespeare's Sonnets." *Shakespeare's Sonnets: Critical Essays*. Ed. James Schiffer. New York: Garland, 1998. 305-24.

Sedgwick, Eve Kosofsky. *Between Men: English Literature and Male Homosocial Desire*. New York: Columbia UP, 1985.

Seymour-Smith, Martin, ed. *Shakespeare's Sonnets*. London: Heinemann, 1963.

Smith, Barbara Herrnstein, ed. *Shakespeare's Sonnets*. New York: NYU P, 1969.

Smith, Bruce R. *Homosexual Desire in Shakespeare's England: A Cultural Poetics*. Chicago: U of Chicago P, 1991.

———. "I, You, He, She, and We: On the Sexual Politics of Shakespeare's Sonnets." *Shakespeare's Sonnets: Critical Essays*. Ed. James Schiffer. New York: Garland, 1998. 411-29.

Smith, Hallett. *The Tension in the Lyre: Poetry in Shakespeare's Sonnets*. San Marino: Huntington Library, 1981.

Sobran, Joseph. *Alias Shakespeare*. New York: Free Press, 1997.

Spurgeon, Caroline. *Shakespeare's Imagery and What It Tells Us*. Cambridge: Cambridge UP, 1935.

Stallybrass, Peter. "Editing as Cultural Formation: The Sexing of Shakespeare's Sonnets." *Modern Language Quarterly* 54 (1993): 91-103.

Rpt. in *Shakespeare's Sonnets: Critical Essays*. Ed. James Schiffer. New York: Garland, 1998. 75-88.

Steevens, George, ed. Preface. *The Plays of William Shakespeare*. London, 1793.

Sterling, Brents. *The Shakespeare Sonnet Order: Poems and Groups*. Berkeley: U. of California P, 1968.

Sutphen, Joyce. "'A dateless lively heat': Storing Loss in the Sonnets." *Shakespeare's Sonnets: Critical Essays*. Ed. James Schiffer. New York: Garland, 1998. 199-217.

Swinburne, Algernon C. *A Study of Shakespeare*. 1879. London: Chatto and Windus, 1895.

Taylor, Gary. *Reinventing Shakespeare: A Cultural History from the Restoration to the Present*. Oxford: Oxford UP, 1989.

———. "Some Manuscripts of Shakespeare's Sonnets." *Bulletin of the John Rylands University Library* 68 (1985-86): 210-246.

Thorpe, Thomas, ed. *Shake-speares Sonnets*. London, 1609.

Traub, Valerie. "Sex without Issue: Sodomy, Reproduction, and Signification in Shakespeare's Sonnets." *Shakespeare's Sonnets: Critical Essays*. Ed. James Schiffer. New York: Garland, 1998. 431-52.

Valbuena, Olga L. "'The dyer's hand': The Reproduction of Coercion and Blot in Shakespeare's Sonnets." *Shakespeare's Sonnets: Critical Essays*. Ed. James Schiffer. New York: Garland, 1998. 325-45.

van den Berg, Sara. "'Mutual ordering': Subjectivity and Language in Shakespeare's Sonnets." *Contending Kingdoms*. Ed. Marie-Rose Logan and Peter L. Rudnytsky. Detroit: Wayne State UP, 1991. 173-201.

Vendler, Helen. *The Art of Shakespeare's Sonnets*. Cambridge: Harvard UP, 1997.

———. "Reading, Stage by Stage: Shakespeare's *Sonnets*." *Shakespeare Reread: The Texts in New Contexts*. Ed. Russ McDonald. Ithaca & London: Cornell UP, 1994. 23-41.

———. "Ways into Shakespeare's Sonnets." *The Hilda Hulme Lecture*. London: U of London, 1990.

Vickers, Brian. *Shakespeare: The Critical Heritage*. Vol. 6 (1774-1801). London: Routledge and Kegan Paul, 1981.

Wait, R. J. C. *The Background to Shakespeare's Sonnets*. London: Chatto and Windus, 1972.

Wheeler, Richard P. "'... And my loud crying still': *The Sonnets, The Merchant of Venice*, and *Othello*." *Shakespeare's "Rough Magic": Renaissance Essays in Honor of C. L. Barber*. Ed. Peter Erickson and Coppélia Kahn. Newark: U of Delaware P, 1985. 193-209.

―――. *Shakespeare's Development and the Problem Comedies*. Berkeley: U of California P, 1981.

Wilde, Oscar. "The Portrait of Mr. W. H." *Blackwood's Edinburgh Magazine* 146 (1889): 1-21. [Expanded version: 1921; rpt. *The Artist as Critic: Critical Writings of Oscar Wilde*. Ed. Richard Ellmann. Chicago: U of Chicago P, 1969. 152-220.]

Willen, Gerald, and Victor B. Reed, eds. *A Casebook on Shakespeare's Sonnets*. New York: Crowell, 1964.

Wilson, John Dover. *An Introduction to the Sonnets of Shakespeare for the Use of Historians and Others*. Cambridge: Cambridge UP, 1963.

Wilson, Katherine. *Shakespeare's Sugared Sonnets*. London: Allen and Unwin, 1974.

Wolff, M. J. "Petrarkismus und Antipetrarkismus in Shakespeares Sonetten." *Englische Studien* 49 (1916): 161-89.

Wordsworth, William. "Essay, Supplementary to the Preface [to Poems, 1815]." *Literary Criticism of William Wordsworth*. Ed. Paul M. Zall. Lincoln: U of Nebraska P, 1966. 158-87.

―――. [Margin Comments.] *A Complete Edition of the Poets of Great Britain*. Vol. 2. Ed. Robert Anderson. London: John and Arthur Arch; Edinburgh: Bell and Bradfute and L. Mundell. 1792-95. [Folger MS n.b. 53-64]

Wright, George T. *Shakespeare's Metrical Art*. Berkeley: U of California P, 1988.

―――. "The Silent Speech of Shakespeare's Sonnets." *Shakespeare and the Twentieth Century*. Ed. Jonathan Bate, Jill A. Levinson, and Dieter Mehl. Newark: U of Delaware P, 1998. 306-27. Rpt. in *Shakespeare's Sonnets: Critical Essays*. Ed. James Schiffer. New York: Garland, 1998. 135-58.

Wyndham, George, ed. *Poems of Shakespeare*. London: Methuen, 1898.

WORKS CONSULTED (SELECTIVE LISTING)

Allen, Michael J. B. "Shakespeare's Man Descending a Staircase: Sonnets 126-154." *Shakespeare Survey* 31 (1978): 127-38.

Bate, Jonathan. "Ovid and the Sonnets; Or, Did Shakespeare Feel the Anxiety of Influence?" *Shakespeare Survey* 42 (1989): 65-76.

Berryman, John. "Shakespeare at Thirty." *Hudson Review* 6 (1953): 175-203.

Burckhardt, Sigurd. "The Poet as Fool and Priest." *ELH* 23 (1956): 279-98.

Cox, C. B. "Bisexual Shakespeare?" *Hudson Review* 40 (1987): 481-86.

Crutwell, Patrick. *The Shakespearean Moment*. New York: Columbia UP, 1955.

Dollimore, Jonathan. "Desire is Death." *Subject and Object in Renaissance Culture*. Ed. Margreta de Grazia, Maureen Quilligan, and Peter Stallybrass. Cambridge: Cambridge UP, 1996. 369-86.

Douglas, Lord Alfred. *The True History of Shakespeare's Sonnets*. London: Secker, 1933.

Engle, Lars. *Shakespearean Pragmatism*. Chicago: U of Chicago P, 1993.

Feinberg, Nona. "Erasing the Dark Lady: Sonnet 138 in the Sequence." *Assays* 4 (1987): 97-108.

Felperin, Howard. "The Dark Lady Identified, or What Deconstruction Can Do for Shakespeare's Sonnets." *Shakespeare and Deconstruction*. Ed. G. Douglas Atkins and David Bergeron. New York: Lang, 1988. 69-93.

Fraser, Russell. "Shakespeare at Sonnets." *Sewanee Review* 97 (1989): 408-27.

Freinkel, Lisa. "Shakespeare and the Theology of Will." *Graven Images* 2 (1995): 31-47.

Gardiner, Judith Kegan. "The Marriage of Male Minds in Shakespeare's Sonnets." *Journal of English and Germanic Philology* 84 (1985): 328-47.

Giroux, Robert. *The Book Known as Q*. New York: Atheneum, 1982.

Graziani, René. "The Numbering of Shakespeare's Sonnets: 12, 60, and 126." *Shakespeare Quarterly* 35 (1984): 79-82.

Green, Martin. *The Labyrinth of Shakespeare's Sonnets: An Examination of Sexual Elements in Shakespeare's Language*. London: Skilton, 1974.

Hammond, Gerald. *The Reader and Shakespeare's Young Man Sonnets*. Totowa: Barnes and Noble, 1981.

Jackson, MacDonald P. "Punctuation and the Compositors of Shakespeare's Sonnets." *The Library*. 5th Series. 30 (1975): 1-24.

Klause, John. "Shakespeare's *Sonnets*: Age in Love and the Goring of Thoughts." *Studies in Philology* (1983): 300-24.

Kott, Jan. "Shakespeare's Bitter Arcadia." *Shakespeare Our Contemporary*. Trans. Boleslaw Taborski. New York: Norton, 1974. 237-92.

Kreiger, Murray. *A Window to Criticism: Shakespeare's Sonnets and Modern Poetics*. Princeton: Princeton UP, 1964.

Laqueur, Thomas. *Making Sex: Body and Gender from the Greeks to Freud*. Cambridge: Harvard UP, 1990.

Levin, Richard A. "Shakespeare's Sonnets 153 and 154." *Explicator* 5 (1994): 11-14.

Lewis, C. S. *English Literature in the Sixteenth Century*. Oxford: Clarendon, 1954.

Lukacher, Ned. *Daemonic Figures: Shakespeare and the Question of Conscience*. Ithaca: Cornell UP, 1994.

Mehl, Dieter, and Wolfgang Weiss, eds. *Shakespeare's Sonette in europäischen Perspeckiven*. Hamburg: LIT, 1993.

Mischo, John B. "'That use is not forbidden usury': Shakespeare's Procreation Sonnets and the Problem of Usury." *Subjects on the World's Stage: Essays on British Literature of the Middle Ages and the Renaissance*. Ed. David G. Allen and Robert A. White. Newark: U of Delaware P, 1995. 262-79.

Neely, Carol Thomas. "Detachment and Engagement in Shakespeare's Sonnets: 94, 116, and 129." *PMLA* 92 (1977): 83-95.

Novy, Marianne. *Engaging with Shakespeare: Responses of George Eliot and Other Women Novelists*. Athens: U of Georgia P, 1994.

Person, Jr., James E., and Sandra L. Williamson, eds. *Shakespearean Criticism*. Vol. 10. Detroit: Gale, 1990.

Ransom, John Crowe. "A Postscript to Shakespeare's Sonnets." *Kenyon Review* 30 (1968): 523-31.

Richmond, Hugh. "The Dark Lady as Reformation Mistress." *Kenyon Review* (1986): 91-105.

Sagaser, Elizabeth Harris. "Shakespeare's Sweet Leaves: Mourning, Pleasure, and the Triumph of Thought in the Renaissance Love Lyric." *ELH* 61 (1994): 1-26.

Simonds, Peggy Munoz. "Eros and Anteros in Shakespeare's Sonnets 153 and 154: An Iconographic Study." *Spenser Studies* 7 (1986): 261-323.

Sinfield, Alan. *Cultural Politics—Queer Reading*. Philadelphia: U of Pennsylvania P, 1994.

Spiller, Michael R. G. *The Development of the Sonnet: An Introduction*. London: Routledge, 1992.

Sprung, Andrew. "Chary Charity: Mother Love and Infant Need in Shakespeare's Sonnets." *American Imago* 47 (1990): 365-82.

Waddington, Raymond B. "The Poetics of Eroticism—Shakespeare's 'Master Mistress.'" *Renaissance Discourses of Desire*. Ed. Claude J. Summers and Ted-Larry Pebworth. Columbia: U of Missouri P, 1993. 1-12.

Wall, Wendy. *The Imprint of Gender: Authorship and Publication in the English Renaissance*. Ithaca: Cornell UP, 1993.

West, William N. "Nothing as Given: Economies of the Gift in Derrida and Shakespeare." *Comparative Literature* 48 (1996): 1-18.

Williams, Gordon. *Shakespeare, Sex and the Print Revolution*. London: Athlone, 1996.

Winters, Yvor. "Poetic Styles, Old and New." *Four Poets on Poetry*. Ed. Don Cameron Allen. Baltimore: Johns Hopkins UP, 1959. 44-75.

SHAKE-SPEARES

SONNETS.

Neuer before Imprinted.

AT LONDON
By *G. Eld* for *T. T.* and are
to be folde by *Iohn Wright,* dwelling
at Chrift Church gate.
1 6 0 9.

Figure 2. The title page of the 1609 Quarto from *SHAKE-SPEARES SONNETS: A Facsimile in Photo-Lithography* [of the copy in the British Museum] (London: C. Praetorius, 1886). Reproduced courtesy of the Rare Book Division of the Library of Congress.

PART II

Recent Essays on Shakespeare's Sonnets

Editing as Cultural Formation
The Sexing of Shakespeare's Sonnets

Peter Stallybrass

I have recently been trying to understand the work of bibliographers and editors. I undertook this "retraining" for two contradictory but related reasons. The first was that as I became increasingly engaged in the teaching and organization of Cultural Studies courses, I began to wonder what the strengths of specific disciplinary trainings might be. That is, one of the obvious dangers of interdisciplinary work is that one ends up doing history, anthropology, economics—badly. It is hard to gather the technical skills of another discipline on the side: the historical skills, for instance, of finding sources, let alone knowing how to read them. I began to wonder what exactly the technical skills of someone teaching in a department of English might be. Whatever they were, I didn't seem to know about them, or have them. (By contrast, I did have at least the rudiments of an historical training through having worked with various historians in England.) I found that the librarians at the University of Pennsylvania had an extraordinary range of skills which, as someone who worked on and with books, I felt I should know. The second reason for my turn to editing and bibliography was that I came to believe that the material culture of books was central to any cultural analysis of "literature" and therefore to one aspect of Cultural Studies.[1] Questions of, for instance, the formation of

Reprinted by permission of Duke University Press and Peter Stallybrass from *Modern Language Quarterly* 54.1 (March 1993), pp. 91-103. Copyright University of Washington.

nationalism (and national languages), of the construction of the individual, of the making of genders and sexualities are materially embedded in the historical production and reproduction of texts.

A further reason for attending to the production and reproduction of books was to interrogate a notion of historicity which emphasized the *punctual* emergence of its objects of study. That is, a course on the seventeenth century would be about writers who wrote ("on time") in the period one was studying (Milton, Donne, Behn, for instance). In such a course, one might incorporate "precursors" or earlier writing as "background," but that only reproduces the notion of a series of punctual moments which can be related chronologically through their dates of origination. It is precisely this view which Margreta de Grazia powerfully challenges in *Shakespeare Verbatim*.[2] She argues that the "Shakespeare" which we still study is the construction of the late eighteenth century and, above all, of the editorial labors of Malone. In other words, "our" Shakespeare is (or at least was until recently) the contemporary of the French Revolution rather than of the Armada. What I attempt to do here is to give a working example of the implications of such a proposition. I argue that there is an important sense in which, if we take seriously the *labor of production* (editorial work, theatrical stagings, critical commentary, the production and distribution of books on a global scale, the incorporation of texts into the educational apparatus), Shakespeare is a central nineteenth-century author. But *what* is being authored remains a question. In the case of the Sonnets, which I shall be examining, I think that we can read the inscription of a new history of sexuality and of "character." But that new history emerges unpunctually, dislocated by its need to write itself over the culturally valued but culturally disturbing body of the Sonnets.[3]

Until Edmond Malone's 1780 edition, the history of the publication of the Sonnets was that of the reproduction of John Benson's edition of 1640, in which Benson had radically reordered the sonnets, given titles to individual sonnets, conflated sonnets to create longer poems, changed at least some pronouns so as to render the beloved female rather than male, and added many other poems that modern editors do not regard as Shakespearean.[4] In returning to the 1609 quarto of the Sonnets, Malone was intent upon rescripting Shakespeare's poems to show the contours of the man behind them. That is, Malone was inventing the character "Shakespeare" as he is still now visible to us. And in inventing this character he turned above all, as de Grazia has argued, to the Sonnets, which he believed gave a crucial key to Shakespeare's inner life.[5] And now, much to Malone's credit, the "boy," the "friend," "he" appear as central figures. But they do so as what can only be described as the site of moral panic. Having created the "authentic" character of Shakespeare, that character steps into the spotlight as a potential sodomite.

The 1821 edition of Malone prints the Sonnets together with the remarks of John Boswell Jr., who presents the characters of Malone's new edition (Shakespeare, the young man, the rival poet, the dark lady) *and* the panic that attends their presentation. Boswell seems appalled at the prospect of what the reader will make of Malone's Shakespeare: the Bard has been given a newly rich interiority but at the cost of having impugned his character. The final page of Boswell's introductory remarks on the Sonnets are dedicated to proving that Shakespeare was not a pederast. In the process he produces, as hysterical symptom, the lines of defence that have governed nearly all subsequent readings of the Sonnets:

1) In the Renaissance, male/male friendship was expressed through the rhetoric of amorous love.
2) Shakespeare didn't love the young man anyway, because he was his patron, and the poems are therefore written in pursuit of patronage.
3) The poems are not really about love or friendship because sonnets are *conventional*. The Sonnets are, then, less about a young man or a dark lady than about Petrarch, Ronsard, Sidney etc. (A boy's club but not *that* kind of boy's club.)
4) Malone was wrong, and the Sonnets are, after all, a miscellany. They "had neither the poet himself nor any individual in view; but were merely the effusions of his fancy, written upon various topicks for the amusement of a private circle."[6]

Now there is nothing necessarily *wrong* with any of these readings. I'm not concerned here with their "truth" or their scholarly credentials but with how they emerge as attempted solutions to a *crisis*. As these critical readings get established, the crisis which produced those readings gets progressively buried, only to re-emerge at junctures like the trial of Oscar Wilde in the 1890s.

At the moment of the formation of "Shakespeare" through a reading of the Sonnets in the 1780s and 1790s, it is striking how *nakedly* the issues are presented. Malone, for instance, prints his commentary at the bottom of the page, but his own remarks are frequently framed as a response to the criticisms of George Steevens, who thought that the Sonnets should not be published at all. Malone's footnote to sonnet 20, for instance, beginning with a long quote from Steevens, reads as follows:

> —the MASTER-MISTRESS of my passion;] It is impossible to read this fulsome panegyrick, addressed to a male object, without an equal mixture of disgust and indignation. We may remark also, that the same phrase employed by Shakespeare to denote the height of encomium, is used by Dryden to express the extreme of reproach:
> "That woman, but more daub'd; or, if a man,
> "Corrupted to a woman; thy *man-mistress.*"
>
> *Don Sebastian.*
>
> Let me be just, however, to our author, who has made a proper use of the term *male varlet*, in Troilus and Cressida. See that play, Act V. Sc. I. STEEVENS.
>
> Some part of this indignation might perhaps have been abated, if it had been considered that such addresses to men, however indelicate, were customary in our author's time, and neither imported criminality, nor were esteemed indecorous. See a note on the words—"thy deceased *lover*," in the 32d Sonnet. To regulate our judgement of Shakespeare's poems by the modes of modern times, is surely as unreasonable as to try his plays by the rules of Aristotle.
>
> *Master-mistress* does not perhaps mean *man*-mistress, but *sovereign* mistress. See Mr. Tyrwhitt's note on the 165th verse of the Canterbury Tales, vol. iv. p. 197. MALONE.[7]

In the most literal sense, character assassination precedes the construction of character: Malone's justification of Shakespeare comes after (both temporally and upon the printed page) Steevens's assault.

Nor did Malone's response satisfy Steevens, who, in his 1793 edition of Shakespeare wrote:

> We have not reprinted the Sonnets etc. of Shakespeare, because the strongest act of Parliament that could be framed, would fail to compel readers into their service; notwithstanding these miscellaneous Poems have derived every possible advantage from the literature and

judgement of their only intelligent editor, Mr. Malone, whose implements of criticism, like the ivory rake and golden spade in Prudentius, are on this occasion disgraced by the objects of their culture.[8]

The passage is a paradoxical mixture of the direct and indirect: the word "sodomy" nowhere appears and yet it everywhere underpins the argument in a curiously inverted form. The acts of Parliament by which sodomites were persecuted and punished are here magically displaced by imaginary decrees which, however strong, will have no force to make the reader turn to Shakespeare's Sonnets. The reader cannot be "compel[ed]" to the "service" of these poems: that is, the reader will refuse to be seduced, corrupted, sodomized. As Jonathan Dollimore has argued elsewhere, this is the familiar strategy by which the coercions of the state apparatus are displaced by an imaginary scenario in which the state's *victims* are represented as the *agents* of oppression.[9] But Steevens limits the danger of those demonic agents by transforming them into the "objects of *culture*," by which Steevens surely means excrement, the excrement which contaminates even that distinguished "culture-critic," Edmond Malone, despite the long handles of his ivory rake and golden spade.

Culture as contamination. The gentle Shakespeare as contaminater and corrupter of youth. But if this character is reiterated throughout the nineteenth century, it is above all as a *character that is denied*. Critics, in other words, worked *from* what they imagined as character assassination (e.g., Shakespeare as pederast) *to* character. But how many character assassinators are there to be reproduced and ritually denounced? In the nineteenth century, as for Malone at the end of the eighteenth, Steevens is virtually alone as the assassinator who must be endlessly named, denounced, put straight. From this distance, the repeated act of putting straight appears as a form of cultural hysteria, but its excesses inscribe a crisis in the attempt to form a normative character and sexuality through Malone's Shakespeare.

One of the most drastic responses to Malone's edition of the Sonnets was the forgery by William Henry Ireland of a letter purporting to be from Elizabeth I to Shakespeare, thanking him for his sonnets.[10] The Sonnets, in other words, were addressed neither to a male beloved nor to a common woman but to the monarch herself. The forgery was only one of several by Ireland, so what is perhaps more remarkable is that the supposition that Shakespeare's beloved was Elizabeth I was justified at great length (and with considerable learning) in two books by George Chalmers.[11] In the latter, *A Supplemental Apology* (1799), Chalmers marvels at the assumption of Steevens and Malone that "Shakespeare, a husband, a father, a moral man, addressed a hundred and twenty six *Amorous* Sonnets to a *male* object!" (p. 55). Chalmers, rightly noting that Malone was the first editor to posit a male beloved, sets out to erase that supposed defamation:

> every fair construction ought to be made, rather than consider
> Shakespeare as a miscreant, who could address amatory Verses to a
> man, "with a romantic *platonism of affection.*" But I have freed him, I
> trust, from that stain, in opposition to his commentators, by shewing,
> distinctly, his real object. This object, being once known, darkness
> brightens into light, order springs out of confusion, and contradiction
> settles into sense. (pp. 73-74)

If Chalmers's position gained little support, the structure of Chalmers's argument was endlessly repeatable. First, the claim that Shakespeare is heterosexual is always *supplementary.* Indeed, heterosexuality is itself constructed as a back-formation from the *prior* imagination of pederasty and sodomy. Secondly, it is simply assumed that the taint of male/male love will destroy the character of the national bard. So just as heterosexuality is the belated defence against sodomy, so "character" is the belated defence against an imagined character-assassination that has preceded it. The Sonnets thus produce in the nineteenth century a formidable apparatus to *invent* a new self: the interiorized heterosexual, projected back onto (or formed in opposition to) Shakespeare.

That apparatus can be seen at its most spectacularly troubled in the writing of Coleridge. On "Wed. morning, half past three, Nov. 2, 1803," Coleridge picked up a volume of Wordsworth's set of Anderson's *British Poets.* The volume contained Shakespeare's Sonnets, and in the margin he found a pencil note by Wordsworth, objecting to the *later* sonnets (that is, to the sonnets addressed, according to Malone, to the dark lady and thus "heterosexual"). Coleridge wrote:

> I can by no means subscribe to the above pencil mark of W.
> Wordsworth; which, however, it is my wish should never be erased.
> It is *his*: and grievously am I mistaken, and deplorably will
> Englishmen have degenerated if the being *his* will not in time give it

a value, as of a little reverential relic—the rude mark of his hand left by the sweat of haste in a St. Veronica handkerchief.[12]

Wordsworth is wrong about Shakespeare; but his error is encoded in the enduring, sexualized mark of his hand, a mark that Coleridge reveres as a "relic" that preserves the physical presence of his friend (a "rude mark," capturing the "sweat of haste," so that the paper on which he writes becomes the handkerchief which, like St. Veronica's, immortalizes his physical being). Writing as masturbation with eternal effects. In response to Wordsworth's comments on the later sonnets, then, Coleridge fetishizes the material trace which homoerotically binds him to his friend.

But it is as if, at this point, Coleridge forgets that Wordsworth is writing about the *later* poems—as if what names his relation to Wordsworth is the name that Steevens silently attributes to the *earlier* sonnets and to the relation between Shakespeare and the young man. Abruptly, Coleridge veers from his meditations upon his friend to an apostrophe to his own son, Hartley, who is being christened that very day:

These sonnets thou, I trust, if God preserve thy life, Hartley! thou wilt read with a deep interest. . . . To thee, I trust, they will help to explain the mind of Shakespeare, and if thou wouldst understand these sonnets, thou must read the chapter in Potter's *Antiquities* on the Greek lovers —of whom were that Theban band of brothers over whom Philip, their victor, stood weeping; and surveying their dead bodies, each with his shield over the body of his friend, all dead in the place where they fought, solemnly cursed those whose base, fleshly, and most calumnious fancies had suspected their love of desire against nature. This pure love Shakespeare appears to have felt—to have been in no way ashamed of it—or even to have suspected that others could have suspected it. Yet at the same time he knew that so strong a love would have been more completely a thing of permanence and reality, and have been more blessed by nature and taken under her more especial protection, if this object of his love had been at the same time a possible object of desire—for nature is not soul only. In this feeling he must have written the twentieth sonnet; but its possibility seems never to have entered even his imagination. . . . O my son! I pray that thou may'st know inwardly

> how impossible it was for a Shakespeare not to have been in his
> heart's heart chaste. (p. 455)

Wordsworth writes about the late sonnets; Coleridge responds by
writing about the early sonnets, and, moreover, the early sonnets as
they had been read by Steevens and Malone. And Coleridge's reading
is a tortuous and tortured reading of the possibily/impossibility of a
sexual relation between men. But it is as if every move by which he
attempts to erase the specter of sodomy conjures it up. To set one's
mind at rest, one needs, of all things, to read a commentary on the
Greeks (a commentary by no less a person than the Archbishop of
Canterbury, and this despite Coleridge's denunciation of christening in
the same note as "unchristian . . . foolery"), as if the "purity" of the
Greeks were sufficiently secure to secure the "purity" of Shakespeare.
Even more strange is Coleridge's attempt to *deny* the function of the
"imagination" to the poet to whom he attributed it in the highest degree.
The possibility of sodomy "seems never to have entered even his
imagination"; he could not "have suspected that others could have
suspected" his love.

   Which makes it the more remarkable that later, in a note of May
14, 1833 (published in *Table Talk* [1835]), Coleridge decided not only
that all the Sonnets were written to a woman but also (more strangely
still) that Shakespeare inserted the twentieth sonnet to *obscure* his
heterosexuality (and thus to raise, seemingly unnecessarily, the thought
of pederasty, which before he could not "have suspected that others
could have suspected"). Again, the movement of Coleridge's thinking
is revealing. His note in 1833 begins with the reflection that "it is
possible that a man may under certain states of the moral feeling,
entertain something deserving the name of love towards a male
object—an affection beyond friendship and wholly aloof from
appetite."[13] When he turns to the friendship between Musidorus and
Pyrocles in Sidney's *Arcadia*, it looks as if he is preparing his way for a
restatement of Malone's position on the Sonnets. "In Elizabeth's and
James's time," Coleridge remarks, "it seems to have been almost
fashionable to cherish such a feeling" (p. 178). But Malone's "defence"
of Shakespeare is no longer adequate as a defence for Coleridge.
Shakespeare must be purified even of the "rhetorical" male/male love
which is said to characterize his age. To the extent that Shakespeare's
Sonnets are "sincere," they must be heterosexual: "It seems to me that
the sonnets could only have come from a man deeply in love, and in

love with a woman; and there is one sonnet which from its incongruity, I take to be a purposed blind" (pp. 180-81). Shakespeare, in other words, disguises himself as a pederast as a ruse to avoid detection as a man "deeply in love" with a woman.

If Coleridge's later interpretation of the Sonnets seems incredible, it testifies to the formidable *obstacle* that those poems formed in the smooth reproduction of the national bard. That there *should* be such a smooth reproduction was, of course, increasingly important as Shakespeare was inscribed within a national and colonial pedagogy. If strategies as desperate as Coleridge's could not command assent, what could one do with the Sonnets? Steevens had a rare follower. Henry Hallam, in his *Introduction to the Literature of Europe in the Fifteenth, Sixteenth, and Seventeenth Centuries*, described Coleridge's "heterosexualizing" of the Sonnets as "absolutely untenable."[14] But Hallam, like Steevens, consequently finds the "frequent beauties" of the Sonnets "greatly diminished" by the supposed "circumstances" of their production. "It is impossible," Hallam concludes, "not to wish that Shakespeare had never written them" (p. 264).

What Hallam and other nineteenth century critics wanted to unwrite was the primal scene in the modern production of Shakespeare: the scene conjured up by Steevens's denunciation. Strangely, Steevens's denunciation, which was directed not at Benson's edition but at the Quarto and at Malone's edition, came to color even the Benson edition, which continued to be reprinted in the early nineteenth century. In 1808, there appeared an edition of *Love Poems* by "William Shakspere" (the spelling of the author's name itself testifying to the influence of Malone).[15] The second volume of the poems included Benson's edition of the Sonnets, but many of the notes of Steevens and Malone were incongruously affixed to these significantly different poems. Even stranger perhaps is the case of Dr. Sherwin of Bath who, sometime after 1818, wrote a series of marginal comments in his 1774 copy of the *Poems* (i.e., the Sonnets in their pre-Malone, Benson form).[16] Dr. Sherwin, in other words, was reading an edition of the Sonnets from which it would have been *impossible* to abstract the story of Shakespeare, the young man, the rival poet, and the dark lady, since the Sonnets had been totally reordered, sometimes run together so that two or more sonnets were made into a single poem, and given titles that pointed in quite other directions, as well as occasionally having had their pronouns changed. Moreover, the poems Sherwin read in his copy were explicitly entitled "*Poems on Several Occasions*."

Yet what Sherwin responded to was not the text before him but the mode of interpretation which Steevens and Malone had instituted. He responds, that is, to what he calls "the unaccountable Prejudices of the late Mr. Steevens":

> When Mr. Steevens compliments his Brother-Commentator [Malone] at the Expence of the Poet, when he tells us, that his Implements of Criticism are on *this Occasion disgraced by the objects of their Culture*, who can avoid a mingled Emotion of Wonder and Disgust? Who can, in short forbear a Smile of Derision and Contempt at the folly of such a declaration?[17]

Steevens and Malone between them had constructed and passed down an impossible legacy: a legacy from Malone of the Sonnets as crucial documents of the interior life of the national bard; a legacy from Steevens of that interior life as one that would destroy the life of the nation. The effects of this impossible legacy were complex. David Lester Richardson, for instance, publishing his *Literary Leaves* in Calcutta in 1840, blamed the "flippant insolence of Steevens" for the neglect of the Sonnets (which Richardson still refers to as "a volume of Miscellaneous Poems").[18] Yet even as he promoted the Sonnets, he was embarrassed by them. A registering of the beauty of the poems is, he writes, "accompanied by [a] disagreeable feeling, bordering on disgust" at the "indelicate" expressions of love between man and man (p. 26). And he writes of sonnet 20 that it is

> one of the most painful and perplexing I ever read. It is a truly disagreeable enigma. If I have caught any glimpse of the real meaning, I could heartily wish that Shakespeare had never written it. (p. 38)

A hundred years later, it was this same sonnet which, according to Walter Thomson, "threatened to mislead us and sent us searching for almost twelve months," until he could reassure himself that the word "passion" in the sonnet meant "emotional poem" rather than "amorous desire":

> "Passion" is the crucial word, the foundation whereon the fantastic edifice is built in which it is alleged that Shakespeare was perverse in his morals. No more subversive mis-statement could be disseminated

about any author or man, and not its least pernicious feature is that it places in the minds and mouths of the perverse a defence of their perversities. . . . We have it from a doctor of wide experience that it is no uncommon thing for perverse persons to cite Shakespeare as their exemplar.[19]

Thomson's last claim is not, I think, as wild as it may first appear. For as Alan Sinfield has argued, one of the effects of the Oscar Wilde trial was to help to constitute a gay subculture with its own privileged texts and modes of reading.[20]

What particularly frightens Thomson is the connection between that new subculture and the uses of Shakespeare as a colonial text. In 1840, Richardson could write from Calcutta of the Sonnets as an unread text,[21] but the educational apparatus of imperialism transformed that. The *Sonnets* by the late nineteenth century were being reproduced in school editions which quoted Dowden as saying that "in the Renascence epoch, among natural products of a time when life ran swift and free, touching with its current high and difficult places, the ardent friendship of man with man was one."[22] It was precisely such an interpretation of the Sonnets which Thomson found unacceptable. "We have information," Thomson complains, "which justifies the statement that about 40 per cent of the people who buy and read Shakespeare entertain the belief that he was a moral pervert" (p. 9). "The supreme literary ornament of our race" (p. 12) had become a contaminated source that subverted the colonial project:

what, for instance, of the many tens of thousands of students who, since Lord Macaulay's day, have come to our universities from India? They are frequently of literary bent and Shakespeare strongly attracts them. How many of them must return to India with these fallacies planted in their minds? (p. 7)

But it is, of course, the "fallacy" of "perversity" which drives the writing of Thomson (as of Malone and Chalmers before him). The justification of Shakespeare is always subsequent to the charge of deviation—just as the concept of the "heterosexual" is a belated response to the *prior* concept of the "homosexual."

The Sonnets, I believe, played a central role in the constitution of a new "history of sexuality." Since Foucault, we have been accustomed to trace such a history through religious confessions, through medical discourse, through architecture. But the post-Enlightenment formation of "literature" was itself a primary site in the formation of sexualities. If the Sonnets were themselves crucial to that new formation of "literature," in their post-Steevens-and-Malone form they lent themslves to intense critical and editorial labors that produced narratives of "normal" and "deviant" sexualities. The two great spurs to such narratives were the Steevens-Malone debate (and the Malone edition) at the end of the eighteenth century and Oscar Wilde's "The Portrait of Mr. W. H." and his trial at the end of the nineteenth century. Wilde published his "Portrait" in *Blackwood's* in 1889 after Frank Harris's *Fortnightly Review* had rejected the piece. As Harris notes in his biography of Wilde:

> "The Portrait of Mr. W. H." did Oscar incalculable injury. It gave his
> enemies *for the first time* the very weapon they wanted, and they used
> it unscrupulously and untiringly with the fierce delight of hatred.[23]

Balfour and Asquith, to whom Wilde sent the story, advised against publication on the grounds that it would corrupt English homes.[24] Wilde created a specter which produced, by reactionary back-formation, not only the "normal" Shakespeare but "normality" itself.

That "normality," I have been arguing, was itself an hysterical symptom which accompanied Malone's construction of a unified character attributable to Shakespeare (and to the "characters" in his writing). But the narrative of characterological unity which Malone produced was ideologically fruitful. That is, it did not merely erase the prior text of the Sonnets, but constructed the site of a new kind of struggle. For the drive towards unity of character (Shakespeare's character, the characters of the Sonnets) produced more and more dramatic consequences at the level of sexual identity. The Sonnets, previously a marginal aspect of Shakespeare's corpus, became a crucial site on which "sexual identity" was invented and contested. If we need now to reconstruct the cultural history of Shakespeare, it is to understand how the imaginary terrain of our own bodies came into being.

NOTES

1. Formative work in this field has been done by Roger Chartier, Jerome J. McGann, and Donald F. Mckenzie. See, for instance, Chartier, *The Cultural*

Uses of Print in Early Modern France, trans. Lydia G. Cochrane (Princeton, N. J.: Princeton University Press, 1987) and ed. Chartier, *The Culture of Print: Power and the Uses of Print in Early Modern Europe*, trans. Lydia G. Cochrane (Princeton, N. J.: Princeton University Press, 1989); McGann, *A Critique of Modern Textual Criticism* (Chicago: University of Chicago Press, 1983) and *The Textual Condition* (Princeton, N. J.: Princeton University Press, 1991); McKenzie, *Bibliography and the Sociology of Texts* (London: British Library, 1986).

2. Margreta de Grazia, *Shakespeare Verbatim: The Reproduction of Authenticity and the 1790 Apparatus* (Oxford: Clarendon Press, 1991). My whole argument can be seen as an extended footnote to de Grazia's book.

I am also indebted to conversations with her and to her "The Scandal of Shakespeare's Sonnets," *Shakespeare Survey* 46 (1994), pp. 35-49, which is also reprinted in this volume.

3. For other work on the Sonnets to which I am indebted, see Gregory W. Bredbeck, *Sodomy and Interpretation: Marlowe to Milton* (Ithaca: Cornell University Press, 1991), pp. 167-80; Bruce R. Smith, *Homosexual Desire in Shakespeare's England: A Cultural Poetics* (Chicago: University of Chicago Press, 1991), pp. 228-70.

4. *Supplement to the Edition of Shakespeare's Plays Published in 1778 by Samuel Johnson and George Steevens* (London: Bathurst, 1780); John Benson, *Poems: Written by Wil Shake-speare. Gent.* (London, 1640).

5. De Grazia, pp. 132-76.

6. John Boswell, "Preliminary Remarks," in *The Plays and Poems of William Shakspeare*, ed. Edmond Malone, vol. 20 (London, 1821), p. 220.

7. *Shakspeare*, ed. Malone, vol. 20, p. 241.

8. George Steevens, "Advertisement," in William Shakespeare, *Plays*, ed. Samuel Johnson and George Steevens (London, 1793), vol. 1, pp. vii-viii.

9. "Transgression and Surveillance in *Measure for Measure*," in *Political Shakespeare: New Essays in Cultural Materialism*, ed. Jonathan Dollimore and Alan Sinfield (Manchester: Manchester University Press, 1985), pp. 72-87.

10. *Miscellaneous Papers and Legal Instruments under the hand and seal of William Shakespeare* (London: Egerton, 1796), p. 30.

11. *An Apology for the Believers in the Shakespeare Papers* (London: Egerton, 1797); *A Supplemental Apology* (London: Egerton, 1799).

12. *Coleridge's Miscellaneous Criticism*, ed. T. M. Raysor (Cambridge, Ma.: Harvard University Press, 1936), p. 454.

13. Samuel Taylor Coleridge, *Table Talk* (London: Murray, 1835), vol. 2, p. 178.

14. p. 263n.

15. William Shakespeare, *Love Poems* (London: Cundee, 1808).

16. William Shakespeare, *Poems* (London: Etherington, 1774). Dr. Sherwin's copy, with his marginalia, is in the Folger Shakespeare Library.

17. Flyleaf, vol. 2.

18. *Literary Leaves* (Calcutta: Thacker, 1840), pp. 1, 3.

19. *The Sonnets of William Shakespeare and Henry Wriothesley* (Oxford: Blackwell, 1938), pp. 2-3.

20. Alan Sinfield, lecture delivered at Georgetown University, April 23, 1992. For related considerations, see his *Faultines: Cultural Materialism and the Politics of Dissident Reading* (Berkely: University of California Press, 1992), pp. 290-302.

21. *Literary Leaves* p. 1.

22. *Shakespeare's Sonnets*, ed. W. J. Rolfe, school edition (New York: Harper, 1883), pp. 15-16.

23. Frank Harris, *Oscar Wilde* (East Lansing: Michigan State University Press, 1959), p. 69. My emphasis.

24. Richard Ellmann, *Oscar Wilde* (New York: Knopf, 1988), p. 298.

The Scandal of Shakespeare's Sonnets

Margreta de Grazia

Of all the many defences against the scandal of Shakespeare's Sonnets—Platonism, for example, or the Renaissance ideal of friendship—John Benson's is undoubtedly the most radical. In order to cover up the fact that the first 126 of the Sonnets were written to a male, Benson in his 1640 *Poems: Written by Wil Shake-speare, Gent.* changed masculine pronouns to feminine and introduced titles which directed sonnets to the young man to a mistress. By these simple editorial interventions, he succeeded in converting a shameful homosexual love to an acceptable heterosexual one, a conversion reproduced in the numerous reprintings of the 1640 *Poems* up through the eighteenth century. The source for this account is Hyder E. Rollins's authoritative 1944 Variorum Sonnets, the first edition to detail Benson's pronominal changes and titular insertions.[1] Subsequent editions have reproduced his conclusions, for example John Kerrigan's 1986 edition which faults Benson for inflicting on the Sonnets 'a series of unforgivable injuries,' above all 'a single recurring revision: he emended the masculine pronouns used of the friend in 1 to 126 to "her," "hers," and "she." '[2] With varying degrees of indignation and amusement, critical works on the Sonnets have repeated the charge.

The charge, however, is wrong. Benson did not attempt to convert a male beloved to a female. To begin with, the number of his alterations

Reprinted by permission of Cambridge University Press and Margreta de Grazia from *Shakespeare Survey* 46 (1994), pp. 35-49.

has been greatly exaggerated. Of the seventy-five titles Benson assigned to Shakespeare's Sonnets, only three of them direct sonnets from the first group of the 1609 Quarto (sonnets 1-126) to a woman.[3] Furthermore, because none of the sonnets in question specifies the gender of the beloved, Benson had no reason to believe a male addressee was intended. As for the pronominal changes, Rollins himself within nine pages of his own commentary multiplies the number of sonnets 'with verbal changes designed to make the verses apply to a woman instead of a man' from 'some' to '*many*.'[4] Rollins gives three examples as if there were countless others, but three is all there are and those three appear to have been made to avoid solecism rather than homoeroticism. In only one sonnet are pronouns altered, though even there not uniformly. In Benson's printing of sonnet 101, masculine pronouns are altered to feminine in lines 11 and 14, but the masculine (or neutral) pronouns are retained in lines 6 and 9.[5] The alteration may have been made to distinguish the personification 'Truth' from the person of the beloved. In sonnet 104, 'friend' is emended to the more conventional 'fair love,' apparently for consistency: the 'fair love' of sonnet 104 corresponds to the twice repeated 'my love' of 105, the sonnet with which it is grouped (along with sonnet 106) to form a single poem entitled 'Constant Affection.' The only other alteration may also have been for the sake of consistency: the emendation of sonnet 108's nonce 'boy' to 'love' avoids the anomaly of a single sonnet addressed to a boy.[6]

Indeed the 1640 collection hardly seems concerned with covering up amatory poems to males. The very first fourteen lines printed in the 1640 *Poems* contain eleven male pronouns, more than any other sonnet, in celebrating an emphatically male beauty. If Benson had wished to censure homoerotic love, why did he not omit the notoriously titillating master-mistress sonnet (20)? Or emend the glamorizing sonnet 106 that praises the beloved—in blazon style, part by part—as the 'master' of beauty? Or the sexually loaded sonnet 110 that apologizes to a specifically male 'god in love' for promiscuity of a decidedly 'preposterous' cast?[7] The same question applies to the numerous sonnets in which references to a male beloved as 'my love,' 'sweet love,' 'lover,' and 'rose' are retained.

It is not Shakespeare's text, then, that has been falsified by Benson but rather Benson's edition that has been falsified by the modern tradition.[8] The question is, why has so patent an error not been challenged before? Certainly it is not for scarcity of copies: while only twelve copies exist of the original 1609 Sonnets, there are that many of the 1640 *Poems* in the Folger Library alone.

I wish to propose that modern treatments of the Sonnets have displaced onto Benson a singularly modern dilemma: what to do with the inadmissible secret of Shakespeare's deviant sexuality?[9] Benson is described as having put an end to that dark secret in the most radical way imaginable, by altering the sex of the beloved and thereby converting an ignominious homosexual passion into a respectable (albeit still adulterous) heterosexual one. In attributing such an act and motive to Benson, modern criticism curiously assumes—indeed posits—the secret it then reviles Benson for concealing. Quite simply, Benson's alleged act of editorial suppression presupposes something in need of suppression: there *must* be something horrible at the heart of the sonnets—the first 126 of them—to compel such a dire editorial manoeuvre.

I have dwelled on Benson only parenthetically to set the factual record straight. My real interest is not in factual error but in the kinds of cultural imperatives that motivate such errors. I see Benson's error as a glaring instance of the need to bury a shameful secret deep within the Sonnets. The need was not Shakespeare's. It has been rather that of Shakespeare criticism which for the past two centuries has been repeating variants of the repression it obsessively ascribes to Benson. This repression has, as I will proceed to argue, produced the very scandal it would deny. At the same time, it has overlooked the scandal that *is* there, not deep within the text but right on its surface.

I

This has been the case from the time the Sonnets were first edited: by Edmond Malone in his 1780 edition.[10] Or, to be more precise, from the time the Sonnets were first not edited: by George Steevens who reprinted the 1609 Sonnets in a collection of early quartos in 1766 but refused to edit them for his 1793 edition of Shakespeare's complete works. While he could justify their publication as documents, he refused to honour them with an editorial apparatus, the trappings of a classic.[11] Though he maintained that it was their literary defects that disqualified them, his response to sonnet 20 points to something more visceral: 'It is impossible to read [it] without an equal mixture of disgust and indignation.'[12] Surely it is this kind of aversion that prompted his condemnation of Malone's decision to edit them:

Malone's 'implements of criticism, like the ivory rake and golden spade in Prudentius, are on this occasion disgraced by the objects of their culture.' For Steevens, Malone's attempt to cultivate such soiled objects as the Sonnets defiled the tools of editing. It was Steevens then and not Benson who first attempted to conceal the scandal of Shakespeare's dirty sexuality, not by changing pronouns but by reproducing the Sonnets in the form of a dusty document rather than of a lofty classic.

Malone, by providing the Sonnets with a textual apparatus in 1780 and then by including them in the canon proper in his 1790 edition of Shakespeare's plays and poems achieved precisely what Steevens had dreaded: he elevated the Sonnets to the status of literature. But the filth that embarrassed Steevens remained—remained to be covered up. In fact, as we shall see, Malone's major editorial ambition in regard to the Sonnets—to establish the connection between the first person and Shakespeare[13]—made the cover-up all the more urgent: if the Sonnets were in Shakespeare's own voice, what was to be done with the fact that the majority of them expressed desire for a young male?

Malone's driving project of identifying the experience of the Sonnets with Shakespeare's own is evident in all his major editorial interventions. Unlike Benson who expanded their contents to accommodate the experience of all lovers by giving them generic titles, Malone limited them so that they applied exclusively to Shakespeare.[14] His first step was to restrict the Sonnets to two addressees by introducing a division after sonnet 126. With only two beloveds, the task of identifying particulars could begin. First the young man was identified on the assumption that he was the same as the dedication's Mr W. H. Other identifications followed suit: of persons, time, things, circumstances. The dedicator's T. T. was Thomas Thorpe, Spenser was the rival poet, the 'now' of the sonnets was early in Shakespeare's career, the gift referred to in 122 was a table-book given to Shakespeare by his friend, sonnet 111's 'publick means, which publick manners breeds,' referred to Shakespeare's own lamentable ties to the theatre, the unfaithful lover of sonnet 93 was Shakespeare's own wife. All of these efforts to give particularity to the Sonnets contributed to Malone's project of personalizing them. His attempts to identify their abundant deictics, what Benveniste has called 'egocentric markers'— their hes and shes, thous and yous, this's and thats, heres and theres— fastened the Sonnets around Shakespeare's 'I.'[15] Thus the experience they recorded could be recognized as that which Shakespeare lived.

The identification proved, as might be anticipated, highly problematic, for there was one connection that could not be allowed: as Malone's own division emphasized, most of the Sonnets were addressed to a male. At each of the three points where Malone insisted upon the division at 126, circumlocutions betrayed his unease: although he referred to the addressee of the second group as a 'lady' and 'female,' the addressee of the first group was no man or male, but rather 'this person,' the majority of the Sonnets are '*not* addressed to a female.'[16] The unspeakable, that 126 sonnets were addressed to a male, remained literally unspoken; at the same time, the basic division according to the beloved's gender proclaimed it.

Within the text too, Malone had to dodge the implications of his own specification, indeed whenever any of the first 126 sonnets were explicitly erotic or amatory. Footnotes then must strain to distance Shakespeare from their content, as did the note to the notorious sonnet 20: 'such addresses to men, however indelicate, were customary in our author's time, and neither imported criminality, nor were esteemed indecorous' (p. 207). Even more belaboured was Malone's rationalization of Shakespeare's references to himself as the 'lover' of the male youth. Here, too, it is not Shakespeare who offends, but rather the custom of his age: and the customary offence was even then not at the level of conduct but at the level of speech. It was 'Such *addresses* to men,' '*expressions* of this kind,' as well as 'the general *tenour* of the greater part of them' that were 'common in Shakespeare's time, and . . . not thought indecorous' [my emphasis] (pp. 219-20). For Malone, nothing separated his present from Shakespeare's past more than the 'strange' custom among men of *speaking* of other men as their 'lovers.'[17] The offence was linguistic and literary and not behavioural; to censure the Sonnets would, therefore, be as 'unreasonable' as faulting the plays for violating Aristotle's *Poetics*—an anachronistic literary judgement (p. 207). Thus for Malone the greatest difference between his late eighteenth century and Shakespeare's late sixteenth century was that in Shakespeare's time, male/male desire was a manner of speaking and not doing, whereas in Malone's more enlightened time it was neither: not done, not even spoken of (hence his repeated euphemisms and circumlocutions).

There is another remarkable instance of how Malone embroils himself in his own editorial commitments. While wanting to read the Sonnets as personal poems, he must impersonalize what his edition foregrounds as their most salient feature: that most of them are addressed to a young male. His longest footnote stretching across six pages pertains to sonnet 93, 'So shall I live supposing thou art true,' a sonnet on sexual jealousy. He fastened on this sonnet in full conviction that Shakespeare, in the Sonnets as well as in the plays, wrote with particular intensity on the subject of jealousy because he himself had experienced it; it was his 'intimate knowledge' of jealousy that enabled him to write on the subject 'more immediately *from the heart*' (p. 266). Malone avoids the scandal that Shakespeare experienced sexual jealousy for a boy by replacing Shakespeare's *boy* to Shakespeare's *wife*, thereby violating his own ascription of the first 126 sonnets to a male, or rather 'not a female.' This weird displacement freed Malone to talk comfortably about Shakespeare's sexual experience—in heterosexual (Shakespeare as cuckold) rather than homosexual terms (Shakespeare as pederast). A digression on his wife's infidelity provided the additional benefit of justifying the adulterous liaison that the second group of sonnets recorded—Shakespeare was unfaithful to his wife because she had first been unfaithful to him. Realizing the danger of such inferences, Steevens (in the notes he contributed to Malone's edition) attempted to block it by insisting that the poem reflected not Shakespeare's *experience* but his *observation*, an impersonal rather than a personal relation (pp. 266-8). Malone stuck fast to his position, finding grounds for Shakespeare's experience of jealousy in documents, anecdotes, and the plays themselves.

James Boswell the younger, when he completed Malone's edition of *The Plays and Poems* in 1821, sided with Steevens, ruling Malone's conviction as 'uncomfortable conjecture.'[18] The judgement was unusual for Boswell, for throughout the twenty-one volume edition he rarely contradicted his friend and mentor. Yet his comments on the Sonnets opposed Malone with astonishing frequency. Indeed it would be fair to say that Boswell dismantled all of the connections Malone had worked so hard to forge between the Sonnets and Shakespeare's experience. The reason is clear: Boswell wanted to counteract the impression that Malone's 1780 edition, reissued in 1790, had produced: it is 'generally admitted that the poet speaks in his own person' (p. 219). Boswell, in the preliminary and concluding remarks with which he bracketed Malone's edition, as well as in scattered internal notes, attempted to stifle all autobiographical possibilities, beginning with Malone's opening identification of 'the individual to whom they were principally addressed, and the circumstances under which they were written.' The Sonnets could not have been addressed to any real nobleman for none, according to Boswell, would have tolerated such effeminizing verse. Any 'distinguished nobleman' would have taken offence at the 'encomiums on his beauty, and the fondling expressions' appropriate only to a 'cocker'd silken wanton' (p. 219). Thus such amorous language could not have been 'customary' between men in Shakespeare's time, as Malone had insisted, for it would have implied that men were effeminate. For Boswell, male desire for males could not have been an acceptable way of even speaking, even back then. For him, male/male desire existed nowhere (in England anyway), not in Shakespeare's past, not in his own present; not in language, not in deed. It was sheer make-believe: what Boswell terms, not unsalaciously, 'effusions of fancy . . . for the amusement of a private circle' (p. 220).

To establish their status as 'fancy,' Boswell must sever all the connections Malone had forged between the Sonnets and Shakespeare's life. And so he does, one by one: Shakespeare was as young as thirty-four or at most forty-five when writing the Sonnets so how could it be he who is represented as old and decrepit in several sonnets? Of course, it is not the association with old age (or with the theatre) that disturbed Boswell, but the logical extension of *any* connection: 'If Shakespeare was speaking of himself in this passage, it would follow that he is equally pointed at upon other occasions' (p. 220). More specifically, if it was Shakespeare who was old then it was also he who was 'grossly and notoriously profligate,' the perpetrator of '"harmful deeds,"' whose '"name had received a brand,"' and whose reputation suffered from the '"impression which vulgar scandal stamped upon his brow."' Such identifications were, Boswell insisted, absurd, for among the extant biographical materials 'not the slightest imputation [was] cast upon his character.' This is not surprising, for Malone and Boswell in their *New Life of Shakspeare* had rejected as factually inaccurate the numerous scandalous anecdotes that had cast him in the shady roles of poacher, adulterer, and carouser.[19]

If Boswell found any fault at all in Shakespeare, it was for his 'selection of topics,' his representation in any form of male/male desire. But Boswell legitimized this choice by attributing it to Shakespeare's altogether admirable 'fondness for classical imitation' (p. 221). Boswell now is at last able to name the unspeakable topic, though only in simultaneously disavowing it: and not in his own words, but in words properly removed from his own by quotation marks and from standard English by sixteenth-century old spelling. The quotation is from Webbe's *Discourse of English Poetrie* that defends Virgil's second eclogue by insisting that the poet 'doth not meane . . . any disordered loue, or the filthy lust of deuillish Pederastice' (p. 221).[20] Boswell keeps a clean distance from the 'filthy' object as if afraid of dirtying his ivory rake and golden spade. Having dismantled all of Malone's connections, Boswell can conclude with a discussion of the Sonnets' literary merits, the only relevant consideration after they have been wrenched from toxic reality and consigned to innocuous fancy.

I have discussed the Malone (1780, 1790) and the Malone/Boswell (1821) editions because it is with them that the modern history of the Sonnets begins, and since no full edition of the 1609 Quarto was printed prior to Malone's, that belated history can be considered their only history.[21] They have the further importance of having established the two critical approaches that have repeated themselves for two centuries now—sometimes ingeniously, sometimes hysterically: (1) Malone's—the Sonnets are about Shakespeare but not as a lover of young men or, (2) Boswell's—the Sonnets are not about Shakespeare or anything else, especially not about Shakespeare as a lover of young men. Though these approaches are antithetical and mutually exclusive, it must be stressed that both are motivated by the same urgency to deny Shakespeare's desire for a male.

In this regard the history of the Sonnets' reception provides a stunning example of the phenomenon Jonathan Dollimore has recently identified: the centrality of homosexuality in a culture that denounces it.[22] The denial of homosexuality in the Sonnets has produced the two polarized approaches by which they have been traditionally read for two centuries. Furthermore, what has been denied (by evasions, displacements, circumlocutions, suppressions, abstractions, etc.) has slipped into the text itself producing (as if from the Sonnets themselves) an hermeneutical interior capable of concealing a sin, a crime, a pathology. The unspeakable of Sonnets criticism has thus become the unspoken of the Sonnets—to the exclusion of, as has yet to be seen, what they quite forthrightly say.

II

I now wish to turn to one of Malone's major editorial acts, his division of the sonnets into two gendered groups, 126 to a young man, the remaining twenty-eight to a woman. The division has been generally accepted. It seems, after all, quite obvious: none of the first 126 sonnets are addressed explicitly to a woman and none of the remaining twenty-eight are addressed explicitly to a male. *Explicitly* is the key word, for what Malone's clear-cut division has obscured is the astonishing number of sonnets that do not make the gender of the addressee explicit.[23] Shakespeare is exceptional among the English sonneteers (Sidney, Spenser, and Daniel, for example) in leaving the beloved's gender unspecified in so many of the sonnets: about five-sixths of them in the first 126 and just less than that in the collection entire. The uncertainty of the beloved's gender is sustained by other types of ambiguity, most notoriously in the 'master-mistress' sonnet 20, but also in sonnet 53 in which the youth is described as a paragon of both masculine and feminine beauty, of both Adonis and Helen; similarly, a variety of epithets recur that apply to either sex: rose, friend, love, lover, sweet, fair.

The little evidence we have of how the Sonnets were read before Malone strongly suggests that the first 126 sonnets were not read as being exclusively to a male. Benson assumed that the Sonnets were to a female unless otherwise specified, as the titles he assigned to his groupings indicate.[24] So too did the numerous eighteenth-century editors who reprinted Benson: Gildon (1723) referred to them as 'being most to his Mistress' and Sewell (1725) believed them to have been inspired by 'a real, or an imaginary Lady.'[25] Independent of Benson, there is further and earlier evidence. Gary Taylor has discussed five manuscript versions of sonnet 2 from the early decades of the seventeenth century with the title 'To one that would die a maid';[26] there is also a 1711 reprint of the 1609 quarto that describes the collection as '154 Sonnets all of them in Praise of his Mistress.'[27] The eighteenth-century antiquarian William Oldys who possessed a copy of the quarto assumed that some of the first 126 sonnets were addressed to a female, and George Steevens defended his logic: 'From the complaints of *inconstancy*, and the praises of *beauty*, contained in them, [the Sonnets] should seem at first sight to be addressed by an inamorato to a mistress' (Malone and Boswell, p. 306). Malone's preliminary note announcing the division at 126 literally prevented such a 'first sight,' precluding the possibility open to earlier readers of assuming the ungendered sonnets to a female.

This is not, however, to say that Malone got it wrong: clearly no sonnets are addressed to a female in the first 126 and none to a male (except Cupid) in the subsequent twenty-eight. Just as clearly, the poet abandons the young man in 126 and declares his allegiance to a mistress in 127 and the formal irregularities (twelve pentameter lines in couplets) may punctuate that shift.[28] Nor is there any reason not to take 144's announcement—'Two loves I have': 'a man right fair' and 'a woman, colour'd ill'—at face value. Some kind of binary division appears to be at work.[29] The question is whether that division is best described in terms—or *only* in terms—of gender difference: in terms, that is, of the object choices that have lent themselves so readily to the modern distinction between homosexuality and heterosexuality.[30]

For that construction of desire—as Foucault's expansive history of sexuality as well as Alan Bray's concentration on the Renaissance have demonstrated[31]—depended on a construal of the body and of the psyche that postdated Shakespeare, like Malone's edition itself, by about two centuries. It may then be that Malone's overly emphatic division of the Sonnets into male/female appears more in keeping with the cultural preoccupations at the turn of the eighteenth century than of the sixteenth. It may be symptomatic of a much later emphasis on sexual differentiation, one that has been fully charted out recently in Thomas Laqueur's *Making Sex: Body and Gender from the Greeks to Freud.*[32]

According to Laqueur, 'Sometime in the eighteenth century, sex as we know it was invented.'[33] What he means by this bold pronouncement is that until then there was essentially one sex rather than two. According to the classical or Galenic model, the female possessed an inverted, interior, and inferior version of male genitalia; as countless anatomical drawings attest, the uterus was imagined as an inverted scrotum, the vagina an inverted penis, the vulva an inverted foreskin. Reproductive processes as well as parts were also on par, so that conception required orgasm from both male and female. Not until the eighteenth century were male and female typically divided into two discrete sexes with distinct reproductive parts and processes: hence the invention of 'sex as we know it.' The shift is reflected in an array of verbal and graphic representations: the construction of a different skeleton for women than for men; anatomical drawings representing incommensurate reproductive structures rather than homologous ones; the division of formerly shared nomenclature into male and female so that once ungendered sperm, testicles, and stones are gendered male and differentiated from female eggs and ovaries. In short, a reproductive biology was constructed based on *absolute* rather than *relative* difference. It is only then, Laqueur notes, that the expression 'opposites attract' is coined, suggesting that 'natural' sexual attraction is between unlikes rather than likes.[34]

As Laqueur points out, this reconstrual removed sexuality from a vast system of metaphysical correspondences based, like society itself, on hierarchical order and situated it firmly in the body or 'nature.' That a woman was previously imagined to possess less perfected versions of male genitalia legitimized her subordination to man. Biology thus upheld social hierarchy. Once difference was grounded in the body rather than in metaphysics, once male and female anatomy was perceived as incommensurate rather than homologous, then sexuality lost its 'social' bearings and became instead a matter of 'nature.' As Laqueur insists repeatedly, and as his characterization of the shift as an *invention* rather than as a *discovery* suggests, the change represents no empirical or scientific advance—'No discovery or group of discoveries dictated the rise of the two-sex model'[35]—but rather a cultural and political reorientation. Malone's division of the Sonnets may best be understood in the context of this reorientation.

There is another shift that strangely corresponds to both Malone's twofold division and biology's two-sex model, and it occurs at roughly the same point in time. In eighteenth-century grammars and discussions of grammar, a new attention to linguistic gender binaries appears. The hierarchy preserved in the one-sex model had also applied in questions of grammatical agreement: male gender prevailed over female because it was the 'more worthy' gender. In his popular rhetoric (1553), Thomas Wilson considered natural order violated when women preceded men in a syntactic construction, since man was clearly the dominant gender. In his official Latin grammar (1567), William Lyly assumed the same principle in explaining that an adjective describing both a male and female noun must agree with the male ('Rex et Regina Beati') because 'The masculine gender is more worthy than the feminine.'[36] In the eighteenth century, however, this ontological and grammatical hierarchy has ceased to be self-evident. And the reason appears to be that grammar now looks to biology rather than to metaphysics for its lead. New discoveries in biology are brought to bear on grammar, so that it is maintained that the discovery that plants have sexes introduced inconsistency into classical grammar's classification of plants as neuter.[37] In highly gendered languages like German, a general rethinking of conventional grammatical gender occurs. In English that possesses no conventional grammatical gendering, the problem took a more focused form. Towards the end of the eighteenth century, the first call for an epicene or gender-neutral pronoun is heard, in response to what is only then perceived as a problem: what to do

with constructions like '*everyone* should go to *his* place' where a
female and male antecedent is represented by the male 'his.'[38] As in
biology, grammar can no longer assume an hierarchical relation
between male and female to justify the predominance of male gender.

It is not only in relation to the third person that hierarchy
disappears; in English, it had also by the start of the eighteenth century
disappeared from the second person. In standard English, *thee/thou* had
been dropped in favour of *you*, collapsing the complexly nuanced range
of distinctions based on class relations. It is curious that Malone, who
took great pride in noting philological difference in Shakespeare's age,
ignored the second person pronoun while focusing on the third. Several
recent critics, however, have discussed it, noting that the first 126
sonnets vacillate between *you* and *thou*, while the second twenty-eight
consistently stick to *thou*.[39] Their explanations have been varied,
contradictory and incomplete; the highly complex code remains
unbroken. What can be ventured, however, is that the unwritten rules
governing second person usage in the Renaissance were social and
hierarchic.[40] They originated in social rank, though clearly were
complicated by a calculus of differentials that included age, gender,
education, experience, race, ethical worth, emotional stake, etc.[41]

This is not to propose a new division, the first 126 to 'you/thou,'
the next twenty-eight to 'thou'[42]—but rather to suggest that gender
difference is not the *only* way to differentiate the Sonnets' 'Two loves.'
There are other forms of otherness that the Malonean or modern
tradition has ignored. Sexual difference is only one differential
category in these poems; class is another; so is age, reputation, marital
status, moral probity, even physical availability. In each of these
categories, the poet is more like the mistress than like the youth; love of
like would, therefore, incline him more to the mistress than the boy. It
is because Joel Fineman's awesome *Shakespeare's Perjured Eye: The
Invention of Poetic Subjectivity in the Sonnets* limits difference to
sexual difference that its argument is so troubling. For more relentlessly
and consequentially than anyone since Malone, Fineman has
emphasized the distinction between male and female; indeed, it is
fundamental to his Lacanian account of the constitution of subjectivity.
The rupturing transition required by this account occurs, for Fineman,
in the move from homosexual love of the same to heterosexual love of
the other, from the ideal specularity of the youth to the false linguistics
of the mistress, a move that readily translates into the Lacanian break
from the imaginary into the symbolic. In short, Fineman bases what

may be the vastest claim ever made for the Sonnets—that they invent poetic subjectivity for the western tradition—on sexual difference, on that rupturing but constitutive transition from a like and admired object to an unlike and loathed one.[43] Yet in light of the biological and grammatical phenomena we have been attending, Fineman's construal of sexual difference is premature. The 'Invention of Poetic Subjectivity' he attributes to Shakespeare must await 'the invention of sex' Laqueur sees as an eighteenth-century phenomenon. Until male and female can be seen as two discrete sexes rather than variants on one sex, how can subjectivity be constituted in the break between the two?

It is because Fineman overstresses the gender division at sonnet 126 that his study might be seen as the culmination of the Malonean tradition. Focus on male/female difference lends itself too readily to a psychosexuality that excludes the psychosocial. If social distinctions like class or even age were introduced, for example, the entire Lacanian progression would be turned on its head, for the poet would experience the youth's aristocratic otherness *before* the mistress's bourgeois sameness, his extreme junior *before* his approximate peer. How, then, would it be possible to make the transition Lacanian subjectivity requires from imaginary identification to symbolic dislocation? I've put the burden of two centuries of criticism on Fineman's massively difficult book in order to make a very simple point: tradition has postulated (and concealed) in the Sonnets a sexual scandal that is based in the personal abstracted from the social, on a biology of two-sexes rather than on an epistemology of one-sex, on a division according to a gendered third person rather than a ranked second person. As I will show in the remainder of this paper by turning—at long last—to the Sonnets themselves, this has been a mistake . . . so *big* a mistake that the real scandal has been passed over.

III

The ideological force of the imperious first line of the Sonnets has gone virtually unnoticed: 'From fairest creatures we desire increase.'[44] In the first seventeen poems which have traditionally (and rather preciously) been titled the procreation sonnets, there can be no pretence of fair being either an abstract value like the Platonic Good or a disinterested one like the Kantian Beautiful. *Fair* is the distinguishing attribute of the dominant class, not unlike Bourdieu's *taste* that serves both to distinguish the dominant class and, by distinguishing it, to keep it

dominant.[45] The first seventeen sonnets urging the fair youth to marry
and beget a son have an open and explicit social function: to reproduce,
like an Althusserian state apparatus, the *status quo* by reproducing a
fair young man, ideally 'ten for one' (6). The preservation of the youth
preserves his aristocratic family line, dynasty or 'house': 'Who lets so
faire a house fall to decay?' (13). If such houses are allowed to
deteriorate, the social formation would itself be at risk: hence the
general (and conservative) desire to increase 'fairest creatures' and to
convince those privileged creatures that the repair of their 'beautious
roofe' should be their 'chiefe desire' (10). Were these houses and roofs
*un*fair, there would be no cultural imperative to maintain them, just as
there is none to reproduce *un*fair (homely) persons: 'Let those whom
nature hath not made for store, / Harsh featurelesse, and rude, barrenly
perish' (11); while the youth is 'much too faire, / To be deaths conquest
and make wormes thine heire' (6), the 'Harsh, featureless, and rude'
can return to dust unlamented. 'Increase' is to be desired only from
those whom Nature has 'best indow'd' with 'bountious guift' (11); and
those gifts are not simply physical or spiritual riches but the social and
material ones that structure society from the top. For this reason, it is
only the fair lineaments of fair lineages that should be reproduced for
posterity—'Thou shouldst print more, not let that coppy die.'

Underscoring the social concerns of this first group is their origin
in pedagogical materials designed to cultivate fair young men. As has
long been noted, these sonnets derive from Erasmus's 'Epistle to
persuade a young gentleman to marriage,' Englished in Thomas
Wilson's widely influential 1553 *The Arte of Rhetorique*.[46] The treatise
was used in schools as a rhetorical exercise in persuasion. Languet
repeated it in a letter to the young Sidney and Sidney in turn echoed it
in his *Arcadia*, that consummate expression of aristocratic ethos. The
treatise's tropes and arguments attained commonplace status, as is
suggested by the seventeenth-century popularity of the sonnet that
deploys the most of them, sonnet 2, copies of which survive in twelve
early manuscripts.[47] It seems likely, then, that these opening sonnets
would have evoked the pedagogical context which prepared fair young
men to assume the social position to which high birth entitled them.
The 'private friends' among whom according to Francis Meres these
sonnets circulated as well as the patron to whom the collection is
ostensibly dedicated can be assumed to have recognized this rhetoric as
a blueprint for reproducing the fair values of the dominant class.[48]
Shakespeare's 'Two loves' relate to this opening set piece quite

explicitly: after sonnet 17, it is through his own poetic lines rather than the youth's generational loins that fair's lineaments are to be reproduced, fair's lineage extended.[49] The fair line ends, however, at 127 with the shocking declaration that 'now is blacke beauties successive heire.' As if a black child had been born of a fair parent, a miscegenating successor is announced, one who razes fair's lineage ('And Beautie slandered with a bastard shame') and seizes fair's language ('beauty hath no name')—genealogy and etymology. Desire inverts its object at this breaking point: from an embodiment of a social ideal to an embodiment of a social atrocity. In praising the youth's fair lineaments, social distinction had been maintained; in praising the mistress's dark colours, social distinction is confounded. This reverses the modern ranking of the 'Two loves' that has found one unspeakable and the other simply regrettable. For the love of the youth 'right fair' which tradition has deemed scandalous promotes a social programme while the love for the mistress 'collour'd ill' which tradition has allowed threatens to annihilate it.

This is a sign, I think, that there is something misleading about the male/female categories by which Malone divided the collection: they too easily slip into the post-Enlightenment categories of homosexual and heterosexual which provoke responses that are precisely the inverse of what the Sonnets themselves call for. I would like to propose instead that the two groups be reconsidered under rubrics available in the period, appearing in E. K.'s note to the *Shepherdes Calendar* defending Hobbinol's passion for young Colin Clout on the grounds that 'paederastice [is] much to be preferred before gynerastice, that is the love that inflameth men with lust toward womankind.'[50] Unlike homosexual and heterosexual, the terms better correspond with Shakespeare's 'better' and 'worser' loves, his pederastic love of a boy ('my lovely Boy,' 126) and gynerastic love of a womb (the irresistible 'waste of shame,' 129).[51] As E. K. specifies, pederastic love is 'much to be preferred' over gynerastic, and the Sonnets demonstrate why: because it does not imperil social distinction.

Indeed the poet's main task in the first group is to protect those distinctions, a task that takes the specific form of preserving the youth's lineaments from Time's disfigurations. Shakespeare's 'pupil pen' is in contest with 'Times pensel' (16). In his own verse lines, he would transcribe the youth's fair features before 'confounding Age' unfairs them by cross-hatching his physiognomic lineaments with 'lines and wrinkles' (63), cancelling or deleting the youth's fair copy, rendering

him thereby 'featurelesse' like those consigned to perish barrenly—as
if to make him indistinguishable from the 'Harsh' and 'rude.' In the
gynerastic group, however, it is not Time but Lust that threatens
distinction. Lust mars not through the sharp incisions of Time's
stylus—its pen-knife—but through the obscuring adulterations of 'a
woman colour'd ill.' While Time's deadly scriptings disfigure what is
seen, Lust's murky adulterations confound what is known. Once a
black mistress preempts the fair youth, a whole range of
epistemological distinctions collapse: between black and fair (131, 132)
to be sure, but also between truth and lies (138); private and public
(137); first person and second, first person and third (135-6); past,
present, and future (129); is and is not (147), worst and best (150),
angel and friend (144). In the first group, though aging himself
('Beated and chopt with tand antiquitie' (62), the poet sets himself up
as Time's adversary, his own glamourizing lines counteracting Time's
disfiguring marks; in the second group, however, Lust and Will are
familiars rather than adversaries, so much so that Will is literally
synonymous with Lust in 135 and 136, and Lust personified blurs into
Will's person in 129. The pederastic 'pupil pen' reinscribes the
pedagogical ideal with which the Sonnets begin; while the gynerastic
'waste of shame' adulterates even the most black and white
distinctions.

This is not to say that love of the youth is altogether 'of comfort.'
The majority of the sonnets to him register intense longing,
humiliation, loss felt and anticipated, betrayal, and even worse, self-
betrayal—all the result, perhaps, of a cultural overinvestment in 'fairest
creatures.' Yet the cost is nothing in comparison with what gynerasty
exacts.[52] As the promiscuous womb threatens social order, so too
gynerasty threatens psychic stability. Will himself takes on the
hysterical attributes of the womb that obsesses him, in the breathlessly
frantic copulatives of 129, in the semantic confusions listed above
which in sonnet 147 he calls 'mad mans' discourse. There could be no
more shocking manifestation of his hysteria than sonnet 136 in which
every word could be said to signal his desire, homonymically or
synonymically.[53] This maniacal repetition is audible in '*Will*, will fulfill
the treasure of thy loue, / I fill it full with wils, and my will one,' but it
is present in all the sonnet's phonetic variables as well, reducing their
signification to the tautological deadlock of 'Will wills will.' Nor is
Will ever released from this uterine obsession; like all men in sonnet
129, he does not know how to avoid the sulphuric pit (144), how 'To

shun the heauen that leads men to this hell' (129); hence the fatal return in the final two Anacreontics to his mistress's genital 'eye,' her inflammatory and unquenchable 'Well.'[54]

But the real horror of gynerasty is social and general rather than personal and particular. Edgar in *Lear* contemns Goneril's royal womb adulterated by the bastard Edmund as 'indinguish'd [*sic*] space of Womans will.'[55] It is precisely this failure of discrimination that characterizes the dark lady's sexual capacity, as is evidenced by her indiscrete admission of Wills. In these sonnets it is not only common names that lose distinction, but also proper. Men named Will are indistinguishable: Will Shakespeare would be among them, and perhaps Will of the dedication's Mr W. H., and perhaps the mistress's husband is also Will, but what difference does it make when Will like *Homo* (like 'sausie Iackes' too) is a common name to all?[56] Repeatedly in these sonnets the indiscriminate womb is contrasted with that exclusive treasured 'place' or 'viall' (6) in which the youth's purely aristocratic seed would be antiseptically distilled or 'pent in walls of glasse' (5). The 'large and spacious' place that is the focus of desire in the second group is no such discerning 'seuerall plot': it is 'the wide worlds common place' (137) and primarily an incontinently liquid one—'the baye where all men ride' (137) and 'sea all water, [that] yet receiues raine still' (135)—in which all distinctions of blood bleed into one another.

As the law itself under Elizabeth confirmed by more severely prosecuting fornication between men and women than between men, nothing threatens a patriarchal and hierarchic social formation more than a promiscuous womb. By commingling blood-lines, it has the potential to destroy the social fabric itself. The gynecrasty of the Sonnets, then, needs to be considered in terms of the range of sexual practices Alan Bray has foregrounded (among them, bestiality, adultery, rape, and prostitution) that were in the period termed 'sodomy' and associated with such crimes against the state as sorcery, heresy, and treason.[57] There is good reason, therefore, to credit Jonathan Goldberg's recent suggestion that in Renaissance terms, it is Shakespeare's sonnets to the dark lady rather than those to the young man that are sodomitic.[58]

The dark lady's indiscriminate womb images social anarchy no less than Lear's invocation of cosmic cataclysm: 'all germains spill at once.'[59] The germains spill serially in the mistress rather than all 'at once,' but with the same helter-skelter randomness, *including those of the fair youth*, so that his noble seed is intermixed with that of common 'sausie Iackes' (128) and of unnumbered intercoursing 'Wills.'[60] The patriarchal dream of producing fair young men turns into the patriarchal nightmare of a social melting pot, made all the more horrific by the fact that the mistress's *black* is the antithesis not just of fair but of *white*. Tradition has been ever slower to entertain the possibility that these poems express desire for a black woman rather than desire for a boy. But the important work that is being done on England's contact with Africa and on its cultural representations of that contact is making it increasingly difficult to dissociate in this period blackness from racial blackness—black from blackamoor—promiscuity from miscegenation, especially in a work that begins by arguing for the perpetuation of pure fair blood.[61]

This paper began with one traditional error and ends with another. The first was minor, an erroneous representation of Benson's publishing efforts. The last, however, is quite major. The scandal in the Sonnets had been misidentified. It is not Shakespeare's desire for a boy; for in upholding social distinctions, that desire proves quite conservative and safe. It is Shakespeare's gynerastic longings for a black mistress that are perverse and menacing, precisely because they threaten to raze the very distinctions his poems to the fair boy strain to preserve. As with the Benson falsification, it is the motive behind the error that is worth thinking about. And I will end by doing so.

　　Since the eighteenth century, sexuality has been seen in biological and psychological terms rather than social.[62] Perversion, therefore, is seen as pathological rather than subversive. But in a period in which the distribution of power and property depended on orderly sexuality, it remained imperative that sexuality be understood and judged in social terms. The social consequences of sexual arrangements (whether male-female marriages or male-male alliances) and derangements (male-female adultery or male-male sodomy) were too basic to allow them to become merely personal matters—to become, that is, what they have become in modern sexual discourse: the precondition of personal identity. Modern readings of the Sonnets (the only kind we have) have skewed the relation of Shakespeare's 'Two loves' to conform with this classification. The result is quite topsy-turvy: readings of the young man sonnets have concealed a personal scandal that was never there; and readings of dark mistress sonnets have been blank to the shocking social peril they promulgate. A category mistake lies at the bottom of this odd hermeneutic: the Sonnets' 'Two loves' have been misclassified, the 'love of comfort' avoided as abnormal and unnatural and the 'love of despaire' countenanced as normal and natural. This essay has argued that a reclassification is in order according to a different system altogether, one that would replace the personal categories of normalcy and abnormalcy with the social ones of hierarchy and anarchy—of desired generation and abhorred miscegenation.

NOTES

1. *A New Variorum Edition of Shakespeare: The Sonnets*, 2 vols. (Philadelphia, Pa. and London, 1944), vol. 2, p. 20, n. 1. Sidney Lee in his introduction to a 1905 facsimile of the Sonnets noted Benson's changes but without itemizing them or speculating on Benson's motives: *Shakespeare's Sonnets: Being a Reproduction in Facsimile of the First Edition* (Oxford, 1905), pp. 57-8.

2. *The Sonnets and A Lover's Complaint* (Middlesex and New York, 1986), p. 46.

3. Benson gives the title 'Selfe flattery of her beautie' to sonnets 113-15, 'Upon receit of a Table Booke from his Mistris' to sonnet 122, 'An intreatie for her acceptance' to sonnet 125. See Rollins, vol. 2, pp. 20-1 for a list of Benson's titles.

4. Cf. Rollins, pp. 20 and 29.

5. Benson alters the pronoun from male to female only in the last four lines of the sonnet: 'To make *her* much out-live a gilded tombe'; 'To make *her* seeme, long hence, as *she* showes now' (emphasis added). The masculine pronoun is retained in lines 6 and 9: 'Truth needs no colour with *his* colour fix'd'; 'Because *he* needs no praise wilt thou be dumbe?' (emphasis added). Benson, *Poems: Written by Wil. Shake-speare. Gent.* (London, 1640), E[v].

6. The only other sonnet referring to the beloved as 'boy' (sonnet 126, 'O thou my lovely boy') was with seven others dropped from the 1640 collection, perhaps by accident.

7. See Stephen Booth's gloss to sonnet 110, lines 9-12, pp. 356-7 as well as to sonnet 109, lines 9, 10, 13, 14, pp. 352-3 in *Shakespeare's Sonnets* (New Haven, Conn. and London, 1977).

8. For accounts of how Benson's printing-house and editorial practices have also been maligned, see Josephine Waters Bennett, 'Benson's Alleged Piracy of *Shakespeares Sonnets* and of Some of Jonson's Works,' *Studies in Bibliography*, 21 (1968), pp. 23S-48. See also Margreta de Grazia, *Shakespeare*

Verbatim: The Reproduction of Authenticity and the 1790 Apparatus (Oxford, 1991), p. 49, n. 1, pp. 163-73.

9. On the hysterical response to this problem in modern readings of the Sonnets, see Peter Stallybrass, 'Editing as Cultural Formation: The Sexing of Shakespeare's Sonnets,' *Modern Language Quarterly*, 54 (March, 1993), 91-103, reprinted in this volume.

10. *Supplement to the Edition of Shakespeare's Plays Published in 1778 by Samuel Johnson and George Steevens*, 2 vols. (1780), vol. 2.

11. *Twenty of the Plays of Shakespeare*, 4 vols., ed. George Steevens (1766).

12. Quoted by Rollins, vol. 1, p. 55.

13. See de Grazia, p. 154.

14. See de Grazia, pp. 155-6.

15. For the profusion of deictics in the Sonnets, see Joel Fineman, *Shakespeare's Perjured Eye: The Invention of Poetic Subjectivity in the Sonnets* (Berkeley, Los Angeles, London, 1986), pp. 8-9, p. 311, n. 6.

16. *The Plays and Poems of William Shakspeare*, 10 vols. (1790; facs. rpt., New York, 1968), vol. 10, pp. 191, 265, 294. Subsequent references to this volume will appear in text.

17. On 'lover,' see Booth, p. 432.

18. *The Plays and Poems of William Shakspeare* (1821; facs. rpt., New York, 1966), vol. 20, p. 309. Page references to this volume will henceforth appear parenthetically in text.

19. For Malone's invalidation of the inculpatory anecdotes, see de Grazia, pp. 104-7, pp. 135-41.

20. Boswell corrects Webbe for referring to the eclogue as the sixth ('by a slip of memory, or the printer's mistake') when it should be the fourth (p. 221). Bruce R. Smith situates this eclogue in Renaissance pastoral in 'The Passionate Shepherd,' *Homosexual Desire in Shakespeare's England: A Cultural Poetics* (Chicago and London, 1991), pp. 79-115.

21. The 1609 Sonnets were reprinted but without an apparatus by Bernard Lintott in 1711 and by George Steevens in 1766.

22. *Sexual Dissidence: Augustine to Wilde, Freud to Foucault* (Oxford, 1991).

23. See Booth's scrupulous account of the division, p. 430.

24. Rollins aligns the 1640 titles with the 1609 sonnet numbers, vol. 2, pp. 21-2.

25. See de Grazia, p. 155, n. 57.

26. 'Some Manuscripts of Shakespeare's Sonnets,' *Bulletin of The John Rylands University Library*, 68, I (1985), 217.

27. Bernard Lintott, *A Collection of poems in Two Volumes . . . Being all the Miscellanies of Mr William Shakespeare, which were Publish'd by himself in the Year 1609 . . .*, 2 vols.

28. In the 1609 quarto, the irregularity is rendered typographically conspicuous by two sets of empty brackets in place of the final couplet.

29. On the possibility that the Sonnets were organized according to a tripartite structure (152 Sonnets, 2 Anacreontics, a Complaint) based on generic rather than gender difference following the model of Daniel, Spenser, Lodge, and others, see Kerrigan's Introduction to *Sonnets*, pp. 13-14 and the bibliographic references on p. 66.

30. On the taxonomy of 'homo' and 'hetero,' see Eve Kosofsky Sedgwick, *The Epistemology of the Closet* (Berkeley and Los Angeles, 1990).

31. Michel Foucault, *The History of Sexuality*, vol. I: *An Introduction*, trans., Robert Hurley (New York, 1978) and Alan Bray, *Homosexuality in Renaissance England* (London, 1982).

32. (Cambridge, Mass. and London, 1990).

33. P. 149. Laqueur notes the agreement of Michel Foucault, Lawrence Stone, and Ivan Illich in identifying the late eighteenth century as the point at which human sexuality was reconceptualized, p. 5 and n. 14.

34. Ibid. p. 152

35. Ibid. p. 153.

36. *A Short Introduction of Grammar* (London, 1530), p. 47.

37. See Dennis Barron, *Grammar and Gender* (New Haven, Conn., 1986), p. 35.

38. Ibid. pp. 190-1.

39. See G. P. Jones, 'You, Thou, He or She? The Master Mistress in Shakespearian and Elizabethan Sonnet Sequences,' *Cahiers Elisabéthains*, 19 (1981), 73-84 and Andrew Gurr, 'You and Thou in Shakespeare's Sonnets,' *Essays in Criticism*, 32 (1982), 9-25. Arthur F. Marotti is sensitive to the tonal effects of such positionalities in his discussion of how Shakespeare's artistry can compensate for his inferior social rank, in 'Love Is not Love: Elizabethan Sonnet Sequences and The Social Order,' *Journal of English Literary History*, 49 (1982), 413-16.

40. On the origins of the distinction between *tu/vos* in Latin and *thou/you* in English, see R. Brown and A. Gilman, 'The Pronouns of Power and Solidarity,' in T. A. Sebeok, ed., *Style in Language* (Amherst, Mass., 1960), pp. 253-76.

41. The same perplexing instability of address characterizes another male/male couple divided by rank, not to mention age, experience, and size: Falstaff and Hal, who shift constantly from one form to the other as they

uneasily jockey for position in a relationship characterized by jockeying, a relationship in which male/male erotic desire is, as Jonathan Goldberg has recently argued, not entirely absent; 'Hal's Desire, Shakespeare's Idaho,' in *Henry IV, Parts One and Two*, ed. Nigel Wood (Philadelphia, Pa., 1995), 145-75. I wish to thank him for letting me read the typescript.

42. Sonnet 145 is the sole exception; it substitutes 'you' for 'thou' in the interest of preserving rhyme: 'I hate, from hate away she threw, / And sau'd my life saying not you.'

43. The book's overinvestment in gender binaries raises troubling political and hermeneutic questions. Its argument that subjectivity is attained through the renunciation of the imaginary realm of homosexual sameness bears a disturbing resemblance to a pseudo-Freudianism that perceives homosexuality as stunted or incomplete development. It also requires that sonnets 1-126 be read as univocal and 127-52 as equivocal, though Fineman later revises this programme by maintaining that equivocation is present in both groups, though only latently in the first.

44. The Sonnets will henceforth be quoted from the facsimile of the 1609 *Shake-speares Sonnets* printed in Stephen Booth's edition. Lars Engle has recently discussed this first line as inaugurating the Sonnets' concern with 'human value in time,' but without noting the specific class inflection of this value, 'Afloat in Thick Deeps: Shakespeare's Sonnets on Certainty,' *Publications of the Modern Language Association*, 104 (1989), 832-43.

45. Pierre Bourdieu, *Distinction: A Social Critique of the Judgement of Taste*, trans. Richard Nice (Cambridge, Mass., 1984).

46. For the influence of this epistle on Shakespeare and others, see Rollins, *Variorum* I, p. 7 and II, p. 192, T. W. Baldwin, *The Literary Genetics of Shakespeare's Poems and Sonnets* (Urbana, Ill., 1950), pp. 183-5, and Katharine M. Wilson, *Shakespeare's Sugared Sonnets* (London and New York, 1974), pp. 146-67.

47. See Taylor, pp. 210-46.

48. This is not to say that the Sonnets unequivocally reproduce aristocratic value. As Thomas M. Greene points out, the thrift and husbandry urged upon the young man in the first seventeen sonnets is decidedly bourgeois ('Pitiful Thrivers: Failed Husbandry in the Sonnets,' *Shakespeare and the Question of Theory*, ed. Patricia Parker and Geoffrey Hartman [New York and London, 1985], pp. 230-44). Furthermore, the socially inferior poet (sonnets 25 and 110) by taking on the youth's responsibility for reproducing fair in effect assumes aristocracy's genetic privilege: his inky poetic lines preempt the youth's fair genealogical ones: 'His beautie shall in these blacke lines be seene' (63).

49. For the semantic and homonymic connections between lines and lineaments, see William Empson, *Seven Types of Ambiguity* (New York, 1947), pp. 54-5, cited by Booth, p. xiii. For the line/loin resonances, see Additional Notes to Booth's 1978 edition, p. 579.

50. Kerrigan brings E. K.'s gloss to bear on the Sonnets to conclude that the Sonnets register a 'profound homosexual attachment of a scarcely sensual, almost unrealized kind,' p. 51; Stephen Orgel comments briefly on the psychological and legal advantages of 'paederastice' over 'gynerastice' in 'Call Me Ganymede,' *Impersonations: The Performance of Gender in Shakespeare's England* (Cambridge, 1996), p. 71. See also Smith's discussion of the quote in relation to Virgil and Spenser, pp. 95-8.

51. On the identification of woman with womb, see Richard Verstegan: 'And as Homo in Latin doth signifie both man and woman, so in our toung the feminyne creature also hath as we see the same of man, but more aptly in that it is for due distinction composed with womb, *she being that kynde of mann that is wombed*, or hath the womb of conception, which the man of the male kynd hath not,' *The Restitution of Decayed Intelligence* (Antwerp, 1605), p. 194.

52. Stephen Orgel, in commenting on the 'all but axiomatic' love of men for boys in the period, refers to the Sonnets as evidence that 'the problem of sex between men involves a good deal less anxiety' than between men and women, 'Call Me Ganymede,' p. 71.

53. No special case has to be made for 'loue' or 'loue-sute' as synonyms for will, and Booth's commentary supports the equivalence of the sonnet's other nouns ('soule,' 'things of great receit,' 'stores account,' 'treasure,' 'number,' 'one,' 'nothing,' and 'none'), pp. 469-73. Verbs also relate to lust: 'come' to climax; 'check' to its deferral; 'knows,' 'proved,' 'reckon'd' to forms of carnal knowing; 'fulfill' and 'fill' to orgasm; 'is admitted' and 'hold' to sexual entry. Adjectives express sexual desirables—'sweet,' 'great,' 'blind'—and adverbs modify the sexual act, 'so neere,' 'thus farre,' 'with ease.'

54. On eye as vulva, see Booth, p. 521.

55. *The Tragedie of King Lear*, The Norton Facsimile *The First Folio of Shakespeare*, prepared by Charlton Hinman (New York, 1968), TLN 2724.

56. Paul Ramsey notes that 22 1/2 per cent of all Englishmen were named Will at the end of the sixteenth century, *The Fickle Glass: A Study of Shakespeare's Sonnets* (New York, 1979), p. 23.

57. See Smith, esp. pp. 41-53 and Jonathan Goldberg, *Sodometries: Renaissance Texts, Modern Sexualities* (Berkeley, 1992), pp. 18-23.

58. 'Hal's Desire,' p. 41.

59. *The Tragedie of King Lear*, TLN 1663.

60. The promiscuous dark lady is not unlike Spenser's miscegenating Acrasia ('bad mixture') who razes the estates of her noble lovers in *FQ*, Bk. II, 12.

61. On the racial inflections of fair/dark and black/white in the early modern period, see Ania Loomba, *Gender, Race, Renaissance Drama* (Manchester and New York, 1989), pp. 42-5 and Kim Hall, *Things of Darkness: Economies of Race and Gender in Early Modern England* (Ithaca and London, 1995), pp. 6-15.

62. This paragraph owes much to Dollimore, pp. 23-40 et passim.

"Incertainties now crown themselves assur'd"
The Politics of Plotting Shakespeare's Sonnets*

Heather Dubrow

I

Indeterminate in their chronology, destabilized by their textual cruxes, and opaque in much of their language, Shakespeare's Sonnets have nonetheless attracted curiously positivistic claims. In particular, critics who differ on many interpretive problems are nevertheless likely to agree that the direction of address of these poems can be established with certainty: the first 126 sonnets refer to and are generally addressed to the Friend, while the succeeding ones concern the Dark Lady. The past thirty years have witnessed trenchant challenges to many assertions in John Dover Wilson's book on these lyrics, such as his identification of the Friend with William Herbert; but his observation that "most readers . . . will not be disposed to deny authority to . . . [the] division into two sections" remains accurate.[1]

The axiom that the first 126 poems involve the Friend and subsequent lyrics concern the Dark Lady generates assumptions about the presence of a linear plot: poet meets Friend, and they enjoy a period of happiness; their joy is, however, shadowed by a period of absence and by the fault alluded to in sonnet 35 ("No more be griev'd at that which thou hast done") and elsewhere. The entrance of the Dark Lady,

Reprinted by permission of *Shakespeare Quarterly* and Heather Dubrow from *Shakespeare Quarterly* 47.3 (Fall 1996), pp. 291-305.

who is as untrustworthy as she is attractive, disrupts the idyll celebrated in the joyous sonnets. She, the poet, and the Friend become embroiled in a triangle of jealousy and deceit. To be sure, critics disagree on the details of this plot, such as the exact nature of the "sensual fault" (35.9).[2] And, indeed, many students of these poems admit that their narrative line is sometimes obscure or submerged. Moreover, practitioners of gay and lesbian studies and queer theory have recently reformulated the story in question in order to emphasize the moments acknowledging homoerotic attraction.[3] But, despite such interpretive debates and doubts, the basic assumptions about structure and plot that I have identified are still widely and firmly accepted.

On the surface at least, it is surprising that those assumptions have been interrogated so rarely. Their pedigree is far from reassuring: the division at sonnet 126 ("O thou, my lovely boy, who in thy power") was established by Malone, whose work on Shakespeare's lyrics has been challenged from many perspectives during the final decades of the twentieth century.[4] Moreover, the most obvious evidence on which to base claims about direction of address—gendered pronouns or other clear referents—is scanty; Margreta de Grazia rightly points out that about five-sixths of the first 126 sonnets and a slightly smaller proportion of the entire collection do not specify an addressee through a gendered pronoun.[5]

If it is puzzling that the conventional wisdom about the Sonnets has been challenged only intermittently, it is even more puzzling that occasional challenges to it have had so little impact on most critics of these poems or, in some cases, even on the challengers themselves. The handful of scholars who raise questions about the bipartite division typically retreat from the most radical implications of those questions. Hilton Landry briefly questions "the myth of two groups," arguing that the sequence lacks the narrative continuity generally associated with such a structure, but proceeds implicitly to accept it by gendering the addressees even when the texts do not specify whether they are male or female.[6] One of the most perceptive students of these poems, Stephen Booth, observes with his customary skepticism that "we have no strong reason to assume the 1609 order to be either the order of their writing or the order in which Shakespeare would have wanted them read." But he also states that "there is . . . some basis for the widespread critical belief that sonnet 126 is intended to mark a division between sonnets principally concerned with a male beloved and those principally concerned with a woman."[7] Notice the judicious reservation in "some basis"; notice, too, that the statement tilts toward accepting the division. Gregory W. Bredbeck acutely notes that the procreation sonnets and sonnet 20 often deflect erotic interpretation by concealing gender; he does not, however, explore at any length the implications of this argument for the sequence as a whole.[8] In earlier work on these poems, I myself contended that critics impose a narrative and dramatic framework on a sequence that resists those modes, yet I implicitly accepted the conventional assumptions about addressees and the plot outlined above.[9]

Finally, an extensive defense of the division into two groups and of the type of plot that results from it has recently issued from the same scholar who has offered the most trenchant evidence for attacking that division. Having previously traced Malone's division of the Sonnets to an Enlightenment agenda and demonstrated that many readers before Malone did not assume that the first 126 poems were exclusively directed to a male, de Grazia writes, "This is not, however, to say that Malone got it wrong. . . . Some kind of binary division appears to be at work."[10] The primary scandal of the Sonnets, her thought-provoking essay proceeds to assert, is neither the sexual preference of the Sonnets' speaker nor the plot their critics have falsely assigned to them. It is rather their transgressive approach to class: praising the youth supports social distinctions while praising the Dark Lady threatens them, and sonnet 126 demarcates the divide between those two very different activities.

In order to interrogate the conventional wisdom about the Sonnets' addressees more radically than de Grazia and others have done, one must first disentangle a range of issues connected with these knotty poems. Critics have long debated the biographical background, if any, of the sequence, but the relationship between that question and the challenge of identifying addressees is more complex than Shakespeareans sometimes acknowledge. Even if historical personages corresponding to the Friend and Dark Lady existed and inspired particular sonnets, it remains possible both that other lyrics in the cycle allude to neither of them and that some of the poems they originally sparked cannot ultimately be associated with corresponding fictive characters. Thus, for example, a sonnet composed in response to a male figure might have been reshaped to allude to the woman in the sequence instead.

Another important epistemological distinction involves the issue of sequence: whether the poems now exist in the order their author intended is closely related to, but separable from, the likelihood of determining their addressees. Some argue that the arrangement of the 1609 edition closely corresponds to the author's intentions, one being to distinguish poems concerning the Friend from those about the Dark Lady. Others contend that, though some individual poems may be out of order, the basic two-part structure determined by Shakespeare survives intact and indicates the direction of address. I will assert instead that the collection published by Thorpe is imperfect in many ways and does not necessarily prove that its author intended a bipartite division. Moreover, even if Thorpe's edition mirrors Shakespeare's own design, we would not invariably know the addressees. Influenced by the resistance to narrativity that characterizes a number of sonnet sequences, the author did not arrange these sonnets in a way that tells a clear story and unmistakably signals the direction of address of each lyric.[11]

The consequences of my assertions are extensive: many other claims about the sequence are revealed as no less unstable, and perhaps even no less self-serving, than the emotions the sequence chronicles. Other possibilities open, though they are as impossible to establish as they are intriguing to consider. For example, what if we were to admit the possibility that one of the highly erotic poems after 126 refers to the Friend? To do so is not to deny that some assumptions about the addressees of these poems remain highly probable. It is not at all likely (though conceivable) that more than one woman with dark hair and darker morals lies behind sonnets 127–52.[12] But even this issue cannot be definitively resolved; more to the point, the addressees of a few poems in sonnets 127–52 and of many sonnets that precede that group are far harder to determine than Shakespeareans usually admit. Often there is no way of being reasonably confident whether a given poem involves the Friend, the Dark Lady, or some third party, and this uncertainty has many implications for the imputed narrative of the sequence as a whole.

Acknowledging and exploring such indeterminacies about plot and direction of address can illuminate the workings of this sequence and of sonnet cycles in general, notably their approaches to narrativity. Such an attack on the conventional wisdom can also illuminate the workings of our own profession, explaining why otherwise incisive critics retreat from some (though by no means all) of the most transgressive consequences of their skepticism. To put it another way, the plot that

Shakespeareans impose on Shakespeare's sequence reveals the plots—
in the several senses of the term—that attract the academy.

II

To support the constellation of presuppositions questioned in this essay,
critics variously adduce the status of sonnet 126, literary and
biographical tenets about Shakespeare's process of composition, and
influential interpretations by earlier critics. To begin with, the stanzaic
irregularities of sonnet 126 function for some as signposts of a change
in addressees: this is, after all, a poem of only twelve lines, and the
closural function established by that prosodic variation is intensified by
an emphasis on termination, notably in the word "quietus" (1. 12) and
the climactic allusions to death and loss. Such evidence is strong but by
no means conclusive. Sonnet 126 is not unique in its structural
irregularity; sonnet 99 ("The forward violet thus did I chide") has
fifteen lines. Indeed, given that Shakespeare's Sonnets include a
repeated couplet, several paired poems that may well be drafts of each
other, and many other apparent irregularities, it is tricky at best to
assign thematic significance to the fact that sonnet 126 deviates from
standard sonnet structure.

Even accepting that sonnet 126 may serve special closural
functions signaled by its twelve-line structure does not establish
irrevocably that the poems preceding it involve the Friend and the ones
succeeding it concern the Dark Lady. Whether or not the poems can be
clearly divided into two large groups, it is obvious that the sequence as
a whole includes a number of subdivisions or clusters. Brents Stirling
goes so far as to assert that most of the poems initially formed discrete
groups;[13] sonnet 126 might originally have been intended to conclude
one of those groups rather than all the poems about the Friend.
Certainly it would be at least as appropriate as a conclusion to the
procreation sonnets. Like those poems, it focuses on Nature and
emphasizes that the passage of time threatens even, or especially, the
lovely youth. Several other poems might seem like equally appropriate
conclusions to a series of sonnets focusing on the Friend. We might
assume, for instance, that sonnet 87 ("Farewell, thou art too dear for my
possessing"), which opens with a word signaling leavetaking and
concludes "Thus have I had thee as a dream doth flatter: / In sleep a
king, but waking no such matter" (ll. 13–14), plays that role. And even
if one grants that sonnet 126 does establish a bipartite division, there is

no reason to assume that the 1609 order reproduces that division; it remains possible that some poems intended for one group or the other slipped out of place.

Another premise sometimes lies behind the belief that we can determine the poems' direction of address and construct a plot built on that determination: namely, the presupposition that they have an immediate relationship to biographical experiences with two persons who correspond to the Friend and Dark Lady. This theory of straightforward mimeticism involves dubious assumptions about the biographical background to the sequence. Among the soundest observations on that subject is John Kerrigan's: "The text is neither fictive nor confessional. Shakespeare stands behind the first person of his sequence as Sidney had stood behind Astrophil—sometimes near the poetic 'I,' sometimes farther off, but never without some degree of rhetorical projection."[14] As this statement suggests, the Sonnets probably exemplify a wide spectrum of connections to biographical events. The many readers who have sensed some such episodes behind the intensity of these lyrics are operating from a sound instinct: the immediacy and force of many sonnets hint that they are written by someone whose knowledge of their events could only be firsthand. Yet all the poems need not have the same genesis. Some may, with little mediation or correction, record an episode with a person who corresponds closely to the fictive characters we now know as the Friend or Dark Lady; others may initially have been written in response to historical people or events but later have been revised in relation to this sequence or, alternatively, incorporated into this group without any revision; and yet others may well have been composed by Shakespeare with no mistress—or master—save his muse in mind.[15]

Conceivably, Shakespeare drafted some sonnets unconnected to the Friend and Dark Lady early in his career, perhaps even a discrete group of them, and then affixed them to his later sonnets; this could account for one or more of the groupings, such as the poems on absence.[16] The popularity of *Astrophil and Stella* when it was published in 1591 inspired a tidal wave of imitations; arguably Shakespeare responded by crafting some contributions to the genre shortly after Sidney's sequence appeared. Critics who accept the possibility of two *Lears* should surely be willing to entertain the possibility of radically revised and superimposed groups of sonnets coalescing into what we now know as Shakespeare's Sonnets. If so, it remains more than possible that many poems within the sequence do refer to the same events, whether experienced biographically or not; but again, to demonstrate that many do so is not to prove that all do so. As Stephen Booth has persuasively argued, Shakespeare's Sonnets both support and undermine a search for coherence.[17] Certainly the presence of sonnets 94 ("They that have pow'r to hurt, and will do none"), 116 ("Let me not to the marriage of true minds"), and 129 ("Th' expense of spirit in a waste of shame"), a group of poems that generalizes about love and lust without referring to a particular lover or relationship, invites us to ask whether the sequence includes other, similar poems which readers have associated with the Friend and Dark Lady without adequate evidence.[18] For example, references to reputation and faults in sonnet 121 ("'Tis better to be vile than vile esteemed") may tempt some critics to read it in relation to events in the narrative about the Friend which they have found—or inserted—in the sequence; but those issues are general ones that do not require presupposing a commentary on a particular relationship. Such speculations suggest that we cannot determine the direction of address of some sonnets because these poems were never intended to involve the Friend or Dark Lady or, alternatively, were adapted cursorily and ambiguously in order to do so. In either case the reader would be less likely throughout the sequence to encounter clear, consistent renditions of character and of characters.

But even critics who reject the idea of mimetic correspondence with experiences outside the sonnet cycle may nonetheless attribute to it an intellectual coherence that permits, indeed encourages, assumptions about to whom the poems refer. According to this reading, whatever the biographical events behind the poems, Shakespeare the dramatist evokes coherent if fictional personages throughout this sequence. The first 126 poems involve the young man and the rest involve the woman because the lyrics paint consistent portraits. Surely this argument holds for certain poems; even the most committed skeptic might hesitate to assert that the procreation sonnets are discrete lyrics that address a cohort of handsome young men, fictive or otherwise, all of whom are reluctant to marry. Yet the assumption that the Dark Lady and Friend are marked by characteristics that regularly allow us to categorize a given poem as pertaining to one or the other of them depends not only on a belief in stable identities (a point to which I will return) but also on a disregard for the perils of circular reading. That is, we assume that a given poem evokes one or the other of those personages, deduce certain traits from the text, and then assign lyrics concerned with the same traits or issues to the same character. For

example, though sonnet 48 ("How careful was I, when I took my way")
nowhere establishes the gender of its addressee, its emphasis on that
personage's preciousness and on the topos of absence substantiates our
assumptions that the poet sees the Friend as praiseworthy and that one
or more episodes of absence complicate their relationship. Hence it
seems more likely that other poems with those preoccupations refer to
the Friend as well, and the cluster of absence sonnets in the first part of
the sequence buttresses the conviction that the earlier poems in the
group do indeed concern the Friend. If, however, we admit that this
lyric could refer to the Dark Lady, then the argument that references to
praiseworthiness or absence in other sonnets flag their addressee
becomes more problematical.

Another reason many Shakespeareans have accepted the premises
challenged in this essay is that these notions have been the underlying
presuppositions of certain highly influential articles or books and the
explicit theses of others. These studies have not, however, established a
definitive case for the addressee of each poem; indeed, in some
instances their analyses can be redirected to support the indeterminate
readings for which I am arguing. For instance, Joel Fineman's
Shakespeare's Perjured Eye argues that the Sonnets establish two
alternative worlds corresponding to two principal groups: the poems
involving the young man celebrate idealized specularity, while those
concerning the Dark Lady lament duplicities occasioned and
represented by language's replacement of vision.[19] But just as the
Lacanian model underlying Fineman's analysis assumes the
interpenetration and coexistence of the Imaginary and Symbolic,
Fineman, throughout the book, stresses the imbrication, conflation, and
erosion of his two categories: "Yet the sequence as a whole refuses to
be . . . discriminated into two distinct and isolated parts. Assuming we
read them both, the two parts of the sequence cannot be kept separate
from each other, for when we begin to compare them each with each
the second sub-sequence retroactively undoes the first, with the latter
'forswearing' the former in a definitive revisionary way."[20] Fineman
himself traces this undoing to the instability of the subjectivities
attributed to the Friend and Dark Lady. To Fineman one may respond,
less subtly but no less persuasively, that the structure of the sequence
itself is unstable: each section may contain poems that are out of place,
referring to characters or values customarily associated with the other
section. Clearly one explanation does not preclude the other.

Longstanding defenses of the sequence's order, which typically carry with them presuppositions that we know about the poems' characters, recently culminated in an important and learned essay by Katherine Duncan-Jones. In it she attempts to defend the structural integrity of the sequence on the basis of the professional integrity of its publisher and the unity of its design.[21] Her points on thematic connections within the sequence are certainly well taken. But the contention that Thorpe was too reliable to publish an unauthorized edition assumes that he was quite atypical of Elizabethan publishers; Duncan-Jones admits that he was responsible for one unauthorized edition, and her effort to dismiss this publication as a prank, "a deliberate piece of mischief," has negative implications for his behavior elsewhere.[22] She cites the outbreak of plague in 1608–09 and the subsequent closing of the theaters as a reason for Shakespeare to have sold this text to Thorpe;[23] but, as G. B. Evans points out, it is also possible that an unauthorized edition would have seemed less risky to Thorpe if, because of the plague, Shakespeare had left the city. In addition, Evans questions whether, given the sexual overtones of the relationship with the young man, Shakespeare would have chosen to publish poems about it.[24]

Duncan-Jones's argument assigns to the sequence a four-part structure: she posits an introductory group of procreation sonnets, followed by 108 sonnets on friendship, the envoi in sonnet 126, and the poems to the Dark Lady. Even if Shakespeare, like Sidney, Fulke Greville, and other writers, does take pains to construct a unit of 108 lyrics, that pattern would suggest but not prove structural unity in other respects. However, as is often the case in numerological analyses, arriving at the proper number involves some special pleading. It is not clear that the sequence does indeed contain a unit of 108 poems. Did Shakespeare really intend to include poems that seem to be versions of each other, such as sonnets 57 ("Being your slave, what should I do but tend") and 58 ("That god forbid that made me first your slave"), in a final manuscript, as he would have had to do to achieve the number 108?

The assertion that the 1609 version is a coherent collection in the order its author intended, the argument offered by Duncan-Jones and many other critics, provides another justification for assigning the first group to the Friend and the later group to the Dark Lady. One of the principal limitations of this position should by now be clear. As many readers have noted, the 1609 version of the Sonnets contains manifold imperfections, such as the repetition of a couplet in sonnets 36 ("Let me confess that we two must be twain") and 96 ("Some say thy fault is youth, some wantonness"), the extra line of sonnet 99, and poems so similar—especially the pair to which I referred earlier, sonnets 57 and 58—that to some they have seemed drafts of the same lyric. One could conceivably attribute a couple of these flaws to printers' errors or attempt to justify others on aesthetic grounds by arguing that the repetition of couplets draws attention to other differences between the sonnets in question.[25] Yet the presence of so many fault lines in the sequence has encouraged an alternative interpretation: that the 1609 edition represents not that dream of traditional textual editors, the author's final intention, but rather a set of poems in various stages of composition. If this is so, the division between poems to one addressee and those to another is not likely to be perfect.

Moreover, the belief that Thorpe's 1609 edition reproduces the poems in a coherent order is often associated with two dubious assumptions about how structural order functions in this sequence and in Petrarchism generally: the expectation that all the poems in a collection will involve a specified addressee with clearly defined characteristics and that many or most of these lyrics will participate in a discernible plot connected with that addressee. To be sure, one can make a case that certain English sequences, notably *Astrophil and Stella*, function in just that way.[26] (Even in that instance, some critics have speculated that Sidney wrote the trochaic songs before he conceived of the sequence and then inserted them within it.[27]) In many other sonnet sequences, such as Samuel Daniel's *Delia*, the lady is so vaguely defined that only the title establishes the principle that all the poems refer to a single mistress, and little plot is perceptible. Other books juxtapose sonnets that refer to a clearly specified addressee and build a plot with poems that could appear in virtually any sonnet sequence. Barnabe Barnes's extraordinarily violent *Parthenophil and Parthenophe*, for example, culminates in a rape, yet it includes many lyrics that might have been lifted from any miscellany. Similarly, Lady Mary Wroth's *Pamphilia to Amphilanthus* defines the speaker carefully and attributes a few salient characteristics to her lover, but within this cycle a large number of poems are lyric meditations unrelated to any plot line. Other cycles make no pretense of a coherent plot or a single beloved; indeed, the Scottish Petrarchan Alexander Craig addresses a large number of presumably fictional ladies in his *Amorose Songes, Sonets, and Elegies*. In short, Petrarchism offers a wide range of models for the structure of a sequence. Its norms and forms do not enjoin a poet to connect every lyric to the mistress constructed by the sequence or even to construct a single mistress; nor do they mandate a clear plot. Because English sequences approach their addressees and plots in such varied ways, an early modern reader would not have assumed that a given cycle included one mistress and a readily discerned narrative. And Shakespeare's sequence, as I have argued at length elsewhere, eschews the narrative and dramatic modes more than most contemporaneous sequences do. A few incidents and events can surely be discerned, but most of the Sonnets are internalized meditations unconnected to a narrative line. Even if Duncan-Jones is right that the 1609 edition reproduces the poems in the order their author intended, his arrangement of them was likely to have been loose and at some points arbitrary—and perceived as such by many Elizabethan readers.

III

What, then, are the consequences of questioning the assumption that we know the addressees of virtually all the Sonnets and can construct on that basis a plot? To begin with, certain interpretations survive intact; as I have already indicated, I am arguing neither for a set of totally discrete poems nor for an infinite number of addressees. Shakespeare's use of masculine pronouns and repeated references to ideal beauty and youth encourage the reader to posit a single male addressee for such lyrics as the procreation group and sonnets 22 ("My glass shall not persuade me I am old"), 42 ("That thou hast her, it is not all my grief"), 54 ("O how much more doth beauty beauteous seem"), 63 ("Against my love shall be as I am now"), and 67 ("Ah, wherefore with infection should he live"). Similarly, the gendered pronouns and references to intertwined physical and moral darkness support the conventional wisdom that many of the poems after sonnet 126 concern the Dark Lady. (This does not, however, preclude the possibility raised above: perhaps even some of these sonnets were originally written with a different addressee, real or fictive, or with no particular addressee in mind and then incorporated into the sequence.)

Yet the questions I pose result in far fewer firm assertions and far more interpretive options. On the one hand, because of the paucity of narrative in this sequence and the possibility that some of the poems traditionally associated with the Friend or Dark Lady do not involve the

personage in question, it is even harder to extract a clear plot line than
many readers have admitted. On the other hand, once the direction of
address is thrown into question, many alternative plot lines become
credible. I do not propose these possibilities as definitive
reinterpretations: the aim of this essay is hardly to substitute one set of
positivistic readings for another. At the same time, these alternatives
invite some intriguing and disturbing speculations about the sequence.

First, then, recognizing that some sonnets among the first 126
could refer to the Dark Lady implies much about that figure, the
speaker, and the culture that contributed to constructing them. There is
no overriding reason to assume that poems such as sonnets 50 ("How
heavy do I journey on the way") and 51 ("Thus can my love excuse the
slow offense"), which concern an absence, describe separation from the
Friend rather than from the Dark Lady. Absence is, of course, a very
familiar topos in Petrarchism. Nor should one assume that the defense
of an unchanged mode of writing in sonnet 76 ("Why is my verse so
barren of new pride?") alludes to creating sonnets about the Friend; if it
would be tellingly appropriate to respond to his constancy, real or
imputed, in a constant style, it would be tellingly ironic to react in that
way to the Dark Lady's many versions of inconstancy.

But what if one extends this analysis to the more celebratory
poems in the first part of the sequence? Suppose, for example, the
generations of undergraduates who have assumed a female addressee
for the frequently anthologized lines of sonnet 18 ("Shall I compare
thee to a summer's day?") are right and it is the Dark Lady who is
celebrated as "lovely and . . . temperate" (l. 2)? The tortured and
tortuous love staged in the later sonnets may be but one of several
responses to her. And the image of the Dark Lady herself which
emerges from the final group of sonnets—that she is attractive but
duplicitous—may be one of several contradictory or at least
contestatory images in the sequence. Our assumption that she is
unremittingly evil would be complicated if we were to envision her as
the subject of a sonnet such as 38, which nowhere definitively
establishes its addressee: "How can my Muse want subject to
invent / While thou dost breathe, that pour'st into my verse / Thine own
sweet argument" (ll. 1–3).

Depending on the critical perspective from which one approaches
them, such possibilities have a number of consequences. From a
characterological viewpoint, the sequence testifies to what might be
described as the Dark Lady's infinite variety. Like Cleopatra, she is a

quick-change artist. This viewpoint would reinforce the duplicity frequently ascribed to her throughout the sequence. Hence the apparent contradictions among the various images of the Dark Lady might also be adduced to dismantle traditional concepts of stable character and support instead an emphasis on destabilized subjectivities.[28] These readings undermine expectations of consistency and wholeness; conceived in Lacanian mirrors, the subjectivity of the Dark Lady is further splintered in the "wilderness of mirrors" that is this sequence.

These apparent contradictions in the construction of the Dark Lady may also testify to how the subjectivities of the speaker and the poet behind him operate. Arguably desire, anger, misogyny, or some volatile admixture of all these potent chemicals prevents Shakespeare the character within the sequence, Shakespeare the poet, or both from constructing a consistent portrait of the Dark Lady. The sequence itself contains lines that buttress this possibility: "For I have sworn thee fair, and thought thee bright" (147.13), for example, might refer back to the brightness mentioned in earlier sonnets. Such contradictions not only exemplify but also clarify the workings of misogyny in the speaker, the poet, and English Renaissance culture. In Tudor and Stuart England the ideologies of gender are consistent in almost nothing save their inconsistency: the careful reader of texts in which such ideologies are expressed finds not a monolithic and hegemonic position but rather a series of contradictions within the works of a single writer and among treatises by different writers on such issues as the amount of authority the wife should have in marriage. Misogyny is often part of a never-ending cycle in which respect, admiration, and attraction generate reactive distancing, and vice versa. In no discourse is this more true than Petrarchism; witness, among a host of many other examples, Spenser's *Amoretti*, which juxtaposes with its most respectful lyrics poems so fiercely hostile toward the mistress that some critics nervously and unpersuasively attempt to assign them to an abortive earlier collection, another lady, another country. It would not be surprising if even a Dark Lady were praised in a poem such as sonnet 18.

Although the majority of poems after sonnet 126 are addressed to a woman, some intriguing revisionist readings are permitted by other texts in the group. The bitter denunciations of lust in sonnet 129 are sometimes read as general but sometimes, because of its placement in the sequence, read in relation to the Dark Lady. They might, however, refer specifically to the male youth as well as to everyone. The repeated references to his "sensual fault" lend some credence to that reading. Sonnet 143 ("Lo as a careful huswife runs to catch") figures the relationship between its speaker and its addressee as that between a harried parent and her child. Whereas the phrase "play the mother's part" (l. 12), as well as the simile of the housewife in which the poem is grounded, encourage the reader to assume a female addressee, a male lover could also be the protagonist of the drama evoked in this poem. (It would hardly be Shakespeare's first or only experiment with crossdressing.) Indeed, this reading opens the possibility that covert antagonism leads to representing a male as the hapless housewife in the poem; reduced to childishness by love and neglect, the speaker on the one hand declares his affection and on the other retaliates by charging his beloved with the effeminacy so feared in his culture.[29]

The most unsettling possibilities, however, involve sonnet 128 ("How oft when thou, my music, music play'st"), which turns on a series of conceits about music. This lyric nowhere genders its addressee, nor does the poem contain references to darkness that ally it with the Dark Lady poems. Though women often played the virginal, sixteenth-century allusions to that instrument testify that men did so as well,[30] and the young man is indirectly associated with music in an earlier poem that is clearly addressed to him, sonnet 8 ("Music to hear, why hear'st thou music sadly"). It is conceivable that the youth is the addressee of sonnet 128. If so, the sequence includes a poem more openly erotic than those that practitioners of gay and lesbian criticism and queer theory have sedulously examined, especially when one considers the sexual innuendos Booth has uncovered in the poem:[31]

> How oft, when thou, my music, music play'st
> Upon that blessed wood whose motion sounds
> With thy sweet fingers when thou gently sway'st
> The wiry concord that mine ear confounds,
> Do I envy those jacks that nimble leap
> To kiss the tender inward of thy hand,
> Whilst my poor lips, which should that harvest reap,
> At the wood's boldness by thee blushing stand.
> To be so tickled they would change their state
> And situation with those dancing chips,
> O'er whom [thy] fingers walk with gentle gait,
> Making dead wood more blest than living lips:
>   Since saucy jacks so happy are in this,

.   Give them [thy] fingers, me thy lips to kiss.

Some critics, notably Bruce R. Smith, discern in the cycle a linear
progression from struggle against homoerotic responses to
acknowledgment of them in sonnet 20 ("A woman's face with Nature's
own hand painted");[32] these Shakespeareans might well argue that the
progression culminates in the open eroticism of sonnet 128. Or, if one
questions that sort of linear movement, then the sequence might seem
to juxtapose poems that ostensibly deny or express ambivalence about
homoeroticism, such as sonnet 20, with lyrics like sonnet 128, which
openly revel in the relationship. From another perspective, accepting
that poems such as sonnet 128 refer to the male friend complicates the
homosocial bonds that Eve Kosofsky Sedgwick traces in the sequence,
adding other points on the spectrum she describes: desire in the Sonnets
includes not only relations with women serving the needs of male-male
love but also expressions of that love more overtly erotic than the
poems normally associated with it.[33] All these are options permitted,
but by no means established, by my revisionist approach to the issue of
addressees.

As even the few examples I have examined suggest, questioning
the conventional wisdom about the addressees of the Sonnets overturns
presuppositions about their story line as well, opening the possibility of
episodes very different from the ones critics have seen in the sequence,
though these, too, remain only speculative. For instance, if sonnets such
as the absence poems and sonnet 55 ("Not marble nor the gilded
[monuments]") do concern the Dark Lady, one might posit a period of
idyllic happiness with *her* followed by disillusion. One need no longer
interpret the sequence in terms of a narrative movement from the
idealized Petrarchism expressed in the first group of sonnets to the
virulent anti-Petrarchism of the poems addressed to the Dark Lady.
And should we necessarily assume that the discovery of betrayal
chronologically succeeds poems that evoke a happy relationship?
Surely this sequence, perhaps more than any other text in the language,
demonstrates ways to disguise and deny what one knows, excuse what
one abhors, embrace what or whom one rejects. This text, then, need
not rest on a plot in which actions generate consistent and logical
reactions. Again, my aim is neither to advocate any of these alternative
readings nor to dismiss more familiar ones out of hand—indeed, I have
stressed throughout this essay the difficulty of arriving at an objective

and definitive plot—but to suggest that the sequence permits a reader to construct any number of narratives.

IV

Why, then, have so many critics accepted debatable assumptions about the addressees and the plot of Shakespeare's Sonnets? The attraction to such interpretations is overdetermined and requires a number of explanations. The least subtle one is not the least significant: it is easier to discuss these poems critically if one can determine to whom they refer and what story they tell. This motive, though a longstanding one, may have become more urgent in the past few decades: quite possibly the privileging of drama over lyric in Renaissance studies has fueled an interest in reading even a sonnet sequence in terms of plot and of clearly defined characters, despite the recent emphasis on subjectivity. In any event, definitively connecting some poems to the male Friend and others to the Dark Lady facilitates the projects of feminism and cultural studies in particular because the assumption that this sequence can be neatly divided into two parts allows a critic to find in them allusions to a society divided by gender and class.

Furthermore, the map of misreading that I have been describing smooths the process of interpretation in another way as well, charting a pattern very like those sometimes enacted in Petrarchism. Critics often take Thomas Wyatt's narrative in "They flee from me" as an objective account of sequential events: once the woman or women in question were loving, and now they reject the speaker. This reading is plausible; alternatively, however, perhaps Wyatt or his speaker or both, unable and unwilling to cope with behavior perceived as simultaneously loving and deceitful, chooses to resolve the problem by creating a temporal narrative. In other words, Wyatt suggests that loving hate was at first love and then hate, thus firmly separating the entwined terms of the oxymoron. Petrarch adopts a comparable strategy when sharply distinguishing the way Laura speaks in the "*in vita*" an "*in morte*" sonnets (though the specific point of division between these groups remains problematical). Similarly, rather than acknowledging the possibility that the Dark Lady has some of the positive qualities attributed to the Friend or the proposition that the Friend was always inscrutable and unreliable, many readers have adopted a plot in which a Golden Age of loyalty between the Friend and the poet is destroyed when the Dark Lady seduces the Friend. Thus critics, like poets, attempt to resolve the coexistence of contradictions: they unchain the synchrony of an oxymoron and project its respective components onto the diachrony of narrative.[34]

Arguably a more general impulse towards linearity and even teleology is also at work when literary critics so confidently impose a two-part structure on Shakespeare's sequence. *Pace* Lyotard, certain master narratives do survive; for instance, attraction to an equivalent of the Whig view of history still structures many critical narratives. Witness the assumption that the so-called Shakespearean sonnet was the ideal form toward which earlier English experiments with Petrarchan rhyme schemes were groping (an assumption, incidentally, that is reminiscent of theories of manifest destiny and, like those theories, demonstrates how models of narrativity can both justify and mask political agendas),[35] or the belief that poststructuralism is the culmination of less sophisticated modes of analysis. This impulse toward linearity and teleology, then, may also intensify critics' attraction to narratives of Fall and apocalypsis—narratives, in other words, in which a seemingly fair dark snake enters the garden where the poet and Friend had been happily tending the roses and "forward violet[s]."

Critics' urge to impose a plot on the sequence, while impelled by an interest in modes of narrativity, is intensified by certain reactions to this text in particular. Stephen Booth rightly points out that the Sonnets offer just enough evidence of coherence, notably in the procreation sonnets, to encourage us to seek for more.[36] Peter Brooks relates the narrative drive to Lacan's concept of an "unsatisfied and unsatisfiable" desire.[37] The inconsistencies and indeterminacies of Shakespeare's lyrics increase precisely that drive in many of their readers; whereas Booth connects our wish to impose order on the sequence to the hints of order already present there, the signs of disorder provide an even greater impetus. In other words, in a sequence whose geometry is based on triangulation, the reader becomes the Rival Poet.

But narrative involves a desire to exclude as much as to order, a wish to rule out other stories that often persist, submerged and struggling, as traces of alternative genres, intertextual allusions, and so on. Critics' unacknowledged anxieties about the possible homoerotic undertones in this text may have led them to replicate one of the most common narratives our culture scripts: the regendering of guilt. That is, by imposing on the Sonnets the plot I have outlined, Shakespeareans can deflect onto the Dark Lady's corruption anxieties about homoerotic corruption and betrayal. Certainly in reading these poems, critics have located evil primarily within one person rather than claiming that it is pervasive and systemic. Thus they create clear moral categories, performing the very process that sonnet 144 ("Two loves I have of comfort and despair") itself vainly attempts to enact. And in doing so, they gender and in a sense localize transgression. I am not denying that, even if one relies only on the poems that deploy pronouns unmistakably to gender their addressee, the sequence paints a picture more critical of women than of men. But many readers collude in this process by assuming that sonnets without a clearly marked direction of address refer to the Friend if they are largely positive and to the Dark Lady if they are negative. Just as sonnet 129 first deflects guilt about desire from the subject to the abstract force of lust and subsequently to the woman, so in reading the sequence as a whole, a number of Shakespeareans repeatedly identify a frailty whose name is woman.[38]

The gendering of evil is, then, but one example of the unfortunate consequences of transforming uncertainties about this sequence into dubious certainties. Although the Sonnets have benefited from incisive, even brilliant critical analyses on occasion, too often Shakespeareans impose their own presuppositions on and script their own narratives for a sequence that offers at best ambiguous support for such interpretations. They do so in the hope that the uncertainties of the poems and the anxieties of their readers will crown themselves emplotted, resolved, assured.

NOTES

*This essay is based on a paper I delivered at the 1992 annual meeting of the Shakespeare Association of America in Kansas City, Kansas. I am grateful to the audience for useful comments, and I would also like to thank David Loewenstein for his incisive commentary on an earlier version.

1. John Dover Wilson, *An Introduction to the Sonnets of Shakespeare for the Use of Historians and Others* (Cambridge: Cambridge UP, 1963), 14.

2. All citations of the Sonnets follow *The Riverside Shakespeare*, ed. G. Blakemore Evans (Boston: Houghton Mifflin, 1974). I identify each sonnet by number and initial line the first time I refer to it and thereafter by number only.

3. Bruce R. Smith, for example, discerns a crucial break after sonnet 20; see *Homosexual Desire in Shakespeare's England: A Cultural Poetics* (Chicago and London: U of Chicago P, 1991), esp. 256.

4. The most influential recent challenge appears in Margreta de Grazia, *Shakespeare Verbatim: The Reproduction of Authenticity and the 1790 Apparatus* (Oxford: Clarendon Press, 1991); see also Peter Stallybrass, "Editing as Cultural Formation: The Sexing of Shakespeare's Sonnets," *Modern Language Quarterly* 54 (1993): 91–103, reprinted in this volume.

5. See de Grazia, "The Scandal of Shakespeare's Sonnets," *Shakespeare Survey* 46 (1993): 35–49, esp. 40–41. De Grazia's essay is reprinted in this volume.

6. Hilton Landry, *Interpretations in Shakespeare's Sonnets* (Berkeley and Los Angeles: U of California P, 1963), 4–5, esp. 5.

7. Stephen Booth, ed., *Shakespeare's Sonnets* (New Haven, CT, and London: Yale UP, 1977), 545 and 430.

8. Gregory W. Bredbeck, *Sodomy and Interpretation: Marlowe to Milton* (Ithaca, NY, and London: Cornell UP, 1991), 167–80.

9. Heather Dubrow, *Captive Victors: Shakespeare's Narrative Poems and Sonnets* (Ithaca, NY, and London: Cornell UP, 1987), 171–90. In a more recent book I allude to the possibility of questioning the direction of address but do not develop the point; see Dubrow, *Echoes of Desire: English Petrarchism and Its Counterdiscourses* (Ithaca, NY, and London: Cornell UP, 1995), 122–23.

10. De Grazia, "Scandal," 41. De Grazia's critique of Malone appears in *Shakespeare Verbatim*, 152–63.

11. On Shakespeare's approach to narrative and dramatic elements, see Dubrow, *Captive Victors*, 171–90, and the article on which this section of the book is based, "Shakespeare's Undramatic Monologues: Toward a Reading of the *Sonnets*," *Shakespeare Quarterly* 32 (1981): 55–68.

12. For a similar position, cf. Booth, ed., 549.

13. This argument is explored by Brents Stirling in *The Shakespeare Sonnet Order: Poems and Groups* (Berkeley and Los Angeles: U of California P, 1968). Though I have reservations about all attempts to reorder the sequence, Stirling's is in my opinion the most responsible effort in that direction.

14. John Kerrigan, ed., *The Sonnets and A Lover's Complaint* (Harmondsworth, UK: Penguin, 1986), 11.

15. A few critics have touched on the possibility of multiple addressees. See, for example, C. L. Barber, "An Essay on the Sonnets" in the Laurel *Shakespeare Sonnets*, ed. Charles Jasper Sisson (New York: Dell, 1960), 7-33; Barber notes that the poems might have been written to more than one young man (8), a hypothesis that seems to me conceivable but less probable than those explored in my essay.

16. Dover Wilson briefly mentions the possibility that the sequence may include some sonnets not originally composed for it (18).

17. See Booth, ed., 545; and Booth, *An Essay on Shakespeare's Sonnets* (New Haven, CT, and London: Yale UP, 1969), 1–28.

18. These three poems are discussed from a different perspective by Carol Thomas Neely in "Detachment and Engagement in Shakespeare's Sonnets: 94, 116, and 129," *PMLA* 92 (1977): 83–95.

19. Joel Fineman, *Shakespeare's Perjured Eye: The Invention of Poetic Subjectivity in the Sonnets* (Berkeley: U of California P, 1986); a useful overview of his complex argument appears on page 15.

20. Fineman, 132.

21. Katherine Duncan-Jones, "Was the 1609 *Shake-speares Sonnets* Really Unauthorized?" *Review of English Studies* 34 (1983): 151–71. Duncan-Jones develops her thesis about the 1609 edition in her discussion of sonnet 126 in "Filling the Unforgiving Minute: Modernizing SHAKE-SPEARES SONNETS (1609)," *Essays in Criticism* 45 (1995): 199-207, esp. 205–6. I am grateful to the author for making this second essay available to me while I was writing this article. These points are also developed in the Introduction to her edition of the poems, which appeared after the original version of my essay was published (*Shakespeare's Sonnets*, ed. Katherine Duncan-Jones [Nashville: Thomas Nelson, 1997], 29-45).

22. Duncan-Jones, "Was the 1609 *Shake-speares Sonnets* Really Unauthorized?" 163.

23. See Duncan-Jones, "Was the 1609 *Shake-speares Sonnets* Really Unauthorized?" 162.

24. See the New Cambridge Shakespeare *Sonnets*, ed. G. B. Evans (Cambridge: Cambridge UP, 1996), 114. I thank Professor Evans for sharing his work with me prior to publication.

25. For that and other arguments about this repetition, see Booth, ed., 313.

26. Such readings of Sidney are propounded in David Kalstone, *Sidney's Poetry: Contexts and Interpretations* (Cambridge, MA: Harvard UP, 1965); and Neil L. Rudenstine, *Sidney's Poetic Development* (Cambridge, MA: Harvard UP, 1967).

27. On the status of the songs, see, for example, William A. Ringler Jr., ed., *The Poems of Sir Philip Sidney* (Oxford: Clarendon Press, 1962), xlvi.

28. Such labels as "traditional" are, however, as dangerous as they are tempting in the current critical climate; in this instance it is important not to oversimplify earlier analyses of character. The role of the unconscious and the conflicts among ego, superego, and id, for example, indicate that Freud's concept of character is less unitary than casual allusions to it might suggest.

29. Many recent studies have traced a fear of effeminacy in early modern England; see, for example, Laura Levine, *Men in Women's Clothing: Anti-*

Theatricality and Effeminization, 1579–1642 (Cambridge: Cambridge UP, 1994).

30. *The Oxford English Dictionary*, 2d ed., prepared by J. A. Simpson and E.S.C. Weiner, 20 vols. (Oxford: Clarendon Press, 1987), 19:667.

31. See Booth, ed., 437–41.

32. See Smith, 245–57.

33. Eve Kosofsky Sedgwick's highly influential analysis of the sequence appears in *Between Men: English Literature and Male Homosocial Desire* (New York: Columbia UP, 1985), 28–48.

34. Compare my discussion of what I term "temporal displacement" in *Echoes of Desire*, esp. 111–13 and 78–79.

35. This view of Petrarchism appears in many sources, notably J. W. Lever, *The Elizabethan Love Sonnet* (London: Methuen, 1956), 12–13.

36. See Booth, *Essay*, 1–4.

37. Peter Brooks, *Reading for the Plot: Design and Intention in Narrative* (New York: Alfred A. Knopf, 1984), 55.

38. It is tempting to speculate that at least some of the critics attracted to this misogynistic reading impose on the sequence an allegory for developments in our own profession during the past two decades. That is, they construct the fantasy that an Edenic period of homogeneous and harmonious male faculties was shattered by the intrusion of outsiders, darkly ambitious ladies and dark-skinned ladies and men. These intruders, the myth goes, proceeded to confound the distinction between fair and foul, canonical and noncanonical, male and female, acceptable and repugnant sexual preferences.

The Silent Speech of Shakespeare's Sonnets

George T. Wright

> Then others for the breath of words respect,
> Me for my dumb thoughts, speaking in effect.
> >   —Shakespeare, Sonnet 85

> O learn to read what silent love hath writ.
> >   —Shakespeare, Sonnet 23

ABSENCE, SILENCE

> O absent presence *Stella* is not here
> >   —Sidney, *Astrophel and Stella*

> He is not here
>
> >   —Tennyson, *In Memoriam*

> Non c'é.
>
> >   —*Madama Butterfly*

Reprinted from *Shakespeare and the Twentieth Century*, eds. Jonathan Bate, Jill A. Levenson, and Dieter Mehl (Newark: University of Delaware Press, 1998) by permission of George T. Wright, the editors, and University of Delaware Press.

In his rich study of *The Portrait in the Renaissance*, John Pope-Hennessy observes that the painting of portraits, even collective ones, provided a record through which families and communities could "salvage the data of physical appearance on the threshold of the tomb."[1] The motive reminds one of Shakespeare's arguments in the first seventeen sonnets, urging the young man to marry "And your sweet semblance to some other give" (S. 13)[2] as a means of enabling his beautiful image to survive his own aging and death. Perhaps because we live in an era of photography some scholars find this argument and these sonnets trivial; we have ceased to feel anxiety over preserving pictures of those we admire or are close to, which are all too likely to clutter our closets and the closets of our own survivors. Yet *all* the sonnets written to the young man have a related motive. Some of them openly claim the power to keep his image alive "When all the breathers of this world are dead" (S. 81); many of the others are designed to imagine his presence during periods or hours of absence. Absence here is mourned as a kind of death, and the return to the friend's presence, or even to the thought of it, is celebrated as an achievement of "wealth" and "state" (S. 30, 29). What may also seem striking is that considerations of absence are usually mingled with considerations of silence, so that the art of the sonnet seems to be an art of "silent thought" (S. 30), in which the very act of conjuring up the young friend's vivid presence in the face of his palpable absence can only be managed through eloquent words that, at least to begin with, go unvoiced, unheard, that *we* read as silently as the unspeaking speaker speaks them.

Of course, we may choose to sound them. But they have their origin, and they often discourse on their origin, in a "time removed" (S. 97), when the young man's absence deprives the poet-speaker of his friend's highly valued presence and makes him suspicious about where the friend is and in what company. To be sure, this absence has its consolations, especially in providing "sweet leave / To entertain the time with thoughts of love" (S. 39). If it weren't for this separation, the Sonnets would never have come to exist; in a sense, there would be no subject, for these sonnets, unlike many others by other writers, are more about absence than presence, more about the absence—experienced, feared, or forecast—of their radiant center than about the enjoyment of its presence, though there is enough testimony about its presence to make its absence seem all the more poignant.

Hardly any of the first 126 sonnets seems likely to have been written in the friend's presence, though we can imagine certain lines as having been generated there (e.g., "If I could write the beauty of your eyes" [S. 17]). The poet confesses, in fact, to being "tongue-tied" before his friend (S. 80, 85, and 23, and cf. 66, 140), as if his best "speech" required the injury of "distance" (S. 44) and the "torment" of absence (S. 39), as if, unlike much portrait and landscape painting, writing could be done only when its subject is not physically present. Some poems we can imagine the speaker writing and then reading or reciting to his friend at their next meeting, or presenting for his friend's own silent (or spoken) perusal. Sonnet 38 perhaps, yet its tone is very much like that of sonnet 39, which speaks directly of—and *to*—absence. Many of them seem so ruminative in tone that we can easily take them to be not really spoken to anyone but as having been produced during those "sessions of sweet silent thought" (S. 30) that seem habitual with this speaker and familiar from our own experience. Indeed, we can imagine all of these poems (including the first seventeen) as unsounded, silent meditations, capable of being voiced by the poet or by the person addressed (or by any of us) but at least equally appropriately read without sound.

Speech without speech—is that what the Sonnets are: speech that comes not after but as long silence? This deeply reflective speaker—is he really a speaker at all? Isn't it more accurate to hear the Sonnets, and much other lyric poetry that shows the same reflective depths, as, primarily, language of silent thought, unvoiced, unsounded, unperformed, the words of a consciousness (his then, ours now) silently addressing itself sometimes and sometimes an absent other? It may even be claimed that this unsounded speech, perfectly familiar to all of us because we generate it constantly every day of our lives, is the basic "voice" of the Sonnets, at least of 1-126, and a great range of other lyric poetry, and that by scrutinizing this dimension of language we can understand better not only what sort of poems the Sonnets and later English lyric and meditative poems are but how thoughtful speech of a different kind—sounded and public—appears in Shakespeare's dramatic writing. Both modes use speech as their main verbal material, but they work it differently. To watch Shakespeare's mastery of both is, to say the least, instructive.

Of course, the speech of Shakespeare's plays may also be, and often is, read silently. But our usual view of it in this century is that its proper condition is as speech spoken and heard. We do not usually take that view of the language of the Sonnets.

TWO KINDS OF SPEAKING

> Why do you never speak.
> —T. S. Eliot, *The Waste Land*

My curiosity about this topic grows out of a longstanding fascination with how the verse of the plays sounded, especially with its metrical design, with how actors spoke the lines and with how audiences heard them, with whether and to what extent dramatic writing like Shakespeare's is "oral literature," and with corresponding questions for lyric poetry: how do poets think of their work (if they do) as being spoken and heard, and how do we actually hear it when we read it from the page? These seem to me pertinent questions to ask of all poetry, and trying to answer them may help us understand a little better these puzzling Sonnets of Shakespeare.

The phrase "sweet silent thought" intrigued me when I used to teach a course in poetic meter, form, and sound and would try to persuade students to pronounce the syllables in a way I believed was consistent with Shakespeare's probable metrical practice—not emphasizing the first adjective more prominently than the second (swéet silĕnt thóught), which would trip the meter of the line into a four-stress dactylic pattern that is rare in Shakespeare's iambic pentameter verse. Such a misreading also, to my ear, distorted the meaning of the phrase. No comma separates the two adjectives, whether we use Renaissance punctuation practice or our own, for "silent thought" is a compound substantive characterized here as "sweet." "I sometimes enjoy moments of delicious reflection," Shakespeare is saying, "sweet silent-thought." (Compare these examples from Shakespeare poems that are probably contemporary: "sweet bottom grass," "sweet coral mouth," "sweet friendship's oath" [*Venus and Adonis*, 236, 542; *The Rape of Lucrece*, 569].) Meter and meaning both ask us to recognize the first syllable of the compound phrase as requiring more stress than "sweet":

Whén tŏ | thĕ sés | siŏns ŏf | swèet sí | lĕnt thóught

Shakespeare is identifying a mode of thinking, of reflecting, unusual enough in his time to merit being the subject of special notice here and elsewhere (S. 29, 85, 119, etc.)—almost an oxymoron, since for Renaissance people a stretch of words, to be recognized as such, would usually have to be spoken. But more of this later.

But the matter of silent thought is more important than that: it has come to seem to me crucial to the lyric poetry we and our predecessors have been reading almost since Shakespeare's time and still read today, though our custom of referring to a poet's "voice" or a poem's "tone" has obscured the fact that we usually read poetry in silence.[3] In pursuit of this idea, several years ago I wrote an essay that tried to explore this question as it was raised by the poetry of T. S. Eliot,[4] whose protagonists often ruminate as they amble about the evocative landscapes of a ruined or aging world. In *The Waste Land* many of the lines that purport to represent the "speaker's" thoughts are presented as silent words that pass through the brain of the ruminating Tiresias but are not meant to be taken by the reader as sounded. One clear indication of this intention appears in the poem's second section, "A Game of Chess," where dialogue of a sort takes place between the lady at the dressing table and a man, presumably her husband. Her lines appear in quotation marks, his do not, and this suggests that there must be a difference in the way we take in the two sets of words:

> "My nerves are bad to-night. Yes, bad. Stay with me.
> "Speak to me. Why do you never speak. Speak.
> "What are you thinking of? What thinking? What?
> "I never know what you are thinking. Think."
>
> I think we are in rats' alley
> Where the dead men lost their bones.
>   (*The Waste Land*, 111-116)

Similar distinctions between voices we are meant to understand as speaking aloud (the hyacinth girl, the typist, Rhine maidens, and others), whether we read them silently or not, and a more muted or silent voice of the protagonist can be noted throughout the poem, and I suggested in that essay that much of Eliot's most impressive poetry is written in this "sub-vocal" register (the term is Susanne Langer's), one that we hear without sound within some internal chamber, a vocal mechanism that "hears" words without speaking them, a "voice of no speech," as Eliot called it in another poem. This is not, however, one of "The Three Voices of Poetry" he identified in an important essay, where he was more concerned with the possible audiences for different kinds of poems, and he never, to my knowledge, wrote in prose about the kind of distinction I have been pursuing here. It is worth noting, however, that when Eliot turned from lyric poetry to verse written for the stage, despite the frequent critical praise for the so-called dramatic qualities of his nondramatic verse, his use of this ruminative voice in his plays is rarely successful—mainly, I speculated, because that deep inner voice, so seductively solipsistic as it processes everyone else's speech in his poems, cannot convincingly overawe other voices when they meet as equals in the theater. The chronological pattern of Shakespeare's career, of course, was exactly opposite to Eliot's: before he wrote his Sonnets he was already an experienced playwright and an actor accustomed to speaking lines from a stage. It is so much the more curious, then, that, as the only playwright among those Elizabethans who participated in the sonnet-writing vogue of the 1590s, he alone should have written sonnets in a style that stresses the solitude of the poet-speaker and the silence of his speech, probably because he had a sharper insight into the peculiar powers of speech and silent thought, and into the differences between them.[5]

ON POEMS AS MESSAGES

> To thee I send this written ambassage,
> To witness duty, not to show my wit.
> > —Shakespeare, Sonnet 26

> Your letter comes, speaking as you,
> Speaking of much, but not to come.
> > —W. H. Auden, "The Letter"

Sonnet 26 seems to say that the poet-speaker is sending this poem, this sonnet, to his friend, to be read by him. This implies what is true of most letters—that it has been written in the recipient's absence and will be read in the writer's absence. Letters may be intoned by writer or reader, but it was probably as true for Shakespeare as it was for W. B. Yeats when, "after long silence," he received a letter from a later Shakespear, that such letters are usually written and read in silence. (Like Auden, he sensed that the letter might be called "Speech" or

"Speaking.") The typical assumption of the written message or lyric is that the writer will not be present when it is read but that the letter acts as his surrogate, sets up a supposed situation ("as if I were with you") that resembles the fiction of theater ("as if these persons were here before you, moving and speaking"). Suppose, the personal lyric says, that I am there with you, speaking to you, there where *you* are: then this is what I say. A large number of Shakespeare's sonnets to the young man imagine this situation, for love messages, letters, or poems not only wish for the presence of an absent lover but (as the further side of a reciprocal design) request the recipient to imagine the absent writer as present. They arrive, as Auden puts it, "speaking as you." The lover's letter is not the lover's presence, but it is something; as one gentleman observes (insincerely) to another, "Thy letters may be here, though thou art hence" (*Two Gentlemen of Verona*, 3.1.250). Each sonnet offers to both its intended and unintended audience—its immediate addressee and centuries of half-invited listeners-in—an occasion to hear the words spoken as the author might speak them if he were present. It offers, as it were, a play without a play.

But normally when we read the poem, we simplify the possibilities. We don't trouble to wonder whether the poet is to be supposed as speaking the poem directly to "you," or recites it to "you" the next day, or sends it or gives it to be read silently or aloud by "you." We just accept the words as supposed or virtual speech, as words addressed by "I" to "you," whether "you" is present or not. We don't inquire too curiously into the dramatic situation because we have no difficulty with it. We know from our own experience what it is to address someone who is absent. We know what it means to say what the speaker of these sonnets is constantly saying to the absent friend: Be yourself, be beautiful, be young, be here, love me. We know what silent thought is, and fruitless address; knowing they can't hear us, we have all addressed (quietly or loudly) stuck windows, headaches, yapping dogs, fools or hypocrites on television, and absent lovers. And when we read one of Shakespeare's sonnets to the absent friend, we know that mode of silent speech—its fluency, its readiness "To leap large lengths of miles when thou art gone" (S. 44), the "wealth" it "brings" (S. 29) on some occasions, how it breaks now and then into voice, and the ultimate pathos, poignancy, frustration, and grief of it.

This is so because what we find in lyrics or love poems is a sort of suspended speech—not the direct, actual speaking of genuine conversation, not even (except rarely) one-sided talk, but a measure of "speech" that is slowed down and prolonged and muted and indefinitely available for reference. It is inner talk turned to stone, as it were, speech that has never fully made it into sound but has been formed and preserved all the same, like those first sacred writings used by a newly literate people to transcribe and preserve the wisdom formerly kept in the songs, chants, and sayings of an oral culture.[6]

IMAGINING VOICES

> Hearing you praised, I say, "'tis so," "'tis true,"
> And to the most of praise add something more;
> But that is in my thought
>
> —Shakespeare, Sonnet 85

> Heard melodies are sweet, but those unheard
> Are sweeter
>
> —Keats, "Ode to a Nightingale"

In our efforts to identify different speakers, selves, or tones, we sometimes lose sight of what we mean when we speak of voice in nondramatic poetry. We all use the term, and we know more or less what it signifies, but we seldom acknowledge that the voice we have in mind, the voice we suppose to be speaking from the page in any silent reading (which is our usual way of reading) is not really a voice; it does not speak, it makes no sound, it does not share with actual voices (or even whispers) the physical characteristics of pitch, volume, timbre, and accent. It is "unheard," like the music that hides in the shrubbery of "Burnt Norton" and echoes the unheard "melodies" played in "soft" silence by the pipers on Keats's Grecian urn. Such melodies, Keats tells us, are "sweeter" than the ones we actually hear, because it is "to the spirit" that they "Pipe . . . ditties of no tone." Keats's phrase gives a very high value to unsounded verse, even when the verse is as sensuous as Keats's own.[7]

We know the ruminant voice of *The Waste Land* not only through our experience of unsounded but formulated thought but also through our acquaintance with printed English poetry, which has trained us to read poems silently. We do not need to say the words aloud to capture their rhythms, or move our lips to savor the words. When we speak of them as sounded by a voice, we probably mean, among other things, that as we follow the phrases and clauses on the page, our own vocal apparatus is at some low level *set* to speak them, and/or that our hearing apparatus is set to hear a voice actually saying the lines—our own voice, Olivier's, Burton's, or Eliot's. Such imagined speaking may include the imagination of variations of stress between syllables, pauses, hesitations, natural pacing, effective strategies of emphasis, shrewd management of pitch, along with paralinguistic gestures, facial expressions, and body language. We are tempted to think that we hear (or see) all this in our heads, but we actually hear (and see) none of it. We are only *prepared*, set, to hear it if a voice materializes and speaks it. Silent reading, however muscularly persevered in, is silent reading. When engaged in it, we are *ready* to perform an action (in this case, to speak words) or to perceive a sense impression (in this case, to hear words) without actually doing it, though in reading poetry you may have the same experience I have of following the words silently for a time and then, occasionally, being so caught up in the eloquence of a passage that (at least if we are alone) we actually voice a phrase or a word without quite having realized that we were going to do so.

REHEARSING THE VERSE

> To write is not to be absent but to become absent; to be
> someone and then go away, leaving traces.
> —Michael Wood, *The Magician's Doubts*

> They but thrust their buried men
> Back in the human mind again.
> —W. B. Yeats, "Under Ben Bulben"

The two dimensions of speech that I have been trying to discriminate here—spoken, and unsounded—cross over so easily, our passages between them are so fluid, that we hardly notice them or pay attention to their differences. Words form in our minds before we speak, as Montaigne observed even during Shakespeare's lifetime: "the sense of hearing . . . is related to that of speech . . . so that what we speak we must speak first to ourselves, and make it ring on our own ears inwardly, before we send it to other ears."[8] Later, as Eliot says (in "Burnt Norton"), "Words, after speech, reach / Into the silence," but they also have a way of following us: "My words echo / Thus, in your mind." This is the dimension of experience that is permanently lost when we forget it a moment or a day later—or, if we keep reverting to

it, when we die, unless it is preserved in someone else's memory or in
art, as Proust and Virginia Woolf steadily observed. So Time, with its
"millioned accidents" (S. 115), ripples these waters, altering,
reckoning, and rendering the changes that occur between what we plan
to say, what we say, what we remember saying (the next moment, the
next day, years later), what people report us as saying. Writing, of
course, fixes what the poet "says." At least that is the case, by and
large, with published lyric poetry, though even the most scrupulously
edited text of an older poet (not to speak of an Auden or a Lowell) can
fail to establish the authenticity of canonical versions of poems. The
playtext, as students of Shakespeare know only too well, is even less
reliable; if some of the quartos were, at least in part, the product of
memorial reconstruction, that suggests a checkered history, indeed:
from written playtext to spoken drama to partly remembered lines to
printed version. But some such mixture of sources probably lies behind
even the most hurriedly composed poem, as the poet writes down, in
horizontal rows, the "lines" that have "popped into his head" or "just
came to me out of the blue," speaks them aloud to test their sound, adds
some more in silence perhaps, revises a phrase here and there, forgets
them while he goes to lunch, falls asleep, or puts them in a drawer for
years, and hears them chime together silently again as he gives them a
more privileged textual life on the computer screen, the disk, the page,
the book.

And there they stay, ready for posterity's inspection, just as he
claimed, even if, after writing them down, he lifted not a finger to help
them survive. What did the claim amount to, if, in the spirit of this
inquiry, we interrogate it closely? In all of Shakespeare's sonnets that
promise to preserve the young man's image and to make it "eternal" or
"immortal" in the "monument" of his own verse (S. 15, 17, 18, 19, 60,
63, 65, 81, 101, 107), there is no claim that the lines that offer this hope
will be spoken aloud again, only the claim that the young man's image
presented in them will be preserved and wondered at. Only sonnet 81
could be taken as pressing a stronger claim:

> Your monument shall be my gentle verse,
> Which eyes not yet created shall o'er-read,
> And tongues to be your being shall rehearse,
> When all the breathers of this world are dead,
>   You still shall live—such virtue hath my pen—
>   Where breath most breathes, ev'n in the mouths of men.

But as I read these lines, they may not suggest more than that later readers will be so astonished at the beauty of the young man as it is praised in the poet's sonnets that they will talk about it, as this poet refers to earlier poets' "descriptions of the fairest wights" in sonnet 106. Even if we understand "rehearse" to mean "recite" and not just "recount" (see Booth on this line, p. 278), the recitation sounds very private, a mere whispered breathing of the words in which the young man, so resurrected, is sure to be buried and disinterred and buried again.[9]

INNER VOICE ON THE PUBLIC STAGE

> I see a voice: now will I to the chink,
> To spy an I can hear my mistress' face.
>   —Bottom, in *A Midsummer Night's Dream*

> Why couldn't a character carry on an external monologue
> that was in fact an internal monologue just coming out?
> And why couldn't it be off the wall or exploratory, the way
> the inner monologue really is?
>   —Sam Shepard

To sound a lyric phrase or line is to flesh it out, to bring it from what seems disembodied existence to physical embodiment—just the opposite of what the sonnet-writer wishes could happen in sonnet 44: "If the dull substance of my flesh were thought"—to turn the bodied substance into silent, unsounded but articulated thought and nullify "Injurious distance." Far from succeeding in this enterprise, all that the speaker of sonnet 44 has to show for his exercise are his "moan" and "heavy tears," the voiced longing and the material "badges of . . . woe." That is, his thought has turned into just the physical and material stuff that he began by wishing he could bypass. The wish is not father to this thought. But that *is* what happens in poetry, which does succeed in turning absence into virtual presence, bringing the absent here, using metaphors, imagery, narrative to transport that "world elsewhere" to wherever we happen to be. If *Henry V* can do this for its audience in the theater, can count on their imaginations to

> deck our kings,
> Carry them here and there, jumping o'er times,

>Turning th'accomplishment of many years
>Into an hour-glass (Prologue, 28-31)

and to do all this "within the girdle of these walls" (19), poetry silently read does it all the time. Whether or not the reading is silent, it amounts to a granting of this wish: the substance of imagery—kings, lover, moan, and tears—becomes inwardly present, at least as shadow. Neither thought nor verse nor letter can bring the lover physically here, but all of these can bring his "shadow" or "shade" within the purview of our "unseeing . . . sightless eyes" (S. 43).

As some critics have pointed out (notably, Heather Dubrow, in *Captive Victors*[10]), the Sonnets in many ways almost compel the reader to re-enact the feelings of the poet-speaker: his confusion, his uncertainty, his ambivalence. They also make us experience an absence, a distance from the speaker, similar to that which the speaker experiences from his friend. He cannot hear or see his friend, or make him hear his own voice. If we must imagine the speaker (Shakespeare's persona, however we define it) as saying the poem (or as imagining his friend reading or hearing it), even if we grant that Shakespeare has done as he promised ("To make him seem long hence as he shows now" [S. 101]) and has kept the image of his friend alive for all these centuries, we understand (as he does) that the image is in most respects dim and blurred and that we can get no closer to him than that. Fortunately, perhaps: not naming his name blesses an ill report. Even if we speak the lines ourselves, or listen to a teacher or an actor read them (live or recorded), we shall never hear the voice of that speaker or the poet.

The theater offers us a different setting: there, as Bottom realizes, we see a voice, we hear a face. We have no text before us, no lines, no "black ink." All the words we are to hear have been written for human actors to con, to speak, and to forget, and those actors (or their modern counterparts) are present now physically. Some of them may pretend not to hear what is being said by others—in asides or soliloquies, or when they are supposed to be drunk or asleep or dead—but *we* hear everything spoken aloud. But we also hear—and have heard in plays for centuries, ever since Shakespeare returned to the theater, after his time out, during the plague, for writing his narrative poems and probably most of the sonnets—a kind of speech that is different from earlier dialogue. In speeches written after this time for some of his characters at certain dramatic moments, we hear what sounds in some ways like the voice that speaks the Sonnets—a ruminative, private voice that deepens our sense of the dramatic character's inner self. We can hear it in Richard II's moving meditations or in Hamlet's or Claudius's; as I have suggested elsewhere, such characters "often take us into the psychic council chambers" where they reach their decisions.

> Their feelings take form on the stage or give signs of having been anxiously arrived at. The language in which they admit to divided feelings or disturbing passions is the language of "silent thought," now for the first time conveyed from the sonnet to the theater, in dialogue as well as in soliloquy. . . . The quiet voice of reminiscence or experience, the muted tones, the pyrrhic dips, the spondaic gravity, the metaphoric and figurative surface, all the stylistic regalia of troubled reflection familiar from the *Sonnets* make their presence deeply felt in the plays that follow.[11]

In short, an authentic inner voice becomes available after 1593 or so to many of Shakespeare's characters, who speak this private or intimate language from the stage as no one had ever done before. To convey what is going on inside a character, a playwright need no longer resort to flamboyant rhetorical gestures and postures, histrionic breast beating, or demonstrative actions; a person in emotional trouble can speak of his distress before an audience as if he were talking to himself. In the soliloquy, as Wolfgang Clemen observes, "monologue becomes dialogue"—in Arnold's phrase, "the dialogue of the mind with itself."[12] The inner discourse that at least some persons carry on is acknowledged by being represented convincingly on the stage, and it gives us the illusion that we are seeing deeply into their souls or selves. If the ruminative, private voice is more eloquent than our own or than we suspect our neighbor's is, it still is of a kind we recognize as coming from a realm we have visited, and the ease and force of its speech may seem at least genuine, at times uncanny—in Sam Shepard's words, "an internal monologue just coming out."

WITHIN BE FED

> [T]o possess a double mental personality has long ceased
> to be the sort of trick that only lunatics can bring off.
> —Robert Musil, *The Man without Qualities*

> Yond Cassius has a lean and hungry look,
> He thinks too much; such men are dangerous.
>
> —Shakespeare, *Julius Caesar*

But did Renaissance people read or think this way? Anne Ferry makes a compelling case for the view that they did not have the concept of an inner life in the sense of "a consciousness of leading a continuous internal existence."[13] If *inward* meant the opposite of those near homonyms *outward* or *uttered*, that which was unuttered, silent, usually appears to have been "inward states" (63-70) or "secrets" (55-59) or "hidden thoughts" (59), not a continuous wordstream; and when you looked into your heart, it was to find not what was personal and individual, your own private and particular version of reality, but the universal truth of man's fallen condition (40-43). But Shakespeare, following Sidney, moves toward the charging of an inner verbal current, with what sounds like authentic "autobiographical material" (29), a strain that we find first in the speaker of the Sonnets and later, most notably, in the character Hamlet, whose soliloquies and asides do suggest that the words he speaks issue from a personal consciousness continuously wording its thoughts, that many of these thoughts are not spoken, and that they compose a hardly interrupted inner discourse, which may appear to be independent of his outer behavior and ambiguously related to his uttered words.[14]

This is a reading of Hamlet worth considering, for it illuminates the difficulty other people in the play have in understanding Hamlet's behavior. It suggests that he has access to an inner mental life, which was thought to be characteristic of people who were notably devious or deviant. Gertrude and Ophelia think Hamlet mad; Polonius judges there is more to it than that: "Though this be madness, yet there is method in't" (2.2.205-6), and he suggests that if Hamlet is mad, it is the madness of love. Claudius, more astute and better informed, comes closer to the truth: "There's something in his soul / O'er which his melancholy sits on brood" (3.1.164-65). Like Cassius in Caesar's view, it appears to Claudius that Hamlet thinks too much, and too much to the purpose. For those who, unlike Claudius, cannot read the clues to Hamlet's behavior, he seems mad—which he is, in a sense: after all, he converses with a ghost.

In effect, anyone whose inner discourse gives signs of being intricate and continuous is likely to arouse suspicion in others: "such men are dangerous." The continuous inward and private consciousness that we now regard as common to the experience of almost everyone (or at least of the verbal people we are and know) could be taken by Renaissance observers as an indication of an aberrant personality, of someone who, whether mad or merely calculating, needed to be watched.[15] It suggested an uncanny, even inhuman, capacity for carrying on two lives, two discourses, simultaneously, one inner and private, the other outer and public, an accomplishment that seemed to them perhaps as difficult and burdensome as a chess champion's playing simultaneous games of chess seems to us: something, that is, that only specially gifted people (a Hamlet, for example) can do. Joyce's *Ulysses*, of course, shows us that ordinary modern people do it, too—not only intellectuals like Stephen Dedalus, but humdrum couples like the Blooms.

This idea may have some explanatory power for *Hamlet*. For the Sonnets, despite the speaker's occasional anxieties over madness (S. 119, 129, 140, 147, and elsewhere), the hypothesis of madness in the poet-speaker is hardly a promising one.[16] More to the point, perhaps, is the possibility that Shakespeare recognized the dangerousness of the Sonnets' "inward" language: that their speaker is to be suspected of being not so much a sexual as an epistemological deviant, of thinking too precisely on every event. Whether or not that recognition had anything to do with his failure to supervise or authorize their publication we cannot know. But Shakespeare may well have perceived that inwardness of speech, that continuous "silent thought," conducted not in fits and starts but in extended "sessions," as a new mode of discourse, which his plays would learn to exploit, in heroic and comic protagonists, by conveying their inward speech to the stage's public spectacle—in effect giving it a public audience that could hear it speaking to itself, sometimes in tones so intimate and appealing that we are drawn to sympathize even with the most appalling villains.

From this time on, any secretive person who follows a hidden agenda may use this private speech to review strategies and anxieties. To some extent, this quiet, confiding stance derives not only from the silent speech of the Sonnets but, more directly, from the dramatic voice of the medieval Vice, who traditionally informs the audience of his malevolent plans—in Shakespeare's early plays, most notably in the person of Richard III, and later in Iago, Edmund, and the Macbeths. But now the asides and soliloquies of these and other villains acquire a reflective tone that can hardly help suggesting that their evil plotting is an activity they carry on steadily all the time. That tone, that vocal bearing—befitting less an orderly program perhaps than a personal taking of stock—is audible as well in some speeches of other characters with restless minds, like Hamlet, Prince Hal, Henry IV, Cassius and Brutus, and perhaps Jaques, Juliet, Viola, and Imogen; and in some of those, and in the language of other personages as well (e.g., Ulysses, Camillo, Prospero), that reflective voice seems to carry as well a wisdom that comes less from the mouthing of sententiae than from long experience and meditation, or, in the young, from genuine thoughtful insight. But it is evil or guilty characters especially who appear to be endowed with an almost uninterrupted conscious or nightmare life, those intrigue-ridden humans in whom mischief never sleeps and against whom average mortals like ourselves or their unsuspecting victims hardly stand a chance: Imogen against the unsleeping Iachimo; Duncan and his grooms sleeping and Macduff unwary against the insomniac and ruminative Macbeths; Hermione against Leontes, who complains, "Nor night, nor day, no rest" (*The Winter's Tale*, 2.3.1); and Hamlet's ghostly father, "Sleeping within my orchard" (*Hamlet*, 1.5.59), against "that incestuous, that adulterate beast" (1.5.42), who even while the Ghost speaks to Hamlet "doth wake tonight and takes his rouse" (1.4.8). Claudius's tormented argument in 3.3.36-72 ("O, my offense is rank") seems an excerpt from speech of the most private kind, thoughts he must be in the habit of revolving within his own innermost self, like some of the frequently "rapt" (1.3.142) Macbeth's: "I have liv'd long enough" (5.3.22-28) as well as "To-morrow and to-morrow and to-morrow" (5.5.19-28). Even Lady Macbeth, her husband's trusty accomplice and instigator, though she shares with him "these terrible dreams / That shake us nightly" (3.2.18-19), cannot share his inner discourse with an invisible dagger, with accusing voices of drugged grooms, with Banquo's ghost, weird sisters, and prophetic visions, as he cannot see into her "mind diseas'd" (5.3.40) or her sleepwalking terrors. All too often it is these demonic characters whose private utterances sound most like the "silent thought" of the Sonnets, though their beleaguered victims also can sometimes adopt a reflective tone. But that only makes their position, and ours and the audience's, more treacherous. This new language, available especially to corrupt and wicked characters, allows the seventeenth-century Shakespeare to impress on us more powerfully than before the unexpected realization that such figures do not enter our world entirely as outsiders, from an unfamiliar cosmos of fallen and foreign angels, that they have motives and words and a habit of inner discourse like our own, only more fluent, more nuanced, and probably more dangerous. The gifted evil creature—Claudius, Iago, the Macbeths, and Milton's Satan—is all too fearfully like us, even *in* us, even *is* us.

To put it another way, that inner language, deeply ambivalent, becomes even more richly implicated, through its use in Shakespeare's plays, in guilt and sin—"subdued," as it were, "To what it works in, like the dyer's hand" (S. 111)—and this is a language, voiced in drama, silent in lyric, that much of later English poetry inherits. For many of us the figures of Shakespeare's mature plays have become defined very largely by those utterances of theirs that we think of as coming from these inner depths—the self-declarations, tainted by the "black and grained spots" (*Hamlet*, 3.4.90) of an indelible guilt, of Richard II, of Henry IV and his son, of Hamlet, Claudius, and Gertrude, of both Macbeths, and of Othello and Lear at their moments of self-absorbed distraction. After the Jacobeans, English drama leaves that language behind in favor of couplets and prose, neither in this period capable of carrying the language of luminous meditation on the stage. But much of English poetry, in contrast, follows Shakespeare's dramatic verse into a speech that we usually experience as potentially sounded yet silent.

The silence of this speech probably makes it different from most earlier English verse—from Chaucer, Gower, and Lydgate, much of whose work was still presumably intended for recitation to a live court audience. The advance of printing would eventually make private reading more common. But Skelton invites expressive performance, much of Wyatt's verse was sung, and it seems likely that Tudor poems, like those we meet in the miscellanies, were often recited. Donne's love poems, too, seem grounded in speech; with their strong colloquial base, they appear to be meant for recitation and sometimes song, for lively entertainment, as do many poems by Herrick, Lovelace, and Suckling, and by some later writers, especially those who write frequently in other meters than iambic or pentameter, and in lively or racy stanzas.

But printing itself, by the sixteenth century, must have made it more and more impracticable for longer poems to be read or heard aloud by most readers. The very accessibility of poetic texts must soon have made silent reading (with all its concomitant options such as skipping, skimming, repeating, speeding and slowing, breaking off or looking back) more convenient, congenial, and solitary, and the physical situation of reading would presumably have led readers to find it more and more natural for the verse they encountered in their private sessions to sound like the same inner discourse they could recognize from their own silent experience.[17]

So in the prayerlike poems of Herbert they could hear the quiet, reflective tones of a lively but not necessarily sounded devotional verse. Milton makes the same kind of silent speech majestically audible in elegy and epic, and by the nineteenth century, after the more public narratives and essays of Dryden and Pope, a different rhythmic pattern of blank verse lines, casting Augustan symmetries and balances aside, leads through a generalized eighteenth-century reflectiveness to the self-dramatizing and usually solitary wordstreams of Wordsworth, Coleridge, and Keats—poets whose "inward eye" is "the bliss of solitude" and whose "musèd rhyme," touching "the sad heart" amid "alien corn," finds its cadence in the silent bell of the word "forlorn." That later lyric poetry is often of this kind, that its readers feel comfortable reading it silently, even perhaps that they enjoy its apparently inherent character of guilty or anxious or ambivalent rumination and reverie, seems likely enough. It seems equally likely that Shakespeare's Sonnets, though they lead to the classic dramatic expression in English of personal anguish, also provide the language for English poetry's chronic mourning of absence (or at least marshal it the way that it was going), through eloquent—one wants to say fallen—words that we mainly hear in a deeply charged silence.

In effect, the language of inner thought and feeling in English might be described as having this kind of history: first appearing with force perhaps in Sidney's *Astrophel and Stella*, it finds its most trenchant expression in Shakespeare's Sonnets, migrates from there to his plays, survives powerfully in Milton's poetry, and then, after being approached in verse for much of the eighteenth century, is redramatized (but silently) in Wordsworth and later nineteenth-century lyric poetry, however widely this poetry varies in tone: from the controlled rhapsodies of Tennyson to the jaunty but unspoken (often, unspeakable) monologues of Browning, the musical reveries of Swinburne, the suppressed outbursts of Hopkins, and the moody meditations of Yeats. In modernist poetry it sometimes takes to disjunctive forms in order to foreground neurosis, dream, and trauma, and at last reemerges, blocked and all but silenced, barely voiced, in the stylized drama of Beckett and Pinter.

THE POEM AS BOOK

> I am to wait, though waiting so be hell,
> Not blame your pleasure, be it ill or well.
>
> —Shakespeare, Sonnet 58

But surely poets for centuries—even those who appear in Shakespeare's plays—have been in the habit of reading their poems aloud to each other or to larger audiences, and lovers of the poems of Tennyson, Kipling, and Yeats, of Longfellow, Poe, and Frost, have been reciting them in public or private for generations. Even if we grant that this poetry of silence has taken the route I suggest and has come to dominate the poetic earscape for much of the last two centuries, there has surely always been a strong countermovement that has run through Dryden and Pope, those public poets who constantly engage us as immediate listeners to their full-voiced verse; through prosodic dissenters like Smart, Blake, and Whitman; and gathering momentum in poets still of the silent tradition perhaps but moving toward open talk, blues, jazz, or rock—Pound, Williams, Langston Hughes, Ginsberg, and a host of others. But, except for anomalies like Vachel Lindsay or Dylan Thomas, not in our century till the late 1950s do poems convincingly requiring to be *sounded* come to be composed, partly inspired by popular-music "poets" like the Beatles and Bob Dylan. The poetry of open or free forms, indebted to rap, reggae, or other contemporary musical forms, committed to performance, associating poetry with ritual occasions, celebrations, and even Dionysian joy in plenitude, and usually intensely hostile to the more silent Apollonian verse of tradition, serves in our time as its chief challenger.

But that tradition remains strong. I would guess that even today most American poetry is read silently and is written by poets with the understanding that it usually will be unsounded but, they hope, silently "heard," an eminently speakable verse that normally goes unspoken. Even if they think of their work as, ideally, read aloud by an excellent reader (themselves or another), they know that most of the time it will be read without sound from the page, that the poem, in effect, is a book.

We recognize that the language of Shakespeare's Sonnets is not entirely confessional, distressed, aggrieved. We should notice at least one other voice we "hear" in these poems, the voice in which, as in lyric poetry of all ages and many languages, the poet, like Hamlet or

Iachimo, consigns or confides his thoughts, observations, and insights to writing, as a means of preserving them, delayed messages for himself or others. Sonnet 77 recommends this procedure to the friend, whose thoughts, committed to the pages of his writing tablet, can be retrieved at a later time "To take a new acquaintance of thy mind." In the Sonnets, however, as in much earlier and later lyric verse, material of this kind is likely to have a personal edge, as it typically does in the plays. Wisdom (or foolish generalization) is not to be detached from the person who speaks it, and from his or her personal predicament or character. The sententiae that precede and modulate into John of Gaunt's impressive description of England's greatness are those of an ill and foolish old man who wants the sense or self-control to save his eloquence for Richard's ear. Similarly, the expression of general truths in sonnets 66, 94, 129, and others can hardly be detached from the situation of their implicated speaker, whose local experience often leads to general statements about life (e.g., in S. 25, 39, 54, 57, 59, 60, 70, 84, 116, 119, 121). Later English poetry, too, includes many poems that serve as delayed and indefinitely delayable messages of general reflection to whoever is disposed to hear them—the poet, an absent lover, or anyone at all. The resource of writing offers a poet the opportunity to transfer the silent, unspoken thoughts of his brain, however inflected with personal feeling, to the equally silent register of, say, a sonnet.

Unlike plays, which offer us a sequence of voices actually heard and normally irreversible and unrecoverable, poems provide a continuous silent speech, which is easily recoverable from the writing or printing in which it is coded. In a sense, the page is always speaking, though at any moment no one may be listening; the paper has kept, in effect, the property of silence it had in the forest as a tree. Or to put it in an opposite image: "All verbal expression, whether put into writing, print, or the computer, is bound to sound forever."[18] The page, the poem, the book is always carrying on its inner discourse, like one of the driven characters in Renaissance plays, or like the electrical current that keeps running through our houses though all the lights have been turned off. In a literate culture, the library preserves the common wisdom, even when the doors are locked for the night; the book itself is an emblem of this feature of the culture. But of all books, the poem best epitomizes this relation of books to a culture, partly because of all writings poems are most recently (and most anciently) oral, even to the extent that their acoustical features (such as rhythm, assonance, alliteration, and phonological contrasts and balances) are still prominent in this silent medium; and partly because its language is often, even usually, imitative of the language we use in speaking to ourselves or in imagining our speaking with others. The poem is a quintessential book, always ready to be silently (or even vocally) read, as the book is a quintessential library. The poem may not always explicitly mourn an absence, but it waits, like a letter, in its permanently tuned silence—or like the lover of sonnets 57 and 58—not for its own but for its reader's presence:

> Being your slave, what should I do but tend
> Upon the hours and times of your desire?
> . . . .
> O let me suffer, being at your beck,
> Th' imprisoned absence of your liberty—
> . . . .
> Be where you list, your charter is so strong
> That you yourself may privilege your time
> To what you will

From this point of view, confined to the page, denied its voice, what is poetry but silent speech that aspires to the condition of sound? But therein lie both its limitation and its strength, as an image of perpetual desire, like those figures on Keats's Grecian urn, or like Yeats's image of Keats as "a schoolboy" who

> made—being poor, ailing and ignorant,
> Shut out from all the luxury of the world
> . . . .
> Luxuriant song.[19]

The emphasis of many of the Sonnets on separation and absence, on silent and patient waiting, on the "ever-fixed mark / That looks on tempests and is never shaken" (S. 116), even in the face of life events that exhibit clearly all the evils of alteration and inconstancy, should not surprise us. Art always depends on negations, on frames that mark it off from what it isn't. If Renaissance portraits provide images that mime the living force they lack, drama offers a voiced enactment of actions that must not be violated by the actual. That Shakespeare understood how art thrives on such conventions, and on their deliberate ruptures, appears in the silence of the Sonnets (which may always break into sound), in the imagery, the supposes, and the intricately coded mirrorings of plays from *A Midsummer Night's Dream* to *The Tempest* (which greatly amplify the apparent range of events represented on the stage), and is nowhere made more manifest than when, almost at the end of his career, he authorizes the statue of Hermione, a likeness without life, to shatter the barrier between nature and art and from her stony sixteen-year absence step once more into life.

NOTES

1. John Pope-Hennessy, *The Portrait in the Renaissance* (Princeton: Princeton University Press, 1966), 9.

2. All quotations from the Sonnets are from *Shakespeare's Sonnets*, ed. Stephen Booth (New Haven: Yale University Press, 1977).

3. Later New Critical analysis made a point of stressing that "a poem is a dramatic fiction no less than a play" (Reuben Brower, *The Fields of Light*, quoted from *Perspectives on Poetry*, ed. James L. Calderwood and Harold E. Toliver [New York: Oxford University Press, 1968]) and "its speaker . . . no less a creation of the words on the printed page" (98). What Brower and others knew but didn't think necessary to say was that the "voice" and "tone" of a poem are also fictions. They are what we would hear if the poem on the page were to be read aloud, but in the usage of many critics this necessary qualification is not made, probably because the point is unimportant in the classroom, where the poem or the parts of it being discussed usually *are* read aloud. The contradiction becomes evident only on written examinations, when students are urged to write in virtual silence about such matters as voice, tone, and rhythm.

But as Barbara Herrnstein Smith insists in *Poetic Closure* (Chicago: University of Chicago Press, 1968), a poem is not an actual but "only a *possible* utterance" (16); "poetry is a *representational* art and . . . each poem is the representation of an act of speech" (17). Smith never forgets that any poem we read or hear may or may not be read aloud, and that what she claims for its form must be valid for both possibilities.

4. "Voices That Figure in *Four Quartets*," in *The Placing of T. S. Eliot*, ed. Jewel Spears Brooker (Columbia: University of Missouri Press, 1991), 152-62.

5. In *T. S. Eliot's Silent Voices* (New York: Oxford University Press, 1989), John T. Mayer studies the extent to which the "voices" composing the psychological dramas of Eliot's early verse represent internal, often

fragmented, elements in his speakers' psychic consciousnesses, not their spoken words. Mayer shows how these silent voices differ from the voices of comparable nineteenth-century poems in, for example, their disjunctive syntax. But, relevant as his subject is to mine, he does not discuss whether we, the audience for this poetry, are to hear its words silently or aloud.

6. For more on this subject, see my "An Almost Oral Art: Shakespeare's Language on Stage and Page," *Shakespeare Quarterly* 43 (1992): 159-69; and "Blank Verse in the Elizabethan Theater: Language That Vanishes, Language That Keeps," in *The Elizabethan Theatre XII* (1993), ed. A. L. Magnusson and C. E. McGee (Toronto: P. D. Meany, 1993), 1-18.

7. This paragraph, and the one that follows, are based on passages in my "Voices That Figure in *Four Quartets*," 154, 157.

8. Michel de Montaigne, "Apology for Raymonde Sebond," in *The Complete Essays of Montaigne*, trans. Donald M. Frame (Stanford: Stanford University Press, 1958), 336.

9. As Booth suggests, the parallelism between "o'er-read" and "rehearse" in lines 10-11 encourages us to understand "your being" and "my gentle verse" as equivalent. Still, line 11 "provides its own object for *rehearse—your being* (future tongues shall rehearse your being, i.e. recount your life, tell about you" (279).

10. Heather Dubrow, *Captive Victors: Shakespeare's Narrative Poems and Sonnets* (Ithaca: Cornell University Press, 1987), 254-56.

11. *Shakespeare's Metrical Art* (Berkeley: University of California Press, 1988), 89.

12. Wolfgang Clemen, *Shakespeare's Soliloquies*, trans. Charity Scott Stokes (London: Methuen, 1987), 6. The Arnold quotation is on page 3.

13. *The "Inward" Language: Sonnets of Wyatt, Sidney, Shakespeare, Donne* (Chicago: University of Chicago Press, 1983), 61.

14. In Ferry's view, developed in persuasive detail in *The "Inward" Language*, Sidney and Shakespeare "explode the boundaries of poetic convention" (28) as they "work through and beyond depiction of the lover's heart struck first by Cupid's dart, then by the lady's scorn, to an exploration of 'how hard true sorrow hits' [S. 120] when lovers injure one another's feelings" (28). Their sonnets' "more than usual intimacy of address, their elaboration of the lover's involvement in causing pain to himself and to his beloved, their dramatization of his imaginative entrance into another person's heart, make these poems radically different in kind from a representative sixteenth-century complaint" so that they become "intimate, private explorations of autobiographical material" (29). Sidney and Shakespeare are "the only two love poets to make central to their sonnet sequences the issue of showing in verse

what is truly in the heart" (29), instead of seeking within for a reflection of the divine love or the conventional imagistic representation of human love.

15. Cf. Katharine Eisaman Maus's view that "in late sixteenth- and early seventeenth-century England the sense of discrepancy between 'inward disposition' and 'outward appearance' seems unusually urgent and consequential for a very large number of people" *(Inwardness and the Theater in the English Renaissance* [Chicago: University of Chicago Press, 1995], 13). Such a discrepancy is explored insistently and intensely in the Sonnets and with deepening subtlety in the plays that follow. Maus seems to me to argue very cogently against those critics who either "claim that a conception of personal inwardness hardly existed at all in Renaissance England" or "acknowledge that the rhetoric of inwardness is highly developed . . . but maintain that these terms inevitably refer to outward, public, or political factors" (2); and she notes that Ferry, in denying an inwardness in the love poetry of poets other than Sidney and Shakespeare, does so "without, apparently, sharing the philosophical agenda that motivates" these other critics of subjectivity (27n.).

16. Still, the need of the speaker to defend himself against the *imputation* of a vileness that may amount to a kind of behavioral madness is evident in sonnet 121 and seems parallel to Hamlet's defensive tactics against Rosencrantz and Guildenstern. Carol Thomas Neely's study, "Documents in Madness: Reading Madness and Gender in Shakespeare's Tragedies and Early Modern Culture," *Shakespeare Quarterly* 42 (1991): 315-38, is helpful here: "Shakespeare . . . dramatizes madness primarily through a peculiar language more often than through physiological symptoms, stereotyped behaviors or iconographic conventions. . . . Shakespeare's language of madness is characterized by fragmentation, obsession, and repetition, and . . . 'quotation.' . . . The mad are 'beside themselves'; their discourse is not their own" (323).

17. See David M. Bergeron, ed., *Reading and Writing in Shakespeare* (Newark: University of Delaware Press, 1996), and especially Bergeron's helpful introductory essay; and Gerd Baumann, ed., *The Written Word: Literacy in Transition* (Oxford: Clarendon Press, 1986), a volume in which two essays are particularly pertinent: Walter J. Ong, "Writing Is a Technology That Restructures Thought," 23-50; and Keith Thomas, "Literacy in Early Modern England," 97-131.

18. Ong, "Writing Is a Technology That Restructures Thought," 31.

19. W. B. Yeats, "Ego Dominus Tuus," in *The Poems*, ed. Richard J. Finneran (New York: Macmillan, 1983), 161-62.

Figure 3. Dedication and sonnet 1 from *Shakespeare's Sonnets* (London: Hacon and Ricketts, 1899). Illustration by C. S. Ricketts. Reproduced courtesy of the Rare Book Division of the Library of Congress.

PART III

New Essays on Shakespeare's Sonnets

Shakespeare's Petrarchism

Gordon Braden

Petrarch's name, like Seneca's, appears once in Shakespeare. Mercutio glosses Romeo: "now is he for the numbers that Petrach [*sic*] flowed in: *Laura* to his Lady, was a kitchin wench, marrie she had a better love to berime her" (*Romeo and Juliet* 2.3/1096-98). We can deduce a conviction that Petrarchan love brings with it a lot to be made fun of, though also a sense that Petrarch's standing as a poet is not directly under attack. The concession, however, hardly suggests real familiarity. In the records of Shakespearean *Quellenforschung*, there has been to my knowledge one serious suggestion (Rollins 1: 276) of a direct borrowing from Petrarch: that the opening of sonnet 110 deliberately mimics a famous effect in the opening poem of his *Canzoniere*:

> Alas 'tis true, I have gone here and there,
> And made my selfe a motley to the view

> Ma ben veggio or sì come al popol tutto
> favola fui gran tempo, onde sovente
> di me medesmo meco mi vergogno

[But now I see well how for a long time I was the talk of the crowd, for which often I am ashamed of myself within myself.][1]

"Motley to the view" is credible as a theater man's equivalent to "al popol tutto / favola" (and for reasons I will be discussing later, "'tis true" would be an especially appropriate translation for "ben veggio"); within such a similarity of statement the comparable alliteration of "m"s looks almost like evidence. But the trail stops here, and without other examples there is no reason to take the parallel as anything other than uncanny coincidence. We cannot be sure Shakespeare did not read Petrarch, but he might as well not have.

It is only slightly easier to link Shakespeare's own Sonnets to those of other practitioners of that genre. Source-hunting in connection with his sequence has seldom led with any specificity to other Petrarchan lyrics.[2] When it has done so, there is often something funny in the air. Our best evidence that Shakespeare read Watson's *Hekatompathia* is the likelihood that it supplied the specific text being mocked in sonnet 130 (Cruttwell 18-19). Sonnet 99 is the only poem in Shakespeare's sequence for which a specific anterior sonnet is regularly cited as a source,[3] and the very closeness of the connection looks like part of a complicated joke: the sonnet has fifteen lines. A few verbal parallels and tricks of phrase from other Elizabethan sonneteers have been detected, but nothing as ample and unguarded as the traces of North's Plutarch or Golding's Ovid in the plays.

Evidence of this sort, however, is only part of what bears on a writer's relation to tradition; here the apparent slightness of Shakespeare's interest in particular poems serves not to establish his disengagement from the tradition in which they were written but to define the nature of that engagement. There can be no serious doubt that Shakespeare read the Elizabethan sonneteers; they loomed too large to be ignored, and the existence of his own sonnets is inconceivable without the precedents set by this busy, unevenly talented guild. The work of that guild is in turn promiscuously dependent on a range of Italian and French practice whereby specifically Petrarchan topics and conventions were systematized, altered, and supplemented in the course of the sixteenth century to create an international poetic idiom corresponding to no particular writer's own *parole*. What Shakespeare would appear to have taken from his reading of individual sonnets was an encounter with this general and even anonymous idiom; we register its presence in themes and conceits that can be illustrated equally well from a number of different practitioners. Shakespeare would in most cases have been ignorant of their specific pedigree; even modern scholarship has had trouble monitoring and sorting out their corporate history.

One of the largely unmet challenges of Shakespearean source study—an enterprise whose monument is entitled *Narrative and Dramatic Sources*—is for an informed assessment of the relation of the

Sonnets to what with due caution I will continue calling the Petrarchan lyric tradition.[4] It is unmet partly because of the difficulty involved in mastering the relevant material, and also, I think, because of a certain lack of imagination as to just what the options might be. Parody is a common suspicion, sometimes a full-blown theory: "It is as if [Shakespeare] meant to say, 'sugar is very well, but not the stuff to make real love out of'. He leaves us to draw the deduction, trusting that he has made his point, and that we shall now think [sonnets such as 153-54] funny" (Wilson 144). But that is the voice of a modern sensibility that has, for its own good reasons, never been under the spell of Petrarchan sonneteering. Major bodies of Renaissance poetry are unintelligible without at least some responsiveness to such a spell, and a compelling account of Shakespeare's place in this tradition cannot merely make him (like us) superior to it. Something more complicated is called for.

The most ambitious recent attempt has been Fineman's. His thesis is, in its way, a version of the parodic thesis, but claiming greater than usual historical reach and consequence:

> I argue that Shakespeare rewrites the poetry of praise by employing (implicitly in the sonnets addressed to the young man, explicitly in the sonnets addressed to the dark lady) in an unprecedentedly serious way the equally antique genre of the mock encomium. . . . Shakespeare rewrites praise through the medium of epideictic paradox and in this way invents, which is to say comes upon, the only kind of subjectivity that survives in the literature successive to the poetry of praise. (2)

The poetry of praise "is regularly taken to be, from Plato and Aristotle through the Renaissance, the master model of poetry per se," but finds a specially important embodiment in the poems of Shakespeare's Petrarchan predecessors:

> it can be shown that the assumptions of epideixis determine in particular ways not only the techniques and conceits of the praising poet but also his literary personality, i.e., the way the poet presents poetic self. This is evident in traditional lyric poetry even when such poetry only casually refers to praise. It is more especially the case in the Renaissance sonnet, however, for this is a literary form in which

an epideictic purpose is regularly developed as primary thematic
motive of poetic first person. (1)

Deforming Petrarchan precedent, Shakespeare is not just revealing
modern sensibility but inventing it.

The reading of Shakespeare's sequence that results has real virtues.
Fineman's key question is not unprecedented, but he asks and pursues
it with a boldness to which no other commentator has risen: "what
happens to the sonnet when its poet ceases to admire that which he
desires?" (55). That desire is fully capable of surviving the death of
admiration is the experiential testimony of Shakespeare's sequence; in
Fineman's view it also gives this notoriously discontinuous collection
its unity when read in the otherwise puzzling order in which we have it.
The poems about the dark lady, where the divorce between desire and
admiration is openly decreed, are the fearful climax of a long story; she
is "the material conclusion of an originally immaterial imagination, the
loathsome heterosexual object of an ideally homosexual desire" (58).
Yet the relation of the last 28 poems to the first 126 is not merely one
of contrast; what manifests itself at the end is stirring from the
beginning: "much of what the young man sonnets do implicitly is
preparation for what the dark lady sonnets subsequently say explicitly,
the latter thus articulating directly in their matter what is indirectly
present in the manner of the former" (160). From this perspective, the
poet's persistent excuse-making for the young man—"No more bee
greev'd at that which thou hast done, / Roses have thornes, and silver
fountaines mud" (35.6-7)—is important not for being heartfelt or
gullible or ironic (though it is all those things), but as a muted version
of what will later be revealed as an insoluble and tragic fact about
desire.[5]

Fineman's cogency here, however, is not matched in his handling
of the lyric precedents that are said to provide Shakespeare's starting
point and against which his activity is defined. Fineman's knowledge of
this tradition looks skimpy and secondhand. Only a handful of specific
poems are cited, in most cases very briefly. Petrarch, Sidney, and
Spenser are the usual sources; Drayton's title, *Ideas Mirrour*, makes
numerous appearances. Aside from one sonnet by Michelangelo, the
continental tradition intervening between Petrarch and the Elizabethans
is almost wholly unrepresented. Stray generalizations do not inspire
confidence. It is true only in a specialized sense to say that
"Shakespeare in his sonnets invents the poetics of

heterosexuality"(18);[6] if Sidney does not count, what of Ronsard? More damagingly:

> in Petrarch, as in the sonnet tradition as a whole, if the lover is
> divided by his love, or if the poet is sundered by his poetry, this is but
> one temporary moment in the course of a potentially complete—even
> if it is a currently postponed—progress toward total self-fulfillment.
> Either the grace of the lady will eventually bring the poet to herself,
> and therefore bring the poet to himself, or, when the sonnet grows
> more self-consciously literary, it will be the poet's poetry that
> resolves the difference between his real and his ideal. (227)

The first of those resolutions very rarely occurs in Renaissance sonneteering (even in Ronsard). The second is primarily a guerdon to be bestowed by the reader; as an explicit boast on the part of the poet it is far more likely to occur along the way (as it does at several points in Shakespeare's sequence) than at the end. Neither alternative characterizes the end of Petrarch's *Canzoniere*. Fineman generalizes about material with which he does not seem to have spent much time.

The most consequential of these generalizations in practical terms concerns the "visual" character of Petrarchan praise. Fineman establishes this point in the main not by citation of Petrarchan texts but by deducing it from the very nature of praise:

> The epideictic is epiphanic because, like light itself, this speech
> displays its referent by self-displaying itself. . . . This is to speak
> figuratively, but the point to recognize is that these are constitutive or
> enabling figures *of* the poetical, necessary or inevitable figurations
> through which a poetics based on *effective* likeness will think its own
> semiotic coherence. Only by imagining itself in terms of such figures,
> in terms of a light whose showing and showing forth are one and the
> same, does epideictic speech "bring to light" the *phάos* or light that
> emanates out of the *phai-nomena* about which it speaks. (103)

This argument justifies giving privileged emphasis to anything that could be construed as a reference to the operations of seeing or light: "'Suspicion' is the right word here, for what is put into question in Shakespeare's sonnets is, truly *sub-spicere*, the ideality of a perennially visual language of admiration" (243). Some neo-Derridean puns mark the limit here—"the 'light' that shines in 'delight'" (94)—or rather, suggest that the category has no limits. Including almost from the start any reference to ideas and the ideal (by way of its Greek etymology from *idein*), the phenomenon being noted risks being indistinguishable from perception and thinking generally. The most important alternative is language, which counters the visionary ideal in manifesting "the 'languageness' of language" (243), a category that also does not inspire confidence; the last several decades of critical practice have shown that pretty much any textual specimen can be so characterized.

The grid pays off at times, particularly with the dark lady poems:

> the way the lady *looks* is precisely like the "belying" double way that language *speaks*, which is why the lady's raven eyes are such that they will thrust the poet out of the poetics of a simulating vision and into the poetics of a dissimulating speech, making him, as at the end of sonnet 127, not a poet of the "eye," but, instead, a poet of the "tongue": "Yet so they mourn, becoming of their woe, / That every tongue says beauty should look so." (23)

The benefits of noticing the eye-tongue polarity, however, are lessened by the way in which it distracts attention from the more deliberate instances in which Shakespeare writes of the operations of the eye in opposition to those of another faculty. Sonnets 46 and 47 on the "mortall warre" between the eye and heart rate a couple of pages' notice (72-74), though less out of interest in the topic itself—a "Petrarchan commonplace"—than for the sake of noting the choreography of its development: "the first sub-sequence tends to derive similarity out of difference, the second [i.e., the dark lady sequence] instead tends to derive difference out of similarity" (74). Sonnet 113—"Since I left you, mine eye is in my minde"—is cited only once, almost in passing (159), though its terms duplicate those in one of Shakespeare's best-known formulations of the perverse connection between desire and subjectivity:

> Through *Athens*, I am thought as faire as shee.
> But what of that? *Demetrius* thinkes not so:
> He will not knowe, what all, but hee doe know.
> And as hee erres, doting on *Hermias* eyes:
> So I, admiring of his qualities.
> Things base and vile, holding no quantitie,
> Love can transpose to forme and dignitie.

> Love lookes not with the eyes, but with the minde:
> And therefore is wingd *Cupid* painted blinde.
> > (*Midsummer Night's Dream* 1.1/227-35)

Fineman does not cite this passage, though he does remember "Tongue loose thy light" (*Dream* 5.1/2000; Fineman 302). I suspect theoretical predilections that deny status to "heart" and "mind" (while granting it to "speech" and "tongue") keep Fineman from attending to the readiest terms in which Shakespeare states something quite close to Fineman's own thesis. In the process, I think, an important window on Shakespeare's relation to the originator of Renaissance sonneteering is smudged.

A better model for the work needed to produce reliable results in such matters is Leishman's; his book on Shakespeare's Sonnets, unsystematic and even rambling by contemporary standards, seems to me still the best of its kind. The method is, over and over, to compare Shakespeare's handling of "a few large general topics" (11) with specific treatments of the same topics by his lyric predecessors. It is from the cumulative feel for the material that such comparisons make possible that usable generalizations about the character and course of the tradition are most likely to develop. That tradition is not so much a stable set of conventions as a repertoire among which particular writers pick and choose, and the history of the tradition is the history of that selecting, some of it at the prompting of individual talent and some of it shaped by less personal trends and pressures. Within this history, specific topics mutate, occasionally beyond recognition; new ones enter and develop; others fade and even disappear. A moment of special interest in Leishman's discussion is his somewhat surprised detection of the dog that does not bark in Shakespeare's sequence. There is no instance of the call to present pleasure as a response to the pressure of time: either the generalized topic of *carpe diem* or the specifically erotic *carpe florem*. The latter is a particularly familiar feature of sixteenth-century sonneteering, one the classic seducer's arguments—"Cueillez dés aujourd'huy les roses de la vie" (Ronsard, *Sonets pour Helene* 2.24.14 [Gather today the roses of life]); "coged de vuestra alegre primavera / el dulce fruto" (Garcilaso, sonnet 23.9-10 [gather the sweet fruit of your happy spring])—though not the exclusive preserve of male poets: "Qui coglieremo a tempo e rose e fiori, / ed erbe e frutti" (Stampa, *Rime* 158.12-13 [Here we will keep time gathering roses and flowers, herbs and fruits]). Shakespeare does not say anything like this, even when context would seem to welcome it. In the procreation sonnets, the poet stresses the productiveness of the imagined union, not its pleasure.

> We do not find Shakespeare reminding his friend that he will only be young once, that the time will come when those Maids of Honour will no longer be casting such melting glances upon him as they are doing today, and that he will regret that he did not 'gather the Rose of love whilst yet was time'. In fact, nowhere in Shakespeare's sonnets is there anything approaching an invitation to pleasure. (Leishman 100)

Leishman writes well of this absence as a matter of conviction and personality—"Shakespeare always speaks of Time as an enemy to be defied, never as a power whose laws are to be accepted and submitted to" (100)—but omits to note something of, I think, comparable interest: among the other sequences from which this topic is missing is Petrarch's *Canzoniere*.[7] Shakespeare's anomaly is also a return to origins.

Mainstream Petrarchism has in its own time a lascivious reputation, which it often deserves; a seducer's arguments are cheerfully at home in seducer's poetry:

> You must lay Lime, to tangle her desires
> By walefull Sonnets, whose composed Rimes
> Should be full fraught with serviceable vowes.
> > (*Two Gentlemen of Verona* 3.2/1461-63)

Petrarch himself, in comparison with most of his followers, is notably muted in this regard. There was even debate within the substantial body of criticism on the *Canzoniere* as to whether his interest in Laura had any relation to the ordinary interest that men have in beautiful women. Decisive arguments that it did were assembled in the late sixteenth century and effectively have the last word;[8] but the prooftexts are only two (*Canzoniere* 22.31-36, 237.31-36), and neither of those is a direct address to Laura. Such is the lover's reticence that a reader may reasonably doubt whether any open profession of desire occurs within the implied narrative of the sequence; in the heyday of European Petrarchism this sort of thing opened itself to serious mockery,[9] and many imitators adjusted their practice accordingly. On this level, the lack of persuasions to enjoy in Shakespeare testifies less to the suppliant's shyness than to the innovative character of his situation: writing love poems to another man, with whom sexual consummation is not in any of the ordinary ways an option,[10] and writing love poems to a woman with whom a physical affair appears underway almost from the start. The effect of these very different causes (if that is what they are) is nevertheless the same, the quiet absence from the mix of something sanguine and predatory.

This point of resemblance connects with others; I want to argue that Shakespeare's sequence is in certain ways one of the most Petrarchan sequences of the age—that some of its most distinguishing marks are not mockeries or refutations of Petrarchism, but fulfillments of some of that movement's original potentialities. This is not a common stance;[11] I feel justified in taking it partly because I am thinking of some of Shakespeare's best-known poems:

> When to the Sessions of sweet silent thought,
> I sommon up remembrance of things past,
> I sigh the lacke of many a thing I sought,
> And with old woes new waile my deare times waste:
> Then can I drowne an eye (un-us'd to flow)
> For precious friends hid in deaths dateles night,
> And weepe a fresh loves long since canceld woe,
> And mone th'expence of many a vannisht sight.
> Then can I greeve at greevances fore-gon,
> And heavily from woe to woe tell ore
> The sad account of fore-bemoned mone,
> Which I new pay as if not payd before.
>   But if the while I thinke on thee (deare friend)
>   All losses are restord, and sorrowes end. (30)

Petrarch's name does not appear in commentary on this poem. The closest thing to a source that has been proposed is in Catullus (Rollins 1: 87)—a poet whom there are good reasons for remembering in connection with Shakespeare's sequence, but who here serves mainly to point out some contrasts:

> Si quicquam mutis gratum acceptumue sepulcris
>   accidere a nostro, Calue, dolore potest,
> quo desiderio ueteres renouamus amores

> atque olim missas flemus amicitias,
> certe non tanto mors immatura dolor est
> Quintiliae, quantum gaudet amore tuo. (*Carmina* 96)

[If anything welcome or pleasing can be passed on to the silent grave
by our grief, by which we renew old loves with desire and weep for
friendships long gone, certainly early death does not grieve Quintilia
as much as she rejoices in your love.]

The common ground is the sense of loss and sorrow from which both
poets seek relief, but Shakespeare's search and the consolation he
affirms are perceptibly more solitary. No relief for the precious but lost
friends is imagined, nor does the present friend (the first time the young
man is so called in the sequence) appear to be a sharer in the grief that
needs comforting; the sonnet's addressee, he is not part of its occasion
in the way in which Calvus is in the Latin elegy. The consolation itself
is austerely denoted, in comparison both to Catullus's poem and to the
otherwise similar conclusion to the previous sonnet: "thy sweet love
remembred such welth brings, / That then I skorne to change my state
with Kings" (29.13-14). The turn comes simply with "I thinke on
thee"—phrasing so modest that we may miss the force of its pivotal
word, one that reaffirms the scene-setting of the opening line: "the
Sessions of sweet silent thought." The whole episode, from despair to
recovery, occurs within the terrain of the isolated thinking mind.

We can imagine some alternative version of the poem, a version
that casual modern readers might hear in Shakespeare's poem, whereby
the young man's sensitivity to his lover's moods enables him, like a
good friend, to intervene in those moods and turn them around. But that
is exactly what Shakespeare's poem does not affirm; the young man
does not intervene, does nothing at all in fact except serve as an object
of thought. Even the stronger claim of the previous sonnet veils the
beloved's intervention with the mind's retrospection: "thy sweet love
remembred." The scene of love is one which might theoretically be
asserted for almost all lyric poetry but which Petrarch's *Canzoniere*
repeatedly makes explicit: "Solo et pensoso i più deserti campi / vo
mesurando a passi tardi et lenti" (35.1-2 [alone and filled with thought,
I go measuring the most deserted fields with steps delaying and slow]);
"Di pensier in pensier, di monte in monte / mi guida Amor, ch' ogni
segnato calle / provo contrario a la tranquilla vita" (129.1-3 [From
thought to thought, from mountain to mountain Love guides me; for I

find every trodden path to be contrary to a tranquil life]). Entries on *pensare* and related words supply 205 entries in the Accademia della Crusca concordance. By word count, there are more *pensieri* in the sequence than *sospiri*; Petrarch's most passionate utterances are repeatedly mixed with the language of meditation and recall: "O passi sparsi, o pensier vaghi et pronti, / o tenace memoria, o fero ardore" (161.1-2 [O scattered steps, O yearning, ready thoughts, O tenacious memory, O savage ardor]). Such usage descends from the intellectualism of the *stilnovisti*, and looks forward to the recovered Neoplatonism with which some later Petrarchists will seek an alliance; in the comparatively unphilosophical context of Petrarch's own sequence it centers on something simpler, more immediately experiential, but also thematically momentous: the solitude of the act of literary composition, the lot of "uom che pensi et pianga et scriva" (129.52 [a man who thinks and weeps and writes]):

> Dentro pur foco et for candida neve,
> sol con questi pensier, con altre chiome,
> sempre piangendo andrò per ogni riva,
> per far forse pietà venir ne gli occhi
> di tal che nascerà dopo mill' anni,
> se tanto viver po ben colto lauro. (*Canzoniere* 30.31-36)

[Inwardly fire, though outwardly white snow, alone with these thoughts, with changed locks, always weeping I shall go along every shore, to make pity perhaps come into the eyes of someone who will be born a thousand years from now—if a well-tended laurel can live so long.]

The coincidence of sexual desire and literary ambition is realized in the pun of Laura and *lauro*, the mortal woman and the crown of poetic achievement which are all but indistinguishable throughout the *Canzoniere*. That pun and its implications are one of the most important twists that Petrarch gives to the lyric inheritance which he received from his Occitan and Italian predecessors. With this twist, the dominant theme of passionate longing for a distant and unattainable object makes a whole new kind of sense; the human love story has the same structure as a writer's lonely desire for a posthumous fame that can only be secured when he can no longer experience it. Shakespeare rounds off one of his best-known poems with Petrarch's coincidence, so offhandedly as almost to escape notice—"If this be error and upon me proved, / I never writ, nor no man ever loved" (sonnet 116.13-14)— clinching an argument whose Petrarchan contours are I think even more deeply lodged if even less likely to be recognized. To the modern world sonnet 116 is an affirmation of successful mutuality in love, a favorite to read at wedding ceremonies; Shakespeare encourages us in this direction by echoing the Anglican rite—"Let me not to the marriage of true mindes / Admit impediments" (1-2)—but proceeds without apparent disruption to anchor love somewhere other than on achieved reciprocity:

> love is not love
> Which alters when it alteration findes,
> Or bends with the remover to remove. (2-4)

Alteration and removal on the part of the beloved change nothing; constancy is a predicate of the lover rather than of the relationship. Asserting the durability of a desire independent of all circumstance is one of the points at which Petrarchan love becomes proudly Stoic:

> ponmi in cielo od in terra od in abisso,
> in alto poggio, in valle ima et palustre,
> libero spirto od a' suoi membri affisso;
> ponmi con fama oscura o con illustre:
> sarò qual fui, vivrò com' io son visso,
> continuando il mio sospir trilustre. (*Canzoniere* 145.9-14)

[place me in Heaven or on earth or in the abyss, on a high mountain, in a deep and swampy valley; make me a free spirit or one fixed in his members; place me in obscurity or in illustrious fame: still I shall be what I have been, shall live as I have lived, continuing my trilustral sighing.]

Or in Surrey's version: "Yours will I be, and with that onely thought / Comfort my self when that my hape is nowght" (3.13-14). Imagining (with good reason) that the changes of circumstance may include betrayal and desertion, Shakespeare inflects his wedding poem with the prospect of Petrarchan solitude taken to a new level of intimacy. The key word in his first line is not "marriage" but "mindes"; the true minds being celebrated are not necessarily marrying each other.[12]

The mode of the true mind's operation is set out three poems earlier:

> Since I left you, mine eye is in my minde,
> And that which governes me to goe about,
> Doth part his function, and is partly blind,
> Seemes seeing, but effectually is out:
> For it no forme delivers to the heart
> Of bird, of flowre, or shape which it doth latch,
> Of his quick objects hath the minde no part,
> Nor his owne vision houlds what it doth catch:
> For if it see the rud'st or gentlest sight,
> The most sweet-favor or deformedst creature,
> The mountaine, or the sea, the day, or night:
> The Croe, or Dove, it shapes them to your feature.
>   Incapable of more, repleat with you,
>   My most true minde thus makes mine eye untrue. (113)

It is here that Shakespeare comes his closest to writing a recognizable version of a specific poem of Petrarch's:

> Pien di quella ineffabile dolcezza
> che del bel viso trassen gli occhi miei
> nel dì che volentier chiusi gli avrei
> per non mirar giamai minor bellezza,
> lassai quel ch' i' più bramo; et ò sì avezza
> la mente a contemplar sola costei
> ch' altro non vede, et ciò che non è lei
> già per antica usanza odia et disprezza.
> In una valle chiusa d'ogn' intorno,
> ch' è refrigerio de' sospir miei lassi,
> giunsi sol con Amor, pensoso et tardo;
> ivi non donne ma fontane et sassi
> et l'imagine trovo di quel giorno
> che 'l pensier mio figura ovunque io sguardo. (*Canzoniere* 116)

[Full of that ineffable sweetness which my eyes drew from her lovely face on that day when I would gladly have closed them so as never to look on any lesser beauties, I departed from what I most desire; and I have so accustomed my mind to contemplate her alone that it sees nothing else, and whatever is not she, already by ancient habit it hates and scorns. In a valley closed on all sides, which cools my weary sighs, I arrived alone with Love, thoughtful and late; there I find not ladies but fountains and rocks and the image of that day which my thoughts image forth wherever I may glance.]

Shakespeare's development of the mind-eye conceit is his own, but its germ is there in lines 5-7 of the Italian poem. The pleasure that the conceit explicates—the pleasure of erotic repletion at a distance—is almost exactly the same in both sonnets, and is a pleasure of particular importance for Petrarch: there is arguably no greater contentment in the *Canzoniere*, a sequence far better known for its turmoil and melancholy. The experience at such moments is of the mind's power to contradict reality: "et quanto in più selvaggio / loco mi trovo e 'n più deserto lido, / tanto più bella il mio pensier l'adombra" (129.46-48 [and in whatever wildest place and most deserted shore I find myself, so much the more beautiful does my thought shadow her forth]).

Putting it that way dramatizes the sublimity of the experience—"se l'error durasse, altro non cheggio" (*Canzoniere* 129.39 [if the error should last, I ask for no more])—but also forecasts a decisive judgment on it: an error is an error, and will ultimately be proved upon its author. The emotions in Shakespeare's sequence unfold at closer quarters than in Petrarch's, and the most important contradiction in play is not between the image and the deserted landscape but between the image and the beloved's behavior; the overlay of idealism and disillusion is eerier, the state of mind more extreme. But the happiness toward which the lover strains is similarly a self-deception that calls itself that: "So true a foole is love, that in your Will, / (Though you doe any thing) he thinkes no ill" (57.13-14). A true mind is a true fool; happiness that recognizes itself as a blessed subjectivity knows the terms of its own destruction: "O cunning love, with teares thou keepst me blinde, / Least eyes well seeing thy foule faults should finde" (148.13-14). In the dark lady poems, the contentedly untrue eye of 113 reasserts enough of its proper function to cast the lover's inexpiable offense as a crime against the simple perception of objective reality:

> My thoughts and my discourse as mad mens are,
> At randon from the truth vainely exprest.
> For I have sworne thee faire, and thought thee bright,
> Who art as black as hell, as darke as night. (147.11-14)

This harsh accounting is the *telos* of Fineman's argument, the key to his sense of the unity of Shakespeare's sequence, but it marks less a radical break with Petrarchan precedent than a ferocious replication of the moral crisis that begins the second movement of Petrarch's sequence and predicts its conclusion: "Quel ch' i' fo veggio, et non m'inganna il vero / mal conosciuto, anzi mi sforza Amore" (*Canzoniere* 264.91-92 [I see what I am doing, and I am not deceived by an imperfect knowledge of the truth; rather Love forces me]). The arena is once more that of thought—"I'vo pensando" (1 [I go thinking])—but thought that now leads the lover "ad altro lagrimar ch' i' non soleva" (4 [to a weeping different from my accustomed one]).[13] He weeps now not in despair at Laura's failure to reciprocate his desire, but in fear that the joint endeavor of love and literary ambition puts his soul at mortal risk; the sin in both cases is adoration of an inferior object: "mortal cosa amar con tanta fede / quanto a Dio sol per debito convensi" (99-100 [to love a mortal thing with the faith that belongs to God alone]). The poem's harrowing discovery is that the poet's clear knowledge of his self-destructiveness gets no secure purchase on his actions:

> et da l'un lato punge
> vergogna et duol che 'ndietro mi rivolve,
> dall'altro non m'assolve
> un piacer per usanza in me sì forte
> ch' a patteggiar n'ardisce co la Morte. (122-26)

[and on one side I am pierced by shame and sorrow, which turn me back; on the other I am not freed from a pleasure so strong in me by habit that it dares to bargain with Death.]

The canzone's last line is simpler and bleaker: "veggio 'l meglio et al peggior m'appiglio" (136 [I see the better but I lay hold on the worse]). Clarity of sight is love's utterly ineffectual opponent.

That sharpened focus on sight is Petrarch's contribution to his Ovidian source: "uideo meliora proboque, / deteriora sequor" (*Metamorphoses* 7.20-21 [I see and approve the better, I follow the worse]). The darkly Pauline resonance of the Latin lines did not escape notice (Pontanus 247); they braid with Petrarch's adaptation to form a recurring topic in Renaissance erotic literature.[14] Boiardo's Orlando, on the verge of the most expansive errancy in Renaissance narrative, quotes the Italian version almost verbatim (*Orlando innamorato* 1.1.31.8); Cariteo (*Endimione*, sonnet 35.13), Garcilaso (sonnet 6.7), and Michelangelo (*Rime* 135.10-12) among others adapt it into their lyrics. It is part of the distinction of Shakespeare's sequence to enact Petrarch's *sententia* more fully than any intervening practitioner; love's capacity to see what it wants to see is not, finally, a gift, but an addiction whose toxins cumulate:

> My love is as a feaver longing still,
> For that which longer nurseth the disease,
> Feeding on that which doth preserve the ill,
> Th'uncertaine sicklie appetite to please:
> My reason the Phisition to my love,
> Angry that his prescriptions are not kept
> Hath left me, and I desperate now approove,
> Desire is death, which Phisick did except. (147.1-8)

Not the beginning of the story nor an observation along the way, this is an awareness towards which the whole sequence moves as to a sinner's damnation. Even Petrarch forecasts a happier ending; the terror in 264 is answered by a turning from Laura in the last poems of the *Canzoniere* and a final prayer to the Virgin Mary. The only comparable moment in Shakespeare's sequence is 146 ("Poure soule the center of my sinfull earth"), but that poem is neither a last word nor really addressed to the poet's most acute anguish, the discovery that disillusion is not a cure: "All this the world well knowes yet none knowes well, / To shun the heaven that leads men to this hell" (129.13-14). The sequence ends with no clear sense of where we go from here.

NOTES

1. References to the Sonnets are from the original-spelling edition of Shakespeare's complete works, edited by Wells and Taylor. Translations from Petrarch's sequence are Durling's, with occasional modifications. Unattributed translations are mine.

2. The standard canvass is still Lee's (177-95); the most vigorous subsequent attempt is Wilson's. In view of the unpopularity of the topic, it is possible, indeed likely, that scholarship is missing things.

3. Sonnet 1.9 in Constable, sig.B5ʳ. The linkage has been recently contested by Lengeler.

4. The best recent contributions are Ferry's analysis of Shakespeare's dealings with *Astrophil and Stella* (170-214, 251-55) and Pearlman's discussion of Shakespeare and Watson. Kennedy's two articles give a fresh sense of the density of the material at hand: not only Petrarchan poems from Petrarch to Shakespeare, but also the voluminous commentaries on Petrarch that inevitably influenced poetic practice. Scrutinizing these texts, however, yields little confidence about specific points of contact, and the conclusions Kennedy does draw are often rarefied and elusive.

5. These excuses are also central to Dubrow's less systematic but in some ways more satisfying reading of Shakespeare's sequence (*Captive Victors* 206-13); she eventually diagnoses them as "passive-aggressive behavior" (253).

6. That specialized sense is captured in Fineman's most memorably aggressive moment: "heterosexual, and therefore misogynous" (188). The connection is reaffirmed in a concluding summary: "After Shakespeare, all poetry, if it is to be called poetry, will be a poetry . . . of misogynistic heterosexuality not idealizing homosexuality" (296).

7. The key classical text for the *carpe florem* topic—"collige, uirgo, rosas" (49 [gather roses, virgin]) from the pseudo-Vergilian "De rosis nascentibus"— is, I think, at work in Petrarch's sequence, but its terms have been rearranged into something more contemplative:

> Se mai candide rose con vermiglie
> in vasel d'oro vider gli occhi miei
> allor allor da vergine man colte,
> veder pensaro il viso di colei
> ch' avanza tutte l'altre meraviglie
> con tre belle eccellenzie in lui raccolte. (127.71-76)

[If my eyes ever saw white with crimson roses in a vase of gold, just then gathered by virgin hands, they thought they saw the face of her who excels all other wonders with the three excellences gathered in her.]

8. See Cresci. First published in 1585, his essay is reprinted at least a dozen times in the next half century. Unlike some polemicists, he maintains that the

obvious truth that he is pointing out is no stain on Petrarch's reputation but simply an *affetto naturale* (sig. b7^r).

9. For instance, in Marguerite de Navarre's *Heptameron*: "because of ignorance and some sort of stupid timidity there are men who miss many a good opportunity in love. Then they attribute their failures to their lady's virtue, even though they never get anywhere near testing it" (119).

10. My reasons for maintaining this relatively conventional position should be clear from the rest of this essay, but a few more things may be said here. Fear that the young man sequence records an active homosexual affair has long been a factor in commentary (Rollins 2: 232-39); recently the fear has become a boast, worked out in its fullest form by Pequigney. His most telling arguments concern the temporizing of earlier critics and the feebleness of attempts to sanitize the young man poems of sexual feeling; his positive case, however, is based almost wholly on the possibility of previously unrecognized puns in the text. Critics have long enjoyed themselves, here and elsewhere, finding such references to heterosexual activity, and there is no reason that the range of that pleasure should not grow; but doing so does not in itself generate the kind of evidence we need to be even moderately sure we are cracking a code rather than just finding what we are looking for. I see no reason not to call the emotions on display in the young man poems "homosexual" in a fairly simple sense of the term, or to deny that they manifest at least as much sexual longing as Petrarch's poems on Laura; but I also think that in conceding, as he does in connection with sonnet 20, "Sonneteers are . . . notoriously capable of sustaining themselves in a worshipful state of ungratified desire" (41), Pequigney is conceding more than he realizes.

11. Roche assimilates Shakespeare's sequence to Petrarch's as an Augustinian critique of cupidinous desire, but Petrarch's name and poetry largely disappear from the Shakespearean part of his discussion (380-461). Dubrow has revisited the topic to affirm that "these sonnets are deeply engaged with their primary tradition and source: they are at once intensely Petrarchan and insistently anti-Petrarchan" (*Echoes of Desire* 121). The elements that she tracks as "Petrarchan," however, tend to the abstract ("the problematics of agency," etc.) and the resulting formulations are not very telling: "the sonnets of Petrarch and Shakespeare share an obsessive fear of impending harm and a slippage between success and failure" (129). The most important discussion to insist on the largely Petrarchan character of Shakespeare's Sonnets remains Wolff's; it is still useful for its review of the specific features of continental Petrarchism that show up in Shakespeare's sequence—including a number of precedents for "der männliche Empfänger" (172-77).

12. Against the poem's popularity at wedding ceremonies may be set its role in Alfred Hitchcock's *The Trouble with Harry* (1955), where it is recited, to no one in particular, by the myopic, tweedy rural doctor who spends most of the movie wandering around the landscape with his head in a book, oblivious even to the corpse over which he twice trips. He is also fond of Marvell's "The Garden," a poem even more openly about the erotic joys of solitude, but Shakespeare's sonnet he knows by heart.

13. Fineman concedes at several points that, "for all its novelty," the disjunction between praise and object in Shakespeare "is something both the conventional Renaissance sonnet and, speaking broadly, conventional literature anticipate in very specific ways" (89), though it is a concession without much detail or conviction. Fineman specifically cites Petrarch, but asserts the anticipation "remains in [the *Canzoniere*] something that is insinuated and latent. It is only in the *Secretum* . . . that Petrarch gives explicit voice to a set of suspicions that are powerfully but, again, only tacitly suggested by the verse" (122). The key elements of the moral self-arraignment in the *Secretum* are present and memorably dramatized in *Canzoniere* 264; the subtlety of Fineman's distinction obscures his haste with the material.

14. In addition to the examples to follow, see the collection assembled around Garcilaso's poem by his imitator and annotator Fernando de Herrera (Garcilaso 326-27). In a rewriting of Petrarch's *Canzoniere* as a virtuous sequence of replies to Petrarch, Laura formulates the normative version: "Che'l peggior lascio, & al meglior m'appiglio" (Colonna sig. N5ᵛ [I relinquish the worse, and lay hold on the better]). When Adam in *Paradise Lost* feels challenged to defend the rectitude of his uxoriousness, he assures Raphael that "[I] Approve the best, and follow what I approve" (8.611).

WORKS CITED

Accademia della Crusca. *Concordanze del Canzoniere de Francesco Petrarca.* 2 vols. Florence: Accademia della Crusca, 1971.

Boiardo, Matteo Maria. *Opere.* Ed. Ferruccio Ulivi. I Classici Italiani. Milan: Mursia, 1986.

Cariteo. *Le rime di Benedetto Gareth detto il Chariteo.* Ed. Erasmo Pèrcopo. 2 vols. Naples: Biblioteca Napoletana di Storia e Letteratura, 1892.

Catullus. *C. Valerii Catulli Carmina.* Ed. R. A. B. Mynors. Oxford Classical Texts. Oxford: Clarendon, 1958.

Colonna, Stefano. *I sonetti, le canzoni, et i triomphi de M. Laura in risposta di M. Francesco Petrarcha.* Venice, 1552.

Constable, Henry. *Diana.* London, 1594. Fac. rpt. Menston: Scolar, 1973.

Cresci, Pietro. "Discorso sopra la qualità dell'amore del Petrarca." *Il Petrarca*. Venice: Giorgio Angelieri, 1585. Sigs. b6^v-12^r.

Cruttwell, Patrick. *The Shakespearean Moment and Its Place in the Poetry of the 17th Century*. New York: Columbia UP, 1970.

Dubrow, Heather. *Captive Victors: Shakespeare's Narrative Poems and Sonnets*. Ithaca: Cornell UP, 1987.

————. *Echoes of Desire: English Petrarchism and Its Counterdiscourses*. Ithaca: Cornell UP, 1995.

Ferry, Anne. *The "Inward" Language: Sonnets of Wyatt, Sidney, Shakespeare, Donne*. Chicago: U of Chicago P, 1983.

Fineman, Joel. *Shakespeare's Perjured Eye: The Invention of Poetic Subjectivity in the Sonnets*. Berkeley: U of California P, 1986.

Garcilaso. *Garcilaso de la Vega y sus comentaristas*. Ed. Antonio Gallego Morell. 2nd ed. Madrid: Gredos, 1972.

Kennedy, William J. "Commentary into Narrative: Shakespeare's Sonnets and Vellutello's Commentary on Petrarch." *Allegorica* 10 (1989): 119-33.

————. "'Sweet Theefe': Shakespeare Reading Petrarch." *Annals of Scholarship* 6 (1989): 75-91.

Lee, Sidney. *A Life of William Shakespeare*. Rev. ed. New York: Macmillan, 1916.

Leishman, J. B. *Themes and Variations in Shakespeare's Sonnets*. 2nd ed. London: Hutchinson University Library, 1963.

Lengeler, Rainer. "Shakespeares *Sonett 99*. Text und Kontexte." *Shakespeares Sonette in europäischen Perspektiven*. Ed. Dieter Mehl and Wolfgang Weiss. Studien zur Englischen Literatur. Munster: Lit, 1993. 129-49.

Marguerite de Navarre. *Heptameron*. Trans. P. A. Chilton. Harmondsworth: Penguin, 1984.

Michelangelo (Michelangiolo) Buonarroti. *Rime*. Ed. Enzo Noè Girardi. Scrittori d'Italia. Bari: Laterza, 1960.

Milton, John. *The Complete Poetry*. Ed. John T. Shawcross. Rev. ed. Garden City, NY: Anchor, 1971.

Ovid. *P. Ouidii Nasonis Metamorphoses*. Ed. William S. Anderson. Bibliotheca Scriptorum Graecorum et Romanorum Teubneriana. Leipzig: Teubner, 1985.

Pearlman, E. "Watson's *Hekatompathia* [1582] in the *Sonnets* and *Romeo and Juliet*." *English Studies* 74 (1993): 343-51.

Pequigney, Joseph. *Such Is My Love: A Study of Shakespeare's Sonnets*. Chicago: U of Chicago P, 1985.

Petrarch (Francesco Petrarca). *Petrarch's Lyric Poems*. Ed. and trans. Robert M. Durling. Cambridge: Harvard UP, 1976.

Pontanus, Jacobus, ed. *Ex P. Ouidii Nasonis Metamorphoseωn libris xv. electorum libri totidem, ultimo integro.* Antwerp, 1618. Fac. rpt. New York: Garland, 1976.

Roche, Thomas P., Jr. *Petrarch and the English Sonnet Sequences.* New York: AMS, 1989.

Rollins, Hyder Edward, ed. *A New Variorum Edition of Shakespeare: The Sonnets.* 2 vols. Philadelphia: Lippincott, 1944.

Ronsard, Pierre de. *Les Amours.* Ed. Henri Weber and Catherine Weber. Classiques Garnier. Rev. ed. Paris: Garnier, 1993.

Shakespeare, William. *The Complete Works: Original-Spelling Edition.* Gen. eds. Stanley Wells and Gary Taylor. Oxford: Clarendon, 1986.

Stampa, Gaspara, and Veronica Franco. *Rime.* Ed. Abdelkader Salza. Scrittori d'Italia. Bari: Laterza, 1913.

Surrey, Henry Howard, Earl of. *Poems.* Ed. Emrys Jones. Oxford: Clarendon, 1964.

Vergil [supposed author]. *Appendix Vergiliana.* Ed. W. V. Clausen et al. Oxford Classical Texts. Oxford: Clarendon, 1966.

Wilson, Katharine M. *Shakespeare's Sugared Sonnets.* New York: Barnes and Noble, 1974.

Wolff, Max J. "Petrarkismus und Antipetrarkismus in Shakespeares Sonetten." *EnglischeStudien* 49 (1916): 161-89.

"I am that I am"
Shakespeare's Sonnets and the Economy of Shame

Lars Engle

Shame, a strongly social affect, has a major role in education. In the education of children, perhaps even more than today, shame was an element in Renaissance pedagogy, especially moral pedagogy. Erasmus, in "On the Education of Children," comments that "Shame is fear of just criticism and praise is the foster-mother of all accomplishments; these must be our instruments for bringing out our children's natural abilities" (332).[1] Shakespeare's Erasmian procreation sonnets to some degree mobilize shame in this way.[2] But later sonnets in the young man sequence focus on shame as an educative element in a more reflective adult context. Their treatment of shame prefigures the reflective moral approach to shame taken by Bernard Williams and Richard Wollheim in philosophic texts I discuss below. Shame in the Sonnets is often insistently referred from general social occasions to the particular relationship: "You are my all the world, and I must strive / To know my shames and praises from your tongue," Shakespeare comments in sonnet 112.[3] So while shame is an interesting disembodied agent in the disciplinary process by which early modern subjects were formed, it is also, I will suggest, a component of the reflective adult self-consciousness, the moral-psychological complexity, for which the Sonnets are justly famous.

Shame is strongly social. The notion that it is in some sense primitively or naively social, a denial of this reflective interior complexity, has recently been disputed by Bernard Williams in a discussion of classical tragedy and epic in *Shame and Necessity*.

Having argued effectively that Greek *aidos* includes a number of
aspects (mostly intentional or reflective ones) of modern "guilt" as well
as "shame," Williams then turns to the question of what our own
possession of the two apparently distinct terms might mean. He
comments:

> we run into a problem . . . of distinguishing what we think from what
> we think that we think. One thing that a marked contrast between
> shame and guilt may express is the idea that it is important to
> distinguish between "moral" and "nonmoral" qualities. Shame itself
> is neutral on that distinction: we, like the Greeks, can be as mortified
> or disgraced by a failure in prowess or cunning as by a failure of
> generosity or loyalty. Guilt, on the other hand, is closely related to
> the conceptions of morality, and to insist on its particular importance
> is to insist on those conceptions. It is said that we make a lot of the
> distinction between the moral and the nonmoral and emphasize the
> importance of the moral. But how far, and in what ways, is this really
> true of our life, as opposed to what moralists say about our life? (91-
> 92)

This essay asserts that Shakespeare interrogates guilt and shame in the
Sonnets (as elsewhere) partly by casting doubt on the existence of a
strong distinction between "moral" and "nonmoral" realms, and that in
so doing he asserts the ubiquity of a social economy in which there are
no immutable or otherwise special values (of the kind philosophers
have sometimes supposed moral values to be), in which moral luck is a
large factor, and from which there is no exit. This is a position I have
argued at length elsewhere, focusing in particular on the treatment of
eternity in the Sonnets as social endurance rather than transcendence, as
value in the *longue durée* rather than an exit from the market-like
mechanisms of human evaluation I see as central in Shakespeare's
writing about most issues.[4] A social economy, as I present it here, is
simply a field of competing interests in negotiation that needs to be
understood by participants if they are to thrive or survive in it. They
thus have a strong incentive to map it as reliably as they can.
Nonetheless, they are mapping something that does not admit of
permanent description and that by its nature does not have a nature, but
rather a set of mutable conventions, nor does it have a fixed structure,
only habits and patterns which can be more or less deep and difficult to

alter. Markets and theaters are, for Shakespeare, the most prominent local instances of such economies.

Before I describe economies of shame and guilt in the Sonnets, let me briefly illustrate this general economic view of the Sonnets by reference to the one sonnet which most clearly invokes a Christian moral psychology, sonnet 146. By virtue of its concern with the soul, this sonnet might be thought to offer a direct challenge to my antifoundational way of talking, just the kind of challenge, in fact, that contemporary secular criticism is most disposed to sweep under the rug.

> Poor soul, the center of my sinful earth
> . . . these rebel pow'rs that thee array,
> Why dost thou pine within and suffer dearth,
> Painting thy outward walls so costly gay?
> Why so large cost, having so short a lease,
> Dost thou upon thy fading mansion spend?
> Shall worms, inheritors of this excess,
> Eat up thy charge? Is this thy body's end?
> Then, soul, live thou upon thy servant's loss,
> And let that pine to aggravate thy store:
> Buy terms divine in selling hours of dross;
> Within be fed, without be rich no more.
>> So shalt thou feed on death, that feeds on men,
>> And death once dead, there's no more dying then.

Far from suggesting that there is a morality separate from prudence, this sonnet applies prudence of an economic kind to the situation of the soul at the prospect of death. Though the soul of the speaker is, as we shall shortly see, only one of a number of agents invoked in the Sonnets as occupants of the speaker's interior space (and not one that receives much attention elsewhere), it is here treated as a proprietor invited to enter into a thriftier set of long-term transactions that will allow it to take full advantage of its special excellence (capacity to survive death). This comment may sound flippant or trivializing, but it is not intended to be, nor to make the sonnet sound that way. One of the problems with an emphasis on the economic layers of meaning in Shakespeare is that the intellectual traditions we still inhabit are on the whole anti-economic and see economic explanations as sticking to shifting shallows rather than mining for deep certainties. The traditions also suggest that *if* there exists a transcendent realm of certainties, it is the reflective duty of human beings to seek it out. Such traditions were alive in the Renaissance, though a number of Renaissance writers bracket them in order to focus productively on this-worldly motives, Machiavelli perhaps most conspicuously. Shakespeare does not often make as much of our putative access to such a transcendent realm as he is making here in 146. Yet even here there is no talk of duty: rather of advantage. The soul is given advice about how to position itself to take competitive advantage of its placement in a long-term struggle with the body or with worldly desires; the self does not commit to the soul, it advises it. "Buy terms divine by selling hours of dross" hardly transcends an economic frame.[5] Stephen Booth has a long monitory note effectively pointing out how many possible reactions we have to forego in order to make this sonnet into *only* an endorsement of Christian moral psychology or *only* a possibly ironic contextualization of it in market terms (507-17). Obviously I am not heeding his admonitions entirely, but neither am I trying to argue away the sonnet's attractive description of the soul's survival of death. You'll have your day—indeed, your eternity—it suggests, and proposes a winning strategy in a set of transactions recommended not only by the fact of mortality but also by the stage of life of this particular body ("why so large cost, having so short a lease / Dost thou upon thy *fading* mansion spend?").

Guilt may be otherworldly or this-worldly in orientation—and is perhaps usually both in a Christian culture. Shame, on the other hand, is distinctively this-worldly. I will, predictably, be suggesting that Shakespeare sets shame in an economic context and that one of the distinctive features of shame in the Sonnets is its negotiability, its availability for redescription in transactions with other people or one's moral environment. Following the quotation from Bernard Williams I began with, I will suggest that Shakespearean guilt cannot be distinguished sharply from Shakespearean shame except insofar as guilt is more internal or covert, shame more external or public. Indeed, in his works generally the word "shame" and its relatives outnumber the word "guilt" and its relatives by 433 to 156 (Spevack 522, 1119-21). The distinction Shakespeare makes between them in the Sonnets is nicely encapsulated in sonnet 36: "I may not evermore acknowledge thee, / Lest my bewailèd guilt should do thee shame." Here the speaker's guilt is something internal that needs to be "bewailèd," brought into the social realm, in order to become a cause of shame to his beloved.

"Guilt" tends to be connected with secrecy and interiority; "shame" with public reactions. But guilt also seeks to expose itself. "So full of artless jealousy is guilt / It spills itself in fearing to be spilt," (4.5.19-20) as Gertrude says in *Hamlet*; Hamlet plans in the play within the play to contrive an appearance to test Claudius, so that, as he says, "if his occulted guilt / Do not itself unkennel in one speech" (3.2.79-80),[6] Hamlet will think him innocent. Of course *Hamlet* is of all the plays the one most preoccupied with secret interiority; but guilt retains this sense both of deep inherency and of outward pressure elsewhere even when just this sense is being denied, as when Lady Macbeth declares that Duncan's drunken guards "shall bear the guilt / Of our great quell" (1.7.72-73) and then gilds them with blood, "for it must seem their guilt" (2.2.61). This superficial notion of guilt's exchangeability is reproved by later consequences in the play—"Out, damn'd spot!" (5.1.33).

It would, however, be a superficial notion of shame that insisted that it is entirely, or even primarily, external, social, and heteronomous. Williams corrects this notion—which he connects with bad progressivist ideas about our moral superiority to the Greeks (that is, the notion that we have achieved a state of moral reflection or moral autonomy they lacked)—with some care in *Shame and Necessity*. The major difference, he suggests, is between the eye and the ear: shame is connected with being seen by a real or potential public when one is in a position of weakness or exposure; guilt with an internal voice that pronounces on what one has done or desired. Shame is thus connected with visible public evaluation; guilt is not. But this raises a question. If the superego is, as psychoanalysis suggests, the introjected voice of parents or other strong early authorities, can there be an internalized eye of shame along roughly the same lines? (Note that the Freudian account of the superego here is what I am calling a map of an economy: something between a description and a myth, which has utility in guiding us but is not really distinct in kind from the phenomena it attempts to describe.)

Richard Wollheim suggests that there can be an internalized eye of shame; indeed, he makes this the basis of his belief that we can develop morally beyond the renunciation of instinctual satisfaction out of mere fear that the superego enforces. Noting that Freud speaks of this internal agent of morality as both the superego and the ego-ideal, he suggests that it may be possible to develop a relation to the ego-ideal in which it is no longer merely a threatening voice:

My suggestion, then, is that the development of, or development beyond, the superego is best understood in this way: that the internal figure, or the group of internal figures, whose phantasised activities regulate the thoughts, feelings, and conduct of the person start off life as merely internalized figures—they 'confront' the ego—but, gradually, or at some rate depending on the circumstances, they come to be figures with whom the person is able to identify. . . . We then have a way of describing the evolution of the moral sense as the growth of the superego into the ego-ideal. A preoccupation with what a person should do gets overlaid by a concern about how he should be. . . . [This] suggests a further development in the moral sentiments. And that is that the sentiment of guilt is now supplemented by a new sentiment, which specifically relates not to actions and how far they fall short of the person's internal prescriptions, but to the condition of the person himself and how far it meets or disappoints the ego-ideal. This sentiment might then be thought of as shame. Perhaps we can come to think of shame as standing to the ego-ideal in the same way that guilt does to the superego. (218-20)

Wollheim goes on to say that if shame is to be thought of in this way, "it must be conceived to be just as much an interiorized sentiment as guilt is" (220). This may seem to contradict my own initial comment that shame is strongly social, but I don't think it really does: Wollheim is, after all, suggesting that moral development of a desirable kind occurs as we put ourselves into a social relation with an ego-ideal, recognizing its strength and our own ambivalence toward its strength, and thus making ourselves capable of shame with respect to it. Shame in this view is recognizing one's low value in the gaze of another, in this case an internal other: as Wollheim puts it, "the essence of shame . . . lies in the look, in the disparaging or reproving regard, whereas the essence of guilt lies in the voice, in the spoken command or rebuke" (220).

Before moving from this to the internalized gaze of the other that is such a feature of the male-male relation in the Sonnets, it is worth pausing over this distinction between the look as the prime mover of shame and the voice as the prime mover of guilt. One interesting feature of this distinction is the way it might seem to play into a programmatic contrast between an idealized poetics of the eye and a reflexive de-idealized poetics of the ear (and tongue and pen)—thus making the idea that we have passed from a shame to a guilt culture parallel, at least structurally, to Joel Fineman's argument that the Sonnets enact a shift from a Petrarchan to a more modern reflexive poetics (88). Of course, I have just been citing Wollheim and Williams *against* this idea about guilt and shame; in fact, both Wollheim and Williams want to insist that there is nothing primitive, inflexible, or unable to capture human interiority about shame; Wollheim in fact wants to play this contrast the other way, and to treat it as an appropriate result of maturation or moral growth to come to a shame relation to the ego-ideal from the prior and more paralyzing guilt relation to the superego. Obviously one thing this shows is that Wollheim's Freudianism is less influenced by Lacan than Fineman's is, but it also shows, I think, the danger of assuming that one can count on all eye/ear binaries to function in parallel with binaries of presence/absence. Those like Wollheim and Williams who wish to see shame as not only more pervasive than guilt, but also sometimes indistinguishable from and in no sense primitive in comparison to guilt, emphasize that the gaze of the community, or of privileged members of it, can be in communication with the internal gazer more fully than the mechanisms of guilt will easily allow. In order for this to happen, shame cannot be only a matter of presence; it must incorporate deferral and reflection. Shame presupposes a social community of mutual regard, rather than a voice of law that addresses persons in isolation, and it presupposes a society of people who wish to be able to look one another in the face and who feel pain when they cannot do so. This suggests that shame is a negative affect more amenable to conversion, development, and exchange than is guilt. Thus Williams on his response to having done something bad:

> *What I have done* points in one direction towards what has happened to others, in another direction to what I am.
>
> Guilt looks primarily in the first direction. . .[i.e., toward the injured victim].
>
> Shame looks to what I am. It can be occasioned by many things—actions . . . or thoughts or desires or the reactions of others. Even where it is certainly concerned with an action, it may be a matter of discovery to the agent, and a difficult discovery, what the source of the shame is, whether it is to be found in the intention, the action, or an outcome. . . . Just because shame can be obscure in this kind of way, we can fruitfully work to make it more perspicuous, and to understand how a certain action or thought stands to ourselves, to

what we are and to what realistically we can want ourselves to be. If
we come to understand our shame, we may also better understand our
guilt. The structures of shame contain the possibility of controlling
and learning from guilt, because they give a conception of one's
ethical identity, in relation to which guilt can make sense. Shame can
understand guilt, but guilt cannot understand itself. (92-93; emphasis
as in original)

While shame in the Sonnets sometimes takes the form of
embarrassment before an audience, it far more frequently focuses on
the external or internal presence of the beloved as the gazer who causes
shame. Indeed, this is why I have quoted Wollheim, who postulates an
ego-ideal in terms close to those with which the speaker of the Sonnets
installs the male beloved in his mind. Thus sonnet 61:

> Is it thy will thy image should keep open
> My heavy eyelids to the weary night?
> Dost thou desire my slumbers should be broken,
> While shadows like to thee do mock my sight?
> Is it thy spirit that thou send'st from thee
> So far from home into my deeds to pry,
> To find out shames and idle hours in me,
> The scope and tenor of thy jealousy?
> O no, thy love, though much, is not so great.
> It is my love that keeps mine eye awake,
> Mine own true love that doth my rest defeat,
> To play the watchman ever for thy sake.
>> For thee watch I, whilst thou dost wake elsewhére,
>> From me far off, with others all too near.

This is a complex sonnet, and as often in the sequence, the speaker's
description of his interior life as reshaped by the beloved conveys some
reproach by declaring an asymmetrical dependence. What I want to
take from it, however, is the way the friend's "image" has joined with
the speaker's "love"; the two combine as a vigilant, beautiful interior
gazer who "find[s] out shames and idle hours" in the speaker. So in the
brilliant couplet, the speaker "watches for" the beloved in two senses:
both as someone who is staying awake thinking about, and someone
who is substituting for—policing his own behavior on behalf of—the
beloved, awake elsewhere but not similarly self-policing.

Writing of the "bonding, interactive, effects of shame" and the character of "the internalized other," Bernard Williams comments that "it is a mistake . . . to suppose that there are only two options: that the other in ethical thought must be an identifiable individual or a representative of the neighbours, on the one hand, or else be nothing at all except an echo chamber for my solitary moral voice. Those alternatives leave out much of the substance of actual ethical life" (83-84).

What Shakespeare does in the many sonnets which analyze the beloved as "internalized other"—or, like sonnet 146, trace the consequences of separating out other kinds of internal agents—is to explore the way "the substance of ethical life" attaches itself to the particular internal agents available. So in sonnet 88, a document in passive-aggressive abjection, the beloved, here both an external agent and the internalized other, is abetted in shaming the speaker:

> When thou shalt be disposed to set me light,
> And place my merit in the eye of scorn,
> Upon thy side against myself I'll fight,
> And prove thee virtuous, though thou art forsworn.
> With mine own weakness being best acquainted,
> Upon thy part I can set down a story
> Of faults concealed, wherein I am attainted,
> That thou in losing me shall win much glory.
> And I by this will be a gainer too,
> For bending all my loving thoughts on thee,
> The injuries that to myself I do,
> Doing thee vantage, double vantage me.
>   Such is my love—to thee I so belong—
>   That for thy right myself will bear all wrong.

The aggressive content comes from the ethical burden it sets on the beloved, and the complex register of a differential in power to hurt suggested by the bland offer of self-sacrifice; justifying his own shame (by producing a narrative of guilt, "a story / Of faults concealed") in order to save the beloved from the shame that should accrue to being "forsworn." But one could also construe this as a sonnet of resistance, one that brings to light a shameful dynamic, or bad economy. Roughly the same bad economic relation is highlighted in sonnet 57, which begins "Being your slave, what should I do but tend / Upon the hours and times of your desire?" In this sense the exploration of shame serves to bring structures of value under scrutiny, and may, as Williams suggests, promote understanding or change. I believe, in fact, that we may see the fruits of such an exploration in the way sonnets 97-125 no longer dwell on a differential in power to hurt between lover and beloved, and more specifically in the way sonnets 117-120 use shame as a starting point for negotiation.

I close with a discussion of sonnet 121, which offers, in my opinion, a demystifying description of the economies of guilt and shame in the Sonnets, one that shows shame operating in the service of understanding. The sonnet suggests how both the subject and his society need the internalized others whose value confers on their gaze the power to shame.

> 'Tis better to be vile than vile esteemed,
> When not to be receives reproach of being,
> And the just pleasure lost, which is so deemed,
> Not by our feeling but by others' seeing.
> For why should others' false adulterate eyes
> Give salutation to my sportive blood?
> Or on my frailties why are frailer spies,
> Which in their wills count bad what I think good?
> No, I am that I am, and they that level
> At my abuses reckon up their own;
> I may be straight though they themselves be bevel.
> By their rank thoughts my deeds must not be shown,
>   Unless this general evil they maintain—
>   All men are bad and in their badness reign. (121)

Williams writes of shame that it

> need not be just a matter of being seen, but of being seen by an observer with a certain view. Indeed, the view taken by an observer need not itself be critical: people can be ashamed of being admired by the wrong audience in the wrong way. Equally, they need not be ashamed of being poorly viewed, if the view is that of an observer for whom they feel contempt. (82)

Sonnet 121 reasons ethically in the direction of Williams's second comment; it also holds up for inspection, as it were, the problem of what can sustain even quite limited ethical autonomy—the autonomy involved in valuing one's own pleasure—in a thoroughly economic conception of social interaction. The value of an action or habit to the agent lies between an audience of internalized others and an external audience of other people. The external audience—the interpretive community—may err, or may be systematically perverse from the view of the agent (may stigmatize his or her favorite acts or desires, for instance). The internal audience may, in ways suggested above, be partial or punitive as well. By understanding and repudiating some of the standard mechanisms of shame—the gaze of recognition, for instance—the speaker tries to clear evaluative space for himself: "I am that I am." We have seen above how such a recourse to "what I am"— the achievement of an ambivalent, ethically productive, shame relation to an ego-ideal—is the profit to be found in the economy of shame.

Sonnet 121 closes by extending this idea, though in a complex way. The last three lines express a conditional imperative: "By their rank thoughts my deeds must not be shown, / Unless this general evil they maintain— / All men are bad and in their badness reign." There is a difference, of course, between knowing in oneself that outsiders cannot understand or properly value one's actions—the sort of knowledge expressed by saying "I am that I am"—and stating that one's actions must not be "shown"—made public, seen, held up for evaluation—in the rank thoughts of others. The only way the second statement can seem anything but a denial of the nature of showing is if the sonnet itself hopes to have had an impact on how others think. Part of that impact should derive from the powerful positive example the sonnet provides: its speaker survives shame and learns from shame through reference to an ego-ideal. But the couplet has further impact by providing a dismaying alternative community, one which would not be moved by the rest of the sonnet because its members lack the internalized gaze of a shaming authority and thus lack shame. Such a community would be one in which "All men are bad, and in their badness reign"; in it the strategies by which one can gain self-understanding through shame would be useless. This alternative community is a version of the nightmare of no difference (suggested in the phrase "they that level"), and it highlights by contrast the way the economies of shame in the Sonnets depend on the existence of the socially admirable, even if only in the form of an internalized other toward which one can direct the kind of self-defense sonnet 121 exemplifies. Such an internalized other helps constitute the idiosyncratic, self-exploratory, resistant interiority Shakespeare here claims as a necessary resource not only for the just pleasure of persons but for the general social good.

To marry a radical metaphor from *Hamlet* to another from *Paradise Lost*, shame plants the mind's eye.[7]

NOTES

1. On Erasmus and other early modern authors of manuals of civility, see Revel, who quotes Erasmus on the shame associated with failures in civility (171). In Erasmus's "On Good Manners for Boys," we find the following: "To expose, save for natural reasons, the parts of the body which nature has invested with modesty ought to be far removed from the conduct of a gentleman. I will go further: when necessity compels such action, it should none the less be done with decency and modesty even if there is no observer present. For the angels, from whom derives that most welcome sense of shame that accompanies and protects the chastity of boys, are always near" (277). So shame is an angelic gift, and we are under angelic gaze even when alone.

2. See sonnets 2, 9, and 10.

3. Sonnets are cited by number from Booth's edition.

4. Engle, chapter 2.

5. For a general argument along these lines which quotes sonnet 146 as an example, see Smith, 145.

6. Plays are quoted from Bevington's edition.

7. See *Hamlet* 1.1.116 ("A mote it is to trouble the mind's eye") and 1.2.185 ("In my mind's eye, Horatio"), and *Paradise Lost* 3: 51-53:

> So much the rather thou celestial Light
> Shine inward, and the mind through all her powers
> Irradiate, *there plant eyes*. . . . (emphasis added)

WORKS CITED

Engle, Lars. *Shakespearean Pragmatism: Market of His Time*. Chicago: U of Chicago P, 1993.

Erasmus. "On Education For Children." *Collected Works of Erasmus*. Trans. Beert C. Vertraete. Ed. J. K. Sowards. Vol. 26. Toronto: U of Toronto P, 1985. 295-346.

————. "On Good Manners for Boys." *Collected Works of Erasmus*. Trans. Brian McGregor. Ed. J. K. Sowards. Vol. 25. Toronto: U of Toronto P, 1985. 273-89.

Fineman, Joel. *Shakespeare's Perjured Eye: The Invention of Poetic Subjectivity in the Sonnets*. Berkeley: U of California P, 1986.

Milton, John. *The Poems of Milton*. Ed. Alastair Fowler and John Carey. London: Longman and W. W. Norton, 1968.

Revel, Jacques. "The Uses of Civility." *A History of Private Life III: Passions of the Renaissance*. Trans. Arthur Goldhammer. Ed. Roger Chartier. Cambridge: Harvard UP, 1989. 167-205.

The Complete Works of Shakespeare. Ed. David Bevington. 4th ed. New York: HarperCollins, 1992.

Shakespeare's Sonnets. Ed. Stephen Booth. New Haven: Yale UP, 1977.

Smith, Barbara Herrnstein. *Contingencies of Value: Alternative Perspectives for Critical Theory*. Cambridge: Harvard UP, 1988.

Spevack, Marvin. *The Harvard Concordance to Shakespeare*. Cambridge: Harvard UP, 1973.

Williams, Bernard. *Shame and Necessity*. Berkeley: U of California P, 1993.

Wollheim, Richard. "The Growth of the Moral Sense." *The Thread of Life*. Cambridge: Harvard UP, 1984. 197-225.

"A dateless lively heat"
Storing Loss in the Sonnets

Joyce Sutphen

At the end of Susan Sontag's short story, "The Way We Live Now," one of the characters says:

> I was thinking . . . that the difference between a story and a painting or photograph is that in a story you can write, He's still alive. But in a painting or a photo you can't show "still." You can just show him being alive. He's still alive, Stephen said. (1179)

And so he is, each time we read those words. Who "he" is, we do not know; his name is never mentioned, even though we learn the names of twenty-six of his friends—one for each letter of the alphabet. We are not told directly what disease he has, but we gather that the situation is quite hopeless. And yet, the words "He's still alive" are somehow affirming; the ending holds off the end, at least in black ink.

The same type of transcendent assertion appears in many of Shakespeare's Sonnets:

> Or I shall live your epitaph to make,
> Or you survive when I in earth am rotten,
> From hence your memory death cannot take,
> Although in me each part will be forgotten.
> Your name from hence immortal life shall have,
> Though I, once gone, to all the world must die.
> The earth can yield me but a common grave,

> When you entombed in men's eyes shall lie.
> Your monument shall be my gentle verse,
> Which eyes not yet created shall o'er-read,
> And tongues to be your being shall rehearse,
> When all the breathers of this world are dead,
>> You still shall live—such virtue hath my pen—
>> Where breath most breathes, ev'n in the mouths of men. (81)[1]

Reading out loud, we breathe breath into the words "You still shall live," even though we have no idea who "You" is or what exactly this person's relationship is to the poet. We do not know why the poet chose to construct such an intimation of immortality, or whether the construction is based on mere convention or sincere evocation.

One thing seems sure: the writer of the Sonnets is interested, in fact, obsessed with memory as a defense against loss. He is at war with time, as he explicitly says in sonnet 15: "And all in *war* with time for love of you, / As he takes from you, I engraft you new" (14-15; emphasis added) and implies in many others:

> Time doth transfix the flourish set on youth,
> And delves the parallels in beauty's brow,
> Feeds on the rarities of nature's truth,
> And nothing stands but for his scythe to mow.
>> And yet to times in hope my verse shall stand,
>> Praising thy worth, despite his cruel hand. (60.9-14)[2]

Time, the poet says, is continually destroying and defacing. Time's hand is "cruel" (60.14), "injurious" (63.2), and "fell"(64.1); among its implements are a "scythe and crooked knife" (100.14), one to mow down everything in sight, and the other to carve and delve the brow or face of beauty (60). Time is "never-resting" (5.5), "bloody" (16.2), and "Devouring" (19.1). Its destruction is fueled by "all-oblivious enmity," and its partner is death (81). But "despite [time's] cruel hand," the poet keeps reinscribing and remembering (analogous and mainly inseparable activities in Shakespeare's time). He composes "eternal lines" (18.12); asserts that his "love shall in [his] verse ever live young" (19.14); and says that his "pow'rful rhyme" shall be a "living record" (55.2, 8), that the beauty of his love "shall in these black lines be seen, / And they shall live, and he in them still green" (63.13-14), and that "in black ink [his] love may still shine bright" (65.14). He claims his pen can make his love "outlive a gilded tomb" (101.11), and proclaims that in spite of death, he himself will "live in this poor rhyme," where his love will also find a place more lasting than "crests and tombs" (107.11-14). He engages overtly in this combat with time, using an array of printing, inscribing, and sealing metaphors that appear intermittently (but once claimed, are always, to some degree, present) . . . *until* the last twenty-eight sonnets. Then something changes.

In fact, one could make a claim similar to one Stephen Booth makes about the sex of the beloved and say that all of the sonnets that are specifically and exclusively concerned with memorializing precede sonnet 126 in the Q order, and that after sonnet 126 the metaphors connected with memory are mostly absent. That is, memorial metaphors having to do with imprinting and inscribing (ones that Mary Carruthers refers to as the "seal-in-wax" family) almost completely disappear, while those having to do with keeping and holding (the "store-house" family) continue to be present, though there is a significant difference in the way they are used.[3]

Sonnet 126 is generally acknowledged to be the last of the poems to the "young man." As Stephen Booth says:

> Although the sex of the beloved is unspecified in most of the sonnets, all those that are specifically and exclusively addressed to a man precede this one in the Q order, and all those specifically and exclusively addressed to a woman follow it. In view of the poem's structural peculiarity, there is therefore some basis for the widespread critical belief that sonnet 126 is intended to mark a division between sonnets principally concerned with a male beloved and those principally concerned with a woman. (430)

Of course the word "principally" should be noted, as well as "some," which is connected with "basis," but certainly Booth notices a demarcation at 126. Indeed, most critics who see a narrative in the Sonnets agree there is a major break at 126.[4] Margreta de Grazia, in an essay reprinted in this volume, wondering whether the "division is best described in terms—or *only* in terms—of gender differences," finds a division runs between "hierachy and anarchy—or desired generation and abhorred miscegenation" (49). Joel Fineman distinguishes "the sub-sequence of sonnets addressed to the young man from the sub-sequence of sonnets addressed to the dark lady," asserting that one is "a poetry of praise and the other a poetry of praise paradox" (86), but rather than examining the ending that 126 makes, he explores the changes made in 127 (280). Lars Engle sees an "economic" difference between the young man and dark lady sonnets, in which "the sonnets to the young man enact an affluent or generative economy of human value, and the sonnets to the dark lady enact a depressed, and consequently an exposed and self-critical, economy of human value" (49-50). In another reading of human economy, Thomas Greene chooses sonnet 125 over what he calls its "somewhat slighter successor, 126," maintaining that "it [125] appears to offer a more substantial, dense, and conclusive instrument of retrospection" (75).[5] Greene is interested in seeing an "outcome of the 'plot' in sonnets 1-126," one that would fulfill the "quest for an adequate economic system which would avoid the 'wast or ruining' and the excessive 'rent' which burden those in 125 who vainly spend themselves" (76). He doesn't find one.

Other critics are less certain about divisions in the kingdom of the Sonnets: John Kerrigan speaks about the order and "plot" of the Sonnets, but he hesitates to declare that there are two "discrete" groups. The young man and dark lady groups, he concludes, "are best regarded as foils of each other, like divergent areas of action in a Shakespeare play. As in the drama, links between the diverse threads of 'story' are ultimately complex yet incidentally explicit" (57). In *Echoes of Desire*, Heather Dubrow questions the customary acceptance of "two distinct groups" of sonnets, especially as regards the addressees:

> Above all, the assertion that the first 126 poems consistently apply to the Friend and the next group to the Dark Lady is a classic illustration of circular reasoning: one chooses a few poems to establish the truism that the Friend is generally fair and the Dark Lady incessantly evil and then deploys that assumption to gender the addressee of other sonnets. (123)

But Dubrow doubts wisely, "not maintaining that the claim that Shakespeare's poems fall into two distinct groups with different addressees is *definitely* fallacious" (122; emphasis added). In the same spirit, she notes that "the stanzaic irregularities of Sonnet 126 do not irrefutably mark it as a turning point," since, as she points out, there are other irregularities in the poems (124).[6]

With growing certainty, however, Dubrow explores the incertainties of the traditional division of the sonnets: "In earlier work on these poems," she says, "I myself contended that critics impose a narrative and dramatic framework on a sequence that resists those modes, yet I implicitly accepted the conventional assumptions about addressees and the plot outlined above" ("Incertainties" 292; also reprinted in this volume).[7] Assumptions about division in the sequence, Dubrow continues, are often supported by the stanzaic peculiarities of sonnet 126, but as in earlier work she asserts that "it is tricky at best to assign thematic significance to the fact that sonnet 126 deviates from standard sonnet structure" (294).

The irregularities in sonnet 126 are, nonetheless, of a particularly interesting sort, especially in light of what Dubrow says in *Echoes of Desire* (and earlier in *Captive Victors*). The usual pattern within an individual Shakespearean sonnet, she says, is to narrate a "process of struggle—struggle between rival narrators, rival endings to the same story, and rival models for sonneteering . . . and the structural function of Shakespeare's couplets . . . often unsettles the very closure they seemingly establish" (*Echoes* 129).[8] Sonnet 126, however, has no "couplet," in the regular sense of the word; in fact, as T. W. Baldwin says, 126 "is not necessarily a sonnet, being twelve lines of heroic verse" (318), but the sonnet pattern is so strongly established in the collection that a twelve-line poem of *any* rhyme scheme is likely to seem incomplete. Despite the fact that we may have been spared an unsettling couplet, we feel unsettled by its absence; the last two lines, that place of unexpected resolution in many of the sonnets, is missing. There is, as John Kerrigan says, a "sense of poetic shortfall, as though the recoiling, inconclusive quality of earlier sonnet couplets . . . had been concentrated in a single poem, consisting entirely of such rhymed endings" (351).

Whatever its technical peculiarities, sonnet 126 does seem to establish a closure between time and the "lovely boy":

> O thou, my lovely boy, who in thy pow'r
> Dost hold time's fickle glass, his sickle hour,
> Who hast by waning grown, and therein show'st
> Thy lovers withering, as thy sweet self grow'st—
> If nature, sovereign mistress over wrack,
> As thou goest onwards still will pluck thee back,

> She keeps thee to this purpose, that her skill
> May time disgrace, and wretched minute kill.
> Yet hear her, O thou minion of her pleasure;
> She may detain but not still keep her treasure.
> Her audit, though delayed, answered must be,
> And her quietus is to render thee.

Every one of the couplets in this unsonnet-like sonnet expresses a paradox, and each of the paradoxes contains a vestige of warnings present in the first 125 sonnets, worn with a difference. Sonnet 126's "time's fickle glass," for example, brings to mind the first two lines of sonnet 3 ("Look in thy glass and tell the face thou viewest, / Now is the time that face should form another"); the second couplet of 126,

> Who hast by waning grown, and therein show'st
> Thy lovers withering, as thy sweet self grow'st— (3-4),

brings to mind the first two lines of sonnet 11,

> As fast as thou shalt wane so fast thou grow'st—
> In one of thine, from that which thou departest (1-2),

although in sonnet 11 the seeming paradox of growing through waning is explained through the principle of procreation, and the bottom line is inferred: everything that moves through time is declining.[9]

In sonnet 126, however, there is no logical explanation for the paradoxical continuance. The "lovely boy" simply seems to have been impervious to the ravages of time: "who in thy pow'r / Dost hold time's fickle glass, his sickle hour" (1-2). All of the warnings from the procreation sonnets,

> That thou among the wastes of time must go,
> Since sweets and beauties do themselves forsake,
> And die as fast as they see others grow,
> And nothing 'gainst time's scythe can make defence
> Save breed to brave him when he takes thee hence. (12.10-14)

are alluded to and undercut.

The next two couplets of 126:

> If nature, sovereign mistress over wrack,
> As thou goest onwards, still will pluck thee back,
> She keeps thee to this purpose, that her skill
> May time disgrace and wretched minutes kill. (5-8)

again "summon up remembrance of things past" (30.1), things once said on a similar subject:

> Let those whom nature hath not made for store,
> Harsh, featureless, and rude, barrenly perish.
> Look whom she best endowed, she gave the more;
> Which bounteous gift thou shouldst in bounty cherish.
> She carved thee for her seal, and meant thereby
> Thou shouldst print more, not let that copy die. (11.9-14)

In both sonnets 126 and 11, the person addressed is the acknowledged favorite of nature, though the relationship is expressed quite differently. In 11, because the person addressed is "best endowed," nature wants to "print more" and thereby through a progression or continuance beat time's ravages; in 126 nature herself "keeps" the person *and* the person's beauty, unnaturally so to speak, since as sonnet 4 claims:

> Nature's bequest gives nothing but doth lend,
> And being frank she lends to those are free.
> Then beauteous niggard why dost thou abuse
> The bounteous largess given thee to give?
> Profitless usurer, why dost thou use
> So great a sum of sums yet canst not live?
> For having traffic with thyself alone,
> Thou of thyself thy sweet self dost deceive.
> Then how when nature calls thee to be gone,
> What acceptable audit can'st thou leave? (3-12)

In sonnet 4, it is nature that "calls thee to be gone" and demands the "acceptable audit."[10] In sonnet 126, this is still true (the "lovely boy" *has* been kept "to this purpose, that her skill / May time disgrace, and wretched minutes kill"); even though the last two couplets indicate that the "audit" is nature's, it is ultimately called in by time:

> Yet fear her, O thou minion of her pleasure;
> She may detain but not still keep her treasure.
> Her audit, though delayed, answered must be,
> And her quietus is to render thee. (9-12)

The seeming "preservation" has only been temporary; stalling can only work for a while, and time's "cruel hand" is simply averted.

As indicated earlier, one of the main projects of sonnets 1-126 seems to have been to hold off that "cruel hand" through various forms of imprint. There is no sense, except in the procreation sonnets, that the person to whom these sonnets are addressed has, personally, any power against time. At first glance, generalizing about memory's project in the sonnets goes like this: after the poet gives up trying to convince the young man to make a physical copy of himself, he (the poet) spends the rest of the sonnets (17-125) more or less engaged in combat with time, first by making copy by means of poetry ("I engraft you new" [15.14]), and then, in the final stages of the memorial battle, by impressing a copy in the book of personal memory ("those tables that receive thee more" [122.12]).

Sonnets that demonstrate this last (and invisible) memorializing strategy include sonnet 122:

> Thy gift, thy tables, are within my brain
> Full charactered with lasting memory,
> Which shall above that idle rank remain
> Beyond all date ev'n to eternity—
> Or at the least, so long as brain and heart
> Have faculty by nature to subsist—
> Till each to razed oblivion yield his part
> Of thee, thy record never can be missed.
> That poor retention could not so much hold,
> Nor need I tallies thy dear love to score.
> Therefore to give them from me was I bold
> To trust those tables that receive thee more.
>   To keep an adjunct to remember thee
>   Were to import forgetfulness in me.

The opening of this sonnet involves a direct reference to the physiological model of memory as well as a (usually noted) reference to the kind of pocket "tables" that people kept to jot down things they wanted to remember.[11] There seems no reason to be certain that the "gift," the "tables," already "contained writings by the friend" (Kerrigan 43).[12] In fact, when one considers the various models for memory, the sonnet is not as problematic as Kerrigan implies. The poet argues that the internal tables of his memory are much more capacious and lasting than the "idle rank" and "poor retention" of external ones, which the poet did not so much lose as not use. The metaphor of memory operating as a surface to receive impressions was so pervasive that it would naturally present itself to the poet.

In that sense, the sonnet grows out of "lived experience," but not in a tightly anecdotal sense. Kerrigan's argument that because of "biography," "Shakespeare found himself tackling a theme [that memory is more lasting than writing] which he could not handle with assurance" is interesting regarding the relationship between poet and subject, but I think that his belief that the sonnet's argument is "counter to Shakespeare's instincts" is mistaken: first, it is based on the assumption that "for Shakespeare recollection was always sadly flawed" (42), an assumption that truncates the concept of memory in a characteristically modern way. Just because "Coriolanus cannot remember the name of the 'poor man' who in Corioli, 'used [him] kindly' and deserved reward (1.9.81)," and "Miranda cannot grapple, from the 'dark backward and abysm of time,' those childhood affairs which most concern her . . . (*Tempest* 1.2.50)" (42), does not at all mean that Shakespeare felt the physical faculty of memory was generally an unreliable one. In those particular instances, memory failed—why? If the reason is simply that memory is "always" flawed, there would be little point in portraying those instances. The other arguable assumption is that heart and brain *will* be wiped clean when the poet dies, or that admitting the possible mortality of the poet's memory "reduces the sonnet which contains it to an awkward, almost sophistical exercise" (43). Both of these points are, in any case, moot regarding the central assertion of the sonnet, which celebrates the making of a lasting personal copy, beyond the book, so to speak.

In sonnet 122, the poet does not "trust" anything but his own brain, does not want to have to be prompted, to rely on "adjuncts." Once it is clear that sonnet 122 is specifically about how this particular poet thinks it best to keep *for himself* what he wants to remember about the poem's addressee, once it is also apparent that the faculty of memory— the *internal* tables—wins out over adjunct means, it should be apparent that there is no contradiction when the poet expresses what is remembered in ink. "Tables" or notebooks are not the same as the poet's verse. He does not create verse to aid memory; verse gives voice to what is in the memory.

In sonnet 123 ("No! Time, thou shalt not boast that I do change"), the poet again opposes the appearance of past and present ("thy records, and what we see" [11]) in favor of a more preserved and constant memory, concluding:

> This I do vow, and this shall ever be,
> I *will be true* despite thy scythe and thee. (13-14; emphasis added)

To see the shift in the memorializing strategy, one has only to think of a sonnet such as 60, which ends: "And yet to times in hope *my verse* shall stand, / Praising thy worth, despite his cruel hand" (13-14; emphasis added).

Sonnet 124 carries on the celebration of the poet's interior keeping by hypothesizing what this preservation would be like if it were based on anything external. *Then* it would be

> As subject to time's love, or to time's hate,
> Weeds among weeds, or flow'rs with flowers gathered. (3-4),

but since it is not,

> It suffers not in smiling pomp, nor falls
> Under the blow of thralled discontent,
> Whereto th'inviting time our fashion calls.
> It fears not policy, that heretic
> Which works on leases of short numb'red hours,
> But all alone stands hugely politic,
> That it nor grows with heat, nor drowns with show'rs.
> To this I witness call the fools of time,
>   Which die for goodness, who have lived for crime. (6-14)

The "love" which the poet claims in sonnet 124, line 1 ("If my dear love were but the child of state") is in sonnet 116, line 9 "not time's fool," and it "alters not with his brief hours and weeks, / But bears it out ev'n to the edge of doom" (116.11-12).[13]

Sonnet 125 continues to express defiance for ever-crumbling outward "shows" and attempts to outlast time in "great bases for eternity / Which proves more short than waste or ruining" (3-4), but again ends with a declaration of triumph, with the proof, so to speak, in the poet. Whatever, whoever the "suborned informer" is—and I suspect time for a number of reasons, including overt connections among sonnets 123-125 in which time is answered for accusations (123.1), threats (123.13-14), general oppression (124.3), and corrupting influence (123.13-14)—these sonnets all end with assertions of "*I* will be true," and proclaim memory's (that is, the actual faculty of memory's) victory over time.

Although sonnets 123-125 are about keeping and preserving, they make no mention of preserving the looks or essence of the person addressed, nor is any assertion made for the memorializing power of poetry. The emphasis is on "mutual render" and ongoing love. These poems assert the constancy of the poet, "In whose confine immured is the store" (84.3), and who seems, at last, to be quite confident that what *he* keeps is out of time's reach. The place for keeping has progressed (regressed? digressed?) from progeny to poetry to poet (though of course the claim of the poet's possession is in the poem).

After sonnets of such increasing subtlety, sonnet 126 sets itself apart in the same way that Prospero's Epilogue stands out from its play, and in both instances the result is usually judged "inferior":

> There seems, indeed, some plausibility in the view . . . that 126 forms
> an Envoy to the poems addressed to the Friend. On the other hand,
> the style is not only greatly inferior to that of the immediately
> preceding sonnets but also no more than a pale reflection of that of
> sonnets 1-17, which it more closely resembles. If the poem be such
> an Envoy, it seems a somewhat deliberate attempt to recapture
> something of the spirit of the opening sonnets in the teeth of
> advancing age. (Ingram and Redpath 288)

As previously demonstrated, sonnet 126 *does* remind and re-enlist a number of the concepts of the poems that preceded it (especially 1-17, it is true), but rather than being a "pale reflection" or a poor "attempt to recapture something of the spirit of the opening sonnets," sonnet 126 can be read as a "state of the young man" address: the dire predictions have not come true, but all the warnings of sonnets 1-17 still hold true. As Stephen Booth suggests, the "sudden *quietus* after twelve lines is—

probably accidentally—an illustrative analogy that demonstrates the justice of the warning the poem offers" (430).

In the sonnets before 126, the poet's main concern is to keep back the hand of time, to store for posterity what is too precious to be lost. In sonnets 122-125, the poet concludes the memorial project by carrying away what he loves, literally inscribing it on his own being. Sonnet 126 then performs service as an envoy in two ways; it acts as a summary and conclusion for a group of poems that were concerned in one way or another with an "old age," in which preserving beauty mattered: "From fairest creatures we desire increase / That thereby beauty's rose might never die" (1.1-2); it sends (or dispatches) the reader into a new group of poems (a new age as opposed to the "old"), in which preserving beauty does not matter, since "beauty" itself is uncertain and "slandered with a bastard shame" (127.4).

Much as I agree with many of the points Heather Dubrow makes about imposed narrativity and debatable assumptions regarding addressees and plots in the Sonnets, I do think it hard to ignore the fact that the word "time," which occurs over seventy times in the first 126 sonnets, never appears again after sonnet 126—nor does "memory." Words connected with the memory motif—"book," "page," "pen," "paper," "pencil," "line," "verse," "copy," "stamp," and "print"—are also absent after 126. Despite Dubrow's cogent arguments against the certainty of the traditional division, there seems to be something more than natural in this pattern.

There also seems to be something worth noticing about the relationship between sonnets 1 and 127. Very rarely are these two sonnets compared, but both are decidedly about beauty and whether or not beauty is worth preserving; sonnet 1 expresses the expectation that "From fairest creatures we desire increase, / That thereby beauty's rose might never die" (1-2). In sonnet 127, reproduction is hardly worth the effort: "But now is black beauty's successive heir, / And beauty slandered with a bastard shame" (3-4). In sonnet 1, preservation of beauty sounds possible: "But as the riper should by time decease / His tender heir might bear his memory" (3-4), but in sonnet 127,

> . . . since each hand hath put on nature's pow'r,
> Fairing the foul with art's false borrowed face,
> Sweet beauty hath no name, no holy bow'r
> But is profaned, if not lives in disgrace. (5-8)

In sonnet 1, the fault seems to be in the person addressed, who is "contracted" to his (or her) "own bright eyes" (5), "Making a famine where abundance lies" (7), "the foe" (8), who "buriest" (11) and "mak'st waste in niggarding" (12) what should be shared with the world (13-14); in 127, the fault is in the world, which is not the good "old age," but a "now" in which beauty is "slandered" (4) and "profaned" (8).

The "world's fresh ornament" and "only herald to the gaudy spring" of sonnet 1 is asked to pity the world lest beauty's line be lost (13-14); in 127, pity for the loss of that lineage seems to happen spontaneously:

> Therefore my mistress' eyes are raven black,
> Her eyes so suited, and they mourners seem
> At such who, not born fair, no beauty lack,
> Sland'ring creation with a false esteem. (9-12)

The beauty in sonnet 1 consumes itself by means of its hidden brightness (5-6), but the mistress in 127 seems to grow in beauty through a display of darkness. She does for herself (though perhaps not on purpose) what the poet has purposed for "beauty" in the sonnets before 127: he wanted to move "tongues to be" (81.11) to praise; now, because of her, "every tongue says beauty should look so" (127.14).

It appears that Sonnet 127 signals a beginning, just as 126 signaled an end, carefully making a distinction between old and new "beauty," an old and new "age," and therefore old and new concerns for the poet. The word "beauty," which is recurrent in the procreation sonnets and in sonnets that are especially concerned with memorializing—sonnets 60, 63, 65, 68, 101, 104, and 106—appears *five* times in sonnet 127, more than it does in any other sonnet. And to what purpose is the idea of beauty invoked? Not, as has been seen, to urge its preservation, but to ask once more its pity. "Pity the world" the poet says to the fairest creature in sonnet 1, but in the sonnets after 126 it is the poet who is in "pity-wanting pain" (140.4).

After 126, it is the poet who is kept and stored, and not, by any means, for posterity. He is simply kept for loss:

> Me from myself thy cruel eye hath taken,
> And my next self thou harder hast engrossed.
> Of him, myself, and thee, I am forsaken—

> A torment thrice threefold thus to be crossed.
> Prison my heart in thy steel bosom's ward,
> But then my friend's heart let my poor heart bail;
> Whoe'er keeps me, let my heart be his guard,
> Thou canst not then use rigor in my jail.
>> And yet thou wilt, for I being pent in thee
>> Perforce am thine, and all that is in me. (133.5-14)

Or lost in being kept, one might say, paraphrasing sonnet 64's description of interchange between ocean and land.[14]

Before sonnet 126, keeping averts loss; preservation of the beloved is accomplished ("such virtue hath [his] pen"), whereas in the sonnets that follow, such as 133, keeping has to do with taking away (as in being kept), and obliteration of the poet's very self is always a possibility. Reading contextually strengthens that impression: sonnet 129 ("Th'expense of spirit in a waste of shame") begins a chain of sonnets that recount loss.

Stephen Booth glosses "expense as (1) expenditure; (2) dissipation, consumption, using up (OED, 1.b,c); (3) loss (as in 30.8); (4) waste (the Folio text of Lear II.i.100 has the 'expense and wast of his Revenues'" (441). This sort of threat is present throughout the procreation sonnets, but in this post-126 sonnet, the waster is not time, but something else (love, lust, desire, life itself?), and so comes the greatest difference in the loss: in the battle against time, what is at stake is substantive, measurable, or visible in some way; loss in this new arena is frustratingly insubstantial, partly because what would be kept is insubstantial to begin with:

> A bliss in proof, and proved a very woe;
> Before a joy proposed; behind, a dream. (129.11-12)

Not only is this loss insubstantial, but it is so interior that is impossible to discern. The waste described in sonnet 129 is not because something cannot be kept in its perfect moment, as in "When I consider everything that grows / Holds in perfection but a little moment" (15.1-2), but because the perfect moment never occurs, though the poet cannot keep himself from continually desiring it.

Another way to follow the difference is to locate where metaphors connected with the "storehouse" model of memory occur and determine how they work now that they are not serving as a way to express a stratagem against time. In sonnet 133, as mentioned, all the "keeping" has to do with being kept: "Me from myself thy cruel eye hath taken" (5), "Prison my heart in thy steel bosom's ward" (9), "for I being pent in thee / Perforce am thine, and all that is in me" (13-14), which, by the way, implies that the "heart that makes [the poet's] heart to groan" (1) is kept as well, since it is part of "all that is in [him]."[15]

Not that the poet is entirely against being kept, stored, admitted, received, enslaved, and consumed. Sometimes he even initiates the offer:

> Myself I'll forfeit, so that other mine
> Thou wilt restore to be my comfort still. (134.3-4),

and the offer is refused: "But thou wilt not, nor he will not be free, / For thou art covetous, and he is kind" (5-6). In the end, the keeper "hast both him and me" (13). Sometimes the poet insists:

> Wilt thou, whose will is large and spacious,
> Not once vouchsafe to hide my will in thine?
> Shall will in others seem right gracious,
> And in my will no fair acceptance shine? (135.5-8)

Notice how small the poet's part (taking "will" as you wish) seems. In fact, in the next two lines, which actually include the word "store," his superfluity is described: "The sea, all water, yet receives rain still, / And in abundance addeth to his store" (9-10).[16]

In sonnet 136, the storehouse metaphors are even more explicit:

> Will will fulfill the treasure of thy love,
> Ay fill it full with wills, and my will one,
> In things of great receipt with ease we prove,
> Among a number one is reckoned none.
> Then in thy store's account I one must be,
> For nothing hold me, so it please thee hold
> That nothing me, a something sweet to thee. (5-12)

"Hold me, keep me, and never let me go"—isn't that the quintessential (and most basic, if sonnet 143 be considered) human longing? Unfortunately, after giving many assurances that he will keep his love, the poet does not reciprocally experience the same sort of certainty, and as a result, he gradually loses himself in various ways, variously expressed:

> My love is a fever, longing still
> For that which longer nurseth the disease,
> Feeding on that which doth preserve the ill,
> Th'uncertain sickly appetite to please. (147.1-4)

> O me! what eyes hath love put in my head,
> Which have no correspondence with true sight!
> Or if they have, where is my judgment fled,
> That censures falsely what they see aright? (148.1-4)

> Do I not think on thee when I forgot
> Am of myself all tyrant for thy sake? (149.3-4)

These lines are explicitly concerned with loss of self, but one could also explore losses of honesty, honor, and discernment (as in 137, 138, 139, 141, 145, 148, 149, 150, 151, and 152). In addition, most of these sonnets call attention to loss of sight (that is, blindness), which even as it misperceives, is aware of true sight. Like a "lucid" dreamer, the poet knows that he does not see, and also knows *what* he does not see, but does not know how he could see otherwise.

In the sonnets after 126, there seems an opposite movement from those before 126. The metaphors of memory from 1 to 125 trace various methods of keeping (in progeny, poetry, and in the poet), culminating with "I will be true" (123.14). The sonnets after 126 pass through stages of loss towards surrender to the "most perjur'd eye" (152.13). These are related, but opposite concerns, related in their opposition: one *can* be "Consumed with that which it was nourished by" (73.12). This, indeed, is the final movement in the Sonnets and why the concern with time's threat is absent. Fire burns quickly what was carefully and slowly stored. One might even say, with Paulina from *The Winter's Tale:* "It is an heretic that makes the fire" (2.3.114). The Sonnets' end is typically Shakespearean, suggesting that "Increasing store for loss, and loss with store" (64.8), though the "thought is as a death" (13), is what life is really about.

NOTES

1. I use Stephen Booth's edition of the Sonnets.

2. In Booth's edition, "time" and "nature" are not capitalized. Kerrigan, Ingram and Redpath, and most other editors retain the Quarto capitalization; Booth explains why he does not (432, xvii-xviii).

3. For a thorough discussion of the two major metaphors of memory (one having to do with inscribing and the other with storing), see chapter 1 of Carruthers.

4. Dante Gabriel Rossetti, himself a writer of a sonnet sequence, had a slightly different division in mind: "There should be an essential reform in the printing of Shakespeare's sonnets. After sonnet CXXV should occur the words *End of Part 1*. The couplet piece, numbered CXXVI, should be called *Epilogue to Part 1*. Then, before CXXVII, should be printed *Part II*. After CLII should be put *End of Part II*—and the last two sonnets should be called *Epilogue to Part II*" (250). Kerrigan seems to agree with the functional equivalency of 126 to 153-154, in principle if not in reforming fervor (61-63).

5. This is another way of detecting a constant concern in the Sonnets to prevent loss, but Greene puts the emphasis on a satisfactory exchange between the young man and the poet, claiming that "our understanding of the outcome of the 'plot' in sonnets 1-126 depends, in part, on our interpretation of the phrase ['mutual render']," which 125 seems to affirm "between the two men" (176). Greene entertains the possibility for this "happy conclusion" for a moment, but the title of the article ("Pitiful Thrivers: Failed Husbandry in the Sonnets") is a prognostication: the young man, in the economy of procreation, fails; the poet, despite claims that his poetry will render its value, fails; and a last possibility—the creation of "equal, direct, unmediated reciprocity" through a "rhetorical economics which would mediate between the two men"—also fails when the contradiction in these definitions plays itself out: "To deny the operation of art requires art, and this art will prohibit the reciprocal affective mutuality toward which the whole work has seemed to want to move" (89).

6. Sonnet 99 has fifteen lines; sonnet 145 is in tetrameter; sonnet 96 repeats the couplet from sonnet 36, and various pairs of sonnets (56 and 58 for example) seem to be drafts of one another.

7. The "conventional assumptions" Dubrow refers to are outlined earlier in the essay (291).

8. For a complete discussion on this subject see *Captive Victors* 213-26.

9. The opening to sonnet 11 presents another possible reading, especially if one holds off the second line, which is a natural, logical explanation for the seeming contradiction expressed in line 1. This reading simply has to do with

seeing things (in Yeatsian fashion) as always containing or storing their opposite action. A modern corollary is found in Bob Dylan's line, "He who is not busy being born is busy dying," from "It's Alright Ma (I'm Only Bleeding)."

10. Booth's note on this phrase not only explains the accent but reminds us that "Q capitalizes and italicizes *audit* here and in 126.11" (140).

11. According to Carruthers, "in memorizing one *writes* upon a surface one has always with one" (30; emphasis added).

12. Ingram and Redpath, in their notes to the Sonnets, agree that it is most likely that the tables given to the poet were blank (280).

13. These lines from "the most universally admired of Shakespeare's sonnets" (Booth 387) seem especially helpful in understanding the phrase "fools of time" (124.13): since what is implied in sonnet 116 is that love, by altering not when it alteration finds, is therefore "not time's fool," one might infer that the fools of time are simply those who alter under altered conditions. And such a one the poet is not.

14. Related themes, duplicated metaphors, and recurrent situations in sonnets before and after 126 are many. Metaphors that display or highlight the interchangeability of cosmic conditions (usually marked by verbal ingenuity and puns) occur throughout the Sonnets and plays, but they have a markedly different focus in the sonnets after 126. In sonnet 64, for example, the "interchange" is in the natural and ideological world and is only observed and recounted by the poet ("When I have seen . . . When I have seen . . . when I have seen") until he gathers his observations into a personal application: "Ruin hath taught me thus to ruminate, / That time will come and take my love away" (11-12). In the sonnets after 126, the poet himself is the location of interchange and loss.

15. The assurance of a sort of "mutual render" (125.12) found in sonnet 31 does not seem to be present here.

16. The soliloquy that Antipholus of Syracuse makes when he arrives at Ephesus comes to mind, especially these lines:

> I to the world am like a drop of water
> That in the ocean seeks another drop,
> Who, falling there to find his fellow forth,
> Unseen, inquisitive, confounds himself.

(Comedy of Errors 1.2.35-38)

The first two lines of this soliloquy, in fact, might serve as a motto for many of the sonnets after 126: "He that commends me to mine own content / Commends me to the thing I cannot get" (33-34).

WORKS CITED

Baldwin, T. W. *On the Literary Genetics of Shakespeare's Poems and Sonnets.* Urbana: U of Illinois P, 1950.

Booth, Stephen, ed. *Shakespeare's Sonnets.* New Haven: Yale UP, 1977.

Carruthers, Mary. *The Book of Memory.* Cambridge: Cambridge UP, 1990.

de Grazia, Margreta. "The Scandal of Shakespeare's Sonnets." *Shakespeare Survey* 46 (1994): 35-49.

Dubrow, Heather. *Captive Victors: Shakespeare's Narrative Poems and Sonnets.* Ithaca: Cornell UP, 1987.

———. *Echoes of Desire: English Petrarchism and Its Counterdiscourses.* Ithaca: Cornell UP, 1995.

———. "'Incertainties now crown themselves assur'd': The Politics of Plotting Shakespeare's Sonnets." *Shakespeare Quarterly* 47 (1996): 291-305.

Engle, Lars. *Shakespearean Pragmatism.* Chicago: U of Chicago P, 1993.

Fineman, Joel. *Shakespeare's Perjured Eye: The Invention of Poetic Subjectivity in the Sonnets.* Berkeley: U of California P, 1986.

Greene, Thomas. "Pitiful Thrivers: Failed Husbandry in the Sonnets." *Shakespeare's Sonnets: Modern Critical Interpretations.* Ed. Harold Bloom. New York: Chelsea House, 1987. 75-92.

Ingram, W. G. and Theodore Redpath, eds. *Shakespeare's Sonnets.* London: Hodder and Stoughton, 1964; rev. ed. 1978.

Kerrigan, John, ed. *The Sonnets and A Lover's Complaint.* London: Penguin, 1986.

The Riverside Shakespeare. Ed. G. Blakemore Evans. Boston: Houghton Mifflin, 1974.

Rossetti, Dante Gabriel. *Recollections.* London, 1882.

Sontag, Susan. "The Way We Live Now." *The Houghton Mifflin Anthology of Short Fiction.* Ed. Patricia Hampl. Boston: Houghton Mifflin, 1989. 1168-1179.

Politics, Heresy, and Martyrdom in Shakespeare's Sonnet 124 and *Titus Andronicus*

John Klause

Near the beginning of the twentieth century, an editor of Shakespeare's Sonnets considered it "pleasant" to report a commentator's forthright admission that the final lines of sonnet 124 were "hopelessly obscure" and that he would add no more to the attempts to explain them (Alden 293). Earlier and later generations of readers, however, have seemed to enjoy the work's obscurities or, as many say, "difficulties," finding in them more a challenge than a source of frustration.[1] In whichever critical direction one's pleasure lies, the poem is not on any count an exercise for impatient minds:

> If my dear love were but the child of state,
> It might for Fortune's bastard be unfathered,
> As subject to Time's love, or to Time's hate,
> Weeds among weeds, or flowers with flowers gathered.
> No, it was builded far from accident;
> It suffers not in smiling pomp, nor falls
> Under the blow of thrallèd discontent,
> Whereto th'inviting time our fashion calls;
> It fears not Policy, that heretic,
> Which works on leases of short-numb'red hours,
> But all alone stands hugely politic,
> That it nor grows with heat, nor drowns with show'rs.

> To this I witness call the fools of Time,
> Which die for goodness, who have lived for crime.[2]

There is one kind of intellectual excitement in seeing a growth from the very first line of the sonnet not only of a "beautiful complexity" but of an air of deliberate and "scornful generality," even "vagueness," that contributes to its "grandeur" (Kerrigan 346, 348; Booth 419). Such was the perception of Arthur Mizener (to be followed by Stephen Booth), who found that in this poem, as not in metaphysical poetry, it is "impossible to read the lines at all without making an effort to keep all the meanings [of single words], all the emergent figures, in view at once"—the poet's purpose being "to make the reader see them all, simultaneously, in soft focus," and the method being "to give the reader just enough of each figure for this purpose" (736). In the word "state," for example, from the opening verse, Mizener recognized seven different senses ("fortune," "status," "wealth," "talent," "pomp," "the body politic," and "statesmanship"), all of them necessary to understand the lines following, but "no single one" adequate to a proper reading. As love's "weeds" and "flowers" give way in the second quatrain to a metaphorical building, which is capable of but resistant to "suffering" or "fall[ing]," and in the third to "Policy," a personified "heretic" (neither building nor plant), before returning to a hint of the original herbal and floral metaphors in line 12 ("nor grows with heat, nor drowns with show'rs") and concluding at the executioner's scaffold, one must either discover grandeur in the "shad[ing]" of tropes into one another or judge the lines "hopelessly defective" (Mizener 740).

A different approach to the sonnet, and the one offered here, would be to allow the poet without much ado the march of his metaphors (which has in fact more of a rationale than, say, the "metaphysical" Donne's in "A Valediction: Forbidding Mourning") and to seek to make *precise* the argument into which all of his figures fit. At first the poem's argument might not seem worth much attention, since its conclusion is radically clear: my love is authentic and constant, born not in policy, subject not to fortune. But the very clarity and definiteness of such an assertion against the background of other sonnets in which the poet confesses himself *in*constant (numbers 110 and 117-119) is provocative rather than reassuring. One should want to know by what right this declaration can be made. If the poet attempts in sonnet 124 to demonstrate something ("To this I witness call . . . "), does he rely only on the analogical proof afforded by "softly focused" metaphors or grandly "vague" abstractions? More specifically and narrowly, does he believe that he can establish his point simply by contrasting his love with the impulses that typically rule the generic "state"? Or does he appeal to a historical politics that allows him to place specific human witnesses on the stand? In recent times it has seemed pointless, even wrongheaded, to follow older commentators in attempting to identify the "fools of Time" whose testimony is crucial to the poet's case. Yet those "Which die for goodness, who have lived for crime" are in such a special predicament, and the witness that they may bear to the rootedness of love in constancy is potentially so "enigmatic" (Evans, *Sonnets* 238), that it is unwise to ignore signs of their identity when these can be made visible either through attention to the poem's own logic or to the author's personal or literary world.

One interested in the sonnet's discursive procedures must first consider the pronoun "this" in the penultimate line. Since the object of testimony, "this," must be at least the truth of all claims made since line 5, and probably all assertions from the very beginning, the "fools'" situation as witnesses must somehow be complexly illustrative. They must demonstrate that love is not spontaneous and fortuitous, but "builded": a self-consciously willed creation, molded in accordance with an ideal of constancy. They must reveal indifference to the pomp of power as well as to the suffering attendant upon political disappointment or punishment ("thrallèd discontent"). Considering opportunism ("Policy") heretical, they yet may endorse a love that survives "alone" and "hugely" opportunistic ("politic"), that is able to maintain an equilibrium in all (emotional and political?) climates. But if these witnesses have such competence to defend constancy, it must be asked why they are labeled "fools," and indeed "fools of Time." The most common answer is that they are "timeservers." Prime exponents of the "policy" that the poem condemns, their crimes have caught up with them and urged them to an expedient repentance—either in a final act of public self-fashioning (on a scaffold) or (on a deathbed) out of a craven fear of eternal punishment. They are, then, not so much "witnesses" as "exhibits," whose careers make up a cautionary tale (Booth 424).

There are, however, several difficulties with this characterization of the "fools of Time." One does not "call" exhibits, but witnesses. It is more likely that the fools are being summoned to testify from beyond the grave than that their ghosts are to be imaginatively "presented," to stand in court in surly silence. If the foolish are to speak, it is to be on behalf of constant love. But while the poet declares that the adaptability of timeservers is reprehensible, he does not consider all adaptability timeserving: love may stand "hugely politic." Thus it should be spoken for by witnesses who themselves have shown a constancy that has lived with inconsistency—like martyrs for ultimate principles (*martyroi* is Greek for witnesses) who have dealt freely with secondary ones. Timeservers could not as "exhibits" offer examples (even negative ones) of this paradox, for theirs has been only an unprinicipled, unparadoxical inconstancy. Nor could they speak as "witnesses" for it, like ghosts from *The Mirror for Magistrates* confessing their shortcomings to promote the opposite virtues, for the testimony must transcend such simple oppositions. Furthermore, timeservers are not likely to "die for goodness," in its *service,* since their lives are grounded in self-interest; and those who feign a noble death may be hypocrites, but have run out of "time" to "serve." Finally, anyone who has "lived for crime" ought not to remain constant in it but repent and testify, if to anything, to the value of change, not of constancy. Surely in a case like this the best endorsements of fidelity come from the faithful. It does not seem right, then, as Booth has done, to *identify* the witnesses with personified "Policy, that heretic" (424), when it is far more likely that Policy (of a certain kind) is deemed heretical by the witnesses' standards and called so by their testimony.

The most plausible identities of those "Which die for goodness, who have lived for crime" are indeed martyrs, those who, as Booth more sagely notes, have experienced "one or another crisis of conscience brought about by clashes between practical considerations and religious conviction" (424). The crime they have lived for is the treason which the "state" and its agent "Policy, that heretic," have declared the practice of their faith; the goodness they have died for is that faith itself, which they refuse to desert in their final hours. If as hunted criminals they have led lives of disguise and dissimulation, if as persecuted believers they have equivocated, and have otherwise shown themselves to resemble the heretics in their policy, theirs has been an honorable adaptiveness which lovers would do well to emulate. If one reads the Sonnets as a drama and not merely as a set of meditations, one can see in the lovers' relationships the same flexibility with the truth, the same providential strategy aimed at keeping a troubled ideal alive, a "huge" policy that attempts to transform waywardness into constancy.[3] In sonnet 124, martyrs are called as witnesses to endorse the congruence between their zeal and the love between persons that is indifferent to the excitements and tribulations of the world, that is "builded" by strenuous effort because serendipity is unreliable, and that is both politic and constant unto death.

The problem remains, however, that the epithet "fools of Time" may seem odd given to witnesses of such stature. In sonnet 116, which declares love "an ever-fixèd mark," love is decidedly *not* "Time's fool" (its victim or plaything). Can fools of Time be credible spokesmen for steadfastness? They can in the moral or religious universe of the martyr, whose self-confessed folly is notorious. Paul in his first letter to the Corinthians preached the doctrine of the cross, which to the Greeks was "foolishnesse" (1:23), and described himself and other missionaries "as men appointed to death," as "a gasing stocke unto the world, and to the Angels, and to men . . ., fooles for Christes sake" (4: 9-10). To the world, or in biblical terms "Time" (Hebrew *olam*, Greek *aion*, Latin *saeculum*, all of whose meanings conflate the temporal with the mundane), the martyr's carelessness of or contempt for its values seems preposterous. And where Time can "hate" as well as "love" (124.3), it is inevitable that those who resist its mutations will find their "folly" punished. But martyrs will have chosen a foolish goodness over a wise compliance that would have saved them from crime. In the fatal choice they evoke admiration in a poet who feels that their love in some way establishes a precedent for his own.

This reading gives sonnet 124 a logic, onto which a host of connotative ambiguities may be grafted. In the process, however, Shakespeare is taken into a political and religious realm where few have seen fit to place him. It is not at all unusual to see him reflecting on the illegitimacy of productions of "state" (bastards "unfatherèd" by "Fortune") and dramatizing the operations of "bare and rotten policy" (*1H4* 1.3.108). It is quite rare to find the suggestion that he sympathized with martyrs who died for goodness in violating the government's laws. T. W. Baldwin once proposed that Shakespeare had modeled the character Egeon in *The Comedy of Errors* on a Catholic missionary priest executed near the Shoreditch playhouses not long after the defeat of the Spanish Armada. The playwright was said to have sympathized with the sufferings of a man of principle, although he endorsed the government policy that had led to his death (129-42). Among annotators of sonnet 124 whose speculations were noted in Rollins's *Variorum*, only Gregor Sarrazin (writing in 1914) recognized that the "fools of Time" were in any way admirable, leading him to the

conclusion that they were "the Catholic priests executed in 1594-5 . . .,
[who] died for goodness, since they held faithfully to their religion"
(Rollins 1: 314). The Jesuit Peter Milward took a similar view
(Milward 59-60). But Russell Fraser has probably spoken for the
majority of those who have considered the matter by claiming that
"Martyrs, Protestant or Catholic, were only grist to Shakespeare's mill"
(Fraser 84).

To prove that the truth is quite different, that Shakespeare's
interest in martyrs and the politics of martyrdom was genuine and
profound, would require a study of much more than a single sonnet, a
study that can only be begun in this essay. Yet even in a short space,
enough of a historical context may be drawn to confirm the "logic" of
sonnet 124 as it has been set forth, and to introduce the possibility that
Shakespeare looked upon "the fools of Time" with far from an
indifferent or impartial eye.

Baldwin's attempts to link Shakespeare personally to the spectacle
of an Elizabethan martyrdom have not been taken as seriously as they
have deserved to be: perhaps because he tried to prove too much, and
because his view of Shakespeare as a single-minded chauvinist has left
even the most impressive aspects of his study open to mistrust. As
improbable as it may seem, however, *The Comedy of Errors* when
studied closely does reveal Shakespeare occupied with the martyr's
plight.[4] Even more pertinent to a consideration of "the fools of Time" is
a play that has not been considered as a "martyrial" drama, *Titus
Andronicus*. This work is of course as bloody as a public execution; it
is imbued with the politics of religious warfare as well. The most
striking evidence of its political character resides in a scene that has
seemed to many little more than comic relief (Metz 121)—even though
it ends with a clown's being dragged off to the gibbet.

By the fourth act of the play, Titus has a mind as steeped in blood
as any of Shakespeare's characters. An inveterate soldier, he has lost
more than twenty of his sons in warfare and has killed one of them
himself. He has ordered the ritual sacrifice of a son of his enemy. Two
of his own sons have been executed for a murder they did not commit.
His daughter has emerged from a wood, "her hands cut off, and her
tongue cut out, and ravish'd" (s.d. 2.4.1). Titus has given up one of his
hands in a vain attempt to save the lives of his falsely accused boys.
When he learns that his daughter has been raped and mutilated by the
sons of the Empress, the Goth Tamora, he becomes desperate for
"justice," but in such an antic way that he will become an impresario of

comic horror. One of his most puzzling schemes is to send a message to the Emperor Saturninus through a "Clown," who had been going, with pigeons in hand, to one of the tribunes of the people to settle a domestic dispute. Titus diverts him:

> *Tit.* Sirrah, come hither, make no more ado,
> But give your pigeons to the Emperor.
> By me thou shalt have justice at his hands.
> Hold, hold; mean while here's money for thy charges.
> Give me pen and ink. Sirrah, can you with a grace
> deliver up a supplication?
> *Clo.* Ay, sir.
> *Tit.* Then here is a supplication for you; and when you come to him,
> at the first approach you must kneel, then kiss his foot, then deliver
> up your pigeons, and then look for your reward. I'll be at hand, sir,
> see you do it bravely.
> *Clo.* I warrant you, sir, let me alone.
> *Tit.* Sirrah, hast thou a knife? Come let me see it.
> Here, Marcus, fold it in the oration,
> For then hast made it like an humble suppliant. (4.3.102-117)

When the Clown approaches Tamora and then Saturninus with letters and pigeons, the Emperor reads and immediately orders his guard to take the suppliant away "and hang him presently" (4.4.45).

It is quite probable that Shakespeare found inspiration for this strange episode in the story of one Richard Shelley, a Catholic layman who, in 1585, put into Queen Elizabeth's hand "at such time as she walked in her parke at Greenewitch" a petition on behalf of his persecuted coreligionists, and for his efforts "was promptly thrown into prison by [the Queen's minister] Walsingham and left to die there" without trial (Bald 72). Shelley's fate was mentioned in another attempt at such a petition, a pamphlet written by his kinsman, the Jesuit Robert Southwell, in late December of 1591. Its title was "An Humble Supplication to Her Majestie," its purpose to defend English Catholics against scurrilous accusations made against them by a government proclamation and to protest against the unjust treatment of Catholic clergy and laity under the regime's penal laws. One is immediately struck by the parallel between Shelley's and the Clown's naive and hapless innocence in delivering their messages (both asking for redress of grievances), as well as by the apparent allusion to Southwell's piece in Titus's "supplication" and "humble suppliant."[5] But there is much more to connect the play, the pamphlet, and the political context.

When the Clown wishes on Empress and Emperor the blessings of "Saint Steven" (4.4.42), he unwittingly associates himself with the Christian protomartyr (Acts 7: 57-60). When he swears "by [our] Lady" (48), he evokes a Catholic world which in all its anachronism seems deliberately, at various points, worked into the play's pagan Roman setting. Titus prays to Jupiter and Pluto, sends his sons across Styx, imagines diving into Acheron, and sanctions human sacrifice to infernal *manes* (4.3.13-54; 1.1.96-103). But his world also features, besides the Clown's saints, "priest and holy water" for wedding ceremonies (1.1.323), "hermits in their holy prayers" (3.2.41), "popish tricks and ceremonies" (5.1.76), "limbo" (3.1.149), and a "ruinous [that is, "ruined"] monastery" (5.1.21). The word "martyr" and its cognates appear in *Titus* more than in any other work of Shakespeare; and there are signs that he intended them to have a special significance for his contemporaries, especially for those who would have had an interest in, even if they had not been able to read, Southwell's *Humble Supplication*.

The influence of the Jesuit's petition on the play is discernible in more than in the similar fates of Shelley and the Clown. Just before the Clown's fatal mission, Titus, pretending to ask for justice from the heavens, had messages sent to the Court on arrows, one of which had gone into "Virgo's lap" and another "beyond the moon" to Jove himself (4.3.65-67). The vision here is doubled. "Virgo" is both Astraea (the goddess of Justice who has left the earth [4.3.4]) and the decidedly unvirginal and wicked Empress Tamora (in the Court where the arrows really land); "Jove" is both god and the undivine Emperor Saturninus (who in the next scene enters carrying the shafts in his hand). Southwell seems to have suggested to Shakespeare at least part of these theatrics.[6] Defending "Priests and Catholiques" against the vilifications of government wordsmiths, which he compared to "arrows" shot at the innocent, Southwell warned the Queen that because of their outrageous messages those same "arrows [might] hit [her] Majesties honor in the way" (2). That is, they might land in the lap of the "Virgin Queen," and (to continue with Shakespeare's image, which implies what Southwell says later in his essay) would certainly travel beyond the "moon" (Elizabeth as the virgin "Diana" or Raleigh's "Cynthia") to God himself, who knew the injustice of their accusations.

Southwell pleaded with Elizabeth that she show herself on earth an agent of justice at least, and more, a source of mercy. He imagined her "bounding [her] desires to the limitts of vertue, and measuring [her] Regality more by will to save then by power to kill" (25). The language is paralleled in Titus's wish that "into limits could I bind my woes" (3.1.220), and in Tamora's early prayer to him that he "Draw near [the gods] in being merciful: / Sweet mercy is nobility's true badge" (1.1.118-19). Elizabeth was addressed by the politic Jesuit as a "mighty ... Princesse ... the only shoot-anker of our last hopes," a monarch of "sacred hand guided by [virtuous] thoughts" (1, 39). The Gothic-Roman ruler was styled, even by a vengeful Titus, as a "proud empress, mighty Tamora"; she wished to have rather than to be an "anchor" in a stormy world (4.4.38); and her lover found in her a "sacred wit" (2.1.120). The Jesuit describes his fellow Catholics as "at the bottome of a helples misery" (1), just as Titus complained that his "sorrow" was "deep, having no bottom," there being no reason for his "miseries" (3.1.216, 219). A list of simple echoes might be extended; for example:

Supplication:	*Titus:*
neither any greatnes should beare downe Justice, nor any meanesnesse be excluded from mercy (1)	rather comfort his distressed plight Than prosecute the meanest or the best (4.4.32-33)
[criminal] words and actions . . . remitted (27)	I do remit these young men's heinous faults (1.1.484)
our death, the end of evills (27)	were there worse end than death (2.3.302)
languish in . . . lingring Combers (33); languishing away . . . with . . . lingring miseries (40)	ling'ring languishment (2.1.110)
poore Farmers . . . Cattell (43)	poor men's cattle (5.1.132)
are drawen nearer to the brinke (45)	I have no strength to pluck thee to the brink (2.3.241)

There are, however, more impressive and intriguing verbal parallels than these, pointing to political issues that Southwell considers openly. but Shakespeare only in dramatic obliqueness.

Well into his supplication Southwell recalls that the first British ruler to be converted to Christianity was "King Lucius," and laments that after the 1,400 years since his time, in which Catholic Christianity had flourished in England, "all Monasteries [were] now . . . buried in their owne ruynes" (29). The play's "ruinous monastery" (5.1.21) of course comes to mind, but more important, Titus's son Lucius, who becomes Emperor in the final scene. Shakespeare's Lucius is a warrior from ancient Rome, and at the same time a Roman Catholic. The atheistic villain Aaron is willing to accept Lucius's promise to save his child because, as he says,

> I know that thou art religious,
> And hast a thing within thee called conscience,
> With twenty popish tricks and ceremonies,
> Which I have seen thee careful to observe. . . . (5.1.74-77)

(Compare Southwell's emphasis on the moral fastidiousness of English Catholics, which their enemies were alert to take advantage of: "many that see, are willing to use the awe of our Consciences for their warrant to tread us downe" [26].)

Why the telescoping of centuries and the blurring of distinctions between antique and contemporary "Romans"? Jonathan Bate has argued that a "Reformation" theme is embedded in the play, a theme meant to illustrate the concept, as Samuel Kliger has studied it, of the *translatio imperii ad teutonicos* (the transfer of empire to the German peoples):

> The *translatio* suggested forcefully an analogy between the breakup
> of the Roman empire by the Goths and the demands of the humanist
> reformers of northern Europe for religious freedom, interpreted as
> liberation from Roman priestcraft. In other words, the *translatio*
> crystallized the idea that humanity was twice ransomed from Roman
> tyranny and depravity—in antiquity by the Goths, in modern times by
> their descendants, the German reformers. (Kliger, qtd. in Bate 20)

At a time, Bate declares, when Elizabeth's age and childlessness had made "the issue of succession" most urgent, and "the preservation of the Protestant nation" a deep concern, Shakespeare wrote into his play a form of reassurance: the Goths who accompany Lucius into a Rome that is really England "are there to secure the Protestant succession," to ensure that the monasteries would stay ruined, and that no more Lavinias would be mutilated to provide matter for another Foxe's *Book of Martyrs* (20-21).

Although there are good reasons for imagining the Goths as Protestants, it is difficult to credit this interpretation of their role in the play. One can hardly forget that the Goths Demetrius and Chiron, with the connivance of their Gothic mother, were Lavinia's butchers; that the young woman was a "Roman" martyr as Alarbus was a Gothic one; that the Queen of the Goths had an atheist as a paramour; and that it was the "popish" Lucius (like an Elizabethan Catholic exile in flight from a persecuting government then returning to overthrow it) who won over the Gothic army, not they who converted him. Shakespeare may well have composed *Titus* with the irenic sentiments expressed by the King in the last act of *1 Henry VI*: "I always thought / It was both impious and unnatural / That such immanity and bloody strife / Should reign among professors of one faith" (5.1.11-14). If so, he presents a picture of reconciliation under Roman auspices—even if the reconciler Lucius (who first proposed the "sacrifice" of Alarbus [1.1.96-100]) is hardly an ideal peacemaker. And if a strain of historical allegory is to be seen in the play, it must be read in the context of its Catholic sources, Southwell's *Supplication* and (as will be shown) his other writings.

Turning back to sonnet 124, one can see that just as the *Humble Supplication* has left a considerable mark on *Titus Andronicus*, so it has significantly influenced the poem. The remarkable coincidence of vocabularies suggests as much. The pamphlet includes parallels with most of the sonnet's important words, concepts, and images: "dearest Frends," "child," "State," "fortunes," "Fathers of . . . infamous Orphans," "tyme," "love," "build," "accidents," "suffer," "enthralled," "fashion," "Pollicy," "Apostata" (cf. "heretic"), "howerly," "huge," "pollitique," "drowne," "calling God and Angels for witnesses" (also "witnessed," "is our witnes," "bear witnes"), "God Almightyes fooles," "who . . . would rather not die . . . than live," "at our deaths we all protest upon our soules, our Clearnes from Treason," "good," "Crymes."[7] It is not the words by themselves, of course, that demonstrate influence, but the contexts in which they are used.

Southwell writes about the "Constancy" (34) of his persecuted and martyred fellows, celebrating its heroic character and defending those constant souls against charges that their loyalty to a faith is "Treason" to the "state." Scoffers may believe them to be "God Almightyes fooles" for not yielding to the state's temporal power, but their folly is "meere . . . Conscience" (42). While they stand firm against the government's "Pollicy," formulated by heretics and carried out by apostates, they are, many of them, "in pollicy . . . noe Punies" themselves (27). But they are politic "in honesty" (36), not, as the state's propagandists claim, guilty of "huge Treasons" (31). As the sonneteer would say, they are instead "hugely politic"—to keep the faith. Their wise prudence keeps them, even though "enthralled . . . in unhappiness," distant from discontents like Babington (16), whom grievances (and government manipulation) have transformed into criminals. When they go to their deaths on the scaffold, they will in protesting their "Clearness from Treason" hardly spend their "last breath in bootles perjuries" (27). They call "Almighty God and his Angells for witnesses" that they are not "Traytors" (11); and though the state insists that they "suffer nothing for Religion" (42), they "[suffer] in proofe all punishments for nothing ells" (45). These are the martyrs—principled and cunning, active and immovable, Time's victims and Time's conquerors—whom Shakespeare's poet calls as witnesses to characterize and commend his "dear love."

This testimony is given, however, in a court where evidence of pure idealism is credible. It is not the world of *Titus Andronicus*, over which clouds of irony and cynicism darken somewhat the glory of the martyr's sacrifice. To understand more about Shakespeare's attitude towards the "fools of Time" it is necessary to anatomize that sanguinary drama in the light offered by another work of Southwell, one much more extensively devoted to the theme of martyrdom than is his *Humble Supplication* and much less infused with worldly prudence: *An Epistle of Comfort, To [those] Restrayned in Durance for the Catholicke Fayth* (1587).[8] Since Southwell addresses the work to those marked for martyrdom themselves and not to those who have the power to take away their lives, he sees no need to speak diplomatically to or about the Queen whose ministers command the courts, the torture chambers, and the sites of execution. The political establishment as a whole is unprincipled and barbaric, and will in God's good time reap what it has sown. His purpose is not primarily, as in the *Supplication*, to win toleration or a respite for the afflicted, but to confirm them in their determination to give up their property, their freedom, or their blood. He makes little of the delights of earthly existence and much of its tribulations. In the warfare that is life, he declares, "How muche more ought we to glorye in our martyrdomes, and not only condemne, but highlye prayse our heavenly Captayn, for exposing us to these bloody frayes" (132^v). In the scale of virtues,

> All must of force yelde to martyrdome, whose glory is unvalewable, whose measure infinite, whose victory unspotted, whose vertue honourable, whose tytle inestimable, whose triumph exceding great. To our blood the gates of heaven flye open, with our blood the fyre of hell is quenched, in our blood our soules are beautifyed, our bodyes honoured, the divel suppressed, and God glorified. (159^v)

And not the least of its consequences is that martyrs "shedd their bloode . . . for newe offspring to arise" (145^r)—their blood is the seed of the Church.

Shakespeare knew this book,[9] which made its way into *Titus*. Indications of this fact are of several kinds. Of the dramatis personae found in the play, for example (only three of whose names are in the chapbook), the following appear in the *Epistle*, sometimes fully spelled out, sometimes abbreviated, sometimes implied as the praenomen of a Roman character: Aaron (11^v); Titus, Lucius, Quintus, and Marcus (64^v-66^r); Valentinus (81^v); Kinges of the Gothes (86^v) (cf. Queen of the Goths); Caius (Plinius [90^v]); Mutius (that is, Mutius Scaevola, the loss of whose hand is more notorious than Titus's [124^r]); Publius (Valerianus [200^r]); and Nurces (152^v)—as well as the "Saint Steven" (123^v, 137^r, 156^v, 163^r, 164^v) so important to the Clown, and Asdrubal (126^v), suggestive of Alarbus. This list is even more impressive than the one from Plutarch's *Life* of Scipio Africanus, usually considered a "source" of Shakespeare's nomenclature (Bullough 25). The *Epistle*'s grouping together the names of the Andronici in close proximity, and its mention of the ruler of the "Gothes" and of Mutius the handless are especially noteworthy. Its allusion to Aaron is intriguing as well; for if one may detect in the name of *Titus*'s Moor a reminiscence of Marlowe's *Jew of Malta* (the name of Ithamore in that play, who in some ways resembles Shakespeare's Moor, may derive from Ithamar, son of the biblical Aaron [Numbers 4: 28]) (Bullough 20), Southwell's reference to the biblical priest is pertinent to Shakespeare's tale in a different way. In his *Epistle* he tells of the "murmuring" of Aaron and his sister Miriam against Moses for marrying an Ethiopian woman (Numbers 12), thus perhaps associating the priest's name with the play's miscegenation.

There are a number of scattered passages in which *Titus* echoes the *Epistle*. Southwell describes the emperor Constantine's kissing the scars of martyrs (155ʳ), as Titus kissed the wounded mouth of his "mart'red" daughter (3.1.81, 120). The Jesuit maintains that the "swordes" of persecutors, which have disemboweled saints for centuries, have but "plowed and tilled" the Church rather than destroyed it (123ᵛ, 149ᵛ, 157ᵛ). Aaron threatens with his sword to "plough . . . the bowels" of anyone who would harm his child (4.2.87). "The Jewes and Gentiles" of antiquity, says Southwell (quoting Psalm 106: 37-38) offered up as sacrifices "their sonnes and theyr daughters to divels" (173ᵛ). Titus and his sons (as they do not in the chapbook) sacrifice Tamora's son to the shades (*manes*) of their dead family (1.1.98). Southwell reports that "Flaccus the Prefect," after he had martyred a bishop, was "stroken by an Angell [and] did vomit out his intrailes" (200ᵛ; preceded by "For why" [that is, "because"] on 199ʳ). In an agony of grief Titus cries out: "For why my bowels cannot hide her woes, / But like a drunkard I must vomit them" (3.1.230-31).

The most striking set of parallels is to be found between the *Epistle*'s language on a few pages that begin at chapter 7, and that of the scene in *Titus* of the violated Lavinia's discovery by her uncle Marcus (2.4). The astonished Marcus ("If I do wake, some planet strike me down, / That I may slumber an eternal sleep!") asks his niece to

> Speak . . . what stern ungentle hands
> Have lopp'd and hew'd and made thy body bare
> Of her two branches, those sweet ornaments. . . .
>   Why dost thou not speak to me?
> Alas, a crimson river of warm blood,
> Like to a bubbling fountain stirr'd by the wind,
> Doth rise and fall between thy rosed lips,
> Coming and going with thy honey breath.
> Be sure some Tereus hath deflow'red thee,
> And lest thou shouldst detect him, cut thy tongue. . . .
> And notwithstanding all this loss of blood,
> As from a conduit with three issuing spouts,
> Yet do thy cheeks look red as Titan's face. . . .

> Shall I speak for thee . . . ?
> Sorrow concealed, like an oven stopp'd,
> Doth burn the heart to cinders where it is. . . .
> One hour's storm will drown the fragrant meads,
> What will whole months of tears thy father's eyes? (14-55)

With many of these words and images Southwell defines the stern necessities of the martyr's lot. "The loppinge time has come," he says to those who will soon know the sight of their own "blood and slaughtered limmes"; the "branches . . . of full growth are lopped"; bodies are "hewed" so that the tree of the Church may sprout more abundantly (93ᵛ-94ʳ, 126ʳ). Changing the metaphor, as Shakespeare does, the Comforter declares, "Your veynes are conduittes, out of which [God] meaneth to drive the streames" (93ᵛ),[10] and the streams become a scarlet river: "martirdome is the ryver Jordan" (141ʳ). Now is the time, "whyle this wind [of crisis] is stirring," when the winnower comes with his fan to separate chaff from wheat (97ʳ⁻ᵛ)—or rather from "sweet roses," for such martyrs are (114ᵛ), sweet with "Sampsons honicombe . . ., taken out of the Lyons mouth" (94ᵛ). A host of other words are shared by the two passages, among them "dreames," "plannetes," "eternal," "sleepe," "sterne" (a homograph), "ornamentes," "buble," "fountaine," "cutt," "tongue," "red," "cheeke," "storme . . . drown," and (comparable to the oven of the heart turned to cinders by suppressed grief) "the chimneye of our fleshe" wherein the flame of virtue, hidden in the "ashes" of "memorye" may be "quenched" by our iniquity.[11] The phrase "whole months" occurs only here in Shakespeare's works, probably because he read "whole monethes" in that part of the *Epistle* that contributed so much else to Marcus's aria (98ᵛ).

The effect of Southwell's writings on *Titus* is of such extent and quality (and evidence of more influence could be provided from the Jesuit's poems and other prose) that one must imagine Shakespeare deliberately seeking them out for inspiration; and he had to seek them where they were to be found. It must be assumed that the *Humble Supplication*, distributed in manuscript and not printed until 1600 (Bald ix-xvii, 47-49), was available to the playwright only through the Catholic underground. The *Epistle of Comfort* had been printed without license on a secret press by Southwell himself; it was eventually taken into "custody" by the government (Devlin 145), and, like the *Supplication*, must have come to Shakespeare surreptitiously (perhaps through the Catholic Southampton circle). [12] Surely the martyrs about whom he took the trouble to read were no mere "grist" for his "mill." He wrote of them with admiration and sympathy. He also wrote of martyr-*makers*, however, and in such a way as to complicate his development of the entire theme of martyrdom.

In sonnet 124 "the fools of Time" suffer resolutely at the hands of a "state" whose creed is only "Policy," a "heretic[al]" and murderous expediency no more legitimate than other creations, or "bastard[s]," of Fortune. In *Titus* the lords of state are equally unprincipled and vicious, but they are not the only martyr-makers. It is Roman piety, "cruel" and "irreligious," expressed in "Roman rites," that creates the first sacrificial victim:

> Alarbus' limbs are lopp'd
> And entrails feed the sacrificing fire,
> Whose smoke like incense doth perfume the sky. (1.1.130-145)

Alarbus's execution, combining features of Mary Tudor's burnings for heresy and Elizabeth's disembowelings and quarterings for treason, is appalling from either perspective; and it is ultimately the doing of Titus, "surnamed" (only in Shakespeare) "Pius" (1.1.23). The name is Virgilian, like Lavinia's; but it is also papal. The militant Pius V was the pope who excommunicated the English Queen in 1570, beginning the transformation of the English Catholic community into a church of martyrs. Like Titus, then, he believed in the necessity of sacrificing his children to maintain the purity of Roman principle. A figure of great austerity and reformist zeal, Pius had been Inquisitor General of Christendom before his election to the papacy. As pope he contributed his own forces to the European victory over the Turks at Lepanto, just as Titus's military prowess saved Roman civilization from the depredations of the Goths. Like Titus, Pius was at his election offered (but, unlike Titus, did not reject) the white *pallium* (Shakespeare's "palliament" [1.1.182]), which popes had come to wear in imitation of the Roman emperors. And as Titus saw his son Lucius off into exile, from which he might return to recover Rome from criminals and infidels, Pius encouraged his British sons into exile on the Continent, that they might recall their brothers and sisters, now ruled by heretics and politicians, to communion with Rome. [13]

Titus is not Pius, of course, but suggests him, revealing some affinities between ancient and modern "Romanness." And the suggestiveness of plot, character, and allusion rather than any set of allegorical correspondences indicates that Shakespeare's mind in composing *Titus Andronicus* was engaged by the bloody history of Europe's and especially England's religious conflicts. Hence the extremes of mutilation in the play, not hyperbolically expressive but mimetic of the tortures inflicted in houses and dungeons, of the hacking and hewing at Tyburn and elsewhere, and of the inquisitorial fires. Hence the veiled reference to "limbo" (3.1.149) (a prison where many Catholics died after their arrests) (Caraman 224, 243); and the allusion to a dispute, at least as old as that between Tyndale and Thomas More, between Catholics and Protestants over the difference between "charity" and "love" (4.2.43) (More 199-203). Hence the "ruinous monastery" and (so styled by the atheist Aaron) the "popish tricks and ceremonies" (5.1.21, 76).

Ovid and Seneca, one might say, provided a public playwright political cover with their convenient analogues, in the tales of Philomela and Thyestes, of the the hatred and gruesome slaughter that Shakespeare needed no literary tradition to know. It would have been rash for him to make more explicit than he did his sympathy for the martyred and his contempt for an unprincipled state and its "martyrquellers" (as Southwell called them [*Epistle* 212ᵛ]). Even so, the play that he wrote must have spoken with a special force to a certain part of his audience, moderate lay Catholics who might have seen the play even in its initial productions by the acting company of Lord Strange, a suspect Protestant whose ambience was Catholic.[14] For many of them, who wished to preserve an integrity of conscience but did not yearn for the glory of martyrdom, both the Machiavellianism of the Goths and the austere *Romanitas* of Titus were cause for dismay in reminding them of the religious politics of their own time. Fully aware of their government's manipulations, oppressions, and butcheries, they also knew that Rome was fierce and bloody in its ideals, that its martyrs were sometimes, like Lavinia before her ravishment (2.3.66-84), self-righteous, or like the Clown in his opportunistic use by Titus, naive (a pigeon was a lure placed in a "train" to catch a hawk). They listened to Roman voices like Southwell's and knew them to be sincere. The Jesuit missionary risked his life every day for the doctrine he preached and was to "witness" to it himself by his own martyrdom. But his ideal was preternaturally hard:

a glorious martyr of our dayes [Richard White], having well understood, when the sentence of his condemnation was red that he should be drawen upon a hurdle to the place of execution, then hanged till he were halfe dead, afterwarde unboweled, his head cut of, his body quartered, his quarters boyled, and sett upp in such and such places, he turned unto the people, & with a smiling countenance sayd, And all this is but one death. (*Epistle* 123ᵛ)

In some sense Titus's dry laughter after his daughter's martyrdom, his sons' execution, and his own mutilation ("I have not another tear to shed" [3.1.264, 266]) is a perverse analogue of the religious and almost incomprehensible joy in White's "smiling countenance." It is the first stage of Titus's transformation from a Roman of antique, inflexible, and in some ways alarming principle into the maniacal revenger who at play's end is a feral comedian little better than the criminals he wittily disgusts and slaughters. The old Roman's sufferings evacuate his soul, to make room not for beatific grace, but for a savage prosecutorial passion. When he kills his already "mart'red" daughter, whether or not to annul her shame (as he says) and to kill his own sorrow (5.2.46-47), the act, as Hamlet would say, has "no relish of salvation in it." Southwell would surely not have endorsed Titus's murders and his proleptic mockery of the Eucharistic feast. "Their mother daintily hath fed," gloats the satisfied avenger, "Eating the flesh that she herself hath bred" (5.3.61-62)—as after Christ's death the Virgin Mary, Southwell noted in a poem, would "drink" in the sacrament her son's "dearest blood" and eat his flesh too (*Poems*, "Sinne's heavie loade" 31). The cook who grinds, bakes, and serves the flesh, blood, and bones of criminals is no different from persecutors of the early Christians, who turned them, as Southwell reported, into "the wheate of Christe . . . to be ground with the teeth of wilde beasts" so that they became "pure and cleane bread" (*Epistle* 197ᵛ). As a priest of Christ, Southwell could not but affirm his master's injunction to forgive one's enemies. Catholics, he promises, will pray "for their good that torment us" (*Supplication* 35); saints, "Though they be stroken . . ., stande not to reveng" (*Epistle* 114ᵛ).

But a priest who lives daily with the thought of his own torture and death, and who must frequently endure the report or sight of what he considers the judicial brutalization and murder of the innocent may not always remember the ethos of the Sermon on the Mount. Southwell warns the persecutors who send God's servants to heaven that there they shall be "continuall soliciters with God for revenge against theyre murderers" (*Epistle* 199ᵛ). Revenge is only justice, he believes. And he finds in the Old Testament a vision of a punishing God adequate to his own anger, a God whose thoughts are as fierce as those of Titus, though the deity seems to have a better right to them:

> You which feede in blood, and lifte upp your eyes to your uncleanesse, & shedd innocent blood: thynke you to possesse the lande by inheritance? Nay rather I will deliver thee over unto blood and blood shall persecute thee . . . Yea and I will meat [that is, "feed"] the enemyes of my church with theyre owne flesh, and they shall be dronken with theyr owne bloode, as it were with newe wyne. (Ezekiel 33: 25-26; 35: 6; Isaiah 49: 26-27; qtd. in *Epistle* 209ᵛ-210ʳ)

Southwell is scrupulous to leave "revenge" in the hands of the Lord. But history shows that the Lord works through fallible or wicked human agents—or crazed ones. There is a wisdom that is woe; but there is a woe that is madness. Those insane with grief or grievance will sometimes try to find sanction in religion for the violent redress of their wrongs, as the Gunpowder Plot would prove. Not all, then, who suffer for "truth" or "justice" will become martyrs; some will become only psychological and political casualties, and perhaps executioners themselves. Shakespeare knew this very well, and would understand the problem even more deeply in writing *Hamlet*. He saw both martyrs and the "merely" persecuted as victims of a war in which one side found the shedding of blood expedient and the other found it a moral retaliation or heroic sacrifice. In either case, despite the fervor and even the exaltation of the parties, he seems to have felt that their attitude towards the spilling of blood was either too casual or too enthusiastic. The comic tone that informs much of the violence in *Titus*—in the visual jokes made of severed limbs, for example, the silly debate about who will deprive Titus of his hand, the cartoonish glee that Titus shows in his role as "pasty" chef—is intended to protest complacent acceptance of butchery of any kind. An audience may laugh at the spectacle of Lavinia's carrying away in her teeth the severed hand of her father, not because the action is pointlessly and cruelly farcical, but because the characters seem too much at home in a world of quotidian horrors and are blind to their own preposterousness. From this point of view (and of course there are others in the play, more sympathetic to those who suffer), *Titus* is a tragic satire.

Shakespeare may admire, then, the "fools of Time" who appear in (and out of) sonnet 124. But there he tells only the part of their story that can speak to the pieties of love, which are in some ways more simple than those of religion as it attempts in the world to survive the embrace of "Policy."

NOTES

1. See Rollins's historical collection of various confident but often hopelessly conflicting readings (from the 1780s to the 1940s) of the sonnet's syntax, vocabulary, logic, and allusive background (1: 311-14).

2. This sonnet and others are cited from the Sonnets edition of G. Blakemore Evans. Other quotations from Shakespeare's works are from *The Riverside Shakespeare*, 2nd edition, edited by Evans et al.

3. See my essay, "Shakespeare's *Sonnets*: Age in Love and the Goring of Thoughts." In sonnet 115 the poet speaks of his love's well-intentioned dissimulation. In 118 he acknowledges that "policy in love" is sometimes too clever for its own good.

4. I have undertaken to show this in a comprehensive study of Shakespeare and Southwell.

5. Editors of *Titus Andronicus* have suspected compositorial problems in the text of 4.3.95-107, seeing signs that a "false start" was not removed in printing. Eugene Waith in his edition of the play would eliminate the lines that refer to "supplication," leaving only those in which Titus speaks of an "oration"—and thus discarding a purposeful allusion (211-12). Jonathan Bate notes that the entire passage has worked well in performance (102).

6. In the chapbook version of Titus's story, which many scholars believe derives from Shakespeare's major "source" for the play, arrows are shot randomly into the air without messages attached. Shakespeare is likely to have had Southwell's word-carrying and virgin-queen-seeking shafts in mind, whether or not he was thinking of a different tale. For various reasons, I agree with the conclusions of Mincoff, Hunter, Jackson, and Bate (see Bate 83-85) that the play preceded the chapbook narrative; but I will not in this essay assume the priority of one or the other work.

7. Pages 15, 39, 23, 32, 41, 22, 34, 20, 32, 15, 16, 8, 23, 20, 14, 31, 23, 20, 11 (also 12, 13, 9), 26, 15, 27, 14, 27.

8. It has been suggested before that Shakespeare read the *Epistle* (Brownlow 27), but the manifold implications of this fact have not been explored.

9. The evidence for this claim is too extensive to be presented here. It will be offered in the study referred to in note 4.

10. As Bate points out, in Golding's Ovid, Pyramus's "bloud did spin on hie / As when a Conduit pipe is crakt" (188). Critics have commented on the Ovidian character of this speech. But it breathes the breath of contemporary as well as ancient Rome.

11. Folios 106^r, 96^v, 109^v, 116^v, 96^v, 124^v, 118^r, 106^v, 96^r, 108^v, 139^v, 140^v, 105^v, 119^v.

12. Southwell was related to the Southamptons through the marriages of his siblings into that family, and indeed to Shakespeare himself through the families of Arden, Throckmorton, and Vaux (Devlin 15, 264). E. A. J. Honigmann, in *Shakespeare: The "Lost Years,"* has investigated Shakespeare's connections with Catholics from Stratford and with Catholic gentry in Lancashire.

13. On the historical points, see Meyer, and Cross and Livingstone.

14. The title page of the 1594 Quarto of the play lists the "Servants" of the "Earl of Darbie" (Lord Strange after his succession to the title) as the first of several companies that "plaide" the work. This seems to imply that the companies acted the play in succession, although it may mean that several companies pooled their resources for a large production. See Bate, 73-77. Honigmann has made much of evidence for Shakespeare's association with Strange's Catholic connections.

WORKS CITED

Alden, Raymond Macdonald, ed. *The Sonnets of Shakespeare*. Boston: Houghton Mifflin, 1916.

Bald, R. C., ed. *An Humble Supplication to Her Majestie*. By Robert Southwell. Cambridge: Cambridge UP, 1953.

Baldwin, T. W. *William Shakespeare Adapts a Hanging*. Princeton: Princeton UP, 1931.

Bate, Jonathan, ed. *Titus Andronicus*. London: Routledge, 1995.

Booth, Stephen, ed. *Shakespeare's Sonnets*. New Haven: Yale UP, 1977.

Brownlow, F. W. "Shakespeare and Southwell." *KM 80: A Birthday Album for Kenneth Muir*. Liverpool: Liverpool UP, 1987.

Bullough, Geoffrey, ed. *Narrative and Dramatic Sources of Shakespeare*. Vol. 6. London: Routledge and Kegan Paul, 1966.

Caraman, Philip, ed. *The Other Face: Catholic Life Under Elizabeth I*. London: Longmans, 1960.

Cross, F. L., and E. A. Livingstone, eds. *The Oxford Dictionary of the Christian Church*. 2nd ed. Oxford: Oxford UP, 1974.

Devlin, Christopher. *The Life of Robert Southwell*. London: Longmans, Green, 1956.

Evans, G. Blakemore, ed. *The Sonnets*. Cambridge: Cambridge UP, 1996.

Evans, G. Blakemore, et al., eds. *The Riverside Shakespeare*. 2nd ed. Boston: Houghton Mifflin, 1997.

Fraser, Russell. *Young Shakespeare*. New York: Columbia UP, 1988.

The Geneva Bible. London, 1640.

Honigmann, E. A. J. *Shakespeare: The "Lost Years."* Totowa: Barnes and Noble, 1985.

Kerrigan, John, ed. *The Sonnets and A Lover's Complaint*. Harmondsworth: Penguin, 1986.

Klause, John. "Shakespeare's *Sonnets*: Age in Love and the Goring of Thoughts." *Studies in Philology* 80 (1983): 300-24.

Kliger, Samuel. *The Goths in England*. Cambridge: Harvard UP, 1952.

Metz, G. Harold. *Shakespeare's Earliest Tragedy: Studies in Titus Andronicus*. Madison: Fairleigh Dickinson UP, 1996.

Meyer, A. O. *England and the Catholic Church under Queen Elizabeth*. Trans. J. R. McKee. 1915. New York: Barnes and Noble, 1967.

Milward, Peter. *Shakespeare's Religious Background*. Bloomington: Indiana UP, 1973.

Mizener, Arthur. "The Structure of Figurative Language in Shakespeare's Sonnets." *Southern Review* 5 (1940): 730-47.

More, Thomas. *The Confutation of Tyndale's Answer*. Ed. Louis A. Schuster et al. *The Complete Works of St. Thomas More*. Vol. 8. New Haven: Yale UP, 1973.

Rollins, Hyder Edward, ed. *A New Variorum Edition of Shakespeare: The Sonnets*. 2 vols. Philadelphia: Lippincott, 1944.

Southwell, Robert. *An Epistle of Comfort*. English Recusant Literature, 1558-1640. Vol. 211. Ilkley: The Scolar Press, 1974.

———. *An Humble Supplication to Her Majestie*. Ed. R. C. Bald. Cambridge: Cambridge UP, 1953.

———. *The Poems of Robert Southwell, S. J.* Ed. James H. McDonald and Nancy Pollard Brown. Oxford: Clarendon, 1967.

Waith, Eugene, ed. *Titus Andronicus*. Oxford: Oxford UP, 1984.

The Name of the Rose
Christian Figurality and Shakespeare's Sonnets

Lisa Freinkel

"From fairest creatures we desire increase, / That thereby beauties *Rose* might neuer die, / . . . But thou contracted to thine owne bright eyes, / Feed'st thy lights flame with self substantiall fewell" (1.1-2, 5-6).[1] The entire story of Shakespeare's Sonnets—if we can attribute a story to a text whose sense of order and sequence is cast in doubt by the mystery behind its production[2]—is told in the first nineteen sonnets. The story concerns a world where desire exists because the natural succession of one generation to the next has ceased to exist; a world where, given that disruption in the natural order of things, poetry is offered as a solution to the ravages of time, filling in the "lines" carved in "my loues faire brow" (19.9-10) with "eternall lines" (18.12) of verse—grafting on to the disrupted lines of filial succession the compensating likenesses and "sweet semblance[s]" (13.4) no longer afforded by offspring. Niggardly prodigal, the young man addressed in these poems withholds himself from propagation, and thus consumes himself to death, destroying himself by failing to produce others like him. In this context, the poet offers metaphors to preserve the beloved's beauty—poetic likenesses which themselves resemble the filial likeness of children. Like lines of heirs, the lines of verse will serve to maintain the young man's identity—his likeness to himself—despite the ravages of time. And yet, in the world these poems portray, poetry is itself also subject to time—to decay, wrinkling and oblivion; in the "age to come," the poet warns, "So should my papers (yellowed with their age) / Be scorn'd, like old men of lesse truth then tongue" (17.7, 9-10).

In this context of time's universal waste, the poetics of praise that the late Joel Fineman characterized as the central feature of the Renaissance sonnet tradition has itself fallen into disrepair: a poetry centered on creating the ideal and idealizing likeness of its addressee can only reveal the ways in which time makes all things, poetry included, *unlike* themselves. "[E]uery faire from faire some-time declines" (18.7): verse, as well as "any mother's child" (21.11), must fall subject to a law so universal. And yet despite the obvious, explicitly thematized failure of the poet's task in the face of time's fundamental unfairness, the first nineteen sonnets do not reveal the death of praise—instead, they proclaim its birth: "Yet doe thy worst ould Time dispight thy wrong, / My loue shall in my verse euer liue young" (19.13-14). A poetics based in metaphoric likeness and the promise of immortality emerges in these nineteen poems amid the very sense of its own impossibility.

For Fineman this sense of impossibility marks the way in which Shakespeare writes in the "aftermath" of a poetics of praise. Reading within a tradition which dates back to the 1780 Malone and Steevens edition of the poems, Fineman examines the work's division between "young man" and "dark lady" sonnets. Fineman argues that the first 126 poems play out the logic of an epideictic tradition, implicitly revealing the ironies and paradoxes of praising. Such ironies finally become explicit in the dark lady poems. The sequence of sonnets thus falls neatly into two halves collectively expressing what comes before, and what comes after, the collapse of a poetics of praise. In this way, by means of a retrospective distinction between praise and its aftermath, the poems manage to "consummate, by representing or reenacting, the original intentions of a bygone poetry" (51).

The retrospective, before-after structure which Fineman reads into these poems is itself part of a centuries-old tradition. Here the Sonnets are narrativized in a manner analogous to Petrarch's *Rime sparse*, divided by its fourteenth-century editors into poems written before and after the death of Laura. Ultimately, however, such narrativizing hearkens still further back, to the Christian allegorizing interpretive mode which Erich Auerbach famously described as "figural" and which was first rendered current by the apostle Paul's treatment of the Hebrew Bible. What Fineman and other sonnet readers share with Paul is their commitment to the figural creation of a narrativized textual unity.

Pauline allegory is a hermeneutic and not a poetic or rhetorical mode. It founds itself upon the effort to construct a unified sense of textual reference despite a disruption in textual reception. The early Christian appropriation of the Hebrew Bible—now restyled the "Old" Testament—masks itself in allegory. As allegorical figures—*figurae*, as the Latin fathers will call them—the events and people of Jewish scripture become legible signs of a future Christian lesson. And in the process, the division between Jew and Christian has both been defined and reconciled by the redemption narrative according to which Judaism is fulfilled in Christ.

Any reading, like Fineman's, that seeks a narrativized, figural coherence for Shakespeare's Sonnets commits those poems in advance to the very conceptions of time, textuality, and language that the early Christians developed through their practice of figural interpretation. However, as we shall see, the Sonnets are poems whose novelty lies in their decisive rejection of any such allegory. Indeed, in this way, the Sonnets are marked by their unique cultural moment. Regardless of their author's personal piety, the Sonnets, I argue, are fundamentally Reformation—even "post"-Reformation—texts. That is, these are poems that bear witness to the devastating challenge for Christian allegory that Reformation doctrine at its most acute poses.[3]

At its base, Christian allegory relies on the Pauline distinction between the *flesh*—which comes to be identified not only with mortality, but also with Judaism and the supposed literalities of its testament with God—and the *spirit*: both Christian faith and the figural substance of Christian revelation. For Paul, the strife between flesh and spirit is essential to the human world, for it defines our sinful distance from God. At the same time, however, allegory reconciles this strife: once we realize that the flesh prefigures the spirit, their contention dissolves into narrative. In this manner, Pauline Christianity comes to understand itself as the spiritual heir to Jewish revelation: it succeeds Judaism by redeeming the letter of Jewish law. However, in defining itself as spiritual successor, Pauline Christianity transforms the notion of succession itself. Thus, the allegory that distinguishes flesh from spirit only in order to reconcile the two through narrative also distinguishes between two principles of inheritance: one based on birthright and generation; the other understood in revisionary and figural terms. Where Judaism, according to Paul, defines its sense of tradition in the fleshy sense of a "genetic" succession of father to son, Christianity understands itself as the spiritual successor to the flesh itself.

In a master trope that becomes central to Shakespeare's imagination in the Sonnets, Paul defines the relation of Christianity to Judaism in terms of grafting. As he explains to his Roman readers, the gentile, wild branch has been grafted on to the true Patriarchal root of God's olive tree:

> [T]hough some of the branches be broken off, and thou being a wild Oliue tree, wast graft in for them, and made partaker of the roote and fatnesse of the Oliue tree: Boast not thy selfe against the branches. . . . Thou wilt say then, The branches are broken off, that I might be graft in. Well, through vnbeliefe they are broken off, and thou standest by faith: bee not high minded, but feare. For if God spared not the natural branches, *take heede* lest he also spare not thee. . . . And they also, if they abide not still in vnbeliefe, shall be graffed in: for God is able to graffe them in again. . . . (Romans 11: 19-23; emphasis as in original)

The hybrid tree Paul envisions here—a cultivated olive with grafted wild branches—emblematizes the figural, revisionary logic by means of which Christianity lays claim to a Jewish heritage precisely by rejecting a filial notion of inheritance. In Romans Paul speaks not to those of his flesh—not to his fellow Jews—but to Gentiles, and he highlights the strangeness of this address, by reminding his readers of the way in which Christianity is founded upon a fundamental rejection of the flesh. A religion, in Paul's eyes, based in conversion and proselytism rather than in familial identity, Christianity disrupts the claims of nature in order to "graft" Gentiles into a tradition which is, at its patriarchal "root," Jewish. Contrary to nature, the wild olive branches usurp the place of the cultivated limbs; simply through their faith, and thus following a logic of spirit and not of the flesh, Gentiles can become heirs to God's covenant with the Hebrews. Indeed, they can become the rightful successors to the Jewish patriarchs, not insofar as they, like Paul, are of the same flesh as the patriarchs, but insofar as a spiritual notion of succession has now supplanted a fleshly one. Even if one is a Jew, succession now obeys the hybrid logic of grafting rather than the "natural" logic of genetics; to have a place on Paul's olive tree even the "real" branches would have to be engrafted. The fleshly, natural sense of succession that defined Judaism as tribal religion has itself been succeeded by the notion of a purely spiritual inheritance.

As the master figure for the Christian principle of succession, Paul's grafted olive serves as a figure of figure. It articulates the figural understanding that simultaneously assimilates and differentiates Jew and Christian, flesh and spirit by means of a revisionary narrative of before and after. When Martin Luther, however, returns to this master trope in his crucial early lectures on the book of Romans, he will reject the possibility of any such narrative. Instead of highlighting the difference of Jew and Christian in order to establish the two poles of a figural narrative, Luther collapses the distinction. Even the cultivated olive [*olea*] is not tame by nature, Luther reminds us, for from the seeds of "the tame olive nothing is produced by nature except the wild olive [*oleaster*]." And yet, he tells us, "the branch of the wild olive through grafting becomes the branch of the tame olive, which the tame could not have done by nature" (25: 101).[4]

For Luther, "ingrafting grace" [*gratia inserens*] serves as the difference between *olea* and *oleaster*; however, this is now not the difference *between* Jew and Christian, but rather the difference that both share in staking their claim to God's inheritance. Where Paul distinguished between two religions and two inheritances, linked together as flesh to spirit, Luther highlights the singular importance of grace. "Just as the wild olive does not by nature but by the art of ingrafting become the branch of the tame olive tree, so the Gentiles become the people of God through the ingrafting grace, and not through the righteousness or virtue of their own nature" (101). If all olive trees are wild "by nature," then the Jews no longer serve as a privileged point of origin in a narrative of succession. They, too, became the people of God through ingrafting grace; they too could not rely on the righteousness of their own nature. For Luther, there is no original and ungrafted tame olive tree since righteousness per se is never natural.

Written in 1515-16, Luther's lectures on Romans reflect the breakthrough insight of the years just preceding his schism with Rome. In these lectures Luther develops the doctrine of justification by faith alone. *Iustitia*, righteousness, Luther argues, must not be understood as the justice with which God judges man's actions, but rather as the mercy by means of which man is justified in God's eyes through faith.[5] There is no righteousness for Luther that does without the "ingrafting grace" of God—a grace without which we lack even the capacity for faith. Luther's true olive tree, thus, is itself a hybrid; incapable of producing on its own, it is always already engrafted. As such it resists the narrative of before and after; instead this hybrid tree bespeaks a constant, ineradicable tension between the works of man—which can never achieve salvation—and the justifying faith freely given by God. The opposition of flesh to spirit so central to Christian allegory thus reemerges for Luther in the context of the conflict between our works and our faith. At the core of his doctrine of justification lies the conviction that the strife between flesh and spirit knows no end in this life: even the saints must reckon with it. Our salvation does not rely on our holiness. It does not depend upon the eradication of sin but rather upon the infused graft of faith. We are beasts of burden, Luther will tell us in his treatise *On the Enslaved Will*, ridden either by Satan or God, and we have no choice in the matter. But our lack of free will does not obviate our moral responsibility: we can no more evade our guilt than we can renounce our flesh.

Below I argue that Shakespeare's Sonnets investigate the poetic stakes of the absolute, Lutheran strife between flesh and spirit—a strife which can neither be resolved temporally nor left unresolved, but which must be lived and renewed in each moment of our lives. Time—as Shakespeare evokes it in the form and content of his poetry—only stutters, broken into discrete and fruitless moments. As we shall see when we examine one of Shakespeare's privileged figures—the figure of the rose—no redemptive logic enriches Shakespearean temporality, ensuring the fulfillment of before in after, of flesh in spirit. But even so (and here, too, the insight is Luther's), every second counts.

Ultimately at issue in the poems is the traditional conjunction of figuration and temporal narrative. Any story like Fineman's which ascribes to these poems a narrative sense of order—a before and an after—will be inadequate. Instead of such narrative coherence, what we will discover is the way in which Shakespeare's "sequence" precisely founds itself on the impossibility of sequentiality. This is not just to say that the Sonnets "resist" narrativity in the manner of a rhetorical choice,[6] but rather that the poems are founded on the *impossibility* of any such choice. Their sense of story is built out of the suspicion that stories can no longer be written. Recounting, primarily, "time's waste"—a genitive that reveals at once the problem of corrosion as well as the sense of an expanse of time which is entirely empty (so that the complex picture here is of an emptiness "filled" with decay)— Shakespeare's figures tell over and over again the failure of narrative succession: "For as the Sun is daily new and old, / So is my loue still telling what is told" (76.13-14).

FROM OLIVES TO ROSES

It is hard to mistake the centrality of the rose in Shakespeare's writings of the 1590s. Presuming, as most critics have, that his Sonnets were written in this period, their first sustained image—the rose of beauty which animates our desire in sonnet 1 ("From fairest creatures we desire increase, / That thereby beauties *Rose* might neuer die")—echoes the mingled red and white of the beloved's face that heralds Shakespeare's Petrarchism in *Venus and Adonis* and *Rape of Lucrece*, even while "[t]his silent war of lilies and roses" (*Rape* 71) also evokes Shakespeare's decade-long preoccupation with the dynastic and dramatic implications of roses in English history. Shakespeare's roses flourish in a context at once erotic and combative, personal and political. But the figure's multivalence should not surprise us. As erotic figure for poetry's erotic figures, the rose has been conventional since the Song of Songs, and its politics have been apparent at least since Tillyard's discussions of the "Tudor Myth" of English history. Behind the damasked roses of Shakespeare's Petrarchism we have long been accustomed to see that emblem of the Tudor dynasty: the double rose, white superimposed on red. Ultimately, however, Shakespeare's roses are striking not so much for the way they foreground their own status as signs—for the way in which they draw attention to their own activity of figuration—but rather for their simultaneous ability to insist upon themselves as *things*. When Juliet famously proposes that "a rose / By any other word would smell as sweet" (2.2.43-44), she cites the flower as the consummate *thing*, the referent whose essential qualities, whose very roseness is indifferent to an order of language. For Juliet the rose works paradoxically as a figure that denies the import and weight of figures.

Of course, Juliet's nominalist insight is itself as conventional as it is mistaken, given its context in a play that demonstrates precisely the tragic force of names. In the figure of a figuration independent from the world of things, Juliet wishfully invokes a conception of language's mere conventionality that dates back in the Christian West to Augustine—but at the same time, by her very effort to offer a figure for the arbitrariness of figure, Juliet belies her own claim, asserting the coinvolvement of signs and things even while she denies it.[7]

Juliet's rose is a trope, but only insofar as it denies the possibility of ever distinguishing—or reconciling—literal and figural uses of language. Juliet's "rose" names nothing; she is citing the word in isolation from its referent—that which we call a "rose," she says, would smell as sweet by any other word; her "rose" is just a word, inadequate as any other. But that nothing which "rose" names does itself name the emptiness of language—and further, thus emptied, the rose serves as trope for the fullness of a world outside language. In this way, Juliet's rose is catachretic, offering a figure without offering a name.[8] In the Sonnets, we find this catachretic rose again—and, as with the flower's catachretic centrality in the contemporaneous *Henry VI* plays, where the sliding referentiality of Lancastrian red and Yorkist white seems both to reflect and to cause the problem of dynastic succession, in the Sonnets catachresis is also from the start tied to the question of an heir. As we have said, the young man's refusal to procreate, "[t]hat thereby beauties *Rose* might neuer die," leads to poetic likenesses—likenesses that remain in a crucial sense *unlike* their subject. Thence the ironies of Shakespeare's most widely reproduced poem: "Shall I compare thee to a summer's day? / Thou art more louely and more temperate. . . " (18.1-2). At first glance the poem declares the inadequacy of its likenesses—the young man is not like a summer's day—but, as I have discussed elsewhere,[9] it is precisely insofar as the young man *is* like a summer's day, like the "eye of heauen" (5), that he like "euery faire from faire some-time declines" (7) and is in need of verse to begin with. The poem, precisely by negating its similes, fails to give the proper image of the young man—and yet produces nonetheless images of perfection: likenesses which, however unlike the young man, will remain forever like themselves. In this way, the poem's failed similes survive as successful catachreses: there is no proper name for the young man's beauty because, like all beauty, it fails to remain like itself.

Indeed, the catachretic nature of the verse inaugurated in these sonnets ultimately reveals that it is impossible to blame the young man's problem on his own refusal to procreate. The problem which these poems confront lies not with the prodigal young man, but with a time which is itself prodigal. "Looke what an vnthrift in the world doth spend / Shifts but his place, for still the world inioyes it / But beauties waste hath in the world an end, / And kept vnvsed the vser so destroyes it" (9.9-12). In the world's economy nothing is gained, and nothing is lost. What is spent merely "shifts" places, redistributed and still enjoyed. But beauty is somehow different; its waste amounts to an actual loss, a true end, because it is itself inextricably bound to time, achieving its perfection on the very road to decay.

When I consider euery thing that growes
Holds in perfection but a little moment.

. . . .

When I perceiue that men as plants increase,
Cheared and checkt euen by the selfe-same skie:
Vaunt in their youthfull sap, at height decrease,
And were their braue state out of memory.
Then the conceit of this inconstant stay,
Sets you most rich in youth before my sight,
Where wastfull time debateth with decay
To change your day of youth to sullied night,
 And all in war with Time for loue of you
 As he takes from you, I ingraft you new. (15)

The ultimate prodigal, time spends, but its wealth doesn't merely shift places: what it wastes is permanently lost. It is because time, as imagined in these sonnets, is itself a waste that the arguments for procreation are doomed to fail: the notion of succession they invoke presumes that time moves toward fulfillment, the old redeemed in the new. In fact, such succession presumes precisely that time wastes nothing—that its expenditures are always recuperated, its beginnings preserved in its ends. In the Sonnets, however, time only ripens on the path to rotting. Beauty's rose thus can never be preserved, even when reproduced in the "liuing flowers" (16.7) of offspring, since what is reproduced will be not beauty itself, but its waste: each flower will only repeat the truth of time's law that fairness cannot remain fair, that no thing can remain like itself.

It is in this context of a wasteful time that Shakespeare imagines his poetry as "ingrafting." Just like Paul's graft of the spirit, Shakespeare's graft of verse means to supplant a succession based on filial generation. A spiritual procreation will supplant a merely fleshly one.[10] And yet, significantly, where Paul's vision of the grafted tree defined the very logic of time, producing an allegorical narrative of fulfillment and right succession, here the graft works against time, seeking to fill in the lines drawn by time with lines of verse. Indeed, in sonnet 18 the image is taken to a further extreme: "Nor shall death brag thou wandr'st in his shade, / When in eternall lines to time thou grow'st" (11-12). As Booth points out in his commentary, these eternal lines invoke the cords that hold a grafted shoot in place: here the graft is attached to time itself. Bound to time in the eternal lines of verse, the young man, it is hoped, will flourish, rather than decline, as time passes. And yet, the young man's problem is already that he is too bound to time—that his beauty, itself a thing of time, cannot remain itself. "O that you were your selfe, but loue you are / No longer yours, then you your selfe here liue" (13.1-2). In binding the young man's image to time the poet promises not the eternal truth of beauty but rather the eternal repetition of the way beauty necessarily belies itself.

Here we return to the problem of praise. For Joel Fineman, the language of the Sonnets verges on paradox because of the paradoxical structure of idealization: finding their poetic necessity in the young man's praiseworthiness, the poet's true words ultimately belie both their subject and themselves. Either praise is superfluous, in which case as "mere painting" it cheapens its subject—or the praise is needed, and thus merely flatters a young man who fails to live up to his ideal. Indeed, in the so-called "rival poet" sonnets (78-86) Shakespeare suggests that these two possibilities converge: there, a purely superfluous praise ("I neuer saw that you did painting need," [83.1]) reveals the young man's one true flaw: his vanity. "You to your beautious blessings adde a curse, / Being fond on praise, which makes your praises worse" (84.13-14). However, as we have seen, the problem with Shakespeare's young man lies deeper than the question of idealization. Certainly Shakespeare responds to the paradoxes of a tradition of epideixis when he imagines a young man who is simultaneously idealized and nonideal. But Shakespeare goes further in these poems. He uncovers the temporal assumptions behind idealism: "beauty's rose"—that is, beauty's exemplar—seems to require a world in which succession is possible. "From fairest creatures we desire increase, / That thereby beauties *Rose* might neuer die, / But as the riper should by time decease, / His tender heire might beare his memory" (1.1-4). Succession, after all, resolves the fundamental dualism of a Christian world—the dualism of flesh to spirit—by enabling the flesh over time, in the *fullness* of time, to serve as the figure of the spirit. Each tender heir "bears" the burden of the past in much the same way that Paul's grafted branches come to bear, after the fact, the burden of the patriarchal root. But in Shakespeare's post-Reformation world, time is no longer full; instead its wastes can only recount the continually renewed decline of flesh from spirit. Here the ideal—the essence of the rose—can only by disappointed by its material, fleshly embodiment. And yet, even so, such a world does not lack for beauty—although its beauty, as such, as precisely *ideal*, can only fail itself.

It is in this context that we must consider the poems that seek to preserve the young man's truth.

> Oh how much more doth beautie beautious seeme,
> By that sweet ornament which truth doth giue,
> The rose looks faire, but fairer we it deeme
> For that sweet odor, which doth in it liue:
> The Canker bloomes haue full as deepe a die,
> As the perfumed tincture of the Roses,
> Hang on such thornes, and play as wantonly,
> When sommers breath their masked buds discloses:
> But for their virtue only is their show,
> They liue vnwoo'd, and vnrespected fade,
> Die to themselues. Sweet Roses doe not so,
> Of their sweet deathes, are sweetest odors made:
>   And so of you, beautious and louely youth,
>   When that shall vade, by verse distils your truth. (54)

In terms of show the canker blossom is as fair as the rose, but its "tincture" lacks that sweet ornament, that perfume, which tells the true rose from the false. However, the poem also suggests that such truth remains hidden as long as the rose lives; odor here is figured as that essence (both scent and spiritual reality) which remains tucked inside— "which doth in it liue"—until the flower is blown and dead. Of course, if such essence is indeed hidden, we must imagine that a rose even by the name of canker would smell indifferent sweet, since its hidden scent would have no smell at all. And yet, the difference between the two flowers—the very difference between a flower and a weed—is, precisely, *essential.* Unlike the rose, cankers have beauty without truth—a beauty which is not "beautious"; when they fade, they "die to themselues." "Unwoo'd" and "vnrespected," the beauty of the canker is inessential, odorless, and thus utterly lost with the passage of time: mere fleshly appearance, it lacks the durance of spirit.

The situation that the poet here ascribes to the lowly canker echoes exactly the description of the young man's plight in the procreation sonnets. Without an heir, the flower of youth will die "vnlok'd [unlooked] on" (7.14)—will die to himself—to his own "sweet selfe too cruell" (1.8). Like the canker, the young man's beauty will prove untrue once it fades, unless somehow distilled in the grafting supplements of progeny or verse. "But flowers distil'd though they with winter meete, / Leese but their show, their substance still liues sweet" (5.13-14). Without the possibility of distillation, the young man is exactly like the canker: only his death, and *not* his beauty, will prove eternal. Presumably, however, the young man is a rose and not a canker. Presumably his beauty is true—and true precisely insofar as it withstands the test of time. Sweet roses do not die to themselves; "Of their sweet deathes, are sweetest odors made: / And so of you, beautious and louely youth, / When that shall vade, by verse distils your truth" (54.12-14).

What sonnet 54 reveals, however, is the ineradicable problem of beauty in a world where time itself is prodigal. The difference between rose and canker is essential, but it can only emerge after death, by means of the graft that fills out "vaded" or departed beauty—that fleshes out time's waste. Such a graft—here figured as the sweet perfume distilled from faded flowers—will tell the difference between rose and canker, but only after the two are gone. As such, the verse that distills pure essence will be indistinguishable from the verse that tells pure lies. Indeed, the problem in these poems is that it will never be clear whether beauty exists as the rose's truth, or as the canker's lie. Roses, like cankers, do indeed die to themselves; the truth of their beauty is a truth which, like the eternal summer's day of sonnet 18, belies their life. Every fair from fair sometime delines.

The consequences of sonnet 54—of a world where the essential difference between roses and cankers verges on a lie—are elaborated in the poems that explore, like the rival poet sonnets, the flattering nature of praise, and in poems like 95 that consider the young man's failings. "How sweet and louely dost thou make the shame, / Which like the canker in the fragrant Rose / Doth spot the beautie of thy budding name?" (95.1-3). Here the problem of beauty becomes internal to the rose itself; rather than understood as that weed indistinguishably, but essentially, different from the flower, the canker here is that worm which blemishes the name of beauty itself. Indeed, that name—which the first sonnet has seemed to identify, through italics, as the proper name of the young man, *Rose*, himself (and according to Rollins's *Variorum*, industrious readers have heard a pun on the Earl of Southampton's family name, *Wriothesley*)—that proper name of Rose here seems to have become improper by "bless[ing] an ill report" (8). The young man's name seems at once to name beauty as *Rose*, and to name the canker which disrupts that beauty, turning flowers into weeds. "That tongue that tells the story of thy daies, / (Making lasciuious comments on thy sport) / Cannot dispraise, but in a kinde of praise, / Naming thy name, blesses an ill report" (5-8). The poem alludes to this ill report, but does not tell us what it consists of—what precise shame or ill-mannered "sport" lascivious tongues have recounted. Instead the poem focuses upon the fact that beauty's name refers equivocally both to rose and to canker. "[B]eauties vaile doth couer euery blot, / And all things turnes to faire. . . " (11-12). What the young man has done literally makes no difference since any report of beauty is an "ill" report. Whether we maintain beauty's fairness in the face of time or declare its cankerous waste at the hands of time, we have done beauty wrong. As these poems imagine it, to be beautiful is necessarily to decline; we cannot help but mistake the canker for the rose.

In other poems Shakespeare considers the cost of equivocal beauty on the poet himself. Given the nature of fairness, the poet's words cannot avoid being, in some measure, unfair:

> No more bee greeu'd at that which thou hast done,
> Roses haue thornes, and siluer fountaines mud,
> Cloudes and eclipses stain both Moone and Sunne,
> And loathsome canker liues in sweetest bud.
> All men make faults, and euen I in this,
> Authorizing thy trespas with compare,
> My selfe corrupting saluing thy amisse,
> Excusing their sins more then their sins are:
> For to thy sensuall fault I bring in sence,
> Thy aduerse party is thy Aduocate,
> And gainst my self a lawfull plea commence,
> Such ciuil war is in my loue and hate,
> That I an accessary needs must be,
> To that sweet theefe which sourely robs from me. (35)

Here we begin with the rose's pricking thorns, but move quickly, and more radically, to the canker that consumes the flower but fails to change beauty's name. All men make faults, but these true words only work to transform invective into praise, trespass into a comparison which, however true, authorizes falsehood itself. The poem's metaphors work in a direction opposite to the similes of sonnet 18. There the poet produced unlikenesses—the summer's day, the eye of heaven—similes that described the young man's beauty only by failing to compare with it. But those unlikenesses, we will recall, were lies;

what animated the poem was instead the recognition that the young man's summer is just as transient as a summer's day. Nonetheless sonnet 18—which failed to tell us what the young man was like—did finally offer us an improper trope of beauty: an image of beauty that would remain ever true, ever like itself; an "eternall Sommer" (9) that would never fade. Sonnet 18 is a poem, as we saw, that lies—but it lies like truth.

In sonnet 35 ("No more bee greeu'd"), however, the poet's comparisons are apt. The young man is indeed like a silver fountain stained with mud, like the sweetest bud eaten by a loathsome canker. Here, the likenesses the poet offers are truthful—and yet, their very truth only renders fault itself lovely: a thing of beauty, a thing of nature. Thus, many critics have emended line 8 in terms of a conflict between natural and moral faults: "Excusing *thy* sins more than *thy* sins are," the poet corrupts himself by exculpating the young man's moral failure as if it were more intrinsic to the young man's identity than it is. The poet's mistake, such readings assert, is to take the young man's sin as if it were a fault *of* his beauty—that is, a fault indispensible to and inextricable from his beauty as such—rather than to take it as a fault *in* his beauty; a fault that mars fairness in the manner of an avoidable blemish. Such readings, however, miss the extent to which even so-called "moral" fault is a natural feature of the post-Reformation world; such fault exists as the inevitable and unconquerable schism (the faultline, as it were) between our fleshly nature and our spiritual heritage.

Because of its grammatical opacity, line 8 will remain difficult and undecidable, although its function within the poem may be clarified. Beauty, as it seems to be defined in these poems, is more a formal category than it is a substantive physical property. The relative absence of blazons in the young man poems should alert us to this fact.[11] In place of the specific catalogue of the young man's features, his beauty seems to consist merely in his *fairness,* in the brutest sense of the word's meaning as *equality* or *parity.* The young man is beautiful because he remains constant, self-identical, equal to himself. He is "fair, kinde and true" (105.9).[12] "O that you were yourself!" (13.1) as the poet exclaims in his arguments for procreation. To be fair is to be one's self, simply, perfectly, eternally. "Who is it that sayes most, which can say more, / Then this rich praise, that you alone, are you" (84.1-2). The height of praise is to assert one's self-identity. In these terms, beauty becomes for Shakespeare that privileged natural feature that time particularly enables and attacks; time makes us who we are, but it also makes us decline from ourselves. In short, for Shakespeare beauty would seem to be something like the name for our particular temporal predicament.

Thus, in sonnet 35, fault does seem to be the inevitable concomitant of beauty—the unavoidable spoilage of the ideal in a world ravaged by time. Such fault is also unavoidable for the poet, whose comparisons only idealize the very nature of sin itself by rendering it the universal property of man. And thus we might approach a reading of line 8: "All men make faults, and even I in this. . . / Excusing *their* sins more than *there* sins are." In making figures, comparisons for fault, the poet has made fault beautiful, a thing pertaining to all beauty—and further, a thing of all flesh, as if flesh itself were beautiful precisely insofar as it fails to live up to the ideals of spirit. He has excused the sins of man too broadly, excusing more generically than he should. The risk the poet runs here is the same risk of complacency that the doctrine, Lutheran at its core, of the will's bondage is always at risk of running. Because the chasm between flesh and spirit is decisive, sins of the flesh are inherent, natural; given such unavoidable fault, to what extent can beauty ever be said to fail—or can failure ever fail to be beautiful? "Oh in what sweets doest thou thy sinnes inclose!" (95.4). With such assumptions about beauty, how can sin as such be thought even to exist?

Erasmus argued in similar terms against Luther in the 1524 diatribe *On Free Will*: if we conclude that man's will is bound, that by nature man is sinful, then we can no longer hold him responsible for his errors. But Luther's vision of man's nature, like Shakespeare's vision of beauty, was more complex than Erasmus realized. For Luther, man does not act by compulsion. In no sense, when he sins, does he do so involuntarily; instead, when man does ill, he does so "spontaneously" and of his own accord. Furthermore, Luther tells us, it is precisely this willingness to sin—this consent to do evil—that man cannot alter. Indeed, as willing creatures, Luther argues that we can *only* do what we want: our desires are the one thing about which we are unwilling. At the heart of us as willing creatures, our wills, *as such*, are unwilling.

In sonnet 35, the poet seems to articulate a similar insight. His fault consists in his idealization—his idolatry, even—of sin: "For to thy sensuall fault I bring in sence" (9), he writes, acknowledging the rationalizing work of poetry, although many readers have also smelled out the worshipful *incense* behind this claim. Through his comparisons the poet has more beautified fault than he has acknowledged the fault in beauty. He has thus failed to realize that one cannot be exonerated on account of unfreedom; rather such unfreedom amounts to the very willful error for which we stand accused. Hence, the ambivalence which this poem records: "Such civill war is in my loue and hate, / That I an accessary needs must be, / To that sweet theefe which sourely robs from me" (12-14). Accessory to the young man's fault insofar as he cites the beauty of that fault—and the fault of beauty—the poet cannot help but possess a will torn between love and hate.

In the dark lady sonnets, of course, this ambivalent will comes entirely to the fore in terms of a poet who loves against his conscience. Further, like the young man sonnets, these poems also begin by invoking the need for succession:

> In the ould age blacke was not counted faire,
> Or if it weare it bore not beauties name:
> And now is black beauties successiue heire,
> And Beauty slanderd with a bastard shame,
> For since each hand hath put on Natures power,
> Fairing the foule with Arts faulse borrow'd face,
> Sweet beauty hath no name no holy boure,
> But is prophan'd, if not liues in disgrace.
> Therefore my Mistersse eyes are Rauen black,
> Her eyes so suted, and they mourners seeme,
> At such who not borne faire no beauty lack,
> Slandring Creation with a false esteeme,
>   Yet so they mourne becomming of their woe,
>   That euery toung saies beauty should looke so. (127)

How are we to understand this poem? For Fineman the sonnet heralds the "after" image of a poetics of praise, but as we have seen, it is precisely the logic of before and after that the young man sonnets devastate in their vision of a wasteful time. Indeed, rather than imagine that the sonnet declares a new beginning, that the succession it envisions succeeds on the ideality of the young man poems, the poem seems to take us back again to the problem of the canker and the rose: the problem of a beauty that cannot help but belie itself.

Here beauty is understood as slandered—as falsified by the hand that has faired the foul. This is the hand that paints—at once the makeup artist and the poet, whose comparisons falsify beauty in the very process of preserving it. This beauty has no name; equally canker and rose, a beauty understood as fairness has only an improper, catachretic place in the world of Shakespeare's Sonnets. Nonetheless, in this world filled with time's waste, such slander constitutes the only words of truth. In these terms the sonnet re-invokes the problem of succession with which the sequence began. There the ideal of beauty— beauty's rose—was endangered by a fairness that was turning foul and needed to find compensating likenesses to sustain itself. Here, the problem is also the foulness of the fair, but the compensations themselves—the grafts and painting that would fair the foul—are now imagined not as solution, but as the dilemma itself. And, in consequence, the spiritual, poetic succession, which the procreation poems finally announced as solution for time's waste, is here declared as nothing but bastardy. "Therefore my Mistersse eyes are Rauen blacke": as heir to a slandered beauty, the dark lady's blackness would stand, presumably, as beauty's legitimate heir, but as such it succeeds beauty not by supplanting it nor, still less, by fulfilling it. Rather such blackness succeeds the fair by mourning its loss.

Yet by the poem's last two lines we realize that this mourning of the fair has been the precondition for our desire all along. "Yet so they [her eyes] mourne becomming of their woe, / That euery toung saies beauty should look so." Desire in Shakespeare's Sonnets appeared, from the first, as the desire for beauty's successor; the starting point of such desire was the recognition that the fair was being wasted without reprieve. From the start our desire for beauty has been predicated on its loss. Here the dark lady invokes, again, our desire for beauty's successor but in slightly different terms: if the dark lady is called beautiful, she is so because she allows the mourning for beauty to take beauty's place.

"I haue seene Roses damaskt, red and white, / But no such Roses see I in her cheekes. . . . / And yet by heauen I thinke my loue as rare, / As any she beli'd with false compare" (130.5-6, 13-14). Unlike the efforts of sonnet 18, the famous anti-Petrarchism of sonnet 130 refuses to go beyond the falseness of comparison in order to speak the truth of beauty. These damasked roses are not catachretic images of a beauty that cannot equal itself; nor, like Juliet's rose, do these flowers insist on the indifference of the world of things to language. The false comparisons that comprise the poem do not simply repeat the lessons of Juliet's nominalism (what's in a name?); instead they are, precisely, belied by the dark lady. She is no rose of beauty—but nor are roses clearly beautiful. Indeed, sweet beauty no longer hath a name.

Throughout Shakespeare's Sonnets, mourning has been everywhere: it has been "our" position from the start, in our desire for beauty's increase. At stake has been a position of amorous interest in a world that is already dying. But here in the dark lady poems we find Shakespeare's fullest picture of such mourning:

> Poore soule the center of my sinfull earth,
>
> . . . .
> Why dost thou pine within and suffer dearth
> Painting thy outward walls so costlie gay?
>
> . . . .
> Shall wormes inheritors of this excesse
> Eate up thy charge? is this thy bodies end? (146.1, 3-4, 7-8)

Ultimately, for Shakespeare, the split between flesh and spirit can offer only one unproblematic image of succession: that of the Diet of Worms convoked upon our fleshy remains.[13] All the same, as long as we are in the flesh, our mourning of beauty and our ability to give up its name will remain incomplete and ambivalent. "I doe betray / My nobler part to my grose bodies treason, / My soule doth tell my body that he may, / Triumph in loue, flesh staies no farther reason, / But rysing at thy name doth point out thee, / As his triumphant prize" (151.5-10). In the end, the conflict between flesh and spirit makes mourning impossible: the flesh, as they say, has a will of its own. And it is this Will, this will of Shakespeare's bawdy no less than body, that inevitably betrays us as it hearkens to the name of the rose.

NOTES

1. Citations of the Sonnets throughout are from the reproduction of the 1609 Quarto in the Booth edition.

2. Since at least 1841, the prevailing critical view has been that Thomas Thorpe's 1609 publication of the poems was unauthorized. For recent discussions of this view, see James Schiffer's introduction to this volume. See also my discussion of authority and intentionality in the procreation sonnets: Freinkel, "Shakespeare and the Theology of Will."

3. My argument, thus, offers no comment on Shakespeare's biographical faith or conscious intention. Instead, I consider the way in which his poems

seem to recast Petrarchism within a Lutheran universe. The Sonnets, I argue, transform and renew a traditional poetics of praise insofar as they register the implications—for notions of language, time, and text—of their era's most powerful cultural movement. Furthermore, of all Protestant reformers, Luther is most central to my account because it is in his early formulations that the profoundly anti-allegorical nature of Reformist thought is most clearly revealed.

4. For Latin see the Weimar Ausgabe (WA) of Luther's works (WA 56: 113). Here Luther cites Augustine's *Ad Valerium de nuptis et concupiscentis* 1: 19 where Augustine discusses the tame olive's failure to produce, of its own nature, other tame olives. See *Patrologiae Cursus Completus, Series Latina* (PL) 44: 426.

5. Luther discusses his breakthrough discovery—often referred to as the "Tower experience"—in the autobiography that appeared as the preface to the first edition of his Latin works (cf. WA 54). Many critics still accept Erich Vogelsang's argument that this breakthrough can be tracked as far back as Luther's 1513-15 lectures on the Psalms.

6. Heather Dubrow's essay "'Incertainties now crown themselves assur'd': The Politics of Plotting Shakespeare's Sonnets," reprinted in this volume, takes precisely this tack.

7. For Augustine's highly influential definition of the literal (*proprium*) and figurative (*translatum*) sign, see *On Christian Doctrine* (2.10 ff.).

8. In terms resonant for our purposes, Roland Barthes has defined the rhetorical figure "catachresis": "there is no other possible word to denote the 'wings' of a house, or the 'arms' of a chair, and yet 'wings' and 'arms' are instantly, already metaphorical." For Barthes, catachresis is the perfect figure of beauty because it establishes the logic of an "object of comparison whose existence is altogether transferred to the language of the object to which it is compared." A beautiful thing cannot be explained except by way of comparison with other beautiful things which in themselves are compared to. . . . Catachresis bespeaks the way in which language constructs its meaning around the holes in reference. See Barthes 34.

9. See Freinkel, "Shakespeare and the Theology of Will."

10. It is no accident that my terms here invoke Diotima's distinction between spiritual and natural procreation in Plato's *Symposium*. The Platonic discussion of procreation as a means to immortality enters Petrarchism both through the impact of Ficino's Neoplatonism on Renaissance poetics, and—even more profoundly—it is implicit in the Johannine distinction between flesh and spirit itself: the distinction upon which Paul bases his notion of Christian allegory.

11. The only real exception is sonnet 99, where the poet accuses flowers of having stolen the "purple pride" of the young man's cheeks and "marjoram" of his hair. But even in this poem the floral catalogue of the young man's beauties seems to serve as mere prelude to the canker in line 13 that consumes flowers, beauty and all.

12. See Fineman's brilliant discussion of this poem (254-55).

13. We are not far here from the famously Lutheran overtones of Hamlet's reference to the dead Polonius at "supper . . . [n]ot where he eats, but where 'a is eaten; a certain convocation of politic worms are e'en at him" (4.3.18-19). Hamlet's mourning—forestalled by his melancholia—is directly relevant to this reading of the Sonnets.

WORKS CITED

Auerbach, Erich. "Figura." *Scenes from the Drama of European Literature: Six Essays*. Trans. Ralph Mannheim. New York: Meridian, 1959. 1-76.

Augustine. *On Christian Doctrine*. Trans. D. W. Robertson Jr. New York: Macmillan, 1958.

Barthes, Roland. *S/Z: An Essay*. Trans. Richard Miller. New York: Hill and Wang, 1974.

Dubrow, Heather. "'Incertainties now crown themselves assur'd': The Politics of Plotting Shakespeare's Sonnets." *Shakespeare Quarterly* 47 (1996): 291-305.

Erasmus, Desiderius. *De Libero Arbitrio Diatribe*. Trans. and ed. Gordon Rupp with A. N. Marlow. *Luther and Erasmus: Free Will and Salvation*. Philadelphia: Westminster, 1969. 33-97.

Fineman, Joel. *Shakespeare's Perjured Eye: The Invention of Poetic Subjectivity in the Sonnets*. Berkeley: U of California P, 1986.

Freinkel, Lisa. "Shakespeare and the Theology of Will." *Graven Images* 2 (1995): 31-47.

The Geneva Bible: The Annotated New Testament Edition. Ed. Gerald T. Sheppard. New York: Pilgrim, 1989.

Luther, Martin. *Lectures on Romans*. Trans. Walter G. Tillmann. *Luther's Works*. Gen. ed. Jaroslav Pelikan. Vol. 25. St. Louis: Concordia, 1955-.

———. *D. Martin Luthers Werke. Kritische Gesamtausgabe*. [Also known as the "Weimar Ausgabe" or WA.] Weimar: Böhlau, 1883-.

Patrologiae Cursus Completus, Series Latina. [Also known as "Patrologia Latina" or PL.] Ed. Jacques-Paul Migne. Paris: Migne, 1844-91.

Rollins, Hyder Edward, ed. *A New Variorum Edition of Shakespeare: The Sonnets*. 2 vols. Philadelphia: J. B. Lippincott, 1944.

Shakespeare, William. *The Riverside Shakespeare*. Gen. Ed. G. Blakemore Evans. 2nd ed. Boston: Houghton Mifflin, 1997.

Shakespeare's Sonnets. Ed. Stephen Booth. New Haven: Yale UP, 1977.

Vogelsang, Erich. "Die Anfänge von Luthers Christologie." *Arbeiten zur Kirschengeschichte* 15 (1929).

What's the Use?
Or, The Problematic of Economy in Shakespeare's Procreation Sonnets

Peter C. Herman

> [A]ll the world choppeth and changeth, runneth and raveth after
> Marts, Markets and Merchandising, so that all thinges come into
> Commerce, and passe into traffique (in a manner) in all times, and in
> all places. . . .
> —John Wheeler, *A Treatise of Commerce* (1601)

In *Shakespeare's Perjured Eye*, Joel Fineman argues that the Sonnets
begin in a predominantly untroubled language of homogeneous vision
and then fall (in every sense) into a whirlpool of heterosexual and
linguistic difference:

> In Shakespeare's sonnets, we can say, linguistic difference predicates
> sexual difference. Thus the young man is "'fair,' 'kind,' and 'true'"
> (105), and the sonnets addressed to the young man regularly invoke
> visual imagery of identificatory likeness when they characterize their
> poet's desire for the young man. In paradoxical contrast, the lady, as
> she is given to us, is foul because both fair and foul, unkind because
> both kind and unkind, false because both true and false. So too the
> sonnets addressed to the lady regularly associate the lady with a
> disjunction occasioned by verbal duplicity. . . . (16-17)

While I concur with his overall analysis, nonetheless I think that
Fineman significantly understates the degree of "linguistic difference"

in the opening sonnets. The "visual image of unity" does more than seem "to some extent, divided" (145), and in this brief essay, I will suggest how the complexities and aporias throughout the opening twenty sonnets both arise from and intervene in the economic developments of the early 1600s. To paraphrase Don E. Wayne's depiction of Ben Jonson's *The Staple of News*, the opening sonnets reflect the "embourgeoisement" of the sonnet form.[1] In other words, they exemplify the reduction of human subjects to the status of things or commodities "that occurs when commodity exchange comes to dominate social relationships and when the circulation of social energy is expressed as the circulation of money" (153-54).

Furthermore, redating the composition and/or revision of the Sonnets to the early 1600s allows us to align these texts with the later Shakespeare's general interest in the deconstruction of cultural and generic forms as well as his particular interest in the conflation of economics and biology in *Troilus and Cressida* (1601-02) and *Timon of Athens* (1607-08).[2] If Shakespeare's Sonnets discover a new form of subjectivity, as Fineman suggests, they explore the subjectivity resulting when the speaker is no longer defined by either courtly values (e.g., Wyatt) or Neoplatonic philosophy (e.g., Petrarch), but by the marketplace, and just as Jonson's work reflects the transition from an ideology based on status to one based on contract (Wayne 145), the Sonnets register the dehumanization implicit in an ideology of commodity.[3]

I

Shakespeare's "obsessive concern with metaphorical wealth, profit, worth, value, expense, 'content'" (Greene, "Pitiful Thrivers" 176) has of course been well-noted, as has his reliance on Erasmus's "Epistle to Persuade a Young Gentleman to Marriage" (Booth 135). Yet critics have not noted just how much Shakespeare "economizes" Erasmus's letter, which would have been widely available from Thomas Wilson's translation in *The Arte of Rhetorique* (1560). In this text, the speaker tries to convince a young man to marry and have children, and as one perhaps might expect from Erasmus, the primary impetus is religious:

> Matrimony is even as honorable as the name of a heretic is thought shameful. What is more right or meet than to give that unto the posterity, the which we have received of our ancestors? What is more

> inconsiderate than under the desire of holiness to eschew that as
> unholy which God himself, the fountain and father of all holiness,
> would have to be counted as most holy? (qtd. in Wilson, *Arte* 81)

Not marrying is clearly unnatural, but even this argument is enfolded
within a religious context, and in an interesting analogy, Erasmus
equates not marrying with acting "like giants," that is to say, fighting
nature is being "a rebel to God himself" (86, 87).

In Shakespeare's sequence, however, the primary referent shifts
from religion to economics. The addressee is guilty of "niggarding" (1);
his beauty deserves "use" and not procreating is "thriftless praise" (2);
Nature "lends" beauty and the addressee is a "Profitless usurer" (4)
who ought to fear Nature's "audit" (4). As Greene says, "The
procreation sonnets display with particular brilliance Shakespeare's
ability to manipulate words which in his language belonged both to the
economic and the sexual/biological semantic fields: among others,
'increase,' 'use,' 'spend,' 'free,' 'live,' 'dear,' 'house,' 'usury,'
'endowed,' along with their cognates" ("Pitiful Thrivers" 176).

Shakespeare signals this alteration in the fundamental orientation
of the argument as well as the consequences of "economizing" the
matter of procreation in the first line of the sequence: "From Fairest
creatures we desire increase / That thereby beauties *Rose* might neuer
die."[4] This opening couplet sounds traditionally Neoplatonic: we want
beautiful people to procreate so that the essence of beauty ("beauties
Rose") will never be lost, the distillation of the multiple world of
becoming to the unity of the ideal nicely suggested by the conflation of
the plural and the possessive in the original spelling ("beauties" = both
the plural of "beauty" as well as the possessive "beauty's," an overtone
lost in modernizing the orthography) leading to the italicized and
capitalized Rose. Lars Engle summarizes the argument thus: the
opening lines refer to "a general social hope or purpose: to achieve a
permanence or stability in beauty that will successfully oppose death"
(27). The poem proceeds to criticize the addressee for his narcissism,
his self-infatuation ("contracted to thine owne bright eyes"—the verb,
"contracted," marvelously conflating an allusion to a marriage contract
and to shrinking), and concludes by enjoining him not to deny "the
world's due," that is, a child.

Fair enough. Yet Shakespeare alters these otherwise unexceptional
sentiments by casting the argument in explicitly *economic* terms that
pull away from and distend the neoplatonic suggestions of "beauties

Rose." "Fairest creatures" certainly means "the most beautiful creations," and "Fairest" denotes the most equitable, yet to call somebody a "creature" slightly diminishes him or her. While the OED records uses of "creature" that refer to people (although the Shakespearean example is from *Richard III*: "There is no creature loves me" 5.3.200 [3.a]), and to endearment (3.b), the word often refers to animate beings "*as distinct* from man" (2.a; my emphasis) and another usage is "expressing reprobation or contempt" (3.c), which is how Othello employs the term when he exclaims "O curse of marriage! / That we can call these delicate creatures ours, / And not their appetites!" (3.3.267-69). Significantly, the next direct reference to Desdemona further demotes her to the status of a "thing" (3.3.271).[5] "Creature" thus puts into play a set of meanings that runs against the idealization most often seen in this line, and the next clause amplifies this counternarrative.

To "desire increase" implicitly reduces the act of procreation to a curiously bloodless phrase (imagine the romantic consequences of saying "I desire increase with you"). More important, however, are the word's manifold resonances. Like "creature," "increase" in some cases can and should be read positively, yet all the definitions of "increase" as a noun in the OED add a dark overtone to this line. Definition II.6, for instance, conflates human and animal progeny; II.7 refers to "that which grows or is produced from the earth"; and II.7.c is "that which is obtained or gained; profit; interest on money" (the citation from the Geneva Bible is apposite: "Thou shalt not . . . lend him thy vitailes for increase" [Lev. 25: 37]. To desire "increase" therefore picks up on and further emphasizes the implicit reification of "fairest creatures" by putting children in the same category as animals, crops, or money. Consequently, the different connotations of "increase" and "creature" disrupt the "homogeneous poetics of vision" that Fineman detects in the young man sequence (147). But in addition to the introduction of linguistic polysemy and therefore interpretive ambiguity, if not undecidability, the use of "increase" coupled with "creature" in the very first line of his sequence implies that the speaker considers procreation as an economic matter and children as the objects of a market economy, and the concatenation of the two terms also serves to associate procreation with agriculture and usury.

Shakespeare's pun on "husbandry" further amplifies the agricultural theme: "For where is she so faire whose vn-eard wombe / Disdaines the tillage of thy husbandry" (3). The argument recasts

Erasmus's simile between not having children and letting fertile land go to waste:

> If that man be punished who little heedeth the maintenance of his tillage (the which although it be never so well manured, yet it yieldeth nothing else but wheat, barley, beans, and peasen), what punishment is he worthy to suffer that refuseth to plough that land which being tilled yieldeth children? and for ploughing land, it is nothing else but painful toiling from time to time, but in getting children there is pleasure which, being ordained as a ready reward for painstaking, asketh a short travail for all the tillage. (qtd. in Wilson, *Arte* 92)

Like Erasmus, Shakespeare's speaker also equates having children with ploughing a field, the "un-eard wombe" being, as Booth notes, equated to "one that is untilled (literally 'unploughed'—from Old English 'erian,' to plough" [139]). But there is one major difference. Erasmus bases his argument on an ideology that does not regard human beings in purely economic terms, and thus he balances this dehumanization of the potential "plough-ee" by immediately following this paragraph with an encomium of companionate marriage:

> If we compt that great pleasure which we receive of the goodwill of our friends and acquaintances, how pleasant a thing is it above all others to have one with whom you may break the bottom of your heart, with whom ye may talk as freely as with yourself, into whose trust you may safely commit yourself, such a one as thinketh all your goods to be her charge. (qtd. in Wilson, *Arte* 92)

Erasmus's metaphor of the field is exactly that, a metaphor, no doubt distasteful today, but a relatively minor part of the overall argument, and immediately qualified (or redeemed) by a section insisting upon the full humanity and equality of the marriage partner. Yet in Shakespeare, the quite literal objectification of both partner and progeny constitutes the entire relationship.

First, the partner. Max Weber has remarked that the "market community [is] the most impersonal relationship of practical life" because of the market's "matter-of-factedness, its orientation to the commodity and only that" (636), and Lukács has argued that commodity structure penetrates "society in all its aspects and [remolds] it in its own image" (85). Significantly, both aspects of reification are manifested in how the procreation sonnets treat women. As perhaps one would expect, given the market orientation of procreation, women are reduced to commodities, to passive vessels of the man's seed. The "husbandry" pun in sonnet 3, for instance, literally transforms the woman, a full-fledged agent and partner in Erasmus, to a field, devoid of any human qualities, who also produces things (crops, in this case). True, the speaker calls the addressee "thy mother's glass" (8), but his own progeny will carry no marks of his (the sonnets assume a son) mother: "Die single and *thine* Image dies with thee" (14; my emphasis). In sonnet 16, the field contracts somewhat to "maiden gardens" (6), and sonnet 6 enjoins the young man to defeat time by making "sweet some viall" (3). Two points on this line: first, once more the speaker reduces the proposed partner to the status of a thing, a vial in this case, which, like a field, passively receives whatever the male decides to put into it and is defined by what it produces; second, the pun on "vial/vile" that is sweetened by semen foreshadows the rampant misogyny of many later sonnets, sonnet 129 in particular, with its depiction of the vagina as "hell."

Other sonnets turn procreation into an almost autoerotic activity. In sonnet 2, for instance, the speaker asks, "How much more praise deseru'd thy beauties vse / If thou couldst answere this fair child *of mine* / Shall sum my count, and make my old excuse / Proouing *his* beautie *by succession thine*" (9-12; my emphasis); and in sonnet 13 he declares: "O none but vnthrifts, deare my love you know, / You had a Father, let your Son say so" (13-14). In these lines, one also finds manifest the second definition of reification; that is, the erasure of the means of production in the object itself. And in sonnet 11, Nature "caru'd thee for her seale, and ment therby, / Thou shouldst print more, not let that coppy die" (13-14). Not only does the speaker entirely occlude the partner's role, but the child is himself now an endlessly reproducible commodity. Moreover, while the couplet begins with an older meaning for printing (making an impression) that has aristocratic overtones (the addressee is Nature's seal), the concatenation of "print" and "coppy" moves the sense into the still relatively novel discourse of publishing. By doing so, Shakespeare once more underscores the mercantilizing of sexuality, an overtone perhaps less immediately accessible today, given the conventionality of print publication.

As Wendy Wall has recently pointed out, early modern poets after Sidney tried to shed the stigma of print publication, with its associations of the marketplace, by trying to make their works seem like manuscripts that somehow ended up in a publisher's hands (54-55). That is to say, to legitimize the text's entry into the marketplace, authors tried to deny (rhetorically and artfully) that this was their intention in the first place. Sonnet 11, however, moves in the opposite direction by explicitly associating procreation with the *de*legitimizing, because mercantile, arena of printing, depicting the work of generation in the age of mechanical reproduction, as it were.

All of these strands come together in Shakespeare's insistence on situating the addressee's beauty and his responsibility to propagate it in the discourse of usury.[6] As we have noted, Shakespeare foreshadows the presence of usury in the first line of sonnet 1, one of "increase's" meanings being interest on money, and although usury is not the primary meaning of sonnet 2's "How much more praise deseru'd thy beauties vse" (9), the cognate anticipates sonnet 4's multiple puns on "use" and "usury":

> Vnthrifty louelinesse why dost thou spend,
> Vpon thy selfe thy beauties legacy?
> Natures bequest giues nothing but doth lend,
> And being franck she lends to those are free:
> Then beautious nigard why doost thou abuse,
> The bountious largesse giuen thee to giue?
> Profitles vserer why doost thou vse
> So great a summe of summes yet can'st not liue?
> For hauing traffike with thy selfe alone,
> Thou of thy selfe thy sweet selfe dost deceaue,
> Then how when nature calls thee to be gone,
> What acceptable *Audit* can'st thou leaue?
>   Thy vnus'd beauty must be tomb'd with thee,
>   Which vsed liues th'executor to be.

Usury is equally central to sonnet 9—"Looke what an vnthrift in the world doth spend / Shifts but his place, for still the world inioyes it / But beauties waste hath in the world an end, / And kept vnvsed the vser so destroyes it" (9-12)—and sonnet 6:

> Then let not winters wragged hand deface,
> In thee thy summer ere thou be distil'd:
> Make sweet some viall: treasure thou some place,

With beauties treasure ere it be self kil'd:
That vse is not forbidden vsery,
Which happies those that pay the willing lone;
That's for thy selfe to breed an other thee,
Or ten times happier be it ten for one,
Ten times thy selfe were happier then thou art,
If ten of thine ten times refigur'd thee,
Then what could death doe if thou should'st depart,
Leauing thee liuing in posterity?
    Be not selfe-wild for thou art much too faire,
    To be deaths conquest and make wormes thine heire.

One critic has suggested recently that in the procreation sonnets, Shakespeare "not only acknowledges the necessity of usury ... [but] even comes to celebrate usury as consonant with the Christian concept of *caritas*" (Mischo 162).[7] The invocation of usury, however, like the multiple resonances of "increase" and "creature," renders any easy, unclouded interpretation of these poems untenable as the term once again effects the dehumanization that occurs when the marketplace governs human relationships.[8] Furthermore, the prominence of usury in the procreation sonnets' argument needs to be seen as part of a number of overlapping contexts: the general economic problems of late Elizabethan, early Jacobean England, the intensification of the usury debate during this period, and Shakespeare's own developing concern for this issue, as evidenced by the marked increase in his employment of "usury" and its cognates beginning in 1599-1600, not one of which is even vaguely positive.[9] Usury may denote a specific economic practice, yet by the early seventeenth century it also connoted all that seemed destabilizing and threatening in the socioeconomic developments affecting early modern England. Finally, usury destabilizes the subject of the Petrarchan sonnet sequence itself by introducing overtones of unauthorized sexualities.

II

As Norman Jones writes, "By the time Elizabeth had died people had become thoroughly confused about usury" (175). On the one hand, the anti-usury bias was enshrined in statute law. The Bill against Usury of 5 & 6 Edward VI, c. 20 (1552) banned usury altogether, and although the usury statute of 1571 allowed for loans with 10 percent interest (forbidding any rate higher or lower) under certain circumstances, it did so grudgingly, as "all Usurie being forbydden by the Lawe of God is synne and detestable" (Jones 63; Nelson 83-84). Yet as Jones also suggests, the period between 1571 and the passing of the next usury statute in 1624 witnessed a slow change in the definition of usury from something abominated on religious grounds to a necessary economic practice whose use and abuse was left to the individual conscience (145). Significantly, however, the attacks on usury "reached a crescendo in the early seventeenth century, a conservative response to hard economic times and new economic thought" (146). As many literary critics and historians have pointed out, the later 1590s witnessed terrible economic dislocation, partly as a result of inclement weather and dearth, and also social dislocation, as the feudal economy gave way to capitalism and the older notions of society's structure no longer seemed adequate or appropriate. With inflation and worsening economic times came of course increased bankruptcies and increasing need for liquid capital. Popular resentment against moneylenders grew in rough proportion to their centrality (Jones 176), and the failed attempts by Parliament to pass a new usury statute in 1604 and 1606 demonstrate both the increasing necessity of usury and the strength of the anti-usury forces.[10]

It is not accidental that this intensification of the usury debate coincided with an upsurge in Shakespeare's own usage of this term, and redating the composition and/or revision of the Sonnets to the early seventeenth century allows us to see Shakespeare's concern for usury as both a result of and an intervention into this ongoing controversy. According to Spevack's concordance, while Shakespeare uses this term three times towards the beginning of his career (*1 Henry VI* [1589-90; rev. 1594-95], *Romeo and Juliet* [1595-96]; and *The Merchant of Venice* [1596-97]), it occurs six times in the later plays. In addition, "usurer's," "usurers," "usuries," and "usuring" do not occur at all in the earlier plays, but collectively occur nine times in the post-1599 plays: *Much Ado about Nothing* (1598-99), *Measure for Measure* (1604), *King Lear* (1605), *Coriolanus* (1607-08), *Timon of Athens* (1607-08), *Cymbeline* (1609-10), and *The Two Noble Kinsmen* (written with John Fletcher, 1613).[11] In toto, we have fifteen usages in the later plays versus three in the earlier (which in itself lends further support to the theory of later composition and/or revision).[12] Consequently, Shakespeare wrote (Foster) or revised (Hieatt, et al.) the Sonnets in about the middle of this process, when for many, including

Shakespeare himself if *Timon* is any indication, usury constituted a deeply unsettled and deeply unsettling issue that in many ways crystallized all the disturbing currents of this period.

Even given the Renaissance penchant for strong rhetoric, the denunciations of usury were particularly uncompromising. The Elizabethan divine, Henry Smith, for instance, writes in 1591 that "Usurie is a kinde of crueltie, and a kinde of extortion, and a kind of persecution, and therfore the want of love doth make Usurers: for if there were love there would bee no Usurie, no deceit, no extortion, no slaundering, no revenging, no oppresion, but wee should live in peace and joy and contentment like the Angels" (sig. B5ᵛ). Thomas Wilson, whose *Discourse upon Usury* became a kind of bible for the anti-usury party, has his preacher desire that government should make usury a capital offense:

> And therefore for my parte, I will wyshe some penall lawe of death to be made against those usurers, as well as agaynste theeves or murtherers, for that they deserve death much more than suche men doe, for these usurers destroye and devour up, not only whole families, but also whole countreys, and bring all folke to beggerie that have to do wyth them, and therefore are muche worse than theefes, or murtherers, because theire offence hurteth more universallye and toucheth a greater nomber, the one offedynge for neede, and thother upon wilfulnesse. (232)

Nicely demonstrating the imbrication of usury with Elizabethan characterizations of the Other, in a 1605 Star Chamber perjury trial, the Lord Chancellor denounced all lending at interest as "judaisme" and all usurers as "mercatores Judaizantes" (cited in Jones 170). As this comparison would suggest, Wilson and Smith, among others, argue that there is no "use" that is *not* forbidden because, as Philippus Caesar writes, "the forbiddyng of Usury, is an article of our faithe" (sig. A.iii).

More specifically, however, popular writers and the government not only blamed usury for the general economic instability marking this period, but they also accused it of bankrupting the aristocracy. The 1570 Act asserted that usury "hath exceedingly abounded to the utter undoing of many gentlemen" (quoted in Draper 26). In *An Alarum against Usurers* (1584), Thomas Lodge asserts that such are the "domesticall practices" of merchants that "not only they inrich themselves mightelye by others missfortunes, but also eate our English

Gentrie out of house and home" (13), and the bulk of his pamphlet is a fictional illustration of how the "young Gentleman" falls into the hands of the usurer, who brings him to financial ruination (and himself to financial gain).

What makes the imbrication of usury and procreation in the Sonnets even more bizarre is that the speaker is urging the addressee to have children in order to keep his presumably aristocratic line from disappearing: "For thou art so possest with murdrous hate, / That gainst thy selfe thou stickst not to conspire, / Seeking that beautious roofe to ruinate / Which to repaire should be thy chiefe desire" (sonnet 10) and "Who lets so faire a house fall to decay, / Which husbandry in honour might vphold" (sonnet 13). Shakespeare thus associates the means of saving the line from extinction with precisely the economic practice that many blamed for the aristocracy's decay. As Draper writes, "Usury seemed the cause that enriched the new families and destroyed the old" (25). Granted, sonnet 6 ("That vse is not forbidden vsery") seems to carve out an exception by alluding to the allegorization of usury in interpretations of the Parable of the Talents (see Haskin 74-88). Roger Fenton, for instance, distinguishes between financial usury and[13]

> the usury of nature, that most innocent and primitive increase which the earth yeeldeth in fruite unto man for his seede sowne . . . . Neither are we to meddle with that supernaturall usury which passeth betweene God and man: where sometimes man plaieth the Usurer, lending unto God by giving to the poore that he may receive an hundred folde. . . . Sometimes God himselfe is the Usurer, lending tallents unto men to lay out that hee may receive his owne againe . . . *with advantage*, as wee translate it. (sigs. D3-D4ᵛ; emphasis as in original)

However, Fenton's comparison between the earth's fecundity and usury also serves to underscore Shakespeare's comparison between a woman and a field or a vial. That is to say, whereas Fenton describes nature's fecundity as "innocent and primitive increase," Shakespeare's comparison dehumanizes the woman as much as Petruchio does in *The Taming of the Shrew* when he (in)famously reduces Kate to "my field" (3.2.231).

Given that Shakespeare does not have one positive, or even neutral, reference to usury in his plays, one can safely assume that he had some sympathy for the anti-usury forces. When, therefore,

Shakespeare yokes together procreation and usury in the Sonnets, the comparison puts together terms that many in his culture—indeed, his own class—found destabilizing and iniquitous, even, it must be admitted, as they practiced it. The homology between usury and procreation thus instantiates a hermeneutic dilemma, an aporia, that is difficult if not impossible to resolve.

Usury's two kinds of sexual overtones render this homology even more problematic (if that is possible). First, the common association between usury and prostitution. Sir Thomas Overbury, for instance, describes a usurer as someone who "puts his money to the unnatural act of generation; and his scrivener is the supervisor bawd to't"; Dekker is more blunt: "the Usurer lives by the lechery of mony, and is bawd to his owne bags"; and in *The Revenger's Tragedy*, Castiza says she will "prostitute [her] breast to the Duke's son, / And put [her] self to common Usury" (4.4.103-4; all three quotations cited in Pearlman 220-21). Shakespeare also invokes this connection in *Timon of Athens*, in which Apemantus calls the usurer's men dunning Timon "bawds between gold and want" (2.2.61-62). Usury is thus connected to the commodification of both sex and women, and as such, it reinforces the reification of women by reminding the reader, if latently, of how they are at best reduced to passive vessels in this sequence.

Usury was also generally associated with unnatural reproduction. In his *Politics*, Aristotle condemns usury in specifically biological terms that will reverberate for centuries afterward: "The most hated sort [of wealth-getting], and with the greatest reason, is usury, which makes a gain out of money itself, and not from the natural object of it. For money was intended to be used in exchange, but not to increase at interest. And this term interest, which means the birth of money from money, is applied to the breeding of money" (1.10.1141). And as numerous critics have noted, Elizabethans made Aristotle's repugnance at the concept of like breeding with like a central element in their polemics against usury (e.g., Chorost 358; Soellner 117-18; Pearlman 218-23). In 1598, Louis Leroy translated Aristotle's comments as: "It seemeth contrary to nature that a dead thing as money should engender" (quoted in Soellner 117). During the debate over the 1606 Act for the Further Repressing of Usury (which, according to the Commons' Journal, was "much disputed"), Sir Nathaniel Bacon remonstrated that usury was "against Morality, namely, that money should begett money" (quoted in Jones 177). Finally, Shakespeare registers his awareness of this tradition in *The Merchant of Venice*, when Shylock says that he makes his money "breed as fast" as "ewes and rams" (1.3.96).[14]

Shakespeare's association of the term "breeding" with usurious, that is, unnatural, reproduction is key because he also returns to it in *Timon*, when the Second Lord says, "no gift to him / But breeds the giver a return exceeding / All use of quittance" (1.1.277-79). Shakespeare's usage in this play gives an entirely different cast to the speaker's urging the addressee to "breed." That is to say, Shakespeare deliberately uses a term that is not only more usually reserved for animals, but also associated in his earlier works with usury, and hence with unnatural reproduction. But in addition to the oxymoronic quality of describing natural childbirth using a term associated with its opposite, there is another latent connotation that will become central to the development of the sequence. The anti-usury tradition also recoiled at the idea of like breeding with *like*, money with money, which creates a further homology between usury and homoeroticism, a practice medieval and early modern discourse also figured as a fundamentally "unnatural." Aquinas, for instance, classified sodomy (meaning same-sex intercourse) as one of the sins against nature (*peccata contra naturam*), and Dante placed homosexuals in the Inferno, the only "unnatural" vice so honored (Pequigney, "Sodomy" 23), and this view of homosexuality clearly continued unabated through the early modern period. In 1611, for instance, John Florio gave this definition in his Italian/English dictionary: "*Catamito*, one hired to sin against nature, an ingle, a ganymede" (cited in Bray 53); and du Bartas, in Joshua Sylvester's translation, writes:

> Die villains die, O more than infamous
> Foul monsters . . .
> Drown, drown the hell-hounds, and revenge the wrong
> Which they have done our Mother Nature long[.] (cited in Bray 59)

Like usury, homosexuality was often considered an abomination that threatened the very order of the universe, and like usury, homosexuality was denounced in the most unrelenting, uncompromising terms.

How, then, does this equivalence inflect the procreation sonnets? To be sure, the analogy between usury and unnatural sexuality infiltrates and destabilizes the putatively heterosexual economy urged by the speaker, the resonances of usury thus giving these sonnets precisely the linguistic doubleness that Fineman finds so pronounced in the middle and later poems. Yet the concatenation of usury and homoeroticism seems, at first reading, far removed from the topic of the procreation sonnets, where usury is a metaphor for heterosexual procreation. Yet, paradoxically, Shakespeare also creates an implicit homology between usury and homoerotic attraction by positing an inverse relationship between the two, since the homoerotic relationship between the speaker and the addressee gradually replaces the economic relationship. As already noted, economic language dominates the sonnets in which the speaker urges the addressee to procreate. Sonnet 1 accuses the "tender chorle" of making "wast in niggarding" (12); sonnet 2 argues that "beauties vse" will "sum [the addressee's] count" (9, 11); sonnet 9 asserts "Looke what an vnthrift in the world doth spend / Shifts but his place, for still the world inioyes it / But beauties waste hath in the world an end, / And kept vnvsed the vser so destroyes it" (9-12); sonnet 13 numbers the addressee among the "unthrifts" (13), and so on. Yet as the erotic attraction between the speaker and the addressee becomes more overt, the economic language and the references to beauty's use and usury drop away, and they are replaced, significantly, by an increasing insistence on the *exegi monumentum* theme and homosexually charged puns.

The shift starts in sonnet 10, when the speaker shifts the focus from procreation to introducing himself and their relationship as an issue:

> O change thy thought, that I may change my minde,
> Shall hate be fairer log'd then gentle loue?
> Be as thy presence is gracious and kind,
> Or to thy selfe at least kind harted proue,
>> Make thee an other selfe for loue of me,
>> That beauty still may liue in thine or thee. (9-14)

Sonnets 11, 13, and 14 return to the economic theme, and these sonnets make no mention of the addressee's sentiments or his poetry. But starting with sonnet 15, the speaker moves from urging the addressee to procreate to proposing *his* poetry, which proceeds from his "love" for the addressee, as the means of defeating time: "And all in war with Time for loue of you / As he takes from you, I ingraft you new" (13-14). As Booth notes, until this point in the sequence, the speaker "has previously called no attention to the power of his verse or to himself as a writer" (158), which suggests that poetry and the sentiments behind the poetry are meant to replace or supplant procreation. The thematic emergence of poetry thus overlaps with the emergence of homoeroticism, very vaguely hinted at in sonnet 10, as a major theme.

Granted, the assumption that the addressee is masculine has no basis within the poem itself due to the lack of gendered pronouns. The poem, therefore, is strictly speaking, indeterminate in its sexual orientation. Yet sonnet 20 alters this indeterminacy in two ways. First, the poem, as Pequigney has argued (*Such Is My Love* 30-41), makes the homoeroticism as explicit as possible:[15]

> A Womans face with natures owne hand painted,
> Hast thou the Master Mistris of my passion,
> A womans gentle hart but not acquainted
> With shifting changes as is false womens fashion[.] (1-4)

Second, the poem's conclusion raises once more the issue of "use," only this time "use" is explicitly tied to sexuality and, equally explicitly, subordinated to the homoerotic relationship: "But since she prickt thee out for womens pleasure, / Mine be thy loue and thy loues vse their treasure" (13-14). In this couplet, the speaker plays on the shifting definitions of "thy love." As Pequigney has suggested, the conclusion "proposes a distribution of the friend's favors" (35), the speaker receiving the addressee's "love," which could be nonsensual or homoerotic. Women, however, who are referred to by the nonspecific "their," which recalls their marginal status throughout this sequence, are to receive the "use," that is, sexual enjoyment but also usurious interest, which will be their "treasure," meaning both progeny and financial gain. Significantly, then, the final use of "use" in the procreation sonnets manages to invoke all of the various meanings hinted at so far while ironizing the earlier usages, since it is clear that the couplet both renders explicit the connections between economics and procreation as well as subordinates procreation to the homoeroticism latently connoted by usury.

Yet if Shakespeare upsets convention by casting the argument of the procreation sonnets in economic terms, be it usurious procreation or homoerotic pleas for patronage, and by privileging homoerotic attraction over heterosexuality, it is important to remember that Shakespeare illustrates a *failed* economy in the procreation sonnets insofar as there is no evidence suggesting that the addressee ever heeds the speaker's advice to engage in usurious procreation. And failed economies permeate the entire sequence as well; despite the sunniness of sonnet 18, the majority of the remaining sonnets in the young man sequence concern a breakdown in relations between the speaker, his male beloved, and the speaker's mistress. As Greene writes, "the sequence to the young man has provided very little by way of stable exchange systems" ("Pitiful Thrivers" 176). And the dark lady sequence is infamous for its breakdowns in the exchange systems between the speaker and his "love." Moreover, it is possible that the final configuration of poet/youth/lady supplies the concretization of the demands the speaker made in the first group of sonnets (Sedgwick 33). Shakespeare thus modulates from the *im*plicitly troubling beginning into the *ex*plicitly homoerotic sequence of the young man poems and then into the explicitly troubled and heterosexual dark lady poems, and each movement is marked by the failures of exchange and problematizations of economy underlying the initial sequence.

To conclude, in the procreation sonnets, Shakespeare uses language that is entirely inappropriate (and would have been recognized as such by Shakespeare's readers) to its subject matter. Thus there is a constant neurotic oscillation, to use Eric Mallin's nice phrase (135), between what Shakespeare enjoins the young man to do and the inevitable resonances of the language he uses to do this. The economic language thus infiltrates the act of procreation and even the linguistic universe of the poem itself, and just as the poems' language invokes an inflationary, destabilized economy of meaning, the poems' homology between usury and procreation creates shifting and often incoherent meanings. Similarly, the homoeroticism of the latter part of the sequence serves to *deform* the expectations of Petrarchan sonneteering. The Sonnets treat Petrarchism in much the same way, I believe, that the idealization of the body in Michelangelo's early and mid-period work is transmuted into the distended, warped forms of the Tomb of Guiliano de Medici. Just as "each of these figures is trapped in a contrapposto pose that defeats the very meaning of contrapposto" (Hartt 138), so does each section of Shakespeare's sequence include elements defeating the generic expectations of Petrarchan verse. Furthermore, several of Shakespeare's plays of this period specifically concern themselves with the problem of capitalism's growth, a development that clearly worried Shakespeare even as he profited from it.[16] The Sonnets continue this interrogation of capitalism by demonstrating what ensues when commodification infects the poetry of praise.[17]

NOTES

1. On economic metaphors in later sixteenth century poetry, see Southall 50-75, and in the Sonnets, see Melchiori 27.

2. Recently, Katherine Duncan-Jones, Joseph Pequigney, Donald Foster, Anne L. Prescott, A. Kent Hieatt, and Charles Hieatt have collectively put into question the commonly accepted wisdom of Shakespeare's composing the Sonnets during the early 1590s and Thorpe's pirating them in 1609. Differences remain, however, as to whether Shakespeare wrote these poems in the years just previous to their publication (Foster), or significantly revised works produced during the early 1590s, as Hieatt et al. suggest.

3. While Grady discusses the relations between the later Shakespeare and reification, he does not discuss the Sonnets.

4. Because of the thematic possibilities foreclosed by modernizing spelling and punctuation, all references are to the reproduction of the 1609 Quarto in Booth's edition. See Greene, "Anti-Hermeneutics," on the problems of modernization.

5. I am grateful to James Schiffer for bringing this reference to my attention.

6. Greene suggests that the "umbrella-pun" for the poem's concatenation of economics and sexuality is "husbandry," because this term "emerges as a universal, existential concern that transcends the addressee's marital status" ("Pitiful Thrivers" 177).

7. See also Melchiori 22-28.

8. Starting with Hubler, critics have often had recourse to the "Renaissance doctrine of increase" to explain away the multiple and contradictory resonances of the economic language (e.g., Mischo 266-67, 277 n. 18; Pearlman 230; Fischer 30). However, no one can cite a sixteenth-century source for this doctrine, and much of the evidence adduced for it, such as Vincentio's opening speech to Angelo in *Measure for Measure* and Marlowe's *Hero and Leander*, works only if one ignores the ironic contexts, which suggests that this doctrine, like Malone's Renaissance cult of friendship, is an invention to keep unwanted interpretations at bay.

9. See below and note 11.

10. The statute would be debated twice more (1614, 1620-21) before finally being passed in 1623-24. Obviously, the latter debates could not have affected the Sonnets, yet they indicate that anyone invoking usury during this period would be drawing on a highly controversial issue.

11. In *The Winter's Tale*, for instance, Autolycus offers a ballad on "how a usurer's wife was brought to bed of twenty money-bags," in response to which the gullible shepherdess, Dorcas, exclaims: "Bless me from marrying a usurer!" (4.4.63, 68); in *Measure for Measure*, Pompey decries the legal toleration of usury: "'Twas never merry world since of two usuries, the merriest was put down, and the worser allow'd by order of law" (3.2.6-7; see Pearlman's fine article on this line), and Timon instructs Alcibiades to kill everyone, because everyone is corrupt: "Pity not honor'd age for his white beard, / He is an usurer. Strike me the counterfeit matron, / It is her habit only that is honest, / Herself a bawd" (*Timon* 4.3.112-15).

12. Along the same lines, the brothers Hieatt and Prescott point out that the noun "audit" "is used in six plays of the second half of the career but in no well-dated work of the first half" (81-82).

13. Fenton also argues that the presence of usury in the Parable of the Talents in no way justifies its use because sometimes the Scriptures will compare a positive to a negative in order to make an allegorical point: "Those delicate wits then, who have from hence extracted conclusions, as if God, by such parables and allusions, did somewhat favour usury; they must by the same reason justify unrighteousnes, because the example of the unjust Steward is commended unto us; and withall conclude that even theft it selfe is therefore santified, because Christ hath compared himself unto a theefe in the night" (sig. D4ᵛ).

14. Shylock, of course, is trying to justify usury by naturalizing it, but given the cultural context, his arguments further erode his credibility.

15. See also Waddington.

16. See, for example, Chorost on *Timon* and Bruster on *Troilus*.

17. I am grateful to Douglas Bruster, Don Foster, James Schiffer, and Don Wayne for their help in writing this essay.

WORKS CITED

Aristotle. *Politics*. Trans. Bejamin Jowett. *The Basic Works of Aristotle*. Ed. Richard McKeon. New York: Random House, 1941. 1127-1316.

Bray, John. *Homosexuality in Renaissance England*. London: Gay Men's Press, 1988.

Booth, Stephen, ed. *Shakespeare's Sonnets*. New Haven: Yale UP, 1977.

Bruster, Douglas. *Drama and the Market in the Age of Shakespeare*. Cambridge: Cambridge UP, 1992.

Caesar, Philippus. *A General Discourse against the Damnable Sect of Usurers*. London, 1578.

Chorost, Michael. "Biological Finance in Shakespeare's *Timon of Athens.*" *English Literary Renaissance* 21 (1991): 349-70.

Draper, John W. "The Theme of *Timon of Athens.*" *Modern Language Review* 29 (1934): 20-31.

Duncan-Jones, Katherine. "Was the 1609 *Shake-Speares Sonnets* Really Unauthorized?" *Review of English Studies* 34 (1983): 151-71.

Engle, Lars. *Shakespearean Pragmatism: Market of His Time.* Chicago: U of Chicago P, 1993.

Fenton, Roger. *A Treatise of Usury.* London, 1612.

Fineman, Joel. *Shakespeare's Perjured Eye: The Invention of Subjectivity in the Sonnets.* Berkeley: U of California P, 1986.

Fischer, Sandra K. *Econolingua: A Glossary of Coins and Economic Language in Renaissance Drama.* Newark: U of Delaware P, 1985.

Foster, Donald. Letter to the author.

Grady, Hugh. *Shakespeare's Universal Wolf: Studies in Early Modern Reification.* Oxford: Clarendon, 1996.

Greene, Thomas M. "Anti-Hermeneutics: The Case of Shakespeare's Sonnet 129." *The Vulnerable Text: Essays on Renaissance Literature.* New York: Columbia UP, 1986. 159-74.

———. "Pitiful Thrivers: Failed Husbandry in the Sonnets." *The Vulnerable Text: Essays on Renaissance Literature.* New York: Columbia UP, 1986. 175-93.

Hartt, Frederick. *Art: A History of Painting, Sculpture, Architecture.* Vol. 2. Englewood Cliffs: Prentice-Hall, 1976.

Haskin, Dayton. "Tracing a Genealogy of 'Talent': The Descent of Matthew 25: 14-30 into Contemporary Philanthropical Discourse." *Wealth in Western Thought: The Case for and against Riches.* Ed. Paul G. Schervish. Westport, CT: Praeger, 1994. 65-102.

Hieatt, A. Kent, Charles W. Hieatt, and Anne Lake Prescott. "When Did Shakespeare Write *Sonnets* 1609?" *Studies in Philology* 88 (1991): 69-109.

Hubler, Edwin. *The Sense of Shakespeare's Sonnets.* Princeton: Princeton UP, 1952. Rpt. Westport, CT: Greenwood, 1976.

Jones, Norman. *God and the Moneylenders: Usury and Law in Early Modern England.* Oxford: Basil Blackwell, 1989.

Lodge, Thomas. *An Alarum against Usurers. The Complete Works of Thomas Lodge.* 1584. Vol. 1. Rpt. New York: Russel & Russel, 1963. 13-52.

Lukács, Georg. "Reification and the Consciousness of the Proletariat." *History and Class Consciousness: Studies in Marxist Dialectics.* Trans. Rodney Livingstone. Cambridge: MIT P, 1971. 83-148.

Malin, Eric. *Inscribing the Time: Shakespeare and the End of Elizabethan England*. Berkeley: U of California P, 1995.

Melchiori, Giorgio. *Shakespeare's Dramatic Meditations: An Experiment in Criticism*. Oxford: Clarendon, 1976.

Mischo, John B. "'That use is not forbidden usury': Shakespeare's Procreation Sonnets and the Problem of Usury." *Subjects on the World's Stage: Essays on British Literature of the Middle Ages and the Renaissance*. Ed. David G. Allen and Robert A. White. Newark: U of Delaware P, 1995. 262-79.

Nelson, Benjamin N. *The Idea of Usury: From Tribal Brotherhood to Universal Otherhood*. Princeton: Princeton UP, 1949.

Pearlman, E. "Shakespeare, Freud, and the Two Usuries, or, Money's a Meddler." *English Literary Renaissance* 2 (1972): 217-36.

Pequigney, Joseph. "Sodomy in Dante's *Inferno* and *Purgatorio*." *Representations* 36 (1991): 22-42.

——. *Such Is My Love: A Study of Shakespeare's Sonnets*. Chicago: U of Chicago P, 1985.

Sedgwick, Eve Kosofsky. *Between Men: English Literature and Male Homosocial Desire*. New York: Columbia UP, 1985.

Shakespeare, William. *The Riverside Shakespeare*. Ed. G. Blakemore Evans. Boston: Houghton Mifflin, 1974.

——. *Shakespeare's Sonnets*. Ed. Stephen Booth. New Haven: Yale UP, 1977.

Soellner, Rolf *Timon of Athens: Shakespeare's Pessimistic Tragedy*. Columbus: Ohio State UP, 1979.

Southall, Raymond. *Literature and the Rise of Capitalism: Critical Essays Mainly on the Sixteenth and Seventeenth Centuries*. London: Lawrence and Wishart, 1973.

Spevack, Marvin. *The Harvard Concordance to Shakespeare*. Cambridge: Belknap, 1973.

Waddington, Raymond B. "The Poetics of Eroticism: Shakespeare's 'Master-Mistress.'" *Renaissance Discourses of Desire*. Ed. Claude J. Summers and Ted-Larry Pebworth. Columbia: U of Missouri P, 1993. 13-28.

Wall, Wendy. *The Imprint of Gender: Authorship and Publication in the English Renaissance*. Ithaca: Cornell UP, 1994.

Wayne, Don E. "The 'exchange of letters': Early Modern Contradictions and Postmodern Conundrums." *The Consumption of Culture 1600-1800*. Ed. Ann Bermingham and John Brewer. London: Routledge, 1995. 143-65.

Weber, Max. "The Market: Its Impersonality and Ethic (Fragment)." *Economy and Society*. Vol. 1. Ed. Guenther Roth and Claus Wittich. Berkeley: U of California P, 1978. 635-40.

Wilson, Thomas. *The Arte of Rhetoric (1560)*. Ed. Peter E. Medine. University Park: Pennsylvania State UP, 1994.

―――. *A Discourse upon Usury*. 1572. Ed. R. H. Tawney. Rpt. London: Frank Cass, 1963.

70

THat thou are blam'd shall not be thy defect,
For slanders marke was euer yet the faire,
The ornament of beauty is suspect,
A Crow that flies in heauens sweetest ayre.
So thou be good, slander doth but approue,
Their worth the greater beeing woo'd of time,
For Canker vice the sweetest buds doth loue,
And thou present'st a pure vnstayined prime.
Thou hast past by the ambush of young daies,
Either not assayld, or victor beeing charg'd,
Yet this thy praise cannot be soe thy praise,
To tye vp enuy, euermore inlarged,
    If some suspect of ill maskt not thy show,
    Then thou alone kingdomes of hearts shouldst owe.

71

NOe Longer mourne for me when I am dead,
Then you shall heare the surly sullen bell
Giue warning to the world that I am fled
From this vile world with vildest wormes to dwell:
Nay if you read this line, remember not,
The hand that writ it, for I loue you so,
That I in your sweet thoughts would be forgot,
If thinking on me then should make you woe.
O if (I say) you looke vpon this verse,
When I (perhaps) compounded am with clay,
Do not so much as my poore name reherse;
But let your loue euen with my life decay.
    Least the wise world should looke into your mone,
    And mocke you with me after I am gon.

72

O Least the world should taske you to recite,
What merit liu'd in me that you should loue
After my death(deare loue)for get me quite,
For you in me can nothing worthy proue.
Vnlesse you would deuise some vertuous lye,

To doe more for me then mine owne desert,
And hang more praise vpon deceased I,
Then nigard truth would willingly impart:
O least your true loue may seeme falce in this,
That you for loue speake well of me vntrue,
My name be buried where my body is,
And liue no more to shame nor me, nor you.
    For I am sham'd by that which I bring forth,
    And so should you, to loue things nothing worth.

73

THat time of yeeare thou maist in me behold,
When yellow leaues, or none, or few doe hange
Vpon those boughes which shake against the could,
Bare rn'wd quiers, where late the sweet birds sang.
In me thou seest the twi-light of such day,
As after Sun-set fadeth in the West,
Which by and by blacke night doth take away,
Deaths second selfe that seals vp all in rest.
In me thou seest the glowing of such fire,
That on the ashes of his youth doth lye,
As the death bed, whereon it must expire,
Consum'd with that which it was nurrisht by.
    This thou perceu'st, which makes thy loue more strong,
    To loue that well, which thou must leaue ere long.

74

BVt be contented when that fell areast,
With out all bayle shall carry me away,
My life hath in this line some interest,
Which for memoriall still with thee shall stay.
When thou reuewest this, thou doest reuew,
The very part was consecrate to thee,
The earth can haue but earth, which is his due,
My spirit is thine the better part of me,
So then thou hast but lost the dregs of life,
The pray of wormes, my body being dead,
The coward conquest of a wretches knife,

Figure 4. E3 Verso/E4 Recto from the 1609 Quarto of *SHAKE-SPEARES SONNETS* (from the Folger Shakespeare Library copy STC 22353). Reprinted by permission of the Folger Shakespeare Library.

Sonnets 71-74
Texts and Contexts

Joseph Pequigney

"That time of year," number 73, is the centerpiece of this run of four sonnets. Their numbering and sequentiality are those established by the first edition, the 1609 Quarto, wherein the title appears on the title page as *SHAKE-SPEARES SONNETS*. Of all 154 of those sonnets, the seventy-third is among the most widely recognized and highly acclaimed, and, whether as cause or effect of its renown, few if any have more often been reprinted. Anthologists, however, almost invariably print it out of context, unyoked by violence from its neighbors, and they thereby deprive it of its connective function and a dimension of its meaning.

Even the sonnets chosen for study here do not constitute a wholly autonomous set, but they do collectively present such a striking instance of a problem and its elegant resolution and play such variations on the shared and recurring motifs of love, death, and poetry as to demand, on these grounds alone, critical scrutiny. But, as will be seen, these poems do more; they reach beyond their seriate confines to touch on at least two of the broader and fundamental questions raised by the entire love-sonnet sequence: the homoerotic character of the love exchanged between the older and the younger friend, and the affinity between the historical author and the poet inscribed in the text.

I

Sonnet 71 addresses the beloved, as the next three poems do also, and begins by urging him not to "mourn for me when I am dead," or at least to do so "No longer . . . "

> Than you shall hear the surly sullen bell
> Give warning to the world that I am fled
> From this vile world with vildest worms to dwell.[1] (1-4)

The "bell," with the onomatopoetic accompaniment of the repeated "l" sounds, is the death knell that tolls as a "warning" to all when a death occurs. The "world" (signifying "earth" in the third verse, "everyone" in the second) that is "fled" may be "vile," but the destination is even worse, that worm-ridden dwelling the grave. In the next quatrain the true motive and import of the discourse begin to emerge, though obliquely:

> Nay, if you read this line, remember not
> The hand that writ it, for I love you so,
> That I in your sweet thoughts would be forgot,
> If thinking on me then should make you woe. (5-8)

The "I"-persona would rather "be forgot" himself than subject the other to the pangs of grief, and would, to spare him, even go so far as to relinquish his one happy prospect of an afterlife, that in "your sweet thoughts." No other survival will be possible for him once in his grave, where he must suffer, besides the worms, coming to be "compounded . . . with clay" (10). A return of love is affirmed in line 12, "let your love even with my life decay," though along with advice to terminate it. Then in the couplet the tone changes, taking on a needling note:

> Lest the wise world should look into your moan,
> And mock you with me after I am gone. (13-14)

The "wise world" refers to the cynical, "knowing" public apt to scorn the youth for bemoaning his scorned lover, and he is admonished to "not so much as my poor name rehearse" (11) in order to steer clear of the mockery, to watch out for himself and never mind loyalty to a dedicated friend.

The argument made overtly and directly is to "forget me once I die." However, what is literally said is heavily qualified, even ironically reversed, by the rhetoric of saying it. Verbal detail throughout is calculated to move the foremost reader and to elicit his sympathetic response. There is, for example, the tender solicitude for his well-being discernible in the wish to spare him "woe," and the piteousness of the two allusions to an abhorrent grave. The bell, accordingly, is "surly" and "sullen" because warning of something bad. Then "your sweet thoughts" alone confer a posthumous existence, and it would be lost were they withdrawn. How can the simple declaration "for I love you so" (6) fail to touch an already affectionate heart? And a passing reminder of "your love" follows in line 12. The "if" clauses at lines 5 and 9 are cunning invitations to future readings of the verse, and how impossible it would be for "you [to] read this [handwritten] line" and "remember not / The hand that writ it." Finally the counsel at the close is at once generous in its protectiveness and wry in its intimation of a reproving attitude toward yielding to the mockers. All this adds up to a persuasive appeal to be recalled, loved, and lamented. This appeal, a covert counterthesis, turns out to be the primary message the verse-writer means to convey. The apparent content that bears and both disguises and bares the rival subject serves less to make it more compelling or palatable than to reveal the mental disposition of the persona. He does not wish the beloved to suffer grief (8) while wishing to be grieved for, nor to suffer mockery (the couplet) while prodding him to risk it. His qualms as an older man and as a lover about making future emotional demands on someone younger and precious to him are what dictate the discursive indirection.

The opening of sonnet 72 takes off from the couplet of 71—and especially does line 1 here echo line 13 there—to create the impression of a continuity:

> O lest the world should task you to recite,
> What merit lived in me that you should love
> After my death, dear love, forget me quite,
> For you in me can nothing worthy prove. (1-4)

The two poems are comparable in style and topic. Both are virtually devoid of figurative language, aside from the faint personifications of "bell" at 71.2 and "truth" and "name" at 72.8, 11-12; there is also a possible allusion to the funereal custom of hanging eulogistic poems on biers at 72.7. The youth is instructed in each poem on how to deal with the world, the verse, and the memory of the poet when dead. But differences overshadow these similarities. The poet in 72 is far more dejected than before, regarding himself as deficient in "merit," worth, "desert" (2-6). He now concedes that the world is after all wise in its scornful estimation of him. Therefore the friend should make no doomed effort to defend his memory with the oxymoron of "some virtuous lie"—"virtuous" as motivated by "your true love" but yet a "lie" as divergent from "the niggard truth" (5-9). Does the poet here take such a dim view of himself for deeming himself generally undeserving or for a particular defect? The unqualified self-indictment of lines 1-12 does suggest the former but the couplet posits the latter alternative:

> For I am sham'd by that which I bring forth,
> And so should you, to love things nothing worth. (13-14)

The worthless "things" brought forth that should make the beloved ashamed are the very love sonnets devoted to him. Whereas 71 guardedly importunes him to read the verse and be sadly mindful of the deceased poet, 72 takes another tack. Now the friend should allow the persona's name to "be buried where my body is" rather than live on to "shame" them both. Although adverted to late, verse becomes the focal point. The self-disdain arises from a depressing sense of having failed as a sonneteer. That the perceived failure is so extremely upsetting makes us realize how great an investment of ego goes into the practice of this lyric art.

Sonnet 74, to pass over 73 for the moment, finds the poet in quite another mental-emotional state, with his attitudes toward his death, his verse, and the friend in relation to both dramatically altered. Death itself implicitly figures as a policeman whose "fell arrest / Without all bail shall carry me away" (1-2). Now a flesh-spirit dichotomy is adduced. The "body" is conceived of in traditional fashion as the inferior of the two components of human nature and in contemptuous terms: as "earth [which] can have but earth" (7) in burial, "his due" (7), and as "the dregs of life" (9), "prey of worms" (10), and "Too base . . . to be rememb'red" (12), and also, more puzzlingly, as "the coward conquest of a wretch's knife" (11). The "wretch" in line 11, though variously glossed as "confounding age" that wields a "cruel knife" at 63.10, Time with a "fell hand" at 64.1, or Death itself, as at 6.14, more likely refers to the kind of knavish back-stabber who may strike anywhere and at any time and whose "conquest" is "coward" because he catches the corporal victim unawares and defenseless. The "spirit" is "the better part of me" (8) but otherwise conceived of in more heterodox terms: as "the very part" that formerly "was consecrate to thee" (6) and still "thine . . . my body being dead" (8, 10) and as that which "thou reviewest" whenever "thou does review" this "line" (5, 3) of poetry. While the poet's spirit will live on, it will do so in no other way than in verse, and even then exclusively in these love sonnets. What valorizes this verbal medium of immortalization is its power to perpetuate the lover in the living memory of the beloved:

> My life hath in this line some interest,
> Which for memorial still [always] with thee shall stay. (3-4)

And in the couplet, "The worth of that [my body] is that which it contains [my spirit)], and that [spirit] is this [sonnet], and this [sonnet] with thee remains" (13-14). The spirit imparts its inherent "worth" to the body when alive and forever to the poem, to abide thereby with the youth. The argument explains why he might "be contented" (1), rather than mournful as before, when death removes the poet, and why the poet might be content to be removed. And one may note that the public "world" that intrudes in 71 and 72 seems to have become extraneous and inconsequential, for it is never mentioned in 74.

Sonnet 74 contrasts more subtly with 71 and more starkly with 72. The poet in 71 could envision postmortal subsistence in the friend's "sweet thoughts" (7), and does twice suggest that he "look upon" (9) the sonnets, though with the suggestions diffident and stated hypothetically. But the poet in 72 altogether repudiates this kind of survival by urging the other both "to forget me quite" and to disregard the embarrassingly poor sonnets. Then in 74 a turnaround occurs. A conception of afterlife, a new and more elaborate conception and one now avidly entertained, reemerges with the introduction of the "spirit" that can exist as both "thine" (8) and as "this [poem]" (14). It is exalted not for its powers of reason or will but as the faculty able to write poetry and embody and memorialize itself therein. One finds here a wish and confident expectation that the youth will be regularly perusing the sonnets, now "things" of great "worth" and deserving of his "love" (cf. 72.14), for the reason that they are repositories of, and so keep present to him, the spirit of his departed lover.

This astonishing revaluation by the poet of himself, his death, and his sonnets is patently problematic. Sonnet 73 (printed below) will deliver a resolution, though an unexpected one, and one that depends on such formal elements as the internal organization, figurative language, and polysemous conclusion.

> That time of year thou mayst in me behold,
> When yellow leaves, or none, or few do hang
> Upon those boughs which shake against the cold,
> Bare ruin'd choirs, where late the sweet birds sang.
> In me thou see'st the twilight of such day,
> As after sunset fadeth in the west,
> Which by and by black night doth take away,
> Death's second self that seals up all in rest.
> In me thou seest the glowing of such fire,
> That on the ashes of his youth doth lie,
> As the death-bed whereon it must expire,
> Consum'd with that which it was nourish'd by.
> > This thou perceiv'st, which makes thy love more strong,
> > To love that well, which thou must leave ere long.

Each of the quatrains commences by directing the "thou" addressed to observe something "in me"; that something, never made explicit, is inferable as age, which remains the metaphorical tenor through the first twelve lines. In the analogous figurative patterns of the three quatrains, where age and its concomitants remain the fixed, tacit subject, the metaphorical vehicles are express and variable, being first the winter "time of year," next "the twilight of [some] day," and finally a "glowing . . . fire." These vehicles, in turn, become tenors that serve to generate additional tropes, those whose vehicles are "ruin'd choirs," "Death's second self," and "[spent] youth" and "the deathbed." Moreover, between the primary tenor and each second vehicle, some kind of significant relation obtains.

The "time of year" referred to at the beginning, and which stands, as "in me" indicates, for the persona's time of life, goes unnamed, being identified as winter or almost winter only by the "boughs" bare or nearly so and windy "cold" of the metonymy within the metaphor. While depicting himself as being at a late stage of life's year, the poet at line 4 alludes to his younger days in troping on the "boughs" as "bare ruin'd choirs." These are the choir stalls, also wooden and in the open air, to be found at the sites of monastic ruins, and these as well were once the seat of song, the liturgical chanting of monks, who then correlate with the "sweet birds."[2] In this second vehicle the tree branches of the first are evoked as they were of "late," when intact and still in warm air, leafy, and the perch of the aviary singers. These wintry and summery states, whose contrast pivots on "boughs," connote, respectively, the poet's present decline in bleak old age and his former young vigor in the summertime of life. "When I look back I seem to remember singing": that—from a girlhood poem of Doris Lessing and endorsed by her in later years (404)—is an apt comment on line 4.

In the second quatrain age in its proximity to death (the tenor) corresponds to the twilight—sundown to darkness—of an expiring day about to be displaced by "black night" (vehicle). Then in the simile of line 8 this "night" (now as tenor) is made "Death's second self" (vehicle), and the two are alike in that each "seals up [closes, shuts up as in a casket] all [animals as well as men and all the wakeful consciousness of each] in rest [the *requiescant* of sleep and of death]." As in the previous quatrain, a second trope issues from the first: a referent in the first vehicle, "night," now serves, as "boughs" did before, to hinge the two tropes—only here the second is a striking reversal of the first. Death, at first tacit and conceived of as an individual human demise (lines 5-8) is then named and conceived of as a personified universal (lines 8-9): thus does the literal but implied death as "night"-like become translated into that same "night" as "Death"-like.

In the third quatrain age with youth past and death near (the tenor) is represented by the "glowing" of a "fire" reduced to the embers dying on its "ashes" (vehicle). The vehicle generates two further figures of speech: one a metaphor, wherein the "ashes of his youth" refers to the fuel burnt to cinders; and the other a simile, wherein the bed of ashes is likened to the "deathbed wherein [the fire] must expire." Line 12 elucidates both figures with a metaphor *cum* paradox based on eating/being eaten: the fuel that at first "nourish'd" the fire gets used up and turns into the ashes that consume it. Hence the aged person of the tenor and the personified fire of the vehicle turn out to mirror each other, with the youth of both wasted away and both awaiting death; or, to put it another way, the implicit literal human situation is made explicit as the situation of the metaphoric fire.

The figuration exhibited in 73.1-12 is masterful, and yet the conceits are commonplaces. The year, a day, or even a fire seem to be natural and almost inevitable analogues of human life. The poem is not distinguished by innovative *discordia concors*, aside from the "boughs" as "choirs" and perhaps the "ashes" as made to represent both "youth" and "deathbed." Rather it is the imaginative and deft adaptation and juxtaposition of these familiar tropes that make the quatrains so impressive.

They are nontransferable and significantly arranged. Each successive figure, for example, shortens the life span, from a year to a day to the duration of a fire, and accordingly brings death ever closer, from a few months away, to an hour or so away, to perhaps minutes away, those it would take for the glowing embers to go out. In the first quatrain the old self glances back to his summertime of youth; in the second he looks ahead to nocturnal death; in the third he looks in both directions, at the past of youth now in ashes and toward the future that will bring a deathbed. In the first quatrain seasonal time runs backward; in the second late diurnal time goes forward; in the third human-life time records the fire's past and future, from its once blazing "youth" to its imminent expiration on a bed. If line 2 had read, "leaves, or few, or none" it could have suggested the progressing fall; instead we get "leaves, or none [at all], or [just a] few," so that the quantity of leaves and even the exact time of year are left indefinite. This incertitude runs counter to the discursive formality of the rest of the poem. The effect is not so much that of briefly injecting a conversational tone (as with "Nay, if you read" and "O if, I say" at 71.5, 9), as that of compositional irresolution. Then again, the first quatrain offers images of "cold" at line 3 and a suggestion of summer warmth at line 4; the second contains images of light and darkness; and the third catches up both kinds of imagery in the fire's heat which lessens and its brightness which dims as it dies down. Also the two colors specified, "yellow" in line 2 and "black" in line 7, possibly anticipate the fire and ashes of lines 9-10. Incidentally, the sole sound image is the bird song of line 4; the rest is silence. And while the sonnet postpones its volta until line 13, still the ninth line does introduce a "turn" of sorts. The prior vehicles picture outdoor scenes of natural phenomena, to which the new vehicle offers the contrast of a fire presumably manmade and indoors, as in a hearth.

The couplet, the two-line sentence that furnishes the volta of the argument and closure, is brought into alignment with the quatrains—

each one also a sentence—by starting "This thou perceiv'st," which recalls the way each of them started: ". . . in me behold" (line 1) and "In me thou seest" (lines 5, 9). The indefinite pronoun "This" refers to all that had been said above, or, more precisely, to the condition that the subject had been directing attention to, namely, his having reached the winter, twilight, and dying-ember stage of life. Perception of this will somehow "make thy love more strong." Readers ordinarily take this strengthened love to be for the poet, since, as someone who is too old to last much longer, he is then one whom "thou must leave ere long." Here "leave" may signify "forgo" or "depart from," and if the latter the verb intimates that life is a journey on which the ongoing living must leave the dead behind. Except for this faint glimmer of a possible metaphor, the language of the couplet, unlike that of the quatrains and like that of the adjacent sonnets, is nonfigurative. Now to seek to bolster received love because of (rather than in spite of) being old can strike one as rather odd, notwithstanding the strategy of depicting age with images disconnected from its symptoms and blemishes (as distinct from the depiction in, say, sonnets 62 and 63). On the other hand, the versifying mind exhibits an enticing vitality.

The final line admits, though, of an alternative reading, as a number of commentators have noted, and does so by reason of the relative pronouns "that . . . which." "That" can refer to the present condition of the young man for whom the utterance is intended, to his summer and noontime of life and his "flaming youth." That youth is a temporary state which "thou must leave [i.e., forgo, give up] ere long," for as you perceive sadly exemplified in me, age like mine is your future lot.[3]

Two distinct and incompatible but equally plausible ideas turn out to thematize sonnet 73. Either the poem (1) argues for devotion to an elderly lover based on the fact that he won't be around much longer, or (2) urges the other to relish his fleeting youth—*carpe diem* (cf. quatrain 2). Either way an action must be taken, and it will entail a loss, that of the friend or that of youth. Readers aware of these two messages are unable to choose between them because they have equal semantic validity.[4] The analysis here seems to have uncovered an aporia, wherein two meanings are contradictory and undermine each other, and thus to have accomplished a deconstruction of the text.[5]

That would be so if the analysis were to stop at this point. Then the impression might register that the author lost control of his language, or that the language managed on its own to escape intentionality.

Actually, Shakespeare could have eliminated the alternative reading simply by substituting "me . . . who" for "that . . . which," a change that without disturbing the meter would render the sense univocal. It is hardly conceivable that so obvious a move would not have occurred to him, and that reflection lends support to the idea of the closing ambiguity as a conscious artistic choice.

Since the two readings work equally well, the plausible next step would be to look for an interpretation that can encompass both. Such a one will be supplied by William Empson's fourth type of ambiguity, which "occurs when two or more meanings of a statement do not agree among themselves, but combine to make clear a more complicated state of mind in the author" (133). The two meanings of the couplet are not only discordant but they propose divergent programs for the friend to follow. That the poet should hold two such proposals simultaneously in mind becomes comprehensible in the light of the two preceding sonnets, 71 and especially 72.

Sonnet 71, too, seems to deliver two discrepant signals: (1) the overtly expressed one, "do not grieve for me or love me after I am gone," and (2) the covert, implied, and contrary one, "grieve for and love me then." These meanings, though, are not held in suspension, as in the case of 73, but the latter overwhelms and deactivates the former. Yet by making the request for continued devotion in a circuitous manner rather than straightforwardly, the poet betrays a hesitant, unconfident, and anxious attitude toward the amity. Then in sonnet 72 he presents himself as more downcast: his sonnets are worthless, he is a failure, and after his death the loving beloved should forget both them and him.

These sonnets enable us to comprehend the frame of mind that finds expression in sonnet 73. The older poet may desire "love more strong" from the younger man but feels, as 72 discloses, that he does not deserve it. This psychological conflict explains why the couplet hovers equivocally between the conclusions "to love me," which the persona cannot bring himself to ask for outright, and "to love your youth," the impersonal alternative exacted by his self-contempt. Hence the two discrepant meanings of that final statement *do* combine to illumine a complication in the mind of the poet, in accord with the Empsonian fourth type of ambiguity. This, moreover, puts the focus where it rightly belongs, on the psyche of that "I" that is the subject of the sonnets from first to last. And to find that 74.14 is logical and intelligible is to undercut or deconstruct the deconstruction.

"But" at the opening of 74 links the sonnet to 73: "But be content when that fell arrest / Without all bail shall carry me away" (1-2). The "arrest" is made by death and carries off the body, and the concept is different from but not incompatible with that of one reading of 73.14, wherein death means that "thou must leave [me]." The ambiguity at the end of 73 is resolved, or dissipated, in 74, wherein the friend's love is conceived of as directed not toward his own youth but outward toward the older poet, and now he can "be contented" for the reasons given in 74.3-14.

The sea-change in the sonneteer's attitude toward self and other and toward his poetic art and pending death between 71-72 and 74 cannot be accounted for unless by the intervening sonnet. And 73 does contribute an explanation, though one that derives far less from its written contents than from the quality of the writing.

The excellence of sonnet 73, incontestable I believe, has been attested to extensively and for a very long time by such witnesses as the editors and anthologists I noted at the outset, as also by commentators and ordinary readers. And someone whose critical judgment would be preeminent in this case, more authoritative than anyone else's, seems also to have held the sonnet in high regard; he is identified below. My own exegetical project has endeavored to make manifest some of the attributes of the poem that cause it to excel. I might add that the close reading considerably utilized so far, which is common to New Critics and deconstructionists and which, though a crucial skill in literary studies, is fast disappearing, has been required by the texts of this study to accommodate evaluative criticism.

The textually inscribed poet cannot go back to, and cannot creditably go on with, denigrating "what I bring forth" after just having finished that masterpiece of sonneteering, 73. If the poem is to fulfill its destined transitioning function, it must be deemed a poetic performance of unusual merit. That the performer so views it is made evident as it snaps him out of the doldrums brought on by his prior sense of artistic inadequacy. He had been composing "things nothing worth" when suddenly, or at least unexpectedly, this classic of sonnet-making takes shape under his pen. Is it any wonder that he then has a change of heart, from a mood of depression to one of contentment and confidence about his art apropos his death and his friend? Thus does sonnet 73 manage to solve the problem of its surrounding sonnets by giving perceptible form to the set of four that had otherwise been incoherent.

Once this development is apprehended, it can generate the following corollaries. First, only when sonnet 73 is read in context will its effect on 74 be discernible; otherwise part of its signification will inevitably be missed. Second, this linkage of sonnets on the basis of the artistic superiority or aesthetic value of one of them is unique both *within* and *to* Shakespeare's Sonnets, and I seriously doubt that such a principle of connection will be found anywhere else among the many love-sonnet sequences of the English Renaissance. And third, Shakespeare himself, by virtue of the conjunctive role he invented for 73 and the sonnets he placed on either side of it, clearly signified that he, too, recognized the great merit of the poem, and the high esteem in which he apparently held it both accords with and sanctions the critical estimate of posterity.

II

The two questions of considerable importance for Shakespeare's Sonnets mentioned in the introduction are questions that I have elsewhere discussed at length. I did so in *Such Is My Love: A Study of Shakespeare's Sonnets*, and there concluded (1) that the exchange of love between the poet and the handsome younger man is represented as erotic in thought, word, and deed; and (2) that the extent to which the inscribed "I"-subject may be identified with William Shakespeare cannot be definitely determined, and that only through weighing textual and other evidence pertinent to identification can one reach a degree of probability on the matter.[6] I have no intention, of course, of going over the same ground again. What I wish to do here is to ascertain in what ways sonnets 71-74 can illumine these several topics.

That the male-male love is mutual, the four serial sonnets make plain, and they adumbrate its erotic character as well. As a matter of fact they allude more to the friend's love than to the persona's, doing so six times, as follows: the reciprocation of "your love" at 71.12; "your true love" and "you for [on account of] love" at 72.9, 10; and "makes thy love more strong / To love that [as *me*] well" at 73.13-14. In the two other instances the friend's love is conceived of not as interpersonal but as directed toward a nonpersonal object, whether an abstract one, the "merit . . . in me that you should love," or a concrete one, "to love things [bad sonnets]" at 72.2, 14. These instances are both analogous to, and pave the way for, one horn of the terminal ambiguity of 73, "to love that [as *your youth*] well."

Only twice does the poet make specific reference to his own love, though both times tellingly: first with the moving avowal "for I love you so" at 71.6, and again with the tender vocative "dear love" at 72.3. To so address the beloved as "love" is a usage that nowhere occurs between males outside the Sonnets, either in Shakespeare or in the early modern period. This amorous appellation otherwise peculiar to heterosexual lovers should be sufficient in and of itself to confirm the amorous nature of the poet's love.[7]

But that is not all. The poet, expecting to die first because he is older, shows the kind of fervent and anxious concern for the other who will live on that is more typical of spouses, parents, or gay lovers than of male friends unconnected by blood or desire. And such an age differential is classic in homosexual loves. Through all the successions and dramatic reversal of feelings voiced by the persona, from the crisis of near despondency in 72 to a calm and contented resolution in 74, what never wavers is his preoccupation with his dearly beloved. Nothing matters to the poet about his own death except how it will affect him, about the sonnets except in relation to him, or about an afterlife except insofar as it entails remaining with him. Then along with this obsession goes a kind of exclusiveness of attention. The poems are written as if only two people count in the world. Yes, anonymous outsiders do intrude into the thoughts at the end of 71 and beginning of 72, but they are viewed as inimical to one or both of the lovers and soon fade from consciousness altogether. The kind and intensity of the mental-emotional reactions recorded in these sonnets would have to belong to someone in love, here a male attached to another by eros rather than philia.

Homoeroticism is not conspicuous in sonnets 71-74, and so they can serve to illustrate how subtly suffusive a presence it can be in the first and longer part of the cycle, the 126 poems to and for the young man. While no reference to the beloved's dazzling beauty occurs in this group, the sonnet immediately before dwells on his beauty, with its attendant dangers and power. And while no reference to sexual acts appears in this group, the very next sonnet emphatically remedies that lack, for 75 is, as I have evinced in *Such Is My Love* (47-49), one of the most densely and richly referential of all to the impassioned sex relations engaged in by the pair of lovers.

III

In this quartet of sonnets the subjective "I" writes "my name." He had not done so before and does so now twice—at 71.11 and 72.11. What "name" is that and who is the "my" that it belongs to? These are the questions to be addressed from now on. So far in speaking of the poet I have been referring to the first-person persona presented in the text, and not, except in a few places where he is specifically mentioned, to William Shakespeare. But now I must discard that distinction in order to speculate on the relationship between the one and the other in the light of the phrase "my name."

Either the name is William Shakespeare and the Sonnets are autobiographical, or else the poet is a character of his invention. But "autobiographical" has to be qualified here. If self-depiction, Shakespeare restricts it to just the part of himself involved in a same-sex romance (sonnets 1-126) and an opposite-sex affair (127-154), and even then we do not know whether or to what extent he may blend fiction into the self-exposure. As for the places to go looking for pertinent evidence, they may be prioritized thus: first and foremost, the text of the Sonnets themselves; second, the 1609 Quarto (hereafter Q), the first edition, the only one to date from the writer's lifetime, and the only one that he could have had some control over; and lastly, anything located anywhere else that may be germane. I am limiting this inquiry to the first two sources.[8]

On several occasions in the sequence the poet discloses that he is called Will. He does so prior to 71-72, at 57.13, and afterwards in 135-136, two sonnets addressed to the mistress: most elaborately all through 135 (where it turns out that the young man also has this agnomen, as he does again at 143.13), and most patently in the couplet of 136,

> Make but my name thy love, and love that still,
> And then thou lov'st me for my name is *Will.* (13-14; italics in Q)

Thus the poet is in possession at least of a nickname, the one for William, and this is a factor that points in an authorial direction, but it is not by itself decisive.

The phrase "my name" shows up six times in the sonnet cycle: the last two times in the above couplet, the first two in 71-72, and in between at 76.7 and 111.5. On these occasions something transparent to the author transpires. In sonnet 111, for example, the goddess of fortune is to be chided

> That [she] did not better for my life provide
> Than public means which public manners breeds.
> Thence comes it that my name receives a brand,
> And almost thence my nature is subdued
> By what it works in, like the dyer's hand. (3-7)

Inside the Sonnets these details are opaque. They make no sense with respect to the persona, but they make perfect sense with respect to the author. Editors invariably have recourse to his "work" in the theater, as actor or playwright, in their glosses. At no other point, perhaps, does the text exert such pressure to seek an outside explanation. Hence "my life" as well as "my name" here advert in an unusual way to Shakespeare himself. And then in 76, a close neighbor of 71-72, the poet, considering why his verse style is so old-fashioned and unchanging, writes "That every word doth almost tell my name, / Showing their birth and where they did proceed" (7-8). The distinctive style, even if imputed to another, is the giveaway, being identifiable and an identifier of the writer, who of course is, as the title of Q makes plain, Shakespeare. What other "name" do the words "tell" and from whom else do they originate? The authorial presence keeps haunting "my name," and most indubitably at 136.14, "for my name is *Will*." Does it likewise haunt the earliest sites of the phrase, in sonnets 71 and 72?

The argument requires a move here from the poetic contents to the book that originally contained them. We do not know how *SHAKE-SPEARES SONNETS* came to be the title of Q,[9] whether it was chosen by the publisher Thomas Thorpe[10] or by the author. Even if he did not choose it, he may have authorized it, and there is no evidence that he objected to it. The title as given admits of two different but compatible constructions. Everyone would agree, I suppose, that Shakespeare's name is in the possessive case, despite missing the apostrophe only later introduced into English punctuation, and so would agree that one sense of the title designates him as the maker and the Sonnets as his on that account. But they may be his for another reason as well. This sonnet sequence is unlike any other in its time and place for being denominated with the surname of the writer. The ordinary practice was for the title character(s) to be a central figure in the sequence, most often the lady to whom the sonneteer is passionately devoted, such as Daniel's *Delia*, or, in the case of Sir *Philip* Sidney's *Astrophil and Stella*, the poet and his inamorata whose love affair constitutes the subject.[11] Seen in the light of these nomenclatural practices, the title of Q is anomalous. It might designate Shakespeare as the leading personage in the work, which then would be *about* him as well as *by* him. Such a decoding of the title opens up a possibility that can be neither proved nor disproved.

An interesting feature of Q is that at the top of every two facing pages the title is repeated, with *SHAKE-SPEARES* (again hyphenated, followed at times by a period, and the first S larger than the other block letters) on the verso and *SONNETS.* (with the first S larger and a period following) on the recto. Whoever reads the Sonnets "Never before Imprinted"—as it says on Q's title page—will see the author's name in block capitals above the verse on each and every left-hand page (see Figure 2 and Figure 4 in this volume). Thus "my poor name" at 71.11 is underneath *SHAKE-SPEARES*, and "let my name" at 72.11 is below and diagonally across from *SHAKE-SPEARES*. This fascinating phenomenon of the names of the author and of his book kept constantly in view above the sonnets is omitted in nearly all later editions.

For sonnets 71, 72, and 73 to have any bearing on the persona-author conundrum, they must first be visualized as they appear on the (unnumbered) pages of Q opened to where they are printed. Under *SHAKE-SPEARES* on the left is 71, and its phrase "my poore name" (Q's spelling) occurs about three-quarters of the way down; 72 bridges the pages, and its clause "My name be buried" is in the sixth line down on the right-hand side. That clause brings up "my name"—and as potentially "buried"—for the second time and repeats it from the sonnet before in the corresponding eleventh verse. The text could be giving off some kind of signal. Then six verses later, including the first three of 73, we come across the word "shake"! It echoes *SHAKE-*, prominent above as the initial word on this pair of pages, and a word, too, especially as divided by the hyphen, that might be construed as a verb. The clause at 73.3 is "boughes which shake."[12] The "boughes" are made, as are spears, of elongated wood, and if the word is plural, so is the spelling of *SPEARES* without the possessive apostrophe. The juxtaposition of the phrasal "shake-speares" with "boughes which shake" produces a kind of chiastic effect. Under the circumstances may one venture the inference that those words are transposable into "shake-boughes"? The concentration of these data, into two facing pages of Q and twenty-one lines over three sonnets, is striking. In that brief space we pass from the hyphenated verb-noun proper name *SHAKE-SPEARES*, to "my poore name," to "My name be buried," which may be a pointer to a hidden name and which seems more likely to be one when "shake" crops up, and in conjunction with "boughes," to invite the inferred verb-noun name of "Shake-boughs."[13] Insofar as "my name" is disinterred, even partially, in the turnabout sonnet of the series, the phrase becomes referential to the author in its initial as well as in its subsequent advents.

If "Will Shake-boughs" were to be William Shakespeare's personal signature within the Sonnets, it would allay suspicions of pure fictionalization and would go far toward certifying the view of the persona as a (signed) portrait of the artist as an older lover. The verbal events in 71-73 form a pattern too distinct to be readily dismissed as coincidence. Yet the nominal "Shake-boughs" is too conjectural to serve as a secure basis for affirming the poetic representation as that of a special and circumscribed area of the author's private life. It would, then, seem reasonable to conclude that the probability of such an affirmation is herewith increased in direct proportion to the plausibility one may grant the evidence set forth above.

At any rate, by focusing in on "my name" in 71 and 72, I have come upon yet another kind of linkage—and again one hitherto unnoticed—among the poetic texts examined here in the context of one another.

NOTES

1. *Shakespeare's Sonnets,* ed. Stephen Booth. Quotations from the Sonnets, except for some citations from the 1609 Quarto, will be from this edition, with an occasional silent emendation.

2. William Empson gives a famous reading, and overreading, of 73.4, and one that includes most of the details of my explication, in *Seven Types of Ambiguity* 2-3. He notes "the protestant destruction of monasteries" as a connotation of the line, and this is the one reference to a historical event in all four of the sonnets, and one of the very few in the entire sequence. George Steevens in 1780 was the first to connect "this image" with "our devastated monasteries" (Rollins 1: xi, 190).

Since "quiers" is the spelling of "choirs" in Q, commentators sometimes hold that the word may also import a gathering of manuscript or book "leaves"—the pages here yellowed with age. Do they "hang" on the quiers, which would somehow be "bare" and "ruined"? The vagueness of it all only serves to point up the precision of the choir metaphor. This book notion is intrusive, disruptive of the sense, and disallowed by the context.

3. Booth, in his editorial comments on 73.14, glosses "that" as "(1) me or my love; and perhaps, secondarily, (2) your youth or life." He glosses "leave" as "(1) depart from; (2) give up, forgo." Kerrigan takes "that" as "(the poet. But also . . . your life)," and "leave" as 'forgo' but "'depart from' also . . . registers."

4. Such a reader is Anthony Hecht. Recognizing the two meanings of "the deeply unnerving couplet," he subjects each one separately to his special and creative brand of criticism, which is to report the reflections on morals and life that the verse sets off in his mind. He does not inquire into a function for the coordinate messages (7-9). Nor does he view sonnet 73 in its immediate context, even though Evans in his annotations in the same edition regards sonnets 71-74 as a group in which "the poet considers how, after his death, he wishes to be thought of (or not thought of) by the youth" (177).

5. The deconstruction I have in mind is more American than French, literary rather than philosophical, and less that of Derrida than of Paul de Man. See, for example, his discussion of the last line of Yeats's "Among School Children" in *Allegories of Reading* 11-12.

6. On the first question see especially chapters 4 and 5; on the second, pp. 5, 73, 97, 217-21 and *passim*. I don't know whether the discussion of the poet/author enigma in those pages has been misunderstood or simply ignored, but a number of people who should know better say that I view the Sonnets as autobiography and seek to prove Shakespeare's homosexuality. Confronted with this crude caricature, I cannot refrain from quoting an accurate grasp of my position, that of Robert Crosman: "Pequigney makes a number of forceful arguments for the bisexuality of the persona of the sonnets" while "studiously avoiding any biographical inferences" (482). That is exactly what I do, until near the end when I argue the likelihood, but never the certainty, of authorial self-revelation. The fact that Crosman got it right is gratifying, and not least for so clearly demonstrating that the position I take is *there* and seeable.

7. *Such Is My Love* 76. This occurrence is not among the examples cited there.

8. For a fuller discussion of the topic, and one that takes into account such germane outside factors as the conventions of the sonnet sequences and readers' responses, see *Such Is My Love* 217-22.

9. That is the correct title and properly adopted by Booth and Rollins (in his running headings). But many other editors, Evans and Kerrigan among them, omit the authorial element and revise the title to *The Sonnets*.

10. Katherine Duncan-Jones provides an estimable and persuasive defense of the much maligned Thorpe and his Shakespearean Quarto in "Was the 1609 *Shake-speares Sonnets* Really Unauthorized?" See also Kerrigan 427.

11. There the "-phil" connects hero and author with the familiar form of the latter's given name. Astrophil has as much authority as Astrophel and preserves both the Greek root of "love" and the self-reference (Ringler 458). Shakespeare might have followed Sidney's lead with some made-up name containing "Will," except that in sonnet 135 three men are named Will (Pequigney 144-46). Otherwise the characters are nameless, which is one of the peculiarities of the Shakespearean sequence (Duncan-Jones 153).

12. The verb "shake" appears in two other places, at 18.3 and 28.6, where, however, there can be no question of nominal wordplay because in neither case is the term foreshadowed by or associated with "my name."

13. Could Shakespeare have in some way been thinking of "Shake-scene," the sobriquet that Robert Greene coined for an attack on the young playwright as an "upstart crow" and for being self-important? This, the first critical notice of Shakespeare on record, appeared in Greene's pamphlet *A Groats-worth of Wit Bought with a Million of Repentance* (1592).

WORKS CITED

Booth, Stephen, ed. *Shakespeare's Sonnets*. New Haven: Yale UP, 1977.

Crosman, Robert. "Making Love out of Nothing at All: The Issue of Story in Shakespeare's Procreation Sonnets." *Shakespeare Quarterly* 41 (1990): 470-88.

de Man, Paul. *Allegories of Reading*. New Haven: Yale UP, 1979.

Duncan-Jones, Katherine. "Was the 1609 *Shake-speares Sonnets* Really Unauthorized?" *Review of English Studies* 34 (1983): 151-71.

Empson, William. *Seven Types of Ambiguity*. New York: New Directions, 1947.

Evans, G. Blakemore, ed. *The Sonnets*. Cambridge: Cambridge UP, 1996.

Hecht, Anthony. Introduction. *The Sonnets*. Ed. G. Blakemore Evans. Cambridge: Cambridge UP, 1996.

Kerrigan, John, ed. *The Sonnets and A Lover's Complaint*. Harmondsworth, Middlesex: Penguin Books, 1986.

Lessing, Doris. *Walking in the Shade: Volume Two of My Autobiography*. New York: HarperCollins, 1997.

Pequigney, Joseph. *Such Is My Love: A Study of Shakespeare's Sonnets*. Chicago: U of Chicago P, 1985.

Ringler, William A. Jr., ed. *Poems.* By Sir Philip Sidney. Oxford: Clarendon, 1962.

Rollins, Hyder E., ed. *A New Variorum Edition of Shakespeare.* 2 Vols. Philadelphia: Lippincott: 1944.

Shakespeare, William. *SHAKE-SPEARES SONNETS. Never before Imprinted.* London: By G. Eld for T. T., 1609. [Reproduced in the edition cited above of Stephen Booth, who identifies this as "the Bridgewater copy of the Apsley imprint of the 1609 Quarto" (xviii).]

The Matter of Inwardness
Shakespeare's Sonnets

Michael Schoenfeldt

Soul is only a word for something about the body.
—Friedrich Nietzsche

Amid the contemporary appetite for discovering in the Renaissance prefigurations of modernity, Shakespeare has proven a particularly tempting site. Although the plays, and *Hamlet* in particular, have provided the primary evidence, the Sonnets have played a part in this conversation.[1] In this essay I intend not to forward my own set of claims for the signal modernity of the Shakespearean subject but rather to highlight some of the considerable differences and surprising similarities that exist between the early modern language of interiority and our own, and to show some of the interpretive dissonance that has been generated from our inability to apprehend these differences and to clarify these similarities. I do wish to explore the paradox by which a regime of the physiological and psychological self so different from our own nevertheless teases us with the illusion of modernity. Significantly these differences are often disguised by the fact that our own vocabulary of inwardness is derived in large part from this physiology we have left behind—familiar terms such as "temper," "complexion," "humor," "passion," "heat," "blood," "spirit," and "temperature" all derive from this earlier lexicon of the self, but mean something very different in early modern usage. Whereas our post-Cartesian ontology imagines inwardness and materialism as necessarily separate realms of

existence, the Galenic regime of the humoral self that supplies
Shakespeare with much of his vocabulary of inwardness demanded the
invasion of social and psychological realms by biological and
environmental processes.[2] Dedicated to rendering salutary the
inevitable permeability of bodies and of selves, this regime literally
embodied inner emotion by comprehending these emotions in humoral
terms. Locating and explaining human passion amid a taxonomy of
internal organs, this physiology issues in a discourse in which, to use a
phrase that Slavoj Zizek borrows from Hegel, "the spirit is a bone"; in
which, that is, the purportedly immaterial subject is constituted as a
profoundly material substance.

After sketching an account of the physiological and psychological
self that emerges in the Sonnets, I will turn to sonnet 94, "They that
have power to hurt," a poem which has been particularly troubling for
twentieth-century criticism. I will argue that this trouble derives in part
from the fact that the poem idealizes a kind of imperturbable self-
containment that seems oppressively chilly if not deeply hypocritical to
twentieth-century sensibilities. It is most frequently read as an ironic
epitome of pathological repression rather than a praise of self-mastery.
When viewed against the endorsement of self-control and the suspicion
of unregulated desire that epitomizes early modern accounts of the self,
accounts that locate pathology not in suppressing desire but in
surrendering to it, the poem becomes a far less vexed, if equally
interesting, performance. Close attention to this atypical sonnet allows
us to view the larger collection not just as remarkable articulations of a
desiring subject but also as impressive discussions of the subjectivity
that emerges from the regulation of desire.

Shakespeare turns so frequently to physiological terminology, I
would argue, because the job of the doctor, like that of the playwright
and poet, is to intuit inner reality via external demeanor. Even the
notorious diagnostic examination of urine and feces by physicians was
simply a way, prior to x-rays, to look inside the patient by looking at
what had just been inside the patient, and testing the efficacy of its
internal processes of assimilation and excretion. Lyric poet and medical
doctor, then, are both students of inwardness. The Renaissance cult of
melancholy—marked by a plethora of books defining, diagnosing, and
curing this phenomenon—attests to the widespread search for
physiological explanations and treatments for an extensive
psychological phenomenon.[3] Perhaps significantly, the Shakespearean
play that is most frequently cited in arguments seeking a moment in

which to inaugurate "modern subjectivity"—*Hamlet*—is itself drenched with this physiological vocabulary. The Sonnets, by contrast, invoke this physiological vocabulary only glancingly, but nevertheless ask its principles of regulation to underpin their ideal of the well-balanced self, and to underscore their portrait of desire as a disease that threatens the physical and mental health of this self.

Two poems that do make explicit reference to the humoral vocabulary of Renaissance medicine are sonnets 44 and 45. These poems use the conventional linkage between the four elements (earth, air, fire, and water) and the four humors (blood, phlegm, choler, and melancholy) to confront rather playfully an issue that haunts and blesses the Sonnets: the status of desire when distance separates one from the object of desire. The speaker of sonnet 44 wishes that "the dull substance of my flesh were thought" (1) so that when he thought of his beloved he would be with him.[4] Separated physically by the elements of "earth and water" (11) from his beloved, he is left in despair. Although "nimble thought can jump both sea and land" (7), thought is not flesh. The speaker of sonnet 45 sends his "thought" and his "desire" (2), which he likens to the other two elements of "slight air and purging fire" (1), to be with the beloved, only to discover that "My life, being made of four [elements], with two alone / Sinks down to death, oppressed with melancholy" (7-8). Together, the two poems provide a playfully physiological—although, as Stephen Booth points out, a somewhat medically inaccurate, since earth and water would produce not melancholy but the far less appropriate phlegm (*Sonnets* 207)—explanation for the sadness that afflicts one when separated from the object of desire. Flesh is not thought, then, but thought is afflicted by the material claims of the flesh.

A more solemn model of body-soul relations obtains in sonnet 146, but a similar conceptual pattern linking physiology and psychology emerges. Rather than wishing that his flesh were thought so that he could possess the remote object of his ardent desire, the speaker of 146 aggravates the tension between body and soul, finding ethical comfort in the distance between flesh and thought that the speaker of 44 wished to close. Sonnet 146 ("Poor soul, the center of my sinful earth") deploys a conventional image of body-soul relations to demonstrate the eternal tension between the demands of the body and the aspirations of the soul that is dictated by classical and Christian ethics, and that underpins the imperturbability idealized in sonnet 94.[5] In 146, the soul is imagined as "the center of my sinful earth" (1), a comparatively

impotent monarch surrounded by "these rebel powers that thee array"
(2). This particular image of the self as a fortress under siege,
moreover, familiar from the Castle of Alma in Book 2 of Spenser's
Faerie Queene and its various medieval precedents, deliberately
confuses inward urging and external temptation in order to argue a
politically contestatory model of body-soul relations. (It is, I think,
significant that a poem filled with such commonplace notions includes
one of the unresolvable textual cruces of the sequence, since the
repetition of the phrase "my sinfull earth" at the beginning of line 2
itself indicates a compositor's unthinking repetition of familiar
material. Suggestions for the elided phrase include "Pressed by," "Lord
of," "Thrall to," and "Feeding.") The poem resolves the respective
claims of body and spirit by reversing typical siege tactics, urging the
besieged soul to starve the body in order to banquet itself:

> Then, soul, live thou upon thy servant's loss,
> And let that pine to aggravate thy store:
> Buy terms divine in selling hours of dross;
> Within be fed, without be rich no more. (9-12)

Outward fasting is inward feasting.[6] This moralized anorexia, familiar
from medieval mystical writings as well as early modern health
manuals, is designed to reestablish a hierarchy between body and soul
that the urgent, quotidian hungers of the flesh would deny. As Nicholas
Culpepper observes in the delightfully titled *Health for the Rich and
Poor, by Diet, without Physick*, to indulge in "ill Diet" is "to make thy
soul a slave to the Flesh, a Servant to his Vassal" (124).[7] The sonnet's
concluding couplet—"So shalt thou feed on death, that feeds on men, /
And death once dead, there's no more dying then" (13-14)—makes
even the mundane mystery of consumption, by which life is sustained
by feeding on dead matter, an extension of this restored hierarchy, and
a premonition of the end of time.

But in the subsequent sonnet, 147, this comparatively simple
opposition between the hungers of the body and the aspirations of the
soul receives nightmarish complication. Rather than starving the body
to feed the soul, the speaker of this poem articulates a desire evinced in
its yearning for what at once precipitates and prolongs the illness:

> My love is as a fever, longing still
> For that which longer nurseth the disease,

> Feeding on that which doth preserve the ill,
> Th'uncertain sickly appetite to please. (1-4)

As in sonnet 151, the depth and force of the speaker's desire leads him to "betray / My nobler part to my gross body's treason" (5-6). In sonnet 151, that is, the "rebel powers" of the body have revolted successfully. In response, the soul offers the body a concession, telling him that "he may / Triumph in love" (7-8). The flesh responds to this victory with lofty exaltation; "proud of this pride," it is ready to "stand in [the] affairs" of the beloved or to "fall by thy side" (10, 12). But in sonnet 147, not even such brief phallic victories are allowed the speaker; rather, abandoned by reason, his "physician" (5), for not keeping his "prescriptions" (6), the speaker is "Past cure . . . And frantic mad" (9-10).

Behind the portrait of love's decidedly unhealthy diet in this poem—"Feeding on that which doth preserve the ill" (3)—is a larger meditation in the Sonnets on food, appetite, and identity. This is in part a response to Galenic physiology, which puts immense pressure on the act of consumption, making each meal an occasion that determines the health of mind and body. Diet either feeds or ameliorates the ill.[8] Shakespeare, moreover, links the corollary appetites of food and love in order to explore the relevance of the necessary periodicity of hunger to the ebb and flow of erotic desire. In sonnet 56, for example, the speaker hopes that an apparently sated love will "renew thy force" (1), so that it will be more like gastronomic "appetite, / Which but today by feeding is allayed, / Tomorrow sharp'ned in his former might" (2-4). He is concerned that erotic "fullness" (6) might "kill / The spirit of love with a perpetual dullness" (7-8) rather than provide a moment of temporary satiation. The speaker of sonnet 75 articulates the bulimic patterns of his erotic life, telling the beloved that he is "to my thoughts as food to life" (1):

> Sometime all full with feasting on your sight,
> And by and by clean starved for a look;
> Possessing or pursuing no delight
> Save what is had or must from you be took.
>   Thus do I pine and surfeit day by day,
>   Or gluttoning on all, or all away. (9-14)

The speaker of sonnet 118, by contrast, invokes contemporaneous medical theory in order to describe a strategy for sustaining desire in the face of satiation: "As to prevent our maladies unseen, / We sicken to shun sickness when we purge" (3-4). He refers here to the paradox inherent in the central therapeutic procedure of Renaissance medicine: inducing a symptom of illness—vomiting—in order to rid a patient of the excess humors that would make him or her truly sick. The poem then proceeds to explore the perverse nexus of sickness and health that such treatments assume. In a brilliantly ambiguous phrase, the speaker describes himself as "full of your nere cloying sweetnesse" (5); here "nere" means both "never" and "near," either denying the possibility of satiation or confessing it. The speaker, moreover, is "sick of welfare" (7); that is, at once tired of, and ill because of, a particularly unsatisfying form of health. In the poem's concluding lines, he only discovers that "Drugs poison him that so fell sick of you" (14)—that what he imagined as inducing a cure of the excess that precipitates disease is functioning in fact as an agent of illness.

Rather than following a regimen that might ameliorate if not cure this madness—a regimen which would likely include a kind of therapeutic fasting like that moralized in sonnet 146 as well as the purge recommended in sonnet 118—the speaker of sonnet 147 can only describe the maddeningly divided sensibility that his unregulated desire produces: "For I have sworn thee fair, and thought thee bright, / Who art as black as hell, as dark as night" (13-14).[9] He is like the speaker of the final two sonnets (153 and 154), who is "sick" (153.11), "a sad distempered guest" (153.12), and who seeks a "sovereign cure" (153.8) for "love's fire" (154.10) in the baths (venereal disease, a malady of love often likened to fire [as in sonnet 144], was thought to be ameliorated if not cured by baths, a kind of purge through the skin rather than the alimentary canal). This speaker, though, learns only that "Love's fire heats water, water cools not love" (154.14). Desire is a contagion that is spread by the very act of trying to treat it. The speaker of sonnet 147 likewise discovers no way to subjugate an erotic desire that drives him to a physiological distemper that is both the cause and the symptom of madness.

In sonnet 129, Shakespeare explores with clinical precision the madness intrinsic to the physiology of sexual desire and corporeal satisfaction. Where most erotic poetry since Petrarch had been premised on the unavailability of the love object, Shakespeare in sonnet 129 writes about exactly what happens when you get what you say you want, and demonstrates it is not a consummation devoutly to be wished, but rather a nightmare that cannot be avoided. In this poem, the imagined physiology of sexual intercourse underpins a visceral disgust with the entire enterprise of corporeal hunger and physical satiation:

> Th'expense of spirit in a waste of shame
> Is lust in action, and till action lust
> Is perjured, murdrous, bloody, full of blame,
> Savage, extreme rude, cruel, not to trust,
> Enjoyed no sooner but despised straight
> Past reason hunted, and no sooner had
> Past reason hated as a swallowed bait,
> On purpose laid to make the taker mad;
> Mad in pursuit, and in possession so,
> Had, having, and in quest to have, extreme,
> A bliss in proof, and proved, a very woe,
> Before, a joy proposed, behind, a dream.
>> All this the world well know, yet none knows well
>> To shun the heav'n that leads men to this hell.

The fact that in the act of orgasm a male was thought to expend his vital spirit and so to shorten his life becomes for Shakespeare representative of the larger loss of self that unregulated desire involves. The often-noticed pun on "waste" and "waist" (buttressed by "shame," the English for *pudendum*, the Latin word for female genitalia) demonstrates the unproductive economy of the self that the poem finds essential to the act of sex. Activity centered in the waist is a waste. Where the early sonnets encourage the young man to give himself away as a strategy of self-preservation via reproduction—"To give away yourself keeps yourself still" (16.13)—this poem locates the self in an economy whereby it desires uncontrollably just what weakens it. Erotic attraction here is made treacherous, a "swallowed bait" that makes "the taker" insane, both in pursuit and in possession. Like the unhealthy diet in sonnet 147.3—"Feeding on that which doth preserve the ill"—sexual appetite is imagined in alimentary terms. As Stephen Booth astutely observes, the poem's headlong syntax mimics the compulsion the poem records (*Essay* 150-51).

It is amid such portraits of the deeply physiological and psychological dangers of desire that sonnet 94 must be read. I want to argue that this poem, probably the most discussed of the Sonnets in the twentieth century, vexes us in large part because we unintentionally vex it with an anachronistic model of self and desire. We fail, that is, to see the premium that Shakespeare's own articulations of desire place on self-control, as well as the medical and moral culture from which they derive. In his compelling interpretation of the poem, Stephen Booth asserts that "throughout the poem the reader has to cope with conflicting reactions, impressions and systems of coherence" (*Essay* 167). I do not want to deny that there is conflict in the poem, but I do want to show that our sense of the occasion and depth of conflict is altered by the very different predispositions about self that we unintentionally import into the poem. The poem's urgent endorsement of cool stability can only be understood against the unstable, overheated self, susceptible to the insanities of insubordinate desire, that is depicted in the other sonnets and is a product of the period's medical, theological, and philosophical inheritance. Under this dispensation, modes of constraint we construe as unhealthy repression are coveted as acts of self-government necessary for the protection of self and other.

Like sonnet 129, sonnet 94 posits a general case rather than the particular desires of a yearning individual. What has most troubled contemporary readers of sonnet 94 is the apparent disparity between the emotional coldness of the figures being praised and the divine reward they are said to merit:

> They that have pow'r to hurt, and will do none,
> That do not do the thing they most do show,
> Who moving others are themselves as stone,
> Unmoved, cold, and to temptation slow—
> They rightly do inherit heaven's graces,
> And husband nature's riches from expense[.] (1-6)

It has proven particularly difficult for modern readers to see how being unmoved can be imagined as an avenue to heaven.[10] Critics of the poem sometimes concede that it is good to be "to temptation slow," but not to be "as stone, / Unmoved, cold." Edward Hubler, for example, reads the entire octave as "ironic," and announces that "It is preposterous on the face of things to proclaim as the inheritors of heaven's graces those who are 'as stone'" (103). William Empson's brilliant reading of the poem similarly refers dismissively to those the poem praises as "the cold people" (89-115). Empson intriguingly compares the poem's ideal of emotional aloofness to Angelo in *Measure for Measure*, a man, in Lucio's apt phrase,

> whose blood
> Is very snow-broth; one who never feels
> The wanton stings and motions of the sense.... (1.4.57-59)

But Angelo's problem is not that he is unmoved, but that he is moved beyond his control. Angelo is not a study in repression but in failed suppression. In the course of the play he becomes one of those who has power to hurt and will do so. Being "cold" and "as stone" is a state to be preferred to the seething instability articulated in "My love is as a fever" (147.1), and dramatized in Angelo's cruel abuse of power in the effort to satisfy a desire he fails abysmally to harness.

The coldness the poem praises, moreover, connotes positive physiological and ethical significance, since it indicates that the individual has allowed a cool brain to master the agitated passions that assault it. As Laurentius argues,

> The temperature of the braine must be cold, thereby to temper the spirits of sence and motion, to resist their aptnes to be wasted and spent, and to keep that this noble member (which is commonly imployed about so many worthie actions) should not set it selfe on fire, and make our discourses and talke rash and headie, and our motions out of order, as it befalleth them which are frenticke. (141-42)[11]

The pun on "headie" underscores the crucial linkage between the physiological properties of an organ and the psychological conduct of the organism. The intrinsic coolness of the brain at once refrigerates a system whose natural heat threatens spontaneous combustion and restrains the forces of insurrection and disorder—themselves imagined as heat—which urge the subject to the wasteful expenditure that haunts the Sonnets. Similarly, in *The Examination of Men's Wits*, Juan Huarte explains psychological instability by recourse to the humoral temperature of an individual:

the cause why a man is unstable, and changeth opinion at every
moment, is for that he hath a hote braine: and contrariewise, his being
stable and firme, springs from the coldnesse of his braine. (56-57)

Ethical conduct, moreover, influences (and is in turn affected by)
humoral physiology. "When the understanding overruleth," continues
Huarte,

it ordinarily inclineth a man to vertue, because this power is founded
on cold and drie: From which two qualities, bud many vertues, as are
Continencie, Humilitie, Temperance, and from heat the contrarie.
(143)

For Huarte, the pernicious moral effect of physiological heat on the
brain offers the clearest refutation of the Platonic notion of the
immaterial soul:

Plato held it for matter verie certain, that the reasonable soule is a
substance bodilesse, and spirituall . . . yet for all this, Galen could
never bring within his conceit, that it was true, but held it alwaies
doubtfull, seeing a wise man through the heat of his braine, to dote,
and by applying cold medicines unto him, he commeth to his wits
againe. (88-89)[12]

Although heat was frequently correlated with both masculinity and
vigor, it was a far from equivocal good, and always part of a network of
relational concepts whose ideal involves balance and temperance, not
instability and extremity.[13]

Where the speaker of 147 is "frantic mad with evermore unrest"
(10), the speaker of 94 articulates a mode of conduct intended to apply
the "cold medicines" prescribed by Huarte to the congenital madness
and instability of the body. As is clear from the fact that our current
word for mental health—sanity—is derived from the Latin term for
corporeal vigor—*sanitas*—physical fitness and psychological stability
are in this earlier medical regime two different sides of the same coin.
In *The Anatomy of Melancholy*, that compendium of Renaissance
ethics, medicine, and psychology, Robert Burton contrasts the elite few
who achieve successful self-governance—those who have power to
hurt and will do none—with those many who fail to bridle their desires:

> Some few discreet men there are, that can governe themselves, and
> curb in these inordinate Affections, by Religion, Philosophy, and
> such divine Precepts of meekenesse, patience, and the like: but most
> part for want of governement, out of indiscretion, ignorance, they
> suffer themselves wholy to be led by sense; and are so farre from
> repressing rebellious inclinations, . . . they follow on, wheresoever
> their unbridled Affections will transport them, and doe more out of
> custome, selfe-will, then out of Reason. (1: 255-56)

The result of this failure to allow reason to lead the passions is a vision
of the self completely out of control, like that envisioned in sonnet 129:

> this stubborne will of ours perverts judgement, which sees and
> knowes what should and ought to be done, and yet will not doe it.
> *Mancipia gulae*, slaves to their severall lusts, and appetite, they
> precipitate and plunge themselves into a Labyrinth of cares, blinded
> with lust, blinded with ambition . . . giving way to these violent
> passions of feare, griefe, shame, revenge, hatred, malice, &c. They
> are torne in peeces, as *Actaeon* was with his dogges. (1: 256)

Giving way to one's various passions is a loss of power over the self, a
surrender of sovereignty to a vastly inferior jurisdiction. Torn apart by
conflicting passion, the self loses any sense of its integrity, and
disintegrates into its various undifferentiated appetites.[14]

Giving way to one's various passions, moreover, is to yield the self
to the kinds of inconstancy with which the Sonnets themselves
continually battle on a variety of fronts. Indeed, if there is a theme that
unifies this collocation of frequently disparate fourteen-line poems, it is
their struggle with inconstancy and variability. Haunted by "the conceit
of this inconstant stay," in the words of sonnet 15, the poems aim to
discover something that will abide. Where the early sonnets imagine
progeny and poetry as corollary forms of reproduction that battle the
inexorable ravages of time, other poems idealize a love marked by
permanence, one that is "an ever-fixed mark," and "alters not" (sonnet
116). Both the dark lady sonnets and many of the poems to the young
man imagine inconstancy to be a harrowing betrayal. Sonnet 94 is part
of this effort to locate a site of constancy amid inexorable flux within
the self, even if the rigid control it prescribes leaves little room for the
emotional bonds of love that other poems postulate as effective
bulwarks against the ravages of time.

Sonnet 94 presents difficulties to us, moreover, because it links the successful control of one's emotions with a social elitism we have for the most part abandoned. Those who control their demeanor are "Lords and owners of their faces," the poem declares, granting them titles far superior to those "others" who are "but stewards of their excellence" (7-8). Self-governance, then, is social mastery, protecting one from the dangers of a "base infection" which would make "the basest weed out-brav[e] his dignity" (11-12). Hubler argues that this praise must be ironic, since "They are the owners of themselves, whereas throughout Shakespeare's work self-possession in the sense of living without regard for others is intolerable" (104). But this argument seems to misrepresent not only sonnet 94 but also the virtue of self-possession throughout Shakespeare. Indeed, it is hard to imagine the rule of the cool, impenetrable Henry V—in many ways Shakespeare's most effective monarch—without this virtue. In parts 1 and 2 of *Henry IV*, plays frequently invoked in discussions of this poem, the deployment of monarchical power depends on shrewd self-possession.

By describing the ideal of constancy in terms of lifeless stone, Shakespeare knowingly deploys conventional anti-Stoic terminology. In the first edition of the *Basilikon Doron*, for example, the future King James I decried "that Stoic insensisible stupidity that proud inconstant Lipsius persuadeth in his *Constantia*." Gabriel Powel, a Puritan, similarly attacked "that blockish conceit that would have men to be without affection, howbeit of late it hath been newly furbished by certain upstart Stoics."[15] Shakespeare invokes such denigrating terminology not to render the poem's larger claims for self-control ironic but rather to reclaim this vocabulary from the critics of stoical demeanor, and to remind us of the costs and difficulties of sustaining the ethical stability the poem demands. We need to remember, moreover, that the imagery of stone possesses in other contexts a variety of positive connotations. Indeed, amid the very religious discourses the poem repeatedly invokes, rock functions as a site of stability desired fervently by the tortuously erratic speaker of the Davidic Psalms. In Matthew 16: 18—"thou art Peter, and upon this rocke I will buylde my Church"—a central passage for the Reformation, Christ chooses a similar stability on which to found his church, punning in the process on the derivation of Peter from the Greek *petros*, rock. God, likewise, has traditionally been defined as the unmoved mover, one who "moving others" is nevertheless "unmoved."

Perhaps the improbable bridge the poem asserts linking dispassionate demeanor to heavenly grace is composed of such lithoid materials.

Accounts of the poem have also foundered on the issue of the hypocrisy that the poem seems to endorse in its idealization of those "That do not do the thing they most do show," and who are "the lords and owners of their faces." Empson, for example, argues that the poem provides an ironic comment on "the Machiavellian, the wicked plotter who is exciting and civilized and in some way right about life" (90).[16] It is true that the capacity to control one's demeanor is a mark of Shakespeare's villains; as Hamlet remarks of Claudius, "one may smile, and smile, and be a villain" (1.5.108). But it is also true that Hamlet defiantly defines himself by recourse to a related inwardness: "But I have that within which passes show" (1.2.85). The kinds of disjunction between inner and outer that we might construe as hypocrisy frequently function for early modern England as the foundation of civility. As George Herbert, a poet committed both to sincerity of expression and to the terrors of the heart, observes:

> Surely if each one saw anothers heart,
> There would be no commerce
> No sale or bargain passe: all would disperse,
> And live apart. ("Giddinesse" 21-24)

Social life, Herbert suggests, demands the salutary deceptions of civil conduct. The inherently unstable and unruly self presumed by Herbert and Shakespeare—the "giddiness" of Herbert's title—makes it a necessary good for the powerful not to do the thing they most do show, particularly in a culture in which social prestige was marked in part by the weapons one was allowed to own and display.[17] Inhabiting the anxious continuum that conjoins a prized civility to a despised hypocrisy, sonnet 94 addresses some of the central aporias of Western civilization.

Another apparent aporia in the poem is the leap from the inorganic imagery of the octet to the organic imagery of the sestet. The poem's theme, moreover, seems to alter, from the declaration of a desired stability to protection from a feared contagion. Both sections of the poem, however, are linked by the attention they devote to self-control, and by the way they imagine the social dimensions of such discipline. The purpose of the sestet is to demonstrate how the rigorous self-control the poem endorses not only delimits a superior's efforts to hurt others but also inoculates such a superior against harm from base infection. The sestet, that is, moves from the sturdy, inanimate world of stone to the delicate, ephemeral world of flowers in order to stress the hygienically prophylactic rather than the socially strategic uses of the imperturbable self-absorption the poem praises. Self-mastery, sonnet 94 suggests, is not only the evidence of social status but also a tactic of self-protection:

> The summer's flow'r is to the summer sweet,
> Though to itself it only live and die;
> But if that flow'r with base infection meet,
> The basest weed outbraves his dignity.
>   For sweetest things turn sourest by their deeds;
>   Lilies that fester smell far worse than weeds. (9-14)

In order to render this statement ironic, Hubler contrasts this ideal of self-enclosure with the early sonnets that encourage the young man to abandon his sterile self-absorption (103).[18] But even in those early sonnets, the young man is urged to give himself away in order cunningly to preserve himself through the techniques of heterosexual reproduction, not out of some ethical joy implicit in the virtue of giving. We need to coordinate this ideal of self-enclosure, moreover, with the attitudes articulated in those sonnets in which the speaker laments the processes by which he or his beloved have exposed themselves to an infectious commonality imagined not just as an overt injury of class but also as a contagious social disease. Sonnet 33, for example, "Full many a glorious morning," blames the sun for allowing "basest clouds to ride / With ugly rack on his celestial face." Like the "base infection" and the "basest weed" in sonnet 94, these clouds are guilty of an offense that is at once social and sexual.[19] The speaker of sonnet 110, in turn, laments having "made myself a motley to the view, / Gored mine own thoughts, sold cheap what is most dear" (2-3). The speaker of sonnet 111 complains that his "name receives a brand, / And almost thence my nature is subdued / To what it works in, like the dyer's hand" (5-7). In response to this stain, the speaker says that "like a willing patient I will drink / Potions of eisel 'gainst my strong infection" (9-10). Playing on the various available meanings of *infection*—to dye, stain, tinge, color; to spoil or corrupt by noxious influence; to affect with disease; to taint with moral corruption—

Shakespeare links the social stain of the dyer's hand to an illness that requires bitter medicine.[20]

The relationship between the sestet's language of disease and the emotional temperature that is the subject of the octet is clarified in the surmise of the speaker of sonnet 144 that he will not be able to confirm his suspicions of sexual betrayal "Till my bad angel fire my good one out" (14). Here, "firing out" is at once infusing another with desire and infecting another with venereal disease. It is the festering heat generated by such "base infection" that the solipsistic self-absorption of the "summer's flower" aims to avoid—not through the bitter homeopathy of sickening to shun sickness but rather through rigorous preventative measures. The initially perplexing invocation of the lily in the last line of sonnet 94 likewise adjoins the poem's obsession with disease. In *The Haven of Health* (1584), Thomas Cogan notes that

> The Lillie is hoat and dry of qualitie, both the flowers, leaves and rootes are used in medicine, but not in the kitchen. The flowers are commended in the gospell for beautie, and preferred before the royaltie of King Solomon. They are a great ornament to a garden or in a house, yet the smell of them is discommended and accounted ill for the plague. (51)

A figure of ornamental beauty and fetid stench, a staple of medicine and an accessory to the plague, a biblical figure of purity (they are a frequent motif in Annunciations), and a source of heat, the lily epitomizes at once the comeliness of self-control and the moral stench that arises from the misdeeds of those who misuse their power to hurt.[21] Assuming a world rife with contagion from without and putrefaction from within, the poem prescribes an uneasy combination of heroic self-control and hygienic solipsism as therapeutic measures for holding such inexorable forces at bay.

John Kerrigan's commentary on the poem emphasizes the impersonality of the poem's chosen mode: "For the first and almost the last time in the sequence Shakespeare writes impersonally, neither addressing the friend nor describing him as explicitly as *he*, and scrupulously avoiding *I* and *me* and *my*" (290). This detached, sententious mode suits perfectly the cool inscrutability the poem praises. But its position in a sequence of poems whose first-person speakers intend the utterance of ardent emotion has encouraged modern readers to ironize the poem's praise of reticence. We need to remember Wordsworth's claim about the Sonnets that "with this key, / Shakespeare unlocked his heart," not to endorse its overt biographical romanticization but to treat it as a symptomatic response to the inwardness the poems seem to promise.[22] Where other sonnets express in manifold ways the involuted curves and wrinkles of the desiring self, sonnet 94 offers a strategy for ironing out these curves and wrinkles, to the benefit of this self and those around it. Rather than depicting the overheated instability of erotic passion, it articulates a mode of self-discipline intended to dampen such passion. It inculcates a "care of the self," to borrow a phrase from Michel Foucault, a practice by which one can become master rather than servant of one's own pleasures and desires. *Contra* Wordsworth, this is a poem not about unlocking hearts but about locking them up tightly. It views such an act, moreover, not as a narrative of bondage to societal norms but of internal liberation from insurgent passions. The discipline it idealizes entails not the repression but rather the constitution of a self. The difficulty we have in reading this poem without ironizing its endorsement of self-discipline measures some of the distance separating the modern fetish of desire from the Renaissance fetish of control. In confronting this difficulty, we learn something about ourselves, and about a writer in whom many still desire to find textual evidence of the birth of the modern self.

NOTES

1. On the Sonnets and a particularly literary form of subjectivity, see Fineman. For the debate about *Hamlet* and modern subjectivity, see Belsey 33-52; Dollimore 173-81; and Barker *passim*. Recent attempts to reclaim for Hamlet the prospect of an authentic proto-modern interiority include Maus, and Kaufman 103-49.

2. For a cogent discussion of the ways that contemporary neurology encourages a rethinking of Cartesian presuppositions about the relationships of selves and bodies, see Damasio. On "how recent and parochial the Cartesian distinction [between mind and body] is," see also Rorty 43-59, and Matson.

3. See, for example, Lyons, and Schleiner.

4. Throughout the essay I will quote the Sonnets from Stephen Booth's brilliant edition, occasionally drawing also on the Quarto facsimile contained therein.

5. Leishman remarks of the poem: "If it were possible to use the word 'conventional' in an unpejorative sense, I think it might be said that this is

Shakespeare's nearest approach to an expression both of conventional Platonism and of conventional Christianity" (120). In his annotations, Booth offers a provocative discussion of the use and abuse of convention to interpret this poem (*Sonnets* 507-17).

6. In a poem entitled "Lent," George Herbert similarly notes that by fasting, one "banquet[s]" the soul (47-48). I discuss this poem, and Herbert's larger meditation on eating and devotion, in Schoenfeldt, "George Herbert's Consuming Subject."

7. The medieval heritage of such conceptions is explored by Bynum.

8. The motto in the top left-hand corner of the recently discovered portrait of Christopher Marlowe in Corpus Christi College, Cambridge is *Quod m e nutruit me destruit* (That which nourishes me also destroys me). In emblem literature, this phrase was often illustrated with a burning torch turned upside-down (see Green 170-75).

9. Fineman sees this maddeningly divided subjectivity as the source of the modern subject.

10. This tension is not peculiar to this poem, but is in fact a critical issue in western Christianity, particularly as it dealt with its Roman inheritance. See the wonderful essay by Bouwsma, "The Two Faces of Humanism: Stoicism and Augustinianism in Renaissance Thought." On the Christian assimilation of Roman ideas, see also Brown, and Foucault, *The History of Sexuality*, vol. 2, *The Use of Pleasure*, and vol. 3, *The Care of the Self*.

11. Laurentius sees himself here as siding with Galen over Aristotle, since Aristotle says that the brain is cold "onely to coole the heart." Leontes describes his onset of irrational jealousy—whose first verbal manifestation is the phrase "Too hot"—as "the infection of my brains" (*Winter's Tale*, 1.2.145).

12. One could perhaps usefully invoke the line from *The Tempest* on how the physical and mental tribulations to which Prospero has subjected Gonzalo, Alonso, Sebastian, and Antonio, have made their "brains, / Now useless, boil'd within [their] skull[s]" (5.1.60). They have literally been overheated by the ordeals they have suffered. This issue of the material underpinnings of behavior, central to Renaissance moral philosophy, has returned in contemporary psychopharmacology, particularly surrounding antidepressants such as Prozac.

13. On the link between heat and masculinity, see Laqueur 27-40, 141-42.

14. Where we tend to discover identity in desire—sexual identity, for example, is constructed out of the object of desire—the Renaissance seems to have imagined identity to emerge from the success one experiences at controlling one's desires.

15. Quoted in Monsarrat 106-07. This passage was dropped in the 1603 edition of the *Basilikon*, perhaps for political reasons. On attitudes to Seneca in Jacobean England, see also Salmon 186.

16. Knights likewise views the poem as filled with "irony" that is "serious and destructive" (146).

17. Significantly, Herbert is the author of a poem entitled "Constancie," which has proven similarly difficult for contemporary readers; see Schoenfeldt, "Herbert's Consuming Subject," 111-13.

18. Ransom concedes that 94 "has proved obscure to commentators, but I think it is clear if taken in context, as an imaginary argument against the friend's relation with the woman, or with any woman, exactly opposite to the argument of the sonnets which open the sequence" (297).

19. See the reading by Pequigney 104-07, which aptly juxtaposes this passage with Prince Hal's soliloquy in *1 Henry IV*, 1.2.

20. In this context, it is important to remember Leontes' description of his mental infirmity in *The Winter's Tale*, 1.2.145, as "the infection of my brains." The word was closely linked to "fester" which means "To putrefy, to rot; to become pestiferous or loathsome by corruption" (OED, citing sonnet 94 and *Henry V*, 4.3.28).

21. The final line of sonnet 94 is quoted in or from the play *The Reign of King Edward the Third* (1596), an anonymous play that may or may not be by Shakespeare, in a scene where a monarch's abuse of power for sexual purposes is being resisted.

22. Wordsworth, "Scorn Not the Sonnet." In "The Motive for Interiority," Margreta de Grazia astutely analyzes the processes by which the character and biography of Shakespeare began to be read into the Sonnets after 1780.

WORKS CITED

Barker, Francis. *The Tremulous Private Body: Essays on Subjection*. London: Methuen, 1984.

Belsey, Catherine. *The Subject of Tragedy: Identity and Difference in Renaissance Drama*. London: Methuen, 1985.

Booth, Stephen. *An Essay on Shakespeare's Sonnets*. New Haven: Yale UP, 1969.

————, ed. *Shakespeare's Sonnets*. New Haven: Yale UP, 1977.

Bouwsma, William J. "The Two Faces of Humanism: Stoicism and Augustinianism in Renaissance Thought." *A Usable Past: Essays in European Cultural History*. Berkeley: U of California P, 1990. 19-73.

Brown, Peter. *The Body and Society: Men, Women, and Sexual Renunciation in Early Christianity*. New York: Columbia UP, 1988.

Burton, Robert. *The Anatomy of Melancholy*. Ed. Thomas C. Faulkner, Nicholas Kiessling, and Rhonda Blair. 2 vols. Oxford: Clarendon P, 1989.

Bynum, Caroline Walker. *Holy Feast and Holy Fast: The Religious Significance of Food to Medieval Women*. Berkeley: U of California P, 1987.

Cogan, Thomas. *The Haven of Health*. London, 1584.

Culpepper, Nicholas. *Health for the Rich and Poor, by Diet, without Physick*. London, 1670.

Damasio, Antonio. *Descartes' Error: Emotion, Reason, and the Human Brain*. New York: Putnam, 1994.

de Grazia, Margreta. "The Motive for Interiority." *Style* 23 (1989): 430-44.

Dollimore, Jonathan. *Radical Tragedy: Religion, Ideology, and Power in the Drama of Shakespeare and His Contemporaries*. Chicago: U of Chicago P, 1984.

Empson, William. "They That Have Power: Twist of Heroic-Pastoral Ideas into an Ironical Acceptance of Aristocracy." *Some Versions of Pastoral*. 1935. Rpt. New York: New Directions, 1974. 89-115.

Fineman, Joel. *Shakespeare's Perjured Eye: The Invention of Poetic Subjectivity in the Sonnets*. Berkeley: U of California P, 1986.

Foucault, Michel. *The Care of the Self. The History of Sexuality*. Trans. Robert Hurley. Vol. 3. New York: Pantheon, 1986.

————. *The Use of Pleasure. The History of Sexuality*. Trans. Robert Hurley. Vol. 2. New York: Pantheon, 1985.

Green, Henry. *Shakespeare and the Emblem Writers*. London: Trubner and Co., 1870.

Herbert, George. *The Works of George Herbert*. Ed. F. E. Hutchinson. Oxford: Clarendon P, 1941.

The Holy Bible, Conteyning the Old Testament, and the New. 1611. Rpt. Nashville: Nelson, 1982.

Huarte, Juan. *The Examination of Men's Wits*. 1594. Trans. Richard Carew. Ed. Carmen Rogers. Gainesville: Florida Scholars' Facsimiles and Reprints, 1959.

Hubler, Edward. *The Sense of Shakespeare's Sonnets*. Princeton: Princeton UP, 1952.

Kaufman, Peter Iver. *Prayer, Despair, and Drama: Elizabethan Introspection*. Urbana: U of Illinois P, 1996.

Kerrigan, John, ed. *The Sonnets and A Lover's Complaint*. Harmondsworth: Penguin, 1986.

Knights, L. C. "Shakespeare's Sonnets." *Scrutiny* 3 (1934): 133-60.

Laqueur, Thomas. *Making Sex: Body and Gender from the Greeks to Freud.* Cambridge: Harvard UP, 1990.

Laurentius, M. Andreas. *A Discourse of the Preservation of the Sight.* 1599. Trans. Richard Surphlet. Ed. Sanford Larkey. London: Oxford UP, 1938.

Leishman, J. B. *Themes and Variations in Shakespeare's Sonnets.* New York: Harper and Row, 1966.

Lyons, Bridget Gellert. *Voices of Melancholy: Studies in Literary Treatments of Melancholy in Renaissance England.* New York: Norton, 1975.

Matson, Wallace I. "Why Isn't the Mind-Body Problem Ancient?" *Mind, Matter, and Method.* Ed. Paul Feyerabend and Grover Maxwell. Minneapolis: U of Minnesota P, 1966. 92-102.

Maus, Katharine Eisaman. *Inwardness and Theater in the English Renaissance.* Chicago: U of Chicago P, 1995.

Monsarrat, Gilles. *Light from the Porch: Stoicism and English Renaissance Literature.* Paris: Didier-Erudition, 1984.

Pequigney, Joseph. *Such Is My Love: A Study of Shakespeare's Sonnets.* Chicago: U of Chicago P, 1985.

Rorty, Richard. *Philosophy and the Mirror of Nature.* Princeton: Princeton UP, 1979.

Salmon, J. H. "Seneca and Tacitus in Jacobean England." *The Mental World of the Jacobean Court.* Ed. Linda Levy Peck. Cambridge: Cambridge UP, 1991. 169-88.

Schleiner, Winfred. *Melancholy, Genius, and Utopia in the Renaissance.* Wiesbaden: In Kommission bei Otto Harrassowitz, 1991.

Schoenfeldt, Michael. "George Herbert's Consuming Subject." *George Herbert in the Nineties: Reflections and Reassessments.* Ed. Jonathan F. S. Post and Sidney Gottlieb. Fairfield, CT: George Herbert Journal Special Studies and Monographs, 1995. 105-32.

Shakespeare, William. *The Riverside Shakespeare.* Ed. G. Blakemore Evans et al. Boston: Houghton Mifflin, 1974.

Zizek, Slavoj. *The Sublime Object of Ideology.* London: Verso, 1989.

"The dyer's hand"
The Reproduction of Coercion and Blot in Shakespeare's Sonnets

Olga L. Valbuena

> In nothing art thou black save in thy deeds,
> And thence this slander, as I think, proceeds.
>
> —Sonnet 131.13-14[1]

The Sonnets continue to elicit from readers the desire for a coherent dramatic narrative, one capable of resolving the web of emotional entanglements among its three presumptive figures. Recent criticism, however, has unsettled certain orthodoxies and created others that deepen these poems' difficulty and interpretive controversy. Less certain now, for example, is the Sonnets' subdivision into the "young man" and "dark lady" sequences, and, by extension, the sex and number of principal addressees in either part of the cycle. Some of the most insightful work in recent years has shown how the "panic" and "hysteria" attendant on confronting Shakespeare as a "potential sodomite" has produced a tortured editorial and critical tradition whose effects are still with us.[2] More recent criticism emphasizing class in relation to sexuality suggests that "the real scandal" of the Sonnets lies not in sodomy but, on the contrary, in the wide indulgence of a "promiscuous womb," the intolerable sexual "gynerasty" implicit in the dark lady sequence.[3] Still other interpretations, conscious of a poetics of race, have read in the dark lady sonnets both a reinforcement and mocking of racial prejudice through the counterdiscourse of the "ugly beauty" tradition.[4]

If nothing else, one can assert with confidence that Shakespeare himself provokes these controversies. He places the self-promoting creative will of sonnet 55 ("this pow'rful rhyme") against the backdrop of disruptive sexualities, which he identifies with his own desire as of sonnet 20 and throughout the sequence ("Loving offenders, thus I will excuse ye" [42.5]). He further praises the dark lady for her proud indifference to conventional beauty, asserting, "Thy black is fairest in my judgement's place" (131.12), but later represents her as "The worser spirit a woman coloured ill" (144.4). And, Iago-like, whether castigating or appearing to excuse "each friend" (144.11), he suffuses every lexical assertion of "truth" about his subject with the pious suspicion of a lie. As contemporary criticism insists, it is neither practical nor beneficial to postulate a narrative of biographical facts or events on the slim evidence of the Sonnets' productive evasions. Categorical resistance to *all* narrative sequencing, however, threatens to foreclose other more productive interpretive possibilities.[5] One such sequence to be explored in this essay involves not the affirmation of an overarching subject but, instead, tells the story of how the formal and material conditions of that subject dissolve in the very ink that writes them. Failing to write the poetry of praise to which the speaker was initially compelled by the young man's beauty or his own financial or emotional circumstances, the poet-speaker nonetheless positions himself within a highly reflexive scene of writing. It is a scene with a narrative logic whose integrity does not depend on those historical persons, fictive characters, or factual events that may haunt it.

Thus, in material terms, the poet's call in the early poems to "Make thee another self" (10.13) concedes an unsuccessful delivery in the middle of the sequence ("Why is my verse so *barren* of new pride?" [76.1; emphasis added]), while in the later poems, the speaker suspends his labor in the dark solution of "lying in" with his unruly mistress (138). In the wake of the first miscarriage, the speaker explores a different route, as it were, moving from land to sea in the dark lady sonnets but carrying with him all the experience and cynicism born of his prior suit's rejection. The ideal of truth and beauty, "But thou art all my *art*" (78.13; emphasis added), fails *within* the young man subsequence. The dark lady's "art," in that word's substantive and indicative senses, absorbs the poet's as well as her own and the young man's "shame" (95.1), "canker" (95.2), "spot" (95.3), and "sins" (95.4), represented in the ink "blot" (95.11) that taints the dark lady subsequence even while giving it material presence. In the second subsequence, instead of asserting that truth and beauty ought to reside in the dark lady, the speaker mockingly approves their disjuncture in a mordant expression of the "pity-wanting pain" (140.4) brought on by her indifference to him.

In the contract offered by the poet, the young man would authenticate "truth and beauty" through his specular identity with the idealizing verses, without introducing personal excess or resistance to the speaker or his project. Pressed into service as both the embodiment of truth and beauty and the eternized subject of the speaker's poetry, the young man's fate turns on his compliance with this role, on a conditional phrase:

> But from thine eyes my knowledge I derive,
> And, constant stars, in them I read such art
> As truth and beauty shall together thrive
> *If* from thy self to store thou wouldst convert:
>> *Or else* of thee this I prognosticate,
>> Thy end is truth's and beauty's doom and date.
>>> (14.9-14; emphasis added)

But as Michael Spiller notes in his historical study of the sonnet, with Shakespeare, "for the first time in the entire history of the sonnet, the desired object is *flawed*, which leads to a new kind of self-questioning, leading in turn to new employment of the sonnet space" (156).[6] The ever more caustic narrative, steeped in and "subdued / To what it works in, like the dyer's hand" (111.6-7), forbids the sequence from justifying and organizing itself through the semantic logic of the workman's craft—the paper, leaves, pen, knife, and ink of the lauding poet. Even so, the narrative achieves substance and coherence in a counterintuitive manner, namely, in the temporal unfolding of its own nonperformance: as the written word materializes, it dis(ap)proves in ink the speaker's claim (and promise) to immortalize the young man. Instead of achieving a chaste and blot-free "fair copy" of the male beloved, the sequence dissolves in the unbounded dark waters of bitterness, the "eisel 'gainst my strong infection" (111.10) of love and lust, the promiscuous dark lady sonnets. It is far from necessary to posit a line of demarcation or "boundary" between the two subsequences, for the speaker attempts to drown his passion for the young man in "the wide world's common place" of that subsequent body (137.10).[7]

The blotted narrative produced by the speaker, "The hand that writ it" (71.6), betrays the rhetoric of coercion organizing the whole. Older, less attractive, and lower in status than the young man, the poet-speaker supposes he at least has one form of persuasion with which to coerce his profligate lover. The speaker claims his language can accelerate or arrest the decaying effects of Time, and so compel the young man's attention.[8] His frustrated desire to possess psychically, if not physically, the one to whom he promises poetic immortality accounts for the speaker's fluctuations in tone. He moves from the officially disinterested exhortation to reproduce, tortuously epitomized by sonnet 16, to the self-abasing tones of sonnets 58 and 61, to the impotent bawdry of sonnets 76 and 78, expressing jealousy about the competitors who "under thee their poesy disperse" (78.4) while the speaker can do no more than waste away alone, "Spending again what is already spent" (76.12).[9] Although the speaker would cherish nothing more than to freeze his beloved "in table of my heart" (24.2) as the endlessly re-invoked static icon of his imagination, he is not above resorting to the "large privilege" (95.13) of condemnatory language when the young man fails to contract or submit himself to the collector of images, the poet-lover.[10] The young man's apparent reluctance to beget a child does not occasion but rather shrouds the speaker's motive for reproving him. Indeed, by sonnet 20, evidently still stinging from some prior rejection, the lover has foregone any realistic hope of being embraced by the young man. He by now seeks only to extort the basest form of respect—pity or fear of scandal—from the young man, to whose "fair flower" (69.12) the poet might inadvertently "add the rank smell of weeds" (69.12), as other observers in "their thoughts" (69.11) have evidently begun to do.

I. CHEAP PRINT VERSUS FAIR COPY

The speaker who seems to act merely as a neutral mediator of inexorable positions—the law of decay against the young man's resistance to his procreative debt—opens the sequence with a collective wish: "From fairest creatures *we* desire increase" (1.1; emphasis added). Yet in the induction or "procreation sonnets" the cunning fusion of irreconcilable subject-positions, of self-absorption (narcissism) and husbandry, ultimately resolves itself in favor of narcissism. Warning the young man, "Die single, and thine image dies with thee" (3.14), the speaker articulates the culture's endorsement of family bonds and lineage but uses the suggestion of marriage only as a ruse. That is, rather than quietly detach himself from the scene of "mutual ordering; / Resembling sire, and child, and happy mother" (8.10-11), the speaker offers the young man an escape from mortality *and* fatherhood in "distillation," a process that could satisfy the beloved's narcissism more than any ordinary act of reproduction (5.9). Ideally, in the preserving hand of the poet the young man would find expressed in verse not a mere "print" but the essence of his "beauty's rose" (1.2), a "liquid prisoner pent in walls of glass" (5.10). The paradox of this project, as the speaker discovers, lies in the fact that his rhyme *is* ineffectual in its bid to eternalize the young man. And though the speaker blames the young man for impairing the speaker's ideal vision, the young man's recalcitrance does not prevent the sequence's progress as such.

The married begetter in any case cannot produce his own beauty exactly, for the "seal" and "print" of beauty can only ever produce a "copy" (11.13-14). The "original" of beauty, if such a thing exists at all, resides in the poetic Idea. But as every poet understands, that "truth" carries no inevitable or intrinsically animating force without the "clothing" of its material formulation (Rosmarin 25-26). Neither does Nature or its accessory, Time, possess the craft to immortalize the young man, for it is in the character of nature to make a singular beauty once—and then to mar its own creation indifferently.

Accordingly, even as sonnet 11 proclaims Nature's "bounteous gift" of beauty to the young man, sonnet 4 has already qualified "thy beauty's legacy," as does sonnet 5:

> Those hours that with gentle work did frame
> The lovely gaze where every eye doth dwell
> Will play the tyrants to the very same,
> And that unfair which fairly doth excel[.] (5.1-4)

If "Beauty's effect" (5.11) should prevail over decay, it will do so only by means of the external agent that draws and preserves nature's creation with "sweet *ornament* which truth doth give" (54.2; emphasis added). Further, while nature has made the young man beautiful, this bounty points more to accident than providential design, despite the speaker's claims about nature's agency in sonnets 1, 4, 11, and 20. Irrespective of marital or parental status, unless specially selected and distilled by the poet, the young man will remain an "unwooed" rose, "that which, withering on the virgin thorn, / Grows, lives, and dies in *single* blessedness" (*Midsummer Night's Dream* 1.1.77-78; emphasis added). Only the branch that the poet "ingraft[s]" (15.4) will survive in time. In sonnet 54, the perfection of the rose, like that of the young man, lies not in its mere occurrence but in being "wooed" by the poet-botanist, preserved as a manufactured product in the sonnet:

> The canker blooms have full as deep a dye
> As the perfumèd tincture of the roses,
>
> . . . .
> But, for their virtue only is their show,
> They live unwooed, and unrespected fade,
> Die to themselves. Sweet roses do not so,
> Of their sweet deaths are sweetest odours made:
>   And so of you, beauteous and lovely youth,
>   When that shall vade, by verse distils your truth. (54.5-6, 9-14)

This comparison between the rose and youth once again plays on the latter's vanity and discloses the poet's fee; for the beauteous youth to be eternalized, his "rose" (1.2) and "bud" (1.11) must be plucked, picked, and distilled in the "sweet deaths" imagined for him by the speaker. The suddenness of this blunt disclosure gives way, as it does elsewhere, to a more "respectable" companion poem, sonnet 55 ("Not marble nor the gilded monuments"), which functions as an envoy to the group that precedes it.[11]

Acting as Time's personified *memento mori*, the speaker chides the young man for his "Unthrifty loveliness" (4.1), the disinclination to see himself "printed" in a child. But the speaker's discomforting reminders of that time "When forty winters shall besiege thy brow" (2.1) insidiously repeal the gesture of these seventeen "induction" sonnets by generating further anxiety in the young man about his impending decay. Because the sequence explores the strained dialectic of reproduction and mortality, the speaker initially compares procreation to perpetual self-renewal—yet not without confronting its discomfortable cousin, heterosexual knowledge, the bearer of despair and death.[12] For if the parent creates in the child the living proof of his own and nature's "bounteous largess" (4.6), that child also heralds the parent's inevitable decay.

As metaphors for a child, the cultural resonance of "print" and "copy" in sonnet 11 further activates the latent apprehension that any attempt to pass the supplement as a duplicate original smacks of suspicious redundancy in one party, producing skepticism in the other. Shakespeare's characters attest to this bias when they call paternity (the only measure of legitimacy) into question. For instance, when the Duke of York plans to denounce his only child, Aumerle, the Duchess protests, "Is he not like thee? Is he not thine own?" to which York quips, "Were he twenty times my son / I would appeach him" (*Richard II* 5.2.94, 101-02). Prospero, too, remarks, "Thy mother was a piece of virtue, and / She said thou wast my daughter" (*Tempest* 1.2.56-57).[13] In legal contexts, as in questions of paternity, the very "seal" of resemblance that authenticates the legitimacy of print and copy concedes the original's susceptibility to imposture or, at the least, acknowledges that supplementarity and difference are inevitable effects of reproduction. The fundamental dissimilarity of the print from the original (Nature's Idea, *paternitas*) reflects not only the Platonic difference between ideas and forms; more locally, this difference illustrates the ambivalence to print among gentlepersons in Shakespeare's day. Aristocrats especially felt that print, by its very commonness—as a reproductive process, as if by wanton female agency—colluded in the real and perceived collapse of distinctions between the traditionally powerful and the aspiring, between court poets and professional writers, and between the genteel and the middling classes.[14] In the Sonnets, the speaker synthesizes these ideas of exclusivity and commonness, of the individuating poetic hand and the common print, and infuses the issue of reproduction in them; so doing he implicitly compares the role of husband and father to a biomechanic process that will, by design, seem unimpressive and precarious when compared to the transcendence of poetic eternization.

With their seeming promise to confer permanence on the young man, writing implements in the Sonnets inscribe or "character" the indelible "record" of the young man's decline to "common grow[th]" (69.14), not in that they produce mock encomium but because they *mock* encomium. Looked at as tropes of poetic composition, when those metonymic instruments of the poet-speaker's trade are not inscribing (engraving) lines and wrinkles, the tables, pen, quill, and paper tend to blot (eclipse, blemish) and "soil" (69.14) the "fair name" of the young man (108.8).

The writing "tables" as well as quill, knife, and ink carry two further characteristics that make them potentially unfavorable to the young man. First, as the poet has become consumed with "love and hate" (35.12), the poet's heart and brain can fairly be said to lack retention; the image of the beloved that overflows from corporeal boundary to paper threatens to disfigure or "mar" the "fair copy" even as the poet-scribe labors to "bring forth" (38.11) the young man. Like one unsure of his writing hand, of his grip on the instruments of his craft, the poet-scribe appears to recognize the inadequacy of his own skill and the need for his outworn (blunt, dull) implements' "repair" (16.9):

> O blame me not if I no more can write!
> Look in your glass, and there appears a face
> That overgoes my *blunt* invention quite,
> *Dulling* my lines, and doing me disgrace.
> Were it not sinful then, striving to *mend*,
> To *mar* the subject that before was well?
>
> (103.5-10; emphasis added)

His pen has become blunted from "striving to mend" and give presence to the absent youth, a project whose failure also threatens the poet's self-image, the specular pleasure he takes in seeing himself (the poems' creator) *in* his subject; his lines, like his quill, have been rendered *pointless* from the same onanism for which he chided the young man in the induction sonnets. The pen or quill, like the paper itself, has become limp with overhandling, tired with overuse, as the rival poet sonnets indicate.[15] The multiplicity of poets, like a brace of merchant scribes stealing the young man's "influence" or impression from the poet-speaker, interferes with his receptive faculty. Incapable now of (re)producing anything both original and faithful, he complains, "But when your countenance filled up his line, / Then lacked I matter, that *infeebled* mine" (86.13-14; emphasis added). The "infeebled" line, like the marred text and the blunt edge of invention, the pen, requires the same instrument of repair, the *knife*, the tool that goes, so to speak, hand in hand with the quill. As Michael Finlay writes,

> The importance to the scribe of his penknife is evident in the frequency with which the writer is shown [in artistic depictions] with the pen in his right hand and his knife, the point holding down any slight undulation in the parchment, but immediately available to *repair* the pen, in his left. Parchment, the prepared skin of animals,

has a number of layers, and the erasure of errors by scraping was the other main function of the scribe's knife. (13; emphasis added)[16]

But as the speaker makes clear in sonnet 95, even though "That tongue that tells the story of thy days / . . . / Cannot dispraise, but in a kind of praise," the effort of "making lascivious comments on thy sport" wears thin on him (5-7). It is at this point that he warns ominously, "Take heed (dear heart) of this large privilege: / The hardest knife ill used doth lose his edge" (95.13-14). The knife will cut striving to repair.

A sonnet sequence that self-consciously dramatizes its failure to achieve immortality for the subject-patron may nonetheless enact the eclipse of the patron *by* the subject. For the reader cannot fail to grasp the sequence's ironic inversion of its own promise, "Your name from hence immortal life shall have, / Though I (once gone) to all the world must die" (81.5-6). Despite successive lapses into rhetorical self-doubt, the speaker asserts for his poetry the power to surpass in timelessness and quality all institutions and edifices. This "pow'rful rhyme" must outlast even the memory of those specifically unnamed personages—including the young man—elevated to give them meaning: "Not marble nor the gilded monuments / Of princes shall outlive this pow'rful rhyme" (55.1-2) and "*Your* monument shall be *my* gentle verse, / Which eyes not yet created shall o'er-read" (81.9-10; emphasis added).[17] The poems may exist ostensibly to immortalize the young man, but the very dynamic of qualified praise on which they are structured blots and eclipses the unnamed figure, and—whether by design or default—cedes "that eternity promised by our ever-living poet" back to the speaker.[18] Taken as a whole, the Sonnets offer more in injury than immortality to the young man whose "present-absent" (45.4) status in the sequence makes him particularly vulnerable to "blot," to being stained with the disgrace of ink by his ostensibly well-intentioned lover whose hand wavers in proportion to his suffering.

On the whole, the sonnet sequence functions as a poetic sampler that contains the range of possibilities in regard to the young man's poetic decay or repair. But as the speaker repeatedly asserts, "repair" of the dissipated young man requires *lying*: "All men make faults, and even I in this, / Authòrising thy trespass with compare, / Myself corrupting salving thy amiss" (35.5-7).[19] Tendering an idealized vision of the young man is of course important to both figures in that each for his own reasons would wish to see the young man ingeniously reproduced. But the speaker claims that the young man's decline to the "soil" of "common" behavior has forced him into the conflictive position of needing to lie about what he sees in order to sustain the writing enterprise at all (69.14). Acting as his own professed adversary, the speaker attests to the illegitimacy *in writing* of his love for the young man:

> Against that time I do insconce me here
> Within the knowledge of my own desert,
> And *this my hand against myself uprear*,
> To guard the lawful reasons on thy part.
>   To leave poor me thou hast the strength of laws,
>   Since why to love I can allege no cause.
>
> (49.9-14; emphasis added)

It must be emphasized that the speaker is *willing* to perjure himself for the young man's sake and that the Sonnets constitute an extended coercive offer to do just that. Sonnet 24, for example, develops the theme of the "imperfect speaker" following the "unperfect actor" of sonnet 23. In sonnet 24, however, an imbricating process of setting "eye" against "heart" and "eye" in apposition to "lie" yields a new and abiding insight in regard to eyes: "They draw but what they see, know not the heart" (24.14). The painter has "stelled" (24.1) the young man and become, literally, so filled by "beauty's form" that, as the speaker asserts darkly, the young man would have to look *through* as well as *beyond* the painter's "windows glazèd" to discover his own faults'/false mystification:

> For through the painter must you see his skill
> To find where your *true* image pictured *lies*,
> Which in my bosom's shop is hanging still,
> That hath his windows glazèd with thine eyes.
>
> (24.5-8; emphasis added)

This strong suggestion that the *eye/I* offers a skewed "perspective" on the young man invites the latter to discover the truth behind the speaker's glazèd shop window, the private lie here on public display. As the patron and privileged addressee, the young man is compelled by textual gaps and ambiguities to read between the lines. He is asked to feel the double "guilt" of the speaker's "Authòrising thy trespass with compare" (35.6) as well as the presumptive absorption of the young man's "blots that do with [the speaker] remain" (36.3). Already by sonnet 35 the speaker's legalisms reveal an internecine battle in which the very act of defending the young man in poetry overrules the speaker's better knowledge:

> Thy adverse party is thy advocate—
> And 'gainst myself a lawful plea commence:
> Such civil war is in my love and hate
> That I an àccessary needs must be
> To that sweet thief which sourly robs from me. (35.10-14)

With just ninety sonnets to go, the speaker laments pathetically, "I may not evermore acknowledge thee, / Lest my bewailèd guilt should do thee shame" (36.9-10). The strife between the famished, will-full eye and the "I" of the unheeded heart, a commonplace in Elizabethan love poetry, produces a feverish split consciousness by sonnet 46:

> Mine eye and heart are at a mortal war,
> How to divide the conquest of thy sight:
> Mine eye my heart thy picture's sight would bar,
> My heart mine eye the freedom of that right.
> My heart doth plead that thou in him dost *lie*
> (A closet never pierced with crystal eyes),
> But the defendant doth that plea deny,
> And says in him thy fair appearance *lies*. (46.1-8; emphasis added)

The sequence itself ensures that despite the effort to identify the young man (or, as some suggest, the poet) as "the onlie begetter of these insuing sonnets," no such spotless Muse can be located, for the poetic enterprise yields, by default, foul papers, "bastard signs of fair" (68.3).

II. HIS INK/HER O: THE MATERIAL REPRODUCTION OF LIES, BLOT, AND COERCION

Margaret. Will you then write me a sonnet in praise of my beauty?

Benedick. In so high a style, Margaret, that no man living shall come over it, for in most comely truth thou deservest it.

Margaret. To have no man come over me! Why, shall I
always keep below stairs?

(*Much Ado about Nothing* 5.2.4-10)

It is significant that Shakespeare uses ink, paper, and blot as emblems
of sexual transgression in two later plays preoccupied with sexual
honesty. In *Othello* and, more caustically, in *Much Ado about Nothing*,
the woman's body is likened to a properly blank writing surface upon
which, it is feared, an unauthorized hand has left its indelible mark. Or,
as the sonnet writer observes in lines worthy of *Othello*:

But what's so blessèd-fair that fears no blot?
Thou mayst be false, and yet I know it not. (92.13-14)

When an "alien pen" (78.3) obtrudes on this inviting and highly
vulnerable surface, the paper loses all worth except as a testament to its
owner's "infamy."[20] Thus, Othello compares Desdemona's body to a
white tablet, asking, "Was this fair paper, this most goodly book, /
Made to write 'whore' upon?" (4.2.73-74). In *Much Ado*, when Claudio
accuses Hero of dishonor "with public accusation, *uncovered* slander,
unmitigated rancor" (4.1.303-05; emphasis added), Leonato
experiences his daughter's blot as part of the larger thematic continuum
of promiscuous "pricking," "noting," and writing comically played on
in the bawdy exchange between Benedick and Margaret, above.

But Hero's abasement surpasses immersion in ink (a superficial
blackening); she embodies for her detractors the infamous "pit" itself.
Thus, when Claudio accuses Hero of foul behavior before the
assembled witnesses to their marriage, the exchange turns on her
name's semantic burden:

Hero. What kind of catechizing call you this?
Claudio. To make you answer truly to your name.
Hero. Is it not Hero? Who can blot that name
    With any just reproach?
Claudio. Marry, that can Hero!
Hero itself can blot out Hero's virtue.

(4.1.78-82; emphasis added)

As Claudio states accusingly, *Her O* comes to stand for the empty "sign
and semblance of her honor" (4.1.32), which now, dilated and black by

force of linguistic circulation, invites confusion between blood and ink, much as Lucrece's body becomes a text that can be multiply interpreted: "Her[o's] blush is guiltiness, not modesty" (4.1.41). When Hero is "smirchèd thus and mired with infamy" (4.1.133), Leonato exclaims:

> Could she here deny
> The story that is printed in her blood?
>
> . . . .
>   —why, she, O she, is fall'n
> Into a pit of ink, that the wide sea
> Hath drops too few to wash her clean again
> And salt too little which may season give
> To her foul-tainted flesh! (4.1.121-22; 139-43)

The anxiety of a daughter's *public*ation turns on the gentleman father's knowledge that he stands to be permanently blotted beside his daughter, as much by the unlettered Borachio's "noting" as Claudio's repudiation of her. For the daughter constitutes the *matrix* of the father's very identity and all his occupation:

> Why had I one?
> Why ever wast thou lovely in my eyes?
> Why had I not with charitable hand
> Took up a beggar's issue at my gates,
> Who, smirchèd thus with and mired with infamy,
> I might have said, "No part of *it* is mine;
> This *shame* derives itself from unknown loins"?
> But mine, and mine I loved, and mine I praised,
> And mine that I was proud on, mine so much
> That I myself was to myself not mine,
> Valuing of her— (4.1.129-39; emphasis added)[21]

Hero's blot is perilous because it involves nothing short of a scribbler's infusion, an "alien pen" discharging its inky blood into "Leonato's Hero's" noble veins. The idea of "blot" links sexual fall to infection and taint of the blood, so that purgation, either through the letting of blood or erasure of the text, must be effected. Under the circumstances, the Friar's advice is notable—"And *publish* it that she is dead indeed" (4.1.204; emphasis added). The comic setting produces temporary forms of blindness, death, and deception so in contrast to the sustained gynophobia of *King Lear*, expressed here in Edgar's assessment of Gloucester's misfortune: "The dark and vicious place where he thee got / Cost him his eyes" (5.3.175-76).[22]

Like the will of the dark lady, it is assumed by her accusers, Hero's wet, salty "Will in overplus" (135.2), once filled, can never be *ful*filled, becoming instead the "indistinguished space" (*Lear* 4.6.275) of unlawful conversation—of cheap print or lowly scrawl—circulated by men.[23] Directly following her swoon, there follows an extended play on Hero's double "dying." The well or "pit of ink" now fitted in her O constitutes an opening through which, in Don John's words, "Leonato's Hero, your Hero, every man's Hero" becomes a sourcebook of bawdy jokes and vengeful hostility, and not only among the spurious miscreants of the city (3.2.100-01).

With paper and ink for her body and blood, the dark lady, too, has been made to blot up and absorb the blunted desires and "black lines" (63.13) of the speaker's "perjured" I (152.13). Like the bitter gall that motivates Don John's slanders, the dark lady subsequence bears the welled-up desires, jealousies, and hostilities the poet-speaker has in store to "convert" to black ink. For their part, the dark lady sonnets oscillate between a mock serious attitude, "Thou blind fool, Love, what dost thou to mine eyes, / That they behold and see not what they see?" (137.1-2), and bitterness—"Oh me! what eyes hath love put in my head, / Which have no correspondence with true sight?" (148.1-2). The shame and bitterness encountered in the young man subsequence become fully realized in the dark lady sonnets. In an act of retrospective anticipation, the dark lady sonnets "bring forth" the young man poems and their issue—the "shifting change, as is false women's fashion" (20.4); a wet and cold *Will* ("false as water" [*Oth.* 5.2.138]); loss through seduction ("Two loves I have, of comfort and despair" [144.1])—the poet-speaker's blunt abasement of his own body and his writing hand.

The composition of black ink itself was common knowledge among the literate in Shakespeare's day and accounts for the poet's preoccupation with its caustic properties. Not only did many writers cut their own quills then, but "careful writers would manufacture their own ink" from readily available substances—oak-galls, vinegar, and alum (Finlay 27-28). Two of Shakespeare's plays indicate familiarity with the composition of ink, and both exploit the secondary meaning of "gall" as productive of bile or bitterness. In *Twelfth Night*, Sir Toby recommends to Sir Andrew a method for galling Malvolio with the challenge of a duel: "Go, write it in a martial hand. . . . Taunt him with the license of ink. . . . Let there be *gall* enough in thy ink, though thou write with a goose-pen, no matter" (3.2.41-49; emphasis added).[24] Sonnet 111 combines the effects of bitterness and tincture in a not unsympathetic image of the artificer (Shakespeare's father was a glover) "branded" in the very process of working with the caustic materials of his trade. As one who requires a bitter (moral) purgative to cleanse him of his labor's corrupting effects, the speaker enfolds a coercive request for patronage, love, and respect in a disingenuous call for pity:

> O for my sake do you with Fortune chide,
> The guilty goddess of my harmful deeds,
> That did not better for my life provide
> Than public means which public manners breeds.
> Thence comes it that my name receives a brand,
> And almost thence my nature is subdued
> To what it works in, like the dyer's hand.
> Pity me then, and wish I were renewed,
> Whilst like a willing patient I will drink
> Potions of eisel 'gainst my strong infection;
> No bitterness that I will bitter think.
> Nor double penance to correct correction.
> > Pity me, then, dear friend, and I assure ye
> > Even that your pity is enough to cure me. (111)

The poet-dramatist, a dyer who works in ink, words and knives ("I will speak daggers to her, but use none" [*Hamlet* 3.2.395]) will view himself with some detachment and self-irony, as the plays on his name in line 9, above, suggest: "*Whilst* like a *will*ing patient I *will* drink." But the evident failure of his suit to the young man spills over in a manner that recommends Heather Dubrow's appeal for "indeterminate readings" that break with the traditional two-part barrier ("Incertainties" 297; also reprinted in this volume). As Dubrow argues, some of the highly impassioned poems of the second subsequence might be addressed to the young man or to the dark lady, or they might be a coercive envoy to both (or neither). Sonnet 140, for instance, threatens to publish the lover's wrongs using the same coercive suit for pity as in the young man poems:

> Be wise as thou art cruel, do not press
> My tongue-tied patience with too much disdain,
> Lest sorrow lend me words, and words express
> The manner of my pity-wanting pain.
>
> . . . .
>
> For if I should despair, I should grow mad,
> And in my madness might speak ill of thee;
> Now this ill-wresting world is grown so bad,
> Mad slanders by mad ears believèd be.
>   That I may not be so, nor thou belied,
>   Bear thine eyes straight, though thy proud heart go wide.
>
> (140.1-4, 9-14)

This poem seems more appropriate to the poet's feelings for the young man than for the dark lady. Even so, if addressed to the dark lady whose eyes "torment me with disdain" (132.2), it still works as a self-ironizing (or desperate or sincere) play for recognition: "Then will I swear *beauty herself* is black, / And all they foul that thy complexion lack" (132.13-14; emphasis added). Even here, the speaker delivers at best a backhand compliment to his mistress, for he treats the quality of blackness (as immorality, ugliness, and insincerity) with mordant wit. After evoking the language of the court only to debase it between sonnets 131 and 142, the speaker tires of the depreciation of language that he himself has brought about since the explicit perjury of sonnets 35 and 46. In the dark lady subsequence, though legalisms still signify *something*, they do so within a universe where the imaginary correspondence between word and idea has been substantially compromised. Though the speaker summons legal language to "prove" that the young man "is thine" (134.1), that concession has not discharged the speaker from his "bond" (134.8) of enslavement to the dark lady's lust: "He pays the w*hole*, and yet am I not free" (134.14; emphasis added). With another ambiguous paean to her beauty, the speaker concludes darkly that "Desire is death / . . . / For I have sworn thee fair, and thought thee bright, / Who *art* as black as hell, as grim as night" (147.8, 13-14; emphasis added).

In Joel Fineman's terms, the "closing" of the young man subsequence marks the end of idealized representation (176-78). The new inky "suits" of chirographic swirls and rhetorical flourishes with which the poet-speaker slanders the dark lady can be traced to the earlier courtship, to the "art" of idealized love that failed to win the young man. The dark lady poems evince a literal and more extravagantly self-referential *carcel de amor*, a prison house of language that becomes at once more rhetorically self-conscious and more openly false than any "art" in the young man subsequence. Not promising the dark lady eternization, the speaker cannot take anything from her that she would not more willingly part with than her reputation and possibly some sex left over from her "store's account" (136.10). Nor, in opposition to Shakespeare's modest heroines, does the dark lady seem to care about the speaker's "publication" of her (in the double sense). "Looking with pretty ruth upon [his] pain" (132.4), her eyes *seem* to mourn his twofold failure as a poet and a lover. In that double sense her "blackness" (ink) spills onto, blots the poet's "fairest wights" (106.2)—"a man right fair" (144.3) and "these waste blanks" (77.10). Wet and blotted, false and fair, indifferent to a fault, the dark lady perforce becomes "beauty's successive heir" (127.3). Refusing traditional categories of objectification, she is literally herself dark *and* composed of "What's in the brain that ink may character" (108.1). The bitter "gall" of the Sonnets has dyed the dyer's hand: it has made, in the words of the speaker, visible inscriptions "Of faults concealed wherein I am attainted" (88.7). And the poet, like a "careful huswife" (143.1), knows when to administer the bitter "eisel" (111.10) and when to pick the common oak gall from the "lofty trees" (12.5): for the same "potions of eisel" that serve as a purgative lend mordancy to the poet's black ink.[25]

NOTES

1. I prefer the enhanced polyvalence of the commas in the final line of sonnet 131, and thus follow here David Bevington, ed., *Complete Works*, based on Q 1609. Unless otherwise noted, however, citations of the Sonnets follow G. Blakemore Evans, ed., The New Cambridge Shakespeare *Sonnets*. Citations of plays are from Bevington's edition of *Complete Works*.

2. See de Grazia, *Shakespeare Verbatim*, "The Scandal" (reprinted in this volume), "The Motive for Interiority"; and Stallybrass (also reprinted in this volume).

3. For a discussion of "miscegenation" and "gynerasty" (not "pederasty") as principal subversions of social order, see de Grazia ("The Scandal" 44-49).

4. Most notably Kim Hall's discussion of "a poetics of color" (*Things of Darkness* 62-122) and in Dubrow (*Echoes of Desire* 163-201).

5. In this connection, I will examine the assertion that "most of the sonnets are internalized meditations unconnected to a narrative line," as exemplarily argued by Dubrow ("Incertainties" 299 [reprinted in this volume]; *Echoes of Desire* 171-90). This position, I believe, obscures the basis of the sonnet as an *externalized* meditation in contained form. I concur with Robert Crosman, who argues for the presence of narrative in the Sonnets (472-74). For a psychoanalytic reading of the narrative, see Hedley 6-7. My argument differs as well from Joel Fineman's in that I trace the origin of the speaker's painful disenchantment and "suspicion of true vision" to the young man sonnets, not the dark lady subsequence (18).

6. For a discussion of the sonnet's prescribed form in relation to personal feeling, see also Spiller 9, 41, 55, 58.

7. For a reading of the second subsequence as Petrarchan, and as "silencing" the figure of the dark lady, see Feinberg and also Schalkwyk.

8. Coming directly after the procreation poems, sonnets 18 and 19 have this demonstrative effect and, as such, provide a sampler of what the poet is *capable* of composing.

9. On the relation between censorship and Shakespeare's bawdy, see Gordon Williams, who observes that "print gave a new vitality to the myth [of the Fall], and conning the forbidden became an issue in much early modern art, both verbal and visual" (47).

10. See also sonnets 76, 105, 108, and Booth's notes on 38.3 for the obscure bawdiness of taking on the young man's "argument."

11. Sonnet 37 thus mitigates the rancor of sonnets 33-36. Sonnet 55 serves as envoy for sonnets 27-54.

12. Though ideas of Christian redemption do not motivate many of the Sonnets, Christian ideas of sin, the decay of all flesh, and death do inform much of the imagery. Foremost among these ideas is the belief that as sex introduces life it also brings death. See also sonnet 146.

13. The same language may also be used to assert the legitimacy of a child, as in *The Winter's Tale* where Paulina defends Perdita against the stamp of bastardy: "Behold, my lords, / Although the print be little, the whole matter / And copy of the father" (2.3.98-100). For a similar context, see *WT* 5.1.124-28, where Leontes greets Florizel with "Your mother was most true to wedlock, Prince, / For she did print your royal father off, / Conceiving you. / . . . / Your father's image is so hit in you, / His very air" (heir).

14. On the issue of tension produced by "an almost strident privileging of matter (*res*) over word (*verba*)," see Rosmarin 24. As Wendy Wall observes, the new mass availability of texts after the 1580s produces a "crystallization of the social tensions that had made print a controversial avenue for mid

[sixteenth] century writers to pursue" (14). For an excellent discussion of the tension between the scribal (chirographic) and printed manuscript, see Love 177-91. For the negative social implications of print, see Saunders 139-64, 140-41. On the ideological implications of the trained (italic) writing hand of European aristocrats, see Goldberg 114-15. For a critique of Goldberg, see Love 154-57.

15. For a related discussion of manuscripts circulating until "literally read out of existence," see Marotti 158.

16. See also Love (106) for a discussion of how scribal erasure (accomplished with a knife) and filigree work (with ink) affect writing paper and the appearance of a text. See Goldberg (59-107) for a discussion of the violence implicit in learning proper letter formation as well as in the instruments and act of writing. Contemporary critics may take exception to Booth's admonition not to "read substance into . . . imperfectly realized connotative networks such as those that inhere in most of the other sonnets where Shakespeare mentions pens and penmanship" (270). It is symptomatic of Booth to devote one page of his commentary to a careful definition of scribal terms in a sonnet even as he downplays their relevance as "logically extravagant and substantially gratuitous webs of pertinence" (270).

17. Also see sonnets 65, 101, 107, 123 and Booth's commentary (227). Of especial interest is Booth's observation that "even as they assert the immortality of the poem these lines [55.7-8] remind a reader of the flimsiness and vulnerability of anything written on paper" (229).

18. See West who compares the Sonnets to Derrida's *Postcards*, noting that "The act of sending obliterates everything but itself. In this absolute destruction, the writer can send letters only to himself—or better, can receive only letters that come from himself, or seem to—through the medium of another whom he destroys with his gift, allowing himself to receive his gift to himself in safety" (11).

19. The word "lie" in the young man sonnets generally carries only nominal innuendo and normally means either "to speak falsely" or "to be contained in" (as "my soul, which in thy breast doth lie" [109.4]—or both. In 101.10 "lies" suggests the above as well as "depends on thee": "Excuse not silence so, for't lies in thee / To make him much outlive a gilded tomb." In the dark lady poems, however, the slippage between meanings comes about because innuendo is granted primacy over "virtuous" signification, as in 138.13-14; on "I lie with her," see Booth 480-81.

20. Here the owner is the husband or father; compare to Collatine as the "hopeless merchant of this loss" in *The Rape of Lucrece* 1660.

21. For the sexual implications of "matrix," "die," "seal," "print," and "copy," see Booth 151 n. 14; see also Finlay 59-60. The phrase "proud on," from "pride" (in heat) still lurks incestuously behind the primary meaning, inasmuch as the linguistic pun is a figure of visual-linguistic incest. For "pride" and "pride in," see Partridge 167, and sonnets 80, 103, 144, and 151. In connection with fathers' burdensome investments in their daughters, see also Capulet's speech in *Romeo and Juliet* 3.5.178-97.

22. Compare Edgar's gynophobic statement about sex, darkness, and (syphilitic) blindness to the pox, burning (lust), and blindness in sonnets 137, 144, and 147.

23. For the association between water and salt in relation to woman, I am indebted to Williams 85-86. Note also that Leander drowned in the Hellespont on his way to visit Hero.

24. See also *Cymbeline*, where Posthumus says to Imogen: "And with mine eyes I'll drink the words you send, / Though ink be made of gall" (1.1.100-01).

25. For instances of purgation, see 111.10-11 and 118.

WORKS CITED

Booth, Stephen, ed. *Shakespeare's Sonnets*. New Haven: Yale UP, 1977.

Crosman, Robert. "'Making Love out of Nothing at All': The Issue of Story in Shakespeare's Procreation Sonnets." *Shakespeare Quarterly* 41 (1990): 470-88.

de Grazia, Margreta. "The Motive for Interiority: Shakespeare's *Sonnets* and *Hamlet*." *Style* 23 (1989): 430-444.

———. "The Scandal of Shakespeare's Sonnets." *Shakespeare Survey* 46 (1994): 35-49.

———. *Shakespeare Verbatim: The Reproduction of Authenticity and the 1790 Apparatus*. Oxford: Oxford UP, 1991.

Dubrow, Heather. *Echoes of Desire: English Petrarchanism and Its Counterdiscourses*. Ithaca: Cornell UP, 1995.

———. "'Incertainties now crown themselves assur'd': The Politics of Plotting Shakespeare's Sonnets." *Shakespeare Quarterly* 47 (1996): 291-305.

Feinberg, Nona. "Erasing the Dark Lady: Sonnet 138 in the Sequence." *Assays* 4 (1987): 97-108.

Fineman, Joel. *Shakespeare's Perjured Eye: The Invention of Poetic Subjectivity in the Sonnets*. Berkeley: U of California P, 1986.

Finlay, Michael. *Western Writing Implements in the Age of the Quill Pen*. Wetheral, Scotland: Plains Books, 1990.

Goldberg, Jonathan. *Writing Matter: From the Hands of the English Renaissance*. Stanford: Stanford UP, 1990.

Hall, Kim. *Things of Darkness: Economies of Race and Gender in Early Modern England*. Ithaca: Cornell UP, 1995.

Hedley, Jane. "'Since First Your Eye I Eyed': Shakespeare's *Sonnets* and the Poetics of Narcissism." *Style* 28 (1994): 1-30.

Love, Harold. *Scribal Publication in Seventeenth-Century England*. Oxford: Clarendon, 1993.

Marotti, Arthur F. "Shakespeare's Sonnets as Literary Property." *Soliciting Interpretation: Literary Theory and Seventeenth-Century English Poetry*. Ed. Elizabeth D. Harvey and Katherine Eisaman Maus. Chicago: U of Chicago P, 1990. 143-73.

Partridge, Eric. *Shakespeare's Bawdy*. 3rd ed. London: Routledge, 1993.

Rosmarin, Adena. "Hermeneutics versus Erotics: Shakespeare's *Sonnets* and Interpretive History." *PMLA* 100 (1985): 20-37.

Saunders, J. W. "The Stigma of Print: A Note on the Social Bases of Tudor Poetry." *Essays in Criticism* 1 (1951): 139-64.

Schalkwyk, David. "'She never told her love': Embodiment, Textuality, and Silence in Shakespeare's Sonnets and Plays." *Shakespeare Quarterly* 45 (1994): 381-407.

Shakespeare, William. *The Complete Works of Shakespeare*. 4th ed. Ed. David Bevington. New York: HarperCollins, 1992.

——. *The Sonnets*. Ed. G. Blakemore Evans. Cambridge: Cambridge UP, 1996.

Spiller, Michael R. G. *The Development of the Sonnet: An Introduction*. London: Routledge, 1992.

Stallybrass, Peter. "Editing as Cultural Formation: The Sexing of Shakespeare's Sonnets." *Modern Language Quarterly* 54 (1993): 91-103.

Wall, Wendy. *The Imprint of Gender: Authorship and Publication in the English Renaissance*. Ithaca: Cornell UP, 1993.

West, William N. "Nothing as Given: Economies of the Gift in Derrida and Shakespeare." *Comparative Literature* 48 (1996): 1-18.

Williams, Gordon. *Shakespeare, Sex and the Print Revolution*. London: Athlone, 1996.

Playing "the mother's part"
Shakespeare's Sonnets and Early Modern Codes of Maternity

Naomi J. Miller

In sonnet 143, "Lo as a careful housewife," Shakespeare's speaker characterizes himself as a neglected infant, and urges his beloved to "play the mother's part, kiss me, be kind" (12).[1] Shakespeare's engagement with "the mother's part" at various moments throughout the sonnet sequence may be read in relation to codes of maternity that marked the early modern period. In a variety of early modern texts, mothers offer the potential for both nurture and rejection, sustenance and destruction. Maternity was associated with a doubleness of identity that only partially coincides with the doubleness commonly associated with femininity at the time. Whereas women in general were directed to be chaste, silent, and obedient in order to counteract the perceived power of their sexuality, mothers in particular emerged as figures who combined the sexuality required for procreation with considerable authority over their offspring, male as well as female. In the enormously popular genre of mothers' advice books, for instance, represented by such examples as *The Northren Mother's Blessing* (1597), Elizabeth Grymeston's *Miscelanea, Meditations, Memoratives* (1604), Dorothy Leigh's *The Mother's Blessing* (1616), and Elizabeth Joceline's *The Mothers Legacie* (1624), women emphasize the dignity and strength that they bring to their roles as mothers, allowing them to direct their children with confidence.

The physicality of women's bodies in the early modern period was frequently defined in terms of maternal functions and responsibilities, resulting in treatises such as Jacques Guillemeau's *Child-Birth, or, The Happy Deliverie of Women* and *The Nursing of Children* (1612). Guillemeau includes explicit descriptions, in some cases illustrated by woodcuts, of women's sexual organs, while addressing the issue of female sexuality apparently only in terms of medical concerns regarding pregnancy, labor, and delivery. Although Guillemeau's nursing text opens with the straightforward recommendation that mothers nurse their own children, substantial space is devoted to discussion of the size, shape, and color of suitable breasts for nursing when wet-nurses must be selected. By contrast, Elizabeth Clinton offers an explicitly maternal perspective on the same issue in *The Countess of Lincolnes Nurserie* (1622), urging mothers to nurse their own children for reasons of spiritual as well as physical nourishment—without concomitant attention to breast size and nipple shape.

Authority and sexuality: a powerful combination in a society that exhibited marked anxieties over the positions of women. Mothers appear as both objects and agents of sacrifice in early modern texts, sometimes represented as madonna and monster at once. Early modern pamphlets that eulogized or condemned individual women construct maternity in particular with heightened metaphors, repeatedly locating a starting point for description in excess. In the case of Elizabeth Crashaw, death in childbirth provided the impetus for a 1620 pamphlet entitled *The Honor of Virtue,* which terms her a "Phoenix" for giving up her own life to bear a child, and praises "her singular motherly affection to the child of her predecessor" (346). On the other hand, a condemnatory pamphlet entitled *A pitiless Mother* (1616) attacks Margaret Vincent—who murdered two of her children in the belief that she could save their souls, since she was being forced by her husband to raise them as Protestants despite her own conversion to Catholicism—as "Tigerous" and "wolfish" for her "unnaturall" violation of the dictates of maternity (363).

In Vincent's case, early modern codes of maternity provide the grounds for the condemnation of a woman "who by nature should have cherished [her children] with her own body, as the Pelican that pecks her own breast to feed her young ones with her blood," but instead behaves more monstrously than "the Viper, the envenomed Serpent, the Snake, or any Beast whatsoever" in taking her children's blood: "nay, her own dear blood bred in her own body, cherished in her own womb"

(364). The pamphleteer accordingly labels Vincent a "Creature not deserving Mother's name" (365). Embedded in the narration of the pamphlet on Vincent is the implication that this tragedy resulted from a woman's misguided attempt to oppose an incipient and subversive maternal authority to her husband's rule. The unsettling figure of Margaret Vincent bears witness to the fact that maternal care, at once contested and contestatory, potentially monstrous and self-sacrificial, could extend to issues not simply of physical reproduction, but of domestic power as well.

Maternal duality marks some of the most notable female characterizations in Shakespeare's plays, extending from the monstrous passion of Lady Macbeth—who challenges her husband's manhood with her asserted willingness to dash her infant's brains to the ground with her milk still in its mouth (*Macbeth* 1.7.49-59)—to the sacrificial love of Hermione—whose ripe sexuality so overwhelms her husband that he orders her baby daughter snatched from her breast, "the innocent milk in it most innocent mouth" [*sic*] (*The Winter's Tale* 3.2.100). Mother's milk is associated with both nurturance and destruction in the minds of Macbeth and Leontes, who prove equally, if differently, unable to stand as men in the face of their wives' sexuality and authority. While the mothers in some of Shakespeare's plays thrive on assertions of desire, resisting direct containment, their notable absence in other plays, from *King Lear* to *The Tempest*, commonly leaves a vacuum in which female sexuality, divorced from maternity, cedes authority to a masculine social order.

Although a number of critics have analyzed issues associated with maternity in the plays (Rose, Adelman, Paster, Willis), Shakespeare's treatment of "the mother's part" in the Sonnets has received less attention. Using D. W. Winnicott's model of ego development as the basis for his discussion, C. L. Barber calls attention to Shakespeare's evocation of "original maternal presence" in the Sonnets (Review 36), and traces the poet's adoption of stances of both infant and parent ("The Family"; Review; *The Whole Journey*). Extending Barber's argument, Andrew Sprung focuses upon "mother love and infant need" in the Sonnets, suggesting that Shakespeare explores "the cherishing parent's use of a child as a transitional object" (366). Along similar lines, Sara van den Berg utilizes post-Freudian object relations theory to explore the ways in which Shakespeare develops the "mother-child motif" in the Sonnets in order to delineate self and language (173). While filled with suggestive insights, these essays uniformly frame the

Sonnets in terms of twentieth-century object relations theory, resulting
in a certain level of idealization of the mother's position as vehicle and
object of desire.

In the present essay, I am concerned not so much to take issue with
readings based on object relations theory as to explore how
Shakespeare's Sonnets at once interrogate and reproduce early modern
codes of maternity, and to what effect. In early modern terms, what
does maternity have to do with the language of desire? Why should the
lovers' passions that govern the sequence be couched in relation to
maternal power or longing? Who plays "the mother's part" in the
Sonnets, and why? I would suggest that Shakespeare's Sonnets play
into and with early modern concerns about maternal roles and
responsibilities, powers and desires, not simply in order to devalue
women or to define male sexual identity in terms of difference, but
rather in order to explore how conflicts between authority and sexuality
frame the progress of desire.

In counterpoising responsibility and neglect, hope and fear,
nurturance and rejection, sonnet 143 offers an overview of issues
associated with maternity that appear throughout Shakespeare's
sequence. Although I will attend to it subsequently in more detail, I
would like to suggest here that sonnet 143 grapples with precisely the
questions of power and unpredictability that make the mother's part
such a compelling touchstone for expressions of desire on the part of
the speaker. As Dorothy Leigh observes in *The Mother's Blessing,* "the
love of a mother to her children is hardly contained within the bounds
of reason" (293). And yet, far from documenting female instability or
weakness, Leigh's claim establishes her right as a mother to speak her
mind, and to inscribe her words so that "my mind will continue long
after me in writing" (294). Suddenly, Leigh's claims and those of
Shakespeare's sonneteer begin to look oddly similar: passion beyond
the bounds of reason, giving life to words beyond the mortality of the
speaker. Moreover, drawing authority for desire from codes of
maternity opens the possibility for both liberating and destructive
excess, grounded in what Shakespeare's speaker identifies as the
mother's "will" (143.13).

As Heather Dubrow points out, sonnet 143, which represents the
relationship between speaker and addressee as that between child and
mother, might be addressed as well to the young man as to the dark
lady. Questioning the interpretive tendency to reify a predictable
narrative pattern in the sequence, Dubrow offers a perceptive caution

regarding "the perils of circular reading," whereby certain traits and preoccupations are assigned to certain characters in Shakespeare's sequence, and consequently perpetuated in readings across a variety of sonnets that might otherwise yield alternative plot lines and interpretations ("Incertainties" 297; reprinted in this volume). In the case of sonnet 143, Dubrow suggests that reading the "housewife" addressee as the young man yields the possibility that, "reduced to childishness by love and neglect, the speaker on the one hand declares his affection and on the other retaliates by charging the beloved with the effeminacy so feared in his culture" ("Incertainties" 302). An alternative possibility, I would add, is that the maternal huswife figures a sexual authority, "hardly contained within the bounds of reason," that designates the addressee, whether male or female, as beyond the logical comprehension and, consequently, the control of the desiring speaker.

Shakespeare introduces issues of maternity from the very start of his sequence by opening with the well-known "procreation sonnets," in which the beloved young man is urged to replicate himself through the vehicle of a woman with a womb, otherwise known as a mother. While some analyses of the procreation sonnets focus entirely upon the "story" of the sequence, reading the mother's part as negligible (Crosman 474), Dubrow argues that the procreation sonnets establish a series of contrasts with Petrarchism, in which sexuality as the means of procreation is played against sexuality as blind and blinding desire, and that love as the fulfillment of social obligations is played against love as narcissistic drive (*Echoes* 131). Interestingly, in an early modern pamphlet such as *The Honor of Virtue,* maternal sexuality and love are praised for the former set of characteristics, associating procreation and social obligations, whereas in the example of *A pitiless Mother,* maternity is attacked and feared for the latter set of characteristics, linking narcissistic drive and blind desire. Both the discourses and counterdiscourses of passion that mark Shakespeare's Sonnets, then, can be associated with early modern codes of maternity.

In the procreation sonnets, the speaker opens with a focus on women's function as wombs—"From fairest creatures we desire increase" (1.1)—which translates not simply into his desire to see the young man perpetuate his beauty in progeny, but also into his recognition of the connection between parent-child bonding and the comfort of affection—"This were to be new made when thou art old, / And see thy blood warm when thou feel'st it cold" (2.13-14). More particularly, the speaker calls attention to the mother's part, from womb to tomb, in advising the young man that his decision not to procreate will "unbless some mother" (3-4):

> For where is she so fair whose uneared womb
> Disdains the tillage of thy husbandry?
> . . . .
> Thou art thy mother's glass, and she in thee
> Calls back the lovely April of her prime,
> So thou through windows of thine age shalt see,
> Despite of wrinkles, this thy golden time. (3.5-6, 9-12)

Whereas van den Berg and Sprung read this moment in terms of Winnicott's "mirror stage" of infant development, in which the mother is mirror to the child,[2] Shakespeare's focus upon the origin of the gaze in the mother, with the child initially as mirror, and then as parental gazer himself, can be linked to early modern notions of maternal love and responsibility.

Elizabeth Grymeston, for instance, advises her son that "there is nothing so strong as the force of love; there is no love so forcible as the love of an affectionate mother to her naturall childe" (A3ʳ), and promises him that in the written advice which she is leaving him "thou maiest see the true portrature of thy mothers minde" (A3ᵛ). Elizabeth Clinton emphasizes that the womb is only the starting point for a mother's responsibility to "*Beare* children, that is, not only to *Beare* them in the wombe, and to bring them forth, but also to *Beare* them on their knee, in their armes, and at their breasts: for this Bearing a little before is called nourishing, and bringing up" (7). And Dorothy Leigh, in *The Mother's Blessing*, promises her sons that no mother can "forget the child of her womb," but rather will "bless it every time it sucks on her breasts, when she feeleth the blood come from her heart to nourish it," even as she will "instruct it in the youth, and admonish it in the age, and pray for it continually" (293). These advice books indicate that early modern mothers were able to offer not simply their gazes, but more lastingly their words, to provide their offspring with the nourishment of instruction as well as affection, from childhood to adulthood. Moreover, the passion of the mother's love for her child extends beyond merely physical reproduction to emotional and spiritual nurturance.

When Shakespeare's speaker plays with the notion of what it means to "unbless some mother," then, such language draws upon the resonance of the "mother's blessing" texts—some of which, like *The Northren Mother's Blessing*, had begun to appear contemporaneously with the circulation of the sonnets, in the late 1590s, while later texts distilled attitudes already in evidence in women's letters and diaries at the turn of the century. Such resonance suggests that the images in the procreation sonnets can be read not only in twentieth-century "proto-psychoanalytic" terms, but more directly in relation to early modern codes of maternity, according to which maternal blessing could extend from the womb to the tomb, sometimes quite literally, when the mothers who authored the advice books died in childbirth. Viewed in this light, the narcissistic discourse of physical vanity that marks sonnet 3, in which an aging mother looks for renewed youth in the face of her son, and the young man is warned of his need to reproduce toward a similar end, may be read against an incipient counterdiscourse of maternal love and responsibility, in which nurturance rather than simply reproduction underlies the "prime" years of the mother, and "blessing" may be reaped by the grown son as well as the mother.

The mother reappears in sonnet 8, in which the speaker urges the young man to recognize in the multiple harmonies of the lute strings a harmonious family group:

> Mark how one string, sweet husband to another,
> Strikes each in each by mutual ordering;
> Resembling sire, and child, and happy mother,
> Who all in one, one pleasing note do sing;
>   Whose speechless song, being many, seeming one,
>   Sings this to thee: "Thou single wilt prove none." (9-14)

In this family group, "sire, and child, and happy mother" are "all in one."[3] The unusual ordering and emphasis of this simile, in which the "happy mother" stands as the culmination of the list, with the adjective applied to the mother rather than the group, underscores the speaker's acknowledgment of the crucial part played by the mother in the harmony of the family. Yet even as the maternal presence in sonnet 3 can be associated at once with narcissism and nurturance, the "happy mother" in sonnet 8 proves capable of striking a note of difference, and dissonance, when she reappears as the "careful housewife" of sonnet 143.

In sonnet 9, the speaker conjures up the figure of a wailing, childless widow, paradoxically produced, just as the "unblessed" mother, by the specter of the young man's refusal to wed and procreate. From the nonexistent blessed and happy mother to the nonexistent weeping widow, Shakespeare's speaker relies upon a process of definition by negation in the procreation sonnets, while establishing an association between maternity and desire that begins to prove problematic only when the mother exhibits a will of her own. As long as the hypothetical mother's sexuality is contained by the young man's refusal to procreate, there can be no children toward whom the mother can exhibit independent affection, or over whom the mother can exert rightful maternal authority. The mother's desire, then, can be channeled in support of the speaker's passion for the young man, enabling the speaker to draw upon the force and intensity associated with "the mother's part" in early modern England in constructing his own play of desire.

The simultaneous presence of discourses of nurturance as well as narcisissism in the procreation sonnets, both linked with maternal desire, sets the stage for the speaker's movement from women as wombs to the birthing of the sonnets themselves, through which the speaker pledges to nurture his beloved as passionately as any mother. The language of the procreation sonnets at moments almost resembles the discourse of the mothers' advice books, in which advice is urged upon a beloved other with passionate force, albeit to different ends. Having established his passion through the first seventeen "procreation advice" sonnets, the speaker claims authority for his desire in sonnet 18 by offering the sonnet itself as the image of the beloved, with the verbal progeny of the poet taking the place of the nonexistent progeny of the young man: "So long as men can breathe or eyes can see, / So long lives this, and this gives life to thee" (13-14).

Playing the mother's part for himself, the speaker proceeds to assert that his love "is as fair / As any mother's child" (21.10-11), and assures his beloved of his readiness to "Bea[r] thy heart, which I will keep so chary / As tender nurse her babe from faring ill" (22.11-12). Even as Elizabeth Clinton affirms mothers' responsibility to "*beare* children" not only in the womb, but also in nourishing and bringing them up, so Shakespeare's speaker promises to nurture his beloved "As tender nurse her babe"—a strategically voiced promise that elevates the speaker to a position of authority over the loved one. Yet in the very next sonnet, the speaker acknowledges his fears of inadequacy for the part that he has claimed:

> As an unperfect actor on the stage,
> Who with his fear is put besides his part,
> Or some fierce thing replete with too much rage,
> Whose strength's abundance weakens his own heart,
> So I, for fear of trust, forget to say
> The perfect ceremony of love's rite,
> And in mine own love's strength seem to decay,
> O'ercharged with burthen of mine own love's might. (23.1-8)

Playing the mother's part proves not to be as easy as it seemed when the speaker was controlling the mother, distanced to the third person, in the procreation sonnets. Now, it is the speaker himself who faces the "burthen of mine own love's might," or the pregnant burden of his verbal progeny. "As an unperfect actor," the speaker fears the responsibility of the mother's part, and fears as well the "strength's abundance" of "some fierce thing," which might be linked to Dorothy Leigh's expression of "the love of a mother to her children," which is "hardly contained within the bounds of reason" (293).

Yet at the very moment that he faces his fears of the potentially overwhelming discourse of maternity, the speaker reclaims his relation to his verbal progeny, embracing both the narcissism and the nurture of the mother's part:

> O let my books be then the eloquence
> And dumb presagers of my speaking breast,
> Who plead for love and look for recompense
> More than that tongue that more hath more expressed. (23.9-12)

Having labored to give birth to his sonnets, the poet resolves to nurse them, in order that his love might be "express'd." The nursing metaphor underlying the "speaking breast" allows the poet to establish a maternal dumb show, in which the sonnets "express" the milk of the poet's love, because they are his own, more effectively than the copious words of others.[4]

On the one hand, narcissism underlies the speaker's exaltation of his own language, even as an assumption of maternal narcissism underlies the description of Margaret Vincent's willingness to take her children's blood, "nay, her own dear blood bred in her own body, cherished in her own womb" (*A pitiless Mother* 364). On the other hand, both desire and capacity for nurture emerge in the speaker's

commitment to "express" his love from his "speaking breast," even as
an affirmation of maternal nurture emerges in Elizabeth Clinton's
observation that "who that judges aright; doth not hold the suckling of
her owne childe the part of a true mother, of an honest mother, of a just
mother, of a syncere mother, of a mother worthy of love, of a mother
deserving good report, of a vertuous mother, of a mother winning
praise for it?" (7-8). And indeed, both obsessed by his words and
willing to offer them up, Shakespeare's speaker has every hope of
winning praise, or "recompense," for his efforts.

In sonnet 59, the speaker once again links poetic invention with
maternal labor, this time questioning the usefulness of playing the
mother's part in order to achieve his desire:

> If there be nothing new, but that which is
> Hath been before, how are our brains beguiled,
> Which, lab'ring for invention, bear amiss
> The second burthen of a former child! (1-4)

Exposing the fiction of the pregnant poet, "O'ercharged with burthen of
my own love's might" (23.8), the speaker admits that the "invention" of
the image of the beloved in his poems comes "second" to the physical
birth of the beloved, who after all is already an adult, or "former
child."[5] And yet, celebrating "this composed wonder of your frame"
(59.10), the speaker closes with an assertion of the legitimacy of his
labor after all, given that others "To subjects worse have given
admiring praise" (14). Acknowledging his own fears of inadequacy, the
speaker chooses to link his worth as a poet to the value of his subject,
even as early modern mothers located their authority in their love for
their offspring.

As the sequence proceeds, the speaker voices his concern that his
verse is "barren of new pride," so predictable that "every word doth
almost tell my name, / Showing their birth, and where they did
proceed" (76.1, 7-8). Here Shakespeare plays ironically with early
modern anxieties about the trustworthiness of maternal sexuality, where
a father must depend upon a mother's word for his claim to his
progeny. On the mother's part, however, no insecurity need arise, since
a mother knows the provenance of each and every child. The gendered
irony in sonnet 76 lurks in the fact that whereas a father should delight
in visual evidence linking his children with himself, the speaker
complains of the visible origins of his sonnets, not needing such

evidence that they are his own. Sounding like an actualized version of the hypothetical mother in the procreation sonnets, worn by the repeated labor required to produce so many poems, all in the service of one beloved, the speaker reenacts the narcissism and nurture of the mother's part in declaring that "you and love are still my argument" (10), as his passion for the loved one fuels the authority of his invention.

In the following sonnet, the speaker urges his beloved to play the mother's part on his own behalf:

> Look what thy memory cannot contain,
> Commit to these waste blanks, and thou shalt find
> Those children nursed, delivered from thy brain,
> To take a new acquaintance of thy mind. (77.9-12)

Once the beloved commits words to the blank page, he shall find "children" of his own. Allied to the impetus of the procreation sonnets, the advice in sonnet 77 is aimed at encouraging the loved one not only to give birth to progeny of another sort, already privileged by the poet's own labors, but also to "nurse" those offspring in order "To take a new acquaintance of thy mind." Here, playing the mother's part offers the opportunity for self-renewal, and links speaker and beloved in a shared endeavor of production.

As in sonnet 23, the failure that repeatedly attends the speaker's efforts can be represented in maternal terms, as well as can the success. In sonnet 86, miscarriage marks the poet's pregnant burden, as the speaker queries the cause that "did my ripe thoughts in my brain inhearse, / Making their tomb the womb wherein they grew" (3-4). From womb to tomb, again the poet rehearses a course of maternity, but this time he focuses upon his own pregnancy. Unlike the "unblessed" mother of sonnet 3, whose unused womb signals the tomb of the beloved's uncreated progeny, the speaker here is pregnant with the beloved's image, yet unable successfully to give birth because the loved one has lent his "countenance" to "[fill] up" the lines of a rival poet (13). In fact, mothers in the early modern period constantly faced the threat of the death of their offspring, whether within the womb or in infancy, even as each pregnancy signaled the concomitant threat of their own mortality. Texts such as the mothers' advice books or correspondence among mothers were filled with language of loss as well as longing. In many ways, early modern codes of maternity could be said to be grounded in mortality, whether of mother or child, offering an identifiable resonance of loss for Shakespeare's speaker to appropriate. Marked increasingly by insecurity and doubt, the speaker's enactment of the mother's part traces a shift from anticipation to anxiety.

Thus in sonnet 97, the beloved's absence counteracts the teeming fertility of the season, now distanced from the poet's production:

> And yet this time removed was summer's time,
> The teeming autumn big with rich increase,
> Bearing the wanton burthen of the prime,
> Like widowed wombs after their lords' decease.
> Yet this abundant issue seemed to me
> But hope of orphans, and unfathered fruit;
> For summer and his pleasures wait on thee,
> And thou away, the very birds are mute. (5-12)

No longer "O'ercharged with burthen of mine own love's might" (23.8), the speaker views the exaggerated pregnancy of the season as a "wanton burthen," suggesting fears regarding the beloved's unfaithfulness. The hypothetical and unimpregnated widow of sonnet 9 is now actualized in the "widowed wombs" of autumn, "teeming" with "rich increase." And yet "this abundant issue" proves only "hope of orphans, and unfathered fruit," given the absence of the loved one, whose presence is needed to complete any family group resembling the "sire, and child, and happy mother" detailed in sonnet 8. Although the mother's part is played metaphorically by the season in sonnet 97, and it is the birds rather than the poet who "are mute," nevertheless the speaker's gloom is associated with the position of an abandoned mother, whose excessive sexuality undermines the authority of her continuing production, even as the speaker's continuing invention loses authority in the absence of reciprocal passion.

Increasingly preoccupied with the mutability of the beloved, the speaker ceases to perform the mother's part, no longer inclined to claim the confident fertility of maternity, given his distance from his love. When the speaker declares in sonnet 115 that "Love is a babe" (13), the reappearance of metaphoric progeny fails to serve as a realization of his desire. Instead, the speaker declines to say "I love you best," in order "To give full growth to that which still doth grow" (10, 13).[6] Playing with the definition by negation that marks the early procreation sonnets, while questioning the validity of those earlier offspring—"those lines that I before have writ do lie" (1)—the speaker reprises the theme of procreation in a minor key, looking ahead to future growth of passion, but no longer with assurance.

When the speaker subsequently suggests that the "child" of his love "might for fortune's bastard be unfathered, / As subject to time's love, or to time's hate" (124.1, 2-3), his use of the term "unfathered" links this sonnet to the "unfathered fruit" of sonnet 97. Whereas earlier in the sequence, the poet uses the paradoxical language of negation to establish a bond with his beloved, at this late point in the sequence terms of negation such as "unfathered" convey the speaker's own fears of abandonment. Casting about for language to convey the shift in his fortunes, as well as the vulnerability of his position, the speaker resorts to juxtapositions of "child" and "bastard," "love" and "hate." Poised on the verge of sonnets that counterpoise longing for the young man with a darker desire for a female other, the poet moves from his illustrative construction of the figure of the "unblessed" mother to a disillusioned reference to the possible bastardy of his own "unfathered" love.

Given Heather Dubrow's caution regarding the application of fixed labels to different sonnets, it seems appropriate to examine Shakespeare's concluding engagement with early modern codes of maternity in sonnet 143 in relation to the possibility of either beloved playing "the mother's part." What is most notable is that where the male speaker himself plays the mother's part in many of the sonnets throughout the sequence, the shift in sonnet 143 to characterizing the unattainable beloved in that role suggests a significant metamorphosis in the enactment of desire. Grounding my reading in early modern rather than psychoanalytic conceptions of maternity,[7] I would argue that the duality of the early modern codes of maternity that mark the sequence allows Shakespeare's speaker to construct a doubled language of desire in order to convey his own ambivalent longing, equal parts narcisissm and nurture, for the beloved, whether young man or dark lady.

As the stakes rise with the interaction of two players in the role of beloved, the speaker appropriates "the mother's part" in the service of his doubled passion one final time. Moving from the construct of mothers as wombs for reproduction in the procreation sonnets, and the usefulness of the mother's part in conveying his own fertile creativity and obsessive passion in sonnets throughout the body of the sequence, the poet here strategically externalizes the mother as agent of desire.

Sonnet 143 clothes the mother in the guise of "a careful housewife," whose care almost immediately is brought into question by her neglect of her wailing infant, who figures the poet's own abandonment:

> Lo, as a careful housewife runs to catch
> One of her feathered creatures broke away,
> Sets down her babe, and makes all swift dispatch
> In pursuit of the thing she would have stay—
> Whilst her neglected child holds her in chase,
> Cries to catch her whose busy care is bent
> To follow that which flies before her face,
> Not prizing her poor infant's discontent:
> So run'st thou after that which flies from thee,
> Whilst I, thy babe, chase thee afar behind;
> But if thou catch thy hope, turn back to me,
> And play the mother's part, kiss me, be kind.
>> So will I pray that thou mayst have thy will,
>> If thou turn back and my loud crying still.

Setting down the babe who had been enclosed in the comfort of her arms, this mother pursues a different object of desire: literally, one of her household responsibilities, but effectively, a competitor to the desires of her child, and metaphorically, as Stephen Booth points out, a "dandified rival" to the poet himself (494).

The opening metaphor of the "careful housewife" which frames the poem employs a figure whose significance and responsibilities were both problematic and contested in the early modern period. Mary Thomas Crane points out that the term "housewife," or "huswife," could mean "simultaneously *both* 'a woman (usually a married woman) . . . who manages her household with skill and thrift' and 'a light, worthless, or pert woman or girl . . . now Hussy.'" Crane examines an array of uses of the term, "in order to trace a pattern of anxiety, first, over working class women's wage-earning potential within the home (with fears of a concomitant sexual independence) and, later, anxiety over upper-class women's increasing idleness (with fears of concomitant sexual freedom)" (1). While the "careful housewife" was expected to conserve all of her husband's assets, ranging from barnyard animals to money, Crane indicates that concerns regarding huswifely independence within the home were associated with worries regarding her independent sexuality (3). Indeed, Crane's study provides a range of examples from Shakespeare's plays as well as from early modern texts like Thomas Tusser's *The Points of Huswiferie United to the Comforts of Husbandrie* (1570), to indicate that a huswife's "power as producer of offspring was, like her potential to augment family income, a quality both desired and feared" (5).

The "careful housewife" in sonnet 143, then, can be read both as a figure of domestic responsibility and maternal authority, and as an agent of her own desires, recalling Iago's mocking characterization of women as "players in your huswifery, and huswives in your beds" (*Othello* 2.1.112).[8] Shakespeare's juxtaposition of huswifery and maternity in sonnet 143 draws upon early modern preoccupations regarding the suspect sexual authority of both huswives and mothers, toward the end of critiquing the doubled passion of the beloved, a "player" who cannot be trusted. Even more explicitly than in the rest of the sequence, maternity operates in sonnet 143 as the subject rather than the object of the metaphor, the touchstone rather than the thing itself. The huswife/hussy dichotomy plays into the duality of the self-sacrificial and yet assertive mother, whose desires prove the most threatening when they cannot be contained, whether within "the bounds of reason" or otherwise.

The mothers' advice books themselves address the concept of huswifery in enabling terms, as when the author of *The Northren Mother's Blessing* advises her daughter to "be huswife good" (E8ʳ) and take the initiative in supervising male laborers in her husband's absence, "for they will do better if thou by them stond" (F1ʳ). Similarly, Elizabeth Joceline follows her recommendation that her infant daughter be brought up to learn "good housewifery" with the observation that "where learning and wisdome meet in a vertuous disposed woman . . . shee is like a well-ballanced ship that may beare all her saile" (B6ʳ). Elizabeth Grymeston's maternal instruction to her son regarding an appropriate wife includes a passage of huswifely advice to "kill bad chickens in the tread, / Fledge they hardly can be catched" (A4ᵛ), that functions as a metaphor for her point that evil thoughts must be cast out, but serves also as a suggestive gloss for Shakespeare's metaphoric reference to the fleeing "feathered creature" that leads the huswife awry in sonnet 143.

The concepts of huswifery in the mothers' advice books, like the other precepts of maternal wisdom, are represented with the aim of benefiting the offspring who are the recipients of the advice. To that end, the mothers remind their children of their authority, "as ever the love of a mother may challenge the performaunce of her demaund of a dutyfull Childe" (Grymeston A5ᵛ), and urge their own children likewise to "take heed to thy children which thou hast born" (*Northren Mother's Blessing* F3ᵛ). Shakespeare inverts that expected focus in sonnet 143 when his "careful housewife" abandons her crying child, "not prizing her poor infant's discontent." This deliberate inversion of early modern codes of maternity functions as a powerful metaphor for the speaker's representation of the beloved's indifference not simply as lamentable but, more forcibly, as a violation of the basic order of human bonding.

Whether the addressee is woman or man makes no difference to the speaker's calculated plea that the beloved "play the mother's part, kiss me, be kind" (143.12). Indeed, the explicit reference to the mother's "part" emphasizes the constructed nature of the role-playing in this scenario. Even if the speaker's "two loves . . . of comfort and despair" (144.1) are pursuing each other, the aim of sonnet 143 is to redirect the focus of the players upon the speaker, who desires the beloved's "will" (143.13) to be himself.[9] The patterns of flight and pursuit, of chasing and catching, of breaking away and turning back that mark this sonnet embed in a single drama the patterns that mark the sequence as a whole, even as the beloved in this sonnet might legitimately be either of the two objects of desire who govern the speaker's affections. Moreover, the invocation of "the mother's part" associates the power and unpredictability of sexual authority with a maternal agent of desire, underscoring the compelling use of early modern codes of maternity throughout the sequence.

Dorothy Leigh identifies those who might be threatened by the power of maternal love early in *The Mother's Blessing*: "Therefore *let no man blame a mother*, though she something exceed in writing to her children, since *every man* knows that the love of a mother to her children is hardly contained within the bounds of reason" (293; emphasis added). As Elizabeth Grymeston observes, "there is no love so forcible as the love of an affectionate mother to her naturall childe" (A3ʳ). Paradoxically, mothers were the figures most empowered, and even expected, to express passionate desire in the early modern period, apart from lovers. Combining the sexuality of generative wombs with the authority of generative words, the authors of the mothers' advice books found a receptive audience not only in their children, but also in an early modern society that called for their words to be printed and reprinted, extending their influence far beyond the boundaries of their immediate families.

Given a sonneteer's burden to authorize his or her passion in terms at once novel and accepted, what better discourse to appropriate than that of a mother? Certainly that choice informs a number of Sir Philip Sidney's sonnets, including the famous opening sonnet in which the speaker proclaims himself "great with child to speake" (*Astrophil and Stella* 1.12). When Sidney's niece, Lady Mary Wroth, draws upon early modern codes of maternity for her sonnet sequence, pregnancy leads to miscarriage within a lyric inscription of the body's betrayal of its fertility, "unaturall to the birth / Of thine owne wombe," that comes to represent the female speaker's recognition of the precarious relation between desire and language (*Pamphilia to Amphilanthus* 40.2-3). While Shakespeare's incorporation of the mother's part in his sonnets is not unique, his extension of maternal metaphors from pregnant wombs to careful huswives expands the range of the tradition.

Shakespeare's Sonnets both reproduce and interrogate early modern codes of maternity in the service of extending the boundaries of the speaker's passion in generative terms. Both risk and release attend Shakespeare's appropriation of the mother's part in a sequence dedicated to the triangulated dynamic between speaker, young man, and dark lady. On the one hand, the risk of feminizing the young man reflects a process already initiated in the Petrarchan rhapsodies of sonnet 18, while the risk of acceding overmuch power to the female role verifies the daunting combination of sexuality and authority attributed to the dark lady. On the other hand, the release of claiming a discourse grounded in passion and framed by the potential for excess, attested to in early modern texts ranging from the mothers' advice books to *A pitiless Mother*, reflects the passionate excess of the desiring speaker, while the release of conjoining authority and sexuality in maternal terms exposes the tensions at the heart of the speaker's obsessions.

To return to the questions that initiated my inquiry: who plays "the mother's part" in the Sonnets, and why? Every character in the sequence plays the mother's part, from the young man who is enjoined both to procreate and to produce "children nursed, delivered from thy brain" (77), to the dark lady who certainly stands as one figure for the "careful housewife" (143), to the poet who acknowledges himself both "an unperfect actor" and a "fierce thing" with "speaking breast" (23). Beyond the identification of these principal players, why might the lovers' passions that govern Shakespeare's sequence be couched in relation to maternal power or longing? One answer might be that the mother's part in early modern terms can be seen to embody a simultaneous capacity for narcissism and nurture, sustenance and destruction, that coincides with the ambivalence of the speaker's desires.

What, finally, does maternity have to do with the language of desire? As evidenced by the early modern texts surveyed above, maternity exhibits the potential to authorize the language of desire "beyond the bounds of reason." Shakespeare's Sonnets are constructed in the apparent service of an obsessive passion that seeks outlets in whatever channels best serve to convey the breadth and depths of yearning and desire. By alternately playing the mother's part or enjoining its performance, Shakespeare's speaker legitimizes the excess of power and/or helplessness, reflective narcissism and/or sacrificial nurture, that attends the progress of his desire.

Berny Grymeston, son to Elizabeth, composes a "Madrigall . . . upon [his mother's] conceit," appended to the published version of Elizabeth Grymeston's advice book, which articulates the dual effects of his mother's passion upon himself: "And yet how oft the strokes of sounding keies hath slaine, / As oft the looks of your kind eies restores my life againe" (D2^r). The son's representation of his mother's words in musical terms, making reference to the "sounding keies" of a virginal, draws upon common early modern tropes connecting auditory and visual beauty, where the spell of musical notes was seen to work in consort with the female gaze at once to devastate and to enrapture male listeners.[10] The passionate relations between woman and man, and mother and child, are here conflated in the words of a son to his mother. Even so, the devastating and yet restorative effects of early modern codes of maternity inform the "speaking breast" of the poet in Shakespeare's Sonnets.

NOTES

1. I use Stephen Booth's edition of the Sonnets and G. Blakemore Evans's 1974 edition of the plays.

2. Van den Berg maintains that "this link of mirror, motherhood, and memory can only be termed proto-psychoanalytic" (183), while Sprung cites sonnet 3 in support of his argument regarding the parent's use of a child as a transitional object (366-67).

3. Fineman finds in the "excess of likeness" in sonnet 8 "the logic, as well as the arithmetic, of . . . a different sameness" (259). Van den Berg, on the other hand, argues that it is Shakespeare's "vision of a 'happy mother' that, in memory or wish, can give a child a sense of self that enables both autonomy and relationship, individual identity and harmony" (185).

4. Sprung emphasizes the reciprocal nature of the nursing metaphor, in which "both the mother's breast and the infant's tongue and lips may be said to 'express' milk; it is in the reciprocal gaze that both express their need-love" (373).

5. Although Fineman terms Shakespeare's imagery in sonnet 59 both "eccentric" and "grotesque," identifying the "former child" as a "monstrous afterbirth . . . whose own mixed-up physicality objectifies the way that repetition ruptures likeness" (263), van den Berg takes issue with Fineman, maintaining that Shakespeare emphasizes "the psychology of the mother who regards her child as unique," and pointing out that the poet is also a "former child" (187).

6. Fineman equates the infant "Love" in sonnet 115 with what he terms the "stillborn, ancient baby" of sonnet 59 (269).

7. Van den Berg argues that "the dark lady sonnets depend on the structure of preoedipal desire," and concludes that "the poet splits the object of his love into an absent, idealized mother and a present woman wholly unlike that ideal" (188).

8. I am greatly indebted to Mary Thomas Crane for her detailed explorations of figures of huswives in a range of early modern texts, including Shakespeare's plays. For a complementary consideration of "husbandry" in the Sonnets, see Thomas Greene.

9. In readings that depend upon identification of the addressee in sonnet 143 as the dark lady, Fineman asserts that "when the dark lady's poet gives voice to his name, he thereby gives expression to the original verbal difference that the sameness of a visionary language is committed to leave out" (295), while van den Berg suggests that "in the life span of human desire, all language echoes that first cry of the child for the absent or abandoning mother, who chooses to pursue her own desires" (192). With a rather different emphasis, Wheeler locates in sonnet 143 a "suspension of primary concern with masculine independence," so that the speaker must forfeit "all claims to autonomous selfhood" in the face of the "mother's part," which Wheeler identifies as "an element of the woman's desired presence" (194-96).

10. Linda Austern provides a detailed analysis of early modern perceptions regarding the auditory and visual powers associated with women and music (esp. 424-27).

WORKS CITED

Adelman, Janet. *Suffocating Mothers: Fantasies of Maternal Origins in Shakespeare's Plays*. London: Routledge, 1992.

Austern, Linda. "'Sing Again Syren': The Female Musician and Sexual Enchantment in Elizabethan Life and Literature," *Renaissance Quarterly* 42 (1989): 420-48.

Barber, C. L. "The Family in Shakespeare's Development: Tragedy and Sacredness." *Representing Shakespeare*. Ed. Murray M. Schwartz and Coppélia Kahn. Baltimore: Johns Hopkins UP, 1980.

———. Review of Stephen Booth's *Shakespeare's Sonnets. New York Review of Books* 25 (6 April 1978), 32-38.

———, and Richard P. Wheeler. *The Whole Journey: Shakespeare's Power of Development*. Berkeley: U of California P, 1986.

Booth, Stephen, ed. *Shakespeare's Sonnets*. New Haven: Yale UP, 1977.

Clinton, Elizabeth. *The Countesse of Lincolnes Nurserie*. 1622. Brown University Women Writers' Project, print version 0.5P.

Crane, Mary Thomas. "'Players in your huswifery, and huswives in your beds': Conflicting Identities of English Housewives in the Early Seventeenth Century." Paper delivered at Renaissance Society of America Annual Meeting, Vancouver, B.C., April 1997.

Crosman, Robert. "Making Love out of Nothing at All: The Issue of Story in Shakespeare's Procreation Sonnets." *Shakespeare Quarterly* 41 (1990): 470-88.

Dubrow, Heather. *Echoes of Desire: English Petrarchism and Its Counterdiscourses*. Ithaca: Cornell UP, 1995.

———. "'Incertainties now crown themselves assur'd': The Politics of Plotting Shakespeare's Sonnets." *Shakespeare Quarterly* 47 (1996): 291-305.

Fineman, Joel. *Shakespeare's Perjured Eye: The Invention of Poetic Subjectivity in the Sonnets*. Berkeley: U of California P, 1986.

Greene, Thomas. "Pitiful Thrivers: Failed Husbandry in the Sonnets." *Shakespeare and the Question of Theory*. Ed. Patricia Parker and Geoffrey Hartman. New York: Methuen, 1985. 230-44.

Grymeston, Elizabeth. *Miscelanea, Meditations, Memoratives*. London, 1604.

Guillemeau, Jacques. *Child-Birth, or, The Happy Deliverie of Women* and *The Nursing of Children*. London, 1612.

The Honor of Virtue. 1620. Reprinted in *Half-Humankind: Contexts and Texts of the Controversy about Women in England, 1540-1640*. Ed. Katherine Usher Henderson and Barbara F. McManus. Urbana: U of Illinois P, 1985. 344-50.

Joceline, Elizabeth. *The Mothers Legacie, To her unborne Childe*. London, 1624.

Leigh, Dorothy. *The Mother's Blessing*. 1616. Excerpted in *Daughters, Wives and Widows: Writings by Men about Women and Marriage in England, 1500-1640*. Ed. Joan Larsen Klein. Urbana: U of Illinois P, 1992. 291-302.

The Northren Mother's Blessing. London, 1597.

Paster, Gail Kern. *The Body Embarrassed: Drama and the Disciplines of Shame in Early Modern England*. Ithaca: Cornell UP, 1993.

A pitiless Mother. 1616. Excerpted in *Half-Humankind: Contexts and Texts of the Controversy about Women in England, 1540-1640*. Ed. Katherine Usher Henderson and Barbara F. McManus. Urbana: U of Illinois P, 1985. 360-67.

Rose, Mary Beth. "Where Are the Mothers in Shakespeare? Options for Gender Representation in the English Renaissance." *Shakespeare Quarterly* 42 (1991): 291-314.

Shakespeare, William. *The Riverside Shakespeare*. Ed. G. Blakemore Evans. Boston: Houghton Mifflin, 1974.

Sidney, Sir Philip. *Astrophil and Stella*. *The Poems of Sir Philip Sidney*. Ed. William Ringler Jr. Oxford: Clarendon P, 1962.

Sprung, Andrew. "Chary Charity: Mother Love and Infant Need in Shakespeare's Sonnets." *American Imago* 47 (1990): 365-82.

Tusser, Thomas. *The Points of Huswiferie United to the Comforts of Husbandrie*. London, 1570.

van den Berg, Sara. "'Mutual Ordering': Subjectivity and Language in Shakespeare's Sonnets." *Contending Kingdoms*. Ed. Marie-Rose Logan and Peter L. Rudnytsky. Detroit: Wayne State UP, 1991. 173-201.

Wheeler, Richard P. "'. . . And my loud crying still': *The Sonnets, The Merchant of Venice*, and *Othello*." *Shakespeare's "Rough Magic": Renaissance Essays in Honor of C. L. Barber*. Ed. Peter Erickson and Coppélia Kahn. Newark: U of Delaware P, 1985. 193-209.

Willis, Deborah. *Malevolent Nurture: Witch-Hunting and Maternal Power in Early Modern England*. Ithaca: Cornell U P, 1995.

Winnicott, D. W. *Playing and Reality*. New York: Basic Books, 1971.

Wroth, Lady Mary. *Pamphilia to Amphilanthus*. *The Poems of Lady Mary Wroth*. Ed. Josephine A. Roberts. Baton Rouge: Louisiana State UP, 1983.

Figure 5. Mary Fitton, maid of honor to Queen Elizabeth, considered by some to have been the Sonnets' dark lady. From Lady Newdigate-Newdegate, *Gossip from the Muniment Room* (London: David Nutt, 1897). Reproduced courtesy of the General Collection of the Library of Congress.

Be Dark but Not Too Dark

Shakespeare's Dark Lady as a Sign of Color

Marvin Hunt

I

Her breasts are "dun" (130.3), her hair a coronet of "black wires" (130.4), her nothing-like-the-sun eyes "raven black" (127.9).[1] The complex overlapping orbits of inverted praise in sonnet 127, the first poem to address her color explicitly, associate her with slander and illegitimacy and shame (4), with anonymity and exclusion from religious sanctuary (7), with profanation and disgrace (8), mourning (10). In 133, she has robbed the speaker of the affection of the fair young man, who is now "slave to slavery" (4); her "cruel eye" has taken "[m]e from myself" (5)—has stripped the subject of subjectivity. The overpowering contrary beauty of Shakespeare's dark lady and the corrosive effects of desire for her are, in part, direct consequences of her color. Yet her darkness has been a matter of persistent difficulty for students of Shakespeare's Sonnets for centuries. The issue is not so much how dark she is but rather how dark we are going to allow her to be.

In this essay I first describe a semiotics of color that emerges from selected commentaries on the dark lady as a means of pointing up the anxiety, revulsion, and covert desire that emerge from discussions of her darkness. In the second part of the essay I discuss selections from a little-known body of lyric poetry from the seventeenth century praising the beauty of African women, attempting to expose some of the ways the poetic strategies for dealing with a fully racialized and eroticized African other in the seventeenth century are prefigured in Shakespeare's sonnets to the dark lady. The history of criticism relating to the dark lady has amply demonstrated the folly and futility of attempting to discover who she was, or even what her racial heritage might be, so I have been careful to avoid such an anachronistic approach, opting instead to consider her as a literary sign to which color values have inevitably been attached.

Historically, the debate over the darkness of the dark lady arrays itself as a ternary semiotics of color, consisting of what I wish to identify as discrete, exclusive somatic values: white, brown, and black.[2] The system can be described briefly as follows. If any given candidate for the dark lady is shown to have been a fair-skinned Caucasian—and this is the fate of most women supposed to have been the dark lady— then she cannot, carrying a white value, signify the mistress of the Sonnets. Even if she is rendered morally dark or foul, most commentators have not been willing to allow a light-complexioned woman—Mary Fitton (see Figure 5 in this volume) is the classic example—to be the dark lady. Her skin must be naturally darker than the typical Englishwoman's; her eyes must be black, her hair black and wiry. There is a threshold of physical color, derived from details of her appearance given in 130, beneath which the dark lady is, in short, no longer a dark lady.

At the next level I assign the value of brown to Caucasian women of dark complexion posited to have been Shakespeare's dark lady— white women who have complexions dark enough to satisfy the darkness registered in 130 but not so dark as to register racial difference. In this brown value most significant historical candidates begin their careers. As a European woman, the brown dark lady is one of the same race and culture as the speaker, the principal difference between them (a large one, of course) being gender. In other words, in her brown value the dark lady is not problematical, at least not from a racial or cultural perspective, because she does not approach the threshold of racial and cultural difference. The darkness attributed to her may signify moral degeneracy but not deeper, more threatening implications for racial and cultural contamination. The major consequence for the champion of any candidate should investigation prove the candidate white, not brown, is that she is not who and what she was announced to be, and her proponent loses an argument of serious personal and professional importance.

At a third level of signification, occupied by the value of black, the dark lady becomes semiotically if not literally a figure of radical cultural and racial otherness. Accordingly, the dark lady as a sign of African or West Indian blackness cannot carry a brown or white value; she has been located in a somatic region beyond these values where she now presents herself as a manifest threat to the racial purity of the sequence and its speaker. Her "blackness," that is, must necessarily signal the operation of radical difference within dominant social, aesthetic, and political discourses of English culture. As I will show, this black value provokes anxiety or revulsion among some commentators and ambivalent desire among others. But whatever the reaction of individual commentators, all who construe or respond to the dark lady as a black value necessarily believe—or fear—that interracial desire motivates the sonnets associated with her.

Because scholarly reputations, not to mention the knit of personal ambition and desire that motivates scholarly work, are at stake in the investigation of the dark lady, candidates for the dark lady who turn out to have been fair-skinned women are especially damaging to their champions. In the nineteenth century Thomas Tyler experienced the prototypical disaster when his dark lady, Mary Fitton, suddenly lost her brown value and became a white woman and so, at least for most of Tyler's readers, no longer a possible candidate for the mistress of the Sonnets. Fitton, one of the Queen's Maids of Honor, disgraced herself by becoming the mistress of William Herbert, third Earl of Pembroke, by this theory Shakespeare's fair young man and the dedicatee of the Sonnets. Tyler discovered that Mary Fitton's monument in Cheshire bore traces of paint indicating a brown-skinned woman. Convinced that his case for Fitton was unassailable, he wanted to see, he wrote in his edition of the Sonnets, "a coloured portrait of Fitton" to compare with Shakespeare's poetic rendering of her (*Sonnets* 80 n.). A "specialist in pessimism," George Bernard Shaw called him, whose translation of Ecclesiastes sold eight copies a year, Tyler should have expected failure. Seven years later, it came. Lady Newdigate-Newdegate, a descendant of Fitton, produced two portraits of Mary that showed a pale-skinned, gray-eyed brunette. Fitton, once a brown lady, was now white, and with this shift of somatic value Tyler's case for the dark lady, his major life's work, was lost. "That settles the question," Shaw wrote, "if the portrait is authentic, which I see no reason to doubt" (109). Despite the definitive weight of this value shift, Tyler maintained his devotion to the Pembroke/Fitton theory, arguing that the

portrait was not of Mary Fitton but rather one of Mary's sister's friends
(*Herbert-Fitton* 18). Few were persuaded by his tortured rebuttal,
however, and Tyler died, Shaw wrote, "dropping unnoted like a stone
in the sea" (112).

A similar disappointing shift from brown to white value, marking
the failure of a project in which huge amounts of time, energy, and
public scrutiny had been invested, awaited A. L. Rowse. In
Shakespeare's Sonnets: The Problems Solved (1973), Rowse
announced that he had discovered the identity of the dark lady. She was
Emilia, daughter of court musician Baptist Bassano and Margaret
Johnson. Orphaned at seventeen in 1587, with a dowry of £100, Emilia
became the mistress of the elderly Henry Carey, Lord Hunsdon, later
Lord Chamberlain, the sponsor of Shakespeare's acting company.
Pregnant by Hundson, who soon died, she married a man Rowse
identified as William Lanier, a court minstrel, whom she despised.
Rowse's identification of Emilia Lanier as the dark lady was based on
his reading of Simon Forman's *Casebook*, in which Forman described a
visit from Emilia in 1593 to have her horoscope read. By the time of
this visit, she had fallen on hard times. Forman claimed she was "now
very needy, in debt and it seems for lucre's sake will be a good fellow,
for necessity doth compel" (*Casebook* 100). Forman tested what a
"good fellow" she might be. After some initial resistance, she sent for
Forman and he seems to have enjoyed "halek" with her, his code word
for sexual intercourse.

Rowse took this suggestion of easy virtue—more likely financial
and emotional desperation—to be an indication of the dark lady's
prodigious sexual appetite. He also noted that Forman described her as
"very brown in youth," by which, Rowse concluded, Forman "means
that she was exceptionally dark" (*Sonnets* xxxiv-xxxv). Together with
the evidence that her husband's name was William, Rowse made the
case that this brown, libidinous, Will-wed girl, Emilia Lanier, was the
dark lady herself. But soon after Rowse proclaimed triumphantly that
he had solved the riddle of the dark lady, his case unraveled. Reviewing
Rowse's evidence, Stanley Wells found that Emilia had not in fact
married William but Alfonso Lanier, and that Simon Forman had not
written that Emilia was "very *brown* in youth" but "very *brave* in
youth" (emphasis added). In the shift from "brown" to "brave" Rowse's
case was effectively lost (see Marder 24).

Yet, characteristic of those who find themselves in such a position,
Rowse refused to let go.[3] In his *Discovering Shakespeare* (1989), a

classic instance of the persecution complex at work, Rowse doggedly advanced his case that Lanier was the dark lady, repeating Forman's remark (silently corrected) about Lanier being "brave in youth" while avoiding the question of her darkness altogether, except to say that she was Italianate. He also complained that in the aftermath of the attacks on his case, his invitation to write the general introduction to the 1974 *Riverside Shakespeare* was retracted: "I was laid off from introducing the volume," he wrote, "and no notice of my work was taken by the contributors." The choice opportunity of writing the general introduction was given, he continued, to "an undistinguished professor content to remain in the rut" (57).

II

A more subtle and interesting negotiation of the dark lady's brown value is provided by George Bernard Shaw, whose little play *The Dark Lady of the Sonnets* (1910) was produced at the Haymarket Theatre to rally support for a national theater memorializing Shakespeare. In it Shaw followed Tyler in identifying Mary Fitton as the dark lady, even though he no longer believed she was. His reasons for employing Fitton were dramatic and polemical, he explained in a well-known preface added four years later. Since he chose to have Shakespeare petitioning Queen Elizabeth, playwright conversing (very rudely) with monarch, the only way to include the dark lady among the dramatis personae was to cast Mary Fitton in that role, since she had once been Maid of Honor to the Queen. But why include the dark lady at all? Why raise troubling issues of gender and color in a play meant to enlist support for a national theater? Why the dark lady and not, say, Ben Jonson or Richard Burbage, or Juliet or Rosalind? Why title the piece *The Dark Lady of the Sonnets* while, in fact, giving her only a minor role? Because the play is brief and unfamiliar to most readers, and since it illustrates the curious attraction and threat that inform Shaw's portrait of her, I offer the following summary.

There are only four characters: the Warder, the Man (Shakespeare, known as Shakespear in the play), the Lady (Elizabeth), and the Dark Lady. On midsummer night outside Whitehall, Shakespeare approaches a palace guard. Following an exchange that echoes the opening of *Hamlet* and depicts Shakespeare busily stealing lines from the guard ("Angels and ministers of grace defend us!"), Shakespeare tells him, "I keep tryst here with a dark lady" (141). To his dismay the naive

Shakespeare discovers from the Warder that he is not the Dark Lady's
only suitor. She has had many others. "I'll not believe it!" Shakespeare
swears. "Now the Lord bless your innocence," the Warder replies. "Do
you think you are the only pretty man in the world?"

Conceding the Warder's point, Shakespeare disconsolately reflects,
"Is it not a strange thing that we, *knowing all women are false*, should
be amazed to find our own particular *drab* no better than the rest?"
(142; emphasis added). After being told that the Earl of Pembroke had
visited the Dark Lady the night before, a reeling Shakespeare confronts
Queen Elizabeth as she comes on stage. Distracted with guilt over the
recent execution of Mary Queen of Scots, the sleepwalking Elizabeth is
a veritable twin sister of Lady Macbeth. "Out, damned spot," she
mutters (144). With Shakespeare repeating and copying down snippets
from *Macbeth* uttered by the Queen, Elizabeth becomes regally
enraged. "Fellow: do you dare mimic me to my face?" (146).

"Tis music," he replies, and we realize that the playwright is
suddenly lovesick. The self-professed "king of words" (146), operating
under "the power of immortal poesy" (147), makes ever stronger love
to Elizabeth, at last attempting to embrace her. "Unmeasured
impudence!" the Queen shouts. "On your life, take your hands from
me" (148). At this point, more than halfway through the action, the
Dark Lady "comes stooping along the terrace" and sees the two in an
embrace. Furious, she runs upon them and breaks the pair apart.
Doffing her cloak to reveal her identity, the outraged Elizabeth shouts,
"High treason!"

"Will: I am lost," cries the Dark Lady. "I have struck the Queen."

"Woman," Shakespeare retorts, "you have struck WILLIAM
SHAKESPEAR."

"And who," Elizabeth asks, "in the name of all the sluts and jades
and light-o'-loves and fly-by-nights that infest this palace of mine, may
William Shakespear be?"

A testy exchange between Shakespeare and Elizabeth over their
respective familial lineages follows. "John Shakespear," he says,
"married but once. Harry Tudor was married six times" (149).
Furthermore, he wonders, "How know you that King Harry was indeed
your father?" Elizabeth cuts him short, crying "Another word; and I
begin with mine own hands the work the hangman shall finish" (150).
But Will will say more. Finally Elizabeth, regaining her composure,
lamely reminds him that "there are things which be true, and yet not

seemly to be said (I will not say to a queen; for you will have it that I am none) but to a virgin."

The scurrilous player replies, "It is no fault of mine that you are a virgin, madam, albeit tis my misfortune." The Queen suddenly turns her attention to the Dark Lady, asking how she came to be involved with such a person. She explains, framing her comments as a warning to Elizabeth, that Shakespeare enchanted her with his language: "He will tie you down to anatomize your very soul: he will wring tears of blood from your humiliation; and then he will heal the wound with flatteries that no woman can resist" (151). Shakespeare denies that charge, "for how can I ever be content with this black-haired, black-eyed, black-avised devil again now that I have looked upon real beauty and real majesty?"

"He hath swore to me," the Dark Lady protests, "ten times over that the day shall come in England when *black* women, for all their foulness, shall be more thought on than fair ones" (151-52; emphasis added). Abruptly, the Dark Lady begs leave of the Queen and departs the stage, not to return. Shakespeare then launches his petition for royal support for a national theater, promising to write plays about capable and accomplished women if Elizabeth will help out. The drama ends with Elizabeth ordering the Warder to lock Shakespeare out, "for I shall scarce dare disrobe until the palace gates are between us" (156) and Shakespeare, unfazed to the end, asking her to "remember my theatre."

"That is my prayer to posterity," she says and the action mercifully concludes.

It is not surprising that "this trifle of a play," as Shaw called it, portraying Shakespeare as a lecherous plagiarist and Elizabeth as a guilt-ridden and possibly illegitimate monarch failed to stir the coals of Bardolatry in the hearts of Shaw's audience. At the end of his preface Shaw laments that his "appeal for a National Theatre as a monument to Shakespear failed to touch the very stupid people who cannot see that a National Theatre is worth having for the sake of the National Soul" (140). He concludes bitterly, asking, "Why was I born with such contemporaries? Why is Shakespear made ridiculous by such a posterity?" As I suggested earlier, Shaw's selection of the dark lady as the titular character of his play, nearly a decade after the Mary Fitton candidacy had been disproved to Shaw's stated satisfaction, when the question of the dark lady's identity enjoyed no particular currency, is itself interesting. It implies the gratuitous nature of Shaw's attraction to the semiotic value of the dark lady as it approaches the condition of otherness, an attraction underscored by the fact that as a figure from the lyric tradition enlisted in the effort to found a dramatic institution she seems miscast. But this attraction is attenuated by Shaw's situating his dark lady within a larger contradictory attitude toward the otherness of women in general, a waffling between disgust with and admiration of the gender itself. While early in the play we are told that "all women are false," we are later promised plays that feature uncompromised stories of skilled and devoted women. This promise is not to be judged, furthermore, without taking into account the context of Shakespeare's verbal abuse of the two women—Dark Lady and Queen—who represent encompassing extremes of the spectrum of class, and perhaps color, difference.

From this muddle of contradictory attitudes toward women, the dark lady emerges with her own uncertainties. There is, to begin with, an unmistakable ambivalence about exactly how dark Shaw's Dark Lady is. The degree of her somatic difference is both obscured and underscored by the darkened stage, the deliberate cloaking of identities, and by the brevity of stage time given to her. While these elements efface her physical characteristics, they also "darken" the play, infusing it with a deliberate indeterminacy that refuses to exclude possibilities, including the possibility of the Dark Lady's carrying what I have identified as a black value, with all the threat to racial and cultural purity that term implies.

At the same time, Shaw is at pains to emphasize her credibility. Even before the Dark Lady appears, his Shakespeare dismisses her as wholly promiscuous, a "drab," Pembroke's "trick." Underscoring her moral darkness, Shaw links this opprobrium to her physical coloring, later describing her as a "black-haired, black-eyed, black-avised devil." Yet her moral degeneracy is countered in the central scene of the play when she speaks for herself, as a woman deeply in love with and genuinely abused by Shakespeare. She strikes an unmitigated note of indignation born of moral superiority when she tells the Queen: "I am ashamed to my very soul that I have abased myself to love one that my father would not have deemed fit to hold up my stirrup—one that will talk to all the world about me—that will put my love and my shame into his plays and make me blush for myself there—that will write sonnets about me that no man of gentle strain would put his hands to" (152). These are hardly the sentiments of a sluttish drab.

It is as a woman more sinned against than sinning that the Dark Lady insists upon the ascendancy of black women. "He hath swore to me," she shouts, "ten times over that the day shall come in England when black women, for all their foulness, shall be thought more on than fair ones." Stripped of its specific reference to the Dark Lady, uttered before an audience that represented England's wealth and power, deeply rooted in the psychology of racial difference in a play devoted to a national cause, her comments acquire a powerful resonance. Subscribing nominally to a debunked case for a brown woman, Mary Fitton, Shaw presses instead a black value in the Dark Lady's final speech, which opposes "black women" to fair ones. It is a prophetic reminder to his audience of the destabilizing potential of the black presence he saw in the Sonnets and, perhaps, in his own time as well.

If Shaw's valuation of the Dark Lady tends finally toward blackness in *The Dark Lady of the Sonnets*, other commentators have explicitly attached a black value to her, arguing that she was a woman of African or West Indian descent. The black version of the dark lady began in 1861 with Wilhelm Jordan who, noting her wiry hair, her skill on the virginal, and her apparent infidelity, proposed that she was "a married woman from the West Indian colonies, of Creole descent with an admixture of African blood" (qtd. in Rollins 2: 243). In 1933 G. B. Harrison subscribed to the same black value and took the case a step further by identifying the dark lady as Lucy Negro of Clerkenwell (301), a proposition that elicited varying degrees of revulsion from some later investigators (see Rollins 2: 272). To Leslie Hotson, for example, the suggestion was preposterous. To Harrison, Hotson noted, belonged the credit of first suspecting that Lucy, the Abbess of Clerkenwell, was the model for Shakespeare's dark lady, "and also the discredit of believing Shakespeare's fair enslaver a blackamoor" (244). "Black Luce," he wrote, "was of course no more an ethiop than the Black Prince." Lucy Negro of Clerkenwell was in fact Lucy Morgan, who had been one of the Queen's gentlewomen during the 1570s and 1580s. For unknown reasons, she was dismissed from the Queen's service and later became the madam of a brothel in St. James Street. There she generously spread the pox and finally, having been deemed a "notorious and lewd woman," was committed to hard labor in Bridewell prison. Hotson believed that Lucy Morgan was the dark lady, even though she appears to have been neither dark-complexioned nor younger (in fact, four years older) than the poet, conditions quite at odds with the evidence of 130 and 138. Moreover, Hotson supplied no connection between Shakespeare and Morgan, no evidence that he knew this particular woman. Even her notoriety would seem to argue

against her candidacy, as Kenneth Muir pointed out, since the dark lady
is mistress rather than whore (156). In any case, Hotson's determined
effort to disprove Harrison's tentative attribution struck Schoenbaum as
plainly racist. "Better," he remarked of Hotson's argument, "that
Shakespeare should take up with a syphilitic brothel-keeper than share
his bed with a West Indian coquette" (232).

III

> I my selfe have seene an Ethiopian as blacke as a coal brought into
> England, who taking a faire English woman to wife, begat a sonne in
> all respects as blacke as the father was, although England were his
> native countrey, and an English woman his mother.
>
> —George Best, 1587[4]

Recent histories of the black experience in England have darkened by
contextualization Shakespeare's dark lady, shifting her value closer to
the threshold of blackness. Paul Edwards traces black people in the
British Isles back to Roman times and concludes that Africans were
present in significant numbers at the Scottish court by the early
sixteenth century when Dunbar's poem "Ane Blak Moir" appeared (19-
21). After John Hawkins initiated the English trade in African slaves in
1563, the population of Africans in Britain seems to have escalated. By
1596, their numbers were sufficient to provoke official concern and
reaction. In that year Elizabeth, "highly discontented" with "the great
numbers of Negars and Blackamoors . . . crept into this realm since the
troubles" with Spain, noted that black people "are fostered and relieved
here to the great annoyance of [my] own liege people that want relief
which those people consume," and also "that the most of them are
infidels, having no understanding of Christ or his Gospel." She ordered
"that the said kind of people should be with all speed avoided and
discharged out of this Her Majesty's dominions."[5] In 1601 she
commanded another deportation of blacks. But despite these attempts
to eradicate black people from England, their numbers, fueled by the
brisk slave trade, continued to rise. Late in the seventeenth century,
when the earliest substantial accounts of the black experience in
England begin to appear, the Royal African Company was clearing
5,000 slaves annually through English ports (Shyllon 8).

As George Best's remark indicates, miscegenational relationships were not unknown to the Elizabethans.[6] Historical circumstances thus doubtless played some part in shaping literary interest in interracial relationships, an interest that appears in Shakespeare's play-writing career both early (*Titus Andronicus*) and late (*Othello*). If to the list of plays that evince an interest in interracial desire we add the discussion of Rosalind's darkness in 4.3 of *Love's Labor's Lost,* noting its striking resemblance to the treatment of the dark lady of the Sonnets, and the less certain miscegenation of *Antony and Cleopatra,* then we have a widespread interest in interracial dynamics among major characters in the Shakespeare canon.[7]

Typically, aesthetic depictions of blackness, especially in the sonnet tradition, have been viewed in the context of the ancient tradition of praising the beauty of black women, originating in the maiden of the Song of Solomon who tells the daughters of Jerusalem, "I am black but comely" (1.5). While the inherent eroticism of the Song was effaced by commentaries allegorizing the bride as the Church and the bridegroom as Christ, and while the tradition of praise that grew from the Song tended to lighten the maiden's darkness as a means of incorporating her difference within a discourse of likeness,[8] these strategies did not succeed in eliminating either the erotic nature of the praise of black woman or her fundamental difference. Indeed, by the mid-seventeenth century there was a full-fledged cult of lyric poetry praising black beauty in explicit terms. As Kim Hall notes, poems in this tradition, twenty-six of which she anthologizes as an appendix to her *Things of Darkness: Economies of Race and Gender in Early Modern England,* become increasingly eroticized and racialized (117). Thus George Herbert's "A Negress Courts Cestus, a Man of a Different Colour" depicts an uncontaminated racial other in the figure of the female speaker:

> What if my face be black? O Cestus, hear!
> Such colour Night brings, which yet Love holds dear.
> You see a Trav'ller has a sunburnt face:
> And I, who pine for thee, a long road trace.
> If earth be black, who shall despise the ground?
> Shut your eyes, and lo, all black is found;
> Or ope, a shadow-casting form you see;
> This be my loving post to fill for thee.
> Seeing my face is smoke, what fire has burn'd

> Within my silent bosom, by thee spurn'd!
> Hard-hearted man, dost still my love refuse?
> Lo, Grief's prophetic hue my cheek imbues.

Herbert's poem, which probably inaugurated the vogue, illustrates that poems praising black beauty in the seventeenth century often did not employ the strategy of lightening the dark lady, washing the Ethiope white, since to do so would be to eliminate her difference, a difference that is essential to the desire manifested in these poems. Rather, "the specificity and abundance" of the common tropes of these poems— associating blackness with the earth, with night and shadows, with eye closing—suggest to Hall "a certain concreteness to blackness that is not found in the sonnet [tradition]" (119). But even poems that employ the typical iconography of Petrarchism, and thus provide a closer link to Shakespeare and the sonnet tradition, present a similarly concretized black female presence. Interracial eroticism is unabashedly celebrated in Eldred Revett's "One Enamour'd on a Black-Moor":

> What strange love doth me invade,
> Whose fires must *cool* in that *dark shade*! (1-2; emphasis in original)

The speaker confronts his black lover asleep and wonders,

> How did my passion find her out,
> That is with *Curtains drawn about*?
> (And though her eyes do cent'nell keep)
> She is all over else asleep. (7-10; emphasis in original)

Stranded in a voyeuristic scene reminiscent of the Second Song of Sidney's *Astrophil and Stella,* the speaker, transfixed by the sight of his reposing lover, enabled by her sleeping to gaze on her at length and at will, remarks that

> This beauty puts us from the part
> We have all tamely *got by hart,*
> Of roses here there Lillies grow,
> Of Saphire, Corall, Hills of snow
> These rivulets are *all ingrost*
> And all in on[e] *Black Ocean lost.* (21-26 ; emphasis in original)

Figuring her contrary beauty as overwhelming the shopworn language of Petrarchism, "This beauty puts us from the part / We have all tamely *got by hart*" (21-22), Revett formulates her blackness as an unknown universe of radical cultural, sexual, and racial difference.[9] She is not only his opposite, but the antithesis of poeticized white beauty he knows from the sonnet tradition as well. She is a vast, unknown, and dangerous region—prefiguring the image of Africa as the heart of darkness—where a man might be lost and destroyed, in which the traditional aesthetics of sonneteering, which fetishized the fair mistress, are subsumed. Roses, lilies, sapphire, coral, hills of snow, these ornaments of sonnet dismembering, "are *all ingrost* / And all in on[e] *Black Ocean lost.*"

As the poem develops, Revett's "contrary swan" is subjected to the same severe anatomizing that entertains Donne in his "Elegy 19: To His Mistress Going to Bed." The speaker's gaze is fixed upon her dark breasts "not as in the *milkie* hue / . . . *broke into Raw streaks of blew*" (68-69), but rather as expressions of elemental beauty, in accord with the treatment of the dark lady in Shakespeare's 130, where the mistress "when she walks treads upon the ground" (12). Revett sees his lover's bosom as a "*Double-headed* Hill":

> Whose tops shade one another still;
> Between them lyes that spicy Nest,
> That the last Phoenix scorch'd and blest[.]
>
> (73-75; emphasis in original)

Compared to the paper women of the sonnet tradition, Revett's dark lady is created from matter rather than art. She is the presence that casts the shadow, not the absent-presence of the shadow itself:

> What fall's [*sic*] from her is rather made
> Her own (just) picture, than her shade:
> And where she walks the Sun doth hold
> Her pourtrai'd in a frame of gold. (77-80)

It is into a similar black ocean, an implacable elemental reality contradicting and subsuming the fair anatomizing of Petrarchism, that Shakespeare plunges at sonnet 127. Images related to drowning—falling into, going under—frequently occur in the final movement of Shakespeare's sequence, especially in poems marked by urgent sexual experience. In 129 the speaker, trapped in the torturous, destabilizing, and self-condemnatory cycle of arousal and satisfaction, likened to the inescapable complex of time itself ("had, having and in quest to have, extreme" (10)), disintegrates into madness, desire consuming him as if it were "a swallowed bait / On purpose laid to make the taker mad" (7-8); and still "none knows well / To shun the heav'n that leads men to this hell" (13-14). Similarly, in 135, where the proliferation of "W/wills" suggests the splintering of subjectivity,[10] the mistress's sexuality—her "will"—is figured as "large and spacious" (5). She is like the "sea" which

> all water, yet receives rain still,
> And in abundance addeth to [her] store;
> So thou being rich in will add to thy will
> One will of mine, to make thy large will more. (9-12)

The speaker plunges irresistibly into his mistress's dark abyss in the next poem which, again displaying the fragmentation of "W/will," puns on the multiple senses of "full" and "fill": "Will will fulfill the treasure of thy love, / Ay, fill it full with wills, and my will one" (136.5-6). Riding unsteadily on the scopic surface in 137, the poet's eyes, "corrupt by over partial looks" (5), are "anchored in the bay where all men ride" (6), this "wide world's common place" (9). In 144, the fair young man, his "better angel" (3), has been lost "in another's hell" (12), sunk into her obliterating sexuality, and the speaker can only wait and hope that he will return to the surface:

> Yet this shall I ne'er know, but live in doubt,
> Till my bad angel fire my good one out. (13-14)

The sequence ends with sonnets 153 and 154, really one poem doubled, that characterize the mistress as a body of water. This time she is a fountain in which Cupid's/the speaker's "brand new-fired" (153.9) is sunk (see Figure 6 in this volume). The suggestion that the speaker seeks a cure for venereal disease in his lover's body underscores the urgent but futile desire to recover his physical and emotional well-being.[11] The speaker,

> sick withal the help of bath desired
> And thither hied, a sad distempered guest.

> But found no cure; the bath for my help lies
> Where Cupid got new fire—my mistress' eyes. (153.11-14)

In 154, the dark lady is similarly a "cool well" (9) promising remedy "for men diseased" (12):

> But I, my mistress' thrall,
> Came there for cure, and this by that I prove
> Love's fire heats water, water cools not love. (12-14)

Like Revett, Shakespeare confronts his lady's darkness head on and drowns in it. The dynamic of these final poems relies upon the fact that as a literary sign she remains the implacable presence of semiotic difference that is manifestly associated with racial and cultural difference, a "black ocean" that engrosses the speaker.

IV

I want to conclude by discussing a contrary pattern of imagery that suggests not the speaker's loss in a black ocean but rather the mistress's captivity within a system that robs her of identity and freedom, a system perhaps alluded to in 127.7: "Sweet beauty hath no name, no holy bower." My discussion begins with the vexed question of the status of black people in England during Elizabeth's reign. Were they slaves or free people? While many black people came to England as free people, most were not. Folarin Shyllon believes that in the mid-sixteenth century "a number of African slaves"—he doesn't estimate how many—"were imported into England and were probably disposed of by private arrangement" (6). Yet they were not unambiguously objects of ownership. In 1569, common law had deemed that "England was too pure an air for Slaves to breathe in" (qtd. in Shyllon 17). Though resolved in the seventeenth century when slavery became an institution in England, the issue was terribly problematic in 1569. Did the law hold that slavery would be illegal in England, thus inviting an influx of slaves seeking freedom there? or did it indicate merely that slaves must not be brought into the country?

The uncertainty over the status of slaves brought into England was complicated by the doctrine, widely supported by the clergy, that upon baptism a slave became free. Slaves were understandably quick to exploit this option, petitioning local ministers for the sacrament of baptism and the conferral of a Christian name.[12] Because many clergymen took seriously their responsibility to baptize all nations, there arose a deep division between the clergy and the slave-owning laity. One side would baptize, christen, and set free a people who were thought by the other side to be property. Masters, for their part, responded to this flight of slaves into the sanctuary of the Church by forbidding them, according to Shyllon, not only "to go through the ritual of baptism, but even prohibit[ing] any form of rudimentary Christian education being given to them" (18). In 1685 Morgan Godwyn supplied examples of such conduct, one involving a slave kept near Bristol who sought baptism from the parish minister. This minister, finding the candidate fit, nevertheless delayed the service long enough for the slave's owner to hear of the plan. Enraged, the owner confronted the minister with "the insolent inquiry, *Whether he would baptize his Horse?*" The owner subsequently chained his man "under the table among his dogs, and there continu[ed] him in that double bondage for sometime" (qtd. in Shyllon 18).

Baptism provides a link with the water imagery I discussed above, of course, but with an inversion. In poems by Revett and Richard Crashaw, "Aethopians" emerge from the waters of baptism with an inner purity shining visibly in dark skin. Revett's candidate is

> *New-risen* from the *Chrystal bed*,
>   All in *Pearl's aparalled*;
> What of *night's* about his skin,
> Skreens, like that too, *Day within*. (9-12; emphasis in original)

Similarly, in Crashaw's poem immersion succeeds in "wash[ing] an Ethiope" (2), in the sense of conferring upon him spiritual purity:

> He's washt, his gloomy skin a peacefull shade
>   For his white soule is made:
> And now, I doubt not, the Eternall Dove,
>   A black-fac'd house will love. (3-6)

I am suggesting that behind the commonplace Petrarchism of 127.7—"Sweet beauty hath no name, no holy bower"—we might detect perhaps if not Shakespeare's mistress herself then the liminal sign of a slave woman who, unbaptized, was also unnamed. The Chrysostom of St. John (Antioch, A.D. 390) explicitly interprets immersion as rescuing the slave from slavery: celebrants are to "embrace" communicants "as they rise from the waters . . . [and] salute them, kiss them, rejoice with them, congratulate them that they, who before had been slaves and prisoners, are now become free men, and sons, and called to the royal table" (Whitaker 33). The Reformed Church understood the liturgy to require the bestowing of a specifically Christian name in the act of baptism. In the Genevan Psalter (1542), according to Old, Calvin interpreted "*on impose le nom a l'enfant*" to mean that un-Christian names were forbidden. "For Calvin," Old writes, "it was not only a matter of giving a name to a child at baptism, but also a matter of giving a Christian name to the child" (256). Thus certain names were proscribed.[13] The preponderance of classical names assumed by or given to black men during the age—Pompey and Scipio were common—may be a trace of resistance, perhaps coerced, to this opportunity to undergo conversion. If so, the namelessness of the dark lady is especially significant, since identifying her has so far proven impossible. In her black value, the dark lady is anonymity itself.

What we might observe in 127.7, then, is a shadow discourse on the circumstances of black people at the time of the sequence, many of whom were slaves who had a means of escaping that terrible yoke. The most recent explications of the verse certainly do not exclude a reading which perhaps they should include. "Hath no name" Stephen Booth glosses as lacking (1) a label or appellation; (2) fame, renown or honor; (3) lineage; or (4) good name or reputation. Booth does not consider that "Hath no name" might apply in a literal sense, though it would seem almost perverse to disallow the self-evident sense of the statement. His reading of "no holy bower" as no "sacrosanct dwelling place" similarly admits a possible reference to the offices of the Church (435-36). G. Blakemore Evans, editor of the New Cambridge Shakespeare edition of the Sonnets, reads in 127.7 "no good repute, no sacred abode or shrine (in which beauty is properly worshipped)" (244). Again, this gloss doesn't exclude, and perhaps ought to include, the obvious as one possible interpretation of the line. Other poems support this suggestion. In 131 the speaker is a victim of his mistress's tyranny, a Petrarchan commonplace. But in 133.4 the fair young man is a "slave to slavery," and in 133.9 the poet asks to be imprisoned in his lady's "steel bosom's ward"; in 133.12 that ward is his "jail." In 141.12 he is a "slave and vassal wretch to her." In the context of physical details of the dark lady—her brown breasts, wiry hair, unblushing cheeks, raven eyes—my reading of 127.7 suggests that in the commonplace imagery of freedom and imprisonment, tyranny and flight, inclusion and isolation, and slavery and liberation of the final movement of his sonnet cycle Shakespeare exploits a discourse of slavery in late Elizabethan England, a discourse that presents the poet-speaker and his fair accomplice, at least at the level of imagery, as slaves of a slave.[14]

In 1994 Margreta de Grazia wrote that "Tradition has ever been slower to entertain the possibility that these poems express desire for a black woman rather than desire for a boy" (48). She might better have written "as well as" for "rather than," but her point is nevertheless compelling. Even Hall, whose work on aesthetic, political, and cultural figurations of the African in English culture is seminal, devotes more attention to Sidney's Stella as a dark lady than to Shakespeare's dark lady. As we approach millennium's end, the dark lady is darker than ever; yet we are still extremely cautious, as de Grazia suggests, about approaching her not only as a sign of womanness, but also of color.

NOTES

1. All citations of the Sonnets are from the New Cambridge Shakespeare edition, ed. G. Blakemore Evans.

2. For a survey of the problems involved in using the terms "black" and "blackness" in studies of early modern England, as well as a justification for using them, see Hall 6-8. My use of these terms is considerably more restricted than Hall's, since I use them to designate semiotic phenomena, in keeping with Saussure's insistence that language consists only in difference.

3. Rowse's work was not entirely futile. He had stumbled upon the author of *Salve Deus Rex Judaeorum.* "Thus, we have looked for a Dark Lady," writes Schoenbaum, whose survey of candidates for the dark lady I have followed, "and instead we find a lady poet. We seek verifiable truth, and settle for the consolations of art" (238).

4. Quoted in Hakluyt's *Principal Navigations* 5: 180.

5. Elizabeth's 1596 order is reproduced in Jones 18-20.

6. Shyllon remarks that "Black men marrying white women was and is the root of Anglo-Saxon racism" (3). See also Newman 143-62; and Hall 11-12.

7. See Evans's comments on the connections between *Love's Labor's Lost* and sonnet 127 (243).

8. For a discussion of the effacement of the maiden's darkness in the Song of Solomon, see Hall 106-16.

9. Cf. Hall's comment that "just as poets begin to depict Petrarchism as an empty and devalued currency, they turn to the language of blackness, which becomes an unexplored and endlessly fertile space for poetic invention" (117).

10. See Joel Fineman's analysis of the complex nature of this disruption (159-78). See also Howard Felperin's deconstructive reading of the dark lady as "an object as dark and different as writing itself" (88).

11. Schoenbaum notes that this imagery suggests venereal disease (225-26).

12. While there is some disagreement among liturgical scholars over just how intimately the rite of baptism and the conferral of names were related (see Fisher, Appendix II, 149-57), the Reformed Church believed them to be inseparable: the act of baptizing a child was accompanied by the naming of the child. Hughes Oliphant Old notes that Abram became Abraham at the moment of circumcision (Genesis 17), and that John the Baptist and Jesus were also named in connection with the rite of circumcision (Luke 1: 59 and 2: 21). "As the Reformers saw it," Old continues, "giving the child his or her own name was surely one of those ancient Christian customs which was quite clearly according to scripture" (256).

13. Among the names Calvin prohibited were Claude, Suaire, and Mama (idolatry); Caspar, Balthazar, and Melchior (connection with superstition); Baptiste, Evangeliste, and Angel (names of offices or ministries). For obvious reasons Emanuel and Jesus were proscribed, as were the names of feast days. Old Testament names were favored at Geneva (Old 256 n. 15).

14. This suggestion is compromised by sonnet 128, which portrays the beloved playing the virginal. While many black people in England were musicians, it is a skill associated rather with court life than the circumstances of slaves. However, noting the absence of gendered pronouns in 128, Heather Dubrow in an essay reprinted in this volume argues that this poem is just as likely a misplaced sonnet written about the fair young man. This would accord with de Grazia's reading (also reprinted in this volume) of the sonnets to the dark lady as preempting "pederasty" by "gynerasty," a preemption that destroys the social superiority of the fair young man: "It is Shakespeare's gynerastic longings for a black mistress that are perverse and menacing, precisely because they threaten to raze the very [class] distinctions his poems to the fair boy strain to preserve" (48).

WORKS CITED

Booth, Stephen, ed. *Shakespeare's Sonnets*. New Haven: Yale UP, 1977.
Crashaw, Richard. *Steps to the Temple*. Menston: Scolar, 1970.

de Grazia, Margreta. "The Scandal of Shakespeare's Sonnets." *Shakespeare Survey* 46 (1994): 35-49.

Dubrow, Heather. "'Incertainties now crown themselves assur'd': The Politics of Plotting Shakespeare's Sonnets." *Shakespeare Quarterly* 47 (1996): 291-305.

Edwards, Paul. "The Early African Presence in the British Isles." *Essays on the History of Blacks in Britain from Roman Times to the Mid-Twentieth Century.* Ed. Jagdish S. Gundara and Ian Duffield. Aldershot: Avebury, 1992. 9-29.

Evans, G. Blakemore, ed. *The Sonnets.* The New Cambridge Shakespeare. Cambridge: Cambridge UP, 1996.

Felperin, Howard. "The Dark Lady Identified, or What Deconstruction Can Do for Shakespeare's Sonnets." *Shakespeare and Deconstruction.* Ed. G. Douglas Atkins and David Bergeron. New York: Lang, 1988. 69-93.

Fineman, Joel. *Shakespeare's Perjured Eye: The Invention of Poetic Subjectivity in the Sonnets.* Berkeley: U of California P, 1986.

Fisher, J. D. C. *Christian Initiation: Baptism in the Medieval West: A Study of the Disintegration of the Primitive Rite of Initiation.* London: S. P. C. K., 1965.

Hakluyt, Richard. *Principal Navigations . . . of the English Nation.* 8 vols. London: Dent, 1927.

Hall, Kim F. *Things of Darkness: Economies of Race and Gender in Early Modern England.* Ithaca: Cornell UP, 1995.

Harrison, G. B. *Shakespeare under Elizabeth.* New York: Knopf, 1933.

Herbert, George. *The Complete Works in Verse and Prose of George Herbert.* Ed. Alexander Grosart. 3 vols. London, 1874.

Hotson, Leslie. *Mr. W. H.* New York: Knopf, 1964.

Jones, Eldred D. *The Elizabethan Image of Africa.* Washington: Folger Library, 1971.

Marder, Louis. "The 'Dark Lady': Demise of a Theory." *Shakespeare Newsletter* (May 1973): 24.

Muir, Kenneth. *Shakespeare's Sonnets.* London: Allen and Unwin, 1979.

Newdigate-Newdegate, Lady. *Gossip from the Muniment Room.* London: David Nutt, 1897.

Newman, Karen. "'And wash the Ethiop white': Femininity and the Monstrous in *Othello*." *Shakespeare Reproduced: The Text in History and Ideology.* Ed. Jean E. Howard and Marion F. O'Connor. New York: Methuen, 1987. 143-62.

Old, Hughes Oliphant. *The Shaping of the Reformed Baptismal Rite in the Sixteenth Century.* Grand Rapids: Eerdmans, 1992.

Revett, Eldred. *Selected Poems Humane and Divine*. Ed. Donald M. Friedman. Liverpool: Liverpool UP, 1966.

Rollins, Hyder Edward, ed. *A New Variorum Edition of Shakespeare: The Sonnets*. 2 vols. Philadelphia: Lippincott, 1944.

Rowse, A. L. *Discovering Shakespeare: A Chapter in Literary History*. London: Weidenfeld and Nicolson, 1989.

——. *Shakespeare's Sonnets: The Problems Solved*. 2nd ed. New York: Harper, 1973.

——. *Simon Forman: Sex and Society in Shakespeare's Age*. London: Weidenfeld and Nicolson, 1974.

Schoenbaum, Samuel. "Shakespeare's Dark Lady: A Question of Identity." *Shakespeare's Styles: Essays in Honour of Kenneth Muir*. Ed. Philip Edwards, Inga-Stina Ewbank, and G. K. Hunter. Cambridge: Cambridge UP, 1980. 221-39.

Shaw, George Bernard. *Misalliance, The Dark Lady of the Sonnets, and Fanny's First Play, with a Treatise on Parents and Children*. New York: Brentano's, 1930.

Shyllon, Folarin. *Black People in Britain 1555-1833*. London, Oxford UP, 1977.

Tyler, Thomas. *The Herbert-Fitton Theory of Shakespeare's Sonnets: A Reply*. London: David Nutt, 1898.

——, ed. *Shakespeare's Sonnets*. London: David Nutt, 1890.

Whitaker, E. C. *Documents of the Baptismal Liturgy*. London: S. P. C. K., 1960.

The Sonnets on Trial
Reconsidering *The Portrait of Mr. W. H.*

Rebecca Laroche

It should be no mystery why an essay on Oscar Wilde is included in a collection on Shakespeare's Sonnets. First, Oscar Wilde's *The Portrait of Mr. W. H.* (1889) charts and negotiates the currents eddying around Shakespeare and the Sonnets in the late nineteenth century. Defying genre categories, Wilde's fictional essay or analytical novella interrogates Edward Dowden's theory, which seeks to integrate Shakespeare's life and art, and it examines and dismantles the ever-continuing W. H. debates, which sought to name the sequence's dedicatee/addressee (see Figure 3 in this volume).[1] Like the library scene in *Ulysses* after it, *Mr. W. H.* makes "academic questions" about Shakespeare's life and works into literature. But beyond its Victorian context, it provides an allegory for literary relations so compelling that its presence is still felt in much current criticism on the Sonnets.

Indeed, one of the most forceful readings of the past twenty years, Joel Fineman's *Shakespeare's Perjured Eye*, declares *Mr. W. H.* "the only genuinely literary criticism that Shakespeare's sonnets have ever received" (28). The praise continues as Fineman notes the parallels between the Sonnets and the novella, writing that "like Shakespeare's sonnets, it too is caught up in the literary problematic that derives from the effort to imagine a visible language . . . in which there would be no difference between the *imago* of presentation (the 'Portrait') and the *sign* of representation ('W. H.')" (28). In this likeness between the Sonnets and *Mr. W. H.*, Fineman recognizes the origins of his own theory. Perhaps as a result of this adulation, Fineman's analysis proves to be the most Wildean of all current criticism. Fineman is no anomaly, however; Wilde inhabits the pages of much turn-of-the-millennium scholarship.

Re-engaging the W. H. debates and in effect analyzing an important context for Wilde's *Mr. W. H.*, Donald Foster's "Master W. H., R.I.P." assesses various lines of argument for the identity of the Sonnets' dedicatee. Was it Thorpe's doing? Is it a misprint? Does it refer to a patron? A fellow actor? But Foster's, like many summaries of the debate, adds Wilde's to the pool of other theories. This reaction is much too literal a reading of the fictional essay, however, and omits the possibility that Wilde may be commenting on the nature of the debate itself rather than participating in it. In effect, Wilde's essay ends in much the same way as Foster's own. Both return to the Sonnets their mystery or—as Foster's more post-modernist argot determines—allow the Sonnets to "exist" as a "symbolic structure in search of a thing signified" (52).

Similarly providing a survey of nineteenth-century sonnet criticism, Peter Stallybrass analyzes the reception history of the Sonnets and maps the appearances of the "specter of sodomy" within these given texts (98; reprinted in this volume). Beginning with the Malone-Steevens debates on the Sonnets (where Margreta de Grazia left off), Stallybrass discusses how the struggle to address sexuality in the Sonnets registers the discursive "formation" of "normative" sexual practices. His analysis ends with the case of Oscar Wilde as a critical moment in the Sonnets' reception history and in this discursive formation. Stallybrass's useful timeline raises the question of whether *Mr. W. H.* fits into this discourse as easily as the reactions to it; whether, that is, its literary evasiveness circumvents many of the categories preceding it. Wilde's is a fictional literary theory, which—as fiction—both comments on and engages with the texts Stallybrass surveys. Its status as fiction makes *Mr. W. H.* a pre-eminent work of modern criticism as well as a consummate Victorian creation.

In his own survey of reactions to the "expressions of homoeroticism" in Shakespeare's poetry, Joseph Pequigney sees Wilde as an "ancestor" of readers willing to see such expressions, in effect putting his project, which interprets the sequence as voicing a physical consummation of male-male passion, in line with Wilde's essay (79). But he is not the first or the last to claim a Wildean inheritance. The advent of queer theory has found several scholars looking at both Wildean writings and Shakespearean verse. Alan Sinfield's theory of dissident reading uses a partly Wildean lens to re-examine canonical Shakespearean texts. Gregory Bredbeck—since his *Sodomy and Interpretation*, which includes an important chapter on Shakespeare's Sonnets—has been looking at the role of Wilde's aestheticism in his "examination of the historicity of Camp as it has been perceived as a gay male political strategy," thus combining the Renaissance and Wilde in one career ("Narcissus" 52). We can add to this list Joel Fineman's work on the Sonnets and on Wilde and, of course, the crucial work of Eve Kosofsky Sedgwick.

Interestingly, Sedgwick does not consider *Mr. W. H.* at any great length in her chapter on Wilde in *Epistemology of the Closet* (1991), though *Mr. W. H.*, like *The Picture of Dorian Gray* and much Wildean drama, involves the mysteries, secrets, and surfaces she discusses. Nor does Wilde's essay receive much examination in her work on Shakespeare's Sonnets in the earlier *Between Men* (1985). The brief mention in her earlier work, however, bears close examination:

> Since the nineteenth century it has been easiest to read the Sonnets as a novel, but the novel had made the claim that its main characters were knowable. Thus Oscar Wilde feels free to extend his authoritative insight into the speaker, toward the lady, as well, as if they were knowable in the same way[.] (36)

By reading the Sonnets, as well as *Mr. W. H.*, "as a novel," Sedgwick can include her remarkable reading of the Sonnets—a reading Jonathan Goldberg calls "the only satisfying reading of the sonnets" (23)— among her readings of novels. But in doing so, Sedgwick occludes *Mr. W. H.*'s status as fictionalized *criticism*. It is not Wilde who projects himself into the desires of the dark lady but rather Wilde's *narrator*. I will be discussing this projection later in this chapter and hope to show how Wilde's fictional frame affords him a stance more anticipatory of Sedgwick's own.

Finally, an analysis of Wilde's narrative will begin to help us answer some of the questions raised in Heather Dubrow's "The Politics of Plotting Shakespeare's Sonnets," which voices concerns about "narratives of Fall and apocalypse . . . in which a seemingly fair dark snake enters the garden where the poet and Friend had been happily tending the roses" (304; also included in this volume). Wilde's narrator may be one of the first of these apocalyptic critics, as he speaks of "the dark woman who, like a shadow or thing of evil omen, came across Shakespeare's great romance, and for a season stood between him and Willie Hughes" (1184). But Wilde's *Mr. W. H.* presents an interesting test case for the "politics of plotting" in that Wilde, who was forced onto the sociopolitical stage, in the end argues for sustaining the narratability of the Sonnets as long as those narratives are recognized as fictions that are never fixed.

This essay examines how Wilde negotiates his own relation to literary history through the Sonnets of Shakespeare. For Wilde, the Shakespearean sonnet serves as the "key" used for opening (not locking) literary relations, and by means of this key, he is able to articulate his own personal relation to literary history. But in other contexts a key may also be a code-breaker, and the same key can be used to confine the reader. As Wilde writes in *The Picture of Dorian Gray*, "from a label there is no escape" (147). That is why *Portrait* is a fiction—as slippery as the Sonnets themselves—about privilege and its undoing, about identification and its dismantling, about narrative fixing and unfixing. In effect, Wilde creates an allegory for the reader's relationship to the poet that develops out of the act of reading Shakespeare's Sonnets. In this allegory, the lover-poet's desire to gain access to and to capture the beloved's heart transmutes into the work of the critic, looking for the "key"—in this case a biographical key—to the private history behind the text.[2]

"THE ONLY PERFECT KEY TO SHAKESPEARE'S SONNETS": THE WILLIE HUGHES THEORY

The Portrait of Mr. W. H. describes a closed circle of critics—Cyril Graham and Erskine and their young follower, the narrator—critics who "uncover" the identity of Shakespeare's young man, the Mr. W. H. of the Sonnets' dedication, as one Willie Hughes, boy actor. Cyril Graham, a student at Trinity, divulges this theory to Erskine, his college fellow, by stating that "we . . . are almost afraid to turn the *key* that unlocks the mystery of the poet's heart" (1155; emphasis added). At first, Erskine is taken by the theory; however, finding no external evidence to substantiate it, he begins to lose faith. With Erskine unconvinced of Willie Hughes's existence, Graham commissions a painting of this lovely boy actor and presents it as an authentic "portrait of Mr. W. H." When the forgery is exposed, Graham kills himself, only after telling Erskine that it is up to him "to present it [the theory] to the world, and to unlock the secret of Shakespeare's heart" (1160). Years later, upon hearing the theory and the story behind it from the non-believer Erskine, the narrator is convinced that it is "the only perfect key to Shakespeare's Sonnets" (1160) and "the only key to the greatest mystery of modern literature" (1161). This key is "perfect" because it is found within the text itself—thus keeping the text untainted by outside forces—and, following Edward Dowden's biographical criticism, it perfectly reveals how the Sonnets were not tangential to but rather "essential to Shakespeare's perfection as an artist" (1162) by uncovering the name and the "profession," boy actor, of the beloved (1163).

What most distinguishes this complex of keys, locks, and mysteries in *Mr. W. H.* from a similar complex in *The Picture of Dorian Gray*, in which Dorian keeps the secrets of his degenerating soul locked up in an attic room, is a specific poetic model, the "source" considered here.[3] This model is an often quoted image from Wordsworth's poem "Scorn Not the Sonnet" (noted in Schroeder 8-9). Wordsworth's opening lines—"Scorn not the Sonnet; Critic, you have frowned, / Mindless of its just honours; with this key / Shakspeare unlocked his heart" (1-3)—state that Shakespeare's Sonnets provide us with a most intimate autobiography, the history of the heart. The poem continues by stating the function of the sonnet for Petrarch, Tasso, Camoëns, Dante, Spenser, and Milton—none of whom, needless to say, is mentioned in Wilde's essay. In effect, whereas Wordsworth ends by extolling Milton, Wilde takes Shakespeare's Sonnets out of their position in Wordsworth's sonnet history, thus claiming his own personal example.

When we compare Wordsworth's idea of the key that is a Shakespearean sonnet to Wilde's of the key that is the theory explaining Shakespeare's Sonnets, we see how Wilde claims agency for the reader where Wordsworth does not. In Wordsworth's sonnet, it had been Shakespeare who "unlocked" his heart through the Sonnets. But Wilde's scholar-readers "are almost afraid to turn the key that unlocks the mystery of the poet's heart." Wilde recognizes that Shakespeare's heart has retained its "riddle" (Hubler); most notably, the name of the beloved remains a mystery, despite sonnet 81's claim that "your name from hence immortal life shall have," a line which G. Blakemore Evans in his edition of the Sonnets sums up as "supremely ironic" (187).[4] Although Wilde's narrator preserves the Wordsworthian possibility of the key, its discovery is not the result of simple reading, the experience of the "common" reader, but rather of rigorous rereading. According to Cyril Graham, those "in-the-know"—literary scholars and other invested readers—can find the key in the text. Within the context of the crowded W. H. debates, each reader seeks the distinction of having proof. Wilde's "secret circle" of readers (Danson, "Unspoken Name of Love" 989) believe themselves to have discovered the *only* key to the Sonnets, and, in holding that key, they have thus distinguished themselves from readers before them.

This sense of holding the key as a type of privilege—a sense not found in Wordsworth's "With this key Shakespeare unlocked his heart"—can be located in Shakespeare's Sonnets themselves. Several of the sonnets figure the heart as a locked enclosure, emphasizing both the poet's desire to keep the beloved for himself and the mystery of the writer's persona. Shakespeare presents this figure most explicitly in sonnet 46:

> Mine eye and heart are at mortal war,
> How to divide the conquest of thy sight:
> Mine eye my heart thy picture's sight would bar,
> My heart mine eye the freedom of that right.
> My heart doth plead that thou in him dost lie
> (A closet never pierced with crystal eyes),
> But the defendant doth that plea deny,
> And says in him thy fair appearance lies. (1-8)[5]

This image of the "closet never pierced with crystal eyes" represents the physical impenetrability of the poet's "inward part" and in so doing registers a desire in both poet and reader to penetrate through exteriors and personae (cf. Ferry 46). On one level, those "crystal eyes" may be read as the poet's, whose heart debates with his eyes for privileged access to the image of the beloved. The eyes can see the portrait of the young man—a portrait present, if forged, in Wilde's essay—but cannot see the idealized image of the beloved's soul held by the heart. In part about privilege (and by what means that privilege may be gained) the poem debates which "part"—the inward or outward—gives the lover the truest relation to the beloved. Upon closer examination, we discover that, on another level, those "crystal eyes" from line 6 might also belong to outsiders. A third person may *see* the beloved, argues the heart, but no one—save the poet—has access to the ideal image held within his breast. The "inward" part of the beloved thus protected, the poet maintains his privilege.

In composing the Sonnets, however, the poet arguably grants admission to this idealized form. Although the beloved is not actually "pictured" within the Sonnets, the Sonnets suggest the beloved's perfections. The sight of these perfections, however, may simply be a fantasy of the reader, who, not having physical access to the actual poet, reads the Sonnets for some hint of the "inward part"—the articulation of which, according to Anne Ferry, is a paradoxical construction—of both lover and beloved.

This trope of enclosure continues in the sequence, as the sense of overprotective hoarding intensifies. In sonnet 48, the lover-poet compares the beloved to jewels "thrust" under "truest bars" and writes that "Thee have I not locked up in any chest, / Save where thou art not, though I feel thou art, / Within the gentle closure of my breast" (9-11). Sonnet 52, in making the poet-lover into a kind of miser, removes the sonnet "economy" from all other economies. The beloved's image is again a type of "up-locked treasure" to which the poet holds the "blessed key" (2, 1). He visits his hoard only rarely so as not to "blunt" his "seldom pleasure" (4). Importantly, these images all occur while the lover and beloved are separate and the beloved is "left the prey of every vulgar thief" (48.8). The trope of enclosure then recurs in the dark woman sonnets, as the poet wishes to "enclose" his "land." In sonnet 137, though his "heart think[s]" her "a several plot," it knows the beloved to be the "wide world's common place" (9, 10). In the end, the poet cannot regulate access to the beloveds when they are "not locked up in any chest."

Through the permutations of this trope of enclosure found in Shakespeare's Sonnets, highlighted by Wordsworth in his "Scorn Not the Sonnet," and further developed by Wilde himself in *The Portrait of Mr. W. H.*, we can see how the evasiveness of language alternately transfers poetic privilege to the readers and keeps it from them. Secrets are locked and unlocked, exposed and obscured, imparted and taken away. First the poet overtly states the impenetrability of his heart, where he imagines he and his beloved are one. He states this impenetrability, however, through confessional verse. According to Wordsworth, the reader of this verse may then assume that the publication of the Sonnets unlocks the poet's heart. With Wilde's text, however, we discover that the object of the poet's love (the occupant of his heart) does indeed remain a mystery. Unearthing the key to this mystery becomes the obsession of Wilde's literary scholar. With both beloved and poet dead and no existing evidence—that is, no portrait—to prove who has the correct answer, the critic holds mere words. In the end, Wilde's narrator must cede his inability to maintain a privileged relationship to the poet simply through the text and admit "that Shakespeare's heart is still to us a closet never pierced with crystal eyes" (1199).[6]

"I HAD LIVED IT ALL": IDENTIFYING WITH THE BARD

Wilde's narrator is destined to become disillusioned as he takes his theory, the "key," "opens" the sonnet's closed form, and writes a story. This narrative, which is drawn from poetry, is also dramatic in its five-part structure. The narrative reaches a climax when by degrees—as if embodying Wilde's assertion that "the highest, as the lowest, form of criticism is a mode of autobiography" (17)—it converges with the narrator's own story. At first the narrator merely effects a kind of textual identification with Shakespeare as he speaks with Shakespeare's "voice" from the Sonnets. For example, the narrator accounts for the procreation sonnets in the Willie Hughes theory by positing that they are a request by the dramatist for Willie Hughes to act upon the stage. Wilde's narrator presents this interpretation by addressing the young man of the Sonnets in the second person, effectually erasing the time that divides young theorist and boy actor. His voice then blends into the language of Shakespeare's sonnet 17:

> Your shade comes to visit me at night, but, I want to look upon your "shadow" in the living day, I want to see you upon the stage. Mere description of you will not suffice:
>
> "If I could write the beauty of your eyes,
> And in fresh numbers number all your graces,
> The age to come would say, 'This poet lies;
> Such heavenly touches ne'er touched earthly faces.'" (1167)

Here seemingly acting the part of Shakespeare, the literary theorist soon completely merges his vision with the poet's. He sees through the poet's eyes. This identification between the narrator and the poet/playwright culminates in the fifth "act" in a passage beginning:

> Yes: I had lived it all. I had stood in the round theatre with its open
> roof and fluttering banners, had seen the stage draped with black for
> tragedy, or set with gay garlands for some brighter show. (1194)[7]

The paragraph continues by elaborating the dress and attitude of young
"gallants" attending the play, descriptions gleaned perhaps from
Elizabethan writings such as Manningham's table-book (1189). The
narrator's research substantiates his fantasy through the physical detail
it brings. Archaeological research, which Wilde describes elsewhere as
a "method of artistic illusion" ("Truth of Masks" 1078), allows him to
know the names of actors and thus to approximate an identification (cf.
Dillon).

This identification can occur because of the fictional figure of
Willie Hughes. Cyril Graham has already named Willie Hughes "the
very incarnation of Shakespeare's dreams" (1156), meaning that
Shakespeare's lifework is perfectly embodied by the figure of Willie
Hughes. The narrator's research takes Cyril Graham's claim one step
further as Willie Hughes appears on the stage, and "the play changed
according to my mood . . . and in each play there was someone whose
life was bound up in mine, who realized for me every dream, and gave
shape to every fancy" (1195). According to the Willie Hughes theory,
this passage is "true" whether the "me" and "mine" refer to the
dramatist or to the literary critic. The body of Willie Hughes on the
stage fulfills the visions of both the playwright—as it "realizes" his
"every dream"—and the critic—as it "gives shape to" or substantiates
the Willie Hughes theory. Furthermore, after the extended fantasy of
the Renaissance theater, the narrator comes to see his own "soul's
romance" in the text. In a passage that Lawrence Danson argues
"speaks" homosexual love without ever naming it ("Unspoken Name of
Love" 986), Wilde's narrator writes—as if looking in a mirror—"How
curiously it had all been revealed to me! A book of Sonnets published
nearly three hundred years ago, written by a dead hand and in honour
of a dead youth suddenly explained to me the whole story of my soul's
romance" (1195). Though Shakespeare's hand is definitely dead, the
"soul's romance" described in the Sonnets is "mine," belonging to the
nineteenth-century critic. The narrator progresses from reciting the
Sonnets to seeing through the poet's eyes and dreaming the poet's
dreams to seeing his own life in the Sonnets. But as Alan Sinfield
reminds us, "What 'Mr. W. H.' suggests is Wilde's interest in
discovering a homosexual identity, but also his scepticism about how

that might be achieved" (*Wilde Century* 19). In this last phase, Wilde betrays this "scepticism" because in it the narrator sees the dead hand of the poet, begins to see a historical divide, and projects anxieties about this divide onto an intruding female body, that of the dark woman.

"AN IDLE DREAM": THE DISSOLUTION OF IDENTIFICATION

Wilde's fictional essay compares the ideal identification between the poet and his beloved with that between the critic and the poet. For Wilde, both poet and critic attempt to enclose their respective beloveds either in sonnet or in theory; however, the need for physical presence will inevitably come between the poet or critic and their objects. The transience of this identification is analyzed by Joel Fineman, who looks through the lens of Lacan's "mirror stage." Fineman records the moments in the Sonnets "when he [the poet] looks into the mirror" and "sees . . . the ways in which his identification and his identity do not coalesce" (*Perjured Eye* 53). Fineman's reading of the Sonnets, however, owes as much to the *narrative* provided by Wilde as to the theories of Derrida and Lacan. The narrator's disillusionment with the Willie Hughes theory—"Willie Hughes suddenly became to me a mere myth, an idle dream, the boyish fancy of a young man" (1196)—may be an analogue for Fineman's theory, in which the poet becomes disillusioned with the powers of his language. The dissolution of identification occurs not only in the Sonnets themselves but also in *The Portrait of Mr. W. H.*, as the narrator, identifying with Shakespeare, in the end "sees . . . the ways in which his identification and his identity do not coalesce."[8]

In Wilde's narrative, as in Fineman's theory, it is the female form that takes on the differences of body, history, and desire that would otherwise keep the narrator from textually identifying with the poet Shakespeare. An instance exemplifying this displacement occurs after the narrator envisions himself as Shakespeare in the theater and after he recognizes his soul's romance in "a book . . . written by a dead hand." At this moment, the narrator

> remembered how once in Egypt I had been present at the opening of a frescoed coffin. . . . Inside there was the body of a young girl swathed in tight bands of linen, and with a gilt mask over her

> face. . . . I had seen that one of the little withered hands held a scroll
> of yellow papyrus covered with strange characters. How I wished
> now that I had it read to me! It might have told me something more
> about the soul that hid within me, and its mysteries of passion. . . .
> Were we to look in tombs for our real life, and in art for the legend of
> our days? (1195-96)

The appearance of a corpse at this point in the narrative reveals some
anxieties about the discovery of the "soul's romance." The "dead hand"
of Shakespeare becomes the "withered hand" of the mummy. But
instead of fixating on mortality so embodied, Wilde's narrator turns his
eyes to the resurrection of the text in her hand. In turning away from
the body, the narrator turns from what it represents: physicality,
mortality, and sexuality.

Prefiguring the narrator, Cyril Graham also turns away from the
decaying body and toward the unsullied, ever-living text. Cyril insists
upon the purity of his theory, which "evolved . . . purely from the
sonnets themselves" (1156). He names himself the "first who, working
purely by internal evidence, had found out who Mr. W. H. really was"
(1153). His fantasy is soon interrupted by Erskine, who, in referring to
the time preceding Graham's suicide, tells the narrator, "I began to see
that before the theory could be placed before the world in a really
perfected form, it was necessary to get some independent evidence
about the existence of Willie Hughes" (1158). In describing the
published theory as the theory in its "perfected form," Erskine
demonstrates how, in order to be published, the theory must account for
both the "perfected form" of Shakespeare's Sonnets and the *perfect*
form of Willie Hughes himself. Erskine entangles publication of a
theory to the "world" with a need for physical confirmation. The
"world" thus intrudes into the theory, which throughout the narrative
circulates among only a trio of men. Erskine's formulation of
publication, placing the theory "before the world," also makes an
analogy between the publication of literary criticism and the
appearance of Willie Hughes to a dramatic audience, "placed before the
world" on the stage. Making Willie Hughes, the beloved, and Willie
Hughes, the theory, so publicly accessible—"the prey of every vulgar
thief"—threatens the enclosed economy which includes the poet, the
beloved . . . and now the literary theorist.

While *Mr. W. H.* represents a "pure" relation to the poet through
the textual alignment between the narrator and the poet/playwright, it

expresses a less pure relation—even a sexualized fixation—through the dark woman, whom the narrative aligns with the mummified young girl. Through this figure, the narrator expresses a sexual desire for Willie Hughes not tied to his own identification with and possession of Shakespeare. The dark woman briefly interrupts his fantasy about the Renaissance theater:

> In the side boxes some masked women were sitting. One of them was waiting with hungry eyes and bitten lips for the drawing back of the curtain. . . . I knew her. She had marred for a season the great friendship of my life. (1195)

Here we see another version of the snake in the garden described by Heather Dubrow, which had "marred . . . the great friendship of my life." The mask worn by the dark woman prefigures the "gilt mask" of the girl-mummy, and physicality and sexuality enter the narrative with this other beloved. That is, the description of her eyes as "hungry" connects the dark woman to what is displaced throughout the narrative, the sexuality of the narrator's desire. Well before this introduction of woman into the narrative, we see the relationship between Shakespeare and Willie Hughes described in pointedly Neoplatonic terms:

> There was a kind of mystic transference of the expressions of the physical world to a sphere that was spiritual, that was removed from gross bodily *appetite*, and in which the soul was lord. (1175; emphasis added)

This "transference" (and my reading of Wilde at this point converges with Sedgwick's of sonnet 144, which states that "both action and sexuality are exclusively female prerogatives" [*Between Men* 45]) requires that "gross bodily appetite" be displaced, and it is the dark woman "for a season" who allows this sexual desire to be expressed, even if it remains "removed" from the poet and critic and their objects.

Wilde's narrator thus posits a dual relation to the public stage, dividing his imagined audience between himself and the woman with "hungry eyes." What is more, this dual relation carries over from the arena of performance into the arena of publication. On the one hand, a disembodied privileged readership—the male scholars—identifies with the author without any mediating principal, and on the other, a public audience—designated female—must ache for the "drawing back of the curtain," barred from connection with the poet. We are reminded of a similar divide between the poet's heart, which encloses the image of the young man, and "every vulgar thief" who may gain access to the publicly circulating beloved. The Neoplatonic pursuits of the scholar are removed from the "base" desires of the collective readership through the gendering of the respective endeavors male and female.

In some ways I follow William Cohen's reading of Erskine's mourning mother as the dark lady, but I do not agree with his assessment that the dark lady in *Mr. W. H* "is so marginal as to be almost unnoticeable" (227), which neglects the importance of where she does appear in the narrative and also neglects the mummy passage. In reading the female into the center of a text where she is thought to be "marginalized," I have tried to articulate the formation of scholarly privilege that occurs through narration in *Mr. W. H.* Since it is the female body that Wilde's narrator excludes from this privilege, understandably, a feminist approach would resist such a narrativization. If we read the Sonnets as does this narrative, as "a great friendship" "marred for a season" by a woman with "olive skin and raven's wing hair," women in general are excluded from any positive identification within the Sonnets. One strategy for addressing this exclusion is Joel Fineman's assessment of the misogynistic subject position occasioned and originated in the Sonnets. Another strategy is that proposed by Heather Dubrow's "The Politics of Plotting Shakespeare's Sonnets," which challenges the narratability of the Sonnets and supports a gender-fluid addressee, not fastened to one, two, or even seven figures (see in particular Dubrow 305 n. 38). Such fluidity does not confine the reader—male or female—within binaries so inscribed. But the case of Oscar Wilde has certain political ramifications worth considering before one adopts any single strategy.

Oscar Wilde's plotting of the Sonnets has a very specific sociopolitical context that complicates the issues related to gendered scholarly privilege heretofore examined. Wilde's narrative is not one that suppresses the female for its own sake. Rather, he displaces overtly erotic desire onto the dark woman in order to circumvent the censorious eyes of the Victorian public. For a homosexual male in 1890, the "wide world" poses a threat that requires the circumvention afforded through this narrative projection.[9] Furthermore, while *The Portrait of Mr. W. H.* seeks to express an "inexpressible" desire (see Danson, "Unspoken Name of Love") through the subterfuges of Neoplatonism and gendered projections, Wilde's identification with Shakespeare the poet takes on a heightened sense of urgency as his own biographical narrative reaches its tragic climax, resulting in the public exorcism of what Stallybrass calls the "specter of sodomy."

"I TRIED THE DOOR AND FOUND IT LOCKED": WILDE ON TRIAL

In 1895, between a rock and a hard place, Oscar Wilde initiates a libel suit against the Marquess of Queensbury, who is the father of Wilde's young man, Lord Alfred Douglas. Not to do so would admit his "guilt" because the Marquess had written a note "For Oscar Wilde posing as somdomite [*sic*]" (Hyde 108).[10] To establish Wilde's "pose," much of the defense's case in the first trial depends on internal "evidence" from Wilde's texts. Wilde uses one of the texts, a letter pilfered by a blackmailer and supposedly demonstrating the "threat" Wilde was to the Marquess's son, to identify himself with Shakespeare and thereby escape through the workings of literary history. The letter reads

> your sonnet is quite lovely, and it is marvelous that those red rose-
> leaf lips of yours should have been made no less for music of song
> than for madness of kisses. Your slim gilt soul walks between passion
> and poetry. (Hyde 112)[11]

Wilde defuses this bit of "evidence," however, by citing its genre, calling the poem a prose sonnet "in the manner of Shakespeare." In fact, Wilde defuses much of the "textual evidence" brought against him, including *Mr. W. H.*, with the claim that the idea was "borrowed from Shakespeare" (Hyde 129). Similarly, as Lawrence Danson points out, "like Shakespeare's sonnets, its purported subject, 'The Portrait of Mr. W. H.', offers a key but withholds the heart it might unlock" (Danson, *Wilde's Intentions* 102). Because Wilde makes the Shakespearean sonnet a "manner" with which to identify, Mr. Carson, the Marquess's lawyer, will no more be able to label Oscar Wilde a sodomite based on internal evidence than Cyril Graham could prove the existence of Willie Hughes simply through the Sonnets.

But the identification between Wilde and Shakespeare ends with the conclusion of this first trial. Unlike Cyril Graham, who could not produce the necessary physical evidence, Mr. Carson is able to produce a young male body, that of a former clerk, "a man named Wood," who had attempted to blackmail Wilde with the above letter. Although

Wilde's soon-to-be-defense lawyers divert Wood's appearance by dropping charges, Mr. Carson's closing statement asserts that Oscar Wilde's secrets will be exposed to the public:

> When I state that, previous to the possession of those letters, Wood had been carrying on certain practices with Wilde, you will have the *key* to the whole situation. (Hyde, 167-68; emphasis added)

Wilde's texts, like Shakespeare's Sonnets, obscure "certain" young male bodies. The reader's desire to uncover the identity of Shakespeare's beloved prefigures the public's desire to know the hidden "practices" of Wilde. In this juridical staging, the figure equivalent to the dark woman with "hungry eyes and bitten lips" is that of the general public denied admission into this crowded courtroom, which Ed Cohen likens to "an oversold opening night" (138). Connecting the excluded public and the privileged legislators are the women who hold the actual *keys*, the maids and landladies who have access to the defendants' (Wilde is tried at the same time as his friend Alfred Taylor) most intimate spaces. Mrs. Grant, landlady to Mr. Taylor and the first woman named in Montgomery Hyde's account of the trials, testifies, "Once I tried the door and found it locked. I heard whispering and laughing and my suspicions were aroused, though I did not like to take steps in that matter" (Hyde 199-200). Whereas the dark lady in Wilde's *Mr. W. H.* waits for the drawing back of the curtain, Mrs. Grant displays a hesitancy in her role as voyeur when public law forcibly enters a private room.

The public prosecutor's assurance that he holds the key to the "whole situation" fixes Oscar Wilde in his role as "sodomite." It is as if Sir Henry's quip, "from a label there is no escape," anticipates the naming of Wilde as sodomite and his consequent imprisonment. Within this limited role, Wilde is scapegoat for what C. L. Barber calls the "Victorian anxieties" (310) about the presence of homoerotic desire in English literary history, anxieties which no "physical evidence" can alleviate or confirm.

But literary history, not ossifiable, provides some solace to the author of *Mr. W. H.* When Wilde next returns to the Sonnets, he writes his own relation to literary history, one different from that sought by his narrator. While Wilde is in prison, his personal literary history embodies more than the object of his desires. It expresses the particulars of his tragedy. Not often considered in current criticism because of its "autobiographical" nature, Wilde's *De Profundis*, a letter written to Alfred Douglas, gives an account of his ruin and abandonment by the young lord. Lord Alfred, of course, is the same young man to whom he had addressed his prose sonnet written "in the manner of Shakespeare." In *De Profundis*, Wilde recognizes the implications of such a "manner." Not only is Shakespeare's poet loved, he is also abandoned. The narrative of *Mr. W. H.* explains this desertion in terms of a defection to another acting troupe; the rival poet is the playwright Christopher Marlowe. In the presence of this rival, the poet writes, "Farewell, thou art too dear for my possessing" (87.1). Wilde's letter asks us to revisit Shakespeare's words when he gives an account of his own abandonment by Douglas. When his beloved Bosie flees to France, Wilde expresses a despair analogous to the Shakespearean lover-poet's.

Aside from giving a first-hand account of his tortured relationship to Douglas, *De Profundis* is in part a philosophical treatise written within a locked prison cell. In the heart of his letter, Wilde puts himself in the place of Coleridge's "myriad-minded Shakespeare" and writes about the processes of identification:

> Art has made us myriad-minded. Those who have the artistic temperament go into exile with Dante. . . . Out of Shakespeare's sonnets they draw, to their own hurt it may be, the secret of his love and make it their own. (926-27)

"And make it their own"—such a phrase suggests a personal relation to literature filled with pathos and "hurt." To occupy literature's secrets is to stay within the indefinite. Perhaps relying on Paterian contentions against theories that "sacrifice" certain elements of "experience" (153), Wilde narrates his own disillusionment through literature's indefiniteness rather than limit literature through his narrative. Wilde's work, especially *The Portrait of Mr. W. H.*, complicates the Sonnets and allows for unacknowledged potentials and suggestive mysteries.

Not claiming to name the players in the Sonnets, *Mr. W. H.* also demonstrates how nineteenth-century critics displace the erotics of their endeavors through a hierarchy of readership. Wilde occupies Shakespeare's Sonnets in order to show the delusory nature of their claim to name and to expose the homoerotics of the critical endeavor. At the same time, he creates a space of his own within literary history.

NOTES

1. See Schoenbaum, who positions *Mr. W. H.* within Shakespearean biography and the W. H. debates of the time. See also Gary Taylor's chapter on "Victorian Values" (162-231) in relation to Shakespearean studies. I follow Hyder Rollins in using italics for the long version of *The Portrait of Mr. W. H.* published in 1921.

2. See William Cohen's excellent reading of this work, which argues that "Wilde's novella displays the inextricability of literature from interpretation" (209). See also Kate Chedgzoy's reading (which I was not made aware of until after completing this essay) of the "key" and Wilde's "appropriation" of Shakespeare.

3. Another possible source for this complex of images is "detective" criticism such as Ignatius Donnelly's *The Great Cryptogram*, printed the year before *Mr. W. H.*, which seeks to prove that the author known as Shakespeare was actually Francis Bacon. Donnelly's preface reads, "The key here turned, for the first time, in the secret wards of the Cipher, will yet unlock a vast history, nearly as great in bulk as the Plays themselves" (vi). I thank Steve Dillon for pointing me to this example. See also Schoenbaum 404-08.

4. See also Fineman, *Perjured Eye* 26-28, and William Cohen 208-09.

5. I use the New Cambridge edition of the Sonnets, ed. G. Blakemore Evans.

6. Cf. Anne Ferry, who writes that along with Hamlet, "the speaker in the sonnets casts . . . doubts on the fundamental assumption that what is hidden in the closet of the heart is describable by the commonest sixteenth-century term, *secrets*" (214).

7. Cf. Bruce Bashford, who writes about this passage that "the narrator is expressing the hermeneutical doctrine that to interpret is to revive the experience implicit in the work" (418).

8. Similarly, Gary Taylor makes an analogy between the Shakespearean critic and the sonnet writer when considering Fineman's analysis of the "exhaustion" of "traditional epideixis." Taylor writes, "This [exhaustion] is also, of course, though Fineman does not say so, the general situation of a Shakespearian critic in the late twentieth century; how do you praise persuasively when so much praise has already been written?" (364).

9. Wilde similarly voices this homoerotic desire through the figure of Salome, as noted by Kevin Kopelson. See also Alan Sinfield discussing J. A. Symond's reading of Shakespeare's *Venus and Adonis* (*Cultural Politics— Queer Reading* 8-12).

10. Although Ed Cohen informs us that Hyde's account is gleaned from newspaper accounts and not from trial transcripts, Hyde's is an interesting cultural fiction nonetheless (Cohen, *Talk on the Wilde Side* 2-3).

11. For a more detailed discussion of this letter, see William Cohen 207-08.

WORKS CITED

Barber, C. L. "An Essay on the Sonnets." *Elizabethan Poetry*. Ed. Paul J. Alpers. New York: Oxford UP, 1967. 299-320.

Bashford, Bruce. "Hermeneutics in Oscar Wilde's *The Portrait of Mr. W.H.*" *Papers on Language and Literature* 24 (1988): 412-22.

Bredbeck, Gregory. "Narcissus in the Wilde: Textual cathexis and the historical origins of queer Camp." *The Politics and Poetics of Camp*. Ed. Moe Meyer. London: Routledge, 1994. 51-74.

———. "Tradition and the Individual Sodomite." *Sodomy and Interpretation: Marlowe to Milton*. Ithaca: Cornell UP, 1991. 141-86.

Chedgzoy, Kate. "'Strange worship': Oscar Wilde and the Key to Shakespeare's *Sonnets*." *Shakespeare's Queer Children: Sexual Politics and Contemporary Culture*. Manchester: Manchester UP, 1995. 135-176.

Cohen, Ed. *Talk on the Wilde Side: Toward a Geneology of a Discourse on Male Sexualities*. New York: Routledge, 1993.

Cohen, William. "Willie and Wilde: Reading *The Portrait of Mr. W. H.*" *South Atlantic Quarterly* 88 (1991): 207-33.

Danson, Lawrence. "Oscar Wilde, W. H., and the Unspoken Name of Love." *ELH* 58 (1991): 979-99.

———. *Wilde's Intentions: The Artist in His Criticism*. Oxford: Clarendon, 1997.

de Grazia, Margreta. *Shakespeare Verbatim: The Reproduction of Authenticity and the 1790 Apparatus*. Oxford: Clarendon, 1991.

Dowden, Edward. *Shakspere: A Critical Study of His Mind and Art*. London: Henry S. King, 1875.

Dillon, Steve. "The Archaeology of Victorian Literature." *Modern Language Quarterly* 54 (1993): 237-61.

Donnelly, Ignatius. *The Great Cryptogram*. Chicago: R. F. Peale, 1888.

Dubrow, Heather. "'Incertainties now crown themselves assur'd': The Politics of Plotting Shakespeare's Sonnets." *Shakespeare Quarterly* 47 (1996): 291-305.

Ferry, Anne. *The "Inward" Language: Sonnets of Wyatt, Sidney, Shakespeare, Donne*. Chicago: U Chicago P, 1983.

Fineman, Joel. *Shakespeare's Perjured Eye: The Invention of Poetic Subjectivity*. Berkeley: U of California P, 1986.

———. "The Significance of Literature: *The Importance of Being Earnest*." *Critical Essays on Oscar Wilde*. Ed. Regenia Gagnier. New York: G.K. Hall, 1991. 108-18.

Foster, Donald. "Master W. H., R.I.P." *PMLA* 102 (1987): 42-55.

Goldberg, Jonathan. *Sodometries: Renaissance Texts, Modern Sexualities*. Stanford: Stanford UP, 1992.

Hubler, Edward, ed. *The Riddle of Shakespeare's Sonnets*. New York: Basic Books, 1962.

Hyde, H. Montgomery, ed. *The Trials of Oscar Wilde*. London: William Hodge, 1948.

Kopelson, Kevin. "Wilde's Love-deaths." *Yale Journal of Criticism* 5 (1992): 52-54.

Pater, Walter. *The Renaissance*. Oxford: Oxford UP, 1986.

Pequigney, Joseph. *Such Is My Love: A Study of Shakespeare's Sonnets*. Chicago: U of Chicago P, 1985.

Schoenbaum, Samuel. *Shakespeare's Lives*. 2nd ed. Oxford: Clarendon, 1991.

Schroeder, Horst. *Annotations to Oscar Wilde, The Portrait of Mr. W. H.* Braunschweig: Privately printed, 1986.

Sedgwick, Eve Kosofsky. "Some Binarisms (II): Wilde, Nietzsche, and the Sentimental Relations of the Male Body." *Epistemology of the Closet*. Berkeley: U of California P, 1991. 131-81.

———. "Swan in Love: The Example of Shakespeare's Sonnets." *Between Men: English Literature and Male Homosocial Desire*. New York: Columbia UP, 1985. 28-48.

Shakespeare, William. *The Sonnets*. The New Cambridge Shakespeare. Ed. G. Blakemore Evans. Cambridge: Cambridge UP, 1996.

Sinfield, Alan. *Cultural Politics—Queer Reading*. Philadelphia: U of Pennsylvania P, 1994.

———. *The Wilde Century: Effeminacy, Oscar Wilde and the Queer Movement*. New York: Columbia UP, 1994.

Stallybrass, Peter. "Editing as Cultural Formation: The Sexing of Shakespeare's Sonnets." *Modern Language Quarterly* 54 (1993): 91-105.

Taylor, Gary. *Reinventing Shakespeare: A Cultural History from the Restoration to the Present*. Oxford: Oxford UP, 1989.

Wilde, Oscar. *The Complete Works*. Ed. Vyvyan Holland. New York: Harper and Row, 1966.

Wordsworth, William. *Poetical Works*. Eds. Thomas Hutchinson and Ernest de Selincourt. Oxford: Oxford UP, 1936.

I, You, He, She, and We

On the Sexual Politics of Shakespeare's Sonnets[1]

Bruce R. Smith

On the subject of homoerotic desire, people are willing to say yes to Shakespeare's plays. But they are inclined to say no to Shakespeare's Sonnets. Playing Antonio as the disappointed lover of Bassanio has become a virtual cliché in productions of *The Merchant of Venice* since the 1980s. More recently, Celia has been cast in the same position vis-à-vis Rosalind in productions of *As You Like It,* notably in Lawrence Boswell's production with the Shakespeare Theater of Washington in 1997. Homoeroticism as a subtext in *Coriolanus* has become so securely established that directors of productions by the Royal Shakespeare Company have been able to pursue increasingly subtle readings: in-your-face leather-and-chains sadomasochism in Terry Hands's direction of Alan Howard in the title role in 1979, an Aufidius (Malcolm Storry) who conveyed "the almost sexual nature of his rivalry with Coriolanus" (bare-chested Charles Dance) in Terry Hands's and John Barton's production of 1989, a psychologically compelling contrast between Aufidius's fervor and Coriolanus's icy detachment in David Thacker's production of 1994 (Osborne 18). With the Sonnets, however, such openly sexual readings still inspire resistance. It has been more than a generation since W. H. Auden wrote his introduction to the Signet edition of the Sonnets (1964), but the position he takes there still informs much contemporary criticism of the poems. Making a play on bed-secrets and Red-secrets, Auden privately told a group of friends that "it won't do just yet to admit that the top Bard was in the homintern"—and acted on those reservations when he wrote his preface later the same year (Pequigney 79-80). Shakespeare, after all, was a married man and a father:

> That we are confronted in the sonnets by a mystery rather than by an aberration is evidenced for me by the fact that men and women whose sexual tastes are perfectly normal, but who enjoy and understand poetry, have always been able to read them as expressions of what they understand by the word love, without finding the masculine pronoun an obstacle. (Auden xxxiii)

Auden spoke, of course, as a man of his own time and place—the terms "normal" and "aberration" belong to a Freudian construction of sexual identity that has been discredited—but more recent critics have found their own ways of keeping the Sonnets safe for heterosexual enjoyment. Anthony Hecht, bringing to the New Cambridge Shakespeare the same credentials as a poet-critic that Auden did to the Signet edition, seems, at first blush, much more willing to entertain the possibility of homosexual desire. The "sexual orientation of the poet, and the quality and degree of his intimacy with the young man" present, Hecht concedes, "a major puzzle that seems beyond the reach of any solution." About these questions "almost no one feels neutral" (10). Hecht's own solution is to take refuge in the traditional exaltation of male-male friendship over male-female desire, as argued, among others, by Montaigne. As a strategy of evasion, this move goes back to the late eighteenth century and Edmond Malone's attempt to assuage George Steevens's indignation over Shakespeare's playful ways with another man's genitals in sonnet 20: "such addresses to men, however indelicate, were," Malone assured Steevens, "customary in our author's time, and neither imported criminality nor were esteemed indecorous" (qtd. in Rollins 1: 55).

In their assumption that an overarching philosophical idea can put into perspective an otherwise troubling, idiosyncratic text, Hecht and Malone speak for a habit of reading that might be called Hegelian. Famous instances are the master trope of *caritas* as deployed by D. W. Robertson and his disciples on medieval texts or Neoplatonist doctrine as the key to all mythologies in Renaissance texts. Critics since Auden have found a variety of other ways to de-eroticize the first 126 sonnets (Gardiner 335-37). The New Criticism, with its strict attention to poems as verbal artifacts, offers one way out: "the sexual undercurrents of the sonnets," in Stephen Booth's formulation, "are of the sonnets;

they probably reflect a lot that is true about their author, but I do not know what that is" (549). Semiotic criticism, with its insistence on indeterminacy, likewise disables any attempt to settle the Sonnets in a particular sexual scenario, as Heather Dubrow argues in an essay included in this volume. The most ingenious ruse of all may be Jonathan Bate's in *Shakespeare's Genius*. Acknowledging an eroticism in the sonnets to the young man quite as palpable as in those to the dark lady, Bate nonetheless wants to keep desire all in the head:

> The sonnets are best thought of as *imaginings of potential situations which might have grown* from the initial Southampton-situation. We will never know exactly which of them are rhetorical transmutations of actual occurrences and which are rhetorical enactments of potential situations that Shakespeare imagined. *And it is of their essence that they deny us this knowledge*: they do so precisely in order to show us that we cannot know whether love is "real" or "imagined." We do not need to know what happened in the bed, because what the sonnets are interested in is how love happens in the head. (53; emphasis added)

It is true enough that readers of Shakespeare's Sonnets can never know whether or not the speaking "I" has acted on the desires he writes about. Pequigney makes the best case, but the only pieces of evidence are, after all, inked letters imprinted on sheets of paper. The difference, in life, between imagining doing something with one's body and physically doing it turns, in Aristotle's terms, on the *material* cause of the action, not the *efficient* cause. In both cases the doer of the action is the same; only the means are different. In fiction, of course, no such material difference exists. In the words of Proverbs 23: 7, "For as he thinketh in his heart, so is he." The bawdy puns anatomized by Booth and que(e)ried by Pequigney bespeak a sensibility in which head and lower body parts are not quite the separate entities Bate makes them out to be. Like all binaries, "head"/"bed" is inherently unstable, a signal instance of what Jonathan Dollimore has called "the perverse dynamic . . . that fearful interconnectedness whereby the antithetical inheres within, and is partly produced by, what it opposes" (33). "Head" needs "bed" in order to *be* "head." In Shakespeare's Sonnets, "bed" penetrates "head," no less than "head" "bed." As it happens, I am personally acquainted with all of the post-Auden critics I have cited, and I know them to be people of good will and liberal convictions. I remain puzzled, therefore, why Shakespeare's Sonnets should still constitute a site of resistance, when homoeroticism in Shakespeare's plays has become a commonplace of stage productions, academic criticism, and classroom discussion.

One obvious answer is that the Sonnets read like autobiographical confessions. However smart we may try to be about not equating the speaking persona with the historical person, there is clearly an uneasiness about attributing such feelings to the greatest playwright who ever lived. Sodomy lodges uneasily in the House of Bardolatry, as witness the eighteenth- and nineteenth-century readers discussed by Peter Stallybrass in an essay collected in this volume. The cause for readers' continuing anxiety is, I believe, more complicated than that. It has to do, at bottom, with pronouns, with transactions among "I," "you," "he," "she," and "we."

By Giorgio Melchiori's calculations, the proportion of pronouns to other words is higher in Shakespeare's Sonnets than in the sonnets of Sidney, Daniel, Drayton, and Spenser: 14.7 percent. The most frequent of these pronouns, among all the sonnet-writers, is first person singular (9-10). To read Shakespeare's Sonnets is, therefore, to acquire a certain identity as "I." The poems' earliest readers seem to have recognized as much. Evidence of how a certain set of these readers made the Sonnets their own is to be found in the twelve surviving manuscript anthologies that contain the sonnet numbered 2 in Thorpe's 1609 Quarto. Most of these collections were put together by students in Oxford colleges in the 1620s and 1630s (Beal 1: 2: 452-53). To judge from the common title that five of the collectors gave the poem, "To one that would die a maid," student readers took "When fortie Winters shall beseige thy brow" to be a poem of seduction out of Catullus, not an argument for procreation out of Erasmus. While it was possible in sixteenth-century English for a sexually inexperienced male to be referred to as a "maid," other poems in these Oxford anthologies suggest that the "thou" of sonnet 2 was construed to be "she," not "he." And that says a great deal about the copying, reading, acting "I." It was perhaps to settle such ambiguities about gender that John Benson changed several instances of "he" to "she" when he edited the Sonnets for the altered social circumstances of the 1640s. (See, however, the essay by Margreta de Grazia collected in this volume.) Facing the same ambiguities with respect to pronouns, the reading "I" of today wants to assume the same sureties: "I" wants to relate to "he" and "she" in reassuringly familiar ways. "I," "you," "she," "he," and "we," because they constitute

constant reference points in English speech, seduce us into accepting
them as somehow "above" history and hence cause us to read our own
experience back into the text of the Sonnets. I want to argue that each
of these reference points—"I," "you," "he," "she," and "we"—is
historically constructed and that they all are interrelated in these poems
in ways that are different—sometimes radically different—from today.
Let us consider the pronouns one by one.

"You"

> To me faire friend you neuer can be old,
> For as you were when first your eye I eyde,
> Such seemes your beautie still: Three Winters colde,
> Haue from the forrests shooke three summers pride,
> Three beautious springs to yellow *Autumne* turn'd,
> In processe of the seasons haue I seene,
> Three Aprill perfumes in three hot Iunes burn'd,
> Since first I saw you fresh which yet are greene.
> Ah yet doth beauty like a Dyall hand,
> Steale from his figure, and no pace perceiu'd,
> So your sweete hew, which me thinkes still doth stand
> Hath motion, and mine eye may be deceaued.
>   For feare of which, heare this thou age vnbred,
>   Ere you were borne was beauties summer dead. (104)[2]

From the standpoint of "I," the most fundamental distinction of all is
"you": the "not me." "You" possesses its own first-personhood, as the
"I" in sonnet 104 may be acknowledging as he reckons love's time in
terms of speech ("when first your 'I' I eyed" or "I 'I'd'" or "I ayed") as
well as sight ("when first your eye I eyed"). In fact, two "you's" are
implicated in these texts: the person being addressed, and the you who
is "overhearing" the poems by reading them outside the immediate
context of "I" speaking to "you." We might distinguish these as the
dramatic "you" and the reading "you." Sonnet 104 recognizes this
distinction, identifying "you" as "fair friend" in the very first line and
invoking at the end the reading "you"—or at least one group of the
reading "you"—in the guise of "thou age unbred." The contrast here
between the friend as "you" and posterity as "thou" substantiates
Andrew Gurr's argument that "you" in the Sonnets usually signals
personal directness as opposed to the literary distance of "thou"—just

the reverse of what we might expect by parallel with *vous* and *tu* in French. Altogether Gurr distinguishes 34 "you" sonnets and 73 "thou" sonnets, with twenty switches from one form to the other in the course of the first 126 sonnets. The fact that the speaking "I" always addresses the lady of sonnets 127 to 152 as "thou," never as "you," indicates for Gurr the more conventionally literary nature of these particular poems (9-25). Misogyny boasts a highly respectable literary pedigree.

It is with respect to the dramatic "you" that Shakespeare's Sonnets differ most remarkably from sonnets written by Sidney, Daniel, Drayton, and Spenser. According to Melchiori, 37.2 percent of the pronouns in Shakespeare's Sonnets are second person, as opposed to just 25.6 percent in sonnets by his contemporaries. "You" at 37.2 percent is, in fact, foregrounded almost as much as "I" at 40.3 percent (Melchiori 15). The reading "you" is just as present in Shakespeare's Sonnets, I would argue, as the dramatic "you." In *Homosexual Desire in Shakespeare's England* I proposed that the mode of Shakespeare's Sonnets is confessional: the reader "takes confession" from the speaking "I" (232-33). The reader's role is suggested by the circumstances in which the poems were first circulated in manuscript and then published, apparently without the writer's permission.[3] "Shake-speares Sonnets. Neuer Before Imprinted": the title given to the 1609 Quarto by its publisher, Thomas Thorpe (see Figure 3 in this volume), invites the reader into the formerly private domain of manuscript culture (Marotti 30-48). A dedication to the mysterious "onlie begetter of these insuing sonnets. Mr. W. H." heightens the effect (see Figure 2 in this volume). The Sonnets are set up as revelations of private experience. The reading "you" is cast as a voyeur, a sharer of someone else's secrets. That makes it very hard for the reading "you" to distance himself or herself from the speaking "I."

"She"

When in the Chronicle of wasted time,
I see discriptions of the fairest wights,
And beautie making beautifull old rime,
In praise of Ladies dead, and louely Knights,
Then in the blazon of sweet beauties best,
Of hand, of foote, of lip, of eye, of brow,
I see their antique Pen would haue exprest,
Euen such a beauty as you maister now.

> So all their praises are but prophesies
> Of this our time, all you prefiguring,
> And for they look'd but with deuining eyes,
> They had not still enough your worth to sing:
>   For we which now behold these present dayes,
>   Haue eyes to wonder, but lack toungs to praise. (106)

In these poems, as in life, "you" is bifurcated into two genders, female and male. The way that Thomas Thorpe has printed the verses seems to privilege this gender distinction—or so it has seemed since Malone abandoned Benson's edition and took the original text in hand in the late eighteenth century. A variety of editors since Malone have tried to rearrange the poems to fit one or another scheme of their own devising, but Thorpe's order and Malone's suppositions about gender as the marker of that order have provided the traditional way of dividing up the Sonnets into two groups, those addressed to "the young man" and those addressed to "the dark lady." Several recent critics have called attention to how arbitrary this division is, primarily by insisting on the gender undecideability that is locally if not globally at work in particular poems. That is not my strategy here. I accept the logical separateness of male and female, but I want to investigate the ways those two categories are implicated in one another. Sonnet 106 may be printed among the poems addressed to "he," but it is full of references to "she." Indeed, "he" has his existence only in terms of "she." Talk of ladies and knights situates the sonnet in the courtly love tradition, and the reference to "*dead* ladies" may specifically invoke Petrarch's Laura. We have in sonnet 106 the desiring male speaker and the desired, unobtainable female object of tradition—but we also have a new, male object of desire: "*lovely* knights." "Lovely" may, of course, carry the force of "loving, full of love," but in most sonnet sequences it is the lady who is lovely and the knight who is dead—or soon will be, if the lady does not grant his desires. Certainly the rest of sonnet 106 is more interested in the knight than in the lady. What follows is a blazon of beauty, a loving catalogue of hand, foot, lip, eye, brow—but shifted in this case from the female object of Petrarchan sonnets to the male object of these poems. The gender of this object is specified in the phrase "such beauty as you *master* now." Self-consciousness about these shifts in gender is perhaps registered in the contrast between *seeing* the male object's beauty and finding the words to *speak* about it:

"For we which now behold these present dayes, / Haue eyes to wonder,
but lack toungs to praise."

The verb "master" in sonnet 106 echoes the phrase "master
mistress" in the more famous crux, sonnet 20. In that sonnet (and in
sonnet 21, with which it forms a kind of diptych), the male is defined as
the "not-she." Nature starts out with a female template. She turns
female into male by the process of addition:

> And for a woman wert thou first created,
> Till nature as she wrought thee fell a dotinge,
> And by addition me of thee defeated,
> By adding one thing to my purpose nothing. (20.9-12)

This is a startling move for post-modern readers who are likely to
assume, with Luce Irigaray writing in "This Gender Which Is Not
One," that in the binary "male"/"female" it is always "male" that acts
as the radical. That is to say, we expect "female" to be defined as the
"not male" (Irigaray 107-10). But that is not the case here. The
erotically desired "he" is defined as the "not she." That, I would argue,
is because the object of desire in most early modern love poems is, in
fact, usually "she." Note all the things "she" is: painted of face, gentle
of heart, acquainted with fashion, false in rolling her eyes, given to
pleasure.

While readers with feminist sympathies would argue that this
misogynist litany is anything but culture-specific to the sixteenth
century, I would like to stress several ways in which the binary does
seem peculiarly early modern. We encounter here some of the same
stereotypical traits we might still recognize, but the underlying reasons
for those traits are different. The difference between male and female is
imagined, first of all, in terms of "outer" versus "inner." Despite their
alluring surface, women hide a frightening "within": fickle,
unpredictable, ultimately unknowable. This idea is rooted in early
modern medical discourse, in the notion of the female body as a leaky
vessel (Laqueur 35-37, 79-96; Paster 23-63). It is the nature of the
vessel that explains hysteria, the changeableness and
polymorphousness of female sexuality. Hence, the way the lustful,
violence-prone male subject tends to identify the irrational impulses
inside himself as female. Lear, for example, is true to early modern
physiology in casting his incipient insanity in biochemical terms, as a
disequilibrium of the body's humors: "O, let me not be mad, not mad,

sweet heaven! / Keep me in temper. I would not be mad" (folio 1.5.45-46).[4] His rising madness he experiences as a "she" within: "O, how this mother swells up toward my heart! / *Histerica passio* down, thou climbing sorrow; / Thy element's below" (2.2.231-33). When Goneril and Regan persist in humiliating him, he locates his disequilibrium in the body, specifically in the blood, and he genders it female. "Thou art a boil," he exclaims to Goneril, "a plague-sore or embossèd carbuncle / in my corrupted blood" (2.2.396-98). Cleopatra is just such a creature of blood. Egypt and its queen are consistently bodied forth in Shakespeare's script as being hot and moist, the very properties of blood as a bodily humor. To keep the body "in temper," the "Cleopatra" within the male subject must be subdued, if necessary by desperate and violent means. When we recall that blood-letting was prescribed by early modern medicine as a cure for almost everything, it is hard not to read physiological effects in the leeching of Cleopatra's breast by the asp. In Shakespeare's Sonnets "he" can maintain "his" integrity only by excluding—or *trying* to exclude—"she." And "she" is imagined in ways quite specific to early modern culture.

"He"

> Beshrew that heart that makes my heart to groane
> For that deepe wound it giues my friend and me;
> I'st not ynough to torture me alone,
> But slaue to slauery my sweet'st friend must be.
> Me from my selfe thy cruell eye hath taken,
> And my next selfe thou harder hast ingrossed,
> Of him, my selfe, and thee I am forsaken,
> A torment thrice three-fold thus to be crossed:
> Prison my heart in thy steele bosomes warde,
> But then my friends heart let my poore heart bale,
> Who ere keepes me, let my heart be his garde,
> Thou canst not then vse rigor in my Iaile.
>   And yet thou wilt, for I being pent in thee,
>   Perforce am thine and all that is in me. (133)

The interconnectedness of "I," "he," and "she" is never more painfully expressed than in sonnet 133. Addressed to "she," who is invoked as "thou," the poem is nonetheless centered on "he": in the poem's central conceit, "he" has his existence inside the poem's "she." Margreta de

Grazia, in an essay collected in this volume, demonstrates how many of the sonnets' sexual anxieties are deflected onto the "she" of sonnets 127 to 152. The situation is registered with peculiar visual power in sonnet 133. The speaker attempts to interpose himself between "she" and "he." "I" and "he" are imprisoned by "she," precisely in her capacity as a female subject who has sexual desires in her own right—and acts on those desires. To "beshrew" in the first line means not only "to cry out against" but to *become* a shrew, to become a woman in the very act of crying out. It is "she" who inflicts "that deep wound," who emasculates both "I" and "he" by turning their closed male bodies into open female bodies. Laqueur has pointed out how Galenic ideas of the female body entail a homology between vagina and throat (35-37). To speak openly, to assume indecorous freedom with the body's upper orifice, was, for a woman, to intimate the same licentiousness with the lower. Ultimately the "I" of sonnet 133 has to acknowledge the literally all-encompassing power "she" possesses: "I" contains "he" (I have his heart inside mine), "you" contains "I" (my heart is prisoner within your "steel bosom"), hence "you" contains both "he" and "I." "You" usurps two subject positions: "his" and "mine." The image of "steel bosom" starts out as image of himself in her "cruel eye," but modulates into a less certain container: her heart? her vagina? her womb?

As "I" proceeds to talk about "my self" and about his friend as "my next self," the phrase "thy cruel eye" begins to sound very much like "thy cruel 'I.'" In the dramatic circumstances of the sonnets addressed to "she," so radically different from the dramatic circumstances of Petrarchan sonnets, "she" can express desire and act on it, but "he" the friend cannot—or so the speaking "I" would wish. In this respect the speaker is typical of homoerotically desiring males in most early modern texts. The desiring male subject has a clear, forceful voice:

> Sweet loue renew thy force, be it not said
> Thy edge should blunter be than apetite,
> Which but too daie by feeding is alaied,
> To morrow sharpned in his former might. (56.1-4)

But the desired male object in the sonnets has no voice. In this respect, "he" is typical of male objects of male desire in early modern texts. Pyrocles/"Cleophila" in Sidney's *Arcadia* offers a good example. When Pyrocles disguises himself as "Cleophila," he gives up not only his proper name but his status as a subject. Under the name of Pyrocles he is a desiring subject who spends most of the revised narrative in pursuit of Philoclea. Under the name of Cleophila he is the object of other's people's desires—the duke's (who thinks "he" is a "she"), the duke's wife's (who knows "she" is a "he"), and Musidorus's (who dances along the boundary between friendship and sodomy when he helps to turn Pyrocles into Cleophila and announces that he has fallen in love, Pygmalion-like, with his own creation):

> sweet cousin, since you are framed of such a loving mettle, I pray you, take heed of looking yourself in a glass lest Narcissus's fortune fall unto you. For my part, I promise you, if I were not fully resolved never to submit my heart to these fancies, I were like enough while I dressed you to become a young Pygmalion. (27)

Others may desire Cleophila, but "she" desires no one. Only Pyrocles can desire. In the words of a song from Rogers and Hammerstein's *Oklahoma!*—with a couple of substitutions—one might sum up the dilemma of Cleophila as, "I'm just a boy who can't say yes."

In the gendered difference between "yes" and "no" consists the specifically early modern construction of "he." The problem with the male object of desire in Shakespeare's Sonnets is that "he" is *not* the usual male object of desire in poems ranging from late antiquity all the way down to *Venus and Adonis*: to wit, a beardless boy with a lovely white neck and a ripe ass. Instead, he is an active subject in his own right, someone who can have sex with the mistress as readily as the speaker can. The erotic male object of the Sonnets is both Pyrocles and Cleophila. In this respect, Shakespeare is developing one particular set of potentialities within the historical construct "he." That "he" is no less a cultural artifact than "she" may be harder for some readers to see, since "he" has usually been taken as the standard against which "she" is judged to be different. Even the standard, however, refuses to stay fixed. In terms of the Galenic model, the "he" of the Sonnets is constructed as "sexual," no qualifier needed (Laqueur 23-35). In post-nineteenth-century terms, "he" is constructed as "bisexual" or, more accurately, as "pan-sexual." If Laqueur is right, that much would be true of *any* sixteenth-century "he." Where the "he" of Shakespeare's Sonnets differs from his peers is in his dual status as both active subject and passive object.

This distinction between subject and object makes all the more contemptuous sonnet 126, the last in the sequence to "him":

> O Thou my louely Boy who in thy power
> Doest hould times fickle glasse, his sickle, hower:
> Who hast by wayning growne, and therein shou'st,
> Thy louers withering, as thy sweet selfe grow'st.
> If Nature (souereign misteres ouer wrack)
> As thou goest onwards still will plucke thee back,
> She keepes thee to this purpose, that her skill.
> May time disgrace, and wretched mynuit kill.
> Yet feare her O thou minnion of her pleasure,
> She may detaine, but not still keepe her tresure! (126.1-10)

"Boy" and "minion" are erotically charged words of contempt, as witness Aufidius's insults of Martius as "boy" at the end of *Coriolanus* (5.6.103 ff.) and the nobles' dismissal of Gaveston as "minion" in Marlowe's *Edward II* (1.4.391 ff. in Marlowe 2: 35). In keeping with Andrew Gurr's argument that "thou" in Shakespeare's Sonnets signals literary distance rather than personal directness, "thou" in sonnet 126 functions as a term of disdain. In his translation of Giovanni Della Casa's conduct book *Galateo* (1576), Robert Peterson explains the difference between "you" and "thou" in public speech acts. "You" implies social or ethical equality; "thou" a difference:

> that is the cause we say: *You*: to euery one, that is not a man of very base calling, and in suche kinde of speach wee yealde such a one, no maner of courtesie of our owne. But if wee say: *Thou*: to suche a one, then wee disgrace him and offer him outrage and wronge: and by suche speach, seeme to make no better reconing of him, then of a knaue and a clowne. (45)

The speaker's final gesture in sonnet 126 is to turn "he" into the traditional object of homoerotic desire: a "boy" who plays the role of a powerless—and voiceless—"minion." "He" in these poems is thus no less a historical construct than "she."

"I"

My loue is strengthned though more weake in seeming
I loue not lesse, thogh lesse the show appeare,
That loue is marchandiz'd, whose ritch esteeming,
The owners tongue doth publish euery where.
Our loue was new, and then but in the spring,
When I was wont to greet it with my laies,
As *Philomell* in summers front doth singe,
And stops his pipe in growth of riper daies:
Not that the summer is lesse pleasant now
Then when her mournefull himns did hush the night,
But that wild musick burthens euery bow,
And sweets growne common loose their deare delight.
    Therefore like her, I some-time hold my tongue:
    Because I would not dull you with my songe. (102)

Implicitly at least, the "I" who speaks in sonnet 102 genders himself both male and female. Philomel is invoked first as a nightingale and hence as male, or perhaps as neuter ("his" in this case having the force of "its"), then in her Ovidian guise as a raped female. The narrative context implies that the occasion for this particular poem is "his" sexual infidelities ("sweets grown common lose their dear delight," "wild music burthens every bough"). The tone here seems to waver between defensiveness and accusation, between politeness and irritation. In this narrative context, "I" casts himself, if only obliquely, in the position of Philomel, sexually violated and unable to speak of his violation. Instead of speaking, Philomel sings—or, more precisely, she greets the season with her lays. The voice the reader hears comes from a space outside the speaker, from the bough of a tree. To use a currently fashionable critical term, "I" is "ventriloquized." And the ventriloquist is "she." "I" is cast in the same position in one of the most famous sonnets of all:

Two loues I haue of comfort and dispaire,
Which like two spirits do sugiest me still,
The better angell is a man right faire:
The worser spirit a woman collour'd il. (144.1-4)

"I" presents himself in sonnet 144 as being constituted by these divergent others: a "he" and "she," each invested with opposing qualities. The word "suggest" carries the force of "propose" or "tempt," as personifications are wont to tempt the hero of a morality play. As with Philomel in sonnet 102, "she" is defined primarily as a sexual being. In the terms provided by sonnet 144, "I," "he," and "she" play out a kind of psychomachia. Ethically speaking, that may be true. But ontologically speaking, the relationship among "I," "she," and "he" is more complicated than that. The implied dramatic situation sets up an ethical opposition between "he" and "she" that fits only too neatly with our rigid post-nineteenth century distinction between "heterosexual" and "homosexual," with all of the prejudices that those terms carry. Confronted with what appears to be a binary opposition between "he" (sonnets 1 to 126) and "she" (sonnets 127 to 152), readers since the eighteenth century have confronted the issue of sexuality and have wanted to see *either/or.* But the whole effect of the poems is to constitute the sexually desiring "I" in terms of *both* "him" and "her." I would argue that "I," "he," and "she" exist ontologically in these texts exactly as three principal characters might in a theatrical script: they have no independent existence, but exist in terms of each other. Each of them may speak and act as if "she" or "he" were an independent "I," but each of them desperately needs the others for "his" or "her" very existence. As Bert O. States observes, "We speak of actors as feeding each other lines, but it would be more accurate to say that they feed each other character" (7). If "he" and "she" are constructed in ways quite specific to early modern culture, then so constructed must be the speaking "I."

By Marvin Spevack's count, forms of the first-person pronoun— "I," "me," "my," "mine"—constitute the single most frequently occurring word group in Shakespeare's Sonnets: 1,062 instances in all. Reiterations of various forms of "I" surpass even the most commonly used conjunctions (489 instances of "and," 163 instances of "but") and articles (162 instances of "a," 431 instances of "the") (2: 1255-287). For all that, the "I" who speaks Shakespeare's Sonnets is much less *there* than "he"/"she" appears to be. "I" depends on a dramatic "you" for its very existence, a "you" that has an existence as both "he" and "she." "I" also depends on a reading "you." And therein arise the political issues that beset contemporary readings of Shakespeare's Sonnets. The reading "I" of today is not at all the same as the writing "I" of 1609 and has no business pretending to be.

"We"

No! Time, thou shalt not bost that I doe change,
Thy pyramyds buylt vp with newer might
To me are nothing nouell, nothing strange,
They are but dressings of a former sight:
Our dates are breefe, and therfor we admire,
What thou dost foyst vpon vs that is ould,
And rather make them borne to our desire,
Then thinke that we before haue heard them tould:
Thy registers and thee I both defie,
Not wondring at the present, nor the past,
For thy records, and what we see doth lye,
Made more or less by thy continuall hast:
   This I doe vow and this shall euer be,
   I will be true dispight thy syeth and thee. (123)

By comparison with "I" (1,062 instances in its various forms), "you" and "thou" (656), "he" (190), and "she" (85), the first-person plural is curiously rare in Shakespeare's Sonnets. Yet the relationship between the speaking "I" and the reading "you" is among the most seductive in all of English verse. There are, in fact, three quite distinct "we's" involved in these transactions. In seven of the sonnets (numbers 36, 39, 40, 89, 102, 120, and 138) "we" is compounded of the speaking "me" and the dramatic "you" or "thou." "Let me confesse that we two must be twaine," the speaker begins sonnet 36, "Although our vndeuided loues are one." The fact that the implicit subject of this sentence is not "I" but "you"—"[you] let me confess"—heightens the syntactic as well as the emotional complications of saying "we." In seven other sonnets the speaking "I" attempts to speak collectively for "me" and "him." The singing of Philomel when "Our love was new" is another example. Only once, it is worth noting, does "I" attempt to speak collectively for "I" and "she." "Therefore I lye with her, and she with me, / And in our faults by lyes we flattered be": the couplet to sonnet 138 seems all the more fragile after the polarities of the three quatrains. She lies about her faithfulness; I believe her. She says I look young; I know I'm past my prime. I lie with her; she lies with me. "Our," in this context, seems tentative indeed. More often, "we" refers to all humankind, as it does in sonnets 1, 53, 54, 60, 118, 121, 123, 124, and 136. "From fairest creatures we desire increase," the speaker begins sonnet 1, and in that gesture he appeals to common opinion to argue his case for procreation. In a third, quite specialized sense, "we" can refer to the speaking "I" and his living contemporaries. Sonnets 59 and 106 both contrast people of former ages with people living now. When in sonnet 106 the speaker reads descriptions of beauty in "antique" writers, he knows that "*they* looked but with divining eyes," whereas "*we* which now behold these present days" see beauty itself in the young man. Sonnet 59 elaborates the same conceit:

> Show me your image in some antique booke,
> Since minde at first in carrecter was done.
> That I might see what the old world could say,
> To this composed wonder of your frame,
> Whether we are mended, or where better they,
> Or whether reuolution be the same. (59.7-12)

First-person plural in sonnet 123—"Our dates are breefe" (5), "therefor we admire" (5), "borne to our desire" ((7), "we before have heard them tould" (8)—can be read in all three senses. The "thou" of this particular sonnet is not "he" or "she," but personified Time. In opposition stand the speaking "I" and the beloved "he." The preceding sonnet, to which number 123 is hinged on that emphatic "No!", certainly encourages such a reading by identifying "thou" as "him": "Thy gift, thy tables, are within my brain / Full charactered with last memory." Yet the sentiments of sonnet 123's second quatrain are set forth as a kind of apothegm, as if "we" were all humankind: because we don't have much time, we admire the used goods Time tries to pass off on us as if they were just what we wanted. In the context of talk about "registers" and "records" from the past, there may also be a sense of "we" as people living "at the present." Where do those multiple possibilities of "we" leave the reading "you"? For Shakespeare's original readers, it was possible to make oneself compact with all three identities of "we": humankind in general, living contemporaries of the poet, the speaking "I" and the beloved "him." A lapse of 350 years has removed the second possibility, but the third and the first remain insistent. And it is the conjunction of the third and the first—the particular and the universal—that accounts for the Sonnets' political volatility.

The pyramids built up by Time in sonnet 123 can be imagined in at least three ways: as crumbling monuments of antiquity along the Nile, as pretentious tombs in churches, or as piles of sand accumulating in the bottoms of hourglasses. About all three the speaker says the same thing: they are "dressings of a former sight," representations of something that happened in the past. It is the folly of humankind not to acknowledge this pastness but to see the representations according to the desires of the present. Critics continue to do just that, I would argue, with Shakespeare's Sonnets: they seize upon the speaking "I" and rush to identify with it as a universal "we." What they seize upon is an illusion. "I" exists only as a function of "you," "thou," "he," and "she." Furthermore, all three parties—"he," "she," and the "I" they constitute—are cultural constructs, products of early modern ways of marking gender and articulating sexual desire. To state it in Lacan's terms, "I" is mediated by language, and language is mediated by culture—in this case, the culture of early modern England.

These contingencies should warn us against identifying with the speaking "I," and yet that is the very thing that has made Shakespeare's Sonnets the last bastion of conservative critical thinking. Too many people have too much personal investment in that "I" to be able to own the desire that "I" expresses for a person of the same sex. It is one thing to acknowledge homoerotic desire in third-person terms: when a character like Antontio in *Twelfth Night* openly expresses his passion for Sebastian, that is, after all, *him* speaking and not *me*, and that's just fine. As a person of liberal politics, I grant him the right to feel those things and say those things. It is something else again, for most people, to read one of the Sonnets aloud, to find themselves saying, "Let me not to the marriage of true minds admit impediments" and imagine expressing those sentiments to someone of their own gender. The "I" of Shakespeare's Sonnets refuses to conform to the sexual dictates of another time and place. If the "I" in these poems is so difficult to locate, then how wary you and I—or you, I, and *they*—should be in presuming to say "we."

NOTES

1. Versions of this paper were delivered as lectures at the universities of Colorado, Kansas, Maryland, and Pittsburgh. I want to thank the colleagues who invited me to speak on these occasions—Ruth Widman, David Bergeron, Marion Trousdale, and Marianne Novy—as well as the listeners whose comments shaped the paper in significant ways.

2. Quotations from Shakespeare's Sonnets are taken from the 1609 Quarto, as reproduced in facsimile in Stephen Booth's edition (1977), and are cited in the text by their number in the sequence.

3. The qualifier "apparently" needs to be emphasized. For an argument that the Sonnets as printed are not the booty of a pirate-printer see Katherine Duncan-Jones's introduction to the new Arden edition of the Sonnets (29-41).

4. Quotations from Shakespeare's plays are taken from *The Complete Works*, ed. Stanley Wells and Gary Taylor (1988) and are cited in the text by act, scene, and line numbers.

WORKS CITED

Auden, W. H. Introduction. *The Sonnets.* Ed. William Burto. New York: New American Library (Signet), 1964, xvii-xxxviii.

Bate, Jonathan. *Shakespeare's Genius.* London: Picador, 1997.

Beal, Peter. *Index of English Literary Manuscripts, 1450-1625.* London: Mansell, 1980.

Booth, Stephen, ed. *Shakespeare's Sonnets.* New Haven, Yale UP, 1977.

de Grazia, Margreta. "The Scandal of Shakespeare's Sonnets." *Shakespeare Survey* 46 (1994): 35-49.

Della Casa, Giovanni. *Galateo . . . Or rather, A treatise of the manner and behaviours, it behoueth a man to vse and eschewe, in his familiar conuersation.* Trans. Robert Peterson, London: Ralph Newberry, 1576.

Dollimore, Jonathan. *Sexual Dissidence: Augustine to Wilde, Freud to Foucault.* Oxford. Clarendon, 1991.

Dubrow, Heather. "'Incertainties now crown themselves assur'd': The Politics of Plotting Shakespeare's Sonnets." *Shakespeare Quarterly* 47 (1996): 291-305

Duncan-Jones, Katherine, ed. *Shakespeare's Sonnets.* The Arden Shakespeare. Nashville: Nelson, 1997.

Gardiner, Judith Kegan. "The Marriage of Male Minds in Shakespeare's Sonnets." *Journal of English and Germanic Philology* 84 (1985): 328-47.

Gurr, Andrew "You and Thou in Shakespeare's Sonnets." *Essays in Criticism* 32. (1982): 9-25.

Hecht, Anthony. Introduction. *The Sonnets.* Ed. G. Blakemore Evans. Cambridge: Cambridge UP, 1996. 1-28.

Irigaray, Luce. "That Gender Which Is Not One." Trans. Claudia Reeder. *New French Feminisms.* Ed. Elaine Marks and Isabelle de Courtivron. Amherst U of Massachusetts P, 1980.

Laqueur, Thomas. *Making Sex: Body and Gender from the Greeks to Freud.* Cambridge: Harvard UP, 1990.

Marlowe, Christopher. *Complete Works.* Ed. Fredson Bowers. 2nd ed. Cambridge: Cambridge UP, 1981.

Marotti, Arthur F. *Manuscript, Print, and the English Renaissance Lyric.* Ithaca: Cornell UP, 1995

Melchiori, Giorgio. *Shakespeare's Dramatic Meditations.* Oxford: Clarendon, 1976.

Osborne, Charles. "Coriolanus as Principal Boy." *The Daily Telegraph* 7 December 1989: 18.

Paster, Gail Kern. *The Body Embarrassed: Drama and the Disciplines of Shame in Early Modern England.* Ithaca: Cornell UP, 1993.

Pequigney, Joseph. *Such Is My Love: A Study of Shakespeare's Sonnets.* Chicago: U of Chicago P, 1985.

Rollins, Hyder Edward, ed. *A New Variorum Edition of Shakespeare: The Sonnets.* 2 vols. Philadelphia: Lippincott, 1944.

Shakespeare, William. *The Complete Works.* Ed. Stanley Wells and Gary Taylor. Oxford: Clarendon, 1988.

Sidney, Philip. *The Countess of Pembroke's Arcadia: The Old Arcadia.* Ed. Jean Robertson, Oxford: Clarendon, 1973.

Smith, Bruce R. *Homosexual Desire in Shakespeare's England: A Cultural Poetics.* Chicago: U of Chicago P, 1991.

Spevack, Marvin. *A Complete and Systematic Concordance to the Works of Shakespeare.* Hildesheim: Olms, 1968.

Stallybrass, Peter. "Editing as Cultural Formation: The Sexing of Shakespeare's Sonnets." *Modern Language Quarterly* 54 (1993) 91-103.

States, Bert O. *Hamlet and the Concept of Character.* Baltimore, Johns Hopkins UP, 1992.

Sex without Issue

Sodomy, Reproduction, and Signification in Shakespeare's Sonnets[1]

Valerie Traub

> For it is of course the case that the threatening sexuality that the dark
> lady represents—outside marriage and promiscuous and dangerous to
> the homosocial order—is closer to sodomy than almost anything
> suggested in the poems to the young man.
> —Jonathan Goldberg, *"Romeo and Juliet*'s Open R's"

> There is good reason, therefore, to credit Jonathan Goldberg's recent
> suggestion that in Renaissance terms, it is Shakespeare's sonnets to
> the dark lady rather than those to the young man that are sodomitic.
> —Margreta de Grazia, "The Scandal of Shakerspeare's Sonnets"

In the early 1990s, a new idea began circulating in Shakespearean
scholarship. Close on the heels of influential readings that highlighted
the homoeroticism of Shakespeare's Sonnets,[2] scholars began
suggesing that sodomy in the Sonnets is not primarily a matter of sex
between men, but rather, of sex between men and women. The remarks
by Goldberg and de Grazia might be taken by some readers as simply a
witty inversion, designed more to shock than to illuminate; other
readers might see in the convergence of their ideas an emerging critical
consensus. Yet, if there is such a consensus in the making, its import
and ramifications have yet to be investigated. For assertions of the
*hetero*sexuality of sodomy in Shakespeare's Sonnets have functioned
primarily parenthetically, embedded as they are in arguments regarding

the transitive erotics of *Romeo and Juliet* (Goldberg) and the disavowal of race in critics' construction of the dark lady (de Grazia).

The following essay investigates sodomy in Shakespeare's Sonnets as simultaneously a construction of and reaction to gender and erotic difference. My analysis addresses both causes and effects: *How is it that sodomy comes to signify heteroeroticism? And what is at stake* in figuring sodomy as a marker of gender and erotic difference? Responding to Margaret Hunt's call for scholarship focused on "the intersections between sodomy fears, the discourse of male friendship, and the domination of women" (373), I have tried to do justice to gay, queer, and feminist investments in a text that poses such investments as conflictual. By locating the sodomy of the Sonnets within material practices of early modern culture, by positioning Shakespeare's treatment of male bonds in diacritical relation to his depiction of women, I hope to gain some intellectual purchase on the elision of women's desires by the category of sodomy; at the same time, I attempt to unravel in historical terms the convergence in Shakespeare's poems of male homoerotic desire and misogyny.

Renaissance sodomy was a diffuse yet flexible prohibitive category, available for deployment in an array of discursive contexts. For the purposes of this essay, it is important to note that as an erotic practice, sodomy was negatively constituted on the basis of various recognitions (or misrecognitions): the human adult marital body is recognized as the only appropriate erotic object; penetration is recognized as the only appropriate activity; the penis is recognized as the only appropriate instrument; and the vagina is recognized as the only appropriate receptacle. In the early modern period, sodomy exists *as an imaginary structure* whenever these recognitions are violated, wherever the boundaries and systems of alliance they attempt to enforce are crossed or confused. Sodomy thus includes, but is not limited to, all sexuality that does not have procreation as its goal.[3] The hazy inclusiveness of sodomy's definition means that there is no cognitive dissonance in the Puritan preacher William Perkins's admonishment that sodomy is a sin that either husband or wife could commit (24, 117), Philip Stubbes's description of an adulterous man and woman "playing the vile Sodomits together" (H6ᵛ), and Sir Simonds D'Ewes's comment that Francis Bacon failed to "relinquish the practice of his most horrible and secret sin of sodomy, keeping still one Godrick a very effeminate faced youth to be his catamite and bedfellow" (cited in Bray, "Homosexuality and the Signs" 54).

In contrast to these broad articulations of erotic sin, however, the discourse of the law increasingly insisted upon a less inclusive definition. In the years between the passage in 1533-34 of the statute that first reinterpreted sodomy as a secular rather than religious crime, and the publication of Sir Edward Coke's authoritative legal scholarship in 1644, a gradual proliferation and codification of legal and social understandings transformed what had for centuries been a general and undefined category of "unnatural acts" into an increasingly precise series of legal and colloquial terms. Despite the sense of unspeakability that the law carried over from religious terminology—Coke called buggery "a detestable and abominable sin, amongst Christians not to be named"—the professionalization of the law demanded more exacting definitions and criteria of proof. Accordingly, even though the number of actual prosecutions remained relatively low throughout the period, the violations of which sodomy was the sign became differentiated according to species, gender, age, and the presence of coercion or force. By the mid-seventeenth century, sodomy required the presence of penetration and/or ejaculation to be legally actionable.[4]

The question remains open whether the law initiated changes in cultural attitudes or merely formalized understandings already widely held. Whichever was the case, the process of legal codification gave official authorization to gender asymmetries already extant in early modern England. With notable, even stunning blindness, English law viewed women as incapable of erotically penetrating others. Despite the increased amplification of discourses of "tribadism" in anatomy texts, midwiferies, and travel accounts over the course of the seventeenth century (see Traub, "Psychomorphology"), and despite the fact that Thomas Blount's vernacular dictionaries of 1661 and 1670, *Glossographia*, include references to "woman with a woman" under the heading of "Buggerie," there was no legal recognition accorded to such a possibility: Coke's *Institutes of the Lawes of England* interprets female sodomy as bestiality, citing an incident of "a great Lady [who] had committed Buggery with a Baboon, and conceived by it, etc." Even so, no English woman was brought to trial under the sodomy statute during this period. The result of legal codification was that women were elided thrice over: within a statutory framework, women's erotic acts with one another were rendered unintelligible; women's nonreproductive erotic acts with men were ignored; and within the judicial exercise of the statute, female bestiality was not prosecuted. Sodomy became a crime between men.

The failure to prosecute women for sodomy is a rare instance of judicial inequality working in women's favor, and I do not mean to fight over the right for women to be victimized by criminal law. Indeed, recent work on the history of female-female eroticism suggests that the disarticulation of women from sodomy may have enabled an unacknowledged space for female erotic autonomy (see Simons; Traub, "(In)Significance" and "Perversion"). But the question remains, why were English women's nonreproductive activities with men conceivable by the populace as sodomitical, and yet, in a culture that increasingly prosecuted women for premarital fornication and adultery, ignored by the authorities?[5] What does the erasure of women from the legal category of sodomy mean, at odds as it is with medical and popular knowledge that women could and did engage in nonreproductive acts with men, as well as erotic acts with other women? What are the historical effects of the gendered deployment of sodomy?

There is nothing intrinsic to the category of sodomy that automatically would exclude women; sodomy statutes were used to prosecute women who engaged in penetrative sex with one another on the continent. Yet, despite the historical distance separating early modern modes of conceptualization from contemporary ones, the elision of English women from the category of sodomy continues today. For despite important differences in recent scholarship on Renaissance sodomy, this work is unified in the assumption that the sodomite is a figure of male desire, and sodomitical erotics are those of the male body. In this regard, most critics take their lead from Alan Bray's *Homosexuality in Renaissance England* which, due to its focus on English law, necessarily omits female sodomy. Bray accurately maintains that "Female homosexuality was rarely linked in popular thought with male homosexuality" (17), a view that is seconded by Smith's *Homosexual Desire in Shakespeare's England*, which explains its focus on men by claiming that in Renaissance culture, "if female sexuality in general has only a peripheral place, lesbianism seems almost beyond notice" (28). Similarly, Bredbeck's *Sodomy and Interpretation* glides over why the category of female buggery admitted in Thomas Blount's 1670 edition of *Glossographia* is omitted in Coke's legal scholarship republished in the same year, judging that question less important than the increasing amplification of sodomitical terms. Finally, although Goldberg focuses our attention on the heteroeroticism of sodomy in Shakespeare's Sonnets, his analysis of Juliet's and Rosalind's sodomitical function depends on a gender transitivity that positions these characters as masculine.[6]

It is not my intent to resurrect gender difference as a critical axiom nor to challenge scholars' interests in erotic practices among men. The pertinent question is not why critics elide women (or femininity) in their analyses of sodomy, but rather how the historical deployment of the category of sodomy has displaced female desire, thus structuring such an elision into discourse. To resist that disarticulation, to pry apart that structure, is to begin to recover its historicity.

Shakespeare's Sonnets provide a way of approaching this problem from an oblique angle, for they defy the historical erasure of sodomitical women at the same time that they disallow the possibility of autonomous female desires. Although the word *sodomy* nowhere appears, its potential to mark erotic practices as illicit and threatening provides a governing structure for the poems' negotiations of gender and erotic difference. As a collection, these poems confront (1) the desirability and significance of male desire for men; (2) the difficulties posed for male heteroeroticism in a society that systematically undervalues women; and (3) the necessity of insuring that women's desires accord with those of men, thus harnessing women to patriarchal reproduction.

Because it condenses these three problems into one, sonnet 20 is pivotal. After conflating masculinity and femininity within the scope of one beloved object—the "Master Mistres" of the speaker's "passion"—the poem reasserts gender difference by elevating the status of the male friend through a series of comparisons to women.[7] Constructing woman as "shifting" and "false" (4), the sonnet concludes by ascribing an apparently natural, physiological inevitability to heteroeroticism: the beloved's penis is "one thing to my purpose nothing" (12); rather, his friend has been "prickt . . . out for womens pleasure" (13). Sonnet 20 has been a battleground for critics intent on proving or disproving the presence of male homoerotic desire; the poet's apparent indifference to his friend's penis is often read as evidence of the poet's lack of erotic investment.[8] My interest in the way the prick is reserved for women's pleasure, however, is not to dismiss male erotic bonds—homoerotic affect is hardly reducible to fetishizing the phallus—but to foreground the strategy at work in the poet's successful refusal to represent male bonds as sodomitical.[9] The male homoeroticism that infuses the first 126 sonnets is less concerned with penetration than procreation, less preoccupied with exploring the male body's interiority than rehearsing the possibility of its duplication. These lyrics are obsessed with the reproduction of the speaker's "love," the word used to denote both the *object* of the speaker's desire and *his own desire*—first, through the physical mimesis of the beloved in his male heirs, and second, through his replication and "posterity" (55.11) in the poet's "eternall lines" (18.12). This strategy brilliantly defends against an emerging ideology: by adopting the dominant discourse by which carnal desire was legitimized—reproduction—the poet authorizes male homoeroticism by placing it outside of the confines increasingly being imposed by legal discourses.

Brilliant, but not without pernicious effects. For gender, as Judith Butler has argued, exists only as a relation; because masculinity and femininity are mutually constitutive, neither exists in any meaningful way without the other. The diacritical work that goes into the construction of gender relations means that those strategies affecting men will produce compensatory strategies affecting women—and vice versa. This ongoing tension between genders is evinced throughout Shakespeare's sequence, beginning with the shift that occurs within the first twenty sonnets: a movement away from an image of woman as pure receptivity and reproductivity, the genital "viall" that impregnation would "make sweet" (6.3), toward an image of man as source of both biological and poetic generation. Through the use of tropes of getting, increase, tillage, husbandry, engrafting, printing, copying, and issue, the collection appropriates the rhetoric of biological and mechanical reproduction for male-male love. "Laboring for invention" (59.3), the poet gives birth to poems which are themselves the progeny of his "love."

The poet's adoption of a rhetoric of reproduction does not merely privilege male over female generation, however. A corresponding result of the exclusion of women from a procreative role is a strategic elaboration of heteroeroticism as sodomical. Sonnet 129 establishes the illicit and terrifying figure of woman-as-sodomite. "Th'expence of Spirit in a waste of shame" figuratively refers to the expenditure of semen—either inside or outside of the vagina, mouth, or anus.[10] If inside the vagina, sonnet 129 constructs the female body as the vile repository of the seed and shame of conventional intercourse. Indeed, the governing pun of the first line works to fix the site of shame as the vaginal orifice, as the Latin *pudenda* enables a series of conceptual equations: "waste" puns on "waist," which conceptually invokes *pudenda*, which itself derives from the word for "shame." This circular tautology constructs the female genitals as always already shameful. But since the amplifying, runaway impulse of the poem works against any effort to circumscribe the eroticism being addressed, "th'expence of Spirit in a waste of shame" can be read to refer, as well, to any penetrative activity, including phallic withdrawal and emission and oral or anal intercourse—especially anal penetration, as "waste" is associated with the orifice for expelling refuse from the body.[11] The defiling sense of profligate consumption that opens this poem constructs erotic encounters as a violation of those recognitions upon which a fantasy of normative sexuality depends. With heteroeroticism rendered penetrative but nonprocreative, with the circle of shame extended to include the man who wastes his semen, the erotic economy of this poem is, *in the terms of Shakespeare's culture*, sodomitical.

This sodomitical economy is reiterated in subsequent sonnets, most notably in the companion poems, "Who ever hath her wish, thou hast thy Will, / And Will too boote, and Will in over-plus" (135) and "If thy soule check thee that I come so neere, / Sweare to thy blind soule that I was thy Will" (136). Given the female promiscuity alleged in sonnet 135, where the lady is "rich" not only in her "Will," but in many other Wills, where the speaker, as Eve Sedgwick notes, seems to luxuriate in a homoerotic sea of seminal fluid, the erasure of female reproductive power compensates defensively for the generative power accorded to male-male love (28-48). For, although the speaker in previous poems has obsessively contemplated his friend's procreative powers, and depends upon the young man's fertility to mimetically reproduce a son in his own "sweet semblance" (13.4), his lack of concern with the similar potential of his mistress suggests that, for him, reproduction is not the purpose of sex with women.[12]

What, then, *is* the purpose of sex with women? The procreative advice given to the young man suggests that desire for women is not itself in conflict with male bonds. Yet, as Sedgwick reminds us, the sequence's urbane suspension of difference between hetero- and homoerotic collapses when a woman as a specific object of desire appears (34-35). Why? Does her entrance simply mark the difference between an idealized concept and a problematic reality? Only partly. For, even as it introduces the presence of a desiring woman, the sequence implements an inversion of reproductive exigencies that attempts to secure and contain that female presence under the sign of sodomy.

We can chart the transformation in psychic affect that takes place. If the young man's first "sensuall fault" (35.9) is excused by the speaker's claim that since he and his friend are one, his mistress "loves but me alone" (42.14), no such rationalization saves later erotic complications from a bitter rhetoric of blame, self-recrimination, and loss. In the early sonnets, love and erotic pleasure are easily, even joyfully, separated, with the poet retaining the youth's love, while women (like their counterparts in anatomy books and midwiferies) enjoy pleasure as part of their reproductive role ("thy loves *use* their treasure" [20.14; emphasis added]).[13] Once marriage, reproduction, and inheritance of name and property are no longer the goal, however, heteroeroticism becomes distinctly unpleasurable, "made" not only "in pursut" but "in possession" (129.9). Increasingly suppressed as the impetus for heterosexual contact, pleasure is replaced with "sicklie appetite" (147.4) and rapacious "will." This displacement of pleasure enforces a corresponding division between love, the name for what the speaker gives and gets from men, and lust, the signifier of what he feels for and projects onto women. This is not to imply that homoeroticism is without erotic energy nor that such energy is anxiety-free. But whereas homoerotic desire is worrisome only to the extent that "the bitterness of absence" (57.7) fosters fear that the poet's love is unrequited, heteroerotic desire is troubling when physical proximity is most imminent and intimate. At issue in both relations is the abjection associated with loss of control, but the materiality of female embodiment renders abjection in relation to a woman intolerable. Evidently, male bonds are not reducible to the "grose bodies treason" (151.6) or lack of free "will" that signifies the "hell" to which men inexorably are led.

Yet, despite the involuntary mechanics of erection expressed in sonnet 151, the inevitability of male desire for women is precisely what has *not* been a given in this sequence: "Nor are mine eares with thy toungs tune delighted, / Nor tender feeling to base touches prone, / Nor taste, nor smell, desire to be invited / To any sensuall feast with thee alone" (141.5-8). Such heteroerotic necessity, rather, is produced—first within the young man by the poet's insistence on progeny, and then in the collection as a whole as a corollary to sodomy. In fact, the idea of women converting what feels unnatural into the inevitable is a good definition of both sodomy and misogyny, and does much to explain their mutually sustaining influence in these poems. The asymmetrical construction of an idealized, if hierarchical, procreative homoerotic love and a compulsive, sodomitical, heterosexual lust instantiates a continuing interpretative difficulty in these poems: the close relation they express between male homoeroticism and misogyny.

This co-incidence, I want to argue, is best approached by a historical account that refuses to predicate its interpretation on a putatively natural, causal link. It is just such a lack of historical analysis that characterizes the psychoanalytic view of the Sonnets' misogyny, with its imputation of the male homosexual's overvaluation of the penis, excessive castration anxiety, and aversion to female genitalia. Finding an etiology in the boy's reaction against a threatening maternal body, psychoanalysis asserts a self-evident link between erotic affect and defensive posture: men hate women because they are homosexual; men are homosexual because they hate women. Not only tautological and homophobic, this interpretation is itself misogynist, premised as it is on the notion of feminine "lack," both as a transhistorical category of being and as constitutive of male homosexuality. On the contrary, homoerotic desire is not a reaction-formation against some putatively natural object choice, nor is misogyny born of an erotic preference for male bodies. Misogyny must be produced, elicited, and supported by historically specific social expectations and structures that construct the female body as inferior, threatening, or loathsome. Shakespeare's Sonnets draw from and reiterate such social codes, but some of his romantic comedies, I have argued elsewhere, do not (see Traub, *Desire and Anxiety*). Why, then, does misogyny seem to accompany male-male love so readily in the Sonnets?

I can advance two historical reasons, the first of which concerns the formal manipulation of genre. Whereas a formal goal of many Shakespearean comedies is to explore homoerotic desires within the safety of an overall heterosexual (en)closure, the Sonnets represent heteroerotic desires within a normative homoerotic economy. As a group of individual lyrics unfettered by demands of coherent character or linear plot, the sonnet cycle may have been less constrained by its Petrarchan models than was the formal structure of comedy, which developed from well-established classical and continental literary antecedents. For, despite the Sonnets' movement from male to female addressee, the collection throughout treats heteroeroticism as a *vehicle* for erotic bonds between men.

As the repeated troping on usury attests, the speaker initially is willing for the young man to lend himself out to women, sure in the knowledge that "To give away your selfe keeps your selfe still" (16.13). The point is to make some "profit" (77.14) on one's loan— namely, an heir. Promoting heteroerotic alliance also allows the speaker to assert indirect control over his friend's erotic circulation; those poems that respond to the youth's "profitles usur[y]" condemn "having traffike with thy selfe alone" (4.7, 9), not only because masturbation is a "waste," a "murdrous shame" (9.11, 14), but because it restricts the speaker's erotic access. As Sedgwick has demonstrated, in these poems the way to erotic congress with other men is in and through the bodies of women. Within this homosocial context, when "nature" pricks the boy out for female pleasure, she functions not as a personification of an essential heterosexual drive—she, after all, has homoerotically fallen in love with her female creation. What her pricking insures is the continuance of male bonds through hetero reproductivity. The problem confronted after this pricking is not that the young man might have sex with women, but that he might desire more from them than domestic, reproductive sex—that he might relinquish his self-ownership and become, in effect, possessed, contained by the very vial he is supposed to fill and contain. Subsequent poems suggest that the friend's erotic circulation has become excessive, expressing fears that he will grow "common" and "rancke" (69.14, 12) or "loose his edge" (95.14)— words that evoke a degraded effeminacy, associated as they are with the lady's genital "common place" (137.10) and the fear of being "ill us'd" (95.14).

One problem with the later erotic triangle is that there is no reproductive issue, no "profit" that would justify either man's erotic "traffike." Having appropriated procreation to authorize male bonds, the sequence preempts the possibility of women's generativity; it is this loss of female reproductive power that further accounts for the coincidence of male homoeroticism and misogyny in these poems. As testified by countless religious, medical, moral, and legal tracts, procreation was the primary means by which early modern women (and marriage) were accorded value. Humanists, Protestant theologians, and writers of conduct books and stageplays contravened misogynist attacks on matrimony by celebrating the necessity of procreation.[14] Even Erasmus, who radically extolled the mutual pleasures of the marriage bed, asserted that "a wife is to be maintained for the purpose of producing offspring not pleasure" (93). The enormous cultural stakes in reproduction cut across class and status lines: from the increase in the working poor's labor power, to the inheritance of vast quantities of wealth and property, to the stability of monarchical government through orderly succession.

With the arrogation of procreation for poetic practice, biological and aesthetic creation become indistinguishable. Indeed, from the first sentence of the first sonnet—"From fairest creatures we desire increase"—the speaker's desire for the young man is figured not only in terms of biological continuity but metaphorical amplification. Part of what makes the "lovely boy" (126.1) such a fascinating object is the potential reproducibility of his fair "coppy" (11.14)—the rights over which are contested by the rival poet poems, where the speaker expresses the hope that his unique spiritual and emotional union with his beloved generates something better and truer than his rivals' "gross painting" (82.13). Indeed, the virtue of male-male love in these poems (as in Renaissance theories of male friendship generally) is that it offers the possibility of mimetic duplication, with the homogeneity of male bodies enabling an infinity of affective and poetic responses.[15] Despite the poet's temporary fretting over his "blunt invention" (103.7), he takes recourse in rehearsing what is, for him, a truism: "How can my Muse want subject to invent / While thou dost breath that poor'st into my verse" (38.1-2). Paradoxically, the Sonnets' homoerotics of similitude depends upon differences of age, status, beauty, and physical location—the contemplation of such differences providing the fertilizing experience for the creation of new poetry. Even when the impulse to "alwaies write of you" (76.9) falls into the repetitive "argument" of "Faire, kinde, and true" (105.9), this "wondrous scope" (105.12) celebrates the linguistic multiplication that the male body engenders.

The homoerotics of similitude generates a poetics of reproduction which, among other things, sanctions the speaker's acceptance of his own encroaching mortality: the "lovely Boy . . . hast by wayning growne, and therein show'st / Thy lovers withering" (126.1, 3-4). As the resemblance between older and younger man enables a productive mimesis, the beloved's youth and beauty compensate for the recognition that both men will age and die. In such lines as "T'is thee (my selfe) that for my selfe I praise / Painting my age with beauty of thy daies" (62.13-14), dread of death is moderated by the poetics of male (re)generation.

The relations between sodomy, reproduction, and signification in the Sonnets rely upon their status as gendered lyrics. Since de Grazia's reminder of "the astonishing number of sonnets that do *not* make the gender of the addressee explicit," the significance of this lack has been debated (40). Heather Dubrow, in an essay reprinted in this collection, notably argues that so many of the poems fail to employ pronouns that we should scuttle the traditional division (the first 126 poems addressed to or about a young man, the subsequent poems addressed to or about a dark lady) as well as narrative sequencing. Acceptance of the Sonnets' indeterminacy, Dubrow asserts, allows for a pluralism of interpretation unhampered by many constraints. In her adjudication of "the issue of addressees," however, Dubrow conflates several separate issues: the textual authority of the 1609 sequence, the structural division of two gendered groups, the fabrication of a linear plot (the love affair) and a corresponding identification of protagonists (303). One need not accept the 1609 Quarto as authoritative nor agree that the collection constructs a diachronic narrative based on coherent characterization (biographical or fictional) to assert that specific gender positions nonetheless are inscribed.

For despite some gender ambiguity in modes of linguistic address, male and female *bodies* are cathected quite differently in these poems; whereas pronouns attached to each erotic object may be absent or indeterminate, the emotional affects attached to their bodies are neither. Specific images of embodiment—fair/dark, angel/devil, kind/covetous, day/night—are mapped onto a gender binary presented as incontrovertible. Other tropes, replete with bawdy meanings, are reserved for the female body: cunning love (148.13), abhor (150.11), hell (129.14, 144.12). Indeed, the investment of these lyrics in multiple and simultaneous erotic objects leads to a compensatory reinscription of gender difference. Rather than celebrating a polymorphously perverse desire that can find satisfaction anywhere with anyone, or a gender transitivity that masculinizes women and feminizes men, the Sonnets apotropaically defend against the possible substitution of women for men.[16]

Sonnet 129 enacts this defensive reinscription. Most of its claims are detached and generalizable, referring to an ostensibly nongendered "lust in action" (2). But the final line slyly genders the source of lust. Read in the context of other sonnets with explicit pronouns or gender markers (i.e., sonnet 144), the hell to which men are led necessarily refers to the "nether parts" of the female body.[17] This articulation of a genital hell, however, extends beyond a general misogyny, given its quintessential Shakespearean expression in Lear's "But to the girdle do the gods inherit / Beneath is all the fiends'. / There's hell, there's darkness, there is the sulphurous pit" (4.6.126-28)[18]—in which the female body, with its rapacious desires, figures the antithesis of heavenly bliss. In the Sonnets, rather, the hell the female body represents is the inversion, even cancellation, of the purpose for which God supposedly made woman.

"Be fruitful and multiply" said God to Adam and Eve, and reproduction thereafter insured in Judeo-Christian cultures a justification of heterosexual alliance. But fruitfulness and multiplication are precisely what are denied to Shakespeare's dark lady, whose sterile body threatens to cancel out the justification for heterosexuality as well as the reproductive poetics of homoerotic similitude. For, in contrast to the speaker's generative union with the young man, "Desire" between men and women, as sonnet 147 bluntly states, "*is* death" (8); it creates not new life but a madness that can only with extreme effort be controlled by the rigid structure of the sonnet form—as attested by the extremity of language in sonnet 129, the masochistic perjury of "When my love sweares that she is made of truth, / I do beleeve her, though I know she lyes" (138.1-2), the self-anatomizing division of the bodily senses from the heart (141), and the careful, oppositional balancing act of "Two loves I have of comfort and dispaire" (144.1).

Indeed, in its attempt to segregate his "better angel" from his "female evil," sonnet 144 epitomizes the poet's effort to produce the two genders as incommensurable opposites. Despite the existence of medical theories that considered the female reproductive body as structurally homologous to the male, Shakespeare's Sonnets figure the terms of female embodiment as the antithesis of male embodiment.[19] The threat let loose by this production of incommensurability, however, is skillfully managed by representing female pleasure as constituted by and for a male erotic economy. If "womens pleasure" (20.13) first appears under the auspices of an allegorical female "nature," the autonomy of this pleasure is foreclosed once woman is embodied with a "will" to which the poet finds himself "morgag'd" (134.2). Thus, in sonnets 135 and 136, the lady's erotic "will" is collapsed into those other "wills" that mix so promiscuously in her body, wills that, in reiterating and amplifying the poet's name, overwhelm and efface her will. If "will" initially functions as a metaphor for the lady's erotic appetite, it ends as a metonym for the poet's identification and union with other men, as an "abundance" of wills subsumes the woman's desire even as it is represented as "large and spacious" (135.5). Whether a synecdoche for vagina, anus, or mouth, the lady's boundless desire becomes identified with a specifically phallic pleasure; and "Will's" pleasure becomes the homosocial measure and merger of all phallic potential: "Thinke all but one, and me in that one Will" (135.14).

In these sonnets Shakespeare transfers the injunction given in sonnet 6 to the young man—"Be not self-willed" (13)—onto his mistress; and his adroit linguistic conflation of male and female wills leaves no space for difference, either between the lady and the poet, or between the poet and other men. Stephen Booth glosses "Thinke all but one" in sonnet 135.14 as "1) consider them a conglomerate; 2) let it all be the same to you; consider it a matter of indifference." This "willed" indifference suggests that heteroeroticism in these poems ultimately involves not an immersion in (or celebration of) gender difference, but an anxious projection of similitude, an attempt to manage difference by reducing it to sameness. The strategy of imposing sameness is reiterated and reinforced: "Will, will fulfill the treasure of thy love, / I fill it full with wils, and my will one" (136.5-6), with the puns on I/Ay and one/won simultaneously expressing the poet's singularity and his victory over all rival desires—including the mistress's desire. The point of all this linguistic repetition and coital filling and merging seems to be a willing away of difference. Expressed within the fantasy of that indifferently phallic "one" is an equally fantastic desire to return to a state of undifferentiation: not the merger of infant with maternal body, but the cramming of the mistress's womb with *male* bodies, and in so doing, eliminating all space for independent female desires.

But without some difference, signification is impossible. By the later dark lady poems, the female body has come to signify a linguistic void, the fantasized capaciousness of her desire a sign of her body's ability to swallow and destroy rather than bring forth. In this vision of sodomy as the erasure of erotic difference, the desiring man literally falls into an endless, dark hole: his sex is used, his self "ingrossed" (133.6), but to no ultimate, redemptive purpose. Rather than conceiving through his erotic activity new life, new words, new poetry, the male body is expended, defeated, wasted. Despite the tight hold it exercises on the poet's imagination, sex with women is linguistically and materially no better than "murdrous" masturbation. And sodomitically shorn of its reproductive potential, the female erotic body becomes equated with the destruction of signification, the end of the reproduction of the signifier. Misogyny thus is not the *pre-existing affect* in Shakespeare's poems, nor is it the cause or result of male homoeroticism. Misogyny here is an *ideological effect* generated from a conflict over who is going to control (discourses of) reproduction.

As sites of negotiation over the gendered meanings of reproduction, sodomy, and signification, Shakespeare's Sonnets resist emerging legal discourses in order to authorize male homoeroticism. While appropriating reproduction for a male homoerotic poetics, the Sonnets correlatively drain heteroeroticism of all procreative promise. With the metaphysical baggage attached to sodomy shifted onto women, the female body becomes the sign of sodomy's potential to disrupt, even end, signification. Whereas the homoerotics of similitude generates an enabling poetic difference, the difference implicit in heteroeroticism is reduced to an overarching masculine sameness. Inverting the status of heterosexuality as originary and natural, the representation of woman-as-sodomite implies that men's desire for women is not axiomatic, but must continually be (re)produced.

Fineman's influential reading of the relations between gender, eroticism, and signification argues that the Sonnets progress from visionary idealization and homologous attraction to linguistic doubleness and heterogenous desire. Assuming the priority of heterosexuality over homoeroticism, and viewing the movement from sameness to difference as a developmental transition recapitulating the movement from the Imaginary to the Symbolic, Fineman reads the dark lady poems as inaugurating a novel poetics of heterosexuality. In contrast, by charting the troubled *production* of heteroerotic desire, I hope to have shown not only that the Sonnets present heterosexuality as a back-formation from homoeroticism, but that anxieties about heterosexual difference are thematized as a threat to creative (re)production.

And yet, the poems keep coming. Specifically, poems keep coming that are obsessed with female duplicity, lies, and ultimately with the impossibility of all previously dependable visual and linguistic codes to tell the truth. Paradoxically, this terror—that lodged within the female body is not only the termination of reproductive heterosexuality, but the end of a poetry equal to the task of representing it—gives rise to more poetry. The intense emotional investment once directed toward the fair true young man is now all for the dark lady whose very body, in the racialized tropes of Western aesthetics, signals false signification. Although the poet attempts to redeem this emotional paradox through the use of further linguistic paradoxes—as in sonnet 138's assertion that both speaker and mistress "in our faults by lyes we flattered be" (14)—and although he acknowledges in sonnet 144 that he must "live in doubt" (13), by sonnet 147 he no longer can play that game. Admitting that his mistress's capacity for duplicity compels his own lies—"For I have sworne thee faire, and thought thee bright, / Who art as black as hell, as dark as night" (147.13-14)—and reiterating that oxymoron through the final couplet of sonnet 152—"For I have sworn thee fair: more perjurde eye, / To swere against the truth so foule a lie"—the speaker expresses the fear that the negative payoff of having defined sodomy as the principal term of female embodiment is the creation of an image of woman powerful enough to stop his own voice.

"OH from what powre hast thou this powrefull might," asks the poet (150.1); and we might well answer: from the equations forged among sodomy, disrupted signification, and the female body. But that is not all. For the impasse he confronts, wherein neither sight can apprehend nor voice can articulate the truth, also derives from the association of sodomy with racial difference. For whether it is the case, as de Grazia contends, that the dark lady refers to a woman of African descent, tropes of light and dark certainly drew from and helped to construct racial and erotic boundaries (see Hall). Sodomy, Mario Digangi opines, "derived its stigmatizing power from threateningly exotic significations: the sodomite was devil, heretic, New World savage, cannibal, Turk, African, papist, Italian" (13). With her darkness potentially contaminating not only the poet, but the youth's fair purity, with her promiscuous unproductivity defying patriarchal reproduction, with her deceit undermining truthful signification, the dark lady embodies many of the most powerful threats to the social order.

This threat, however, is overwritten, and the image of female sodomite elided, by the two poems that conclude the sequence, poems that have so puzzled critics that many have sought to deny their inclusion in the Shakespearean canon. Thematically and stylistically detached from the rest of the sequence, these "anacreontic" poems narrate in two different versions the same story, in which Cupid's "heart inflaming brand" is stolen by a virgin nymph, its fire quenched in a fountain/well (see Figure 6 in this volume).[20] Both lyrics enact the destruction of an emblematic love, symbolized by Cupid, while constructing the origin of a specific heterosexual desire, that of the speaker. Although Cupid's arrow is "disarm'd," by the end of the poems his "love's brand" is "new fired" (9) in the eye of the mistress; the speaker becomes the living embodiment of a lovesickness for which there is no cure. By renarrating the origin of heterosexual desire as a mythological occurrence, by reconfiguring the female body as the originary, natural object of male desire, these surprisingly conventional poems work as a defensive addendum, attempting to cancel what has come before. As the collection draws to a close, the poet, in an effort to bypass the problems engendered by his own aesthetic strategy, attempts to undo by overdoing. His very repetition implies an insecurity about asserting the naturalness of heteroeroticism—understandably enough, given that the previous 152 poems have so insistently troubled appeals to heterosexuality as prior, originary, essential.

Historically, Shakespeare's attempt to reserve sodomy as a signifier of heteroeroticism loses out; since the seventeenth century, sodomy has signified acts performed, legislated, and prosecuted primarily between men. Yet, despite the historical failure of the Sonnets' strategy, their legacy is to demonstrate how intractably the relationship between eroticism, gender, and signification is mediated by desires for and anxieties about "sex without issue." That sex in the Sonnets becomes, in the nineteenth century, conflated with the issue of sodomy—significantly *reattached* to male bodies and bonds and because of this a site of moral panic (see Stallybrass, also reprinted in this volume)—perversely reenacts the historical conditions out of which Shakespeare's Sonnets emerged.

NOTES

1. The genesis of this essay owes everything to a conversation with Peter Stallybrass about the heterosexuality of the Sonnets, and I thank him for his provocative remarks. I also thank Mark Schoenfield for graciously reading and discussing with me all of Shakespeare's Sonnets; his comments on an early draft of this essay, along with those by Jim Schiffer, Mike Schoenfeldt, Carol Thomas Neely, Teresa Goddu, and William Slights were most welcome. I am also grateful to the Shakespeare Association of America, the University of Massachusetts, the University of Florida-Gainesville, and Florida State University for the opportunity to benefit from auditors' responses to this paper, and to the Newberry Library for a fellowship during which I completed revisions.

2. See the groundbreaking work of Eve Kosofsky Sedgwick, Joseph Pequigney, Bruce R. Smith, and Gregory Bredbeck.

3. See Bray, *Homosexuality in Renaissance England.* I am especially indebted to Goldberg, who follows Foucault in describing sodomy as "the word for everything illicit, all that lies outside the system of alliance that juridically guarantees marriage and inheritance, the prerogatives of blood, the linchpin of social order and the maintenance of class distinctions" (*Sodometries* 122). Goldberg's focus on the definitional incoherence of sodomy emphasizes the extent to which reproductive sexuality was crucial to the social order. The limitation of this interpretation, however, is that it fails to take into account the varying deployments of sodomy within different material practices: sodomy was encoded differently in various discourses, changed historically, and only occasionally included female eroticism within its scope.

4. For the political context of the passage of Statute 25 Henry VIII, chapter 6, and subsequent refinements of sodomy legislation, see Smith 43-53. For the proliferation of terms, see Bredbeck 10-20. In the *Third Part of the Institutes of the Lawes of England* (London, 1644), Coke insisted that penetration was necessary, but the Lord Chief Justice in the 1631 Castlehaven case thought that emission alone was sufficient proof; see Herrup 1-18.

5. That the varieties of female sexual sin are condensed into the legal categories of fornication (intercourse before marriage), adultery, and bastard bearing (all under the purview of ecclesiastical justice) and whoredom (under the purview of secular courts) suggests the extent to which the primary frame of reference for both ecclesiastical and secular law was less particular erotic acts than the maintenance of *reproductive sexuality* within the bonds of marriage. Martin Ingram, in *Church Courts, Sex and Marriage in England, 1570-1640*, argues that ecclesiastical prosecutions increased in parishes experiencing economic upheaval, with the purpose of limiting the number of destitute children for whom the parish would be financially responsible. He also demonstrates that litigation over sexual slander was on the rise.

6. Whereas Goldberg's tracking of movements across gender destabilizes hetero normativity, it also tends to evacuate gender specificity.

7. Quotations follow the 1609 Quarto reproduced in *Shakespeare's Sonnets*, ed. Stephen Booth.

8. In this regard, Pequigney's courageous book cedes too much to the heterosexist demand that homoeroticism be ascertained through "proof" of genital "consummation"—a criterion notably missing from presumptions of heterosexuality. In addition, although readings of individual poems are insightful, Pequigney's effort to make the Sonnets tell a story of transhistorical homosexuality, his dependence on the developmental narrative of "the love

affair," and his reliance on Freud in discussing the etiology of homosexuality and male narcissism remain undertheorized.

Conversely, the dismissal of eroticism from male bonds in the criticism of Arthur Marotti and Joel Fineman flaws their important studies. Marotti's assertion that Shakespeare's is a "collection in which erotic love and the affectionate friendship of males are kept strictly separate" enforces an ahistorical dichotomization of desires (412). Fineman's distinction between ascetic homosexuality and erotic heterosexuality likewise is blind to the eroticism suffusing the first 126 poems, and imposes modern identity categories onto early modern eroticism. See *Shakespeare's Perjured Eye.*

Judith Kegan Gardiner helpfully locates the speaker's courtship of the young man within Renaissance discourses of marriage. However, in detailing the ways Shakespeare appropriates marital language, she inadvertently reasserts the binarisms she wishes to displace: emotional commitment (chaste, companionate marital love) is privileged over and against erotic practices. Although her definition of marital chastity includes the possibility of sexuality, her assumption that there is no discernible eroticism between the two men belies this definition. See "The Marriage of Male Minds in Shakespeare's Sonnets."

9. Bray's analysis of the conceptual split between discourses of sodomy and male friendship in "Homosexuality and the Signs of Male Friendship" informs my account.

10. "Spirit" was a colloquial term for seminal fluid, while "spend" referred to ejaculation.

11. My sense that sonnet 129 depends on penetration relies on the all-encompassing enclosure that ends the final couplet: hell. Nor is it fear of conception that impels the sonnet; despite the relative lack of effective birth control and the harsh social consequences for illegitimate births, unwanted pregnancy never arises as a possibility.

12. Despite the fact that the youth is his "mothers glasse" (3.9), the possibility of engendering female offspring seems to be unimaginable.

13. Conception was believed to be dependent upon female orgasm; see Laqueur.

14. In *The Expense of Spirit: Love and Sexuality in English Renaissance Drama,* Mary Beth Rose explores the rise in the prestige of marriage, helpfully bringing humanist and Protestant tracts into dialogue with drama. In addition, in "The Marriage of Male Minds," Gardiner notes that of "the three conventional Renaissance reasons for marriage—legitimate procreation, sinless sexuality, and marital love, Shakespeare stresses only the first" in his addresses to the young man (334).

15. My understanding of the homoerotics of similitude and its relation to rhetorics of male friendship is indebted to Jeffrey Masten, *Textual Intercourse: Collaboration, Authorship, and Sexualities in Renaissance Drama*.

16. I do not mean to imply that all of the Sonnets so gender the object of address, only that enough of them do to create a binary frame of reference. At the same time, the assumption that the collection identifies only four players too narrowly circumscribes erotic possibilities. The references to at least two triangles, the beloved's erotic traffic, and the lady's involvement with multiple "wills" all suggest an overpopulation of possible players.

17. Hell is associated with the young man as a metaphor for anguished waiting (58.13, 120.6), not a bodily trope.

18. Citations of the plays are from Bevington's edition of *The Complete Works of Shakespeare*.

19. Laqueur's contention that the Renaissance body was based on one sex (with hierarchical degrees of difference) too quickly extrapolates from the limited domain of reproductive anatomy to dominant cultural ideology.

20. Booth glosses *fountain* and *well* with numerous references to female genitalia.

WORKS CITED

Bredbeck, Gregory. *Sodomy and Interpretation: Marlowe to Milton*. Ithaca: Cornell UP, 1991.

Blount, Thomas. *Glossographia: Or, A Dictionary Interpreting All Such Hard Words of Whatsoever Language Now Used in our Refined English Tongue*. London, 1661 and 1670.

Bray, Alan. "Homosexuality and the Signs of Male Friendship in Elizabethan England." *Queering the Renaissance*. Ed. Jonathan Goldberg. Durham: Duke UP, 1994. 40-61.

———. *Homosexuality in Renaissance England*. London: Gay Men's Press, 1982.

Butler, Judith. *Gender Trouble: Feminism and the Subversion of Identity*. New York: Routledge, 1991.

Coke, Sir Edward. *Third Part of the Institutes of the Lawes of England*. London: 1644.

de Grazia, Margreta. "The Scandal of Shakespeare's Sonnets." *Shakespeare Survey* 46 (1994): 35-49.

DiGangi, Mario. *The Homoerotics of Early Modern Drama*. Cambridge: Cambridge UP, 1997.

Dubrow, Heather. "'Incertainties now crown themselves assur'd': The Politics of Plotting Shakespeare's Sonnets." *Shakespeare Quarterly* 47 (1996): 291-305.

Erasmus. *Defense of His Declamation in Praise of Marriage*. 1519. Trans. David Sider. *Daughters, Wives and Widows: Writings by Men about Women and Marriage in England, 1500-1640*. Ed. Joan Larsen Klein. Urbana: U of Illinois P, 1992. 89-96.

Fineman, Joel. *Shakespeare's Perjured Eye: The Invention of Poetic Subjectivity in the Sonnets*. Berkeley: U of California P, 1986.

Gardiner, Judith Kegan. "The Marriage of Male Minds in Shakespeare's Sonnets." *Journal of English and Germanic Philology* 84 (1985): 328-47.

Goldberg, Jonathan. "*Romeo and Juliet*'s Open R's." *Queering the Renaissance*. Ed. Jonathan Goldberg. Durham: Duke UP, 1994. 218-35.

———. *Sodometries: Renaissance Texts, Modern Sexualities*. Stanford: Stanford UP, 1992.

Hall, Kim. *Things of Darkness: Economies of Race and Gender in Early Modern England*. Ithaca: Cornell UP, 1995.

Herrup, Cynthia. "The Patriarch at Home: The Trial of the Earl of Castlehaven for Rape and Sodomy." *History Workshop Journal* 41 (1996): 1-18.

Hunt, Margaret. Afterword. *Queering the Renaissance*. Ed. Jonathan Goldberg. Durham: Duke UP, 1994. 359-77.

Ingram, Martin. *Church Courts, Sex and Marriage in England, 1570-1640*. Cambridge: Cambridge UP, 1987.

Laqueur, Thomas. *Making Sex: Body and Gender from the Greeks to Freud*. Cambridge: Harvard UP, 1990.

Marotti, Arthur. "'Love Is Not Love': Elizabethan Sonnet Sequences and the Social Order." *ELH* 49 (1982): 396-428.

Masten, Jeffrey. *Textual Intercourse: Collaboration, Authorship, and Sexualities in Renaissance Drama*. Cambridge: Cambridge UP, 1997.

Pequigney, Joseph. *Such Is My Love: A Study of Shakespeare's Sonnets*. Chicago: U of Chicago P, 1985.

Perkins, William. *Christian OEconomy*. Trans. Thomas Pickering. London, 1609.

Rose, Mary Beth. *The Expense of Spirit: Love and Sexuality in English Renaissance Drama*. Ithaca: Cornell UP, 1988.

Sedgwick, Eve Koskofsky. *Between Men: English Literature and Male Homosocial Desire*. New York: Columbia UP, 1985.

Simons, Patricia. "Lesbian (In)Visibility in Italian Renaissance Culture: Diana and Other Cases of *donna con donna*." *Journal of Homosexuality* 27 (1994): 81-122.

Shakespeare, William. *The Complete Works of Shakespeare*. Ed. David
    Bevington. Updated 4th ed. New York: Addison Wesley Longman, 1997.
———. *Shakespeare's Sonnets*. Ed. Stephen Booth. New Haven: Yale UP,
    1977.
Smith, Bruce R. *Homosexual Desire in Shakespeare's England: A Cultural
    Poetics*. Chicago: U of Chicago P, 1991.
Stallybrass, Peter. "Editing as Cultural Formation: The Sexing of
    Shakespeare's Sonnets." *Modern Language Quarterly* 54 (1993): 91-103.
Stubbes, Philip. *The Anatomy of Abuses*. London: 1583.
Traub, Valerie. *Desire and Anxiety: Circulations of Sexuality in Shakespearean
    Drama*. London: Routledge, 1992.
———. "The (In)Significance of 'Lesbian' Desire." Ed. Jonathan Goldberg.
    Queering the Renaissance. Durham: Duke UP, 1994. 62-83.
———. "The Perversion of 'Lesbian' Desire." *History Workshop Journal* 41
    (1996): 19-49.
———. "The Psychomorphology of the Clitoris." *GLQ: A Journal of Lesbian
    and Gay Studies* 2 (1995): 81-112.

Figure 6. Nymphs Stealing Torch from Cupid (sonnets 153-154). Design by W. Harvey. *The Pictorial Edition of Shakespeare's Works*, vol. 7, ed. Charles Knight (London: C. Knight and Co., 1841). Reproduced courtesy of the Rare Book Division of the Library of Congress.

"That which thou hast done"
Shakespeare's Sonnets and *A Lover's Complaint*

Ilona Bell

For much of this century scholars believed that the first edition of Shakespeare's Sonnets and *A Lover's Complaint* (1609) was a pirated text, published without Shakespeare's knowledge or approval. That raised doubts about the authenticity of *A Lover's Complaint* and the authority of the sonnet order. Over the last decade, however, a consensus has begun to emerge that Shakespeare wrote *A Lover's Complaint*—probably during the early years of the seventeenth century—and revised it just prior to publication, while he was writing *Cymbeline*. New evidence has also emerged making it more than likely that Shakespeare arranged the 1609 sequence of poems for publication.[1]

The bibliography of scholarship and criticism dealing with Shakespeare's Sonnets grows more gargantuan every year. Yet there are still only a handful of essays devoted to *A Lover's Complaint*. Most studies of the Sonnets ignore *A Lover's Complaint* altogether, as this collection itself illustrates. The language of *A Lover's Complaint* is ornate, stylized, dense, and contorted—hard to understand and difficult to love. Apparently, most critics would prefer not to consider another 329 lines of abstruse and virtually unexplicated poetry as they struggle to explain 154 Shakespearean sonnets, with all their famed perplexities.

Thanks to Kerrigan's and Duncan-Jones's editions, it is now possible to read *A Lover's Complaint* without being put off by the genre or stymied by the literal meaning of the lines.[2] Yet, critics continue to ask, why would Shakespeare have written a poem like *A*

Lover's Complaint so late in his career? The answer lies, I believe, in the pervasive and insistent links to the Sonnets. Together, the female complainant's speech and the male lover's persuasion embedded within it provide a commentary on and reader's guide to the drama enacted by and concealed within the Sonnets.

As Kerrigan's introduction reveals, Shakespeare's Sonnets and *A Lover's Complaint* belong to a well-established English Renaissance literary tradition—the sonnet sequence conjoined to and published with a narrative poem. It includes Daniel's *Delia and A Complaint of Rosamond* (1592), Lodge's *Philis and The Tragical Complaint of Elstred* (1593), and Spenser's *Amoretti and Epithalamion* (1595).[3] Shakespeare's literary debts to Daniel are well documented (Schaar; Kerrigan, *Sonnets* 13-17; Muir, *Sonnets* 23-25); my own work on Daniel suggests that the resemblances between the two volumes are even more instructive than scholars have realized.[4]

The first authorized edition of *Delia and A Complaint of Rosamond* appeared in print in February 1592—about the time many scholars think Shakespeare was beginning to write the Sonnets. A shorter, unauthorized version of Daniel's sonnet sequence, containing "the priuate passions of my youth," had been printed five months earlier, along with the pirated edition of Sidney's *Astrophil and Stella*. As the dedication explains, Daniel was distressed to find his "secrets bewraide to the world, vncorrected," and felt "forced to publish that which [he] neuer ment" (9). He quickly set to work to transform his private poetry of courtship and seduction, addressed to an unnamed lady, into public poetry of praise, addressed to a conventional sonnet lady he called Delia. The name, an anagram of the word "ideal," convinced twentieth-century critics that the poems were written not to a real woman but to a Platonic ideal. Daniel removed the most erotic and critical poems and completely reordered the sequence, thereby concealing the courtship the poems originally enacted. He interspersed a large number of new poems designed to eternize and idealize his love. To complete the volume, Daniel added *The Complaint of Rosamond*, in which Rosamond speaks to "Delia" through Daniel so that Daniel can speak to her through Rosamond. Daniel continued to revise the sonnets between 1592 and 1594, interweaving new sonnets and altering key words and phrases, still hoping to win the love of the woman he called Delia. Ten more editions of *Delia* and *Rosamond* appeared, but the later revisions are more stylistic than substantive. As his hopes dwindled, the continuing revisions dampened the original passion and weakened the poetry.

The publication history of Daniel's sonnets and complaint elucidates Shakespeare's. The constant allusions to events unfolding outside the poems combined with the overriding persuasive purpose suggest that Shakespeare's Sonnets, like Daniel's pirated sonnets, comprise one side of an ongoing private lyric dialogue. Yet Shakespeare's sequence begins with idealizing, eternizing poems of praise like those Daniel wrote for the authorized, published edition of *Delia*, suggesting that Shakespeare (unlike Daniel) was conscious of a potential public lyric audience from the outset.[5]

The unauthorized publication of Sidney's and Daniel's poems constitutes an important watershed in English literary history, for it proved that private manuscripts were no longer safe from public exposure. English love poetry from the 1590s and early 1600s is still primarily private poetry, written not for publication but for a particular lyric audience known to the poet. Yet the best love poetry from this period—and that includes Shakespeare's Sonnets as well as Spenser's *Amoretti* and Donne's *Songs and Sonets*—also addresses a potential, wider lyric audience that is eager to discover the "secrets" of the poet's "private passions." Shakespeare, Spenser, and Donne (unlike Daniel) do not conceal the courtships their poems enact; instead, they veil allusions to actual persons or events in ambiguity or obscurity.

Shakespeare's Sonnets begin with an elaborately argued rhetorical persuasion addressed to a beautiful, unnamed young man, urging him not to squander his beauty in self-love but to marry and produce children, "That beauty still may live in thine or thee" (10.14). The young man, who is clearly not at death's door, could presumably produce a copy of himself for a good while to come. Why then does Shakespeare insist that "Now is the time" (3.2) for the young man to marry? This is just one of the many questions the Sonnets leave unanswered.

Since the persuasion to marry constitutes a major departure from sonnet convention, and since the lyric situation remains elusive, many critics have sought explanations outside the poems.[6] Did the young man's mother hire Shakespeare to convince her son to marry because she was eager to have grandchildren? Or did the lady's kin commission Shakespeare to help secure the young man's hand in marriage? There is no indication that Shakespeare's lyric persuasion had any impact on the young man's marital status, but it does accomplish something much more important for the history of English literature: it initiates a private lyric dialogue with the young man.

The expostulations ("O, change thy thought, that I may change my mind!" [10.9]), the gentle prodding ("For shame, deny that thou bear'st love to any" [10.1]), and constant questions ("Music to hear, why hear'st thou music sadly?" [8.1]), are all calculated to provoke a response, and so, it seems, they do. Very quickly, the monologic voice of the sonnet speaker becomes not only intimate—"Make thee another self for love of me" (10.13)—but also distinctly conversational—"Dear my love, you know / You had a father; let your son say so" (13.13-14).

Sonnet 18 begins with a question, "Shall I compare thee to a summer's day?", which combines the sophisticated self-referentiality of the poet with the beguiling flattery of a suitor: "Thou art more lovely and more temperate" (18.2). The simile hints at behaviors that are too "rough" and passions that are "too hot," but it does so in order to shield the young man from reproach: "Sometime too hot the eye of heaven shines, / And often is his gold complexion dimmed . . . But thy eternal summer shall not fade" (18.5-6, 9).

Shakespeare neither explains nor retracts the persuasion to marry; it simply drops out of the picture, displaced by the eternizing power of his own poetry—"So long lives this, and this gives life to thee" (18.14)[7]—and a revised rhetorical purpose: "A woman's face, with Nature's own hand painted, / Hast thou, the master-mistress of my passion; / A woman's gentle heart, but not acquainted / With shifting change, as is false women's fashion" (20.1-4). Has Shakespeare somehow learned that the woman he was trying to persuade the young man to marry is inconstant? Or has Shakespeare decided that male promiscuity and a casual scorn for women are rhetorically advantageous because they enable him to claim the young man's love for himself alone? No answers are forthcoming. The poem's antifeminism is reflexive and unexamined; so too is the male bond that idolizes the young man at the expense of womankind.[8]

Sonnet 20 is a pivotal moment, for it replaces the poems' previous raison d'etre, the persuasion to marry, with an even more radical departure from Renaissance sonnet convention, a lyric campaign to win the young man's love for the poet himself.[9] Critics disagree about whether sonnet 20 initiates or precludes a sexual relationship with the young man, but I would argue that the amphibolous conclusion serves Shakespeare's rhetorical purposes: "But since she pricked thee out for women's pleasure, / Mine be thy love, and thy love's use their treasure" (20.13-14). To the wider lyric audience, the reference to "women's pleasure" affirms the young man's heterosexuality and legitimates Shakespeare's "love" as Platonic. At the same time, however, the double entendre flatters the young man with a witty allusion to his sexual endowment, inviting him to interpret the lines as he wishes, either as evidence of his sexual attractiveness to Shakespeare, or as license to "pleasure" any number of "women" (rather than husbanding his seed for his legitimate heirs).

As the private lyric dialogue with the young man becomes increasingly intimate and complex, Shakespeare goes to considerable lengths to maintain appearances for the wider lyric audience. In sonnet 33, "Full many a glorious morning," Shakespeare reworks the earlier image of "a summer's day," gilding the description with tender praise ("Kissing with golden face" [3]), broaching and then concealing the possibility of moral culpability: "Anon permit the basest clouds to ride / With ugly rack on his celestial face, / And from the forlorn world his visage hide, / Stealing unseen to west with this disgrace" (33.5-8).

The rhyme scheme divides the poem into three quatrains and a couplet, but the rhetoric and syntax divide the argument into an octave that describes many a glorious morning and a sestet that turns the generalized description of nature into a metaphor for a specific moment in the poet's relationship to the young man: "Even so my sun one early morn did shine" (33.9). The octave freely metes out praise and blame, making the sun an active collaborator in its "shame." The sestet attributes agency to the young man only as long as he maintains his "triumphant splendour" (10), rendering him passive at the very moment when the logic of the metaphor calls for his "disgrace": "But out, alack, he was but one hour mine, / The region cloud hath masked him from me now" (11-12). Whatever "[t]he region cloud" refers to, it has so distanced the speaker from the young man that he can only be approached indirectly, in the third person.

The couplet exonerates the young man: "Yet him for this my love no whit disdaineth; / Suns of the world may stain when heaven's sun staineth." Yet the logic of the metaphor implies that he either has lost luster himself ("stain" as "drain light away") or stained someone else ("stain" as "defile or corrupt morally")—before stealing away "unseen" to conceal his "disgrace" from the world. "Stain" (as "color") also echoes the prior description of the young man—"A man in hue all hues in his controlling, / Which steals men's eyes and women's souls amazeth" (20.7-8)—where his dazzling beauty blinds men and women alike to the perils of his promiscuity.

Poems such as this acquire their metaphoric brilliance and rhetorical complexity at least in part from the pressure of writing for a private lyric audience which is already privy to the circumstances underlying the poem, while at the same time writing for a wider, uninitiated lyric audience.[10] The mixture of tones that tempers loving admiration with wariness, the rhetorical effort to elicit signs of the young man's love balanced by the ever-present fear of giving offense—these are some of the ways Shakespeare attempts to woo and placate the young man. At the same time, however, the morally responsible argumentation attempts to satisfy the stringent standards of the reading public, concealing the details of the young man's "disgrace" in clouds of metaphoric verbiage. Shakespeare hedges his words, hinting at what he is loath to tell the public, lest he contribute to the young man's "disgrace."[11]

The ambivalence and contradictions bespeak an intense, ongoing relationship that is evolving even as the poems are being written. As the lyric dialogue continues, it becomes harder to explain—or to explain away—"that which thou hast done" (35.1). In sonnet 94 the famed ambiguities and suppressions of the language make it virtually impossible to distinguish praise from blame: "They that have power to hurt and will do none, / That do not do the thing they most do show, / Who, moving others, are themselves as stone, / Unmovèd, cold, and to temptation slow" (94.1-4). The speaker cannot seem to decide whether "they" are admirably controlled, "to temptation slow," or chillingly hardhearted, "themselves as stone, / Unmovèd, cold."

Much as sonnet 33 moves from the generality of "Full many a glorious morning" (1) to the specificity of "Even so my sun one early morn did shine" (9), sonnet 94 moves from a general category ("They that have power to hurt") to a specific moment in the life of an individual: "The summer's flower is to the summer sweet, / Though to itself it only live and die; / But if that flower with base infection meet, / The basest weed outbraves his dignity" (94.9-12). An expressive theory of the lyric attributes the poem's famed ambiguities to the poet's ambivalence, but a dialogic theory of the kind I have been developing here also attributes the ambiguities to the pressures of the lyric audience. To begin with, the lines offer an empathetic account of the young man's narcissism, implying that even if he fails to marry and have children, his beauty is treasured by Nature and eternized by the poet. As in sonnet 33, the imagery protects the young man from censure, for who would think to blame a flower for an infestation of aphids? Still, it is distressing to see "[t]he basest weed" triumph over "his dignity."

The final couplet takes refuge in the indirection of the plural: "For sweetest things turn sourest by their deeds; / Lilies that fester smell far worse than weeds" (94.13-14). Whose "deeds" are being discussed here? And what has begun to fester and rot? The poet's love? The young man himself? Or other flowers, infected by their intimacy with the young man? The epigrammatic formulae raise more questions than the poet cares (or dares) to answer. By setting up a comparison without explaining the terms of the comparison, Shakespeare can communicate his concerns to his private lyric audience, while publicly protecting the reputation of whomever the metaphor describes. The active verbs, the pointed reference to "their deeds," and the increasingly repellent smell of corruption suggest that whoever is culpable should be held responsible. Yet the poem ends without explaining who has done what to whom—and so it must, if Shakespeare himself is to remain among that great clan of people, "They that have power to hurt and will do none."

The more Shakespeare's rhetoric strains to ease what his imagery can no longer conceal nor yet explain, the more one feels the pressure of events that cannot be kept outside the boundaries of the poems. Shakespeare strives to ameliorate the growing criticism—"Some say thy fault is youth, some wantonness" (96.1)—with self-deprecating remarks about the limits of his own inventiveness: "But that wild music burdens every bough, / And sweets grown common lose their dear delight. / Therefore, like her, I sometime hold my tongue, / Because I would not dull you with my song" (102.11-14). Yet he cannot conceal the imputation that his private lyric dialogue has foundered because the young man himself has "grown common."

Shakespeare has praised the young man's beauty, eternized his name, and criticized his behavior, ever so tactfully and all to no avail. The young man's "deeds" press upon the sonnets, yet there is no indication that the sonnets have any effect upon the young man's character or behavior. The private lyric dialogue culminates in sonnet 103:

> O, blame me not if I no more can write!
> Look in your glass, and there appears a face

> That overgoes my blunt invention quite,
> Dulling my lines and doing me disgrace.
> Were it not sinful then, striving to mend,
> To mar the subject that before was well?
> For to no other pass my verses tend
> Than of your graces and your gifts to tell;
>   And more, much more, than in my verse can sit
>   Your own glass shows you when you look in it. (5-14)

Sonnets 1-103 are classic poems of courtship. Their express purpose is to praise the young man's "gifts" and "graces," his natural abilities, attractive qualities, and charms, in order to win the "graces," the signs of his favor, and the "gifts," the material rewards which poems like these seek to elicit. The young man is not only "the subject" of these poems; he is also the private lyric audience, a "subject" who exists outside the poems. He can be represented in the poems and wooed by the poems, but he cannot be controlled by them because he is not constructed by them.

On the surface, sonnet 103 reiterates Shakespeare's inability to capture the young man's "gifts" and "graces" in poetry. But the language also directs the young man to look below the surface of the poems, into his own glass where he will see "more, much more, than in my verse can sit." Like sonnet 94, this poem contains two contradictory readings, one so eager to flatter the young man that the effort "overgoes my blunt invention quite," the other, so damning that its charges cannot be stated openly enough to be affirmed or denied. Shakespeare cannot continue to write sonnets, the express purpose of which is simultaneously to praise the young man's "gifts" and to win his "graces," because anything the poems could possibly say at this point would only "mar the subject" and "disgrace" the poet. The private lyric dialogue with the young man comes to an abrupt halt, leaving the young man (and us) to think about what the poet is unable or unwilling "to tell."

Sonnet 104 confirms the hiatus, suggesting that a period of time has passed since Shakespeare last addressed the young man in poetry. The remarkably upbeat tone and retrospective point of view suggest that Shakespeare has deliberately set out to write a more positive ending to a lyric dialogue that ended badly. The new sonnets range from gorgeous reminiscences of former intimacies—"To me, fair friend, you never can be old, / For as you were when first your eye I eyed, / Such seems your beauty still" (104.1-3)—to relentless reiterations of flattering (and somewhat suspect) abstractions: "Kind is my love today, tomorrow kind" (105.5).

Like the sonnets Daniel added in 1592, sonnet 104 and those immediately following strive to mask the less seemly aspects of the earlier private lyric dialogue: "'Fair, kind, and true' is all my argument, / 'Fair, kind, and true,' varying to other words" (105.9-10). At first, Shakespeare can only repeat what has been said before—"What's new to speak, what now to register" (108.3)—because nothing new is happening between him and the young man: "I must each day say o'er the very same, / Counting no old thing old—thou mine, I thine" (108.6-7). Before long, they are communicating again: "O, never say that I was false of heart" (109.1).

As nostalgia yields to dialogue, former grievances revive, drawing the poems into a lyric situation that exceeds both the poem's boundaries and the poet's control. Shakespeare strives to make amends by assuming responsibility for whatever it was that went amiss: "You are my all the world, and I must strive / To know my shames and praises from your tongue" (112.5-6). The poetry tries to demonstrate that "ruined love, when it is built anew, / Grows fairer than at first, more strong, far greater" (119.11-12). Yet old wounds still fester, and his imagination soon spins out of control: "How have mine eyes out of their spheres been fitted / In the distraction of this madding fever!" (119.7-8).

Twice now, Shakespeare has set out to build a powerful foundation, but cracks are again beginning to show—"laid great bases for eternity, / Which proves more short than waste or ruining" (125.3-4)—when the sequence comes to another, even more definitive, impasse: "Hence, thou suborned informer! A true soul / When most impeached stands least in thy control" (125.13-14). The slanders remain unconfirmed and unexplained. There is simply nothing more to say since the express purpose for writing these sonnets is "to prove / The constancy and virtue of your love" (117.13-14).

Thomas Whythorne and George Gascoigne both wrote poems of courtship and seduction to numerous Elizabethan women. When Whythorne later decided to circulate the poems to a male coterie, he wrote an autobiographical prose narrative designed to explain the poems' original meaning and purpose: "I do think it needful not only to show you the cause why I wrote them, but also to open my secret meaning in divers of them" (1). When Gascoigne decided to publish his poems in *A Hundreth Sundrie Flowres*, he provided discursive prose titles—"The absent lover (in ciphers) disciphering his name, doth crave some spedie relief as followeth"—designed to entice the reader with clues to the persons and events alluded to in the poem (142). Shakespeare, being Shakespeare, was unwilling to reduce the manifold perplexities of his Sonnets to a few lines of prefatory or explanatory prose. Instead, he appended *A Lover's Complaint*, as if to tell the wider lyric audience, "Why, look you now, how unworthy a thing you make of me! You would play upon me, you would seem to know my stops, you would pluck out the heart of my mystery" (*Hamlet* 3.2.363-66). Why then, you figure it out.

As Shakespeare warns us from the very outset of *A Lover's Complaint*, this is a symbolic universe where words contain veiled allusions and double meanings: "From off a hill whose concave womb reworded / A plaintful story from a sist'ring vale, / My spirits t'attend this double voice accorded" (1-3). "[T]his double voice" describes the formal structure of *A Lover's Complaint*: the male narrator quotes the female complainant who in turn quotes her male lover. It might also be a warning that the female complainant is duplicitous, for when she first comes into view, the narrator immediately dubs her "a fickle maid" (5). Kerrigan therefore associates her with the dark lady whose lies the Sonnets eternize, and with the unreliable female speakers whose plaintive tales occupy conventional male-authored female complaints. The antifeminist stereotyping also recalls sonnet 20, where Shakespeare says the young man is "not acquainted / With shifting change, as is false women's fashion" (20.3-4).

As the introductory narrative frame unfolds, however, the female complainant begins to look "fickle," not in the sense of deceitful or sexually inconstant, but in the sense of changeable or emotionally distracted. Her eyes dart from the heavens to the earth, unable to find a focus or a resting place: "their gazes lend / To every place at once, and nowhere fixed, / The mind and sight distractedly commixed" (26-28). These lines have an uncanny resemblance to the way Shakespeare represents himself at the moment when his lyric dialogue with the young man is dissolving: "How have mine eyes out of their spheres been fitted / In the distraction of this madding fever!" (119.7-8). This is the first of countless parallels between the sonnet speaker and the female complainant.

The internal lyric audience is itself "double," for while the male narrator watches, a "reverend man" approaches and "desires to know / In brief the grounds and motives of her woe" (62-63). Kerrigan suggests that the unconventional presence of this father confessor figure directs us to judge her tale as an unsatisfactory confession and repentance for her sins. Yet this reverend man is a distinctly secular figure: "Sometime a blusterer that the ruffle knew / Of court, of city" (58-59). Whereas the male narrator conceals his presence so as to observe unobserved, the reverend man "sits he by her side" and invites her to relate "her grievance." Unlike the male narrator who immediately describes her as "fickle," the "reverend man" assumes she has legitimate grounds of complaint. He quite literally takes her side, and even more important, he invites us to do likewise.

In response, the female complainant tells "[a] plaintful story" of being enamored, seduced, and abandoned by a beautiful young man— "Small show of man was yet upon his chin; / His phoenix down began but to appear, / Like unshorn velvet, on that termless skin" (92-94)— who bears a remarkable resemblance to the young man of the Sonnets—"A woman's face, with Nature's own hand painted" (20.1). The male lover's beauty captivates his admirers: "Each eye that saw him did enchant the mind; / For on his visage was in little drawn / What largeness thinks in paradise was sawn" (89-91). The young man of the Sonnets enchants the sonnet speaker and others in precisely this way: "But heaven in thy creation did decree / That in thy face sweet love should ever dwell" (93.9-10); "How many gazers might'st thou lead astray" (96.11).

The young man's androgynous beauty "steals men's eyes and women's souls amazeth" (20.8); similarly, the male lover "had the dialect and different skill, / Catching all passions in his craft of will, / That he did in the general bosom reign / Of young, of old, and sexes both enchanted" (125-28). These lines recall sonnet 20, in which Shakespeare turns his rhetorical powers to wooing "the master-mistress of my passion," and sonnet 135, in which Shakespeare tries to work his way into a *ménage à trois* by punning madly on his own name and the dark lady's sexual appetites: "So thou being rich in Will add to thy Will / One will of mine, to make thy large Will more."

Like Donne's quibbles on Ann More's surname, or Sidney's references to Penelope Rich's "rich" husband, the punning allusion to Shakespeare's own "craft of will" hints that the poetic fiction of the complaint is somehow linked to biographical truths concealed in the

Sonnets.[12] The following lines, which tell us that the male lover's admirers "dialogued for him what he would say, / Asked their own wills, and made their wills obey" (132-33), are a brilliant synopsis and critique of Shakespeare's lyric dialogue with the young man. In the Sonnets Shakespeare "dialogued for" the young man, anticipating his response, blurring the identities of poet and lover, expressing his feelings ("my love") so as to imply that the young man ("my love") acts as Shakespeare wills, even though Shakespeare always seems to succumb to the young man's will.

In *A Lover's Complaint* the female complainant not only speaks for herself; she also lets her male lover speak for himself, and he blithely dismisses all his previous affairs, assuming that his lovers are as untrue and unkind as he himself is: "with acture they may be, / Where neither party is nor true nor kind" (185-86). This is perhaps the most chilling of all the many allusions to the Sonnets because these are precisely the qualities upon which Shakespeare grounds his praise of the young man: "'fair, kind, and true' is all my argument" (105.9).[13]

The female complainant is beguiled by her male lover, though unlike the sonnet speaker, she openly acknowledges his perfidy: "For further I could say this man's untrue, / And knew the patterns of his foul beguiling, / Heard where his plants in others' orchards grew, / Saw how deceits were gilded in his smiling . . . " (169-72). The male lover's sexual guilt recalls and exposes Shakespeare's lyric gilt/guilt, for the Sonnets bathe the young man's faults in the purifying light of lyric idolatry, "Gilding pale streams with heavenly alchemy" (33.4), "Gilding the object whereupon it gazeth" (20.6). Furthermore, the male lover's abandoned sexual partners—especially the virgin who forsook her holy vows of single life only to be forsaken by him—provide a narrative analogue to sonnets 1-18, suggesting that Shakespeare urged the young man to marry *immediately* because he, like the male lover, had impregnated a respectable gentlewoman. Indeed, the "bastards of his foul adulterate heart" (175) explain what the Sonnets only imply, ever so discreetly: "You had a father, let your son say so" (13.14).

The male lover woos the female complainant as he himself has been wooed, with poems of courtship: "the annexions of fair gems enriched, / And deep-brained sonnets that did amplify / Each stone's dear nature, worth, and quality" (208-10). Shakespeare woos the young man—"thou, to whom my jewels trifles are" (48.5)—with poems of courtship, which are valuable jewels, or tokens of love, precisely because they reflect the young man's worth, however inadequately:

"Like stones of worth they thinly placéd are, / Or captain jewels in the carcanet" (52.7-8).

The female complainant knows her lover impregnated and abandoned many other women, but she nonetheless believes him when he insists that she is the first woman he ever loved or actively wooed: "And be not of my holy vows afraid. / That's to ye sworn to none was ever said" (179-80). In short, she wants to believe "that strong-bonded oath / That shall prefer and undertake my troth" (279-80). Swayed by his charismatic beauty and rhetorical skills—not stopping to think that he is betraying his former lovers by giving their tokens of love to her— she allows herself to believe that his lover's tokens and "holy vows" constitute a legally binding, clandestine marriage contract.

The poetic connections between the male lover and the young man, the female complainant and the sonnet speaker, reach a climax when the male lover completes his persuasion to love and promptly bursts into tears: "For lo, his passion, but an art of craft, / Even there resolved my reason into tears: / There my white stole of chastity I daffed" (295- 97). The entire force of the poem's logic is overturned by the sheer joy of the male lover's tears, and her resistance dissolves, just as Shakespeare's does: "Ah, but those tears are pearl which thy love sheeds, / And they are rich and ransom all ill deeds" (34.13-14).

The male lover brags shamelessly about his ability to project his "shame" onto his lovers: "They sought their shame that so their shame did find; / And so much less of shame in me remains / By how much of me their reproach contains" (187-89). These lines recall sonnet 34, which continues the imagery of sonnet 33 and even repeats the same damaging rhymes in lines 6 and 8, suggesting that Shakespeare's own "face" bears the marks of the young man's disgrace: "'Tis not enough that through the cloud thou break / To dry the rain on my storm-beaten face, / For no man well of such a salve can speak / That heals the wound and cures not the disgrace / Nor can thy shame give physic to my grief" (34.5-9). Sonnets 33-35 are generally read as meditations on the poet's disappointments with the young man; Booth, Kerrigan, and Duncan-Jones all gloss "thy shame" to mean "thy regret at having done me wrong." If *A Lover's Complaint* is a commentary on and conclusion to the Sonnets, as the correlations I have been tracing suggest, sonnets 34-35 may suggest that Shakespeare is distressed with the young man for deceiving his female lovers, leaving them to suffer the shame he escapes by "Stealing unseen to west with this disgrace" (33.8).

The Sonnets are constantly "confusing the identities of injurer and injured party" (Booth 189), making it virtually impossible to separate the young man's beguiling deceptions from the poet's beguiling evasions. By allowing the young man's tears to "ransom all ill deeds," Shakespeare becomes an accomplice, taking the young man's "shame" and "disgrace" upon himself: "And men make faults, and even I in this, / Authorizing thy trespass with compare, / Myself corrupting, salving thy amiss" (35.5-7). Indeed, the very act of writing a poem of courtship, the express purpose of which is to secure the young man's love by assuming his "faults," means Shakespeare "an accessory needs must be" (35.13). Not surprisingly, Shakespeare makes the same sick bargain all over again when he accepts the young man's conditions for reinstating their lyric dialogue: "and I must strive / To know my shames and praises from your tongue; / None else to me, nor I to none alive, / That my steeled sense or changes right or wrong" (112.5-8). Because the sonnet speaker takes the "shames" upon himself, the young man departs unscathed. So too, the male lover emerges stronger than ever, leaving the female complainant to the dishonor and misery he readily escapes: "Appear to him as he to me appears— / All melting, though our drops this diff'rence bore: / His poisoned me, and mine did him restore" (299-301). Being a woman, the female complainant is far more vulnerable (as the "concave womb" of line 1 hints) than the sonnet speaker, but he nonetheless suffers an analogous fate: "Drugs poison him that so fell sick of you" (118.14).

When the female complainant first begins to speak, Shakespeare describes her lost innocence and independence in terms that recall sonnets 94-95: "I might as yet have been a spreading flower, / Fresh to myself, if I had self-applied / Love to myself, and to no love beside" (75-77). Upon first reading, we may wonder whether *she* is the canker whose festering corruption has spread to her male lover, destroying his sweet innocence just as the dark lady reputedly corrupted the young man of the Sonnets. But after seeing her "fresh" innocence deflowered and destroyed by her male lover, the imagery of sonnet 94 looks quite different, especially when it continues into sonnet 95, in which the young man looks even more like the male lover: "How sweet and lovely dost thou make the shame / Which, like a canker in the fragrant rose . . ." (95.1-2). In retrospect, the resemblances between the male lover and the young man suggest that he used his "power to hurt" his sexual victims—the innocent lilies who were all too ready to be "moved" by his beauty and eloquence.

Of course, we hear the male lover's persuasion only through the female complainant; therefore, we might well wonder whether she can be trusted or whether she belied him to exonerate herself. Does *A Lover's Complaint* give us any reason to think that she is the one who is manipulative and deceitful—or self-deceived? I think not, for she does what *The Complaint of Rosamond* urges Delia to do: she makes a conscious decision to follow the force of her desire. Moreover, she is remarkably willing to accept responsibility for her actions: "Ay, me! I fell; and yet do question make / What I should do again for such a sake" (321-22). It is only in retrospect that she realizes he must have treated his other lovers in much the same way, leaving them to suffer the "shame" and "disgrace" he himself caused: "When he most burned in heart-wished luxury, / He preached pure maid and praised cold chastity" (314-15).

Like sonnets 104-126, *A Lover's Complaint* is deeply retrospective, its conclusions clarified by the passage of time and elaborated by the expansiveness of the narrative form. The seven-line stanzas of rhyme royal (ababbcc) turn the alternating rhyme of the quatrain (abab) into a couplet (bb) which is immediately followed by a summary couplet (cc). The stanza form looks back and sums up in order to tie things together and move on to another reworking of the same pattern. Similarly, the female complainant looks back at her lover's earlier affairs, sees the "patterns of his foul beguiling" (170)— the same pattern that recurs in the Sonnets—and sums it all up, only to begin the cycle all over again, just as the Sonnets do, again and again. Her willing admission that he could "yet again betray the fore-betrayed, / And new pervert a reconcilèd maid" (328-29) explains what sonnets 34 and 95 dramatize: no sooner does Shakespeare the poet represent the young man's "shame" or "disgrace" than Shakespeare the lover finds himself beguiled and reconciled all over again.

The conventional male-authored female complaint subjects the female complainant's vanity and weakness to the male narrator's irony and judgment. Typically, the introductory narrative frame introduces the female complainant, and the concluding narrative frame summarizes the lessons to be drawn from her mea culpa. But Shakespeare's male narrator sets the scene only to subside into silence. The elaborate and unconventional narrative structure—the introductory narrative frame which claims an aesthetic distance it adroitly undercuts, the presence of an internal audience which enunciates an interpretive position that is at once compassionate and proactive, the male lover's lengthy self-incrimination, and above all, the absence of a concluding narrative frame—confirms what the narrative reveals: the unreliable narrator whose sins are revealed by the poem is not the female complainant but the male lover. Shakespeare's male narrator does not reappear to provide an authoritative final judgment; therefore, the female complaint frames and judges the male lover's speech, just as the male narrative conventionally frames and judges the female complainant.

In writing *A Lover's Complaint* Shakespeare may have "reworded" a real-life story told him by someone else (presumably the "reverend man") who heard it from the female complainant herself, or he may have "reworded" the conventional male-authored female complaint to shed light on the events underlying, and unexplained by, the Sonnets. Either way, he exposes the hypocrisy of both genres, which regularly "preached pure maid and praised cold chastity" (315). *A Lover's Complaint* provides a narrative analogue for what the 1609 Sonnets stop short of saying: "Hence, thou suborned informer! A true soul / When most impeached stands least in thy control" (125.13-14). In retrospect, it seems that the informer is the "true soul," and the young man, the false soul, who "stands" even less in the poet's "control" because he, like the male lover, carries off his most breathtaking evasions of responsibility when he is most severely impeached.

Shakespeare seems to have written *A Lover's Complaint* soon after finishing the sonnets to the young man in the early years of the seventeenth century, much as Daniel wrote *The Complaint of Rosamond* as a conclusion to the authorized, published edition of 1592. In preparing the first edition, Daniel revised numerous sonnets, removed the sexiest and nastiest poems, and reordered the sequence. Shakespeare also seems to have revised many of his sonnets. He may have moved some poems around, or inserted a later poem in a group of earlier poems. Shakespeare also seems to have removed some poems or lines that seemed inappropriate for publication. The Sonnets promise to eternize the young man's name, but the published sequence omits his name. Shakespeare may have decided to conceal his identity because *A Lover's Complaint* makes the young man's shame and disgrace so much clearer. At some point, Shakespeare may have been thinking about publishing the sonnets to the young man without the sonnets to the dark lady; if so, *A Lover's Complaint* would have followed the slanders cited in sonnet 125. In the 1609 edition, however, the sonnets to the dark lady intervene, which means that there may well be important connections between those sonnets and the complaint—but that is the subject for another essay.

Shakespeare's Sonnets help to explain the intricate structure and obscure language of *A Lover's Complaint*. Even more important, *A Lover's Complaint* helps to explain the gaps and contradictions that make the Sonnets such a riddle. When read together, Shakespeare's Sonnets and *A Lover's Complaint* provide further evidence that the 1609 text is a brilliantly imagined and intricately interconnected volume of poems. The pervasive and insistent links between the ways the young man beguiles the sonnet speaker and the ways the male lover beguiles the female complainant indicate that Shakespeare conceived *A Lover's Complaint* as the conclusion to and commentary upon Sonnets 1609.

NOTES

1. For further information, see the works cited by Duncan-Jones; Hieatt, Bishop, and Nicholson; Hieatt, Hieatt, and Prescott; Muir, *A Lover's Complaint*; Jackson; Kerrigan, *Sonnets*, Slater.

2. Shakespeare's Sonnets and *A Lover's Complaint* are quoted from Kerrigan's edition.

3. See Kerrigan's introduction to *The Sonnets and A Lover's Complaint*, 13 ff. Kerrigan's notes to *A Lover's Complaint* include numerous references to the Sonnets. His *Motives of Woe: Shakespeare and 'Female Complaint'* is a valuable guide to the tradition. For a feminist critique of the genre, see Harvey 140-42.

4. For a more thorough exposition, see the chapter on Daniel in Bell's *Elizabethan Women and the Poetry of Courtship*.

5. Hieatt, Hieatt, and Prescott use computer dating to argue that Shakespeare (like Daniel) revised his sonnets and complaint prior to publication. For more skeptical views of the sonnet order, see Dubrow's essay reprinted in this volume and Duncan-Jones's introduction to her edition. For further information on the transition from manuscript to print, see Marotti, *Manuscript, Print, and the English Renaissance Lyric*, and Wall, *The Imprint of Gender*.

6. Muir writes, "As far as I know, there is no other group of sonnets consisting of persuasions to marry" (*Sonnets* 35). These poems are generally referred to as "procreation sonnets," but the language is filled with allusions to marriage, as Duncan-Jones's notes point out repeatedly.

7. My understanding of the Sonnets is greatly indebted to Anne Ferry's elegant study, *All in War with Time: Love Poetry of Shakespeare, Donne, Jonson, and Marvell.*

8. See Eve Sedgwick's classic account of the male bond in *Between Men,* 28-48.

9. According to Duncan-Jones, "there is actually only one other Elizabethan sonnet sequence with a male addressee, Richard Barnfield's mini-sequence of twenty 'Sonnets' included in his *Cynthia* (1595)" (47). For a comparison of the two sequences, see Bredbeck.

10. As Barber writes, "A fiction, especially a fiction by Shakespeare, would satisfy our curiosity where the sonnets frequently baffle us by speaking of things which the person addressed is assumed to know but to which we have no key" (16).

11. I take the liberty of referring to both the poet and the sonnet speaker as Shakespeare since the puns on Shakespeare's name, "Will," the references to his professional identity, and the constant allusions to events outside the poems invite us to connect the persona as constructed in the poems to the poet's own life. For example, Colie remarks "how deviant Shakespeare's sonnets are" and "how peculiarly personal" (31). As Robert Crosman argues, "The sonnets are too rich and ambiguous to count as history, but they are something as good or better—a portrait of the artist as lover, painted by his own hand" (485).

12. Judith Anderson, in *Biographical Truth: The Representation of Historical Persons in Tudor-Stuart Writing,* demonstrates that Renaissance writers do not distinguish between fiction and nonfiction.

13. "This is moral Doublespeak of the worst, most complacent kind," Kerrigan comments, for "how can he speak for his abandoned partners?" (*Sonnets* 16).

WORKS CITED

Anderson, Judith H. *Biographical Truth: The Representation of Historical Persons in Tudor-Stuart Writing.* New Haven: Yale UP, 1984.

Barber, C. L. "An Essay on Shakespeare's Sonnets." *Shakespeare's Sonnets: Modern Critical Interpretations.* Ed. Harold Bloom. New York: Chelsea House, 1987. 5-27.

Bell, Ilona. *Elizabethan Women and the Poetry of Courtship.* Cambridge: Cambridge UP, 1998.

Booth, Stephen, ed. *Shakespeare's Sonnets.* New Haven: Yale UP, 1977.

Bredbeck, Gregory W. "Tradition and the Individual Sodomite: Barnfield, Shakespeare, and Subjective Desire." *Homosexuality in Renaissance and*

Enlightenment England: Literary Representations in Historical Contexts. Ed. Claude J. Summers. New York: Haworth, 1992. 41-68.

Colie, Rosalie L. "Criticism and the Analysis of Craft: Shakespeare's Sonnets." *Shakespeare's Sonnets: Modern Critical Interpretations.* Ed. Harold Bloom. New York: Chelsea House, 1987. 29-45.

Crosman, Robert. "Making Love out of Nothing at All: The Issue of Story in Shakespeare's Procreation Sonnets." *Shakespeare Quarterly* 41 (1990): 470-88.

Dubrow, Heather. "'Incertainties now crown themselves assur'd': The Politics of Plotting Shakespeare's Sonnets." *Shakespeare Quarterly* 47 (1996): 291-305.

Duncan-Jones, Katherine, ed. *Shakespeare's Sonnets.* The Arden Shakespeare. Nashville: Nelson, 1997.

——. "Was the 1609 Shake-speares Sonnets Really Unauthorized?" *Review of English Studies* 34 (1983): 151-71.

Ferry, Anne. *All in War with Time: Love Poetry of Shakespeare, Donne, Jonson, and Marvell.* Cambridge: Harvard UP, 1975.

Gascoigne, George. *George Gascoigne's A Hundreth Sundrie Flowres.* Ed. C. T. Prouty. U of Missouri Studies 17, 2. Columbia: U of Missouri P, 1942.

Harvey, Elizabeth D. *Ventriloquized Voices: Feminist Theory and English Renaissance Texts.* London: Routledge, 1992.

Hieatt, A. K., T. G. Bishop, and E. A. Nicholson. "Shakespeare's Rare Words: 'Lover's Complaint,' *Cymbeline*, and *Sonnets.*" *Notes and Queries* (1987): 219-24.

Hieatt, A. Kent, Charles W. Hieatt, and Anne Lake Prescott. "When Did Shakespeare Write Sonnets 1609?" *Studies in Philology* 88 (1991): 69-109.

Jackson, M. P. *Shakespeare's 'A Lover's Complaint': Its Date and Authenticity.* Auckland: U of Auckland P, 1965.

Kerrigan, John, ed. *Motives of Woe: Shakespeare and 'Female Complaint.' A Critical Anthology.* Oxford: Clarendon, 1991.

——. *The Sonnets and A Lover's Complaint.* New York: Viking, 1986; Harmondsworth: Penguin, 1986.

Marotti, Arthur F. *Manuscript, Print, and the English Renaissance Lyric.* Ithaca: Cornell UP, 1995.

Muir, Kenneth. "'A Lover's Complaint': A Reconsideration." *Shakespeare the Professional and Related Studies.* Totowa: Rowman and Littlefield, 1964. 204-19.

——. *Shakespeare's Sonnets.* London: Allen and Unwin, 1979.

Schaar, Claes. *An Elizabethan Sonnet Problem*. Lund Studies in English 28. Lund: Gleerup, 1960.

Sedgwick, Eve Kosofsky. *Between Men: English Literature and Male Homosocial Desire*. New York: Columbia UP, 1985.

Slater, Eliot. "Shakespeare: Word Links between Poems and Plays." *Notes and Queries* (1975): 157-63.

Wall, Wendy. *The Imprint of Gender: Authorship and Publication in the English Renaissance*. Ithaca: Cornell UP, 1993.

Whythorne, Thomas. *The Autobiography of Thomas Whythorne*. Ed. James M. Osborn. Modern Spelling Edition. London: Oxford UP, 1962.

LaVergne, TN USA
10 December 2010
208135LV00002B/52/P